Building English Skills   Orange Level

Contents of the Teacher's Edition

Components of the *Building English Skills* Series . . .

	Student Text	Teacher's Edition	Skills Practice Book	Diagnostic and Mastery Tests	Duplicating Masters
Orange Level Grade 9					
Blue Level Grade 10					
Yellow Level Grade 11					
Purple Level Grade 12					

Student Text

See pages T6–T17 for significant features of the Student Text.

Teacher's Edition

See pages T18–T29 for significant features of the Teacher's Edition.

Skills Practice Book

Thousands of additional skill-building exercises in composition, vocabulary, grammar, usage, and mechanics provide extra reinforcement. Because each page is a self-contained unit offering explanations, examples, and exercises, the workbooks are ideal for independent practice.

Diagnostic and Mastery Tests

Consumable test booklets offer easy-to-use tests: diagnostic tests to help determine the direction of your teaching; and mastery tests to help you check progress throughout the year. The test booklets are available in a convenient Test Packet that contains 35 Test Booklets, an Answer Key, a Class Record, and an Individual Student Record.

Duplicating Masters

The Skills Practice Book exercises are available in duplicating master form.

The Timesaver

The Teacher's Resource Binder offers time-saving instructional aids for reinforcement, evaluation, and record-keeping. Each level contains:

- **Teaching and Evaluating Student Writing** Booklet
- Overhead Transparencies for teaching the Process of Writing
- Copy Masters for students who need extra practice in grammar and usage
- Copy Masters for practice in the Process of Writing
- Copy Masters for practice in applying Life Skills
- Classroom Posters: **SQ3R Study Method**
  The Process of Writing
  Proofreading
  Making a Speech

Significant Features of the *Building English Skills* Series

The 1985 Edition of *Building English Skills* offers up-to-date emphasis on the skills students need today. The series expands its in-depth presentation of the process of writing at every level and continues its dedication to teaching grammar skills as tools to improve composition. Lively, entertaining assignments make writing more enjoyable for students. And new material gives you better coverage of critical thinking, study and research skills, speaking and listening, and life skills. Note these special features of the new *Building English Skills:*

In-Depth Development of the Process of Writing

Building English Skills teaches the process of writing as a circular process of thinking and rethinking, writing and revising (see page T6).

Comprehensive Coverage of Grammar, Usage, and Mechanics

Building English Skills offers an exceptionally clear, thorough presentation of traditional grammar topics (see page T12).

Integration of Composition and Grammar

Composition and grammar are consistently interwoven to show students the practical application of grammar in writing (see page T14).

Related Communication Skills

Separate chapters at each level teach the related skills students need for effective communication and for successful learning in all subject areas (see page T16).

In-Depth Development of the Process of Writing

Building English Skills teaches the process of writing as a process of thinking and rethinking, writing and revising.

Building English Skills provides in-depth, continuous development of the process of writing. While many other programs simply require students to mimic the writing models in the text, *Building English Skills* develops the thinking and writing techniques students need to write independently. Writing is taught as an ongoing decision-making process, so that students learn to make choices in their writing. A special chapter in each text teaches the stages of the process of writing: pre-writing, writing, and revising. Students then apply these skills consistently to every type of writing throughout the composition chapters.

The Philosophy

All teachers are aware of the difficulties some students have when asked to compose a paragraph or composition. The products of such assignments often seem to indicate that the writers have little ability to express thoughts clearly, develop content adequately, or organize ideas into a logical presentation. In reality, the problem is often not one of ability, but of technique. The students may simply never have been taught what writing really is, or the best way to approach it.

One of the biggest handicaps in writing is the tendency to view it in terms of a final product rather than as an ongoing process. In other words, many students are, in effect, beginning the writing process at the end. There is little or no planning of ideas, and only a superficial revision of content. Such an approach invariably results in a poor piece of writing, as well as a frustrated writer.

It is important to make students recognize that few people know exactly what they want to say when they begin a piece of writing. In fact, it is usually the act of writing itself that enables us to discover exactly what it is we are thinking or feeling. As ideas are written down, worked, and reworked, they begin to crystallize in our own mind. Only then are we able to begin developing and organizing them with any confidence.

Since this is the case, writing must be viewed as a thinking process. It is a means of finding out what we want to say and then deciding on the best way to say it. This belief is the cornerstone of the entire writing philosophy of *Building English Skills*. The text teaches students to approach writing with the understanding that writing is a *process* of thinking and rethinking, writing and revising. A summary of the process is provided below.

The Process

1. Pre-Writing. The pre-writing stage can also be called the planning stage. It is one of the most basic and essential parts of the writing process. The purposes of the pre-writing stage are to explore possibilities for topics and presentation, and to begin gathering and organizing the details that will be used to develop the main idea. To help students accomplish these goals, the teacher should encourage them to complete the following pre-writing steps every time they write:

1. Choose and narrow a topic.
2. Decide on the purpose of writing.
3. Identify the audience who will read the final version.
4. Gather details that develop the topic and suit

the purpose and audience.
5. Put the ideas into a logical order.

The teacher should also remind students that pre-writing is only a way to begin sorting through ideas, and that the notes made at this stage of the process may be modified, changed, or deleted altogether.

2. Writing the First Draft. The purpose of a first draft is basically to get some ideas down on paper. Even as they write this draft, students will find that they are discovering new ideas and refining others. This will lead to a need to re-evaluate other aspects of the writing, such as organization and the choice of supporting details. A first draft, therefore, is simply that— the first attempt by the writer to find out what he or she wants to say. A student should be prepared to work through several versions of any piece of writing before reaching a final product.

It is important that students learn not to break the flow of ideas at this point to worry about grammar, usage, and mechanics. There will be time to concentrate on these later, during the revision process.

3. Rewriting, or Revising. Some writers make the mistake of equating revision with proofreading. Although checking for errors in grammar, usage, and mechanics is important, the greatest part of revising time should actually be spent on content. As previously noted, the first draft is primarily a way of discovering the ideas that are to be used. The most crucial part of writing occurs on successive drafts, during the revision process. When revising, a student should do the following:

1. Check to see that all ideas and details are related to the topic and purpose.
2. Refine good ideas, and add any new ones that could improve the writing.
3. Make certain that the purpose is clear.
4. Refine the organization of the ideas.
5. Check to see that the sentences flow smoothly.

6. Check for a consistent tone and mood.
7. Make sure that the language and content are suitable for the audience.
8. Substitute vivid words for vague language.
9. Proofread for errors in grammar, usage, and mechanics.

Students should be made to see that revising a piece of writing is like working with a clay statue—the material is constantly reshaped until the desired result is achieved.

4. Preparing the Final Copy. Only after the first three steps are completed should a student consider making the final copy. This version incorporates all of the improvements of the rest of the process.

One important point needs to be made about the process of writing as taught in this book. To aid student understanding, the process is often presented in a step-by-step manner. However, the teacher should make certain that the students always treat writing as a circular process. In other words, a writer should be prepared to work on any element of a piece of writing at any time.

The Follow-Through

Throughout the student texts, students are called upon to apply the process of writing to all of their writing tasks. Such consistent follow-through is imperative if students are to improve their writing habits. See pages T8–T11 of this Teacher's Edition for examples from the student texts.

Another important aspect of follow-through must be the area of evaluation. Evaluation of student writing is a crucial part of the teaching of writing. See pages T20–T23 for a thorough presentation of **Guidelines for Evaluating Composition.**

For a further, detailed discussion of the teaching of writing, refer to the separate booklet **Teaching and Evaluating Student Writing.**

Pre-Writing

With *Building English Skills*, students learn and apply all pre-writing skills, including choosing and narrowing a topic, determining audience and purpose, researching supporting information, and gathering and organizing ideas.

Choosing a subject

Detailed guidelines and practical techniques help students choose a writing topic.

Narrowing the subject

Students learn to focus on a topic narrow enough to be covered within a specified length.

Determining audience

The series makes students aware of audience as an important pre-writing consideration.

Part 2 Pre-Writing: Deciding on a Subject

The first step in writing a composition is to choose a subject. When you are doing so, keep these three guidelines in mind:

1. *Choose a subject that interests you.* This is important. Without interest on your part, you will have a difficult time creating interest on the part of your readers.
2. *Choose a subject that is familiar to you.* You will then be able to write with confidence about your subject.
3. *Choose a subject that has value for you.* You will then com-
ng of value to your readers.

ubjects that are interesting, familiar, and
clings, ideas, knowledge, and memories.

Part 3 Pre-Writing: Narrowing the Subject

In your study of the paragraph, you learned that an idea must be narrow enough to be developed adequately within the limits of the paragraph. The same holds true for the composition. The topic must be narrow enough to be covered in a few paragraphs.

Sometimes a subject based on first-hand experience does not need to be narrowed if a writer has a specific incident in mind. On the other hand, a subject in which you have a general interest or knowledge may be too broad for a composition. Your hobby may be collecting butterflies, but, unfocused, this subject would be too broad for a short composition. Brainstorming might help you to identify possible composition topics within this subject:

Identifying Butterflies
Capturing and Mounting Butterflies
Catching a Monarch
The Joys of Butterfly Collecting

The subject "Video Games" is also too broad for a composition. Again, the writer must decide on a specific topic. Some possibilities include the time spent on video games, the money spent on video games, the types of video games, or the writer's favorite video game. By choosing one of these specific topics, you could cover the material in a few paragraphs, as did the writer of the following composition.

TOO MUCH MONEY!

Almost anyone could use an extra $100. This is the amount a person would spend in a year by playing video games at the rate of $2.00 a week. If the player regularly spends more than that amount, as many do, the total can skyrocket. Although many people like the games, some are also worried that they are spending too much money on them. They also wonder *why* they spend so much. Actually, there are several simple reasons why players spend more than they should on video games.

189

Part 4 Pre-Writing: Deciding on the Audience and the Purpose

Before you begin to develop a plan for your composition, you must answer two questions.

1. For whom are you writing the composition?
2. What is your purpose for writing?

Your Audience. You should know two things about your readers. First, you should know their approximate age. The need for this information is clear. If, for example, your readers will be very young, you must use simple words, avoid difficult ideas, and explain your ideas very carefully.

Second, you should know the readers' familiarity with your subject. This will influence the amount and difficulty of the information you can include. It will also determine the number and types of explanations and definitions that you must give.

Your Purpose. Before developing a plan for your composition, decide whether you want to tell a story; to describe an object, place, or person; or to explain something. You must decide whether you want your readers to cry, to laugh, or to think seriously about an idea.

A one-sentence **statement of purpose** might help you to clarify your topic and goal. This statement is for your own guidance only. It will not be included in your composition. Here are three examples of such statements:

1. In my composition I will *explain* why it is important to take part in extracurricular activities.
2. In my composition I will *describe* the three most beautiful areas of Yellowstone Park.
3. In my composition I will *tell a story about* a humorous incident that happened on my first day of high school.

Later, when you write the introduction for your composition, you may wish to include a more formal version of this statement. It will then become the **thesis statement** of your composition.

191

Determining purpose

Students learn to identify a purpose for their writing and develop their subject accordingly.

Gathering ideas

Students learn several methods for gathering or researching details to develop a topic.

Organizing information

The text teaches students to look for relationships among ideas and to arrange these ideas in an effective order.

Writing the First Draft

Students explore different approaches and shape their ideas by putting their thoughts down on paper.

Concentrating on meaning

The emphasis in this stage is on content rather than form. Students learn to allow their ideas to flow without concern for mechanical details.

Developing the topic

Students develop the topic by adding relevant details and deleting unrelated items.

Achieving unity and coherence

The series shows students a variety of techniques for achieving unity and coherence in their writing.

Revising

In *Building English Skills*, students learn revision as a two-step process: revising for content and proofreading for errors in mechanics. Checklists provide criteria to guide students in evaluation and revision. Revision techniques become more detailed in the upper grades as students are more able to concentrate on the finer points.

Marking content changes

The revised copy shows the rethinking, replacing, and reorganizing that are all parts of revising.

Part 7   Revising the Composition

This is the stage of the writing process where you are concerned with getting everything just right! At this point, you want to select the most vivid word or phrase, strengthen your organization, and check the unity and coherence.

To keep your concentration focused during this stage, you may find that the best solution is a many-part revision process. Since you will want to check and revise your ideas, word choice, unity, coherence, and level of language, try looking over your draft several times. Correct problems in just one or two areas at a time.

Chapter 7, "The Process of Writing" and the Guidelines for Writing and Revising Compositions on page 212 will help you focus your revisions and do a thorough job.

The writer of "Music: The Universal Language" made many revisions in her rough draft, as shown on the next page.

Analysis of the Revision

The changes that the writer made in her revised draft improved her composition in many ways.

1. Vivid, specific words have been added or have replaced weaker language. For instance, the writer has added "distinctive wails" to modify jazz and "torchy strains" to modify blues.

2. More formal language has replaced informal language. For instance, the writer deleted all uses of "you" in her paper. She also deleted the term "old folks" in paragraph two.

3. Unity has been strengthened. For instance, the word "universal" now appears in the title, the introduction, and the conclusion. The addition of "reflecting all time periods and cultures," to the topic sentence in the third body paragraph ties it more closely to the introduction, too.

4. Coherence is strengthened by adding transitional words and phrases such as "still later in life" in the first body paragraph.

MUSIC: THE UNIVERSAL LANGUAGE

is a unique collection of

Every person has special opinions, tastes, ideas, and beliefs. No two people like the same things or feel the same way. Yet there is one thing that all people enjoy — music. Music is an universal boundaries art that ignores age, culture, and time.

(handwritten revision marks throughout)

Even if you remote a famous composer and even if you don't like orchestra concerts, music is still a part of you. Almost as soon as they are steady on their feet, toddlers begin "dancing" by moving in time to the rhythm of music. As these babies get older, there will be rhythm bands in school campfire singalong or jam sessions with friends. Music on the radio or stereo will become a companion for work around the house or for travel. Finally, for old folks, the strains of certain tunes will recall memories of times gone by.

Music touches us all because it evokes a lot of feeling. One person may be touched by a sorrowful selection of mendelssohn. Another person may get that same feeling when Barry Manilow sings This Song's for you. Music can also bring joy. Who can resist feeling good when a rythmic tune like Jump Shout Boogie bounces across the air waves? And of course, music can effect love. Music edifies the soul. Person long for another. Not only do we all like music, we all take part in it's creation. Some of us can do no more than hum off key, but we have still made a contribution. So have other people. Folk melodies remain with us from a long time ago. Bach and Handel sent us music from Europe. South Americans gave us the tango and rhumba. Black Americans gave us jazz and the blues.

209

Guidelines for Writing and Revising Compositions

As you write a composition, follow the steps in Guidelines for the Process of Writing on page 122. Use the following Guidelines as you revise your first draft.

1. Has the subject been narrowed to a topic that can be covered in a few paragraphs?
2. Does the composition deal with a single topic or idea?
3. Does it have an introduction, a body, and a conclusion?
4. Does the introduction present the main idea? Does it catch the reader's interest?
5. Does the body explain or support the main idea?
6. Does the conclusion restate the main idea, summarize the information, or comment upon it?
7. Do the paragraphs work together to develop a single topic or idea that is the subject of the composition?
8. Is the composition appropriate for the audience for which it is intended? Is the purpose clear?
9. Are the ideas presented in a clear, logical order?
10. Does the composition have unity? Are the supporting ideas in each paragraph related to the topic sentence? Is each paragraph directly related to the main idea in the introductory paragraph?
11. Does the composition have coherence? Are there transitional devices that tie the paragraphs together?
12. Is the title meaningful and interesting?

Revising for content

In revising, students first look at content. They check their drafts several times for ideas, word choice, unity, coherence, and level of language.

Analysis of revised copy

Students analyze the thinking process that goes into any good revision.

Following guidelines for revising

A checklist directs students in checking for interest, clarity, organization, and sense.

Special feature of the Teacher's Edition

Lesson suggestions offer numerous group activities and teacher-directed techniques to use in revising.

Proofreading

Proofreading is presented as a necessary step following revising for content. Checklists help students make sure that the writing will be clear to their audience.

Making a final copy

Students make a final copy, incorporating all changes and corrections.

Proofreading symbols

Students use basic proofreading symbols throughout the revision process.

Guidelines for the Process of Writing

This chart is a handy reference tool for students to use in all their writing.

Proofreading Checklist

The proofreading checklist provides a handy summary of proofreading steps.

Special feature of the Teacher's Edition

A discussion of two types of evaluation (holistic and analytic), and guidelines for evaluation are provided in this Teacher's Edition. (See pages T20–T23 on Evaluating Composition.)

Sample page 210

Proofreading

Many errors in grammar, capitalization, punctuation, and spelling will be corrected during revision. However, you must still proofread your revised draft specifically for these types of errors. Use the proofreading symbols on page 124 as the writer of the sample composition did. The following paragraph shows some of the errors the writer found during this final check.

> Music touches us all because it evokes a multitude of feeling. One person may be deeply affected by a sorrowful selection of mendelssohn. Another person may get that same feeling when Barry Manilow sings This Song's for you. Music can also bring joy. Few people can resist feeling elated when a spirited rythmic tune like Jump Shout Boogie bounces across the air waves. And of course, music can enhance love. How many times has a special song made one person long for another.

When you are satisfied with your composition, make a final, neat copy. Use whatever heading your teacher directs. Below is the final version of the composition on music.

MUSIC: THE UNIVERSAL LANGUAGE

Every person is a unique collection of opinions, tastes, ideas, and beliefs. No two people like exactly the same things or feel precisely the same way about an issue. Yet there is one thing that all people enjoy, and which is an important part of almost everyone's life—music. Music is a universal art that ignores boundaries of age, culture, and time.

Not everyone is a famous composer or an orchestra concert buff, yet music is still important to each one of us, no matter what our age. Almost as soon as they are steady on their feet, toddlers begin "dancing" by moving in time to the rhythm of the music. As these babies get older, they take

210

Sample page 122

Guidelines for the Process of Writing

Pre-Writing

1. Select a topic that interests you.
2. Narrow the topic until it can be thoroughly developed in a specified length.
3. Decide on your purpose.
4. Use your understanding of purpose and audience to determine your type of language and choice of details.
5. Gather and list details that you could use to develop your topic.
6. Evaluate and organize your list of details. Delete unrelated ideas. Add new ones. Put your details into a logical order.

Writing the First Draft

1. Keeping your audience and purpose in mind, begin to write.
2. Let your thoughts flow freely. Modify your initial plans for content and organization, if necessary. Do not be too concerned with grammar and mechanics at this point.

Revising

Read what you have written. Answer the following questions:

1. Did you stick to your topic?
2. Did you include everything you wanted to?
3. Are there any unnecessary or unrelated details?
4. Is each main idea clearly expressed and thoroughly developed?
5. Do your ideas flow smoothly?
6. Is your writing organized logically, with a beginning, a middle, and an end? Are the ideas presented in an order that makes sense?
7. Is your writing interesting and lively? Is there variety in the type and structure of your sentences?
8. Is each word vivid and precise?
9. Do the language and content suit your audience?
10. Have you accomplished your purpose?

Revise as necessary. Then proofread your work, using the checklist on page 123.

122

Sample page 123

Proofreading Checklist

Proofread your paper, by answering the questions below. Additional instruction on each concept may be found in the indicated Sections.

Grammar and Usage

Are there any sentence fragments or run-ons? (Sect. 1, 2)
Have you used the correct form of each pronoun? (Sect. 4)
Have you used verb tenses correctly? (Sect. 5)
Have you used adjectives and adverbs correctly? (Sect. 6)
Do all verbs agree with their subjects? (Sect. 10)
Are compound and complex sentences written and punctuated correctly? (Sect. 11)

Capitalization

Did you capitalize first words and all proper nouns and adjectives? (Sect. 13)
Are titles capitalized correctly? (Sect. 13)

Punctuation

Does each sentence have the proper end mark? (Sect. 14)
Are end marks, such as colons, semicolons, apostrophes, hyphens, and quotation marks used correctly? (Sect. 14)

Spelling

Did you check all unfamiliar words in the dictionary? (Sect. 15)
Are plurals and possessive forms spelled correctly? (Sect. 3, 15)

Form

Were corrections made neatly? (Sect. 16)
In your final copy, is the writing legible?
Have you used the proper heading and margins?
Did you follow all points of good manuscript form?

123

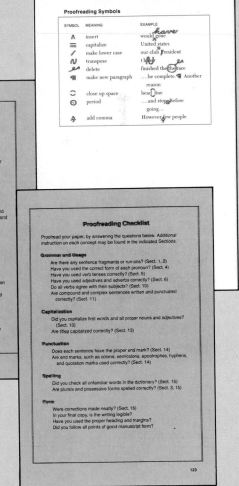

Proofreading Symbols

SYMBOL	MEANING	EXAMPLE
∧	insert	would have gone
≡	capitalize	United states
/	make lower case	our club President
∼	transpose	thier
ℰ	delete	finished the the race
¶	make new paragraph	...be complete. ¶ Another reason
⌒	close up space	head line
⊙	period	...and stop Before going...
⋀	add comma	However few people

Comprehensive Coverage of Grammar, Usage, and Mechanics

Building English Skills offers an exceptionally clear, thorough presentation of traditional grammar topics.

In *Building English Skills,* topics are introduced with precise explanations, illustrated with appropriate models, and immediately applied in practice exercises. The flexible, self-contained format allows for developmental teaching, skills review, or student reference.

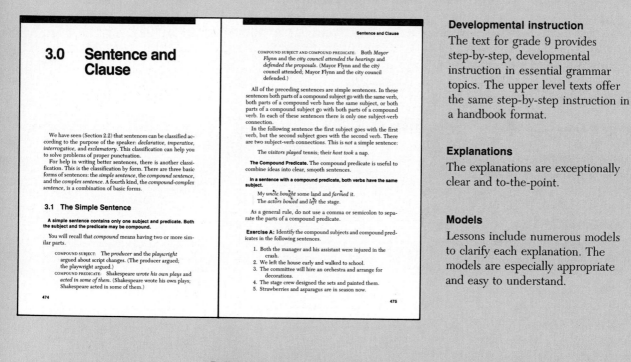

Developmental instruction

The text for grade 9 provides step-by-step, developmental instruction in essential grammar topics. The upper level texts offer the same step-by-step instruction in a handbook format.

Explanations

The explanations are exceptionally clear and to-the-point.

Models

Lessons include numerous models to clarify each explanation. The models are especially appropriate and easy to understand.

Definitions

The text highlights important definitions and rules in boldface type for easy reference.

Abundant exercises

Section parts include two or more sets of exercises that test mastery of the skill being taught.

Success-directed practice

The first set of exercises gives students confidence and practice in applying the skill; following sets provide more challenging practice.

1.1 The Noun

Certain words in the language are used as labels. We use them to identify people, places, things, and ideas.

A noun is the name of a person, place, thing, or idea.

Things include such visible items as *clothes, trees,* and *chairs.* Things may also be items that we perceive with our other senses: *smells, sounds, tastes.* Ideas include all things, such as *beliefs, theories,* and *emotions,* that exist inside the minds of people.

PERSONS	PLACES	THINGS	IDEAS
Matt Dillon	Boston	baseball	love
friend	country	amplifier	charity
priest	arcade	prayer	democracy

A **common noun** is the name of a whole group of persons, places, things, or ideas. It is a name that is common to an entire group: *animal, dish, apple, tent.*

A **proper noun** is the name of an individual person, place, thing, or idea.

A proper noun always begins with a capital letter.

COMMON NOUNS	PROPER NOUNS
dancer	Maria Tallchief
bridge	Golden Gate Bridge
continent	Africa
business	Columbia Pictures
language	Spanish

As the above list shows, some nouns, especially proper nouns, may consist of more than one word. Each word in a proper noun is capitalized.

Any word that can be immediately preceded by *the* is a noun: *the* bridge, *the* dog, *the* language. Most proper nouns, but not all _____ odome, *the* Buick,

---

Exercise A: Find all the nouns in the following sentences.

1. The announcer said that the plane for Minneapolis would leave in thirty minutes.
2. Maria Mayer, an American physicist, won the Nobel Prize.
3. John wanted to change the ribbon on his typewriter, but the ribbon would not cooperate.
4. There was a scream of skidding tires and then a metallic thud, followed by the sound of splintered glass.
5. The tourists gathered together at the foot of the Eiffel Tower for a snapshot.
6. The boys and their mother drove through the desert at night.
7. Helen is president of the class, and her brother Philip is the recording secretary.
8. Al wrote a paper about Babe Didrikson and her life in sports.
9. Half of the people in the world can neither read nor write.
10. Andrew Wyeth is well known for his paintings of rural scenes.

Exercise B: Decide which are common nouns and which are proper nouns. Write the proper nouns, beginning each with a capital letter.

1. german, science, language, english
2. lake, lake erie, mountain, mount everest
3. park, joshua national monument, gulf, cape cod
4. village, fairfield township, country
5. labor, labor day, good friday, birthday
6. senator nancy kassebaum, mayor tom bradley, state representative
7. judge, justice thurgood marshall, judge shirley m. hufstedler
8. uncle harry, bridge, rittenhouse square, gettysburg battlefield
9. cathedral, rabbi, saint patrick's cathedral, church
10. college, purdue university, sawyer business college, vocational school

---

REINFORCEMENT EXERCISES
Adjective and Adverb Usage

A. Use adjectives and adverbs correctly. Correct any errors in the use of modifiers. Three sentences are already correct.

1. A lone swan flew graceful over the marshes.
2. That incoming wave is moving fast.
3. After all of those _____ tasted sourly.
4. Many of the passe _____
5. Your chimney mu _____
6. The baking fish s _____
7. The President's n _____ simultaneous
8. Charlece felt unc _____
9. The team of hors _____
10. Hold tight and try _____

B. Use troublesome _____ graph, correcting all adv _____

My brother and _____
neighbor to let us _____
good together and _____
than some professi _____
we headed to the h _____
told us that we sho _____
we wouldn't have t _____
him, "We want to u _____
handled brushes. S _____
them eight-foot co _____
good when our nei _____
turned to her and _____
the brushes landed _____
get two black eyes _____

622

Reinforcement exercises

Additional exercises appearing at the end of each section can be used for more practice on a specific topic, or as a review.

CUMULATIVE REVIEW
The Sentence (III)

Writing Different Types of Sentences. Rewrite each sentence on your own paper. Follow the directions given in parentheses.

1. The Y.M.C.A. offers several aerobics classes. (Change the active verb to a passive verb.)
2. Some students discovered the bones of a saber-toothed tiger. (Add a prepositional phrase to modify *students.*)
3. Would you like to meet the celebrated author? (Change this simple sentence to a complex sentence by adding a clause beginning with a relative pronoun.)
4. Maria wished a safe voyage to everyone. (Change this N V N sentence to one with a N V N N pattern.)
5. One of the actors forgot his lines. (Change the form of the verb from past to past participle.)
6. Martin's hobby was speleology. Speleology is the scientific study of caves. (Change these two sentences to one sentence by using an appositive phrase.)
7. Barbara likes painting brightly-colored abstract designs. (Change the gerund phrase to an infinitive phrase.)
8. Carl jogged for two miles along the path, and Sandi ran with him. (Change this compound sentence to a simple sentence with a compound subject.)
9. The circus had to refund the money for the tickets. (Add an adverb clause.)
10. The early American pioneers did not have sophisticated tools. They could build a log house in a matter of days. (Change these two sentences into one compound sentence by using the conjunctive adverb *nevertheless.*)

558

Mixed review

Each section includes a mixed review that covers all major concepts taught in that section. The review can be used as independent work or as a test of chapter content.

Cumulative review

Eight cumulative reviews appear at intervals in the grammar half of each text to further reinforce both grammar and writing skills.

MIXED REVIEW
Agreement of Subject and Verb

A. Choose the standard form of the verb for _____

1. A pile of rocks (is, are) blocking Centr _____
2. My backpack, together with its conten _____ over twenty pounds.
3. Each of these towns (has, have) a year _____
4. One of the new cars (gets, get) over si _____
5. Everybody (expects, expect) to be trea _____
6. Fruit or fruit juice (makes, make) a nu _____
7. The editors or the art director (design _____
8. Around the grounds of the park (strut _____
9. There (is, are) many ski areas in Color _____
10. How (does, do) artists make stained g _____
11. Hawaii (is, are) actually several islands _____
12. Creativity and enjoyment (is, are) the _____
13. Les (doesn't, don't) read any magazine _____
14. The choir (sings, sing) at a special spr _____
15. Gymnastics (requires, require) precise _____
16. "Hill Street Blues" (has, have) high vi _____
17. Sixteen dollars (is, are) the price of th _____
18. Three-quarters of an hour (is, are) the _____
19. These boots are made of material that _____
20. Laverne is one of several class officers _____ meeting with the principal.

B. Choose the correct verb for each of the f _____

1. Marc Chagall's *Four Seasons* (was, were) installed in Chicago in 1974.
2. Everyone who (thinks, think) that a reporter's life is romantic should spend time working on a newspaper.
3. There (is, are) some problems that can't be solved without the help of others.

577

T13

Integration of Composition and Grammar

Composition and grammar are consistently interwoven to show students the practical application of grammar in writing.

In order to achieve a logical, developmental presentation of skills, the text divides concepts into two sections: composition and related skills are presented in the first half; grammar, usage, and mechanics skills are covered in the second half.

In the composition section, students are encouraged to refer to useful topics in the grammar section. In the grammar sections, numerous writing exercises allow students to practice the grammar concepts in a practical context.

4.0 Complete Sentences

Through study and practice, you can learn to write effective and forceful sentences. However, you must learn to avoid two kinds of sentence error: (1) the sentence fragment, and (2) the run-on sentence. Both of these errors cause confusion.

Uncompleted sentences are more often a problem in writing than in speaking. If you use an uncompleted sentence in speaking people can interrupt and ask you what you mean. In writing, however, your reader will simply have to wonder what you meant. This is why you must correct all uncompleted sentences during the revision stage of the writing process.

4.1 Fragments Resulting from Incomplete Thought

An uncompleted sentence is called a **sentence fragment**. It is only a part, or fragment, of a sentence.

You can think much faster than you can write. Many of your sentence errors, if you make them, happen because your mind has raced ahead of your hand. You have started to write a second thought before you have finished writing the first. Or, perhaps in haste, you have left out a key word necessary for a complete sentence. Suppose you intended to say something like this:

In 1939, Ike was a colonel. After war broke out, he soon became commander of American forces in Europe. He later led all Allied forces.

507

Complete Sentences

In the hurry to get on with your writing, however, what you put down was something like this:

In 1939, Ike was a colonel. After he soon became commander of American forces in Europe. He later led all Allied forces.

The second group of words is not a sentence. It causes confusion. The reader may suppose that you meant to say Ike was a colonel after he became commander of American forces in Europe.

Exercise A: Writing Find the sentence fragments. Add the words needed to make each fragment a sentence.

1. The same size as a human child and just as curious
2. A program just like several others
3. After reaching the top of the hill
4. Most of the world's great books available in inexpensive paperback editions
5. Mr. Walters, one of the oldest residents in the city
6. The huge trucks rolling along the nation's highways all night long
7. Finally, in a corner of the garage, the missing boxes
8. Nothing in the newspapers about the robbery
9. There is a reward. Anyone who finds the valuable bracelet
10. After working hard all day, a little relaxation

Exercise B: Writing Three of the groups of words in the following paragraph are sentences. The rest are fragments. Rewrite the paragraph. Add words to make the fragments into sentences.

Ghost towns all across the country. Pithole, Pennsylvania, one of the most famous. It flourished for a brief ten years. For a time, 20,400 people in the town. Everyone left quickly when the oil wells dried up. Elsewhere, ghost towns in timber country. Modern ghost towns in the iron-mining regions of Minnesota. The most famous of all in the mining sections of the West. Houses full of furniture and offices with papers in the desks. Wherever the resources gave out, there are ghost towns.

508

Section introductions

Section introductions present grammar concepts in the context of writing to help students understand the relationship between grammar and writing.

Writing exercises

Writing exercises follow grammar lessons to show students how the correct application of grammar concepts can improve their writing.

Using grammar in writing

Writing activities following each grammar section apply the skill or concepts taught in the lesson.

USING GRAMMAR IN WRITING
The Parts of a Sentence

A. Imagine that you are one of the first civilian passengers aboard a space shuttle. You have been asked to write your impressions of the space flight for NASA's archives. Write the first paragraph of this report, describing your take-off. Use all four kinds of sentences: declarative, imperative, interrogative, and exclamatory.

B. Read the following skeleton of a story. Identify the sentence pattern of each of the sentences. Then, expand and finish the story by adding your own infinitive, participial, appositive, gerund, or prepositional phrases. Underline and label each phrase that you add. Notice how much more interesting the story becomes.

The moon was full.
The Arctic air was bitter.
A dog sled crossed the frozen landscape.
No village was in sight.
Suddenly, the driver slumped forward.
The lead husky howled and stopped in his tracks.
The dog escaped from its harness.
It ran for miles.
Eventually, it found our camp.
We followed the dog.
We rescued its owner.

C. Writers must tailor the length and complexity of their sentences to suit different audiences. Write a short magazine article about an interesting subject, such as the Loch Ness monster. Assume that you are writing for a children's magazine. Make all of your sentences short and simple, with no unusual subject-verb order. Now rewrite your article for an adult magazine. This time, vary the subject-verb order. Experiment with starting your sentences using different types of phrases.

473

Using mechanics in writing

Extra pages give students practice in using capitalization, punctuation, spelling, and other mechanics rules in their writing.

Lively writing exercises

A variety of fresh, original writing activities stimulates student interest while reinforcing the concepts taught.

USING MECHANICS IN WRITING
Capitalization

You can quickly gain insights about a person by asking him or her the right types of questions. Interview four people whom you consider to be interesting personalities. Ask these questions:

1. What is your age?
2. What is your occupation or area of interest?
3. What part of the country are you from?
4. Would you describe yourself as ordinary, different, unique?
5. Which modern figures do you most admire?
6. What magazines or newspapers do you read?
7. What two books and two musical recordings would you take with you to a desert island?
8. What is your favorite movie or television show?

Choose the person whose answers most interest you. Write a short composition analyzing his or her interests and background. Do they fit the type of person that you perceived this individual to be? Be sure to capitalize according to the rules presented in this Section.

B. Imagine that you are the winner of a sweepstakes contest. You will be given the foreign vacation of your dreams. The contest rules state that you must submit a letter containing the following information:

1. What two countries would you most like to visit?
2. What languages are spoken there?
3. What geographical features (mountains, rivers, waterfalls, and the like) attract you to these
4. What cities or towns would you like to visit the
5. What sights would you like to see in these coun

Research the countries of your choice in the library. W ter based on this research. One country may be the U

668

Special feature of the Teacher's Edition

In composition chapters, the Teacher's Edition provides suggestions for integrating grammar sections into the composition lessons.

Part 1

Objective

To join two sentences of equal importance with *and, but,* or *or.*

Presenting the Lesson

1. Read and discuss **Joining Sentences** on page 66. Stress the idea that only sentences that express related ideas of equal importance should be joined by and, *but,* or *or.* Refer the students to Section 3.2 in the Handbook for more information on compound sentences.

2. Assign Exercises A and B on pages 66-67. You may wish to have students tell how the pairs of sentences are related in selected items.

Individualizing the Lesson

Less-Advanced Students

1. Call on volunteers to do the first three items of Exercise A on page 66 on the chalkboard. Make sure the combined sentences contain the proper punctuation. Then have students complete the exercise independently.

2. Do items 1 and 3 of Exercise B on page 67 orally.

Advanced Students

Ask the students to write a choppy, monotonous passage like the one on page 65. Then have them exchange papers and combine the sentences so the passage flows smoothly and is interesting.

Optional Practice

Have the students join each of the following pairs of sentences using *,and, ,or,* or *,but.*

66

Part 1   Joining Sentences

Often two sentences express similar ideas that are of equal importance. Such sentences can usually be joined by a comma and the word *and.*

Diane began work at noon. Sue joined her at one o'clock.
Diane began work at noon, *and* Sue joined her at one o'clock.

If two sentences express contrasting ideas of equal importance, they can often be joined by a comma and the word *but.*

I went to bed early. I could not get to sleep.
I went to bed early, *but* I could not get to sleep.

When two sentences express a choice between ideas of equal importance, they can often be joined by a comma and *or.*

Is Greg going to the game? Is he taking you to the movies?
Is Greg going to the game, *or* is he taking you to the movies?

Exercises Joining Sentences

A. Join each pair of sentences by following the directions in parentheses.

1. Will Tom be able to rejoin the team? Will he have to sit out the whole season? (Join with **, or.**)
2. I remembered the eggs. I forgot the butter. (Join with **, but.**)
3. Jane sanded the tabletop. Phil assembled the base. (Join with **, and.**)
4. Would help arrive in time? Would we be stranded on the mountaintop all night? (Join with **, or.**)
5. Rain began to fall in torrents. The players sprinted for the shelter of the dugout. (Join with **, and.**)
6. Lucille is not as fast as Joan. She has more endurance. (Join with **, but.**)
7. Pine is much less expensive than oak. It is not as sturdy. (Join with **, but.**)
8. My parents are on a business trip. I'm staying with Jeff's family. (Join with **, and.**)

66

Related Communication Skills

Separate chapters at each level teach the related skills students need for effective communication and for successful learning in all subject areas.

Part 3   The Levels of Language

"If we spoke as we write, we should find no one to listen; if we wrote as we speak, we should find no one to read."—T. S. ELIOT

No speaker or writer of English uses the language in the same way all the time. Instead, it is often necessary to vary the way [...] articular audience. For example, [...] when you are talking with your [...] are speaking in class, and perhaps [...] a speech or oral report. The same [...] ccurs in written material. The types [...] different occasions are called the [...]

[...] at all times and in all places is called [...] d guidelines of standard English [...] s of the language to communicate [...] fear of misunderstanding. This [...] nd guidelines for using standard [...]

[...] There are two accepted levels of [...] informal. Formal English is found [...]

Part 6   Applying Your Vocabulary Skills

You have now learned several useful methods for determining the meanings of unfamiliar words. The following exercises are much like the vocabulary questions on standardized tests—they will provide practice in using the methods that you have learned.

Section 1: *Learning Word Meanings from Context*. Use context clues to select the best definition for the italicized word in each passage. Write the letter that represents the best definition.

1. Ms. Bell prefers to spend her vacation in a *bucolic* place—a farm or a cabin in the woods.

(A) relating to a vacation, carefree   (C) relating [...] country [...]
(B) friendly   (D) far awa[...]

2. She did have one *idiosyncrasy*, a very od[...] tled new acquaintances.

(A) a foolish act   (C) hobby
(B) peculiar behavior   (D) strange acq[...]

3. Marietta likes the quiet of the library, a[...] *cacophony* of the cafeteria.

(A) clutter   (C) food
(B) crowd   (D) noise

4. The whale came into existence fairly recen[...] a truly *primordial* beast, has been around for mill[...]

(A) ancient   (C) wild
(B) frightening   (D) unknown

5. The minister's living quarters, or *manse*, w[...] the church.

(A) church   (C) pulpit
(B) congregation   (D) home

Part 4   Listening to and Evaluating Speeches

There are many occasions in which you will find it necessary or important to listen to speeches by other people. Some of these speeches will be informal such as lectures or instructions from a coach or employer. Some may be formal such as campaign speeches or church sermons. Whatever the occasion there are a few guidelines for good listening that you should always follow:

Listening Courteously

1. Do not speak when someone else is speaking.
2. Sit upright and direct your attention to the speaker.
3. Give the speaker positive feedback by using appropriate facial expressions and maintaining eye contact.
4. Take notes if appropriate.

Listening for Content

In order to get the most out of a speech, you must learn to recognize important points that a speaker is making. Listen for key words or phrases that signal the introduction of a major idea. Such signals are often similar to the transitional words used in a composition:

first   another   most importantly
next   similarly   in addition

If you are taking notes on the speech, jot down these main points. Then focus on how the speaker supports or develops each idea. This may help you to draw certain conclusions about the material. A strong, well-documented development, for example, may indicate a valid point or an idea worth accepting. A weak development that uses poor methods of argument or support may indicate that you should examine the ideas much more closely.

377

Language

The language strand teaches different levels and types of language. Students learn about language growth and change, dialects, specialized vocabularies, and levels of language.

Vocabulary

Vocabulary development chapters provide transferable skills—a basis for understanding and using new words. Students learn the various ways to determine meaning from context, through the analysis of word parts and by using the dictionary. In addition, application exercises familiarize students with standardized test format.

Speaking and Listening

Students learn to present, evaluate, and appreciate both formal and informal oral presentations. The texts also teach the specialized speaking and listening skills needed for group discussion. At the upper grades, students also learn about public speaking, simple debate, and parliamentary procedure.

Critical Thinking

As students develop critical thinking skills, they learn to analyze what they read and hear so that they can present their own ideas effectively. Skills include establishing facts, distinguishing fact from opinion, dealing with generalizations, detecting errors in reasoning, recognizing emotional appeal, and using inductive/deductive reasoning.

Study and Research Skills

The chapters on study and research skills include following directions, establishing study habits, organizing studies, taking notes, using the SQ3R study method, studying for tests, and taking tests. At the upper grades, special sections prepare students for the SAT and ACT tests, and include sample questions.

Life Skills

In addition to teaching students how to write letters and résumés, and how to fill out forms and applications, the texts provide real-life application of these skills. Students learn how to apply to colleges, look for employment, interview, and assess personal skills, interest, and potential.

Summary and Applications

A special page follows each composition chapter to summarize key concepts taught and to allow students to apply their writing skills across the curriculum.

Part 4 Discovering Errors in Reasoning

Reasoning is the process of drawing a conclusion from known information. Poor opinions often result from errors in reasoning. Such errors are called **fallacies.** The following fallacies are among the most common:

Circular Reasoning

… attempts to prove a statement by sim-
…ment in other words. This is called **cir**-
…tement "team sports are better than
… it's better to play with a team," is an
…ning. The speaker has not provided any
…argument. Instead, the initial statement
…n different words.

…ffect Fallacy

…pens after another event, people some-
…rst event caused the second. They make
…ugh there is no direct evidence proving
…elated. This error is a **fallacy of cause and**
… are based upon just such reasoning. For
…eaks a mirror and then has bad luck might
…irrors causes bad luck. However, the two
… unrelated.

…llacy

…that there are only two alternatives when
…, this is called the **either/or fallacy.** One
…fallacy is the remark "You're either with
…mark leaves out several possibilities. The
…might not have taken any side, or per-
…d points on both sides."

Part 4 Types of Test Questions

Once you understand the general strategies for test-taking, you can concentrate on some more specific ones. These strategies are determined by the types of tests and test questions you are dealing with. If you familiarize yourself with these questions and techniques, you will be able to complete tests more confidently.

The most common sort of examination is the **objective test.** Objective tests may consist of *multiple choice, true/false, matching, completion,* or *short answer questions.* Also common are **essay** questions on examinations. Each type of test question requires particular strategies.

Multiple Choice Questions

On **multiple choice** tests, the student is asked to choose the *best* answer from among a group of answers that are provided on the test. The strategies listed below are useful for completing multiple choice tests:

1. Read through all of the choices before deciding on your answer.
2. Always eliminate incorrect answers first.
3. Choose the most complete and accurate answer.
4. Be wary of choices that contain words such as *totally, ways, never, only,* or *forever.*
5. Pay particular attention to choices such as *none of the ab…* or *all of the above.*

EXAMPLE

Which of the following literary forms did *not* begin as part of the oral tradition?

    a. the epic   c. the ballad
    b. the novel   d. the folktale

304

Part 5 Résumés and Interviews

Writing letters and filling out forms are not the only business skills that you will need to develop. You must also learn to present yourself favorably through written résumés and personal interviews.

Writing a Résumé

A **résumé** is a list of your experience, education, and skills. Many schools and employers require résumés instead of, or in addition to, applications. Résumés serve as tools for narrowing a field of applicants. It is therefore essential for you to learn how to write a résumé that conveys a good impression of you.

As with any piece of writing, you may want to work through several drafts of your résumé. All résumés, however, should include the following information:

Personal Data. This section simply includes your name, address, and phone number, including the area code.

Objective. This is a short statement of your purpose. Are you seeking admission to a college or applying for a job? Your objective can be as broad or as narrow as you like.

  OBJECTIVE: Position as a sales trainee in a retail organization that gives opportunities for advancement to a position in management.

  OBJECTIVE: Salesperson in Sporting Goods Department of Johnson Brothers Company.

Experience. This section should include all paid employment. Also, you may wish to include volunteer jobs that you have held. Names of employers, addresses of the businesses, dates of employment, and job descriptions should be included. Always list your most recent job first, and work back to your first job. Do not be concerned if your experience seems a little sparse right now; you will be surprised how quickly it will increase in the next few years. Put this information in the following order:

352

SUMMARY AND APPLICATIONS   CHAPTER 4

1. Good writers make their work come alive by vividly describing how things look, taste, sound, feel, and smell.
2. Skillful use of the senses can make you a better writer. It will also strengthen your powers of observation in all subjects and situations.
3. Train yourself to be more aware of your senses by concentrating on one sense at a time. Record your sensory experiences in a journal.
4. When you write descriptions, use strong sensory words such as the ones included in this chapter.
5. Depending upon the purpose and the subject of your writing, you may concentrate on one sense or use several senses in combination with one another.

Applications in Other Subject Areas

History. Historians depend upon many sources to learn about the past. Among these, first-hand accounts are extremely important. These accounts often contain vivid sensory details that re-create the atmosphere surrounding an historical event. Find a first-hand account of an historical event in a history text, an autobiography, a journal, or a magazine article. Then list the important sensory details in the account.

Science. A scientist must have the ability to make detailed observations and to record them accurately. Select one of the following subjects or choose one of your own. Observe the subject carefully for at least fifteen minutes, jotting down notes on sensory details. Use as many of the senses as possible.

  a. an ant hill   d. a mixture of oil and water
  b. any animal at a zoo   e. a spider and its web
  c. a constellation   f. any science experiment

81

How To Use the Teacher's Edition

The Teacher's Edition provides clear, well-paced teaching aids for presenting, individualizing, and extending each lesson.

Full-size student pages

For ease in reading, the entire student text is reproduced full size.

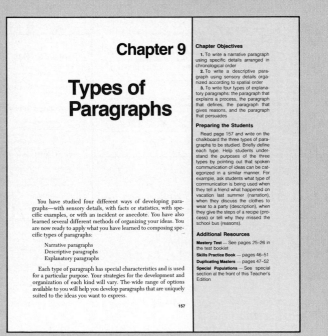

On-page teaching suggestions

All teaching suggestions are printed in the margins beside the student page.

Chapter objectives

Each chapter opener lists the skills to be mastered in the chapter.

Preparing the students

Suggested lessons or activities introduce students to the subject of the chapter.

Additional resources

A detailed list gives page references for extra practice, review, and testing materials.

Lesson objectives

Clear objectives are stated in terms of student performance.

Presenting the lesson

Step-by-step teaching strategies stress points of emphasis and suggest ways to use the exercises most effectively.

Individualizing

Specific teaching approaches are suggested for adjusting the basic lesson to different levels of ability or skill development.

Part 1

Objective

To choose and narrow a subject for a report

Presenting the Lesson

1. Read Choosing a Subject page 238. Stress the enormous amount of guidance students can receive through reference to a book or encyclopedia. Ask students if they can think of any other suitably narrow topics under the general topics "Japanese Culture" or "The Rodeo." Point out that it will be much easier to do research for a paper if the topic is narrowed from the beginning.

2. Assign Exercise A on page 239. Do the first two orally with the class, writing their suggestions for narrowed topics on the board. If the topics they suggest are still too broad, (for example, "famous American architects,") help them limit the topic even further ("Frank Lloyd Wright").

3. Assign Exercise B, page 239. Tell the class to spend time choosing their topics because they will write on one of the topics from this list later on in the chapter.

Individualizing the Lesson

Less-Advanced Students

Explain that some of the ways of limiting a general topic are to choose a specific example (Native Americans—Sitting Bull), to pick a particular time period (the British monarchy in 1603), or to pick a particular place (acupuncture at St. Luke's Hospital).

**Part 1 Pre-Writing:
Choosing a Subject**

When you are not assigned a specific topic for a report, your first step is to choose a subject. Make a list of subjects that interest you and that would be interesting to your readers. Remember that the subject you select should not have you as the main source of information.

Subjects based on learned information may need to be narrowed. In limiting your subject, keep two things in mind:

1. the amount of information available on the subject
2. the length of your report

At this stage, it is sometimes helpful to consult a general encyclopedia article on your subject or the index of a book dealing with your subject. Checking either of these may provide possibilities for limited subjects.

Consider, for example, the subject "Japanese Culture." It is so broad that to develop it would take an entire book at least. Even if the subject were narrowed to "Japanese Culture in the Twentieth Century," it would still be too broad for a short, five-paragraph report.

The general topic "Japanese Culture" does, however, contain a number of possible report topics. Examination of a book or article on Japan might yield the following ideas:

Japanese Family Relationships	A Japanese Garden
The Japanese New Year Celebration	Koto Music of Japan
Residential Architecture in Japan	Japanese *No* Theater

Many more topics could be added to the list. Each could be developed adequately in a short report.

Another example of a subject that is too broad for a short report is "The Rodeo." A little research, however, could provide these topic possibilities:

The Ropers	Steer Wrestling
Bronc Riding	The Bull Ride
Barrel Racing	History of the Rodeo

238

---

3. Use of undefined or unclear terms. Sometimes a word has no one, clear definition. Its meaning may vary depending on the speaker or the situation. Such words should be avoided unless they are clearly defined. Many snarl words and purr words **full** into this category.

WEAK OPINION: Libraries should carry only the *right* kind of books.

ANALYSIS: *Right* in what sense? *Right* for whom? *Right* in what circumstance? Because the meaning of the word *right* is not clear in the context of this sentence, the statement itself has little or no meaning.

In matters of personal taste, everyone is entitled to his or her opinion. Some people like comedies; some people like dramas. Some people like solitude; some people like being in groups. When expressing personal tastes, it is permissible to use snarl words, purr words, and vague, undefined judgment words like *wonderful* or *beautiful*. However, it is important to remember that personal tastes are not facts. You cannot expect other people to share them.

Exercises

A. All of the following statements are opinions. Identify those opinions that can never become facts and those opinions that may eventually become facts.

1. Scientists can find a cure for cancer.
2. Every home needs a computer.
3. Algebra is much easier than geometry.
4. Lilacs smell better than roses.
5. Solar energy is the most efficient and practical energy source to use.
6. Abraham Lincoln was as great a President as Thomas Jefferson.
7. Visiting New York City is more interesting than visiting Washington, D.C.
8. There is life on other planets.

269

C. Ask several students to perform their dialogues with a partner, and have the rest of the class analyze the weaknesses of the arguments.

Optional Practice

Ask the students to rewrite the opinions in Exercise B, eliminating overstatements, "snarl" and "purr" words, and undefined or unclear terms.

Extending the Lesson

Have students write dialogue for conversations they remember that included a difference of opinion. You may also want to tape such conversations from a TV show. Discuss the dialogues, tell whether the opinions were presented as facts or expressions of personal taste.

Optional practice

Additional teaching ideas are provided for drill, review, or reinforcement.

Extending the lesson

The text suggests an enrichment lesson or exercise that applies the concepts outside the English classroom.

Answers

For convenience, exercise answers are printed on or beside the student page.

Guidelines for Evaluating Composition

Adapted from *Teaching and Evaluating Student Writing,*
copyright © 1985 by McDougal, Littell & Company

Most educators would agree that constant, helpful evaluation of student writing is the only way to help young writers develop their skills. For many teachers, however, this "helpful" feedback has come to mean endless amounts of time spent with a stack of papers and a red pencil, marking every incorrect spelling or misplaced comma. Such an evaluation is suffered through for the good of the students. Yet how much does this evaluation system aid the developing writer?

When a child is learning to talk, a parent will accept and respond to single words or incomplete phrases, recognizing that the child has a message to communicate even if the form of the message is undeveloped. Similarly, when a student is learning to write, he or she needs the encouragement of a response to a written message, no matter what the form of that message is. A teacher cannot afford to require correct sentence structure, grammar, capitalization, punctuation, and spelling before looking at the ideas in a piece of writing.

The practical classroom application of these ideas, advanced by recent research into the writing process, is that students should be given opportunities to write as frequently as possible and that they be given some evaluation of the sense and style of their writing as frequently as possible. This emphasis on quantity means that some teachers may need to rethink their evaluation procedures.

Types of Evaluation

In order to give student writers the constant practice and feedback they need, teachers must have a practical method of evaluation. Obviously, if the student will be writing constantly, a teacher cannot be expected to evaluate each piece in a line-by-line, word-by-word manner. Nor would such an evaluation necessarily be useful to the developing writer. It is therefore suggested that a teacher learn to use two different evaluation methods—the holistic method and the more detailed analytic method.

Holistic evaluation of writing is a quick, guided method of rating pieces of writing. It can best be used to evaluate daily writing samples or first drafts of more complex pieces. With holistic evaluation, an evaluator reads the written piece as a whole, considers certain features, and immediately assigns a grade. The grade may be a single rating for the entire piece of writing or a set of ratings for the different features being considered.

The evaluation form provided on page T23 of this Teacher's Edition is of this second type of holistic evaluation, but will also guide teachers who wish to use the single rating evaluation. It lists the major characteristics of content and form that can be identified in most types of writing. When the teacher desires to evaluate a certain type of writing, such as narrative composition, he or she might supplement the general questions about content with more specific guidelines.

Analytic evaluation should occur only when the student has turned in the clean, final copy of a piece of writing. In this detailed type of evaluation, the teacher analyzes each aspect of a piece of writing, including both content and mechanics. By this point, many of the student's errors will have been spotted and corrected during the revision process. Problems that remain in the final copy are likely to be indicative of where the student's real weaknesses lie, and both student and teacher can concentrate on identifying and correcting them.

Evaluators

The evaluation process can be utilized by three types of evaluators: the writer of the piece, other students, and the teacher. Each type of evaluation offers unique benefits to the developing writer.

1. Self-Evaluation. In this type of evaluation, a writer comments on his or her own work, noting which parts were successful and which unsuccessful. During self-evaluation, a student may be guided by a chart such as the one on page T23, as well as by what "feels" right.

It will not always be possible for a student to pinpoint exactly what is wrong in a piece of writing. When this occurs, the writer should be encouraged to underline any sentence or section that doesn't "feel" right, verbalize the problem as he or she perceives it, and then seek further clarification and help from the teacher. This estimation of errors will eventually become more precise as the student learns to recognize similar problems in later writing.

It is very helpful for students to be guided through the evaluation process before they attempt self-evaluation. The teacher might, for example, project a sample composition using an overhead projector, and then guide the class to an understanding of the types of questions they should ask during the revision process. Such guided evaluation helps the young writer develop a sense of when information is incomplete or ideas unclear. This knowledge can then be applied during self-evaluation.

2. Peer Evaluation. Evaluating the writing of others is often a strong learning experience. In peer evaluation, students work together in small groups to improve a piece of writing. Student evaluators should always be given a list of specific criteria that the writing is expected to meet, and should then comment on how well each paper succeeds. Peer evaluation is most effective when the writer is given time to make revisions after the group suggests ways to improve the work.

3. Teacher Evaluation. The teacher's comments and suggestions may be incorporated at any point in the writing process. Studies indicate that evaluation by the teacher is most successful when it is done in combination with self- and peer evaluation. The evaluation form on page T23, therefore, provides for such a combination of evaluation procedures.

Teacher evaluation should also involve direct communication with every student. Such help can be provided in student-teacher conferences. These conferences provide an opportunity for students to ask the questions they develop during self-evaluation. They also give teachers a chance to comment on the strong points of the paper, offer additional suggestions, provide individualized instruction when it is needed.

Teacher evaluation of a final copy should be the last step in the evaluation process. When a student turns in a clean, final copy of a paper, the teacher should require that previous drafts be turned in with it. The teacher should then provide an in-depth analysis of the final copy, judging it not only on its final content, but also on how well the student incorporated earlier suggestions.

Keeping a Record of Improvement

Both the teacher and students benefit when writing folders are maintained throughout the school year. A piece of writing from early in the year, along with its evaluations, can be compared with later pieces. Progress from one piece to the next will be erratic, as the writer takes risks using new techniques and appears to move backwards until gaining mastery of each new technique. However, over the course of the year, progress should be evident.

BIBLIOGRAPHY

Cooper, Charles R., and Lee Odell, eds. *Evaluating Writing: Describing, Measuring, Judging.* Urbana, Illinois: National Council of Teachers of English, 1977.
Graves, Donald H. *Balance the Basics: Let Them Write.* New York: The Ford Foundation, 1978.
Handbook Writing Committee. *Handbook for Planning an Effective Writing Program Kindergarten Through Grade Twelve.* Sacramento: California State Department of Education, 1981, 1982.
Murray, Donald M. *A Writer Teaches Writing: A Practical Method of Teaching Composition.* Boston: Houghton Mifflin, 1968.
Payne, Lucile Vaughn. *The Lively Art of Writing.* Chicago: Follett, 1965.

Using the Evaluation Form

The following form for composition evaluation may be used at any stage of the writing process, and may be re-used after each revision.

The form should be filled out by the student and turned in with the writing. There is also space on the form for peer evaluation, if desired. The teacher may ask students to turn in only final copies, or may ask to see work in progress. The student states whether the submitted writing is the final copy.

On the evaluation form, content may be rated at any point; mechanics should be graded only on a final copy.

Self-Evaluation: Besides the questions on the form, the student can ask himself or herself the questions concerning revising listed in the relevant composition chapter. The student may use 1, 3, and 5 subjectively.

Peer Evaluation: Members of the peer group should rate each feature as objectively as possible. In order to focus on ideas and organization, the group should evaluate content only.

Teacher Evaluation: The following standards for evaluating composition are provided to assist the teacher in rating papers with objectivity and consistency. In a conference, the teacher might discuss one or two of these areas in detail.

Standards for Holistic Evaluation

Content	1—Low	3—Average	5—High
1	Unclear, unimaginative writing.	Understandable but unimaginative writing.	Imaginative, interesting writing.
2	Boring or poorly defined topic.	Topic adequately limited and defined.	Well-chosen, precisely developed topic.
3	Purpose unclear, or not achieved in the writing.	Purpose defined adequately. Not completely achieved.	Clear, well-defined purpose. Writing achieves purpose successfully.
4	Writing so lacking in detail that topic remains undeveloped.	Incomplete development. More information needed.	Topic thoroughly covered. Writing is rich in detail and supporting information.
5	Many irrelevant sentences or details.	Few irrelevant sentences or details.	Well-chosen, relevant sentences and details.
6	Disjointed ideas. No transitional words, phrases, or ideas.	Inconsistent flow. Some transitional devices.	Ideas flow well. Good use of transitional devices.
7	Lack of any logical organization of ideas.	Some organization of ideas evident.	Well-organized ideas. Type of organization suited to topic and purpose.
8	Dull, general words, poorly chosen. Inappropriate to audience.	Suitable but unimaginative language. Generally appropriate to audience.	Specific, vivid language. Appropriate to audience.

Mechanics

1	Many fragments and run-on sentences. Frequent mistakes in the use of nouns, verbs, pronouns, and subject-verb agreement.	Few fragments and run-ons. Some mistakes in the use of nouns, verbs, pronouns, and subject-verb agreement.	No fragments or run-ons. Few mistakes in the use of nouns, verbs, pronouns, and subject-verb agreement.
2	Frequent mistakes in capitalization.	Occasional mistakes in capitalization.	Infrequent mistakes in capitalization.
3	Punctuation marks frequently misused or missing.	Punctuation marks usually used correctly.	Infrequent mistakes in punctuation.
4	Frequent mistakes in spelling, without any indication of awareness of spelling patterns.	Occasional misspellings, usually indicating an approximation of the correct spelling and an awareness of spelling patterns.	Infrequent spelling mistakes.
5	Paragraphs not indented. Writing illegible. Incorrect headings or margins.	Some carelessness or inconsistency in form. Occasionally hard to read.	Correct form. Neat, legible handwriting.

Composition Evaluation Form

Writer _____   Date _____

Title _____   **Circle one:**   Unfinished   Final Copy

Evaluation Symbols
1   Needs a great deal of work
3   Acceptable—could be improved
5   Very good. Needs no further revision.

Content

	Writer's Opinion	Peer Group Opinion	Teacher's Evaluation	Teacher's Comments
1. **Interest.** Is the writing interesting and understandable? Does it hold the reader's attention?				
2. **Topic.** Is the topic a good one? Has it been narrowed sufficiently?				
3. **Purpose.** Is the purpose of the writing clear? Has the writer accomplished this purpose?				
4. **Development.** Has the topic been developed well? Is there sufficient information?				
5. **Unity.** Are all ideas and details related to the topic? Do they all help to develop or strengthen the main idea?				
6. **Continuity.** Do ideas flow smoothly? Has the writer avoided any breaks in thought?				
7. **Organization.** Were ideas arranged in a logical order? Does this order suit the purpose of the writing?				
8. **Language.** Is the language appropriate to the writing? Does it suit the audience? Are the words vivid?				
Additional Guidelines				

Mechanics (to be graded by teacher on final copy only)

1. **Grammar and Usage.** Are there any fragments or run-ons? Is the correct form of every pronoun or verb used? Are adjectives and adverbs used correctly?			
2. **Capitalization.** Are all first words, initials, proper nouns, proper adjectives, and titles capitalized?			
3. **Punctuation.** Does each sentence have the proper end mark? Are all punctuation marks used correctly?			
4. **Spelling.** Are all words spelled correctly? Are plurals and possessive forms spelled correctly?			
5. **Form.** Is the writing legible? Is the heading correct? Are there sufficient margins?			

T23

Checklist for Evaluating Speeches

Throughout both the teacher's and pupil's editions of *Building English Skills*, suggestions are provided for strengthening students' oral communication skills. In order to increase student awareness of the elements of effective speaking, you may wish to duplicate the checklist provided below. This checklist may be used by the teacher, to provide an evaluation of student presentations, or by the students, to provide a means of peer group response.

Content

Introduction
- [ ] gets audience's attention
- [ ] is brief and to the point
- [ ] is appropriate to the topic

Body
- [ ] supports the main idea
- [ ] contains no irrelevant material
- [ ] states supporting ideas clearly
- [ ] develops supporting ideas completely

Conclusion
- [ ] is brief
- [ ] provides a summary of major points or draws attention back to main idea

Presentation

Nonverbal
- [ ] speaker has good posture
- [ ] speaker is relaxed and confident
- [ ] speaker has good eye contact
- [ ] gestures and facial expressions are natural and appropriate

Verbal
- [ ] speaker is not too quiet or too loud
- [ ] speaker's articulation is clear
- [ ] speaker's pace is not too slow or too rapid
- [ ] speaker's pitch is not too high or too low
- [ ] speaker varies volume, pace, and pitch
- [ ] speaker uses pauses effectively

Teaching Special Populations

Most classrooms in our society are likely to contain some students with special language problems or needs. The purpose of this section is to make the classroom teacher aware of these special students and their learning problems. A teacher who is prepared in this way can make certain that these students are not penalized for problems that are beyond their control. He or she will also be better equipped to help them fulfill their potential.

Three of the most common groups of students with special needs are students with learning disabilities (LD), students for whom English is a second language (ESL), and students who speak a nonstandard dialect of English (NSD). These students are apt to have special problems in mastering the concepts and acquiring the skills presented in *Building English Skills*. They may have other difficulties, not shared by the majority of the class, in completing assignments. Below are some general strategies for modifying lessons and assignments so that these students can overcome some of their difficulties.

result of brain damage, central nervous system disfunction, mild cerebral palsy, or other physical impairment. Therefore, what may appear to be inattentiveness or an uncooperative attitude on the part of a student may, in fact, reflect his or her inability to learn through conventional channels. Nevertheless, learning disabled students can compensate for their handicaps and overcome their problems. This is most likely to occur when teachers understand their students' strengths and limitations and are willing to adjust assignments and presentation of material to maximize the chance for success.

Whenever possible, the teacher should work with counselors and special education teachers to determine the specific nature of students' disabilities. Doing so will allow the teacher to devise strategies for circumventing them. Some general strategies that apply to many different kinds of learning disabilities are presented here; however, the teacher is encouraged to improvise other methods and modify materials as seems appropriate for individual students.

Learning Disabled Students (LD)

These students typically have average or above average potential; however, specific areas of deficiency, which vary from student to student, make the processing of information and the acquisition of skills difficult in the traditional classroom. There are many different learning problems classed together under the general heading "learning disabilities." Specific areas of dysfunction include auditory memory, auditory discrimination, visual memory, visual discrimination, fine motor coordination, gross motor coordination, written expression, and oral expression.

It is essential for the teacher to remember, in dealing with any of these problems, that they are beyond the students' control. Learning disabilities may be the

General Areas of Difficulty. Whatever the nature of an individual student's disability, there are certain predictable problems that will impede his or her efforts to learn. These problems include the following:

1. Short attention span
2. Poor memory
3. Difficulty in generalizing
4. Hyperactivity
5. Distractability
6. Low motivation
7. Poor motor coordination

These problems of concentration and memory are usually compounded by low levels of acquired skills:

1. Low reading level
2. Inability to organize work or ideas
3. Laborious and illegible handwriting

A teacher should try both to counter the problems caused by disabilities and to modify the course material to make it more accessible.

General Strategies. There are several strategies for countering the disabilities themselves.

1. Seat the students in front of the classroom where there are no obstructions to sight or hearing.
2. Present essential pieces of information both orally and in writing. Reinforce written material in the text with oral explanation or with tape recordings made by the teacher, the student, or the student's parents. Conversely, write oral instructions and assignments on the board, and provide a written study guide highlighting key points of lectures and oral presentations.
3. Supply visual aids whenever possible to reinforce material from the text. Simple charts, diagrams, and illustrations may help clarify relationships among ideas.
4. To help students compensate for poor short- and long-term memory, repeat important ideas frequently and begin each lesson with a summary of material covered the previous day. Repeat assignments more than once, and give them both orally and in writing.
5. When making an assignment, work one or several problems on the board, demonstrating how students should go about answering them. Break the process down into steps, and be sure that the order of the steps is clear.
6. When grading written work, give one grade for content and another for mechanics, so that the student will receive credit for good ideas in spite of mechanical shortcomings. Do not penalize

students with visual disabilities at all for misspellings.
7. Allow students to answer test questions orally, either to the teacher or with a tape recorder. This practice will eliminate the anxiety caused by the prospect of writing under time pressure.
8. When complete words or sentences are unnecessary, help the students find shortcuts to avoid writing long or difficult words repeatedly. Devise abbreviations for the complicated terms in each chapter. For example, use *D., Int., Imp.,* and *E.* instead of *Declarative, Interrogative, Imperative,* and *Exclamatory* for purposes of completing exercises on the types of sentences. Allow LD students to print rather than write if printing is easier and more legible; you might also suggest that students with writing difficulties learn to type.

Adaptation of Material. In addition to using the strategies mentioned in the previous section, the teacher may find that some modification of the course material in *Building English Skills* will be necessary so that learning disabled students can keep pace with the rest of the class. Some suggestions follow.

1. Break long-term assignments into shorter, individual tasks that can be assigned on a step-by-step, short-term basis.
2. Shorten and simplify all regularly assigned work; these students must put extra time and effort into completing their work. When possible, allow the students to select one, or a few, of several questions, topics, or exercises.
3. Simplify the assignments for written paragraphs and compositions, and allow students to work with partners or to put first drafts on tape.
4. If the reading level of a chapter or section is too advanced, explain important vocabulary words and concepts before asking students to read it.
5. Either supplement or replace difficult terms from the text with simpler ones. For example,

when teaching the types of sentences, supplement or replace the terms *Declarative, Interrogative, Imperative,* and *Exclamatory* with words like *Statement, Question, Command,* and *Strong Feeling.*

6. Review with LD students, several times during the year, Chapter 15, "Study and Research Skills," and Section 17, "Outlining"; both will help them to overcome their difficulties in organizing work and ideas.

English as a Second Language (ESL)

Students whose first language is not English face a number of challenges. These vary in difficulty, depending on their native language and culture and their familiarity with American language and culture. In general, speakers of Indo-European languages, such as German and Spanish, will probably have fewer problems learning English grammar and adapting to American culture than will, for example, speakers of Oriental languages. However, most ESL students share one distinct disadvantage: the lack of their classmates' years of experience with the English language, experience which is necessary to the thorough understanding of most standard textbooks. For these students, the problems of using these textbooks fall into two categories: difficulty with the complexity of language and unfamiliarity with cultural references.

The chapters and sections of *Building English Skills* are written at a level that may be difficult for many ESL students. Moreover, the exercises and assignments require students to analyze and manipulate a language that many ESL students will not yet have acquired fully. Once a teacher is aware of these problems, he or she can implement certain techniques for reducing the difficulties ESL students face.

General Strategies for Countering Language Barriers. To help students overcome the difficulties posed by an unfamiliar language, the following strategies may be employed:

1. Introduce new topics at a slower pace, and provide guided practice with increased feedback and monitoring.
2. Read aloud the essential parts of each chapter, allowing time for explanations, examples, and the answering of questions.
3. In explaining any abstract concept, such as "unity," it is better to go to the specific example first, pointing out the elements that show unity before giving the definition. Beginning from the concrete and particular enables ESL students to follow to the general or abstract.
4. Shorten assignments for these students and allow extra time for the acquisition of concepts.
5. Simplify all activities and exercises linguistically whenever possible. Exercises from intermediate ESL books would be helpful.
6. Build into the activities as many visuals, manipulatives, and concrete experiences as possible. The teacher may have to illustrate and demonstrate meanings as if with small children. However, these aids should not be presented in a condescending manner—the age and intelligence of the students must be respected.
7. Suggest that students work as a group whenever possible. Allowing each student to go through activities with the group before having to do them individually gives him or her enough concrete practice and confidence to try it alone.
8. Correct written exercises and compositions carefully so that students will not continue to practice mistakes.
9. Precede *every* writing activity for ESL students with a similar oral activity; these students must have opportunities to speak and express themselves *before* writing. This procedure provides students with an opportunity to separate the tasks of clarifying ideas and translating them into correct written form.

10. Encourage ESL students to keep journals in English, recording thoughts and impressions without concern for grammar, spelling, and punctuation. It will help them to develop fluency and build confidence and enjoyment in their writing, and it will free them from anxieties about absolute correctness.

11. To reduce the demands on the teacher's time, recruit advanced students to help the ESL students understand written materials and to monitor their practice.

General Strategies for Countering Cultural Differences. The other major problem area for ESL students will be the many cultural references that appear in the text. Some ESL students will have trouble determining gender from proper names alone. They may also have difficulty understanding references to national holidays, sports, individual teams, famous people, geography, foods, and popular culture. Slang, jargon, and idiomatic expressions are tied directly to a specific culture and are often impossible to translate. The following approaches could alleviate these problems:

1. Encourage class discussion to clarify cultural references and provide general information to the whole class. This and other oral work will greatly facilitate the ESL student's acquisition of English.

2. Encourage discussion of differences and similarities between the ESL student's language and English. In covering verb tenses, for example, ask the ESL student to explain how his or her language expresses ideas of time. Such comparisons would benefit the American students by exposing them to aspects of language that are not part of their own linguistic experience.

3. Encourage ESL students to write about their native customs, holidays, geography, celebrities, and foods.

4. Encourage ESL students to read material, at an appropriate level, about specifically American people, places, and events. You might even provide these students with newspapers and popular magazines to read and discuss. This will help them acquire the common stock of information familiar to most Americans.

Speakers of Nonstandard Dialects (NSD)

Everyone speaks some sort of dialect. The speech of Americans in one section of the country differs in at least some aspects of pronunciation, vocabulary, and grammar from the speech of people in other sections. In addition, certain social, ethnic, and racial groups share a distinct way of speaking. Sometimes, however, the dialect common to a particular group departs so much from the more widely used and accepted dialects that it is termed "nonstandard." It is with students who speak such a dialect that this section is concerned.

Teachers must be aware that nonstandard dialects are legitimate language variations. These dialects follow regular phonological and semantic rules and serve the needs of the speech communities that use them. Speakers of "nonstandard" dialects are not necessarily careless speakers of English, nor should the variant features of these dialects be considered "errors." On the other hand, speakers of these dialects should be led to recognize that they cannot participate fully in mainstream American culture and society without understanding and effectively employing its language, standard English.

General Strategies. The teacher of NSD students should bear in mind that one need not, and indeed should not, eradicate one dialect in order to teach another. Instead, the teacher should implement the following strategies:

1. Encourage students to learn the patterns and usages of standard English for use in contexts where it is considered more appropriate (for academic writing and speech; in job applications and interviews; at work, if co-workers or superiors use standard English).

2. Encourage students also to use the dialect that sounds natural to both speaker and listener in informal, casual, and family settings.

3. Tape-record samples of speech from various settings: playing fields, family gatherings, classrooms, committee meetings. Guide students in analyzing the vocabulary, sentence patterns, and grammar used in these different contexts. This practice will make them see that various forms exist within a single language, each form being appropriate in a certain setting. It has proven to be a nonthreatening way to increase all students' awareness of linguistic variation and to demonstrate that shifting from one form of speech to another does not involve a loss of identity.

4. When covering the composition chapters in *Building English Skills*, have the NSD students keep journals in whatever dialect is natural and comfortable, of thoughts, feelings, impressions, and experiences. Read the journals periodically and comment in writing about potential uses for the material in later compositions. Do not "correct" variations from standard usage or point out misspellings. Such nonjudgemental reading, discussion, and subsequent use of the journal entries will reinforce the lesson that writing in standard English is not abandoning one's identity but communicating it to a wider audience.

5. Establish small-group "workshops" consisting of four or five students, and have them collaborate in making suggestions for revision of written work. This strategy educates all of the students about the various dialects spoken in class.

6. Take note of the areas of grammatical variations that appear in the NSD students' written work, and be prepared to help the students with any problems that arise from these differences. Speakers of so-called Black English, for example, may have trouble with verb usage, for some of the principles of standard grammar and usage do not match their speech patterns. For similar reasons, speakers of Hawaiian dialect may encounter difficulties with articles and pronouns. Other groups may have trouble with word order in sentences. Provide extra coaching, more detailed explanations, and additional practice, until the students have mastered the unfamiliar parts of standard dialect.

Special Consultants

Rebecca Benjamin, Educational Consultant, Albuquerque, New Mexico

Grace Massey Holt, Instructor of English as a Second Language, California State University, Sacramento, California

Dr. Eleanor Wall Thonis, District Psychologist, Wheatland School District, Wheatland, California

Karen Bustelo Wehle, S.L.D. Teacher, Leon County School District, Tallahassee, Florida

Virginia Woods, Secondary Resource Teacher, Dripping Springs Independent School District, Dripping Springs, Texas

Additional Levels of the *Building English Skills* Series

Grades 1–8

Building English Skills is the only complete, developmental English program for grades 1–12. The philosophy, terminology, and topical emphasis are consistent throughout the grades, providing for a smooth transition from the elementary grades through high school. Skills are developed sequentially from one grade to the next, with each level reinforcing and extending the skills learned earlier.

Program Components

Student Text

Teacher's Edition

Skills Practice Book

Diagnostic and Mastery Tests

Duplicating Masters

Teacher's Resource Kit

Pink Level
Grade 1

Plum Level
Grade 2
Available in both
hard and soft covers

Brown Level
Grade 3

Aqua Level
Grade 4

Silver Level
Grade 5

Gold Level
Grade 6

Red Level
Grade 7

Green Level
Grade 8

Kindergarten

Building Learning Skills, a comprehensive kindergarten program with a strong language arts development strand, is coordinated with *Building English Skills*.

Other McDougal, Littell Programs

Basic Skills in English

Basic Skills in English for grades 7–12, the companion series to *Building English Skills*, provides composition and grammar instruction for students reading at a 5th–6th grade level. In addition to a controlled reading level, the series features short, highly-structured writing lessons and exceptionally clear definitions and explanations.

The McDougal, Littell Literature Series

The *McDougal, Littell Literature* Series for grades 7–12 provides an in-depth presentation of literary types at every level to give students a strong grasp of the possibilities of each genre. Carefully-chosen selections illustrate the concepts, skills, and literary techniques students need in order to understand and appreciate literature. For each selection, a useful list cross-references writing skills to specific lessons in *Building English Skills*.

Reading Literature Series

Reading Literature is a new literature program for grades 6–12 that combines high-quality literature selections with developmental instruction in reading skills. The texts help students understand and appreciate both traditional and contemporary literature. Through purpose-setting pages and carefully-developed questioning strategies, the program builds skills in comprehension, reading literature, vocabulary, and writing. In addition, related skills such as study and research, speaking and listening, and critical thinking are reinforced throughout.

Building English Skills

Orange Level

Building English Skills

THE McDOUGAL, LITTELL ENGLISH PROGRAM

Building English Skills

Orange Level

Joy Littell, EDITORIAL DIRECTOR

McDougal, Littell & Company
Evanston, Illinois
New York   Dallas   Sacramento

Prepared by the Staff of
THE WRITING IMPROVEMENT PROJECT

Joy Littell, Editorial Director, McDougal, Littell & Company

J. A. Christensen, East High School, Salt Lake City, Utah

Stephen G. Ham, New Trier Township High School East, Winnetka, Illinois

Patricia Phelan, Chairperson, English Department, Hale Jr. High School, San Diego, California

Marcia Baldwin Whipps, East High School, Salt Lake City, Utah

The Staff wishes to thank the more than 1500 students who contributed samples of their writing for analysis.

Consultants

Beth Johnson, English Department Chair, Polk County School District, Lakeland, Florida.

Karen Kutiper, Language Arts Coordinator, Alief Independent School District, Houston, Texas.

Adrian W. McClaren, English Consultant, Memphis City Schools, Memphis, Tennessee.

Julia S. Nichols, English Department Chair, North Area II, Memphis, Tennessee.

Harry H. Raney, Teacher, Memphis School District, Memphis, Tennessee.

ISBN: 0-86609-300-1   TE ISBN: 0-86609-302-8

Acknowledgments: Simon & Schuster: For entries from *Webster's New World Dictionary,* Student Edition; copyright ©1981 by Simon & Schuster, Inc. Macmillan Publishing Company: Chapters 1 and 6 contain, in revised form, some materials that appeared originally in *English Arts and Skills, Grade 9,* by Ronald J. Wilkins et al, copyright ©1965, 1961 by The Macmillan Company. Used by arrangement. (Acknowledgments are continued on page 725)

85 86 87 / 9 8 7 6 5 4 3

Contents

Grammar, Usage, and Mechanics

Chapter 1

Building Your Vocabulary

Why does this English book begin with a chapter on building your vocabulary? It begins this way because your success in school and work will depend to a great extent on your knowledge of words. Words are tools that you use in writing, reading, speaking, and listening. They are the tools that you will use in mastering other subjects—history, science, foreign languages, and so on.

Studies have shown that the larger your vocabulary is, the greater your chances are for success in school and in later life. If you study this chapter seriously, you will indeed enlarge your vocabulary. More importantly, you will acquire the *power* to add to your supply of words.

Learning Word Meanings from Context

Objective

To use context clues to determine the meanings of unfamiliar words

    a. definition or restatement
    b. example
    c. comparison
    d. contrast

Presenting the Lesson

1. Read aloud the introduction to Part 1, **Learning Word Meanings from Context**, on page 2. Define *context* and tell the students that, in fact, they already have the ability to use context clues. To demonstrate, ask the class for at least three definitions of the word *bill* (statement of fees, piece of paper money, advertising poster, beak of a bird, draft of a proposed law). Then, have the students determine the appropriate meaning of *bill* in each of the following sentences:

    a. Some people think a two dollar bill is bad luck.
    b. In social studies we learned how a bill becomes a law.
    c. Our telephone bill comes at the end of each month.

Explain that the sentence—the specific context—in which *bill* appeared led the students to the correct choice in each case.

Tell the students that they can also use context clues to figure out the meanings of unfamiliar words, and to explain them in their own writing.

2. Before reading **Definition and Restatement**, ask the students if they can determine the meaning of *fastidious* and *porringer* from the following sentences:

From reading books or viewing television programs, you know that a detective who is called to the scene of a crime examines the surrounding territory for clues that might help to solve the case. In much the same way, you can often learn the meaning of an unfamiliar word by examining the "surrounding territory"— the context in which the word is used. The **context** of a word is the sentence or group of sentences in which the word appears. Often the context of an unfamiliar word will help you determine its meaning.

Several types of context clues can help you discover the meaning of an unfamiliar word. The most common types, all of which you should become familiar with, are these:

1. Definition and restatement
2. Example
3. Comparison
4. Contrast

Once you have learned to use these clues, you can unlock the meanings of many unfamiliar words. With a large vocabulary at your command, you will be able to master your school subjects more quickly and easily. You will also be able to express your own thoughts and feelings more precisely.

Definition and Restatement

Sometimes a writer will reveal the meaning of a word by defining it for you. At other times, the writer may restate an idea in other words. These types of clues are the easiest to detect. Study the example below. What words give you some indication as to the meaning of the italicized word?

> The long climb up the steep cliff was a *grueling* experience—one that left us utterly exhausted.

According to *Webster's New World Dictionary, grueling* means "very tiring, exhausting." Notice that the phrase following the dash is nearly the same as the dictionary definition.

Here is another example.

> Howard Hughes spent the last few years of his life *secluded* in hotel suites, shut off from personal contact with even his closest associates.

Even if you do not know the word *secluded,* the context of the passage points to the words "shut off from." One dictionary definition for this word is "barred or shut off from the view of or relations with others." Thus the context provides a definition of the word *secluded.*

The most obvious context clue in this category is the **appositive,** a restatement of the same idea in other words. An appositive is often set off by commas, which makes it easy to identify. Here is an example of this type of restatement.

> The directors of the Bay City Zoo have announced the purchase of a pair of *quetsals,* crested birds native to Central America.

Without the appositive phrase "crested birds native to Central America," you might not know whether *quetsals* were animals or vending machines.

Here is another example of an appositive.

> Uncle Ivan is very fond of *kohlrabi,* a vegetable related to the cabbage.

For people unfamiliar with *kohlrabi,* the appositive phrase "a vegetable related to the cabbage" provides a context clue essential to unlocking the meaning of the word.

By skillful use of the context clue of Definition or Restatement, you will be able to unlock the meanings of many unfamiliar words quickly and easily. You will also be able to use these clues in your own writing as a way to introduce a new term or phrase to your reader.

a. Grandfather is a *fastidious* housekeeper, always careful to put everything in its place.
b. Eighteenth century colonial children often ate from *porringers,* small, shallow bowls with handles.

Discuss the students' responses and then read pages 2–3.

3. Tell the students that examples can also be helpful context clues. Read and discuss **Example** on page 4. Emphasize the key words that often signal the use of one or more examples.

To show students how examples can be used, tell the class that a hansom is a horse-drawn covered carriage with two large wheels and a raised driver's seat in the back. Then have the class design a sentence that uses the word *hansom,* a key word or phrase, and examples. Take suggestions from the class on composing the sentence, and write it on the chalkboard. One possibility might be:

On display at the historical society are a hansom and many other horse-drawn carriages.

4. Read aloud **Comparison** on page 5. Review the key words that signal a comparison, and have the students compose a sentence for each of the following words. Each sentence should include a key word and a comparison.

a. armoire (a large, ornate cabinet)
b. talons (the claws of a bird of prey)

5. Read and discuss **Contrast** on pages 5–6. Remind the students that contrasts work by pointing out differences, rather than similarities, between the unfamiliar and the familiar. Ask them to identify the key word in the following sentence and to state the contrast. Many huge dinosaurs were plant eaters, but the *Allosaurus* was a meat eater.

6. Assign Exercises A, B, and C on pages 6–8.

Individualizing the Lesson

Less-Advanced Students

1. Do the first half of Exercise A orally, asking different students to point out the context clues. Then have the students finish the Exercise on their own.

2. Do Exercise B orally. Discuss the possible meanings of the first underlined word, and identify the context clues. Then have one or more students look the word up in a dictionary and read the definition to the class. Continue with this procedure for the entire Exercise.

3. For Exercise C have the students work in pairs or small groups. Let each group use a different brief, high-interest newspaper or magazine article. The articles may be supplied by the teacher or the students. Ask the students to find two unfamiliar words in their article, copy sentences in which the words appear, and use context clues to determine the meanings of the words. Have each group then report the words and the techniques they used to the class.

Advanced Students

1. Ask students to choose from their own vocabularies five words that the rest of the class is not likely to know. The words might be specific to a hobby, skill, or area of interest; drawn from science, history, or other areas of study; or drawn from a certain ethnic culture. Have the students write sentences for

Example

Context can also help to unlock the meaning of an unfamiliar word by giving one or more examples. When several examples are cited, they achieve a "snowball" effect; that is, they pile up so that, with a little thought, you can make a guess at the meaning of the word. In this type of clue, watch for certain "key" words that will help you unlock the meaning of the unfamiliar word.

Be alert for key words in the following example.

> A small museum near Vicksburg, Mississippi, contains some excellent examples of Civil War *memorabilia,* such as flags, cannonballs, maps, guns, photographs, and Union and Confederate uniforms.

In this example, several clues help you determine the meaning of *memorabilia.* The word *examples,* the key words *such as,* and the list of examples, all help you understand the meaning of *memorabilia*—"a collection of things worth remembering."

Here is another example.

> The reading teacher must be prepared to deal with *dyslexia* and other reading problems.

The skillful reader can use the key word *other* to help unlock the meaning of *dyslexia*—"a type of reading problem."

4

Comparison

A third very effective type of context clue is comparison. In this type of clue, the writer compares the unfamiliar word with other, more familiar, words. By paying close attention to these comparisons, you can unlock the meanings of many unfamiliar words.

Certain key words can help you determine the meaning of an unfamiliar word when you use the comparison context clue.

Note how the use of a key word in the following example helps you understand the meaning of the word *dromedary*.

> The *dromedary*, like all other desert animals, can go for long periods of time without drinking water.

Even though the context does not fully reveal that the dromedary is a type of camel, the word *like* helps to point out the dromedary as a type of desert animal. By comparing the unfamiliar word to something more familiar, the writer gives you a key to help unlock the meaning of the unfamiliar word.

Contrast

By contrasting an unfamiliar word with something familiar, the writer of a passage gives you a valuable context clue. Here again,

each of their own words, making sure to include key words and context clues. Then have the students take turns writing their sentences on the board, challenging the rest of the class to figure out the meanings of the unfamiliar words.

Optional Practice

Ask students to determine the meanings of the italicized words in the following sentences. Remind them to watch for key words and context clues. Also, ask them to identify the type of context clue they used to define the word.

a. Mr. Brown finally lost his *equanimity;* he became extremely upset and left the room.
b. On the buffet table were catsup, relish, and other *condiments*.
c. We finally figured out the *cryptogram,* a message written in a secret code.
d. Although the storm has *abated,* some rain is still falling.
e. The dinner speaker could not have been more boring. Many people dozed and others looked at their watches. I suffered silently through the *insipid* speech.

Extending the Lesson

1. Have each student bring in examples of the four kinds of context clues. Encourage them to use a variety of sources (newspaper and magazine articles, science and social studies books, books on technical subjects). Discuss whether the context clues in the examples are sufficient to enable the reader to figure out meanings of familiar words.

2. Have students, individually or as a class, keep a list of new words that they come across in their reading or hear in conversation. Have them add to the list each week.

certain key words will help you determine the meaning of the unknown word.

The contrast in the following example helps to clarify the meaning of the word *archaeologist*.

The *archaeologist,* unlike many other students of ancient history, actually digs in the earth to uncover remains left by former civilizations.

Two context clues help you understand the word *archaeologist* in the example above. The word *unlike* tells you that the archaeologist is being contrasted with someone else. The word *other* tells you that the archaeologist is one student of ancient history. The rest of the sentence tells you that the archaeologist's methods are different from those of the other students of ancient history. Sometimes more than one context clue will be given in a particular sentence.

Exercises Learning Word Meanings from Context

A. The sentences on the next pages contain words with which you may be unfamiliar. Using the context clues that you have just studied, select the *best* meaning for the italicized word in each passage. Write down the letter that you think represents the correct response. After the letter, tell which context clue (or clues) you used to determine the meaning of the italicized word.

6

1. Several *lustrous* objects added to the brightness of the room, especially the glimmering chrome sculpture, the gleaming crystal chandelier, and the sparkling silver doorknobs. example

    A. stolen   B. expensive   <u>C. shining</u>   D. handmade

2. I was simply *petrified* from fright; I couldn't move a muscle. definition

    A. panicked   <u>B. paralyzed</u>   C. thrilled   D. scared

3. Some nations have unwisely *exploited* their colonies, taking as much wealth out of them as they could. restatement

    <u>A. taken advantage of</u>   C. destroyed
    B. enslaved   D. bought and sold

4. Of course this narrative is *fictitious;* it has no basis in fact. definition

    A. colorful   C. important
    B. changeable   <u>D. imaginary</u>

5. The story was too *somber.* I prefer something with a more cheerful setting. contrast

    A. sleepy   <u>B. sad</u>   C. lengthy   D. noisy

6. Paul's *scrupulous* attention to detail, such as dotting every *i,* crossing every *t,* and forming every letter perfectly, makes his handwriting a pleasure to read. example

    A. careless   <u>C. very careful</u>
    B. left-handed   D. occasional

7. SALT, for Strategic Arms Limitation Talks, and NATO, for North Atlantic Treaty Organization, are examples of *acronyms.* example

    A. governmental agencies
    B. important business organizations
    <u>C. words formed from the first letter of other words</u>
    D. words borrowed from foreign languages

8. Although the cheerleaders maintained their usual *exuberance,* the fans silently mourned the team's tenth consecutive loss. contrast

    <u>A. high spirits</u>   C. appearance
    B. embarrassment   D. routine

9. The works of two *prolific* authors, Agatha Christie and William Shakespeare, fill several shelves in most libraries. example

    A. poor   C. respected

    B. <u>producing many works</u>   D. lucky

10. The sign beside the beautiful fountain in Rome contained the warning AQUA NON POTABLE. Those who failed to heed this *admonition* became sick from drinking the water. definition

    A. invitation   B. information   C. sign   <u>D. warning</u>

B. Read the following passage very carefully. Copy the underlined words on a sheet of paper. After each word, write your idea of the meaning of the word. Check your meaning with a dictionary. (You may want to review the types of context clues before you begin.)

Answers will vary somewhat.

Shortly after the *Golden Clipper* left Pago Pago, several of the crew members became ill with <u>enterocolitis</u>. Since everyone who suffered from this intestinal disorder had eaten at the same cafe, the ship's doctor <u>surmised</u> that the crew members had <u>contracted</u> this disease by eating tainted fish.

intestinal disorder   guessed   gotten

The government of the Philippines, however, fearing the spread of a contagion, refused to let the ship dock in Manila Bay. Instead, the entire crew was transferred to a <u>lazaretto</u> floating three miles offshore. A staff of doctors and nurses cared for those who were ill and carefully observed the other crew members for any signs of the <u>malady</u>. When no new cases developed after three days, the Philippine doctors ruled out any possibility of a <u>contagion</u>. The ailing crew members were then transferred to a hospital in Manila, and the others were permitted to return to the *Golden Clipper* and dock in Manila Bay.

floating hospital   disease   epidemic

C. Choose a feature article from a newspaper or a magazine. The article can be about fashion, sports, or any other subject. Read the article carefully. When you come across an unfamiliar word, copy the sentence in which it appears. Using the skills you have learned for unlocking the meanings of new words, write the definition you have determined from the context clue. Be ready to point out the context clue that helped you unlock the meaning of the word.

Part 2   Inferring Word Meanings

The context in which an unfamiliar word appears does not always provide clues as obvious as the ones in the examples you have just seen. Instead of directly stating the meaning of the word, the writer may just imply certain things. The reader must read between the lines to pick up clues. This process of reading between the lines to reach some conclusion is called **inference.** Most of the context clues you used in Part 1 were found in the same sentence with the unfamiliar word. When you are trying to **infer** the meaning of a word, you will frequently have to look elsewhere in the paragraph, or at the paragraph as a whole.

There are five common types of inferences used to determine word meaning from context. These are inferences based on main ideas, stated details, cause and effect relationships, implied comparison, and implied contrast. Each one requires a slightly different approach.

Inference Based on the Main Idea

The main idea of the paragraph that follows concerns the meaning of the term *planned obsolescence.* No doubt, you already know the meaning of *planned,* but you may not know the meaning of *obsolescence.*

> Much of the American economy is based on the principle of *planned obsolescence.* Consumer groups have criticized manufacturers for turning out products that are designed to wear out in a short time, although the technology exists to make longer-lasting products. Criticism has also been directed at the automobile industry for "brainwashing" the consumer into believing that a year-old car is outdated as soon as the new models go on sale.

From the main idea of this paragraph, you can infer that *obsolescence* means one of the following:

A. investment
B. uselessness or outdatedness
C. high prices
D. patriotism

9

Part 2

Objective

To use inference to determine the meanings of unfamiliar words

Presenting the Lesson

1. Read aloud the introduction to Part 2 on page 9. Write *infer* on the chalkboard and define it (to reach a conclusion based on evidence). To help the class understand the concept, ask the students to imagine arriving at the bus stop in the morning and finding no one else waiting for the bus. The other students who are usually there are not to be seen, and there are no other people around. Have the students tell which of the following conclusions is a logical inference:

a. The bus must be late.
b. I have missed the bus.

Discuss the evidence that they used to arrive at the conclusion.

Tell the students that they can use a similar reasoning process to figure out the meaning of an unfamiliar word in a paragraph. Explain that they can infer word meaning by examining the evidence—the sentences and ideas—presented in the paragraph.

2. Read **Inference Based on the Main Idea** on page 9. Analyze and discuss each sentence in the sample paragraph, looking for clues to the meaning of *obsolesence.* Point out words and phrases like "wear out," "short time," "year-old," and "outdated." Remind students that contrast can also present helpful clues, as in the clause, "although the technology exists to make longer-lasting products."

3. Read and discuss **Inference Based on Stated Details** on page 10. Have the students list all the details in the sample paragraph that give clues to the meaning of *impromptu.* Emphasize the unexpected power failure, and the neighbors' responses to this sudden, forced change in their plans for that Sunday.

4. Read **Inference Based on Cause and Effect Relationship** on pages 10–11. Ask students to name the cause and the effect stated in the paragraph.

5. Read **Inference Based on Implied Comparison** on page 11. Identify the implied comparisons, and discuss how they can be used to infer the meaning of *amalgam.*

6. Read **Inference Based on Implied Contrast** on page 11. Ask students to find the statement that provides the basis for the contrast in the sample paragraph (sentence two). Point out that the rest of the description follows from that sentence. Ask the students to state the contrast implied in the phrase, "his eyes, now bright . . ." (that his eyes, used to be dull, but now are alert and bright). Then determine the best meaning for *transformation.*

7. Assign and discuss the Exercise on pages 12–13.

Individualizing the Lesson

Less-Advanced Students

1. These students are likely to have difficulty understanding the concept of inference. Before discussing the five kinds of inference introduced in this Part, give the students more practice in making in-

Inference Based on Stated Details

The various details in the following paragraph help you infer the meaning of *impromptu.*

> It was an intensely hot summer Sunday. Most of the neighbors were indoors with air conditioners and color TVs going full blast. Suddenly, there was a power failure. After about a half hour, most houses had lost their pleasing coolness, and people began to drift outdoors in search of a gentle breeze. Before long, everyone was sharing soda, lemonade, and iced tea. Food began to appear, someone fetched picnic tables, and an *impromptu* block party developed. All around me, people were getting acquainted, and no one seemed to care that the power was still off. Nor did the spirit of the party die with the end of the evening. We have since organized a block softball team and a number of charity projects. Ever since that power failure, our neighborhood has been a more pleasant place to live.—PETER PAGE

From the details stated in this paragraph, you can infer that *impromptu* means one of the following:

A. done without previous preparation
B. carefully planned and organized
C. exciting and lively
D. wooden and uninteresting

Inference Based on Cause and Effect Relationship

You read the following passage in Part 1 to determine by context the meaning of *admonition.* As you read the passage this time, note that the effect, or outcome, of an action is stated in the paragraph. See if you can correctly infer the meaning of the Italian phrase AQUA NON POTABLE.

> The sign beside the beautiful fountain in Rome carried the warning AQUA NON POTABLE. Those who failed to heed this admonition became sick from drinking the water.

10

The cause and effect relationship in this passage leads you to infer that the Italian phrase means one of the following:

A. keep off the grass   C. water for horses only
B. no swimming   D. undrinkable water

Inference Based on Implied Comparison

From the implied comparisons in the following passage, try to infer the meaning of *amalgam*.

Sonia's pleasing personality is an *amalgam* of the most desirable traits of the other members of her family. She has her father's cheerfulness, her mother's sense of humor, and her grandfather's calmness.

From the comparisons in this passage, you can infer that *amalgam* means one of the following:

A. combination   C. mockery
B. denial   D. delight

Inference Based on Implied Contrast

The contrasts in the following passage should enable you to infer the meaning of *transformation*.

Sophia took a hard look at him; an astounding *transformation* had taken place. No longer did he appear lackluster or even middle-aged. His expression sparkled, his clean-shaven face was flooded with color; he had shifted his shoulders about until his coat fitted him the way the tailor had meant it to; he bristled with a youthful zest and energy. . . . But most important for her were his eyes, now bright, clear, knowledgeable, the lids opened wide to let in all the sights the world had to bestow upon an eager and penetrating mind—IRVING STONE

What is the best meaning for *transformation* in this passage?

A. accident   C. movement
B. change   D. sin

ferences. Show them that they use this kind of reasoning in daily life. For example, have them draw inferences from the following situations.

a. You hear sudden cheering coming from your school's football stadium on the day of a game. (We just scored a touchdown.)
b. You see a long line of people outside a movie theater. (The movie is good.)
c. You see a dog with a leash trailing from its collar running down the street. (The dog escaped from its owner.)

2. Give the students extra practice in **Inference Based on Stated Detail.** After reading and analyzing page 10 as suggested, ask students what details they might include in a paragraph that describes an *exuberant* crowd at a rock concert. Remind them that they encountered *exuberant* earlier in this lesson and that it means "high spirited," or "enthusiastic."

3. After reading and discussing the **Cause and Effect** section on page 10–11, have the students imagine other situations that involve information or warning signs (STOP, NO LEFT TURN). Using the following French phrases, have the students write cause and effect sentences modeled on the example in the text.

a. Attention! Méchant chien
   (Beware of mean dog)
b. Entrée Interdit
   (No entrance; do not enter)

4. Allow students to do the first half of the Exercise on pages 12–13 orally or in small groups. Assign the remainder of the problems as independent work.

1. Ask the students to infer tone as well as word meaning for some of the sample paragraphs. For example, for the paragraph on planned obsolescence on page 9, have the students determine whether planned obsolescence seems to be a favorable or unfavorable thing. Ask them to list words and phrases that influence their decision ("criticized," "designed to wear out," "criticism," "'brainwashing'").

For the paragraph on the impromptu block party on page 10, have the students find clues that tell whether the situation was a happy one or an uncomfortable one ("drift," "sharing," "party," "getting acquainted," "spirit of the party" continued, neighborhood cohesiveness developed, "a more pleasant place to live").

2. Ask the students to find five unfamiliar words in the dictionary and then to use each word in a short paragraph that demonstrates one of the inference techniques. In pairs or small groups, have the students try to figure out each other's words.

Optional Practice

Ask the students to infer the meaning of *voracious* in the following paragraph.

Charles is a *voracious* reader. In just one month he read seven novels while still keeping up with several weekly magazines. His friends say that books are Charles's favorite source of entertainment.

Extending the Lesson

Ask the students to find newspaper or magazine articles that require the reader to use inference techniques to determine meanings

Exercise Inferring Word Meanings

Read each of the following passages in its entirety. Then reread each passage, paying particular attention to the italicized word or words. Based on your understanding of the passage, try to infer the meaning of each of the italicized words. Write your inference and check it in a dictionary. Answers will vary somewhat.

1   Many politicians are masters at the art of *circumlocution*. This fact is often best illustrated in press conferences. In response to a controversial question posed by a reporter, some politicians can talk for several minutes without ever really answering the question. wordy evasiveness

2   Most Americans would find it difficult to adapt to the *ascetic* lifestyle of a monk. Garage door openers, dishwashers, garbage disposers, stereos, and color televisions—the luxuries that many pampered Americans consider necessities—are missing from the life of a Franciscan monk. austere

3   The sudden collapse of the Brennan Dam sent a *torrent* of devastation into the St. Thomas Valley. Within a matter of hours, however, numerous organizations and individuals met the *exigency* of the situation with food, clothing, shelter, and medical help. *torrent*-flood, deluge; *exigency*-emergency

4   A true *gastronome* like Julia Child is probably unimpressed by the billions of hamburgers sold by fast food, carry-out restaurants. Better known as "The French Chef," Mrs. Child is the author of a number of books on French cooking. For her, the measure of cooking rests more in the quality than in the quantity of the final product. gourmet

5   The immediate destruction caused by the earthquake was much less than the destruction caused by the *ensuing holocaust*. The earthquake ruptured gas and water lines throughout the city. Without a water supply the firefighters were unable to combat the fires fueled by the broken gas lines. following fire, conflagration

6   The Better Business Bureau is investigating a new product that claims to cure practically every type of human ailment. It

claims to bring immediate relief for arthritis, headaches, colds, vitamin deficiency, low vitality, backache, and sleeplessness. Because of the *preposterous* claims of the new medicine, the suspicions of the medical profession have been aroused.

absurd, ridiculous

Part 3 Analyzing Word Parts To Determine Meaning

In the preceding two chapter parts, you learned to determine the meaning of a word by examining the sentence or paragraph in which it apears. Sometimes, however, the word itself contains all of the information you need to figure out its meaning.

Many large English words are composed of smaller units, called **word parts.** Each word part carries its own specific meaning. If you combine the meanings of the individual parts, you can often determine the meaning of the entire word.

In order to complete this type of analysis, you must first be able to recognize the smaller units that can make up a word. You can begin by learning about three basic types of word parts: base words, prefixes, and suffixes.

Base Words

Base words are shorter English words that lie at the heart of longer words. Other word parts may be added to a base to create new words. What base word was used to make all of the words in the following list?

distrust   trustful
mistrust   distrustful

The word, of course, is *trust.* The beginnings *dis-* and *mis-* were added to it. The ending *-ful* was also added. You can see that adding these parts resulted in new words, each with its own distinct meaning. However, you also know that all of the words still have something to do with the idea of "belief in the reliability of some person or thing." This gives you a starting point for deter-

of unfamiliar words. Have them identify the unfamiliar words and name the technique(s) they might employ to understand the meanings of those words.

Part 3

Objective

To determine word meaning by analyzing word parts

Presenting the Lesson

1. Read the introduction to Part 3 on page 13. Write *certain* on the chalkboard and ask students to define it. Then write *uncertain* and have the students define it. Then write *uncertainty* and ask students for a definition. Tell them that they have just used three basic kinds of word parts to determine meaning. Circle the three parts and label them on the board (*certain*–base word; *un*–prefix; *ty*–suffix).

2. Read and discuss **Base Words** on pages 13–14. Have the students identify the base words in *distasteful, unfortunately, happiness*, and *preschool*. Ask them to think of other base words that can be expanded with additional word parts.

3. Read **Prefixes** on pages 14–15. Ask the students to give additional examples of words that begin with the prefixes listed on the charts. Make certain that these words contain true suffixes, and not simply letters that resemble prefixes. The word *press,* for example, does not contain a prefix.

4. Read the introduction to **Suffixes** on page 16.

5. Remind the students that a noun names a person, place, thing, or idea. Read **Noun Suffixes**, and point out that the endings listed on the charts signal that the new word is a noun. Have the students give other examples of words that contain noun suffixes. To get them started, mention *auctioneer, advisor, scientist, freedom, brotherhood, bombardment, security*.

6. Remind the students that adjectives modify nouns and pronouns. Read **Adjective Suffixes** on pages 17–18, and have the class think of additional examples for each of the three charts.

7. Assign Exercises A, B, and C on pages 18–19.

Individualizing the Lesson

Less-Advanced Students

1. Do the first five items of Exercise A orally. For each word, have the students use dictionaries to determine the meaning of the base word, if necessary. Then have them follow the directions given for the Exercise. Ask student volunteers to write the words on the board, analyze the word parts for the class, and give word meanings. Assign the last ten words to be done independently.

2. Do the first five items in Exercise B as a class. Again, students may need help in determining the meanings of the base words.

3. Assign Exercise C. For each word have students circle the base word and underline the prefix and suffix. Then have them follow the directions given for this Exercise.

mining the meaning of the longer word. You can complete the process if you understand the meaning of the other word parts, prefixes and suffixes.

Prefixes

A **prefix** is one or more syllables placed at the beginning of a base word to change the meaning of the base word. Many new words can be made simply by adding a prefix to a base word. For example:

PREFIX	+	BASE WORD	=	NEW WORD
in-	+	correct	=	incorrect
extra-	+	ordinary	=	extraordinary
mis-	+	manage	=	mismanage

Every prefix has one or more meanings. If you can identify the prefix and the base word, you can often determine the meaning of the longer word. You need only know the meaning of both parts.

The prefixes in the following chart mean "not" or "the opposite of." For example, *appropriate* means "fitting" or "suitable." The word *inappropriate* means "not suitable."

Prefixes That Mean "Not" or "the Opposite of"

PREFIX	EXAMPLE	WORD MEANING
in-	inconsiderate	not considerate
ir-	irregular	not regular
im-	immobile	not mobile
il-	illegible	not legible
dis-	disclaim	opposite of claim
un-	unknown	not known
non-	nonpoisonous	not poisonous

The following prefixes show relationships in time or space. For example, *subsoil* means "the *lower* layer of soil."

Prefixes That Show Relationships in Time or Space

PREFIX	PREFIX MEANING	EXAMPLE	WORD MEANING
sub-	beneath, under, lower	subcommittee	a committee under the control of another committee
pre-	before	prepaid	paid ahead of time
post-	after	postdated	dated after a certain date
super-	over, above, beyond	superstructure	structure built above another
extra-	outside, beyond	extralegal	outside the law

The following prefixes show judgment. For example, *malpractice* means "improper practice."

Prefixes That Show Judgment

PREFIX	PREFIX MEANING	EXAMPLE	WORD MEANING
pro-	in favor of	probusiness	in favor of business
anti-	against	antimissile	a device that acts against a missile
mis-	wrong	misplace	put in the wrong place
mal-	bad or badly, wrong	malnourished	not properly nourished

When you analyze words, be careful not to confuse words that have prefixes with words that contain letters that only resemble prefixes. For example, *prepaid* is a base word with a prefix. *Pressure* is simply a word that contains the letters *p, r,* and *e.*

Advanced Students

1. Have the students write the words in Exercises A, B, and C in complete sentences, using as many list words as possible in each sentence. You might want to direct them to incorporate context clues (see Parts 1 and 2) in several of the sentences.

2. Give the students a list of difficult words to analyze and use in sentences. You might start with the following:

maladroit	dauntless
discredit	resinous
unquenchable	antitoxin
adjournment	infirmity
prehistoric	disrepair
authorship	nonperson
awful	antisocial
humanism	unfathomable

Optional Practice

Have the students give the meaning of each base word, prefix, and suffix in the following words:

postgraduate	unforgivable
malcontent	supermarket
misfire	beauteous
inadequate	relentless
unbiased	nonfiction

Ask the students to use each word on the list in a sentence.

Extending the Lesson

Present the students with short passages from fiction, news articles, and textbooks. Ask them to examine the words in each passage, looking for base words with prefixes and/or suffixes. Identify difficult passages and discuss how the word analysis techniques can help readers to understand the excerpts.

Suffixes

A **suffix** is one or more syllables placed at the end of a base word to form a new word. Each suffix has its own meaning or meanings. When you can recognize suffixes and attach meanings to them, you can use them to determine the meanings of longer words. See how suffixes have been added to the following base words to form new words.

BASE WORD	+	SUFFIX	=	NEW WORD
compose	+	-er	=	composer
friend	+	-ship	=	friendship
fury	+	-ous	=	furious

Notice that the spelling of a base word may change when a suffix is added. In the examples above, the silent *e* was dropped from *compose,* when *-er* was added. The final *y* in *fury* was changed to *i* when *-ous* was added.

Noun Suffixes

Noun suffixes are those suffixes that make nouns out of the base words they are added to. The suffixes in the following chart all change their base words into a particular type of noun.

Noun Suffixes That Mean "One Who Does Something" or "That Which Does Something"

SUFFIX	EXAMPLE	WORD MEANING
-eer	puppeteer	one who operates puppets
-er,-or	computer conductor	that which computes one who conducts
-ist	physicist	one who studies or is experienced in physics
-ian	electrician	one who works with electric devices

The words that you find listed in the following chart are all **abstract words.** That is, they describe a state of being or a quality. For example, *boredom* is the state of being bored. *Cleverness* is the quality that makes a person clever. Remember that the spelling of a base word may change when a suffix is added to it. The *e* in the word *wise*, for instance, is dropped when the suffix *-dom* is added.

Noun Suffixes That Make Abstract Words

SUFFIX	EXAMPLES
-dom	boredom, wisdom
-hood	statehood, womanhood
-ism	patriotism, realism
-ment	settlement, encouragement
-ness	cleverness, kindness
-ship	leadership, friendship
-ty	certainty, frailty
-ity	sanity, rapidity

Adjective Suffixes

Adjective suffixes change base words to adjectives — words that describe or modify other words. Study the following charts to learn about different types of adjective suffixes.

Adjective Suffixes That Mean "Full of"

SUFFIX	EXAMPLE	WORD MEANING
-ous	glorious	full of glory
-ful	graceful	full of grace

The adjective suffixes listed in the chart on the next page mean "relating to" or "pertaining to."

Adjective Suffixes That Mean "Relating to" or "Pertaining to"

SUFFIX	EXAMPLE	WORD MEANING
-al	regional	relating to a region
-ic	angelic	like an angel
-ical	historical	pertaining to history
-ish	stylish	relating to style

The adjective suffixes in the following chart mean exactly what they say.

Adjective Suffixes That Mean What They Say

SUFFIX	EXAMPLE	WORD MEANING
-able, -ible	imaginable	something that one is able to imagine
	digestible	something that is able to be digested
-most	foremost	being at the very fore (front)
-less	blameless	without blame
-like	catlike	like a cat

Exercises   Examining Word Parts

A. Determine the meaning of the prefix in each of the following words. Then write the meaning of the prefix next to the meaning of the base word to find the meaning of each complete word. Answers in margin.

1. imprecise
2. nonbinding
3. superstar
4. antifreeze
5. inaccurate
6. disallow
7. substructure
8. postwar
9. misquote
10. irregular
11. unbound
12. prearrange
13. extraordinary
14. malpractice
15. impractical

B. Determine the meaning of the suffix in each word on the next page. Then write the meaning of the base word next to the meaning of the suffix to find the meaning of each complete word. Answers in margin.

1. not exact
2. not restrictive
3. above (greater than) well-known performer
4. against freezing
5. not precise
6. not permissible
7. under (the) building
8. after (a) war
9. incorrectly repeated
10. not standard
11. not tied
12. organized before
13. beyond normal
14. not done well
15. not sensible

1. auctioneer	6. calculator	11. violinist
2. statistician	7. knighthood	12. consumerism
3. agreement	8. likeness	13. authorship
4. humanity	9. outrageous	14. tactful
5. global	10. curable	15. matchless

C. Determine the meanings of the prefixes and suffixes in each of the following words. Then write the meaning of each complete word by adding the meanings of the prefix and suffix to the meaning of the base word. Answers in margin.

1. inexcusable	6. irregularity
2. impracticality	7. disadvantageous
3. nonconformist	8. precolonial
4. mismanagement	9. malodorous
5. uncontrollable	10. extraterritorial

Part 4 Applying Your Skills

You now have several useful tools for unlocking the meanings of words. The following exercises will allow you to practice using these tools. The exercises are much like those you will encounter in the vocabulary sections of standardized tests. Use the skills you have learned in this chapter to unlock the meanings of the words.

Section 1: *Determining Word Meanings from Context.* Select the best meaning for the italicized word in each passage. Write the letter that represents the best answer.

1. The detective *surmised* that the man was lying. Her guess was right.

    (A) knew   (C) worried
    (B) guessed   (D) solved

2. A rainbow is an *evanescent* thing; it gradually disappears, leaving only a memory.

    (A) temporary   (C) even; balanced
    (B) shaped like an arch   (D) beautiful

1. one who holds public sales
2. one who works with numbers
3. the state of being in accord
4. the quality of being part of mankind
5. relating to the entire world
6. that which computes numbers
7. the state of being a knight
8. the state of being similar
9. full of offensiveness
10. able to be made well
11. one who uses a violin
12. the practice of working with the buying public
13. the state of being a writer
14. full of sensitivity to others
15. without equal

Exercise C

1. not able to be forgiven
2. the state of being not sensible
3. one who does not follow set standards
4. the state of being poorly handled
5. not able to be restrained or directed
6. the condition of not following an established pattern
7. full of unfavorable qualities
8. pertaining to things before the colonial period
9. full of bad smells
10. relating to things outside of a specified area

Part 4

Objective

To apply word analysis skills to standardized test situations

Presenting the Lesson

1. Read the introduction to Part 4, **Applying Your Skills,** on page 19. Assign section 1. Then have students prepare explanations for their answers.

19

2. Assign section 2 on pages 21–23. Remind the students that clues to the meaning of the italicized word in each paragraph will be found throughout the passage.

3. Assign section 3 on pages 23–24. Remind the students to examine the base word, prefix, and suffix to determine word meaning.

Individualizing the Lesson

Less Advanced Students

1. Read the introduction to **Applying Your Skills** aloud. Then review the meaning of *context*. Do the first five items of section 1 of the "test" as a class. Discuss each one, emphasizing key words and other context clues in each passage. Have the students complete section 1 on their own.

2. Assign section 2 and do the first three items orally. Discuss each passage carefully, reviewing the inference techniques that a reader can use. Have the students complete section 2 independently.

3. Assign section 3. For each item, have the students copy the word, circle the base word, and underline the prefix and/or suffix. Do the first three orally, combining the meanings of the different word parts. Have the students complete section 3 independently.

Advanced Students

1. After completing all three parts of the "test," have the students design similar vocabulary questions that cover from ten to fifteen words. They may look for words in textbooks, periodicals, works of literature, dictionaries, and other reference sources.

3. Like any other beginner, a *novice* in the kitchen will make mistakes.

(A) cook   (C) helper
(B) young person   (D) someone new to an activity

4. Places of *egress,* such as the plane's doors and removable windows, must be clearly labeled.

(A) public transportation   (C) exit
(B) mistake   (D) first-aid stations

5. Tell me the *gist* of the movie. I don't have time for a long description right now.

(A) rating   (C) complete explanation
(B) characters   (D) main idea

6. The child was *precocious.* She could read before she started nursery school.

(A) hard to manage   (C) likely to brag
(B) ahead in development   (D) very young

7. *Avarice* is different from other kinds of greed in that its sole object is money.

(A) wealth   (C) greed for food
(B) a sickness   (D) strong desire for money

8. The coach had strict rules for the team. New players had trouble obeying such *stringent* orders.

(A) athletic   (C) rigorous
(B) unfair   (D) limp, like string

9. I like a *succinct* sports announcement, not one that rambles.

(A) brief; clear   (C) wise; well-informed
(B) witty; joking   (D) wordy; repetitious

10. A guinea pig is *vulnerable.* It can't fight well, it can't run fast, and it has no tough hide nor bad scent to protect it.

(A) hopeless   (C) popular pet
(B) lovable   (D) easily hurt

11. Although he isn't handsome, he has a *winsome* manner. Everyone considers him charming and likeable.

    (A) ugly   (C) talkative
    (B) pleasing   (D) conceited

12. Tom Sawyer didn't *cajole* his friends into painting the fence. He made the job look like so much fun that his friends paid him to let them do it.

    (A) lead   (C) coax
    (B) teach   (D) worry

13. Such *heinous* crimes as murder or kidnapping usually receive the harshest punishments.

    (A) rare   (C) very wicked
    (B) against the law (D) improper

14. The agency's activities were *covert*. No outsiders knew anything about them.

    (A) illegal   (C) dangerous
    (B) secret   (D) governmental

15. Backstage, the rock star sulked, complained, and growled at the band. His *petulant* manner, however, disappeared on stage.

    (A) nervous and shy   (C) irritable and bad-tempered
    (B) annoying   (D) too confident

Section 2: *Inferring Word Meanings.* Read each passage. Write the letter that represents the best definition of the italicized word.

1.   The Battle of Antietam was the bloodiest twelve hours of the Civil War; 22,719 soldiers were killed or wounded. Yet Clara Barton did not turn back in horror from the *carnage* of the battlefield. She had taken upon herself the duty of nursing the injured. She did not flinch from stepping across corpses to tend to the mangled survivors.

    carnage

    (A) combat   (C) filth
    (B) enemy   (D) mass killing

When they finish constructing their own tests, students should exchange tests in pairs or small groups.

2. Have each student choose from the three "test" sections ten words he or she finds difficult. Then have students compose paragraphs that include all ten of those words.

Optional Practice

Have the students determine the meanings of the italicized words in the following items.

Using Context Clues:

a. Since Millie's brother has found the *cache* where she keeps her candy, she will have to find another hiding place.

b. In the hallway was a huge crowd, a *multitude* of students waiting for the bell to ring.

Using Inference:

a. My aunt saves string, wrapping paper, and old boxes. In fact, she hardly throws anything away that she thinks could have some use someday. She is the most *frugal* person I know.

Analyzing Word Parts:

a. *superabundance*
b. *irremediable*

Extending the Lesson

Each day, have students present to the class two or three "words of the day." Each presenter should be prepared to help the class determine the meaning of the words. Through context clues, inference techniques, or word part analysis.

The word may then be posted on a bulletin board display that illustrates the three methods of figuring out unfamiliar words. At the end of each week, test the students on these words or assign a writing exercise that requires them to use the words.

2. When news broke that a tanker had spilled tons of oil off-shore, students from the local high school rushed to the beach. There they bathed oil from the feathers of helpless seabirds so that the birds could fly again. The students had *mitigated* at least some of the damage caused by the spill.

mitigated

(A) made worse   (C) caused

(B) made milder or less serious   (D) ignored

3. The letter from home had a *salutary* influence on Ginger. Its effect was like that of a swim on a hot day or a thermos of lemonade during a long hike.

salutary

(A) favorable; good   (C) warming

(B) honorable   (D) unpleasant; uncomfortable

4. Kevin's new *lassitude* worried his family. He no longer dashed cheerfully from task to task or from one pleasure to another. He seemed to have lost his enthusiasm for whatever the day might bring.

lassitude

(A) great tiredness   (C) pep; enthusiasm

(B) a small lasso   (D) loss of self-respect

5. A severe back injury had forced Eileen Gardner into a rather *sedentary* life. For months she did little more than watch television and do light chores around the house. Originally a capable athlete, her muscles were beginning to *atrophy*. Then Eileen Gardner decided to fight back.

sedentary

(A) used to sitting; getting little exercise   (C) sad

(B) used to running; active   (D) angry

atrophy

(A) waste away   (C) strengthen

(B) develop   (D) became tight

6. The damage caused by the testing of the new insecticide has angered local residents. In an attempt to *mollify* its outraged neighbors, the Kental Corporation has offered to make *restitution* for any damage. The offer is not enough. Residents say that no amount of money can make up for the fear, worry, or loss of crops that has resulted from the testing.

mollify

(A) make fun of   (C) accuse
(B) soothe   (D) mislead

restitution

(A) a place of rest   (C) the act of paying or
(B) refusal to be responsible   making up for damage
                                (D) apologies

7. Friday was the *antithesis* of the rest of that whole, miserable week. The sun shone for the first time, the air was warm, and the pools of water began slowly to evaporate. Although the pleasant weather could not really make up for the damage caused by the storm, it could at least *alleviate* the depression of those who had lived through it.

antithesis

(A) cause   (C) last day
(B) opposite   (D) best

alleviate

(A) give a reason for   (C) increase
(B) prepare for   (D) relieve

Section 3: *Examining Word Parts.* Write the letter that represents the best definition for each italicized word.

1. *antislavery*

    (A) after slavery   (C) opposed to, or against, slavery
    (B) before slavery   (D) in favor of, or for, slavery

2. *postdate*

    (A) to occur after   (C) a special occasion
    (B) to occur before   (D) in favor of dating

3. *disquiet*

   (A) a quiet mood   (C) anger; disgust
   (B) the lack of mental   (D) sudden
         peace; uneasiness

4. *illimitable*

   (A) not legal   (C) able to be confined
   (B) one who places limits   (D) without limit; infinite

5. *pro-American*

   (A) not an American   (C) opposed to America
   (B) a professional athlete   (D) in favor of America

6. *nonmetallic*

   (A) not made of metal   (C) an unknown metal
   (B) like metal   (D) a metalworker

7. *supernatural*

   (A) frightening   (C) related to things beyond
   (B) fiction   the natural world
               (D) less than natural

8. *inglorious*

   (A) full of glory   (C) beautiful; magnificent
   (B) dishonorable   (D) someone who wins an honor

9. *mischance*

   (A) luck; fortune   (C) another chance; second try
   (B) misconduct   (D) bad luck; unlucky incident

10. *impracticality*

   (A) that which is im-   (C) involvement in some
         possible to practice   sort of preparation
   (B) perfectly possible   (D) a condition of not
                                   being practical

SUMMARY AND APPLICATIONS

1. One way to determine the meaning of an unfamiliar word is to look at its context. The **context** of a word is the sentence or group of sentences in which the word appears. Context clues include definition or restatement, example, comparison, and contrast.

2. Another method of determining word meaning is **inference**. To infer meaning, the reader must "read between the lines" to reach a conclusion about the word.

3. The meanings of **prefixes** and **suffixes** can help unlock word meanings. Prefixes and suffixes are word parts added to a base word to form new words.

4. These word-attack techniques may be used whenever you come across unfamiliar words. They may also be used in the vocabulary sections of standardized tests. The expanded vocabulary you acquire will help you to speak and write more precisely.

Applications in Other Subject Areas

Science / Math / English. Start a vocabulary notebook. Label several pages with the names of your courses. You may use classes other than those listed above. In this notebook, record the new words and definitions that you learn in your classes. Note with symbols which meanings you were able to determine from context (C), which meanings from the word parts (WP), and which meanings from dictionaries or other formal sources of definitions (D).

○	Biology
	1. antibody— a substance that works against harmful elements (WP)
	2. gene — a unit on the chromosome by which hereditary characteristics are passed on (D)
	3. catalyst— something that causes a process to happen or to be speeded up (C)

Chapter Objectives

1. To distinguish between abridged and unabridged dictionaries, use guide words, and understand the various parts of a dictionary entry

2. To be aware of the multiple meanings of words

3. To increase precision in the use of words through an understanding of synonyms, antonyms, and the thesaurus

Preparing the Students

Have the class read page 26. Ask students to give reasons for using a dictionary. They will probably mention that they use it to look up the spelling or definition of a word. Explain that the dictionary contains a wealth of additional information beyond spellings and definitions.

Put the word *recondite* on the board. Ask if anyone can answer the following questions about the word: What is its part of speech? (adj.) How can it be divided into syllables? (rec on dite) How is it pronounced? (rek′ ən dīt or ri kon′ dīt) What language did it come from? (Latin) What other words are derived from it? (reconditely, reconditeness) What are some close synonyms? (hidden, obscure) Tell the class all of these questions may be answered by consulting a dictionary.

Additional Resources

Mastery Test — See pages 13–14 in the test booklet. Recommended for use after teaching the chapter.

Skills Practice Book — pages 9–12.

Duplicating Masters — pages 9–12.

Special Populations — See special section at the front of this Teacher's Edition.

Chapter 2

The Dictionary as a Key to Word Power

If you were trying to improve your skill in some sport, you would know where to look for help. You could ask your coach to evaluate your skills. You could study the techniques of another player. You could read a book or an article about the subject. You might even study a film or videotape of yourself in action.

As you work to improve your vocabulary skills, you also have several sources to which you can turn. Often, you can ask a friend or teacher to define an unfamiliar word. Sometimes the words themselves or the contexts in which they appear provide helpful information. Your best source, however, is a book that you have used for years, but with which you might not be very familiar even now. This book is the dictionary.

This chapter will teach you how to read and use a dictionary. It will provide the key with which you can unlock this amazing treasure chest of information.

Part 1 Finding Information in a Dictionary

Abridged and Unabridged Dictionaries

There are two main types of dictionaries that you should learn to use—unabridged and abridged. An **unabridged dictionary** is as complete as its writers and editors can make it. It is a huge volume containing information about hundreds of thousands of words. You can find an unabridged dictionary in the reference section of your school or public library. Occasionally you will need to use an unabridged dictionary, but many of the words in an unabridged dictionary are words that people rarely use.

For most of your work, you will use an **abridged dictionary.** The word *abridged* simply means "shortened." The smaller size of an abridged dictionary makes it easier to use. In addition to being aware of these two main classifications of dictionaries, you should also familiarize yourself with the many specialized dictionaries that are available. See Chapter 14, "Using the Library," for a list of dictionaries that you are likely to find useful.

As you examine the different types of dictionaries, remember that no two dictionaries are quite the same. Dictionaries may be organized differently, and they may use different symbols and abbreviations. Try to work with and become familiar with one dictionary. If you work with one dictionary consistently, you will soon find it easy to use and understand.

What You Will Find on a Dictionary Page

Although some aspects of a dictionary vary from book to book, certain elements are standard. Among these are the general design of a dictionary page and the types of information presented. We will begin by looking at the dictionary page as a whole.

On pages 32 and 33, you will find a reproduction of a dictionary page. As you study the information that follows, refer to that reproduced page.

Part 1

Objective

To distinguish between abridged and unabridged dictionaries, use guide words and keys, and understand the various parts of a dictionary entry

Presenting the Lesson

1. Read and discuss **Abridged and Unabridged Dictionaries** on page 27. Arrange to have your library's unabridged dictionary in class. Ask students to look up the following words in their desk dictionaries: *morcellation, komondor, philosophaster, duroy.* The words will probably not be included. Then call on volunteers to find the words in the unabridged dictionary and read their definitions. You might also compare the entries for a word such as *carriage.* The information in the unabridged dictionary will be much more complete.

2. Read and discuss **What You Will Find on a Dictionary Page,** pages 27–28. As part of your discussion of *guide words,* have students locate the section in their dictionaries that explains the principles of alphabetization. Have them put the following pairs of words in alphabetical order:

billet, bill of fare
St. Patrick's Day, sake
McCarthyism, mace
80, 50

3. Have students locate the keys to pronunciation in their dictionaries. Call on students to pronounce the following words: *redoubt, clandestine, sleight, feint, cyst, gnar, legume, patois.*

4. Read and discuss **What You Will Find in a Dictionary Entry**, pages 28–30. Work through each category, referring to the sample dictionary page as you go along. Ask students to see if they can find anything on the sample dictionary page that has not been explained.

5. Assign and discuss Exercises A and B on page 31.

6. Assign Exercise C. Be sure students record the title of the dictionary they use for this exercise. Be aware that answers may vary slightly, depending on the dictionary.

Individualizing the Lesson

Less-Advanced Students

Give additional practice in alphabetizing so that students may use the dictionary efficiently. Ask students to put the following lists of words in alphabetical order:

1. *rack, racing, rage, racket, rag, radish, radio*
2. *tendon, tenant, tepid, terse, tempest, teller, tender*
3. *ace, accurate, acid, accuse, abacus, absolute, add*

Advanced Students

Assign each student a specialized dictionary to investigate and report on to the class. Have them report on dictionaries of etymology, slang dictionaries, bilingual dictionaries, rhyming dictionaries, reverse dictionaries, dictionaries from specialized fields, and other interesting types. Ask them to bring in specialized dictionaries from home if they have any.

1. Guide Words. At the top of each dictionary page are two words in large type. These **guide words** tell you the first and last words that you will find on that page. Beneath the guide words are the words that fall between the guide words. They are listed in alphabetical order. The guide words help speed up the process of locating a word.

Not all dictionaries alphabetize words in the same way. The introduction to your dictionary will explain how words are alphabetized in that dictionary. (This information will help you decide, for example, whether to look for *Mt. Rushmore* under *mt-* or *mo-*.)

2. Entry. An **entry** is the information given about a word. Different dictionaries give different types of information, and may list the information in different orders.

3. Key. In most dictionaries, a **key to pronunciation** is printed on the bottom of each right-hand page. This key explains the symbols used to show how words are pronounced. A fuller set of symbols and abbreviations is printed at the front or back of the dictionary.

What You Will Find in a Dictionary Entry

Different dictionaries may contain different types of information. However, there are certain elements of a dictionary entry that are somewhat standard. These elements are listed below. Refer to the reproduced dictionary page as you study each item. Each entry on that page follows this general pattern:

1. entry word
2. pronunciation (or pronunciations)
3. part of speech
4. etymology
5. definition (or definitions)
6. synonymy
7. words derived from the entry word
8. cross-reference

Not every item is included in every entry.

1. Entry Words. Each **entry word** is printed in dark type and divided into syllables. Sometimes, when you are writing or typing a paper, you may have to divide a long word at the end of a line. The divisions in the entry words show how to divide the word correctly.

Occasionally you will see what appears to be the same entry word listed twice. Each entry is followed by a small, raised number. Such words are **homographs**—words with the same spelling but with totally unrelated meanings. See the entries for *pale* for examples of homographs.

2. Pronunciation. The **pronunciation** of each word is given in parentheses, directly following the entry word. By using the pronunciation key at the bottom of the page, you can determine the pronunciations. If a word has more than one acceptable pronunciation, or if the word is pronounced in different ways at different times (for example, *address*), those differences will be shown and explained. Like the entry word itself, the pronunciations are also divided to show syllables. It is important to notice that pronunciation divisions and end-of-line divisions are not always the same.

3. Part of Speech. Following the pronunciation of the word *palate* is the letter *n*. It indicates that *palate* is a noun. Often a word can function as more than one part of speech. If so, other part-of-speech abbreviations will be found somewhere in the entry. A key to these abbreviations can be found in the front or back of the dictionary. If the plural of a noun is not formed by simply adding -*s* or -*es,* the correct spelling of the plural will also be given at this point.

4. Etymology. Some words are quite new, and others are ancient. However, every word has a history. Many words have been borrowed from other languages. Some were derived from the names of people or places. Still others were invented only this year to describe new ideas or inventions. (See Chapter 3, "Using Language for Different Purposes," for a discussion of how words are created.)

The history of a word is told in its **etymology**, which traces the word back to its origins. In the entry for *palette,* you will find that *palette* comes from a French word spelled the same way, which

Optional Practice

Explain the *Oxford English Dictionary* to the class. If your library has a copy, have it available in the classroom. Show how each entry gives the history of the word by citing examples of its use from the Middle Ages to the modern era. Tell students that this dictionary is useful when they want to know how a particular word has been used in the past as well as how it is used now.

Extending the Lesson

Discuss the use of glossaries in textbooks. Have students compare the information found in a glossary entry to that found in a dictionary entry. Remind students to use their glossaries when they need quick and handy reference.

in turn came from the Latin word *pala*, meaning "a shovel." The symbols and abbreviations used in etymologies will be explained in the front or back of your dictionary.

5. Definition. Following the etymology, you will find the **definition** of the word. For most words, you will find more than one meaning listed in the definition. It is a good idea to read *all* the listed meanings, even if you think you have found the one you want at once. You may find another that is more specific, or more suitable to the context in which it is used.

6. Synonymy. A **synonymy** is a list of words that are similar in meaning to the entry word. Notice the abbreviation *SYN*. after the definition of *pale*[1]. Here you find a discussion of words that are similar in meaning to *pale*. This synonymy points out the slight differences in the meanings of *pale, pallid, wan, ashen,* and *livid*. The abbreviation *ANT*. at the end of the synonymy introduces antonyms for *pale*, words with the opposite meaning. The synonymy can be an invaluable aid when you write. Use it to help you choose the most precise synonym for a term or idea.

7. Derived Words. Following some dictionary entries, you will notice additional words, printed in bold type and divided. These are words that are **derived** from the entry word. These words are so closely related to the entry word that the editors of the dictionary did not feel it necessary to list them as separate entries. See the entry for *paleontology* for an example.

8. Cross-Reference. A **cross-reference** directs you to another entry for more information. At the end of the etymology for *palaver*, the word PARABLE in small capital letters tells you that additional information about the etymology can be found in the entry for *parable*. If you look closely, you will find additional cross-references on this page.

Other Information. Certain abbreviations and symbols provide you with additional information about a word. For example, a star ☆ sometimes marks a usage that first appeared in our country. Check the front or back of your dictionary for a key to other abbreviations and symbols.

Exercises Learning How To Use the Dictionary

A. Answer the questions below. They will help you decide how well you understand what information you can get from a dictionary.

1. What is an etymology? The history of a word
2. What is a synonymy? A list of words with similar meanings
3. What is a derived word? A word closely related to the entry word
4. What is a cross-reference? A direction to another entry for more information
5. What is a key? A pronunciation guide

B. The following questions refer to the sample dictionary page reproduced on pages 32 and 33. Some answers will be found in the pronunciation key.

1. What is the etymology of the word *palliate*? from Latin *palliare* (to conceal) and *pallium* (cloak)

2. Which synonym for *pale* suggests the paleness resulting from a serious illness? wan

3. Would you expect a person who was interested in paleography to be interested in ancient Egyptian hieroglyphics? yes

4. Which of the words below is a palindrome?

        clip   loop   lap   <u>deed</u>

5. What derived form of *Palestine* is listed? Palestinian

6. Where would you find information about the etymology of the word *palatial*? Under entry for *palace*

7. Which definition of *palisade* is an Americanism? #3—a line of steep cliffs

8. List two familiar words that have the same vowel sound as the vowels in *Palawan*. Answers may vary.

C. Use your own dictionary to answer the following questions. Answers may vary.

1. List the abbreviations used in the etymologies for these languages: Latin, Greek, French, Middle English, Hungarian. L., Gr., Fr., ME., Hung.
2. What words are synonyms for *humble*? Lowly, meek, modest
3. Copy the pronunciation for *narwhal*. (när′ wəl)
4. How many meanings are given for *paradox*? four
5. Where could you divide the word *consonant* at the end of a line of writing? con·so·nant

pal·ate (pal′it) *n.* [L. *palatum*] 1. the roof of the mouth, consisting of a hard, bony forward part (the *hard palate*) and a soft, fleshy back part (the *soft palate*) 2. taste [the food was delicious to his *palate*] 3. liking

pa·la·tial (pə lā′shəl) *adj.* [see PALACE] 1. of, suitable for, or like a palace 2. large and splendid; grand; magnificent —**pa·la′tial·ly** *adv.*

pal·at·i·nate (pə lat′′n āt′, -it) *n.* the territory ruled by a palatine

pal·a·tine (pal′ə tīn, -tin) *adj.* [< OFr. < L. < *palatium*, palace] 1. of a palace 2. having royal powers in his own territory [a count *palatine*] 3. of or belonging to a palatine or palatinate —*n.* a medieval vassal lord having the rights of royalty in his own territory, or palatinate —[P-] one of the SEVEN HILLS OF ROME

pa·la·ver (pə lav′ər) *n.* [Port. *palavra*, a word, speech < LL. *parabola*, PARABLE] 1. a conference, as orig. between African natives and European explorers or traders 2. talk; esp., idle chatter 3. flattery; cajolery —*vi.* 1. to talk, esp. idly or flatteringly 2. to confer —*vt.* to flatter or wheedle

Pa·la·wan (pä lä′wän) island in the W Philippines, southwest of Mindoro: 4,550 sq. mi.

pale¹ (pāl) *adj.* **pal′er, pal′est** [OFr. < L. < *pallere,* to be pale] 1. having little color in the face [*pale* after a sunless winter; *pale* with fright] 2. lacking intensity or brilliance; dim; faint: said of color, light, etc. 3. feeble; weak [a *pale* imitation] —*vi.* 1. to become pale; lose color [her face *paled* at the news] 2. to seem weaker or less important [my work *paled* beside his] —*vt.* to make pale —**pale′ly** *adv.* —**pale′ness** *n.* —**pal′ish** *adj.*

SYN.—**pale** is the most general of the words describing an unnatural whiteness or lack of color, often temporary, of the complexion; **pallid** suggests a paleness resulting from exhaustion, faintness, emotional strain, etc.; **wan** suggests the paleness resulting from a serious illness; **ashen** implies the grayish paleness of the skin as in death; **livid** refers to a grayish-blue complexion, as of one in great rage or fear —**ANT.** ruddy, rosy

Pal·es·tri·na (pä′les trē′nä: *E.* pal′ə strē′nə), **Gio·van·ni (Pierluigi) da** (jô vän′nē dä) 1525?-94; It. composer

pal·ette (pal′it) *n.* [Fr. < L. *pala,* a shovel] 1. a thin board with a hole for the thumb at one end, on which an artist arranges and mixes his paints 2. the colors used, as by a particular artist

palette knife a flexible steel blade on a handle, used by artists for mixing, scraping, and applying paints

pal·frey (pôl′frē) *n., pl.* **-freys** [< OFr. < ML., ult. < Gr. *para,* beside + L. *veredus,* post horse] [Archaic] a saddle horse, esp. a gentle one for a woman

PALETTE

Pa·li (pä′lē) *n.* the Old Indic dialect which has become the religious language of Buddhism

pal·imp·sest (pal′imp sest′) *n.* [< L. < Gr. < *palin,* again + *psēn,* to rub smooth] a parchment, tablet, etc. that has been written upon several times, with previous, erased texts still partly visible

pal·in·drome (pal′in drōm′) *n.* [< Gr. < *palin,* again + *dramein,* to run] a word, phrase, or sentence that reads the same backward or forward, as the word *madam*

pal·ing (pāl′iŋ) *n.* 1. a fence made of pales 2. the action of making such a fence 3. a pale, or a number of pales

pal·i·sade (pal′ə sād′, pal′ə sād′) *n.* [< Fr. < Pr. < L. *palus,* a stake, PALE²] 1. any of a row of large pointed stakes set in the ground to form a fence as for fortification 2. such a fence ☆3. [*pl.*] a line of steep cliffs, usually along a river —*vt.* **-sad′ed, -sad′ing** to fortify or defend with a palisade

pall¹ (pôl) *vi.* **palled, pall′ing** [ME. *pallen,* short for *appallen,* AP-PALL] 1. to become tiresome, boring, dull, etc. [his jokes are beginning to *pall* on me] 2. to become tired or surfeited [*his interest in stamps soon palled*] —*vt.* to bore after a time

pall² (pôl) *n.* [< OE. < L. *pallium,* a cover] 1. a piece of velvet, etc. used to cover a coffin, hearse, or tomb 2. a dark or gloomy

pale² (pāl) *n.* [< MFr. < L. *palus*, a stake: for IE. base see PEACE] **1.** a narrow, pointed stake used in fences; picket **2.** a fence; enclosure; boundary: now chiefly figurative [*outside the pale of the law*] **3.** a district enclosed within bounds ☆ **pale·face** (pāl′fās′) *n.* a white person: a term said to be first used by N. American Indians

Pa·lem·bang (pä′lem bäŋ′) seaport in SE Sumatra, Indonesia: pop. 723,000

pa·le·o- [< Gr. *palaios*, ancient] *a combining form meaning an-cient, prehistoric, primitive, etc. [Paleozoic, paleolithic]:* also, before a vowel, **pa·le-**

Pa·le·o·cene (pā′lē ə sēn′, pal′ē-) *adj.* [< PALEO- + Gr. *kainos*, recent] designating or of the first epoch of the Tertiary Period in the Cenozoic Era —**the Paleocene** the Paleocene Epoch or its rocks: see GEOLOGIC TIME CHART

pa·le·og·ra·phy (pā′lē äg′rə fē, pal′ē-) *n.* **1.** ancient writ-ing or forms of writing **2.** the science of identifying or translat-ing ancient writings —**pa′le·og′ra·pher** *n.* —**pa′le·o·graph′ic** (-ə graf′ik), **pa′le·o·graph′i·cal** *adj.*

pa·le·o·lith·ic (pā′lē ə lith′ik, pal′ē-) *adj.* [PALEO- + -LITHIC] designating or of the middle part of the early Stone Age, during which stone and bone tools were used

pa·le·on·tol·o·gy (ān täl′ə jē) *n.* [< Fr.: see PALE(O)- & ONTO- & -LOGY] the branch of geology that deals with prehis-toric life through the study of fossils —**pa′le·on′to·log′i·cal** (-tə läj′i k'l), **pa′le·on·to·log′ic** *adj.* —**pa′le·on·tol′o·gist** *n.*

Pa·le·o·zo·ic (-ə zō′ik) *adj.* [PALEO- + ZO- + -IC] designat-ing or of the era between the Precambrian and the Mesozoic —**the Paleozoic** the Paleozoic Era or its rocks: see GEOLOGIC TIME CHART

Pa·ler·mo (pə ler′mō; *It.* pä ler′mô) seaport on the N coast of Sicily: pop. 659,000

Pal·es·tine (pal′əs tīn′) **1.** region on the E coast of the Mediterranean, the country of the Jews in Biblical times **2.** territory in this region, west of the Jordan River, held by the British as a mandate from 1923 until the establishment of the state of Israel in 1948 —**Pal′es·tin′i·an** (-tin′ē ən) *adj., n.*

covering [*a pall of smoke*] **3.** a cloth, or cardboard covered with cloth, used to cover the chalice in some Christian churches —**vt. palled, pall′ing** to cover as with a pall

Pal·la·di·o (päl lä′dyô), **An·dre·a** (än dre′ä) (born *Andrea di Pietro*) 1518–80; It. architect —**Pal·la·di·an** (pə lā′dē ən, -lä′-) *adj.*

Pal·la·di·um (pə lā′dē əm) *n., pl.* **-di·a** (-ə) **1.** the legendary statue of Pallas Athena in Troy on which the safety of the city was supposed to depend **2.** [p-] anything supposed to ensure the safety of something; safeguard

pal·la·di·um (pə lā′dē əm) *n.* [ModL., ult. < Gr. *Pallas*, the goddess] a rare, silvery-white, metallic chemical element: it is used as a catalyst, or in alloys with gold, silver, etc.: symbol, Pd; at. wt., 106.4; at. no., 46

Pal·las (pal′əs) *Gr. Myth.* Athena, goddess of wisdom: also **Pal-las Athena** —**Pal·la·di·an** (pə lā′dē ən) *adj.*

pall·bear·er (pôl′ber′ər) *n.* [PALL² + BEARER] one of the per-sons who bear the coffin at a funeral

pal·let¹ (pal′it) *n.* [< MFr.: see PALETTE] **1.** a wooden tool consisting of a flat blade with a handle; esp., such a tool for smoothing pottery **2.** *same as* PALETTE (sense 1) **3.** a low, portable platform for storing goods in warehouses, etc. **4.** any of the clicks or pawls in the escapement of a clock, etc. which engage the teeth of a ratchet wheel to regulate the speed: see illustration at PAWL

pal·let² (pal′it) *n.* [< MFr. < OFr. *paille*, straw < L. *palea*, chaff] a small, crude bed or a mattress filled as with straw and used on the floor

pal·li·ate (pal′ē āt′) *vt.* **-at′ed, -at′ing** [< LL. pp. of *palliare*, to conceal < *pallium*, a cloak] **1.** to lessen the pain or severity of without curing; alleviate [*aspirin palliates a fever*] **2.** to make appear less serious or offensive; excuse [*to palliate an er-ror*] —**pal′li·a′tion** *n.* —**pal′li·a′tor** *n.*

pal·li·a·tive (-āt′iv, -ə tiv) *adj.* that palliates, eases, or excuses —*n.* something that palliates, as a drug

pal·lid (pal′id) *adj.* [L. *pallidus*, PALE¹] lacking in normal or natural color or brightness [*a pallid face*] —see SYN. at PALE¹ —**pal′lid·ly** *adv.* —**pal′lid·ness** *n.*

Part 2

Objective

To be aware of the multiple meanings of words

Presenting the Lesson

1. Read and discuss **The Multiple Meanings of Words,** pages 34–35. Ask students to think of other words that have several distinct meanings. See who can come up with a word with the most different meanings. Mention that words like *down,* which can serve as many different parts of speech, often have several different meanings.

2. Assign and discuss Exercises A and B and page 35. In Exercise B, point out that some of the uses of *key* are related. For example, those for a typist/piano teacher, and a person solving a puzzle/student studying pronunciation have elements in common. Ask them if any other pair in the exercise is similarly related.

3. Assign Exercises C and D on page 36. You may wish to do these exercises orally with the class.

Individualizing the Lesson

Less-Advanced Students

Be sure students understand that a word can have several similar meanings, or several different meanings. For example, a word like *bed* has several meanings (furniture to lie on, flower bed, river bed, etc.), but all the meanings are extentions of one basic idea. A word like *bureau,* on the other hand, has two completely different meanings (chest of drawers, division of a business or government agency).

Part 2 The Multiple Meanings of Words

Most of your vocabulary development in school has probably involved learning one meaning and spelling for each new word. For some words, this plan is acceptable. For many other words, however, it does not go far enough. Most words have more than one meaning. By assigning just one meaning to a word you ignore the additional meanings of that word.

Before you read the following sentences, write a definition for the word *court.* Now compare your definition with the uses of that word in these sentences.

1. Helen and Alice are going to the tennis *court* for a game this afternoon at three.
2. The strolling players set up their stage in the inner *court* of the castle.
3. The Queen and her entire *court* attended the gala New Year's Ball.
4. The judge asked the *court* to consider the evidence carefully and impartially.
5. Some politicians *court* the favor of those people who have powerful positions.
6. The King usually held *court* on the first day of the month, to receive the petitions of his subjects.
7. In some areas, a man must still ask permission of a woman's parents to *court* her.
8. Some people are foolish enough to *court* danger.
9. Our home is on a very short street known as Canterbury *Court.*
10. If you feel the ticket is unfair, you can plead your case in traffic *court.*

Did your definition of *court* fit any of the sentences? If not, share with the class a sentence using *court* to fit your definition. The excerpt from *Webster's New World Dictionary* shown on the following page, lists thirteen different meanings for the word *court.*

Dictionary Entry for *court*

word used as a noun	**court** (kort) **n** [OFr. < LL. < L. *cohors:* see COHORT] **1.** an uncovered space wholly or partly surrounded by buildings or walls **2.** a short street, often closed at one end **3.** *a*) an area for playing any of several ball games [a tennis *court*] *b*) a part of such an area ☆**4.** a motel: in full, **motor court 5.** *a*) the palace of a soverign *b*) the family, advisers, etc. of a sovereign, as a group *c*) a sovereign and his councilors as a governing body *d*) any formal gathering held by a sovereign **6.** attention paid
word used as a verb (transitive)	to someone in order to get something **7.** courtship; wooing **8.** *a*) a person or persons appointed to examine and decide law cases, make investigations, etc.; judge or judges *b*) a place where trials are held, investigations made, etc. *c*) an assembly or meeting of the judge or judges, the lawyers, and the jury in a law court **vt. 1.** to pay attention to (a person) in order to get
word used as a verb (intransitive)	something **2.** to try to get the love of; woo **3.** to try to get; seek [to *court* favor] **4.** to make oneself open to [to *court* in-
word used as an adjective	sults] **vi.** to woo **adj.** of or fit for a court **—out of court** without a trial **—pay court to** to court, as for favor or love **—court′er n.**

- 8 meanings of *court*, used as a noun.
- 4 meanings of *court*, used as a verb.
- 1 meaning of *court*, used as an adjective.

Advanced Students

Ask students to think of words with multiple meanings and to give the meanings only. See if the rest of the class can guess the word. Start them off with the following examples:

1. a crustacean
2. a machine for lifting heavy weights
3. a kind of apple
4. an ill-tempered person. *Answer: crab.*

Optional Practice

Have students write sentences that reflect different meanings for the words listed below: The number of sentences they should write is given in parentheses.

case (3)
pat (3)
sharp (4)
rook (3)
nut (3)

Extending the Lesson

Have students look in specialized journals and magazines that deal with a specific interest, hobby, or sport. Have them find examples of words that are used in specialized ways. In a computer journal, for example, the word *bit* or the word *menu* will have a specialized meaning that only readers of the journal are likely to understand.

Put together lists of specialized terms for several areas such as music, sports, the media, science, and medicine. Look up several of these words in a dictionary. Point out that the specialized meanings are often set off with boldfaced or italicized heads within the entry.

From these examples, you can see the need for being aware of multiple meanings. The dictionary is your best tool for learning about all the possibilities of meaning in a single word.

Exercises Words with Multiple Meanings

A. Each of the four words below has more than one meaning. Write at least five sentences for each word. Each sentence should illustrate a different meaning for the word. Use a dictionary.

note   light   round   ring

B. The word *key* may be used differently by each of the people named below. Look up the meanings in a dictionary and show the use of each in an original sentence. Answers will vary.

1. a locksmith
2. a typist
3. a singing teacher
4. a person solving a puzzle
5. a piano teacher
6. a composer of songs
7. a student of the geography of Florida
8. a student studying pronunciations in a dictionary
9. a mathematics teacher

C. Give the meaning of the word *square* in each of the following sentences. Check with a dictionary in cases where you are not sure.

1. A concert will be held in the village *square* tonight after the fireworks display. Open area
2. On Monday we can *square* our accounts. Settle
3. Carpenters use *squares* to test right angles. Ruler that forms 90° angle
4. The *square* of 2 is 4. Product of number multiplied by itself.
5. He *squared* the surface with a straightedge. Test or adjust for straightness
6. The sergeant told the recruits to *square* their shoulders and stand at attention. Make a right angle; straighten
7. What is the formula for the area of a *square*? Figure with 4 equal sides

D. The following sentences contain phrases using forms of the word *book*. Explain the meaning of each italicized phrase. Use the dictionary if necessary.

1. Even though her team had lost the final game, the coach admitted that the referees had called the fouls *by the book*. According to the rules
2. Ms. Carr has *kept books* for our neighborhood food cooperative for many years. Do record-keeping for
3. The officer *booked the man* for suspicion of burglary. Put charges on police record
4. The candidate said he wanted to *make an open book* of his family finances. Make all facts known

Part 3

Objective

To increase precision in the use of words through an understanding of synonyms, antonyms, and the thesaurus

Presenting the Lesson

1. Read the introduction to Part 3 and **Using Synonyms**, pages 36–39. Be sure students understand that synonyms are similar, not identical,

Part 3 Gaining Precision in the Use of Words

The concert singer who is exactly on pitch, the archer who hits the bull's-eye, the sky diver who lands directly on target—all display a precision that marks superior skill. Similarly, speakers and writers who display precision in their choice of words show themselves to be skillful users of language.

Precision in the use of words is essential to achieving word power. Precise use of synonyms and antonyms distinguishes the person with a powerful vocabulary from the person with an ordinary vocabulary.

36

Using Synonyms

Synonyms are words that have similar meanings. They do not usually mean *exactly* the same thing. Each one has a meaning that is slightly different from the others. It is important to have many synonyms in your vocabulary so that you can say exactly what you want to say and understand exactly what you read and hear.

Let's see how synonyms work. If a neighbor asked you if you were a *pupil* in East High School, would you say "Yes"? If she suggested that your ten-year-old brother was *student* at Jefferson Elementary School, would she be right? If she called you a *scholar*, would she be using the correct word?

Here is how one dictionary explains the differences in meaning among these three synonyms.

1. The word *pupil* applies to a child in school, or to someone studying privately with a teacher.

   EXAMPLES: Ruthmarie is a *pupil* of the famous singer Carlo Amato.
   Bobby is a *pupil* at Jefferson Elementary School.

2. The word *student* applies to someone attending a junior high school, a high school, a college, or university.

   EXAMPLES: Several hundred college *students* attended the rally.
   I am a first-year *student* at East High.

3. The word *scholar* is reserved for a learned person who is an authority in some field, or to a student who has earned a scholarship.

   EXAMPLES: Uncle Andrew is a Biblical *scholar*.
   Charlotte is a Rhodes *scholar*.

You can see from these examples that you might feel somewhat insulted if someone said you were a *pupil* at East High. You would probably prefer to be called a *student*. At the same time, you will realize that you probably should not be called a *scholar*. This is exactly what is meant by precision in the use of words. The more careful you are in the choice of synonyms, the more effective your use of the language will be.

in meaning. Stress that with an understanding of the various shades of meaning in a group of synonyms, a writer or a speaker can convey meaning precisely and colorfully. Write the word *cold* on the board. Ask the students for synonyms. Discuss the various shades of meaning and have the students write a sentence for each synonym.

2. Caution students that a thesaurus will only suggest words of related meaning; it is usually necessary to check the exact meaning in a dictionary. Have the class look up the word *party* in a thesaurus. Write the sentence, "My parents have a party every New Year's Eve" on the board. Substitute the synonyms listed under *party* in the sentence. The results will demonstrate the need to check precise meanings of synonyms.

3. Read and discuss **Using Antonyms**, page 39. Check to be sure students understand the idea of antonym by asking for antonyms for the following words: *smooth, friendly, dull, top, east, hurt, clean, dry,* and *tense*.

4. Assign Exercises A and B, page 40. Have several students read their answers aloud.

5. Assign Exercises C and D. You may wish to do these orally with the class, especially with less-advanced students. Point out that Exercise C is much like parts of some college entrance exams.

Individualizing the Lesson

Less-Advanced Students

1. Help students remember the difference between synonyms and antonyms by pointing out that the word *synonym* begins with an *S*, which they may think of as standing for *same*. *Antonym* starts with *A*, which they may think of as *against* (or opposite)

2. Do Exercises C and D as an oral discussion.

3. Instead of assigning exercise E, provide students with several lists of synonyms. Have students work in pairs or groups to write sentences that use each word most effectively (see Optional Practice).

Advanced Students

1. Assign Exercise E, page 41, to be completed individually. Then ask students to read their answers aloud and discuss them.

2. Ask students to write a short paragraph on any topic (descriptive paragraphs may work best). Then have these students revise the paragraphs by replacing words with more effective synonyms.

Optional Practice

Have students look up one of the following words in the thesaurus: *important, fragrant, cheerfulness, plunge.* Ask them to write a separate sentence for each of the synonyms listed. The sentences must make clear the precise meaning of the word.

Extending the Lesson

Ask students to find a passage in a newspaper or magazine that includes description. Have them experiment with substituting various synonyms for adjectives, nouns, and verbs in the passage. If any of the students feels they have improved on the original, have them read their revision to the class.

A good dictionary is a valuable tool for developing precision in the use of synonyms. As you learned in Part 1 of this chapter, most dictionaries contain **synonymies,** listings of synonyms explaining their differences or shades of meaning. Use the synonymy sections of your dictionary carefully, since there are few absolute synonyms in English.

Examine the synonymy entered in *Webster's New World Dictionary* following the word *brave.*

Dictionary Entry for *brave*

synonymy

brave (brāv) **adj.** [Fr. < It. *bravo*, brave, fine, orig., wild, savage < L. *barbarus*, BARBAROUS] **1.** not afraid; having courage; valiant **2.** fine; splendid [a *brave* new world] **—n.** **1.** any brave man **2.** a N. American Indian warrior **—vt. braved, brav'ing 1.** to face with courage [they *braved* the storm] **2.** to defy; dare **—brave'ly adv. —brave'ness n.**

SYN.—brave is the general term that implies fearlessness in meeting danger or difficulty; **courageous** suggests readiness to deal firmly with any dangerous situation because of self-discipline and strong convictions; **bold** stresses a daring nature, whether shown by courage, insolence, or defiance; **audacious** suggests reckless boldness; **valiant** emphasizes a heroic quality in the courage shown; **intrepid** implies absolute fearlessness in facing something new or unknown; **plucky** is usually used of someone who continues fighting even though at a disadvantage **—ANT. craven, cowardly**

To the casual user of the language, the words *brave, courageous, bold, audacious, valiant, intrepid,* and *plucky* are interchangeable. To the precise user of the language, they are not. A precise user of the language might speak of a *brave* or *valiant* warrior or a *bold* or *audacious* robber, but is not likely to describe the robber as either *brave* or *valiant.* Each synonym carries a meaning not present in the other six words.

Synonyms add variety and color to our language. They also help us to avoid boring repetition of the same word. Certain words, particularly colloquial expressions, are overused to such an extent in daily conversation that they lose much of their impact. In your speaking and writing, make a conscious effort to avoid such repetition.

The Thesaurus. A thesaurus is a reference book that can be an invaluable help to a writer. It is a storehouse of synonyms and advice on word usage. Clarity and effectiveness in writing are dependent upon accurate word choice, and a thesaurus can help you find the exact word you need. However, when you use a thesaurus, remember that the differences in meaning among synonyms are of critical importance. Before you use a synonym that you find in a thesaurus, check its full meaning in a dictionary. Be sure that it is the correct word for the use you have in mind.

Here is an entry from *Roget's Thesaurus.*

DANGER.—I. *Nouns.* **danger,** chance, hazard, insecurity, jeopardy, peril, unsafety, risk, pitfall, endangerment; storm brewing, clouds gathering, clouds on the horizon; crisis.
dangerousness, riskiness, touch and go, unsafety, treachery; venturousness, etc. (see *Adjectives*).
[*dangerous person*] **menace,** threat, serpent, viper; dangerous woman, *femme fatale* (*F.*).
II. *Verbs.* **endanger,** expose to danger, hazard, jeopardize, peril, imperil, risk, speculate with, venture, compromise.
[*accept danger*] **risk,** hazard, venture, adventure, dare, stake, set at hazard, speculate.
III. *Adjectives.* **dangerous,** chancy, risky, ticklish, touch-and-go, venturous, venturesome, adventurous, adventuresome, speculative; hazardous, perilous, parlous, precarious, insecure, jeopardous, critical, queasy, unsafe, ugly, treacherous, serpentine, viperous.
See also CHANCE, FEAR, THREAT, WARNING.
Antonyms—See PROTECTION.

Using Antonyms

Antonyms are words with meanings that are the opposite of each other. *Summer—winter, night—day, near—far, happy—sad* are examples of antonyms. Knowing how to use antonyms well will help to make your speech and writing more colorful and more precise. Antonyms are also useful when you need to present a contrast.

You have already seen that antonyms can be found at the end of dictionary entries. A thesaurus may also provide you with antonyms.

Exercises Gaining Precision in the Use of Words

A. Read the following paragraph. Note the monotonous effect of the overuse of the word *fantastic*.

> The Homecoming dance was a *fantastic* affair. The decorations committee did a *fantastic* job. The band, James and Company, was really *fantastic*. The students consumed all of the *fantastic* refreshments. Everyone agreed that this was the most *fantastic* dance ever held at Jefferson High School.

Rewrite this paragraph, substituting other words for the overused word *fantastic*. The rewritten paragraph should give the reader a more precise picture of what the dance was actually like. After you have rewritten the paragraph, check your words in a dictionary.

B. Study the following synonymy for the word *estimate* from *Webster's New World Dictionary*. Write a sentence for each of these four words—*estimate*, *appraise*, *evaluate*, and *rate*—to illustrate the different shades of meaning of each word.

SYN.—estimate refers generally to the forming of a personal opinion or judgment; **appraise** implies the intention of giving an accurate or expert judgment, as of value or worth [to *appraise* a new house]; **evaluate** also connotes an attempt at an exact judgment, but rarely with reference to value in terms of money [let us *evaluate* the evidence]; **rate** implies the comparing of one person or thing with another or others as to value, quality, etc. [he is *rated* the best in his field]—see also **SYN.** at CALCULATE

C. Answer the following. Use your dictionary for help.

1. Could the same person be *uninterested* and *disinterested* in the same project at the same time? Yes

2. Could a person be *healthy* in an *unhealthful* climate? Explain. Yes. A person could be in good health even though the climate is harmful.

3. If someone said you were a *bore*, would you be happy about it? If the same person said you were a *boor*, would you feel better or worse? No. Worse.

4. Explain the difference between *flash, glitter,* and *sparkle*. Use each in an original sentence. Answers will vary.

5. A person with an *irritable* disposition is easily annoyed. A person with an *irascible* disposition has what trouble? quick-tempered

6. Can you be *happy* without being *cheerful?* Could you be *cheerful* without being *happy?* Yes. Yes.

7. *Neat, tidy,* and *trim* are often used interchangeably, but each word implies something different from the others. Use each in an original sentence that will make the distinctions clear. Answers will vary.

8. Could you be *eager* without being *anxious?* Explain. Yes.

D. Answer the following. Use your dictionary if necessary.
Answers in margin.

1. Would you deal with a person who is *unscrupulous?* What word would you use to designate the opposite trait?

2. *Parsimonious* people have few friends. What quality would they have to cultivate to change the situation?

3. Would an *illiterate* person necessarily have to be *uncultured?* Explain.

4. You attend a student meeting; nothing much is accomplished. A classmate says the meeting was *unorganized;* another says it was *disorganized.* Is there a difference? Explain.

5. You find the word *abridged* on the cover of a novel you are about to read. Would you expect a complete telling of the story as the author wrote it?

6. If you found a package of corn seeds marked "atypical," what type of corn would you expect to grow from them?

7. If you were told that doing a certain thing would be a *disservice* to you, would you do it? Give a reason for your answer.

8. What type of person is a *malcontent?*

9. What is the difference between *asocial* and *antisocial?*

10. Would you describe a secret code as being *indecipherable* or *illegible?* Use each word in a sentence.

E. Write down two synonyms for each of the words given below. Use a dictionary or thesaurus if necessary. Then use each synonym in an original sentence that clearly shows the difference in meaning.
Answers in margin.

1. fear	6. hesitate	11. oblivious
2. lazy	7. spite	12. deplore
3. guard	8. injure	13. observe
4. scoff	9. scanty	14. noticeable
5. scold	10. hateful	15. error

Exercise D

1. No. Scrupulous, principled, moral, honest
2. Generosity
3. No. Inability to read and write does not imply unrefined speech or behavior.
4. *Unorganized* implies that there was no plan.
   Disorganized implies that an existing plan was not followed.
5. No.
6. Odd, unusual
7. No. It would be harmful.
8. discontented, unhappy
9. *Asocial*—stays away from others; *antisocial*—harmful to others.
10. *Indecipherable,* which means "impossible to figure out." *Illegible* refers to poor printing or writing.

Exercise E

1. terror, fright
2. idle, indolent
3. defend, protect
4. ridicule, make fun of
5. find fault, complain
6. pause, be unsure
7. hostility, hatefulness
8. hurt, injure
9. sparse, meager
10. malicious, bad
11. unmindful, forgetful
12. regret, lament
13. see, watch
14. conspicuous, visible
15. mistake, fault

Summary and Applications

These summaries are designed to restate the main concepts covered in the preceding chapter. In addition, they suggest ways in which the concepts may be applied in more general situations.

Encourage students to use this summary for review, or as part of the SQ3R method of study (see Chapter 15). Remind them, though, that more specific points can only be reviewed by skimming the chapter itself.

Applications in Other Subject Areas

These high-interest activities are designed to provide challenging opportunities to apply the chapter concepts in other subject areas.

1. For **Foreign Language**, offer examples of foreign words and phrases to help the class get started: *nom de plume, gesundheit, ab ovo, con brio*.

2. To extend the second activity, have the students submit quiz questions *not* related to definitions that can be answered by consulting the dictionary. Here are some possible examples:

Where is Barbers Point?

What does £ mean? Compile the questions into an open-book quiz for the class.

SUMMARY AND APPLICATIONS   CHAPTER 2

1. The dictionary is an excellent source for increasing and strengthening your vocabulary. It can also be used as a reference text for many different subject areas.

2. There are two main types of dictionaries—unabridged dictionaries and abridged dictionaries. You will use the shorter, abridged dictionaries in most of your work.

3. All standard dictionaries contain the following information:

Guide words	Entry words	Etymologies
Entries	Part of speech	Synonyms
Pronunciation	abbreviations	Derived words
keys and respellings	Definitions	

Check your dictionary for additional elements and for symbols and abbreviations.

4. Use a dictionary to discover the precise meaning of a word in a particular context. Also use dictionary synonymies or a thesaurus to choose precise words as you write.

Applications in Other Subject Areas

Foreign Language.   Look through your classroom dictionary. Identify the symbol that indicates foreign words and phrases. Then find at least twenty foreign words and phrases. Write them, along with their pronunciations and definitions.

Speech / Math / Science / Social Studies.   Most dictionaries have special charts at the front or back containing different types of information. Some contain tables of weights and measures, metric conversion tables, lists of colleges and universities, terms and symbols from areas of specialization, and even maps. Find a dictionary that contains such graphic aids. Summarize or list the aids found in one of these. Prepare a brief report for oral presentation to your class.

Chapter 3

Using Language for Different Purposes

Chapter Objectives

1. To recognize that the English language contains many words borrowed from other languages

2. To understand the ways in which new words are created

3. To recognize the different levels of usage in the English language and the appropriate uses of each level

4. To understand the importance of simple and direct language in communicating effectively

Preparing the Students

Point out that the latest edition of Webster's Dictionary contains thousands of new words, such as *videodisc, high-tech, humungus,* and *nouvelle cuisine.* Ask the students to try to determine the origins of these words. Point out that our language is constantly growing as new words are added. Ask students whether these words are appropriate for use in all situations. Are any of them **slang**? Should any be used only in a technical situation?

Read and discuss the introduction on page 43. Emphasize the two main objectives of the chapter.

Additional Resources

Mastery Test — See pages 15–16 in the test booklet. Recommended for use after teaching the chapter.

Skills Practice Book — pages 13-16.

Duplicating Masters — pages 13-16.

Special Populations — See special section at the front of this Teacher's Edition.

Would you be upset if someone accused you of *brangling* too much? Would you be disturbed if you were offered a *nuncheon*? You probably would have no idea how to react. However, an American colonist who lived in the 1700's would understand that you had been accused of quarreling in the first instance, and had been offered a snack in the second. The same colonist, though, would be perplexed by such words as *Skylab, plastic,* and *laser*.

A changing vocabulary is just one example of the adaptability of our language. Sometimes we must change the way we speak or write simply to suit the situation or company in which we find ourselves. We can do this by using different kinds, or **levels**, of language.

This chapter will examine these two aspects of our rich and fascinating language. You will learn how language changes with time. You will also learn how individual speakers and writers adapt language to suit particular situations.

Objective

To recognize that the English language contains many words borrowed from other languages

Presenting the Lesson

1. Read and discuss **Borrowed Words** on page 44. Remind students that America is a country composed of many different native cultures, as well as dozens of ethnic, cultural, and religious groups who brought their languages with them when they emigrated to this country. Point out that, not surprisingly, many words from those different cultures have found their way into the English language. Ask students if they can identify the origins of the following words: *pasta* (It.); *rendezvous* (Fr.); *won ton* (Chi.); *sauerkraut* (Ger.); *opossum* (Algonquin); *lei* (Hawaiian).

2. Discuss the chart on pages 45–46. Ask students to think of additional examples from these or other languages.

3. Assign Exercises A and B on page 44. In Exercise B, encourage students to find words from several different languages. Other reference sources for Exercise B might include the following: *A Dictionary of Word and Phrase Origins* (3 vols.); *The Oxford Dictionary of English Etymology;* Foster, *The Changing English Language;* Pei, *The Story of the English Language.*

Individualizing the Lesson

Less-Advanced Students

1. For Exercise A on page 44, review the location and use of the

Part 1   Borrowed Words

America has been called a melting pot because it is made up of people from many different countries and cultures. In the same way, the English language can be called a melting pot of other languages. Since its beginnings over 1,500 years ago, English has grown to be the largest language in the world, containing over 790,000 individual words. Most of this enormous vocabulary has been borrowed from other languages, especially from Latin, French, German, and Greek.

When another language has a word for which we have no term of our own, we borrow it as it is, or we change it to fit into our language. In colonial America, for example, the colonists did not want to use the monetary terms of the British. Instead, they borrowed the Dutch word *daler*, which meant "coined in the valley," and this became our term *dollar*. When the Texas cowboys of the Old West were learning how to handle angry herds of long-horned cattle, they adopted the Spanish word *estampeda* and changed it to *stampede*. These are but two of the hundreds of thousands of borrowed words that help make up our language.

Refer to the list on pages 45 and 46 for other borrowed words that have enriched our language.

Exercises   Recognizing Borrowed Words

A.   Use a dictionary to discover the language from which each of the following words was borrowed. You will have to refer to the abbreviations key in your dictionary. Copy the definitions of any words that you do not already know.

Italian 1. piano   5. tycoon Japanese   8. opossum American Indian

French 2. ensemble   6. khaki Hindi   9. veldt Afrikaans

Chinese 3. tea   7. mosquito   10. gusto Italian,Spanish

4. jaguar   Spanish, Portuguese

Portuguese

B.   Using a dictionary, encyclopedia, or other source, find fifteen words that came into English from other languages. Note whether these words were changed or left as they were when adopted.

Answers will vary.

Words Borrowed from Other Languages

AFRICAN

tote	gumbo	jazz	canary

AMERICAN INDIAN

moccasin	wigwam	hominy	squash
chipmunk	skunk	raccoon	moose
powwow	pecan		

ARABIC

algebra	mosque	almanac	magazine
zero	mattress		

AUSTRALIAN

boomerang	kangaroo	outback

CHINESE

yen	typhoon	silk	catsup

DUTCH

ahoy	boom	deck	hoist
pickle	wagon	boss	landscape
sketch	yacht		

ESKIMO

igloo	kayak

FRENCH

machine	fiancé(e)	chic	religion
seige	ballad	literature	courage
gentle	liberty	virtue	parliament
charity	bureau		

abbreviation key in the dictionary. Write the first two words, *piano* and *ensemble,* on the chalkboard. Show students how they would locate the origins of these words. Then have the students complete the exercise independently.

2. For Exercise B on page 44, ask the students for two examples of borrowed words. Suggest food words, if necessary *(macaroni, enchilada).* Look these up and discuss them with the students. Ask for five more examples. If necessary, suggest *boutique* (Fr.), *discotheque* (Fr.), *dunk* (Ger.), *bonanza* (Sp.), *barbeque* (Haitian). Then have the students complete the exercise independently.

Advanced Students

Ask each student to find five English words with interesting histories. Have them trace the evolution of each word from its early forms and meanings up through its current form. Suggest that the *Oxford English Dictionary* might be especially useful for this exercise. Have students represent their findings on charts or diagrams to be displayed in the classroom. Direct the students to the introductory pages of the dictionary and to other reference materials for information for this assignment.

Optional Practice

1. After they complete Exercise B on page 44, have the students read their lists of words and word origins aloud. Make a list on the chalkboard showing how many different languages are represented.

2. Have the students find words from languages not represented on

45

the chart or in the exercises, such as Malay: *amok, batik, kapok;* Tonga: *taboo;* Sanskrit: *karma;* Yiddish: *schmaltz, schnook.*

Extending the Lesson

Have each student select a country that he or she is interested in. Then direct students to research their countries, looking for names of foods, cultural terms, and other words that they recognize as having entered the English language. Point out that many words were borrowed from languages that had different alphabets and sound systems (Chinese, Greek, Russian) or no written language (Hawaiian, Algonquin). The English pronunciations and spellings of these words are, therefore, often only rough equivalents.

Words Borrowed from Other Languages

GERMAN

frankfurter	delicatessen	kindergarten	stein
zinc	cobalt	poltergeist	spiel

HEBREW

amen	sabbath	cinnamon	hallelujah

ITALIAN

spaghetti	soprano	violin	cello
volcano	studio	sonata	fresco
balcony	trombone		

JAPANESE

soybean	kimono	judo	haiku

PERSIAN

kiosk	chess	jasmine	lemon
lilac	paradise	jackal	azure
bazaar	spinach		

SCANDINAVIAN

ski	fiord	geyser	viking
smorgasbord	sauna		

SLAVIC

gherkin	babushka	polka	vampire

SPANISH

canyon	cigar	desperado	renegade
comrade	vanilla	alligator	bronco
rodeo	siesta		

Part 2   Created Words

> The new circumstances under which we are placed call for new words, [for] new phrases, and for the transfer of old words to new objects. — THOMAS JEFFERSON

New ideas need new words. Because new concepts and inventions are continually being developed, our language must grow in order to communicate these ideas. In this section we will briefly look at several ways in which new words are created.

Compounds and Blends

A **compound word** is made by combining two existing words to form a new word.

$$\text{night} + \text{shirt} = \text{nightshirt} \qquad \text{foot} + \text{ball} = \text{football}$$

People develop compound words to describe new ideas or things while still using familiar terms. With a little thought, you should be able to explain how and why such new words as *superstar*, *spacewalk*, and *drive-in* were created.

If two words are combined, but some of the letters are dropped, the resulting word is called a **blend**. For example, *walrus* is a blend made from the animal's original name, *whale horse*. The word *laundromat* was made from *laundry* and *automatic*. More recently, *situation comedy* has become the familiar term *sitcom*.

Clipped Words

Sometimes, one or more parts of a word are dropped and the remaining part is used alone as a word. Such words are called **clipped words**. They are commonly used in less formal speaking and writing.

The following are some common clipped words:

gymnasium-*gym*	examination-*exam*	gasoline-*gas*
advertisement-*ad*	teenagers-*teens*	photograph-*photo*

Part 2

Objective

To understand the ways in which new words are created

Presenting the Lesson

1. Read and discuss **Compounds and Blends** and **Clipped Words** on pages 47 and 48. Have students give their own examples of compounds, blends, and clipped words.

2. Assign and discuss Exercises A and B on page 48.

3. Read and discuss **Acronyms** and **People and Place Names** on page 48. Go over the chart on page 49. Have students define the words in the chart by looking them up in a dictionary.

4. Assign Exercise A on pages 49–50. You may wish to do this exercise orally.

5. Assign Exercises B and C on page 50.

6. Read and discuss **Terms from Specialized Areas** on pages 50–51. Point out that jargon is often thought of as unintelligible by people outside a certain profession because of its highly specialized nature. Once jargon enters into everyday speech, however, it loses its specialized quality and ceases to be jargon. Discuss ways in which the words of specialists come into general speech: through newspapers, radio, television, magazines, and even conversation.

7. Ask students to add examples of specialized vocabularies to the chart on page 51, or to think of new categories of jargon. Following are some possibilities:

Astronomy: quasar, pulsar, microwave, zodiac, red dwarf, black hole
Military: squad, junta, hostage, wargame
Sociology: norm, mores, peer group, sanctions, alienation, ethnicity
Biochemistry: octane, enzyme, protein, glucose, cholesterol
Art: collage, mobile, graphic, mosaic, calligraphy, sketch
Theater: ad lib, burlesque, ingenue, pantomime, repertory
Literature: epic, archetype, genre, ballad, allegory

8. Assign Exercises A and B on page 51.

Individualizing the Lesson

Less-Advanced Students

1. Do Exercise A on page 48 orally. Be sure the students know the meaning of each word.

2. For Exercise B on page 48, write the first three words on the chalkboard, showing the word or words from which each was made. Have the students complete the exercise independently.

3. For Exercise B on page 50, assign two or three words to each student. Help students work independently on the research, and ask them to report their findings to the class.

4. Do Exercise A on page 51 orally. See how many meanings the students can come up with before referring to a dictionary.

5. You may not wish to assign Exercise B on page 51 to these students. Make sure, however, that they are part of the class discussion of this exercise.

Advanced Students

1. After the students complete Exercises A and B on page 48, have them write a paragraph using these

Exercises ## Recognizing Compounds, Blends, and Clipped Words

A. Using a dictionary, find the clipped form of each of the following words. Check the definition of any word that you do not know.

1. cabriolet cab
2. laboratory lab
3. fanatic fan
4. omnibus bus
5. airplane plane
6. zoological gardens zoo
7. pianoforte piano
8. pantaloons pants
9. chimpanzee chimp
10. delicatessen deli

B. Using a dictionary, determine whether each of the following terms is a compound, a blend, or a clipped word. Then write the word or words from which each one was made.

1. dorm CL-dormitory
2. splashdown CD
3. splurge BL-splash, surge
4. typewriter CD
5. brunch BL-breakfast, lunch
6. marketplace CD
7. chortle BL-chuckle, snort
8. fence CL-defense
9. phone CL-telephone
10. gasohol BL- gasoline, alcohol
11. wristwatch CD
12. smog BL-smoke, fog
13. sub CL-submarine
14. bookkeeper CD
15. moped BL-motor, pedal

Acronyms

Sometimes a new word is created from the first letters of a group of words. This new word is called an **acronym**. *Scuba,* for instance, is an acronym for "self-contained underwater breathing apparatus." *Radar* means "radio detection and ranging." The computer industry has created the word *Cobol,* which is a specific computer language, from "common business oriented language."

People and Place Names

Many proper names have passed into our language to form new words. The term *mesmerize,* for example, comes from the name of Dr. F. A. Mesmer, an Austrian physician who was known for his work with hypnotism. The word "tuxedo" was originally the name of a country club near Tuxedo Lake, New York. Here are some other words made from names:

	Words from Names
saxophone	from Adolphe Sax, the Belgian inventor of this musical instrument
tantalize	from Tantalus, a Greek mythological king who was condemned to be forever tempted by water and food that he could not reach
sideburns	from Ambrose E. Burnside, a Union general during the Civil War who had very distinctive whiskers
bowdlerize	from Thomas Bowdler, a British editor who, in 1818, published a heavily censored edition of the works of Shakespeare
paisley	from the city of Paisley where wool shawls with colorful, intricate patterns were made
Frisbee	from "Mother Frisbie's" cookie jars, the lids of which were used for a game by Princeton students
silhouette	from Étienne de Silhouette, a French finance minister, much disliked because of his poor economic policies. His name came to be associated with pictures which were, like his abilities, incomplete.

Exercises Using Acronyms and Words Made from Names

A. Give the acronym for each of the following:

1. Cooperative for American Relief Everywhere CARE
2. Zone Improvement Plan ZIP
3. Beginners All-purpose Symbolic Instruction Code BASIC

or other clipped words, compounds, and blends. Direct them to underline each example.

2. After students complete Exercise A on pages 49–50, have them find the words from which these acronyms were made:

CAP (Civil Air Patrol),
UNICEF (United Nations International Children's Emergency Fund), SALT (Strategic Arms Limitation Talks), CHASE (Cut Holes and Sink 'Em, Navy ammunition disposal project), PUSH (People United to Save Humanity).

3. Add the following five words to Exercise B on page 50: *malapropism* (humorous misuse of a word, after Mrs. Malaprop, in Sheridan's play *The Rivals); leotard* (names for French aerialist who first wore the long, tight-fitting garment); *spinnaker* (a large sail on racing yachts, named after the yacht Sphinx); *macadamia nut* (after John Macadam, Australian chemist); *spinet* (small piano, after Venetian Giovanni Spinetti, probably its inventor).

4. Assign and discuss Exercise B, page 51.

Optional Practice

Have the students use the dictionary to find five clipped words, compounds, or blends not already used in the text. Have each student read his or her words aloud.

Extending the Lesson

Select students to find several brief newspaper or magazine articles to read to the class. Encourage them to select articles that deal with other countries or with specialized areas such as science or the arts. Ask the rest of the students to write down any foreign words, acronyms, or jargon they hear.

4. Housing and Urban Development HUD
5. Volunteers in Service to America VISTA
6. North Atlantic Treaty Organization NATO
7. Light Amplification by Stimulated Emission of Radiation LASER
8. Wide Area Telecommunications Service WATS
9. Health Maintenance Organization HMO
10. World Health Organization WHO

B. Research the following words. Do they have their origins in the names of people or of places? Explain how each term was added to our language. Answers in margin.

1. boycott	6. Fahrenheit	11. laconic
2. calico	7. bloomers	12. diesel
3. tangerine	8. turquoise	13. derby
4. July	9. Braille	14. cardigan
5. Wednesday	10. watt	15. quisling

C. The names of things often come from the names of people, but the reverse is also true. People's names often come from the names of things or qualities. Using reference materials, look up the following names and find out what they originally meant:

1. Adam man	6. Vincent conqueror
2. Deborah bee	7. George farmer
3. Robert famous	8. Barbara foreign
4. Thomas twin	9. Mary rebellion
5. Florence prosperity	10. Bonnie pretty

Terms from Specialized Areas

When members of a profession or industry develop their own specialized vocabulary, this vocabulary is called a **jargon.** Jargon can be very useful because it helps people within a profession to communicate efficiently.

Often the terms used in jargon enter everyday speech. Notice how much of the jargon on the following chart has come to be widely used by people outside these areas of specialization:

Exercise B
1. person–after Captain C. C. Boycott who was shunned by his neighbor during the Irish Land League agitation in 1880
2. place–from Calcutta, India, where this cloth was first obtained
3. place–from Tangier, Morocco
4. person–after Roman ruler Julius Caesar
5. person–after Norse god Woden (Woden's day)
6. person–after German physicist G. D. Fahrenheit who developed this temperature scale
7. person–after feminist Amelia Bloomer who advocated the use of these baggy pants for women
8. place–from "Turkish"; the stone was originally brought to Western Europe through Turkey
9. person–after Louis Braille who developed this alphabet for the blind
10. person–after James Watt, a Scottish engineer and inventor
11. place–from Laconia, a region in Southern Greece whose citizens were thought to be brief or terse in speech
12. person–after Rudolf Diesel, inventor of the diesel engine
13. person–after the 12th Earl of Derby who founded a race for 3-yr.-old horses in 1780
14. person–after J. T. Brudnell, the Earl of Cardigan, who developed this style
15. person–after Norwegian traitor Vidkun Quisling

Television/Radio		Sports	
network	commercial	grand slam	icing
channel	prime time	game plan	dribble
transistor	station break	knockout	match point

Automobiles		Music	
convertible	crankshaft	woodwind	cadence
power drive	spark plugs	motif	libretto
carburetor	shocks	counterpoint	crescendo

Computers		Space	
byte	terminal	satellite	skylab
software	input	astronaut	launching pad
disk	printout	blastoff	space shuttle

Sometimes members of different professions use the same word but attach different meanings to them. For example, an electrician *wires* a house; a newspaper reporter *wires* a story to an editor. A reporter sends in a *scoop;* a chef uses a *scoop* to cook.

Exercises Recognizing Jargon

A. Define each of the terms below as it would be used in the two listed professions. You may have to use a dictionary. Answers in margin.

1. trace   (A) *physician*   (B) *police officer*
2. culture   (A) *biologist*   (B) *sociologist*
3. bumper   (A) *farmer*   (B) *auto mechanic*
4. fault   (A) *geologist*   (B) *tennis pro*
5. book   (A) *librarian*   (B) *talent agent*

B. Give two examples of jargon from each field listed below. You may have to consult reference works such as encyclopedias. Answers will vary.

1. painting   4. law   7. teaching
2. religion   5. banking   8. cosmetics
3. medicine   6. carpentry   9. swimming

Exercise A
1. (A) an amount too small to be measured or a line drawn by a cardiograph
   (B) clue, evidence, or to follow the trail of
2. (A) bacterial growth in specially prepared environment
   (B) the characteristics of a given people in a given period
3. (A) unusually large (bumper crop)
   (B) bar across front and rear of an auto to absorb shock
4. (A) a crack in the earth's crust
   (B) an error while serving
5. (A) pages of writing fastened together and put between covers
   (B) to hire

To recognize the different levels of usage in the English language and the appropriate uses of each

Presenting the Lesson

1. Ask the students what they think T. S. Eliot means in the quotation on page 52. Read and discuss the rest of page 52. Make sure students understand the differences between standard/nonstandard and formal/informal. Be certain that they understand that both formal and informal language are acceptable in different situations.

2. Go over the chart on page 53. Ask the students if a person using informal English is using incorrect English. Then ask students to suggest situations that would call for formal English and others where informal language would be more appropriate.

3. Read **Nonstandard English** and **Slang** on page 54. Ask the students for additional examples of nonstandard English and slang. Emphasize that most slang is short-lived, developing from certain popular but temporary trends in lifestyle.

4. Assign Exercises A and B, on pages 54–55. Following are suggestions for revisions of Exercise A:

Sentence 2: change "one most folks know" to "one most people are familiar with"

Sentence 3: Delete "As a matter of fact"

Sentence 4: Change "really neat" to "fascinating"; replace "all the interesting stuff that they do" with "their interesting habits"

Part 3   The Levels of Language

"If we spoke as we write, we should find no one to listen; if we wrote as we speak, we should find no one to read."—T. S. ELIOT

No speaker or writer of English uses the language in the same way all the time. Instead, it is often necessary to vary the way one speaks or writes to suit a particular audience. For example, you probably speak one way when you are talking with your friends, another way when you are speaking in class, and perhaps a third way when you are giving a speech or oral report. The same sort of language variation also occurs in written material. The types of language that one uses on different occasions are called the **levels of usage.**

Standard English

Language that is acceptable at all times and in all places is called **standard English.** The rules and guidelines of standard English enable all speakers and writers of the language to communicate clearly and precisely without fear of misunderstanding. This textbook presents the rules and guidelines for using standard English.

Formal and Informal English. There are two accepted levels of standard English, formal and informal. **Formal English** is found primarily in writing but is appropriate in any circumstance that is serious, dignified, or ceremonial. **Informal English,** also known as colloquial English, is appropriate in most everyday situations. It is the language used in most magazines, newspapers, casual letters, and conversation. Look at these examples:

FORMAL: No written law has ever been more binding than unwritten custom supported by popular opinion.

INFORMAL: Traditions and habits are both hard to break.

Now examine the chart on the following page.

Characteristics of Formal and Informal English

	FORMAL	INFORMAL
Tone	Serious, reserved, academic, ceremonial	Personal, friendly, casual
Vocabulary and Mechanics	Sometimes uses longer or more complicated words Avoids contractions, clipped words, and slang Uses correct grammar, spelling, and punctuation	Uses simpler words Often uses contractions and clipped words Avoids slang Uses correct grammar, spelling, and punctuation
Organization	Longer, carefully constructed sentences	Sentences of a great variety of lengths Similar to conversational English
Appropriate Uses	Reports or serious essays Legal, academic, religious, or other professional documents Formal speeches, debates, or interviews	Writing intended for a general audience Conversations, letters Informal talks
Audience	Readers of scholarly material Readers of professional documents Persons in positions of authority	Friends, co-workers Most general audiences

Sentence 6: Change "a real blast" to "enjoyable"; replace "stuff a lot of food" with "pack large quantities of food"

Sentence 7: Change "Though they sure don't drink much" to "even though they drink very little"

Sentence 9: Delete "give or take a little"

Individualizing the Lesson

Less-Advanced Students

1. Do Exercise A on page 54 orally.

2. For Exercise B on page 55, go over the slang expressions with the students. Then have the class do this exercise orally, with each student contributing one or two sentences that contain the slang terms. Write the conversation on the chalkboard. Ask pairs of students to take turns reading it aloud.

Advanced Students

1. Have each student write a paragraph about a hobby or area of interest in an informal style, as though telling the information to a group of friends. Students should then present the same information in a paragraph written in more formal language, as though they were writing it for a class report.

2. Let the students work in pairs and act out their dialogues from Exercise B on page 55.

Optional Practice

Write nonstandard sentences such as the following on the chalkboard. Have the students change them to standard English.

Al should of brung the wood hisself.
Me and Jody set for a while in the shade.

He don't know there ain't no difference.
We be leaving soon.

Extending the Lesson

Begin a class discussion on some interesting topic, such as a recent news event or an exciting school game. As the conversation continues, tape it on a recorder. The next day, play back the conversation. Have students pick out examples of nonstandard English. Also have them suggest ways of changing the statements into standard English.

Nonstandard English

Language that is not accepted at all times and in all places is called **nonstandard English.** This level of language includes all grammatical forms and constructions that are not widely accepted, such as *He ain't got none* or *Pass me them papers.* Also included are slang and all language containing errors in punctuation, spelling, capitalization, and manuscript form.

Slang. The term **slang** is applied to all words and phrases that are not accepted as standard English. Slang words usually lead brief but colorful lives and then drop out of common usage. For example, American youths in the 1960's developed a large vocabulary of slang that included such terms as *groovy, hip, far out, square,* and *uptight.* Most of these terms now seem quaint and dated. However, some words that originate as slang eventually do become accepted as standard. This is true of most clipped forms and of such now standard words as *hot dog* and *lengthy.*

Slang can be appropriate on occasion. However, you must be careful about when and how you use it. Slang would not be appropriate in a group discussion or in a business letter, but it might help enliven conversation with friends or dialogue in a short story.

Exercises Levels of Language

A. The following report contains several different levels of language. Rewrite the report. Eliminate all nonstandard English and replace inappropriate phrases and slang with formal language.

Answers in Teacher Notes.

Gerbils belong to the scientific family *Cricetidae.* There are approximately one hundred different species of these furry, ratlike rodents, but the one most folks know is the Mongolian gerbil. As a matter of fact, all pet gerbils in the United States are descendants of twenty-two Mongolian gerbils sent to America by a Japanese laboratory in 1954. Gerbils make really neat pets because of all the interesting stuff that they do.

Pet gerbils should be fed commercial gerbil pellets or a mixture of fruits, small seeds, and raw vegetables. Watching them eat is a real blast, because they stuff a lot of food in the pouches of their cheeks. Water should be made available in their cages, though they sure don't drink much. Gerbils obtain water primarily through moisture in the food they eat. If properly cared for, a pet gerbil should live up to four years, give or take a little.

B. As you learned in the preceding section of this chapter, you should avoid slang except for a few special purposes. One such purpose is the writing of realistic, casual dialogue. The following slang expressions were popular during the 1920's. Using these expressions, write a conversation between two young people of 1925.

1. *caveman*—in boxing, a strong slugger with little skill
2. *dive*—a cheap restaurant or public place
3. *give (someone) the gate*—to jilt
4. *lam*—to leave quickly
5. *scrim*—a large dance party
6. *on the shelf*—not interested in getting married
7. *palooka*—a prizefighter
8. *pal*—any close friend; used in the 1920's to refer to women as well as men
9. *raspberry*—a sharp, harsh, scornful comment
10. *the bee's knees*—any excellent or popular thing

Part 4   Writing and Speaking Clearly

The purpose of language is to communicate. The best speakers and writers use language that is simple, direct, and appropriate to their audiences. Sometimes, however, people make their speech or writing unnecessarily difficult. This may occur as they unconsciously, or intentionally, attempt to impress or mislead others. Such writers use unnecessary jargon, complicated sentences, and long or uncommon words. This language is sometimes called **gobbledygook.**

Gobbledygook is often found in professional publications and in public statements made by professional people. Occasionally, it is the result of some writer's attempt to be too precise and

Part 4

Objective

To understand the importance of simple and direct language in communicating effectively

Presenting the Lesson

1. Read and discuss **Writing and Speaking Clearly**, pages 55–56. Be certain that students understand the difference between jargon and gobbledygook. After going over the gobbledygook sentences in the box, ask students if they have ever heard or seen this type of language. Ask for examples.

2. Assign Exercises A and B on page 57. Following are suggested answers for Exercise B:

1. He quit his job because he felt he was not being paid enough for the work he was doing.
2. Even during our busiest time periods, the parking lots for our building are usually adequate.
3. At the end of this disastrous movie, the star gives up his life as a cowboy, agrees to marry the young lady, and then kisses her.
4. Before the stage performance can begin, the lights in the theater must be dimmed.

Individualizing the Lesson

Less-Advanced Students

Do Exercises A and B on page 57 orally. Encourage the use of a dictionary.

Advanced Students

Have students pick a well-known saying like the ones in Exercise A on page 57 and see if they can write a gobbledygook version of it. Then have them read these sentences to the class and ask for translations.

Optional Practice

The following example is from an actual recall letter sent to an automobile owner. Have the students rewrite it in language that is clearer and more direct.

"A defect which involves the possible failure of a frame support plate may exist on your vehicle. This plate (front suspension pivot bar support plate) connects a portion of the front suspension to the vehicle frame, and its failure could affect vehicle

thorough. For example, there are some insurance contracts that sound like this:

> This policy is issued in consideration of the application therefor, a copy of which application is attached hereto and made part hereof, and of the payment for said insurance on the life of the above-named issued.

This passage uses legal jargon and complicated sentence structure to "dress up" its simple meaning: "Here is your insurance policy."

To avoid writing gobbledygook yourself, remember to use simple, direct language. Avoid using jargon that is unfamiliar to your audience, and replace long-winded phrases with shorter, clearer ones. When writing reports avoid trying to "dress up" straightforward statements by padding your sentences or using big words when small ones will do.

Look at the "translations" of gobbledygook in the chart that follows:

GOBBLEDYGOOK	DIRECT STATEMENT
1. We need some help *in the area of budgetary planning considerations.*	1. We need some help planning our budget.
2. He *made inquiry regarding* the letter.	2. He asked about the letter.
3. He *is of the opinion that* . . .	3. He believes . . .
4. The manager hoped *to escalate in terms of* production.	4. The manager hoped to increase production.
5. These machines *have the capability of* flying.	5. These machines can fly.
6. *The accident was caused by a failure to maintain sufficient altitude to avoid neighboring terrain.*	6. The plane crashed.

Exercises Writing Clearly

A. Our language contains many concise, familiar expressions that are models of simple, direct prose. Some examples are "A stitch in time saves nine," and "Time and tide wait for no man." Match the following passages of gobbledygook with the corresponding familiar sayings on the right.

c 1. One photographic exposure merits an appraisal identical to that accorded a ten hundredfold sum of verbiage.

a. A fool and his money are quickly parted.

d 2. Under no circumstances and on no occasion presume to calculate the entirety of those barnyard fowl that are identified as belonging to you prior to the termination of their incubation.

b. All that glitters is not gold.

a 3. He whom one might designate as deficient in understanding is in record time in a state of disconnectedness from his legal tender.

c. A picture is worth a thousand words.

b 4. Objects that scintillate are not necessarily auric in nature.

d. Never count your chickens before they hatch.

B. Translate these gobbledygook sentences into understandable standard usage. Your dictionary will help you with unfamiliar words.

Answers in Teacher Notes.

1. He gave up his employment because he came to the conclusion that the remuneration involved was not commensurate with his performance load.

2. Demand for parking does not appear to exceed significantly the supply of available parking spaces within our building's designated parking lots even during peak demand periods.

3. In the concluding montage of this cinematic debacle, the star foregoes his prior Western equestrian pursuits, accedes to the ingenue's matrimonial ambitions, and proceeds to osculation.

4. Before performance can be initiated on stage, all illumination in contingent areas must be lessened to the maximum extent.

directional control, particularly during heavy brake application. In addition, your vehicle may also require adjustment service to the hood secondary catch system. The secondary catch may be misaligned so that the hood may not be adequately restrained to prevent fly-up in the event the primary latch is inadvertently left unengaged. Sudden hood fly-up beyond the secondary catch while driving could impair driver visibility.

Extending the Lesson

Duplicate copies of George Orwell's widely anthologized "Politics and the English Language" or read it aloud to the class. Discuss Orwell's view of the dangers of gobbledygook.

Review the importance of understanding the nature of language—both its growth and use. Then encourage students to use this summary for review, or as part of the SQ3R method of study (see Chapter 15). Remind them, though, that more specific points can only be reviewed by skimming the chapter itself.

Applications in Other Subject Areas

These high-interest activities are designed to provide challenging opportunities to apply the chapter concepts in other subject areas.

1. Extend the application of the first activity. After students have compiled their dictionaries of jargon, have them quiz each other as a class activity. Try a "jargon bee" using students' dictionaries as your source.

2. To enliven the second and third activities, break the class up into small groups. Have them write and then act out skits in which formal language is used in a playing field or locker room situation or, conversely, slang is used in a government meeting, lecture, interview, or law court. The resulting humor should illustrate quite clearly the importance of using the right level of language.

SUMMARY AND APPLICATIONS   CHAPTER 3

1. As the world changes, language must change with it. Our vocabulary grows as we borrow words from other languages and create compounds, blends, clipped words, acronyms, words derived from people and place names, and jargon.

2. Whenever you speak or write, choose language that is appropriate to the occasion and to your audience.

3. Standard English is language that is acceptable to all audiences on all occasions. The two levels of Standard English are **formal English** and **informal English**.

4. Nonstandard English is language that is not acceptable to all audiences on all occasions.

5. Avoid slang except in casual conversation or in dialogue. Avoid "gobbledygook" altogether.

Applications in Other Subject Areas

Science / Math.   Much of the English language is made up of scientific and technical terms. Most of these terms are borrowed from Latin and Greek. From your science and math texts, begin collecting as many examples of these terms as you can. Look them up in a dictionary to determine their meanings and origins.

All Subjects.   As you go through your next day of school, notice the specialized vocabularies used in different classes. What terms are unique to your gym class? Which are heard only in science? art? music? Choose one class and make a dictionary that defines the jargon used in that subject area.

All Subjects.   Listen carefully to the language you hear during class. Compare it to the type of language used during lunch or out on a playing field during gym. How does the language used in these situations differ? Is each level of language appropriate to the situation in which it is being used? Does the language a speaker uses affect your opinion of that person?

Chapter 4

Using the Senses in Writing

Chapter Objectives

1. To become more sensitive to the senses of sight, hearing, touch, taste, and smell

2. To write vivid descriptions that appeal to all of the senses

Preparing the Students

Read the introduction to Chapter 4 on page 59. Ask the students to name the five senses, and write them on the chalkboard. Then have the students imagine a scene with which they are all familiar—the school lunchroom, the gym, their English classroom, for example. Ask them to suggest words and phrases that describe the scene. Write each response on the chalkboard next to the appropriate sense.

Explain that good writers create vivid descriptions by using words that appeal to the senses.

Additional Resources

Skills Practice Book — pages 17–22.

Duplicating Masters — pages 17–22.

Special Populations — See special section at the front of this Teacher's Edition.

Imagine being a child again and experiencing the world for the first time. How strange and beautiful life would seem, how fascinating and full of wonders! As writers, we must be like children in this respect. We must be aware of the carnival of sensation all around us, and try not to take for granted the extraordinary world revealed by our senses.

Writers have to remember vividly how their subjects look, sound, taste, smell, and feel. Then they must find the right words to make these remembered sensations live in their readers' imaginations. By training yourself to use your senses fully and by learning how to translate your sensory experience into words, you can make your own writing come alive.

Part 1

Objective

To write vivid descriptions that appeal to the sense of sight

Presenting the Lesson

1. Read aloud the first paragraph of **The Sense of Sight** on page 60 and the poem "To Look at Any Thing." Discuss the questions that follow the poem. Moffitt's advice to his reader is to "Be the thing you see." He also says, "You must take your time."

Ask the students if they understand what he means by "Be the thing you see." Suggest that the poet is talking about identifying physically and spiritually with the things you are looking at—in other words, imagining what it feels like to be those things.

There is evidence that Moffitt has taken his own advice because he seems to have imagined what it feels like to be a stem (like a "dark snake") or a leaf (like a "ferny plume"). He also says to really see something you must feel the spaces between objects. He feels the spaces between leaves as "small silences" and says that both the leaves and the spaces between them issue from "peace." His identification with the things he is looking at obviously includes both physical sensations and spiritual ones.

Remind the students that this ability to identify with objects takes time to develop. As Moffitt says, "You must look at it long." Use this idea as a springboard to the first exercise in **Training in Seeing**.

Part 1 The Sense of Sight

Most of our knowledge of the world comes to us through our eyes. This is why the verb *to see* means not only "to look," but also "to know" or "to understand." In the following poem, writer John Moffitt describes the kind of seeing that leads to understanding:

To Look at Any Thing

To look at anything,
If you would know that thing,
You must look at it long:
To look at this green and say
"I have seen spring in these
Woods," will not do—you must
Be the thing you see:
You must be the dark snakes of
Stems and ferny plumes of leaves,
You must enter in
To the small silences between
The leaves,
You must take your time
And touch the very peace
They issue from.

Study "To Look at Any Thing" carefully. What is Moffitt's advice? What evidence is there in the poem that he has taken his own advice? What words does he use to re-create his own visual experience?

Whenever you write, you must observe the world around you as carefully as this poet does. You must learn to "be the thing you see" so that you can become aware of even the tiniest details. You must also learn how to communicate what you see and learn.

You can begin to develop these abilities by "training" your sense of sight. The exercises that begin on the next page will give you practice in using your eyes. They will help you become more sensitive to the world of form and color.

Training in Seeing

You are already a kind of expert at observing the world with your eyes. You notice the color when you pick out your favorite shirt. You notice subtle changes in expressions on other people's faces.

Begin a journal in which you record your work for this chapter. Your first entries will be your responses to the following suggestions for training your sight to be even sharper.

1. Select a small object near you—something on your desk, on the floor, or on the wall. Study it carefully for a short time. Then move so that you can no longer see it. Write a detailed description of the object without naming it. Include specific information concerning its size, color, shape, texture, and unusual characteristics. Compare it to other objects. Is it the size of a walnut? Is it the color of lemons? When you feel you have included all possible details, turn back to see how well your description fits. Share your writing with another person by reading your description of the object without naming it. See if this person can recognize what you are describing.

2. Sit down in a familiar place in a room at home or at school, or outside if you wish. Write down everything you can see without turning or moving your circle of vision. Notice all the things you usually see in this spot; then concentrate on finding something you did not expect to see here. Describe it as specifically as you can, allowing your other senses to affect what you see. Share your experience with someone.

3. Stretch your sense of sight by careful observation on your way to or from school. Going your same familiar way, find ten things of interest that you never noticed before. Be prepared to write out this list of new "sights" to share with the rest of the class.

The lists of "sight" words on the following pages will help you make your descriptions more vivid and exact. Study the words and try to determine how each of the related words is different. Add your own words to the list and record them in your journal.

2. Read **Training in Seeing** on page 61 and assign the journal to be kept for this chapter. Read aloud the directions for the first exercise on page 61 and remind the students to think of Moffitt's advice to "Be the thing you see." Have the students complete the first exercise in class.

3. Have students read to themselves the lists of **Sight Words** on pages 62–64. If they do not know the meaning of a word, they should write it in their journals. Ask the students which words were unfamiliar, and see if other students can help define or explain the word or give an example that illustrates it.

4. Assign Exercises 2 and 3 on page 61 to be completed outside of class. Remind the class to use the words on the **Sight Words** list when they are completing the assignment.

5. Assign Exercise A on page 65 to be completed in class. For each subject, ask several students to read their sentences aloud and compare the variety of ways in which a single object may be perceived.

6. Read and discuss the paragraph in Exercise B. Ask the class to make the lists of strong verbs as well as verbs that appeal to sight.

Sight words: windless, summer, evening, creek, sycamore, stillness, spellbound, stains of lilac, water, cloud, sky, turned on by a switch, reflection, flat, floating, creek bottom, life in the water, water turtles smooth as beans, easy, weightless push-offs, as men bound on the moon, mudbank, last of the swallows, like streamers.

Verbs: stalk, straddle, hunched, starring, lighted, materialized, gliding down with the current trace, scan, follow, trailed.

7. Assign Exercise C. Have the students brainstorm to come up with additional subjects and write them on the chalkboard. Refer students to the paragraph in Exercise B and the effective use of sight words and verbs that the author used to make a vivid picture in her readers' minds. Tell them to refer to the list of Sight Words to find the right descriptive words or phrases for their paragraphs.

Individualizing the Lesson

Less-Advanced Students

1. Do Exercise B on page 65 orally, listing sight words and verbs on the chalkboard.

2. For Exercise C have the students find a picture of a subject to describe in their paragraph. Suggest that they refer to the picture as they right. Compare the visual details in the written descriptions with the details in the pictures.

Advanced Students

Write the following poem on the chalkboard and read it aloud to the class.

The Great Figure

Among the rain
and lights
I saw the figure 5
in gold
on a red
firetruck
moving
tense
unheeded
to gong clangs
siren howls
and wheels rumbling
through the dark city.

—William Carlos Williams

Sight Words

COLORS

Red	Blue	Yellow	Purple
pink	sky	beige	lavender
salmon	sapphire	buff	amethyst
rose	azure	straw	lilac
coral	delft	peach	orchid
raspberry	porcelain	apricot	mauve
strawberry	turquoise	butter	plum
tomato	aqua	buttercup	mulberry
currant	aquamarine	lemon	pansy
cherry	violet	chartreuse	fuchsia
crimson	peacock	citron	magenta
cardinal	teal	canary	
vermilion	cobalt	chrome	
carmine	royal	gold	**White**
flame	navy	topaz	snow
ruby	steel	ochre	milky
garnet	powder	saffron	marble
wine		sulphur	cream
blood		mustard	ivory
maroon	**Brown**	butterscotch	oyster
burgundy	sandy	orange	pearl
	almond	tangerine	silver
	amber	persimmon	platinum
Green	tawny		bone
celery	hazel		bleached
mint	cinnamon	**Black**	
apple	nutmeg	jet	
lime	chocolate	ebony	**General**
moss	coffee	licorice	colorless
pea	copper		rainbow
kelly	rust		drab
emerald	ginger	**Gray**	stark
olive	bronze	ashen	bland
pistachio	walnut	dove	vivid
chartreuse	mahogany	steel	vibrant

Sight Words

MOVEMENTS

Fast			
	careen	bounce	saunter
	rush	swoop	loiter
hurry	race	plunge	stray
run	zoom	swing	slink
scamper	zip	fly	stalk
skip	ram	sail	edge
scramble	chase		sneak
dart	hurl	**Slow**	stagger
spin	swat		lope
sprint	flick	creep	waddle
stride	whisk	crawl	drag
streak	rip	plod	sway
trot	shove	slouch	soar
gallop	swerve	lumber	lift
drive	smash	tiptoe	drift
dash	drop	bend	droop
bolt	plummet	amble	heave

SHAPES

flat	oval	jutting	broken
round	conical	irregular	spindly
domed	cylindrical	proportioned	skinny
curved	tubular	angular	thin
wavy	hollow	triangular	wiry
scrolled	rotund	rectangular	shapely
globular	chubby	hexagonal	winged
rolled	portly	octagonal	shapeless
scalloped	swollen	square	crooked
ruffled	lumpy	pyramidical	curved
frilled	clustered	tapering	straight
crimped	padded	branching	wide
crinkled	tufted	twiggy	narrow
flared	pendulous	split	stretched

Ask the students to point out sight words and verbs. You may also wish to point out words that appeal to the sense of sound. Then have them choose a moment from their journal entries and write a one-sentence poem about it, using "The Great Figure" as a model.

Optional Practice

Have students rewrite these sentences, expressing the ideas more effectively by using descriptive sight words and phrases.

a. It was Monday morning.
b. The man sitting in the doorway looked sad.
c. Flowers bloomed everywhere.
d. Grandpa and Grandma painted their house.

Extending the Lesson

Bring in color charts from a paint store that show hundreds of different colors and the names that paint companies have given them. Discuss with the class the appropriateness of the color names in the charts. How many of the names refer to objects in nature, such as *Oyster, Daffodil, Parrot,* and *Avocado*? How many color names refer to places, such as *Lexington, Paris,* or *Caribbean*? What other sources of color names do the paint companies use to evoke particular associations?

Sight Words

dotted	cheap	muscular	expansive
freckled	ugly	sturdy	imposing
spotted	ramshackle	robust	regal
blotched	tired	stolid	stately
wrinkled	exhausted	hardy	elegant
patterned	arid	strong	statuesque
mottled	awkward	healthy	huge
striped	crooked	frail	immense
bright	loose	fragile	massive
clear	curved	pale	gigantic
shiny	straight	pasty	showy
glowing	orderly	sickly	decorative
glossy	formal	tiny	distinctive
shimmering	crisp	miniature	dazzling
fluid	pretty	timid	jeweled
sparkling	heavy	shy	lacy
iridescent	flat	fearful	lavish
glassy	stout	apprehensive	exotic
flashy	rigid	tearful	gorgeous
glazed	narrow	nervous	radiant
sheer	overloaded	frightened	vivid
transparent	congested	terrified	flushed
opaque	cluttered	hysterical	fiery
muddy	crowded	wild	blazing
grimy	jammed	bold	verdant
drab	packed	dramatic	fresh
dingy	squeezed	tantalizing	clean
dull	bruised	irresistible	tidy
dark	stretched	exuberant	handsome
dismal	erect	energetic	pleasant
rotted	lean	animated	sunny
worn	slender	perky	calm
untidy	supple	attractive	serene
shabby	lithe	arrogant	unruffled
messy	lively	flamboyant	nerveless

Exercises Using "Sight" Words in Your Writing

Here is a chance to practice using specific details in order to help your reader "see" what you are describing as clearly as you do.

A. Write a sentence describing each of these nine things.

the sidewalk	a stone	a button
the sky	a dog or a cat	a leaf
someone's hair	a slice of bread	a piece of soap

B. Here is a paragraph that re-creates a vivid sight impression.

. . . On windless summer evenings I stalk along the creek bank or straddle the sycamore log in absolute stillness, watching for muskrats. The night I stayed too late I was hunched on the log staring spellbound at spreading, reflected stains of lilac on the water. A cloud in the sky suddenly lighted as if turned on by a switch; its reflection just as suddenly materialized on the water upstream, flat and floating, so that I couldn't see the creek bottom, or life in the water under the cloud. Downstream, away from the cloud on the water, water turtles smooth as beans were gliding down with the current in a series of easy, weightless push-offs, as men bound on the moon. I didn't know whether to trace the progress of one turtle I was sure of, . . . or take a chance on seeing the carp, or scan the mudbank in hope of seeing a muskrat, or follow the last of the swallows who caught at my heart and trailed it after them like streamers.

—ANNIE DILLARD

Make a list of all the words or phrases in the paragraph that create especially strong pictures in your mind. Next, make a list of all the words or phrases that create action or movement. Answers in Teacher Notes.

C. You have stretched your sight experiences and are now ready to write your own paragraph. You may use any of the subjects from the following list. You may also use an entirely new idea of your own.

your room	outside the window	a dream
the kitchen	a puddle of water	a quiet or a busy scene

65

To write vivid descriptions that appeal to the sense of hearing

Presenting the Lesson

1. Read the first paragraph of the **The Sense of Hearing** on page 66. Ask the students to mention some school sounds that they expect to hear each day. Then ask them to be silent and listen for at least one new sound.

Discuss the difference between hearing and listening. Point out that hearing is a passive, often unconscious, registering of sounds. Listening on the other hand, is an active attention to sounds that includes interpretation and storing as well as receiving.

2. Read the second paragraph of the introduction. Discuss the sounds mentioned in the quoted passage, and ask the students which of those sounds one would perceive only through especially careful listening. Ask the students which sounds have very personal associations for the writer ("squeaky popcorn," "sand, crisp as toasted linen").

3. Go over the list of **Hearing Words** on pages 67–68 with the class. Ask the students to make distinctions between words with similar meanings (*scream, yell, noise, discord*) and to look up three unfamiliar words in the dictionary. Have them record the new words in their journals.

4. Assign items 1, 2, 3, and 4 in **Training in Listening** to be done over

Part 2 The Sense of Hearing

Have you ever temporarily lost your sense of hearing, perhaps from an ear infection or a bad cold? Only at such times are you likely to be aware of how much you depend on this particular sense as you move through your day, from the alarm clock on waking up, to the sounds of traffic as you cross the street, to the greetings of friends at school, and conversations around the dinner table in the evening.

Notice the vivid sounds recorded by the writer of the following passage:

> I like the quiet crackling of root beer foam; the swish, then flap of the net as the basketball passes through . . . squeaky popcorn; slept-on mattress . . . moccasins treading soft sand, crisp as toasted linen; steel door weightlessly slammed shut; secret roar of sea shell; whirr of a movie reel; the ps-s-s-t of freshly opened coffee . . . whirr and buzz of the WALK signal; a Band-Aid coming off . . . creaky wicker chairs . . . .
>
> —SISTER MARY LOIS GLONEK

Training in Listening

In order to increase your sensitivity to sounds, you may sometimes need to close your eyes and concentrate only on listening, without your sense of sight to distract you. It is possible to develop more acute hearing, to notice more with your ears than you did before? Careful listening to sounds can add a rich new dimension to your life and to your writing. Here are some suggestions for training your ears to hear even more. Record your responses in your journal.

1. Take your journal to bed with you tonight. After you are comfortably settled in the dark room, listen carefully to every sound you hear. Then turn on the light long enough to write down all of the sounds you were able to hear. Take this list with you to school in the morning so that you can share what you heard with someone else. Did this careful listening affect how easy or difficult it was for you to sleep?

2. Listen to three conversations: one at school, one at a store or on the way home, and one at home. Listen to the tone of voice the speakers use and determine how this tone affects the meaning of what is said. Record your findings by re-creating one of the dialogues as well as you can remember it. In your writing, indicate changes in tone of voice and the emotion you think each person is feeling as shown below.

Customer (loudly and angrily): That item is marked a dollar and nine cents.

Cashier (bewildered): Isn't that what I charged you? It's right here on the sales slip.

3. List the sounds that you are so used to at home that you do not ordinarily notice them.

4. List five sounds that you like to hear and five that you do not like to hear.

Following are lists of "hearing" words to study. As you read each word, try to hear the sound each one conveys. Add more words to the list and record them in your journal.

Hearing Words

LOUD SOUNDS

crash	yell	clap	brawl
thud	whistle	stomp	bedlam
bump	whine	stamp	pandemonium
thump	squawk	noise	hubbub
boom	bark	discord	blatant
thunder	bawl	jangle	deafening
bang	bray	rasp	raucous
smash	bluster	clash	earsplitting
explode	rage	caterwaul	piercing
roar	blare	clamor	rowdy
scream	rumble	tumult	blast
screech	grate	riot	yowl
shout	slam	racket	shatter

several days and in the journal. Discuss item 2 in class, and have pairs of students act out the different dialogues.

5. Assign Exercise A on page 68. Have the students share their responses.

6. Read the paragraph in Exercise B aloud. Students should notice the following sound words and phrases: animals under the earth, hissings, groanings, muffled cries that a dying creature might make dislodging the stones of his underground cave, crashing, sharp crackling, monstrous snapping of twigs, roar like the fall of a whole forest of trees, explosion that tore earth and sky, thunders beneath.

Point out how the author uses these sound words and phrases to create an atmosphere of danger and destruction.

7. Discuss the suggestions given in Exercise C and assign the exercise to be completed at home.

Individualizing the Lesson

Less-Advanced Students

1. For Exercise A on page 68, do the first three items orally with the students. Then have students work in pairs to complete any other five items on the list.

2. In place of Exercise C on pages 69–70, have the students brainstorm from their own experience a list of moments in which sound left a strong impression in their memories (a train station, traffic jam, sports event, a heated argument, a crowded hallway). Write the list on the chalkboard. Then, have each student choose one of the moments and write in his or her journal a sentence that anchors the

moment in his or her own experience ("When I was stuck in a traffic jam last Thursday, I could feel myself becoming more and more anxious.") Have the students finish their paragraphs independently.

Advanced Students

Explain to the students that words such as *crash*, *jingle*, and *clink* actually imitate the sound they represent. Tell them that use of words such as these is common with writers and poets, and that the device is called "onomatopoeia." Ask students to think of other examples of onomatopoeia. (*buzz*, *swish*, *tap*, *bang*, *splash*, *whirr*, *clatter*, *ping*, *pop*, *peep*, etc.) Have the students look at the lists of **Hearing Words** and decide which ones are examples of onomatopoeia and which ones are not. For example, *hum* and *gurgle* should be classified as onomatopoeia; *chime* and *melody*, however, should not.

Optional Practice

Show the class pictures that portray different kinds of conversations taking place between two people (friendly, angry, formal, parent-child). Have the students write dialogue for each picture. Ask them to supply appropriate "dialogue tags" to show how each line is being spoken (*yelled*, *hissed*, *whispered*). You can refer them to the speech sounds in the chart on page 68. Then have students read their dialogues aloud with a partner, using appropriate intonation.

Extending the Lesson

1. Obtain a record of sound effects, or make a tape of various

SOFT SOUNDS			
sigh	mutter	gurgle	speechless
murmur	snap	swish	mute
whisper	hiss	rush	faint
whir	crackle	chime	inaudible
rustle	bleat	tinkle	melody
twitter	peep	clink	resonance
patter	buzz	hush	harmony
hum	zing	still	musical

SPEECH SOUNDS			
stutter	sing	bellow	whimper
stammer	yell	growl	talk
giggle	scream	chatter	speak
guffaw	screech	murmur	drawl
laugh	snort	whisper	hiss

Exercises Using "Hearing" Words in Your Writing

A. Here are fifteen sounds you are familiar with. Spend a few minutes "hearing" the sounds in your mind. Write a sentence about each sound that describes it as vividly as you would want your reader to hear it. Record the sentences in your journal.

the wind	a fire
feet walking	the rain
a car starting	a door opening
opening a can of soda	turning on a faucet
a police car siren	a lawn mower
sawing a board	a garbage truck
an ice cream wagon	someone roller skating
a train	a washing machine

B. Read the following passage carefully. List all of the words that are used to describe the terrifying sounds of a city threatened by an erupting volcano. What other sense is appealed to in these paragraphs? Answers in Teacher Notes.

> Then he began to hear sounds. Peculiar sounds, like animals under the earth. Hissings and groanings and muffled cries that a dying creature might make dislodging the stones of his underground cave. There was no doubt about it now. The noises came from underneath . . . .
>
> It was then the crashing began. First a sharp crackling, like a monstrous snapping of twigs; then a roar like the fall of a whole forest of trees; then an explosion that tore earth and sky. The heavens, though Tito could not see them, were shot through with continual flickerings of fire. Lightnings above were answered by thunders beneath. A house fell. Then another. By a miracle the two companions had escaped the dangerous side streets and were in a more open space. It was the Forum. They rested here awhile—how long he did not know.
>
> —LOUIS UNTERMEYER

C. Now put all of your hearing experiences and practice together to write a paragraph in which sound plays an important part. Use an idea from your journal or from the following list:

1. I adjusted the ear plugs to protect my ears, dove into the water, and all of a sudden . . .

2. As I was listening to the radio with my headset on, the strangest thing happened.

3. Without warning, all sound suddenly disappeared. It had become a strange new world in which I did not fit.

4. The elevator dropped swiftly, and the quick descent seemed to plug up my ears.

5. Suddenly, the band leaped on stage and the packed auditorium exploded with noise.

6. Take an ordinary sound that is familiar to you. Exaggerate this single sound in your writing until it takes on a new meaning. It might, for example, become sinister or exciting.

sounds from daily life. Have the students identify each sound with an appropriate word or phrase.

2. Have each student who owns a tape recorder record between five and ten sounds common to one specific place (for example, the kitchen: water faucet, radio, dishes clattering, chairs scraping, silverware being put away). Play the tapes in class and have the audience identify the sounds and the place represented on each tape. Then ask them to recreate the sounds as precisely as possible using words.

3. Especially talented students might work together on writing a simple narrative that can be "told" solely by a sequence of sounds. Detective stories work particularly well for this assignment. After recording their sounds, they can play their "story" for the class. Have the class recreate the narrative verbally, and then discuss the strengths and weaknesses of sound as a conveyer of information.

4. Ask for a small group of students to present a dramatic reading of Edgar Allan Poe's short story "The Tell-Tale Heart" to the class. Be certain to point out especially effective sensory details.

7. Contrast two completely different sounds, or a particular sound and quiet.

8. Describe an event by sound words only. Do not give your reader the final clue as to what you are describing until the last sentence of the paragraph.

9. Go to a place where there is a great deal of noise and activity, such as a store, airport, or carnival. Shut your eyes for a moment and listen. Take notes on what you hear. Now go home and write a paragraph about the place you visited, using as many sound words as possible.

10. Imagine a new invention and the sound it might make. Briefly describe it so that someone else could "see" and "hear" it.

Part 3   The Sense of Touch

Touch is the one sense we can't turn off. We can close our eyes to shut out sight. We can move away from sounds or smells. No matter what we do, however, we will still be touching something.

The things we feel are usually physical objects of some kind. We must make a conscious effort to touch them. Sometimes, however, sensation comes from emotions within us. Read the following passage for an example of this type of feeling.

He was freezing; he couldn't lie there all night. Inch by inch he crawled away. Silent as a shadow he went back across the lake. There was danger everywhere now, every time he moved a muscle. He could feel it all around him, feel a prickling in his scalp and a supernatural certainty that as he was stalking Mathieu, Mathieu was stalking him. Cautiously, with long waits, he approached his camp. The fire was out. His fingers touched the game-bag and drew back. Something was there, something that shouldn't be! *Something was wrong.* Chills went up and down his spine. He whirled toward a deeper patch of shadow, knowing with the certainty of panic that gunfire would belch from that shadow and blind him. His eyes roamed round in his head in the darkness and he waited, turned to stone.

—ELLIOT MERRICK

Objective

To write vivid descriptions that appeal to the sense of touch

Presenting the Lesson

1. Read aloud the first paragraph of The Sense of Touch on page 70. Ask the students for examples of basic touch sensations (hot, cold, sharp, smooth).

2. Point out that touch sensations may also result from internal, emotional sources. Read the passage by Elliot Merrick aloud and ask students to note words and phrases that suggest touch sensations. Have them distinguish between touch sensations that show a response to the external environment and those that show a response to internal stimuli:

External: He was freezing; His fingers touched the game bag and drew back.

Training in Touching

To gain a wider appreciation of your sense of touch, follow the directions given below and record your responses in your journal.

1. List all of the objects you can touch while you are seated in your chair right now.

2. Describe your physical sensations now. Are you cold, hot, warm, cool, comfortable? How do you know?

3. List rough objects in the classroom, then smooth ones.

4. List some things that are cold to the touch, hot to the touch, rough, smooth, wet.

5. List some things you do not feel with your hands, such as the wind or the touch of your clothes.

6. Describe the type of ride you get on different forms of transportation.

7. Imagine that you are sitting in your classroom on a hot summer day. How do you feel? Now imagine you are in the same room on a bitter winter day. How do you feel now?

Below is a list of touch words. Study it and write down an object that you think belongs with each word.

Touch Words

cool	slippery	silky	gritty
cold	spongy	satiny	sandy
icy	mushy	velvety	rough
lukewarm	oily	smooth	sharp
tepid	waxy	soft	thick
warm	fleshy	woolly	pulpy
hot	rubbery	furry	dry
steamy	tough	feathery	dull
sticky	crisp	fuzzy	thin
damp	elastic	hairy	fragile
wet	leathery	prickly	tender

Internal: He could feel it all around him, feel a prickling in his scalp; Chills went up and down his spine; turned to stone.

3. Assign **Training in Touching** on page 71. Have students share their responses.

4. Go over the chart of **Touch Words** on page 71. Clarify the meanings of unfamiliar words. Then have the students write in their journals an object that corresponds to each word.

5. Assign and discuss Exercise A on page 72.

6. Read the paragraph in Exercise B aloud and discuss the questions that follow it:

Babe's feelings: pain was with him, a helpless creep, *hurt like crazy*.
Objects of touch: attached the open nerves, hard, sharp, jammed, penetrate.
Internal reaction: hurt enough to penetrate into his brain deeper than the air against the nerves; Babe hoped it wasn't the broken glass.

7. Read the paragraph in Exercise C aloud and discuss the questions that follow it.

What kind of rain: Rain that carries the seeds or spores of plant life that grows on humans.
Where are these men? On a strange planet or mysterious forest.
Touch words: crawled; trickled; moved down his flesh; cling; he felt the small flowers bud and petal away; pattered; hit; on the rubbery plants.
Overall effect: threatening.

8. Assign Exercise D to be completed at home.

Individualizing the Lesson

Less-Advanced Students

For additional practice, have the students analyze and discuss the following passage, listing the words and phrases that suggest sensations of touch.

> A red pony colt was looking at him out of the stall. Its tense ears were forward and a light of disobedience was in its eyes. Its coat was rough and thick as an airdale's fur and its mane was long and tangled. Jody's throat collapsed in on itself and cut his breath short. —John Steinbeck

Advanced Students

Explain to students that it is often difficult to describe how something feels. One way to do so is by comparing it with something else ("The gentle wind felt like feathers brushing against my face."). Explain that this device is called a *simile*. Ask students to make up ten examples.

Optional Practice

1. Have students make a texture survey of the classroom. Ask them to record and describe in their journals two different textures of wall material, floor surface, desk material, and items used to decorate the room.

2. Have students describe something; such as cotton candy or velvet, that has a distinct and interesting texture. Tell them to see if they can describe the texture clearly enough so that the rest of the class could identify the object without knowing what it is.

Extending the Lesson

Ask students to look through their favorite works of literature for passages that use especially effective touch words and phrases. Tell students that such wording is also called *tactile imagery*. Have volunteers read their selections aloud.

Exercises Using "Touch" Words in Your Writing

A. Write sentences describing how each of these things or activities feels. Record your sentences in your journal.

a piece of cotton	an ice cube	the bark of a tree
an apple	a warm bath	roller skating
a dry leaf	a sunburn	a spring shower

Read what you have written, checking for the use of vivid and precise words. Would another person know what you were describing if the name of it were left out?

B. Read the passage below. Then, answer the questions.

> As he tried to make his inept way, the pain was with him, because every time he tried to inhale, the night air hit the holes in his teeth and attacked the open nerves. The street was hard and filled with sharp dark things and he didn't have shoes on to protect him. He was still in his pajamas, a helpless creep just like the stoop gang always said, staggering along . . . Something jammed into his foot then, something that hurt enough to penetrate into his brain deeper than the air against the nerves. Babe hoped it wasn't the broken glass but only maybe a rock that would hurt like crazy but not lay his foot open to even more serious pain. — WILLIAM GOLDMAN

What particular feelings does Babe have? What particular words are used to describe objects of touch? What particular words are used to describe Babe's internal reactions to these objects of touch?

Answers in Teacher Notes.

C. This paragraph will give you an entirely new feeling about rain.

> There were things that crawled on his skin. Things grew upon him in layers. Drops fell and touched other drops and they became streams that trickled over his body, and while these moved down his flesh, the small growths of the forest took root in his clothing. He felt the ivy cling and make a second garment over him; he felt the small flowers bud and open and petal away, and still the rain pattered on his body and on his head. In the

luminous night — for the vegetation glowed in the darkness —he could see the other two men outlined, like logs that had fallen and taken upon themselves velvet coverings of grass and flowers. The rain hit his face. He covered his face with his hands. The rain hit his neck. He turned over on his stomach in the mud, on the rubbery plants, and the rain hit his back and hit his legs. — RAY BRADBURY

This is not a soft and gentle spring rain. What is it? Where do you imagine these men to be? What specific words and phrases associated with touch are used in the paragraph? What is the overall effect of these words and phrases? Answers in Teacher Notes.

D. Look over your notes and the material in your journal. Choose a topic from these sources or choose one of the topics listed below. Write a paragraph emphasizing touch.

diving into the water of a lake or pool

trudging through the snow on a cold day

walking along a beach or a road on a hot day

playing a sport

Part 4   The Sense of Taste

Unlike your other senses, the sense of taste does not operate well alone. Much of what we experience as taste is a reaction to the way foods look and smell, or the way they feel against the mouth and tongue. Therefore, when describing tastes, it is a good idea to include references to other senses as well.

On Sunday morning Momma served a breakfast that was geared to hold us quiet from 9:30 A.M. to 3 P.M. She fried thick pink slabs of home-cured ham and poured the grease over sliced red tomatoes. Eggs over easy, fried potatoes and onions, yellow hominy, and crisp perch fried so hard we would pop them into our mouths and chew bones, fins, and all. Her cathead biscuits were at least three inches in diameter and two inches thick. The trick to eating catheads

Part 4

Objective

To write vivid descriptions that appeal to the sense of taste

Presenting the Lesson

1. Before assigning Part 4, blindfold two student volunteers and have them hold their noses, thus blocking both the sense of sight and the sense of smell. Then, give them slices of apple, pear, orange, melon, and other kinds of fruit to taste. You might also include cheese, bread, and crackers. After each sample, ask the students to identify what they have tasted and

73

to describe the taste. Chances are, the description will emphasize texture, and in some cases, the students will not be able to identify the food.

2. Read the first paragraph of **The Sense of Taste** on page 73 and discuss its relevance to the tasting experiment conducted in step 1.

3. Read aloud the passage by Maya Angelou and ask the students to point out words and phrases describing specific kinds of tastes (*home-cured, "fried," "crisp," "delicious"*). Discuss how sight and touch words are also used to describe food (*pink slabs, "sliced red tomatoes," "yellow hominy" got cold, gooeyness*).

4. Assign the four journal activities in **Training in Tasting**. Discuss the results in class.

5. Review the list of **Taste Words** with the class. Have them add new words from the their journal writings.

6. Assign Exercise A, page 75.

7. Read the passage in Exercise B, page 75, and discuss the questions.

> *Taste words*: rich, too salty, slightly stale, flavored, sweet, cherry-flavored, sugar.
> *Foods mentioned*: ice cream, popcorn, snow cones, licorice, cotton candy.
> *Other sense words*: smooth, sliding, crunched, melted, sticky, huge pink cloud, spun cotton, gossamer, little wisps.

8. Discuss the questions in the introduction to Exercise C, page 76, and assign.

Individualizing the Lesson

Less-Advanced Students

Do the first three items in Exercise A orally, encouraging the students

was to get the butter on them before they got cold — then they were delicious. When, unluckily, they were allowed to get cold, they tended to a gooeyness not unlike a wad of tired gum. — MAYA ANGELOU

Training in Tasting

Record the following in your journal.

1. At dinner tonight concentrate on your sense of taste. Sort out the flavor of each thing you eat. After dinner make a list of the foods you had. Beside each food write a short phrase that describes the flavor. Make some notes about your tastes in general. Do you like strong or mild flavors? Are there some foods you would eat hot but not cold, and vice versa?

2. Think of one taste you like or don't like. Describe what happened when you last experienced this taste.

3. Make a list of some things you have tasted and their quality of taste. For example: lemons — sour, candy — sweet.

4. Survey your family or some of your friends to see what tastes they like and don't like. Compare your results with those of a classmate.

Here is a list of taste words. As you think about each taste, try to recall your own experience. What things would you relate to each taste? Add more words and record them in your journal.

Taste Words

oily	sugary	tangy	gingery
buttery	crisp	unripe	hot
salty	ripe	raw	burnt
bitter	bland	alkaline	overripe
bittersweet	tasteless	medicinal	spoiled
sweet	sour	fishy	rotten
hearty	vinegary	spicy	
mellow	fruity	peppery	

Exercises Using "Taste" Words in Your Writing

A. The sense of taste differs in each person. Here are some things you may have tasted. Write a sentence for each one, trying to use exact words to describe how it tastes to you. Record the sentences in your journal.

peanut butter	an orange	a pencil
a piece of toast	gum	medicine
a blade of grass	an egg	cola
ice cream		

Reread your sentences. Would every member of your family agree with your descriptions? Compare your sentences with those of someone sitting next to you. Where do you agree and disagree?

B. Read the following passage and notice all of the words that appeal to the sense of taste.

> To me, the memories of the circus will always remain tied to the tastes of the food upon which I gorged myself. My parents warned me about eating too much, and even I knew that these treats were the worst things in the world for a child's stomach. Still . . . I loved the feeling of smooth, rich ice cream coating my lips and sliding down my throat. I crunched happily on bags of popcorn that was usually too salty and always slightly stale. I treasured the flavored ice-crystals of snow cones as they melted into sweet streams of cherry-flavored syrup, and I could chew on a sticky rope of licorice for hours. But my favorite, my absolute favorite, was the cotton candy. What could be better than biting into a huge pink cloud of spun cotton and then feeling the mouthful of gossamer dissolve into little wisps of sugar on your tongue? I was always sick and remorseful for at least a day afterwards, but, after all, wasn't that part of the fun?

What foods are mentioned in the paragraph? What words are used to describe them? How many specifically relate to the sense of taste? What other senses are employed to describe the food? Make lists to record your answers. Answers in Teacher Notes.

to use touch, smell, and sight words as they compose their descriptions. Write some of the suggested phrases on the chalkboard. Have the students choose five other items from the list to finish independently in their journals.

Advanced Students

Have each student write a description of a food without mentioning its name. Ask volunteers to read their paragraphs aloud, and have the audience determine the food being described.

Optional Practice

Obtain the food section of a local newspaper and distribute to the class copies of food articles, recipes, and advertisements. Discuss the words and phrases used by the writers to describe food, ingredients, and prepared dishes.

Extending the Lesson

Have the students bring in magazine pictures that display food in attractive ways. Analyze the pictures for appeals to the sense of taste, and to sight and touch (texture) as well. Ask the students to write captions for these pictures that appeal especially to the sense of taste.

C. Do you think your tastes change with time? Are there some things you like now that you didn't like before? After concentrating on tastes, you are ready to write a paragraph of your own in which you appeal to the sense of taste. Look over the ideas in your journal or try some of the following ideas.

1. Ask someone at home to give you something that is all right to eat, but not to tell you what it is. Close your eyes so that you can concentrate only on the taste. In a paragraph, describe the experience and the taste. Keep the events in the order they happen.

2. What is your favorite taste? Can you remember the first time you tasted it? What was happening at the time? Where were you? Who was with you? In a paragraph, re-create the moment or create a brand new situation in which you might be tasting the same thing.

Part 5 The Sense of Smell

Human beings do not have a highly developed sense of smell. Smells must be particularly strong or near for us to notice them. Even then, we quickly become used to most smells and soon can no longer smell them.

Nonetheless, smells are all around us, and many evoke strong memories, emotions, and moods. What moods are evoked by the sense of smell in the following passage?

There were all the smells of salt and seaweed, of fish and water and wind. There were all the human smells too of the hundreds of people who filled the boardwalk: ladies in print dresses smelling like passing gardens; swimmers with their scents of sun-tan oils and skin lotions; there were the smells of the eating places: of mustard and onions, of hamburgers frying; and the sudden sharp smell of stacks of dill pickles, as brisk in the nose as a sudden unintended inhalation of sea water. There was the smell of frying fish from the many fish grottos. And outside these places, in the middle of the boardwalk like miniature, land-locked seas, the glass tanks, where passers-by might admire the grace and color of their dinners before eating them. It was hard to say who did the

Objective

To write vivid descriptions that appeal to the sense of smell

Presenting the Lesson

1. Write *Fall, Winter, Spring,* and *Summer* on the chalkboard. Ask the students to name definite smells that they associate with each season, and write their ideas on the board. Determine which of those smells are specific to your own geographical region (for example, the smells of a lake or ocean, of indigenous trees and flowers, of especially severe winters, or perhaps of seasonal crops grown locally).

2. Read aloud the introduction to **The Sense of Smell** on page 76 and discuss the passage from Jessamyn West. Point out that the smells mentioned create the effect of a confused, but pleasing, holiday atmosphere.

most looking; fish outward from these sidewalk aquariums, at the strange pale gill-less pedestrians, or pedestrians inward at the finny swimmers. — JESSAMYN WEST

Training in Smelling

Record the following in your journal:

1. List your favorite smells; then list the smells you dislike.
2. Starting when you leave this room, begin to list everything you can smell. Be aware of how the smells change with place, time of day, temperature, or other variables.
3. Choose a room at home or at school and describe all the different smells that are there when you walk in.
4. Think of an outdoor place you like. List all the smells you can recall that are there. If you can go to this place on your way home, check to see how well your nose "remembers."
5. Think of a past experience you have had that has a particular smell connected with it. List what you can remember about the place, such as the time of day, what happened, and the smells you remember.

Below is a list of words related to smell. As you study these words, try to recall vivid experiences with each smell. Add your own words to the list and record them in your journal.

Smell Words

sweet	piney	briny	rancid
scented	minty	acidic	sickly
fragrant	odorous	acrid	stagnant
aromatic	pungent	burnt	moldy
perfumed	tempting	gaseous	musty
flowery	spicy	reeking	mildewed
heady	savory	putrid	damp
fresh	sharp	rotten	dank
balmy	gamey	spoiled	stench
earthy	fishy	sour	stale

3. Assign **Training in Smelling** and discuss the journal entries in class.

4. Read the chart of **Smell Words** aloud, and discuss unfamiliar words from the list. See if the students can add any other words from their journals or from the introductory exercise.

5. Assign Exercises A, B, and C on page 78. Be sure students notice all the phrases in Exercise B that describe smells: scent of man, acrid odor of the clothing, musty smell of an ancient wool coat saturated with a disagreeable stench of sweat and fear, oppressive odor of the man, heavy musky smell of warm skin and racing blood.

Individualizing the Lesson

Less-Advanced Students

1. Do the first half of Exercise A as a group. Write the sentences on the chalkboard, and have the students copy them into their journals. Assign the rest to be done independently.

2. Do Exercise B orally, sentence by sentence.

3. Read Exercise C and have the students brainstorm possible ideas for 1 and 2. Remind them that they also have the option of writing about a personal experience for this Exercise.

Advanced Students

Send the students on a "smell" scavenger hunt, either in groups during class time or as a homework assignment to be done individually. Have them find and bring to class objects that represent each of ten smell words. (You might use *sweet, fresh, minty, spicy, briny, rotten, musty, pungent, perfumed,* and *piney*.)

77

Optional Practice

Bring in an assortment of strong-smelling substances in covered paper cups or in small jars with holes punched in the lids. Have the students work individually to write a detailed description of each smell. Reveal the contents only after the descriptions are complete.

Extending the Lesson

Have each student construct a word picture, in prose or free verse, of a specific place that has identifiable smells associated with it. If necessary, you might suggest such places as a gas station, doctor's office, garden, pet shop, fish market, school wood shop or cafeteria. Remind the students to use vivid smell images, and to refer to the list of Smell Words, page 77, if necessary.

Exercises Using the Sense of Smell in Writing

A. Write a sentence describing the smell of each of the things listed below. Record your sentences in your journal.

a fire	perfume
a flower	toothpaste
food cooking	cookies
wet coats	chalk
rain	popcorn

If the thing you are talking about were not named in the sentence, would your reader still know what you were describing?

B. Read the following paragraph. Then, list all of the smells recorded in the paragraph. Answers in Teacher Notes.

> The wolf wrinkled its nose in disgust, its wary expression contorting into a grimace of distaste. The scent of the man was strong here, much more so than at any time in the past several hours. The acrid odor of the clothing alerted the wolf first — the musty smell of an ancient wool coat saturated with a disagreeable, sickly-sweet stench of sweat and fear. And then there was the oppressive odor of the man himself, the heavy musky smell of warm skin and racing blood. The wolf lowered its head and cast about. Finally it located faint, cow-like traces of thin, grease-caked boots. Hurriedly, nose to the ground, the wolf darted along the trail.

C. Concentrating especially on the sense of smell, write a paragraph using smell as a central idea. Use ideas from your journal, something from the suggestions below, or a new idea.

1. Write the first paragraph of a story that opens with a particular smell. It could be any kind of story, even a mystery, in which the smell plays an important part.

2. Smells often trigger memories. Write a paragraph that begins with a character in the present who is experiencing a smell. Then, describe the character's memories associated with this smell.

Part 6 All of the Senses Working Together

You have spent a lot of time practicing the use of your five senses, concentrating on one at a time and sharpening each one. Now it's time for you to pull together all you have learned. Look over the work you have done thus far on your senses — your lists, notes, and all of the material in your journal. Find the writing that you most enjoyed doing, or the activities that were most satisfying to you. Before you write, study this example of sensory writing in which all of the senses are working together to achieve a unifed effect.

> The evening is lovely.
> True, it is not raining but still is lovely. The puriri stands at the window motionless and shadowy, the forest mysterious and still, and between them the clearing, without the foxgloves which have died down in the winter. Water voices drift up from the river, the tui lets fall an occasional note, his signature to the evening, while from the forest emanates an odor made up of all the winter decomposition and all the summer blooming; exotic, pungent…heady.
> It is the enchanted moment when day faces night, a magic time which holds in itself a capacity for improbability unlikely in the daytime. The fire is still going in the stove with one overlong arm of wood beckoning from the firebox, while moths and other night-winged creatures make a freeway of the window. — SYLVIA ASHTON-WARNER

List the senses used in these paragraphs, with the words and phrases related to them. What one sense is missing? The writer speaks of enchantment, "magic," "improbability." What senses are involved here? What kind of mood does this passage create in the reader?

In the paragraph on the next page, the effect is quite different. Notice, again, the senses to which the writer appeals.

Part 6

Objective

To write vivid descriptions that appeal to all five senses

Presenting the Lesson

1. Read pages 79–80 aloud, and discuss the quoted passages in detail. Ask the students to point out words and phrases that appeal to each of the five senses, such as shadowy (sight), Water voices (sound), pungent (smell), malignant violet (sight), crack and split with a roar (sound), plastering my shirt to my back (touch).

Point out that taste is not represented in these two passages. The mood of the first passage is tranquil and dreamy; whereas the mood of the second passage is violent.

2. Assign the Exercise on page 80.

Individualizing the Lesson

Less-Advanced Students

Before the students begin their compositions, have them list three or four things they might like to "be." Discuss their ideas and have them offer suggestions for each others' topics. Guide students away from abstract or unusable topics. Ask students to consider what this thing would see, hear, smell, touch and taste. How would it get around? What kinds of fears would it have? What would give it pleasure? You may want to brainstorm on one subject as an example. Then assign the composition for homework.

Advanced Students

Bring in copies of in-depth reviews of plays or concerts. Have the class analyze the reviews for the use of sense words and phrases. Then have the students write their own reviews of movies, plays, or record albums. Tell them to emphasize impressions of sight, sound, smell, and touch (including internal sensations).

Optional Practice

Ask the class to analyze the following passage for its use of sensory details.

> On she went. The woods were deep and still. The sun made the pine needles almost too bright to look at, up where the wind rocked. The cones dropped as light as feathers. Down in the hollow was the mourning dove—it was not too late for him.
>
> The path ran up a hill. "Seem like there is chains about my feet, time I get this far," she said, in the voice of argument old people keep to use with themselves. "Something always take a hold of me on this hill—pleads I should stay." —Eudora Welty

Extending the Lesson

Have students invent products and try to "sell" them to the class. To present the new creations persuasively, the students must write a sales pitch using words and phrases that appeal to all of the senses. A food product would be particularly suitable for this assignment.

Above me the clouds roll in, unfurling and smoking billows in malignant violet, dense as wool. Most of the sky is lidded over but the sun remains clear, halfway down the west, shining beneath the storm. Over my head the clouds thicken, then crack and split with a roar like that of cannon balls tumbling down a marble staircase; their bellies open—too late to run now!—and suddenly the rain comes down.

Comes down: not softly, but gently, with no quality of mercy, but like heavy water in buckets, raindrops like lead pellets smashing and splattering on the flat rock, knocking the berries off the juniper, plastering my shirt to my back, drumming on my hat like hailstones, running like a waterfall off the brim.

— EDWARD ABBEY

Exercise All of the Senses Working Together

You are now ready to write about all of the senses working together. Reread John Moffitt's poem "To Look at Any Thing" on page 60. To experience any thing fully, the poet says, you must "Be the thing." If you are a fish, for example, you live in a watery world. Light and dark are shadowy; color is muted. You are cold blooded. You have scales, fins, a tail. Your eyes are on the sides of your head. You have to search for food. Dangers are of a different order. Time doesn't exist as humans know it.

Write a short composition in which you are something other than yourself. Put all your senses to work in your particular world. *Be the thing*.

Here are some suggestions to stir your imagination, but you can be anything else you wish.

a motorcycle	a pillow
a snake	a bird
a bee	an animal
a stone	a window
a rug	a fence
a tooth	a weed

SUMMARY AND APPLICATIONS

1. Good writers make their work come alive by vividly describing how things look, taste, sound, feel, and smell.
2. Skillful use of the senses can make you a better writer. It will also strengthen your powers of observation in all subjects and situations.
3. Train yourself to be more aware of your senses by concentrating on one sense at a time. Record your sensory experiences in a journal.
4. When you write descriptions, use strong sensory words such as the ones included in this chapter.
5. Depending upon the purpose and the subject of your writing, you may concentrate on one sense or use several senses in combination with one another.

Applications in Other Subject Areas

History. Historians depend upon many sources to learn about the past. Among these, first-hand accounts are extremely important. These accounts often contain vivid sensory details that re-create the atmosphere surrounding an historical event. Find a first-hand account of an historical event in a history text, an autobiography, a journal, or a magazine article. Then list the important sensory details in the account.

Science. A scientist must have the ability to make detailed observations and to record them accurately. Select one of the following subjects or choose one of your own. Observe the subject carefully for at least fifteen minutes, jotting down notes on sensory details. Use as many of the senses as possible.

a. an ant hill
b. any animal at a zoo
c. a constellation
d. a mixture of oil and water
e. a spider and its web
f. any science experiment

Summary and Applications

Go over the summary with the class. Emphasize how important the use of their senses will be in all of their writing. Encourage students to use this summary for review or as part of the SQ3R method of study (see Chapter 15). Remind them, though, that more specific points can only be reviewed by skimming the chapter itself.

Applications in Other Subject Areas

These high-interest activities are designed to provide challenging opportunities to apply the chapter concepts in other subject areas. Before assigning the **History** activity, read the following passage from Mary Rowlandson's account of her captivity among the Indians in 1675.

Then I went to another wigwam, where there were two of the English children; the squaw was boiling horses feet; then she cut me off a little piece, and gave one of the English children a piece also. Being very hungry I had quickly eat up mine, but the child could not bite it, it was so tough and sinewy, but lay sucking, gnawing, chewing and slabbering of it in the mouth and hand. Then I took it of the child, and eat it myself, and savory it was to my taste. . . Thus the Lord made that pleasant refreshing, which another time would have been an abomination.

Chapter Objectives

1. To join sentences that express ideas of equal importance

2. To join sentence parts and eliminate repeated words

3. To add single words to one sentence from another

4. To add groups of words to one sentence from another

5. To use the words *who, which,* or *that* to combine sentences

Preparing the Students

Read the first paragraph and the examples on page 82. Have the class discuss the differences between the two examples. Ask them which version they prefer. Finish reading the page. Tell the students that this chapter will help them develop strategies they can use in revising their own writing. Explain that sentence combining will help them produce smoother, clearer sentences.

Additional Resources

Mastery Test — See pages 17–18 in the test booklet.

Skills Practice Book — pages 23–27.

Duplicating Masters — pages 23–27.

Special Populations — See special section at the front of this Teacher's Edition.

Chapter 5

Sentence Combining

An important part of good writing is learning how to write sentences that express your ideas clearly and directly. This skill also involves creating sentences that are interesting to your reader. For example, compare the following two ways of expressing the same ideas.

> Andrea sat at the computer. She sat there for hours. She hunted for the mistake in the program. The mistake had baffled the rest of us.
>
> Andrea sat at the computer for hours, hunting for the mistake in the program that had baffled the rest of us.

The second example contains the same information as the first, but presents it in a much more interesting and efficient way. The first example is a set of short, choppy sentences. The second is a combined sentence that flows smoothly and shows how the ideas are related.

This chapter will give you practice in combining short, related sentences. The skills you learn will be useful as you revise your writing.

Part 1 Joining Sentences

Two sentences that state related ideas of equal importance can usually be combined into a single statement by a comma and the word *and*.

> The storm will pass tonight. Tomorrow will be fair.
> The storm will pass tonight, and tomorrow will be fair.

The sentences could also be joined by a semicolon.

> The storm will pass tonight; tomorrow will be fair.

Two sentences that state contrasting ideas of equal importance can usually be joined by a comma and the word *but*.

> Tomorrow will be fair. Another storm is on its way.
> Tomorrow will be fair, but another storm is on its way.

Two sentences that express a choice between ideas of equal importance usually can be joined by a comma and the word *or*.

> Will the weekend be sunny? Is another storm coming?
> Will the weekend be sunny, or is another storm coming?

Exercises Joining Sentences

A. Join each pair of sentences by following the directions.

1. The car was locked. The keys were inside. (Join with **,and**.) ,and
2. The race was stopped. No one knew why. (Join with **,but**.) ,but
3. Can you meet me at the library? Do you have to go directly home? (Join with **,or**.) ,or
4. Lightning struck. All our lights went out. (Join with **,and**.) ,and
5. The promoters of the concert advertised widely. Attendance was excellent. (Join with **;**.) ;

B. Join sentence pairs using **,and**, **,but**, or **,or**.

1. Many people believe in UFO's. Few have ever seen one. ,but
2. Do I have to wear glasses? Can I wear contact lenses? ,or

Part 1

Objective

To join sentences that express ideas of equal importance.

Presenting the Lesson

1. Read **Joining Sentences**, page 83. Emphasize the different meanings and uses of the three conjunctions: *and* (similar ideas), *but* (contrasting ideas), *or* (alternatives). Discuss the use of the semicolon as a substitute for a conjunction.

2. Assign and discuss Exercises A and B on pages 83–84.

Individualizing the Lesson

Less-Advanced Students

Have each student write sentences that can be combined with *and, but,* and *or.* Ask them to read their sentences. Be sure that they all understand the differences among the conjunctions as well as among the types of sentences that these conjunctions can join.

Advanced Students

Ask students to write an Exercise like Exercise B, page 83. They may look in their literature books or text books for sentences to split up. Have students write their sentences on the board and quiz each other.

Optional Practice

Have students combine sentences such as the following:

a. We were bored by the dull speech. We managed to look interested.
b. Chad is always on time for the movies. He is often late for work.
c. Honesty is the best policy. It is our company's policy.

83

Ask students to bring to class examples of combined sentences from newspaper or magazine articles.

Part 2

Objective

To join related sentence parts using conjunctions

Presenting the Lesson

1. Tell the students that the connecting words, *and, but,* and *or* can also be used to combine parts of sentences. Review the relationships expressed by those words.

2. Read and discuss page 84.

3. Assign and discuss Exercises A and B. Remind the students that they usually will *not* use commas when combining related sentence parts.

Individualizing the Lesson

Less-Advanced Students

Review the difference in punctuation between the following two sentences. Explain that commas are used between complete sentences, not sentence parts.

Harry likes to swim, and he likes to ski.
Harry likes to swim and ski.

Advanced Students

Have students replace the second sentence in each pair in Exercise B with another sentence that can be combined with the first. Challenge them to make their sentence one that could be combined using a different conjunction.

3. The legendary Red Baron flunked his first flying tests/ He ^, but^ became one of the most notorious pilots of World War I.

4. The force of the blizzard increased/ The city was paralyzed. ^and^

5. The team's record must improve/ The coach might be fired. ^, or^

Part 2   Joining Sentence Parts

Two sentences may express ideas that are so closely related that words are repeated in the sentences. It is usually best to combine such sentences and eliminate the repeated words.

Sentence parts with similar ideas of equal importance can often be joined by *and*. (Italicized words are eliminated.)

> Louise stepped onstage. *Louise* walked to the podium.
> Louise stepped onstage and walked to the podium.

> The papers ignored the election. TV stations *ignored it, too.*
> The papers and TV stations ignored the election.

Sentence parts that express contrasting ideas usually can be joined by *but*.

> I arrived late. *I* worked harder than anyone else.
> I arrived late but worked harder than anyone else.

Sentence parts that express a choice between ideas usually can be joined by *or*.

> Is the Shuttle launch scheduled for Thursday? *Is the Shuttle launch scheduled for* Friday?
> Is the Shuttle launch scheduled for Thursday or Friday?

Exercises Joining Sentence Parts

A. Join the related parts in each pair of sentences by following the directions in parentheses. Eliminate the italicized words.

1. Natalie called. ~~Andy *called*.~~ (Join related parts with **and**.) ^and Andy^

2. The software for this system is excellent, ~~*It is*~~ expensive, ~~*though*~~. (Join related parts with **but**.) ^but^

3. The missing hikers may have followed Hurricane Trail. ~~The missing hikers may have~~ left the trail system completely. (Join related parts with **or**.) [or, inserted]

4. Jensen took a quick look toward first base. Then ~~Jensen~~ went into his windup. (Join related parts with **and**.) [and, inserted]

5. Most of the popular musical groups are from England. ~~Many are from~~ Australia. (Join related parts with **or**.) [or, inserted]

B. Combine each of the following pairs of sentences by joining related sentence parts. You decide which parts to join. Answers may vary.

1. Computers fascinate some people. ~~They~~ terrify others. [and, inserted]

2. Searchers never found the plane's tail section. ~~They never found the plane's "black box," either.~~ [or "black box."]

3. A Rubic's Cube is fascinating. ~~It is also frustrating.~~ [but frustrating.]

4. Richard Pryor may be approached for that role. ~~Eddie Murphy may also be asked.~~ [or Eddie Murphy]

5. The bobsled whipped around the curve. ~~Then it~~ plummeted down a big hill. [and, inserted]

Part 3   Adding Single Words

Sometimes the ideas in two sentences are not equally important. However, there may be one word in the second sentence that could add a great deal of meaning to the main idea. The one important word can be added to the first sentence to create a tighter and more effective way of expressing the idea.

Williston was a little town. *It was a* quiet *place*.
Williston was a quiet little town.

Notice that the italicized words were eliminated.

You may be able to combine more than two sentences in this manner. You can do so if one of the sentences states a main idea and each of the other sentences adds only one important detail.

A cloud passed in front of the moon. *The cloud was* dark. *The moon was* silvery.
A dark cloud passed in front of the silvery moon.

85

Optional Practice

Have students join related parts in sentences such as the following:

a. The freshmen will be in charge of the bake sale. They will also run the used book auction.

b. Does the bazaar open in the morning? Does the bazaar open in the afternoon?

c. Fewer adults attended this year's carnival. More students attended.

Extending the Lesson

Have students select a previous writing assignment. This could be a paragraph from the journals they began in Chapter 4. Have them look for sentences that could be combined. Direct them to revise these sentences accordingly.

Part 3

Objective

To add words to one sentence from another

Presenting the Lesson

1. Read and discuss pages 85–86. Discuss the main idea of each example sentence. Emphasize that the main idea of each should not be changed when the sentences are combined; only repeated words or words that do not contribute to the main idea should be eliminated.

2. Assign and discuss Exercises A and B, pages 86–87.

Individualizing the Lesson

Less-Advanced Students

Before assigning the Exercises on

pages 86–87, combine the following sentence pairs on the board. As you proceed, ask students for their suggestions on combining.

    a. Marla tried to shut the door. The door was heavy.

    b. We could barely walk into the wind. The wind howled.

    c. We drove down the street. We were careful.

Advanced Students

    Discuss the effects of merely combining the whole sentences in Exercise B with *and, but,* or *or* (Choppiness, unnecessary repetition, less sophisticated style). Lead students to the conclusion that different combining techniques are necessary in different situations.

Optional Practice

    Devise pairs of sentences such as the following. Have students add the important word from the second sentence to the first.

    a. Marie picked up the dishes. They were broken.

    b. Eric announced that he had finished his paper. He was proud.

    c. The skiers flew down the slopes. Their movements were graceful.

Extending the Lesson

    Write this sentence on the chalkboard: The barn burned.

    Ask students to suggest sentences that are related to the main idea, and write these sentences on the board. Then ask students to combine the first sentence with the others by adding words.

Be careful to choose the right location in the main sentence for each word that you add.

You may have to use a comma when you add more than one word to a sentence.

> Below the falls was a pool of water. *The water was* cool. *The water was* bubbling.
> Below the falls was a pool of cool, bubbling water.

See Section 14 for further discussion on the uses of the comma.

Occasionally, a word does not quite fit into a sentence because of the form it is in. In this case, you may have to change the form of the word slightly. Sometimes you will have to add -*ing* or -*ed*.

> We sang folk songs around a fire. *The fire* blazed.
> We sang folk songs around a blazing fire.

> Pour the batter into a baking dish. Butter *the baking dish.*
> Pour the batter into a buttered baking dish.

At other times you will have to add -*ly*. Often, the word ending in -*ly* can be placed in any of several positions in the sentence.

> Insulation increases fuel economy. *The increase is* great.
> Insulation increases fuel economy greatly.
> Insulation greatly increases fuel economy.

Exercises Adding Single Words

A. Combine these sentences by adding the important word. Eliminate italicized words and follow any special directions.

1. Scott wore a ˄ waterproof watch. ~~*The watch was* waterproof~~.

2. The laser cuts ˄ through ˄ steel. ~~*The steel is* hardened. *The laser cuts* smoothly.~~ smoothly   hardened

3. The ˄ thrilling surprise ending made the movie worth seeing. ~~*The ending was* thrilling. *The ending was a* surprise.~~ (Do not use a comma.)ₛₜᵢₙgᵢₙg

4. Two pairs of eyelashes protect a camel's eyes from the ˄ desert sand. ~~*The sand* stings~~. (End the important word with **-ing**.)

5. The program was ˄ repeatedly interrupted for storm warnings. ~~*The interruptions were* repeated *several times.*~~ (End the important word with **-ly**.)

B. Combine the following sentence pairs by adding important words to the first sentence. You decide how to join the sentences. You may have to change the form of a word before adding it.

1. The boat was caught in a storm. ~~The storm was sudden.~~ *(sudden)*
2. Mary oiled the hinges. ~~The hinges squeaked.~~ *(squeaking)*
3. I saw the light of a TV screen. ~~The light flickered.~~ *(flickering)*
4. Matsuko visits the art galleries. ~~Her visits are frequent.~~ *(frequently)*
5. The framework of the building is steel. ~~The steel is welded to make the framework.~~ *(welded)*

Part 4   Adding Groups of Words

One sentence may contain a group of words that can add important information to another sentence.

> Ken stacked the cartons. They are in the basement.
> Ken stacked the cartons in the basement.

If you can learn to recognize these word groups, you will be able to create stronger, more precise sentences.

Adding Groups of Words Without Changes

Sometimes you can add a group of words without changing it. When the words give more information about someone or something, add them near the name of the person or thing.

> The clouds were alarming. *The clouds were* on the horizon.
> The clouds on the horizon were alarming.

When the words describe an action, add them near the words that name the action.

> Geraldo was waiting. *He was* at the corner.
> Geraldo was waiting at the corner.

When the words add more information to the entire main idea, you may add them at the beginning or the end.

Part 4

Objective

To add groups of words to one sentence from another

Presenting the Lesson

1. Review briefly the three kinds of sentence combining already studied. Then ask the students if any of those techniques could be used to combine the information in these two sentences.

The children were too noisy.
They were on the school bus.

2. Read and discuss the introduction and **Adding Groups of Words Without Changes** on pages 87–88. Point out the importance of positioning the group of words accurately, and discuss the use of commas for setting off groups of words.

3. Read and discuss **Adding Groups of Words with -ing** on page 88. You may wish to refer to Section 9 at the back of the student book.

4. Assign and discuss Exercises A and B on pages 88–89.

We hold a family reunion. *It happens* every summer.
Every summer, we hold a family reunion.
We hold a family reunion every summer.

Sometimes you will have to separate the group of words from the rest of the sentence with a comma or a pair of commas.

The robot is controlled by a microprocessor. *A microprocessor is* an electronic device smaller than a postage stamp.
The robot is controlled by a microprocessor, an electronic device smaller than a postage stamp.

Adding Groups of Words with *-ing*

When you add words to a sentence, you may have to change the form of one of the words. The new word will often end with *-ing*.

Helicopters began arriving in the morning. *They* carried food.
Helicopters carrying food began arriving in the morning.

More than one group of words can be added to a sentence. You may have to use a variety of techniques to combine them.

We saw a ferry. *It* carried hundreds of passengers.
It was just off the coast of Ontario.
We saw a ferry carrying hundreds of passengers just off the coast of Ontario.

Exercises Adding Groups of Words

A. Combine each of the following pairs of sentences by adding a group of words to the first sentence. Eliminate the italicized words. Follow any special instructions given in parentheses. Answers in margin.

1. The gray door leads to the main office. *The door is* at the end of this hall.
2. The call was from Anthony Metrakas. *He is* a newspaper reporter. (Use a comma.)
3. The flight is from Tampa. *The flight is* arriving at Gate 16.

4. The Chesapeake and Ohio Canal was completed in 1850. *The canal* linked Washington, D.C., and Cumberland, Maryland. (Use **-ing** and a pair of commas.)

5. Rescuers plunged out of the burning school. *They* carried children in their arms. (Add **-ing** to one of the words.)

B. Combine each group of sentences.

1. The Pioneer Days celebration will begin with a flapjack breakfast. The breakfast will start at 8:00.

2. Cairo was founded in A.D. 969. Cairo is the capital of Egypt.

3. Brass was first produced in ancient Rome. Brass is an alloy of copper and zinc.

4. Ted will write a column. The column will list plays. He will write the column for the Hinsdale *News*.

5. The historic park contains houses and shops. The houses and shops date back to the 18th century.

Part 5 Combining with *who, which,* or *that*

When you add a group of words to a sentence, you may sometimes find it necessary to add an introductory word to that group. The words *who, which,* and *that* are used for this purpose.

Use *who* to add information about a person or group of persons. If the information is absolutely necessary to the meaning of the sentence, simply add the words as near as possible to the word they refer to. If the information is not absolutely necessary to the meaning, it should be set off with commas.

The newscaster won the award. *She* covered the fire.
The newscaster who covered the fire won the award. (The added information is necessary. It tells *which* reporter.)

The newscaster won an award. *She* is popular with viewers.
The newscaster, who is popular with viewers, won an award. (The added information is not necessary to the meaning.)

89

Part 5

Objective

To use the words *who, which,* and *that* to combine sentences

Presenting the Lesson

1. Read aloud and discuss pages 89–90. Emphasize the difference between essential and non-essential information.

2. Assign and discuss Exercises A and B, page 90.

Individualizing the Lesson

Less-Advanced Students

Present the following sentences on the board before assigning the Exercises. Ask students how these sentences should be combined.

a. The circus was the first to visit our town. The circus had canvas tents and a fine collection of animals.

b. Mario plays the dulcimer. Mario loves all types of stringed instruments. (use **, who**)

Advanced Students

Have students find examples of sentences combined with *who, which,* and *that.* Then, using these sentences as models, have them write several sentences of their own.

Extending the Lesson

Have students look through their textbooks for uses of *who, which,* and *that.* Have them copy and present examples that follow the rules.

Exercise A

1. Tim Hutton, who first became known in *Ordinary People,* has starred in several movies.
2. This type of bicycle, which is used for racing, weighs less than ten pounds.
3. This is the book that I told you about yesterday.
4. The wrench that I need to loosen this tight pipe is in the bottom drawer of the tool chest.
5. The committee member who suggested the project was Terri.

Exercise B

1. The whale that had been caught by the tide had beached itself on the coast of the tiny fishing village.
2. The computer company that had designed one of the first home computers has just gone out of business.
3. The eighty-five-year-old comedian, who is loved by everyone in the entertainment field, was honored with a banquet.
4. The trolley, which ran on this avenue since the early 1900's, has finally been replaced.
5. The astronomer who made the discovery had the new comet named for him.

Which and *that* are also used to add groups of words. When the added information is necessary to the meaning of the sentence, use *that.* When the information is not necessary to the sentence, use *which* and set off the word group with commas.

Here are the guitar strings. You asked me for *them* last week.
Here are the guitar strings that you asked me for last week.

The existence of the Loch Ness monster has yet to be proven. *The monster's existence* has been debated for decades.
The existence of the Loch Ness monster, which has been debated for decades, has yet to be proven.

Exercises Combining with *who, which,* and *that*

A. Combine each of the following pairs of sentences.

Answers in margin.

1. Tim Hutton has starred in several movies recently. *He* first became known in *Ordinary People.*(Combine with **,who**.)
2. This type of bicycle weighs less than ten pounds. *The bicycle* is used for racing. (Combine with **,which**.)
3. This is the book. I told you about *it* yesterday. (Join with **that**.)
4. The wrench is in the bottom drawer of the tool chest. I need *the wrench* to loosen this tight pipe. (Combine with **that**.)
5. The committee member was Terri. *Terri* suggested the project. (Combine with **who**.)

B. Combine each of the following pairs of sentences. Decide on your own whether to use **,who**, **,which**, or **that**. Answers in margin.

1. The whale had beached itself on the coast of the tiny fishing village. The whale had been caught by the tide.
2. The computer company has just gone out of business. The company designed one of the first home computers.
3. The eighty-five-year-old comedian was honored with a banquet. He is loved by everyone in the entertainment field.
4. The trolley has finally been replaced. It ran on this avenue since the early 1900's.
5. The astronomer had the new comet named for him. The astronomer made the discovery.

90

SUMMARY AND APPLICATIONS

1. Related ideas may often be combined into a single sentence that clearly shows how the ideas are related.

2. Sentences and sentence parts that state ideas of equal importance can usually be joined by a comma and the word *and, or,* or *but.*

3. You may be able to combine two or more sentences by adding individual words or groups of words from one sentence to another.

4. Sometimes when you add words to a sentence, you will have to change the form of one of them. In its new form, the word will often end with *-ing* or *-ly.*

5. When you add a group of words, you may need to add the word *who, which,* or *that* at the beginning of the word group.

6. Use these sentence combining techniques when you are writing reports or compositions for your classes. Also use them to make talks and speeches more interesting.

Applications in Other Subject Areas

Literature. The writing styles of many authors are easily identifiable by the types of sentences that are used. Find one short story or novel by Ernest Hemingway and another by John Steinbeck. Which writer tends to use short, simple sentences? Which uses more complex sentences? Copy several typical sentences from each writer's work. See if you can identify any sentence combining techniques. You and your classmates may wish to discuss the effects these different styles have on the reader.

All Subjects. A textbook definition often combines a great many ideas into a single sentence. Find four such single-sentence definitions in your health, science, history, or mathematics texts. Break these statements down into the individual ideas that were combined to produce the definitions.

Summary and Applications

Discuss the summary. Emphasize that all of the techniques learned in this chapter can be used for revision of any written material.

Encourage students to use this summary for review or as part of the SQ3R method of study (see Chapter 15).

Applications in Other Subject Areas

These high-interest activities are designed to provide challenging opportunities to apply the chapter concepts in other subject areas.

For the literature activity, you may wish to use the following passages by Hemingway and Steinbeck as illustrations of their styles.

> Outside it was getting dark. The street-light came on outside the window. The two men at the counter read the menu. From the other end of the counter Nick Adams watched them. He had been talking to George when they came in.
> —Hemingway, *"The Killers"*

> Then the creeping murderer, the octopus, steals out, slowly, softly, moving like a gray mist, pretending now to be a bit of weed, now a rock, now a lump of decaying meat while its evil goat eyes watch coldly. It oozes and flows toward a feeding crab, and as it comes close its yellow eyes burn and its body turns rosy with the pulsing color of anticipation and rage.
> —Steinbeck, *Cannery Row*

Improving Your Sentences

Chapter Objectives

1. To recognize and revise empty sentences

2. To recognize and revise padded sentences

3. To recognize and revise overloaded sentences

4. To recognize and revise illogical sentences

5. To vary sentence beginnings

Preparing the Students

Read and discuss page 92. Emphasize the comparison between strong building materials and effectively written sentences in creating a strong final product. Explain that careful revision shows the writer's concern with how well he or she communicates to an audience.

You may wish to tell the class the following anecdote to illustrate one famous writer's concern with revision. Abraham Lincoln wrote five different versions of his famous Gettysburg Address. He wrote most of the first version in Washington and wrote a second version in Gettysburg. He held the second version in his hand as he spoke, but made some changes during his speech. After the ceremony he made three more copies. His fifth version is the one you see carved on a stone plaque at the Lincoln Memorial.

Additional Resources

Mastery Test — See pages 19–22 in the test booklet.

Skills Practice Book — pages 28–33.

Duplicating Masters — pages 29–34.

Special Populations — See special section at the front of this Teacher's Edition.

A contractor would never construct a building using weak or unsound materials. Timbers might buckle, walls could crumble, and the whole structure might collapse. Similarly, a conscientious writer must be concerned with the building blocks of a piece of writing — sentences. If individual sentences are awkward, wordy, or repetitive, the writing as a whole will lose its impact and have little appeal to the reader.

To avoid producing ineffective materials, a good writer carefully examines and evaluates every sentence he or she produces and revises whenever necessary. This chapter will help you understand how to do such revisions. It gives examples of unsatisfactory sentences and shows you how to go about improving them. It then supplies additional sentences for you to revise on your own.

Almost all of the sentences you will work with in this chapter were written by high school students. They did not have a chance to revise what they had written. You will be doing the revising for them. You will also be training yourself to think and write clearly

Part 1 Avoiding Empty Sentences

The purpose of a sentence is to say something. Unfortunately, words may be put into sentence form and still not say anything. Such a sentence is called an **empty sentence.**

There are two kinds of empty sentences.

1. Those that repeat an idea and end up where they started.
2. Those that make statements but fail to support them with a fact, a reason, or an example.

Sentences That Repeat an Idea

Notice the repetition of an idea in the following sentences.

FAULTY He had no friends, and so he was always alone.
(Omit the second clause. It merely repeats the idea *He had no friends.*)

REVISED He had no friends.

FAULTY I have a minor *crisis* in my life, and to me it presents a *problem.*
(Since *crisis* and *problem* are similar, use only one. Omit the second clause entirely.)

REVISED I have a minor crisis in my life.

Sometimes a whole sentence is repeated. This repetitious style is boring and monotonous to read.

FAULTY My father *complains* that I'm always on the phone, no matter what the time of day. His *complaint* is that I don't give anyone else a chance to use it.

REVISED My father complains that no one else has a chance to use the phone because I'm on it all day.
(Expressing the idea of *complaint* once is sufficient. The father's complaint has two parts: (1) *I'm always on the phone,* and (2) *I don't give anyone else a chance to use it.* Combine these ideas.)

Objective

To recognize and revise empty sentences

Presenting the Lesson

1. Read and discuss **Avoiding Empty Sentences** on pages 93 and 94. Tell the class to listen for weaknesses in the faulty sentences. Point out that although the revised sentences are much shorter, they communicate the ideas more effectively.

2. Before assigning the exercise on pages 94–95, discuss the six suggestions for revision. Tell the students to refer to these suggestions while completing the exercise.

3. Read and discuss **Sentences That Contain Unsupported Statements** on page 95. Tell the students to be alert for statements in their own writing that leave readers with questions in their minds. Such statements weaken the credibility of the writer's ideas.

4. Assign the exercise on pages 94–95. Discuss the two suggestions for revising the sentences. Emphasize that even sentences that are grammatically correct can be ineffective in communicating an idea.

Individualizing the Lesson

Less-Advanced Students

Work with the students to complete the first five revisions in the exercise orally. Referring often to the suggestions for revision.

Have the students write short paragraphs based on some opinion they hold concerning a TV show, song, or famous personality. When they have completed their paragraphs, have them reread them to identify any empty sentences. Ask them to share with the class their original empty sentences and the revised versions.

Optional Practice

Have the students revise the following faulty sentences:

a. When I am in college I will enjoy being a college student.
b. In planning his career he was making plans to work in the computer industry.
c. Exercise is important for a person's health. Everyone should exercise three times a week.
d. Summer jobs are hard to get. Most students generally have trouble finding summer work.

Extending the Lesson

1. Use several samples of unrevised writing, such as student essay tests, to provide further examples of faulty sentences. Duplicate them to distribute to the class, or use an overhead projector to project the samples.
2. Clip several letters to the editor from a local paper. Try to find one or two that contain unsupported statements. Have students compare the effectiveness of the letters.

Exercise (Revised sentences may vary somewhat.)

1. Many people find chess a very interesting game.

FAULTY   From my earliest days I have been an avid reader. I suppose I inherited this love of books from my mother. *She also loves to read.*

REVISED   From my earliest days I have been an avid reader. I suppose I inherited this love of books from my mother. (The second sentence indicates the mother's love of reading in her love of books. *She also loves to read* is unnecessary repetition.)

FAULTY   I asked Tom to stop at my house *for a snack* and *to meet my mother.* After he *met my mother,* we went into the kitchen and *had a snack.*

REVISED   Tom accepted my invitation to stop at my house for a snack and to meet my mother.

Two suggestions will help you avoid this writing fault: (1) read aloud what you have written, and (2) revise.

Exercise Revising Sentences That Repeat an Idea

Revise the following sentences.   Answers in margin.

Suggestions

1—Look for repeated words in the same sentence.
2—Look for repeated ideas in the same sentence.
3—Look for sentences that repeat an idea already expressed.
4—Omit the repetitions wherever possible.
5—Combine two sentences into one, if necessary.
6—Realize that there is more than one way to revise these sentences.

1. Many people are interested in chess because it is a very interesting game.
2. The movie was boring, and I found it very dull.
3. Of course, you can't go on a hike without food. Who would ever dream of going on a hike without food?
4. Dad can't understand why I have to call my friends when I get home from school. He claims that I see my friends all day long in school, so I don't have to phone them as soon as I reach home.

5. At this point I usually burst into a torrent of tears. Mom and Dad usually know the right words to comfort me, however, for I soon feel better and begin to be a little more cheerful.

6. Have you ever watched television in a crowd? If you haven't watched it in a crowd, you can't imagine what it is like to watch television with three hundred people.

7. On Sunday we are going on a trip for the day. I am sure we will have a good time if the weather permits. There are seven of us going on the trip, and everyone is praying that we will have a wonderful day for our trip.

8. When I was small, I was spoiled. It wasn't because I was an only child, because I had two brothers. It was because I was the only girl and the only granddaughter. You see, all my cousins were boys.

9. In our high school, at every lunch period, there is a long cafeteria line. In the cafeteria we can buy yogurt, salad, fruit, hot food, and so on. To buy these items, we must stand in a line.

10. If you have ever been to the zoo, you know what a great time you can have there. The zoo is a place to visit again and again. At the zoo there is always something new, wonderful, and educational.

2. I found the movie very dull.

3. You would not dream of going on a hike without food.

4. Because I see my friends all day at school, Dad can't understand why I have to phone them when I get home.

5. Whenever I burst into tears, Mom and Dad know how to comfort me, and I soon feel more cheerful.

6. If you have ever watched television in a crowd, you can imagine what it is like to watch it with three hundred people.

7. If we have good weather on Sunday, seven of us are going on a trip for the day.

8. I think I was rather spoiled when I was small, because I was the only girl and granddaughter in our family.

9. We have to stand in a long line to buy candy, ice cream, pretzels, and hot food in our high school cafeteria.

10. Because there is always something new, wonderful, and educational at the zoo, it is a great place to visit often.

Sentences That Contain Unsupported Statements

A kind of emptiness in writing results from statements that are not supported by reasons, facts, or examples. The question "Why?" is left in the reader's mind.

Try to find the unsupported statement in this group:

Not only does chess provide players with a challenging and enjoyable pastime, but it also sharpens thinking skills as players plan and carry out strategies.

Chess is becoming popular with people of all ages. Even young children play it. I think it would be good for everyone to learn the game.

The unsupported statement is not difficult to find. Look for the sentence that involves an opinion. *Why* would it be good for everyone to learn chess? The writer should add one or more reasons that support the opinion.

Exercise (Revised sentences may vary
somewhat.)

1. Practical jokes played in school can relieve the monotony of lessons. However,
school is not the place for practical
jokes because they can interfere with
the primary purpose of education.
2. New industries and occupations are now
opening up good job opportunities for
minorities.
3. It is good that Detroit is making more
small cars now because they will use
less fuel.
4. Some people are talking about making
the school year longer. This would be a
mistake because the school year is
already long enough. Teachers and
students need to take the summer off so
that they can rest and have a change of
pace.
5. My parents do not want me to get a
part-time job this year. They think it will
interfere with my studies.
6. Parents and teachers often complain
about how much time young people
spend watching television. However,
many television shows are good for us to
watch, especially educational programs
that deal with subjects we are studying
at school.
7. According to the state law, you have to
be eighteen before you can get a
decent job. The law should be changed
because teenagers need work experience and income.
8. Every year a million Americans go to
Europe. These tourists should first see
their own country in order to appreciate
its history, geography, and culture.
9. I always cheer for the Bears because
they are my favorite team, win or lose.
10. The movie rating system ought to be
changed to effect higher standards.

Exercise Revising Unsupported Statements

Revise the following selections. They contain statements that need more support.   Answers in margin.

Suggestions

1—Locate the statement or statements that need support.
2—Ask "Why?" Then add whatever reasons or facts you think are necessary.

1. You can get a good laugh from practical jokes played in school. They can relieve the monotony of lessons. However, school is not the place for practical jokes.

2. There are more good job opportunities for minorities now because more good jobs are opening up.

3. Detroit is making a lot of small cars now. I think that is very good. I like these small cars and hope to save enough money to own one in a few years.

4. Some people are talking about making the school year longer. This would be a mistake. I think that the school year is long enough as it is.

5. I want to get a part-time job this year. I could work at least two hours after school each day. My parents do not approve of the idea.

6. Parents and teachers often complain about how much time young people spend watching television. However, many television shows are good for us to watch.

7. According to the state law, you have to be eighteen before you can get a decent job. I think this is very bad. I think the law should be changed.

8. Every year a million Americans travel to Europe. I wonder how many of those people have traveled around this country. It seems to me that people should see their own country before traveling to Europe.

9. When I watch a football game on television, I always cheer for the Steelers (or Bears or Jets or Cowboys) because they are my favorite football team.

10. The movie rating system ought to be changed because it isn't effective the way it is.

Part 2 Avoiding Padded Sentences

A padded sentence is one that contains unnecessary words or phrases. Some sentences contain padding such as *the fact that* and *the reason is*. Others contain clauses that could be reduced to phrases without any damage to the thought. Although such padding may not always be considered incorrect, it often clutters the sentences and prevents writers from expressing their ideas clearly and concisely.

Taking Out the Padding

Phrases that puff up a sentence with unnecessary words get in the way of the meaning of the sentence. Getting to the meaning can be like trying to find a path that is overgrown with weeds.

The following expressions usually add little to a sentence and should be avoided:

"FACT" EXPRESSIONS

because of the fact that
owing to the fact that
due to the fact that
on account of the fact that
the fact of the matter is
    that

"WHAT" EXPRESSIONS

what I mean is
what I believe is
what I want is
what I want to say is

OTHER EXPRESSIONS TO AVOID

the point is   the thing is
the reason is   being that

Sentences are smoother and simpler when unnecessary words are omitted.

PADDED   My family did not go to the shore *on account of the fact that* there was a storm.

REVISED   My family did not go to the shore *because* there was a storm.

Part 2

Objective

To recognize and revise padded sentences

Presenting the Lesson

1. Read pages 97 and 98. Briefly discuss the meaning of "padded sentence," emphasizing that ideas should be expressed in as few words as possible. Discuss in detail the commonly used expressions on page 97 that often contribute to poor sentences.

2. Read and discuss **Reducing Clauses to Phrases** on page 98. Point out the difference between a clause and a phrase. (You may wish to refer to sections 9 and 11 at the back of the student book.) Explain that a clause always contains a subject and a verb, but a phrase does not. Also point out that clauses frequently begin with *who, whose, whom, which,* or *that*. Remind students that *who is* or *which is* at the beginning of a clause are often unnecessary words that may be eliminated when the clause is revised to a phrase.

3. Assign Exercises A and B on pages 99 and 100. Encourage the students to refer to the four suggestions on page 99 when revising the sentences in both exercises.

Individualizing the Lesson

Less-Advanced Students

To be sure that the difference between a clause and a phrase is clear to these students, write the examples below on the chalkboard and discuss the difference between them.

Phrases: my oldest brother in New Hampshire
Clauses: who is my oldest brother
which orginated in New Hampshire

Work together with students to complete Exercise A in class. Have students complete Exercise B independently.

Advanced Students

Review the use of *who* and *which* as interrogative pronouns. See Section 4 at the back of the book. Be sure students understand the difference between the use of *who* and *which* in the following sentences.

Who will be you teacher?
Ms. Mell is the gymnast who will be your teacher.
Which is Max's favorite movie?
We rented the videotape of *Fantasia,* which is Max's favorite movie.

Optional Practice

Write the following sentences on the chalkboard for the class to revise.

a. *To Kill a Mockingbird,* which was a popular book written by Harper Lee, was made into a movie.
b. My brother and I are what you might call opposite in our appearance as well as in our temperaments.
c. The thing that excited Spot most about being the fire station dog was the fact that he got to ride on the truck to the fire.

Extending the Lesson

Have the students bring to class examples of padded sentences from magazines and newspapers. Write some of the examples on the board and discuss possible revisions.

PADDED   *What I mean is* that his ideas of summer camp are not realistic.

REVISED   His ideas of summer camp are not realistic.

PADDED   *The reason* I washed my father's car *was* that he hinted that it was dirty.

REVISED   I washed my father's car *because* he hinted that it was dirty.

PADDED   *What I want* is to go to Baltimore to see my grandparents if I don't get a job.

REVISED   I want to go to Baltimore to see my grandparents if I don't get a job.

PADDED   I know *that* if I study hard *that* I can get a scholarship.

REVISED   I know that if I study hard I can get a scholarship.

Reducing Clauses to Phrases

Clauses that begin with *who is* and *which is* can sometimes be simplified to phrases.

LENGTHY   We admired the lights at the airport, *which is across the bay.*

REVISED   We admired the lights at the airport *across the bay.*

LENGTHY   Her latest movie, *which is a modern Western,* has been nominated for an Oscar.

REVISED   Her latest movie, *a modern Western,* has been nominated for an Oscar.

LENGTHY   The swimming meet, *which was the most exciting event of the year,* attracted crowds of students.

REVISED   The swimming meet, *the most exciting event of the year,* attracted crowds of students.
or
The swimming meet was *the most exciting event of the year* and attracted crowds of students.

Exercises Revising Padded Sentences

A. Revise these sentences by reducing and simplifying them.

Answers in margin.

Suggestions

1—Look for "fact" expressions, "what" expressions, and other padding.

2—Look for *who* or *which* clauses that can be simplified.

3—Eliminate as many unnecessary words as possible.

4—Realize that there is more than one way to revise these sentences.

1. What Sarah wants is to be a baseball coach.

2. The thing that nobody could understand was Ann's fear.

3. You must admit that even if you don't admire him that he plays well.

4. The Eiffel Tower, which is located in Paris, is a symbol of France.

5. On account of the fact that she had learned to bowl during the summer, Debbie wanted to join the school team.

6. We immediately called Mrs. Vincent, who is our lawyer, to ask for advice.

7. Due to the fact that the fog was dense, the two huge tankers collided.

8. What I believe is that you succeed largely because of your own efforts.

9. The point is that the study of French has many values.

10. Howie, who will do anything for a laugh, wore a T-shirt that had a formal black tie and ruffles printed on it.

B. Revise these sentences. Answers in margin.

1. The reason that we took the car through the car wash was that it was covered with tree spray.

2. The rocks that extend out into the bay are dangerous.

3. The reason that Venice is fascinating is that many of its streets are all water.

4. Whenever it happens to rain hard, our cellar fills up with water and becomes a lake.

Exercise A (Revised sentences may vary somewhat.)

1. Sarah wants to be a baseball coach.
2. Nobody could understand Ann's fear.
3. Even if you don't admire him, you must admit that he plays well.
4. The Eiffel Tower in Paris is a symbol of France.
5. Debbie had learned to bowl during the summer and wanted to join the school team.
6. We immediately called our lawyer, Mrs. Vincent, to ask for advice.
7. The two ships collided because of the dense fog.
8. You succeed largely because of your own efforts.
9. Studying French has many values.
10. Howie, our class clown, wore a T-shirt with a formal black tie and ruffles printed on it.

Exercise B (Revised sentences may vary somewhat.)

1. We took the car through the car wash because it was covered with tree spray.
2. The rocks out in the bay are dangerous.
3. Venice is fascinating because many of its streets are all water.
4. Whenever it rains hard, our cellar fills up with water and becomes a lake.
5. The excavation of many of the ruins in Rome makes them visible to tourists.
6. I could hear the drone of the planes all night.
7. If I had to change the typewriter ribbon, it would be a hopeless tangle.
8. The fountain of Trevi in Rome is connected with a legend about coins.
9. We finally rehearsed in Mr. Steiner's garage.
10. I bought this ring in Harper's novelty store on Walnut Street.

5. Many ruins in Rome are visible to tourists on account of the fact that much excavating has been done.
6. What I couldn't help hearing all night was the drone of the planes.
7. I knew that if I had to change the typewriter ribbon that I would create a hopeless tangle.
8. The fountain of Trevi, which is in Rome, is connected with a legend about coins.
9. What we finally did about our rehearsals was hold them in Mr. Steiner's garage.
10. I bought this ring in Harper's novelty store, which is on Walnut Street.

Part 3 Avoiding Overloaded Sentences

Long sentences containing a number of ideas, usually connected loosely by *and*'s, are confusing and ineffective. They give the reader a whole series of ideas to sort out without any clue to their relationship. Such sentences violate the principle that a sentence usually contains *one* central thought.

LENGTHY I went into the building, *and* I waited for the elevator in the lobby, *and* when it didn't come I had to walk up eight flights of stairs.

REVISED I went into the lobby of the building and waited for the elevator. When it didn't come, I had to walk up eight flights of stairs.

LENGTHY Horrible faces glared at me from the shelves in the costume shop. All of them were contorted, *and* most of them were scarred, *and* they were a deathly gray with a greenish cast.

REVISED Horrible faces glared at me from the shelves in the costume shop. All of them were contorted, and most of them were scarred. The faces were a deathly gray with a greenish cast.

Part 3

Objective

To recognize and revise overloaded sentences

Presenting the Lesson

1. Read and discuss page 100. Point out that *and* is not the only conjunction used in loosely connected sentences. Other conjunctions such as *but, or,* or *so* may also overload a sentence.

2. Assign the Exercise on page 101.

Extending the Lesson

Let students write sentences like those in the Exercise by having one student begin the sentence, and then asking two or three other students to add ideas to it.

Individualizing the Lesson

Less-Advanced Students

Do the Exercise orally, as a group.

Advanced Students

Have students write a paragraph in which a nervous or excited character relates an incident in one long sentence. Then have students exchange papers for revision.

Exercise **Revising Overloaded Sentences**

Revise the following sentences.   Answers in margin.

Suggestions

1. Separate each sentence into two or three shorter ones.
2. Reduce the number of *and*'s.

1. Debbie got a white bike for her birthday, and it is a ten-speed model and it has a suede saddle.

2. Dad lost his wallet last Saturday with all his credit cards in it, but, luckily for him, it was returned yesterday by a neighbor who found it in the street outside our house.

3. For the Halloween party Luis dressed as Rocky Balboa, and Anna dressed as the Cookie Monster, and several people came as Darth Vader, but the Wizard of Oz won the costume contest.

4. My family picked apples at an orchard, and we learned how to tell which apples were ripe and how to keep from bruising the fruit and how to climb ladders to reach the top branches, and the biggest bonus was the juicy apple pies we made.

5. Some children learn to read at age three or four, and others learn in school, and experts disagree about the value of very early training in reading.

6. Different styles of furniture change the mood of a room. Early American furniture has a comfortable look, and contemporary furniture has a sleek look, and traditional furniture has a formal look, and there are also ethnic styles, like Mediterranean.

7. One tree in our town is six hundred years old, and it has a hole in the trunk, and twenty people can stand inside it, and Indians used the tree long ago as a meeting place.

8. The art department offers classes in ceramics and photography, and this year there will be a printmaking class, and many students are eager to learn about etching and lithography.

9. Hurricanes are tropical cyclones, and they start over oceans, especially near the equator, and the winds can reach 150 miles per hour, and the most destructive hurricane occurred in 1972.

10. The Olympic Games are patterned after an ancient Greek festival, and the first modern games were held in 1896, and since then the number of sports and participants has greatly increased.

Objective

To recognize and revise sentences that are illogical

Presenting the Lesson

1. Point out that there are four common sentence errors in student writing. The next few pages provide practice in identifying and correcting them. Read page 102 as a class and discuss the faulty sentences in **Making Sure That the Verb Has a Subject**. Ask students to suggest other possible revisions.

2. Read and discuss **Avoiding the Use of a Prepositional Phrase as the Subject**, page 103. Explain that only nouns or words that act as nouns can be the subject of a sentence. Explain that the words *setting* and *detecting* in the revised sentence are verb forms that are acting as nouns. (See Section 9 for a discussion of gerunds.)

3. Read and discuss **Avoiding Faulty Comparisons** on page 103.

4. Read and discuss **Making Sure That Necessary Words Are Included** on page 104. Point out that, because we can think faster than we can write, such omissions are not uncommon. Exphasize that careful review of all written work will reduce the frequency of this type of error.

5. Assign Exercise A and B, pages 104–105.

Part 4 Writing Sentences That Make Sense

Sometimes students write sentences that do not make complete sense because they shift from what they started to say to something else. In between, the main idea has become confused or lost. They may also write quickly and carelessly and fail to check what they have written. The result is a hodgepodge, and situations like these occur:

1. A verb has no subject or a subject has no verb.
2. A prepositional phrase is used as a subject.
3. A faulty comparison is made.
4. Single words, necessary to complete the meaning of the sentence, are left out.

Making Sure That the Verb Has a Subject

Study the following examples.

FAULTY If you constantly practice is a help in becoming a better dancer.
      (There is no subject for the verb *is*.)

REVISED Constant practice helps you to become a better dancer.

FAULTY His character was very weak and never did the right thing.
      (There is no subject for the verb *did*.)

REVISED His character was very weak, and *he* never did the right thing.

FAULTY The speech was long and were bored.
      (There is no subject for the verb *were*.)

REVISED The speech was long, and *we* were bored.

You can eliminate this problem by rereading and revising what you have written.

Avoiding the Use of a Prepositional Phrase as the Subject

A preposition is a short word used to show a relationship in time or space. Common prepositions include *to, at, on, with, by, from, of, for, after, until*, and *around*. Prepositional phrases, groups of words that begin with prepositions, should never be used as subjects of verbs.

Study the following examples.

FAULTY   By setting up observation posts near volcanoes and detecting eruptions early can save many lives.
            (A prepositional phrase is used incorrectly as the subject of *can save*.)

REVISED   *Setting* up observation posts near volcanoes and *detecting* eruptions early can save many lives.
            (The italicized words are acceptable subjects for *can save*.)

Avoiding Faulty Comparisons

A special kind of senseless sentence is one in which there is a faulty comparison or one in which two things are treated as though they were similar when they are not.

FAULTY   *Studying biology* in high school is very different from *college*.
            (*Studying biology* should not be compared with *college*.)

REVISED   *Studying biology* in high school is very different from *studying it* in college.

FAULTY   The requirements for the job are an engineer and at least one year of experience.
            (An *engineer* is a person and does not equal the word *requirements*.)

REVISED   The requirements for the job are an engineering degree and at least one year of experience.

103

Making Sure That Necessary Words Are Included

The omission of a single word can make a sentence meaningless. This kind of carelessness can be avoided by rereading and revising your work.

FAULTY　The little Swiss family find themselves comfortably situated as conditions will permit.
(The word *as* has been left out.)

REVISED　The little Swiss family find themselves *as* comfortably situated as conditions will permit.

FAULTY　Elizabeth Barrett, an invalid for many years, knew what she wanted to do but was afraid of her father to attempt it.

REVISED　Elizabeth Barrett, an invalid for many years, knew what she wanted to do but was *too* afraid of her father to attempt it.

Exercises　Revising Sentences That Do Not Make Sense

A. Revise the following ten sentences. Answers in margin.

Suggestions

1. Make sure that every verb has a subject.
2. Make sure that a prepositional phrase is not used as a subject.
3. Correct the faulty comparisons.
4. Make sure that necessary words have been included.

1. The cost of running a small car is less than a big car.
2. The real test of Donna's personality was her older sister.
3. The easier a subject is and the higher marks you can get with little work does not mean you should choose it.
4. To anyone who observes life and the game of football will soon detect many similarities.
5. The only real problem I find I wear out the rug by dancing.
6. Paula's fever has broken and is now feeling much better.

7. You could tell by the expression on my face the anguish I was through.

8. Andy's explanation of scuba diving is clearer than high-diving.

9. By applying for a summer job early is the best way for a student to be hired.

10. The faster the car goes is not the most important reason for buying it.

B. Revise the following sentences.   Answers in margin.

1. Playing football in college is much different from high school.

2. The way I check a person is how he or she acts.

3. The more you have to do and the less time makes you work harder.

4. Some hobbies are so that you can make money out of them.

5. Going to college or a job is a question every student must face before he or she graduates.

6. I burned the hamburgers is why we finally went to McDonald's.

7. Because it's a white dog with black spots all over it is why I'm sure it's a Dalmatian.

8. Any fad that Jerry hears about, he follows it.

9. Radio commercials don't bother me as much as TV.

10. You tell a good friend what he or she wants to hear is not always the kindest thing to do.

Part 5 Varying Your Sentence Beginnings

You want people to enjoy reading what you have to say. You are therefore interested in making your writing lively and effective. One way to achieve this is to vary the beginnings of your sentences, to give them a new look by inverting the order of their parts. You must be careful not to overwork this technique, but it can effectively be used to intensify a situation or an idea, or momentarily to slow down the pace of your writing.

7. You could tell by my expression the anguish I was going through.
8. Andy's explanation of scuba diving is clearer than his explanation of high diving.
9. The best way to be hired for a summer job is to apply early.
10. High speed is not the best reason for buying a car.

Exercise B (Revised sentences may vary somewhat.)

1. Playing football in college is much different from playing it in high school.
2. The way I check a person is to observe how he or she acts.
3. The more you have to do and the less time you have, the harder you work.
4. You can make money from some hobbies.
5. Every student must face the question of going to college or getting a job.
6. We finally went to McDonald's because I had burned the hamburgers.
7. I'm sure it is a Dalmatian because it's a white dog with black spots all over it.
8. Jerry follows any fad he hears about.
9. Radio commercials don't bother me as much as TV commercials.
10. Telling a person what he or she wants to hear is not always the kindest thing to do.

Part 5

Objective

To vary sentence beginnings

Presenting the Lesson

1. Read the introductory paragraph on page 105. Tell the students to pay particular attention to the contrast between the usual order of each sample sentence that follows and the inverted order. Refer to the appropriate grammar sections when helpful.

2. Read **Ways to Vary Your Sentence Beginnings** on page 106–108. When discussing suggestion 1, point out that an adverb placed at the beginning of a sentence is often followed by a comma. (See Section 6 for a discussion of adverbs.) Discuss the sample sentences.

3. When discussing suggestion 2, note that these inverted sentences have a certain dramatic quality. Briefly discuss the appropriate use of this type of inversion and caution students not to use this kind of inversion too frequently. (See Section 1, Parts 6 and 7.)

4. Before discussing suggestion 3, you may wish to put these definitions on the chalkboard.

A *prepositional phrase* consists of a preposition, its object, and any modifiers of the object.

A *participle* is a verb form used as an adjective. A *participial phrase* is made up of a participle and its modifiers or an object or both. The entire phrase is used as an adjective.

An infinitive with modifiers and objects forms an *infinitive phrase*.

See Sections 7 and 9 for a more in depth discussion of these grammatical terms.

5. Read and discuss suggestion 4 on page 107–108. Tell the class that this is one of the easiest and most common structural variations. Point out that when the subordinate clause ends a sentence, no comma is used. When the subordinate clause begins a sentence, a comma is necessary. Refer to Section 11, Part 3 if more information is needed on subordinate clauses.

Ways To Vary Your Sentence Beginnings

1. Put an adverb before the subject.

USUAL ORDER   Butch inched his way *cautiously*.

          (adverb)

INVERTED   *Cautiously*, Butch inched his way.

USUAL ORDER   She stopped *abruptly* and stared at him.

          (adverb)

INVERTED   *Abruptly*, she stopped and stared at him.

2. Put the verb or direct object before the subject.

USUAL ORDER   The *torrents* of rain *poured* down.

          (verb)   **(subject)**

INVERTED   Down *poured* the *torrents* of rain.

USUAL ORDER   *Anchorage was* twenty miles ahead of us.

          (verb)   **(subject)**

INVERTED   Twenty miles ahead of us *was Anchorage*.

USUAL ORDER   I could not tolerate an *insult* like that.

          (object)   **(subject)**

INVERTED   An *insult* like that *I* could not tolerate.

USUAL ORDER   *I* can recall certain *songs* without difficulty.

          (object) (subject)

INVERTED   Certain *songs I* can recall without difficulty.

3. Begin the sentence with a prepositional phrase, a participial phrase, or an infinitive phrase. Be sure the phrase modifies the proper word.

USUAL ORDER   I waited alone *for ten minutes*.

          (prepositional phrase)

INVERTED   *For ten minutes* I waited alone.

USUAL ORDER   Nothing is more beautiful *to me* than a snowstorm.

     (prepositional phrase)

INVERTED   *To me*, nothing is more beautiful than a snowstorm.

USUAL ORDER   James led her into the hall, *taking her gently by the hand*.

     (participial phrase)

INVERTED   *Taking her gently by the hand*, James led her into the hall.

USUAL ORDER   We headed for the dude ranch, *excited about our unusual vacation*.

     (participial phrase)

INVERTED   *Excited about our unusual vacation*, we headed for the dude ranch.

USUAL ORDER   Sharon went to the library *to get information about satellites*.

     (infinitive phrase)

INVERTED   *To get information about satellites*, Sharon went to the library.

USUAL ORDER   Dick must pass a physical examination *to be eligible for the team*.

     (infinitive phrase)

INVERTED   *To be eligible for the team,* Dick must pass a physical examination.

4. Begin the sentence with a subordinate clause.

USUAL ORDER   Paula's mother was at the airport to meet the girls *when they got off the plane*.

     (subordinate clause)

INVERTED   *When the girls got off the plane*, Paula's mother was there to meet them.

6. Assign Exercise A and B on page 108.

7. The Review Exercise on page 109 may be used for a final test on the Chapter or as a graded assignment. Remind the students that there may be more than one possible revision for each sentence.

Individualizing the Lesson

Less-Advanced Students

1. Review grammatical terms with students before beginning this part.

2. Work with the students to revise the first four sentences of Exercise A, page 108 orally. Have the students complete the exercise in pairs.

3. For Exercise B, divide the students into two groups. Have one group complete the first five sentences and the other group complete the last five sentences. Have each group check the revised sentences of the other.

Advanced Students

Have students write a two or three paragraph narrative of an incident they saw or experienced recently. Have them include one of each type of sentence variation in these paragraphs.

Optional Practice

Read aloud several paragraphs from a work of fiction the class is currently reading together. Tell the students to listen for the various ways the author begins his or her sentences.

Extending the Lesson

Ask any students who are studying a foreign language to explain to the class the usual word order of different types of sentences in these languages. Which orders are similar to those in English, which are different?

1. As we walked onto the stage, we tried not to shake.
2. Finally, the clock struck ten.
3. Dressed in his best suit, he looked stiff and unhappy.
4. In the corners of the parking lot, the plow was tossing up huge mounds of snow.
5. Unless I make the first move, nothing will happen.
6. Suddenly the driver was blinded by a flash of light.
7. Out into the rain hurried the frightened people.
8. After the accident, I lost my interest in snowmobiling.
9. To fight against his fear, Paul buried himself in his work.
10. The smell of fish I just can't stand.

1. In the middle of the test, my pen ran dry.
2. Down came the swirling, muddy torrent, dragging tents and equipment with it.
3. Reluctantly, Peter sold his stamp collection.
4. After I reminded my dad that the car was insured, he gave me my first driving lesson.
5. Carrying three new dresses she went off to the fitting room.
6. As he shuffled down Main Street, Joe's problem grew heavier.
7. The suspect was questioned for eight hours by the police.
8. As soon as the game was over, Diana hurried to the locker room.
9. Even though he knew he was gaining too much weight, Andy kept on eating pizza.
10. When our Siamese cat climbs the curtains, Dad climbs the walls.

USUAL ORDER   I felt like a millionaire *as I boarded the ship for France.*

(subordinate clause)

INVERTED   *As I boarded the ship for France,* I felt like a millionaire.

Exercises Varying Your Sentence Beginnings

A. Rewrite the following sentences, varying the positions of the words or word groups in italics.   Answers in margin.

1. We tried not to shake *as we walked onto the stage.*
2. The clock *finally* struck ten.
3. He looked stiff and unhappy, *dressed in his best suit.*
4. The plow was tossing up huge mounds of snow *in the corners of the parking lot.*
5. Nothing will happen *unless I make the first move.*
6. The driver was *suddenly* blinded by a flash of light.
7. The frightened people hurried *out into the rain.*
8. I lost my interest in snowmobiling *after the accident.*
9. Paul buried himself in his work *to fight against his fear.*
10. One of the instruments Leona plays is *the tenor sax.*

B. Rewrite each sentence below. Change the positions of words so that you have an effective variation of the sentence.   Answers in margin

1. My pen ran dry in the middle of the test.
2. The swirling, muddy torrent came down, dragging tents and equipment with it.
3. Peter sold his stamp collection reluctantly.
4. My dad gave me my first driving lesson after I reminded him that the car was insured.
5. She went off to the fitting room, carrying three new dresses.
6. Joe's problem grew heavier as he shuffled down Main Street.
7. The police questioned the suspect for eight hours.
8. Diana hurried to her locker as soon as the game was over.
9. Andy kept on eating pizza even though he knew he was gaining too much weight.
10. Dad climbs the walls when our kitten climbs the curtains.

Review Exercise Revising Sentences with Various Problems

Revise the following sentences. They contain various problems you have dealt with in this chapter.   Answers in margin.

1. I know that if I try that I can get into college.
2. The pen that has the red felt tip leaks.
3. Each time, I went through a routine that was different.
4. Television lets you sit back and let a machine think for you. You don't do any of the thinking yourself.
5. My speech did not go over well due to the fact that I was extremely nervous.
6. What I sometimes wish is people wouldn't behave like sheep.
7. Mr. Russo is completely bald is probably the reason he always wears a cap.
8. The photos of the surface of Mars look just like the Painted Desert of Arizona.
9. I got sick on account of the fact that I ate too many tacos.
10. Disc jockeys at many radio stations are given a "play list" of songs that have been selected by a computer, and these songs are either popular now or expected to be popular soon, and the disc jockey has to play the songs on the list.
11. The reception on my parents' stereo is better than my radio.
12. When you think about it, you realize that death is something that happens to everyone, but most of the time you think it will happen only to other people and that it will never happen to you.
13. In Switzerland, skiing is a popular sport. Many Swiss ski regularly.
14. Make my bed, clean up my room, but put away my barbell is the only thing I forget to do.
15. How to load an Instamatic camera is the thing I have trouble doing.
16. My brother says that microcomputers are going to be the hottest home entertainment industry since television, and he says people are just starting to see how much fun these little gadgets can be, and he predicts that people will soon be bored by television.

Go over the summary with
the class. Emphasize the importance of these revision
techniques to clear thinking
and writing.

Encourage students to use
this summary for review or as
part of the SQ3R method of
study (see Chapter 15). Remind them, though, that more
specific points can only be reviewed by skimming the chapter itself.

Applications in Other Subject Areas

Read and discuss **Industrial
Arts/Home Economics.** Ask if
any students have had any
appliances or new plumbing
installed recently. If not, tell
them to visit any appliance or
department store and ask for
copies of installation instructions. Another place to find instructions is a toy store, or a
pattern in a fabric store. Allow
time for them to show their
findings with the class. Point
out that many people have
spent hours trying to put together a simple object because of unclear and imprecise instructions.

SUMMARY AND APPLICATIONS

1. A good writer reviews his or her work carefully and revises awkward, repetitious, or wordy sentences.

2. Some sentences lack meaning because they either make unsupported statements or repeat the same idea in different words.

3. Padded sentences contain unnecessary phrases and clauses that obscure meaning and decrease readability.

4. Overloaded sentences contain too many different ideas. These sentences should be divided into several shorter statements.

5. Some sentences are illogical because of grammatical errors, faulty comparisons, or missing parts.

6. One way to make writing more interesting is to vary sentence beginnings.

7. Mastery of these techniques will help you write, think, and speak clearly. Try to be aware of them whenever you express your ideas.

Applications in Other Subject Areas

Industrial Arts / Home Economics. Instructions for completing projects, operating tools and machinery, and repairing or checking different items must be extremely clear and precise. Poor sentence construction can weaken such directions. Find an example in which poor sentences have led to muddled instructions. Then revise the instructions on your own.

Speech / Social Studies. Effective speakers, like effective writers, must avoid empty, padded, or overloaded sentences. Listen to speakers in any two of the situations given below. Write down any examples of poor sentences that weaken their speeches. Then revise the sentences so that they express the ideas more clearly.

    a. a class speech or lecture   c. a televised speech
    b. a city or town council meeting   d. an interview

Chapter 7

The Process of Writing

Chapter Objectives

1. To understand and use different pre-writing tehniques

2. To write a first draft based on pre-writing activities

3. To use revision and proofreading to polish a rough draft

4. To understand how to prepare a final copy

Preparing the Students

Read the first paragraph of the introduction. Ask students to describe the steps involved in making a cake, painting a room, or planning a party. Then ask students to name other activities involving detailed processes.

Point out that writing also involves a series of steps. Then tell the students that the purpose of this chapter is to give them practice in the three main steps of the writing process: pre-writing, writing the first draft, and revising. Point out that mastering this process will make their future writing assignments not only better, but also easier.

Additional Resources

Skills Practice Book — pages 34–35.

Duplicating Masters — pages 35–36.

Special Populations — See special section at the front of this Teacher's Edition.

As you bite into a piece of cake, look at a painting, or read a book, you usually give little thought to the processes that were involved in creating each product. For instance, the artist whose painting you are admiring may have considered and rejected several possible subjects. He or she may then have drawn dozens of sketches. Even while actually painting, the artist may have blotted out sections and begun over.

There is another process to which you may never have given much thought. This is the **process of writing**. No matter what you compose, you should follow certain steps of preparation and development. Like the artist in the example above, you plan what you want to do, try out ideas, and then modify or rework those ideas. These are the three stages of the process of writing: pre-writing, writing the first draft, and revising. The better you understand this process, the more satisfying and successful your writing will be.

Part 1

Objective

To understand and use different pre-writing techniques

Presenting the Lesson

1. Read and discuss the introductory paragraph on page 112. Emphasize the importance of prewriting in generating writing ideas and selecting details. Stress the preliminary nature of the pre-writing process.

2. List on the chalkboard the five pre-writing steps discussed in this Part. Read and discuss step 1 page 112. Emphasize the importance of the first step in pre-writing: finding and limiting a topic. Introduce the pre-writing techniques listed in the chart on page 113. Hold a class brainstorming session by starting with a general topic such as "photograph" or "horses." Record on the chalkboard the students' suggestions, drawing lines to show how one writing idea can spring from another. Then ask for suggestions for narrowing several of the topics to sizes suitable for a paragraph.

3. Read and discuss pre-writing steps 2 and 3 (purpose and audience) on pages 113–114. Illustrate the importance of considering purpose and audience. For example, ask students how an entertaining essay written to describe a family's unusual Thanksgiving for an audience of classmates would require a different development than an informative essay written to explain our country's Thanksgiving holiday to students from another country.

4. Read and discuss steps 4 and 5 on page 114 (gathering and orga-

Part 1   Pre-Writing

The pre-writing stage is one of the most valuable parts of the writing process. It is at this planning stage that you decide exactly what you will be writing about and how you can most effectively present your ideas. Careful attention to the pre-writing stage makes the writing that follows much easier. Complete each of the following steps as part of the planning process.

1. Select and limit your topic.

Choosing a topic. Often you will be writing in response to a specific assignment or requirement. Sometimes, however, you will be given the chance to select your own topic. To produce a list of possible writing topics, begin by asking yourself questions such as these:

What do I know about?
What would I like to learn more about?

What do I remember from my reading and past experience?

What is happening to me or around me that I could observe or record?

The answers to these questions may provide you with possible topics for your paper.

The techniques listed in the chart on page 113 may also help you find interesting and enjoyable subjects for writing. Begin a "writing file" with the ideas you gather from these methods. Write interesting facts, headlines, quotations, and other bits of information on note cards. Cut out intriguing stories or articles. Keep all of these topic possibilities in a file box or folder. Refer to this file whenever you need a writing idea.

Limiting a topic. Topics may need to be limited, or narrowed, so that they fit the length of paper you want to write. Your topic is the right size if it can be fully developed in the specified length. If you are writing a long paper, make sure your topic is large enough to provide you with enough information and details so that you do not have to stretch your information or pad your sentences.

Pre-Writing Techniques

Journal Writing. Keep a spiral notebook in which you record interesting ideas, thoughts, feelings, impressions, and experiences. Write in your journal on a regular basis. Such a book can become a treasure-chest of writing ideas.

Reading. Skim magazines, books, and newspapers for intriguing topics, or for stories that trigger your imagination. Keep a list of possible subjects.

Discussions and Interviews. Other people are often a source of fascinating ideas. Listen carefully for the opinions and stories that emerge in conversation. Be aware that everyone has special experiences to share.

Brainstorming. This technique may be done individually or with others. It simply means starting with one idea and then building on it or branching out from it. The topic "railroads," for example, could eventually lead to topics as varied and interesting as "how a train yard works," "building the transcontinental railroad," or "work songs."

Clustering. Clustering is actually a type of brainstorming. Begin by writing a word or phrase on a piece of paper. Circle it. Now, outside that circle, write down any word or idea that you associate with the "nucleus" word. Put each in its own circle and connect it with a line to the nucleus word. Branch out from the new ideas in the same way. When a completely new train of thought strikes you, begin again from your nucleus idea.

2. Decide on your purpose.

Once you have a topic, you can limit it further by deciding exactly what you want to say about your subject. Do you want to analyze it? describe it? explain it? criticize it? defend it?

You must also decide what effect you want your writing to have. Do you want to inform? entertain? persuade? In longer pieces of writing, you may wish to include a statement of your topic and controlling purpose. This is sometimes called a **thesis statement**.

nizing information). Illustrate these steps by writing the following items on the board:

Topic: the meaning of the Fourth of July
Purpose: to inform
Audience: non-American teenagers

Have the class decide what information would be needed for topic development and how such information might be gathered. Refer students to Chapter 14 **Using the Library** for detailed information on material to be found there.

Working from the students' suggestions, list appropriate details on the board. Then ask students if there is any unrelated information that should be deleted; next, discuss what a logical order for presenting the information might be. Emphasize that no decision made at this stage is final.

5. Discuss the sample pre-writing notes on page 115. Try to re-create the process the writer went through from choosing possible topics to selecting specific details. Ask for comments on the sample notes, and discuss possible reasons for the deletion of some of the original details. Ask students if the order the writer has chosen seems logical. Point out that there is no single correct way to organize or develop pre-writing notes.

6. Assign Exercise A on page 116. After students have completed the assignment, discuss possible organizations of the details, reminding students that there is no one correct way. Suggest that details 2 and 9 could be deleted. Details that could be added include the type of sculpture that was being built, the supplies used, and the nature of the arguments that occurred.

Ask the class what order seems most logical for presenting this information. They will probably list details in the order in which they occurred. Tell them this is called "chronological" order.

7. Assign Exercise B on page 116. Remind students that there are many techniques for finding topics and supporting details.

Individualizing the Lesson

Less-Advanced Students

Emphasize the importance of choosing a manageable topic. Write the following general topics on the chalkboard and discuss with students how to narrow each topic.

    high school
    sports
    careers

Then choose one of the limited topics and have students develop pre-writing notes for it as a group.

Advanced Students

1. Many of these students have already experienced success in writing and may therefore be reluctant to spend time on each pre-writing step. Remind them that each step is important and that such attention to detail can turn good writers into outstanding ones.

2. Bring in an informative article or essay for the students to read. Have them look for evidence of the author's pre-writing activities, especially the gathering of details. Discuss their analyses.

Optional Practice

1. Assign a journal to be used for generating writing ideas. The first

3. Identify your audience.

Not only should you determine the effect you wish to create on your readers, you must also pinpoint who those readers are. Your audience will determine whether you write formally or informally. It will also indicate the type of vocabulary and level of language you should use. (See Chapter 3, "Using Language for Different Purposes," for a discussion of the levels of language.) Finally, the audience determines, to some extent, how you will develop your topic. Consider these questions:

> What do my readers already know?
> How familiar are they with my topic?
> What are their attitudes or opinions toward it?

Choose your supporting details accordingly.

4. Gather your supporting information.

There are many ways to gather additional material once you have a specific audience, purpose, and topic in mind. You can generate details through brainstorming, discussing, reading, and observing. Make use of your own personal knowledge and experiences, or use outside sources such as the library. Finally, take notes on your ideas so that you can evaluate them.

5. Evaluate and organize your information.

Looking at your lists and notes, evaluate their content. Are there any unrelated details that should be deleted? Are there any gaps in your information? Should other details be added for clarity? Next, decide how your material can most effectively be organized. What would be a clear order for this particular type of information? What would make the most sense to your readers? The details of a simple story, for example, would probably be organized in the order in which they occurred. The arguments of a persuasive piece would be arranged to build up to the most powerful argument.

Remember that all of these pre-writing steps are designed simply to help you begin writing in a thoughtful, organized way. None of the decisions that you make at this stage are final. Any of them could be adjusted, changed, or completely discarded.

Study this example of pre-writing notes:

1. Possible topics
   my surprise party   Mammoth Cave
   the class dance   roller skating *

2. Narrowed topic
   my five minutes at the roller rink

3. Purpose
   to describe my feelings, thoughts and
   actions as I began to skate

4. Audience
   my classmates

5. Specific details
   ~~new, different skates~~
   ~~blue canvas, size 7~~
   ④ rubberized wheels
   ③ Royal Sport skates
   ~~$3.00 for 2 hours~~
   ⑦ falling
   ⑧ badly sprained ankle
   ~~emergency room~~
   ~~crutches for two weeks~~
   ⑤ no control over arms or legs
   ⑥ earth seemed to tilt
   ① nervous before I began
   ⑨ embarrassed - blushing
   ② worried - add the thoughts going
                    through my head?

6. Order of details
   chronological -- time order

five or ten minutes of class may be set aside for journal-writing each day.

2. Have the students discuss what differences might result from writing on the following topics for the different audiences in parentheses:

programming games on a home computer (English classmates, computer science classmates);

attending a World Series baseball game (elementary school children, your softball team);

student involvement in curriculum planning (student council, PTA).

Extending the Lesson

1. Have each student bring in one magazine, book, or newspaper article. Each article should be one of general interest that has possibilities for future writing topics. Assemble the articles in a class file labeled "Writing Topics."

2. Have students bring in published journals of professional writers. These may be found in any library. Ask them to find in these journals some ideas and topics the writers could have used at a later date.

Exercises Completing Pre-Writing Notes

A. Copy this section of a writer's pre-writing notes. Delete any unrelated details. Add details that you think would make the notes more complete. What might be a good order for presenting the details? Number the details in the order you would present them in a paper. Answers in Teacher Notes.

NARROWED TOPIC

the sand sculpture calamity

SPECIFIC DETAILS

Ted and I arrived at beach
go to beach several times a month
sand sculpture competition going on
entered competition
later, I wanted to throw Ted into lake
couldn't decide on a design
fought as we built
built it too close to the water
people of all ages were competing
gathered supplies from all over the beach
creation began to collapse
waves began to eat at it
Ted tripped and fell into it

ORDER OF DETAILS?

B. Make a pre-writing plan like the one on page 115. You might begin by brainstorming for possible topics for a general category such as those listed below. Save your notes for use later in this chapter.

1. Ten Years From Today
2. Favorite Places/Activities
3. My Most Embarrassing Experience
4. Special People
5. The Best of Days
6. The Real Me

Part 2   Writing a First Draft

Careful attention to the pre-writing steps makes writing a first draft much easier. At this point in the process, simply write to get the ideas from your pre-writing notes down on paper in paragraph form. Do not worry about details such as spelling and punctuation. This would only interrupt your flow of ideas and break your concentration. You will have the opportunity to correct these errors later, during revision. Leave space between the lines to allow you to make corrections.

In a first draft, you are exploring to see whether your writing plan is workable. You are also experimenting with your ideas. Remember, pre-writing notes are not engraved in stone. In fact, you will find that many of your best ideas don't come to you until *after* you begin to write. Add these new details, and delete others that you no longer think are interesting or relevant. Change your organization if it becomes necessary. You may even want to start over as a new approach or more exciting idea occurs to you. As you continue working on your draft, keep your main idea, purpose, and audience in mind.

Remember, a first draft is *not* the final product. Even professional writers complete several drafts of any piece of writing before they are satisfied. You should be prepared to spend just as much time on your writing.

Sample Rough Draft

On the next page is the first draft of a paragraph written from the pre-writing notes on page 115. Read it carefully.

Notice that the writer has expanded the detail of being worried by including the thoughts that were running through his head. The writer has eliminated some details describing the skates and some relating to the consequences of the skating episode. Despite these improvements, however, the paragraph needs a great deal more work before it will seem completely developed and interesting to a reader.

Part 2

Objective

To write a first draft based on pre-writing activities

Presenting the Lesson

1. Read and discuss **Writing a First Draft** on page 117. Explain that writing a first draft can generate ideas in addition to those discovered in the pre-writing stage, so that the first draft takes on a life of its own. Emphasize that the function of a first draft is to get ideas down in sentence form. The draft should by no means be considered the final product. Therefore, students should not spend unnecessary time at this stage on spelling and punctuation.

2. Read the sample first draft on page 118. Ask how the content of the draft is similar to or different from the content of the pre-writing notes. Ask how the draft might be improved, stressing the addition and deletion of specific details that are not spelling errors. You might wish to look ahead to the revised draft for guidance in this discussion.

3. Assign the Exercise on page 118.

Individualizing the Lesson

Less-Advanced Students

These students often feel that they are the only ones whose work needs revision. Make sure they understand that reworking a rough draft is a natural part of the writing process. Also show them changes made on anonymous papers from other students, or from your own writing, so they can see that all writing needs revision.

Work with individuals as much as possible to ensure that they see the first draft as a starting point and not as a piece of writing that cannot be changed and improved upon.

Advanced Students

Have students write a second paragraph on a topic of their own, following the pre-writing and drafting advice given in Parts 1 and 2. Be aware that advanced students often see the need for revision as an indication of failure on their part. Remind the students that a good writer, professional or non-professional, often produces several drafts of a given piece of writing before feeling satisfied with it.

Optional Practice

Provide all students with the same set of pre-writing notes. Ask them to write first drafts based on these notes. Have several students read their drafts aloud. Discuss how many different approaches can evolve from one set of ideas.

Extending the Lesson

Bring to class examples of revised rough drafts done by experienced writers. These may be drafts of your own or those of writers you know. They may also be published examples by professional writers. For example, William Zinsser provides a sample of his revised manuscript for two pages of *On Writing Well* in the book (Harper & Row, 2nd ed., 1980), pages 10 and 11.

As I tightened the laces of the sleek, rented roller skates, I felt nervous. I had not been on skates since I was eight years old. These were Royal Sport skates with rubberized wheels. Could I manage to roll along with my freinds? Would I fall? Would everyone laugh at me? As I took my first steps I lost my ballance. I fell backwards. I had no control. I was so flustered, I felt like an awkward kid. The earth tilted as I hit the floor. The pain in my ankle told me I wouldn't be skating for awhile and my embarrasment told me I didn't want to be.

Exercise Writing a Rough Draft

Using your pre-writing notes from Exercise B in Part 1, write a rough draft of a paragraph. Remember that changes and revisions in your plan are not only possible, but probably necessary at this point.

Ask yourself the following questions:

Are there any unrelated details that interfere with the flow of ideas?

Could I add any details that would make my writing clearer or more interesting?

As I write, am I keeping my topic, audience, and purpose in mind?

Part 3   Revising

Revision is a continuous part of the writing process. Although it is listed as the last stage, it occurs from the moment you begin your pre-writing steps. For instance, you changed and refined your ideas as you worked on your pre-writing notes and as you wrote the rough draft. Now examine your work thoughtfully. Begin by asking yourself these questions:

1. Did I stick to my topic?
2. Did I include everything I wanted to?
3. Are there any unrelated or unnecessary details?
4. Could any details be added to clarify or improve my writing?
5. Have I accomplished my purpose?

Now read aloud what you have written. Often your ears will catch what your eyes do not. Listen to the rhythm of your writing. Is there variety in the type and structure of your sentences?

Check your arrangement of details. Is your writing organized logically? Is there a beginning, a middle, and an end to the development of your main idea? Do the details flow well? You may want to have a conference with your teacher or to have a friend read your work. Are your ideas clear to them?

Finally, polish your writing. Concentrate on every word. Are your ideas expressed in an interesting manner? Did you clearly express to your reader what you wanted to say? Is each word the most precise or vivid word for the situation?

Proofreading

At some time after you have finished your content revisions, perhaps in a second draft, proofread your paper. This is primarily an opportunity to correct mistakes in spelling, capitalization, and punctuation. You will find that many of these types of errors will have been corrected as you worked through your drafts. Use reference texts as well as the sections on grammar, usage, and mechanics in this book to correct any errors that remain. You may also use the proofreading symbols on page 124.

Part 3

Objective

To use revision and proofreading to polish a rough draft

Presenting the Lesson

1. Read **Revising** on page 119. Have the students check the rough drafts they wrote for Part 2 by asking themselves the five questions listed after the first paragraph.

2. Read **Proofreading**, page 119. Emphasize that this is *part* of the revision process, but that content revision should always precede it. Point out that the **Proofreading Checklist** on page 123 gives the appropriate Sections in the second half of the pupil book for discussion of various kinds of grammatical and mechanical problems.

3. Go over the **Proofreading Symbols** on page 124.

4. Do Exercise A, page 120, orally. Students should notice that the word order of the first sentence was changed to emphasize the writer's feelings. A new sentence, giving the name of the Roller Rink, follows the first sentence. The unrelated sentence telling about the skates was deleted. Then the topic and purpose were strengthened through the addition of three sentences telling how the author felt. Three choppy sentences were also deleted.

In the second half of the draft, there are several changes in spelling, as well as the addition of several single words and short phrases that clarify ideas.

Point out that the changes help focus the paper on the writer's feelings of self-doubt and embarrassment. Irrelevant details, such as the

119

kind of skates, were eliminated.

Students should also discover the following two additional mistakes:

1. the word "awhile" should be changed to "a while"
2. a comma is needed after the clause, "As I took my first halting steps."

6. Assign Exercise B, page 120.

Individualizing the Lesson

Less-Advanced Students

If possible, hold individual conferences with students to discuss revisions of their first drafts.

Go over the **Proofreading Checklist** on page 123 and show students where these items are covered in the second half of their books.

Advanced Students

As you hold individual conferences with less-advanced students, have your stronger writers meet in groups of three or four to discuss their drafts.

Optional Practice

Have the students compose prewriting notes and write the first draft of an essay entitled "If I were _____." Have them put the first drafts away for a week and then return to them for revision. Point out how much more objectively writers can view their writing after some time has elapsed.

Extending the Lesson

Have students create a "revision" bulletin board with such items as a chart of proofreading symbols, sample rough drafts with revision symbols, and completed final copies.

Exercises Revising the Rough Draft

A. Look at the rewritten, or revised, paragraph on this page. Compare it with the first draft. What content changes have been made? Why were they made? Several errors in spelling and mechanics have been corrected. Can you find two more mistakes that need correction? Answers in Teacher Notes

B. Revise the rough draft of the paragraph you wrote for the Exercise in Part 2. Then proofread your paper for errors in spelling and mechanics.

Part 4 Preparing the Final Copy

Finally, when you are satisfied that your writing is clear and correct, you are ready to prepare your final copy. Write carefully. Make your work as neat as possible. Be sure to follow the manuscript form that your teacher requires. When you have completed your final copy, proofread your work again.

FINAL COPY

> I was terrified as I tightened the laces of the rented roller skates. What was I doing at the Wacky Wheels Roller Rink? I had not been on skates since I was eight years old. Skating had been easy then, but I was worried now. I knew I wouldn't be trying anything fancy. I'd settle for just staying on my feet! As I took my first halting steps, I lost my balance. I fell backwards and then lurched forward with my arms moving like windmills. The whole rink seemed to tilt. After I hit the hard floor, the sharp pain in my ankle told me I wouldn't be skating for a while. The stifled snickers of my friends and the tingling blush creeping up my neck told me that I was just as glad!

Exercise Making the Final Copy

Prepare the final copy of the paragraph that you revised for Part 3, Exercise B.

Objective

To prepare a final copy

Presenting the Lesson

1. Read **Preparing the Final Copy** on page 121, emphasizing that this is the final step after all revision and proofreading have been completed.

2. Read the sample final copy. Discuss the changes the paragraph has undergone from the pre-writing stage to its final form.

3. Assign the Exercise on page 121.

Individualizing the Lesson

Less-Advanced Students

After the final copy of the paragraph is completed, have students compare their rough drafts to their final copies.

Advanced Students

Have each student construct with his or her own pieces of work a process model that shows the paragraph from its early stages on through to the final copy.

Optional Practice

Have students write a final copy of the paper "If I Were _____." Ask them if their ideas for the paper have changed during the writing process.

Extending the Lesson

Explain that a final copy is not really "final," but a reflection of the writer's decision that he or she has done the best job possible for the project at hand.

Guidelines for the Process of Writing

Pre-Writing

1. Select a topic that interests you.
2. Narrow the topic until it can be thoroughly developed in a specified length.
3. Decide on your purpose.
4. Use your understanding of purpose and audience to determine your type of language and choice of details.
5. Gather and list details that you could use to develop your topic.
6. Evaluate and organize your list of details. Delete unrelated ideas. Add new ones. Put your details into a logical order.

Writing the First Draft

1. Keeping your audience and purpose in mind, begin to write.
2. Let your thoughts flow freely. Modify your initial plans for content and organization, if necessary. Do not be too concerned with grammar and mechanics at this point.

Revising

Read what you have written. Answer the following questions:

1. Did you stick to your topic?
2. Did you include everything you wanted to?
3. Are there any unnecessary or unrelated details?
4. Is each main idea clearly expressed and thoroughly developed?
5. Do your ideas flow smoothly?
6. Is your writing organized logically, with a beginning, a middle, and an end? Are the ideas presented in an order that makes sense?
7. Is your writing interesting and lively? Is there variety in the type and structure of your sentences?
8. Is each word vivid and precise?
9. Do the language and content suit your audience?
10. Have you accomplished your purpose?

Revise as necessary. Then proofread your work, using the checklist on page 123.

Proofreading Checklist

Proofread your paper, by answering the questions below. Additional instruction on each concept may be found in the indicated Sections.

Grammar and Usage

Are there any sentence fragments or run-ons? (Sect. 1, 2)
Have you used the correct form of each pronoun? (Sect. 4)
Have you used verb tenses correctly? (Sect. 5)
Have you used adjectives and adverbs correctly? (Sect. 6)
Do all verbs agree with their subjects? (Sect. 10)
Are compound and complex sentences written and punctuated correctly? (Sect. 11)

Capitalization

Did you capitalize first words and all proper nouns and adjectives? (Sect. 13)
Are titles capitalized correctly? (Sect. 13)

Punctuation

Does each sentence have the proper end mark? (Sect. 14)
Are end marks, such as colons, semicolons, apostrophes, hyphens, and quotation marks, used correctly? (Sect. 14)

Spelling

Did you check all unfamiliar words in the dictionary? (Sect. 15)
Are plurals and possessive forms spelled correctly? (Sect. 3, 15)

Form

Were corrections made neatly? (Sect. 16)
In your final copy, is the writing legible?
Have you used the proper heading and margins?
Did you follow all points of good manuscript form?

Proofreading Symbols

SYMBOL	MEANING	EXAMPLE
∧	insert	would gone *have*
≡	capitalize	United states
/	make lower case	our club President
∾	transpose	th(ie)r
ℯ	delete	finished the (the) race
¶	make new paragraph	....be complete. ¶ Another reason
◡	close up space	head line
⊙	period	....and stop Before going...
⋏	add comma	However few people

SUMMARY AND APPLICATIONS

1. All types of writing—from compositions in English to reports in science or history—become easier and more satisfying when a writer is aware of the stages involved in the process of writing.

2. Careful pre-writing efforts make actual writing much less difficult. This advance work includes choosing and narrowing a topic, deciding on the audience and purpose for the writing, and gathering and organizing ideas.

3. The first draft is simply the writer's initial attempt to get the ideas down on paper. Mechanical details are not important at this time.

4. Revising and proofreading are the final stages of the process of writing. The writer completes one or more drafts of a paper, checking for complete coverage, a precise vocabulary, and sound organization. Finally, the writer proofreads for errors in grammar, capitalization, punctuation, and spelling.

5. Careful attention to the writing process will help train you to think through problems clearly and logically.

Applications in Other Subject Areas

Science. Like writing, scientific research and experimentation is a process involving very specific stages. Look up "Science" or "Scientific Method" in a good encyclopedia. Write a short paper describing the stages in the process of conducting an experiment.

Computer Science. For a good example of careful planning, interview an expert on computer programming. Ask him or her to explain the process of developing the step-by-step instructions that are fed into a computer. Notice especially the care that is taken to include every detail and to organize those details in a logical order.

Summary and Applications

Go over the summary with the class. Emphasize that this orderly approach to writing is a skill that can be applied to any task.

Encourage students to use this summary for review or as part of the SQ3R method of study (see Chapter 15). Remind them, though, that more specific points can only be reviewed by skimming the chapter itself.

Applications in Other Subject Areas

For the computer science activity, invite an expert in computer programming to talk to the class. Ask him or her to illustrate on the chalkboard the use of a flow chart for a simple program and provide the actual printout for that program. Tell him or her to emphasize the need for logical order and detail in programming, by demonstrating what occurs when a logical step or detail is omitted.

Chapter 8

Writing Effective Paragraphs

Have you ever tried to squeeze an important message into a twenty-second recording on an answering machine? If you have, you know how frustrating the experience can be. When you have a complex idea to communicate, you need enough time to express it correctly.

A sentence often has the same sort of limitations. If you want to relate an incident or describe a scene, a single sentence simply may not be adequate. Several sentences together, however, might do the job. When sentences are grouped together for such a purpose, they result in the unit of writing called the **paragraph**.

In this chapter, you will learn to express your ideas in paragraphs. You will also learn to write paragraphs that communicate your ideas clearly and in a variety of ways.

Part 1   What Is a Paragraph?

A paragraph is a group of sentences dealing with a single topic or idea. Usually, one sentence, called the **topic sentence**, states the main idea of the paragraph. All the other sentences are related to this topic sentence. They further explain or support the main idea.

Example 1

Study the following paragraph.

> My father was a master storyteller. He could tell a fine old story that made me hold my sides with rolling laughter and sent happy tears down my cheeks. He could tell a story of stark reality that made me shiver and be grateful for my own warm, secure surroundings. He could tell stories of beauty and grace, stories of gentle dreams, and paint them as vividly as any picture with splashes of character and dialogue. His memory detailed every event of ten or forty years or more before, just as if it had happened yesterday.—MILDRED D. TAYLOR

This is a well organized, well written paragraph. In the first sentence, the writer states, "My father was a master storyteller." In the remaining sentences, she supports that idea by describing the many kinds of stories that her father told.

Example 2

The following is also a well written paragraph.

> The wolverine may well be nature's most fearsome fighter. In battle with an enemy, he is a twisting, slashing blur of sheer fury that bewilders and terrifies an adversary. He has been known to attack a 1,200-pound moose—an animal more than forty times his weight—and is capable of defending himself against an entire pack of wolves.—REED MILLARD

The writer begins with the sentence, "The wolverine may well be nature's most fearsome fighter." In the sentences that follow,

Objective

To understand the characteristics of a well-written paragraph

Presenting the Lesson

1. Write the definitions of *paragraph* (a group of sentences dealing with a single topic) and *topic sentence* (one sentence that states the main idea of the paragraph) on the chalkboard.

2. Read **What Is a Paragraph?** on pages 127–129. Point out how all sentences in Examples 1 and 2 relate to the main idea stated in the topic sentence.

3. Read Example 3 on page 128, showing how sentence 3 is not related to the main idea of the paragraph.

4. Read Example 4 and ask for reactions from the class. If necessary, point out the lack of development of the main idea of the paragraph. Read the revised paragraph that follows, explaining how the addition of specific details improves the paragraph.

5. Assign the Exercise on pages 129–130. Answers appear below.

Paragraph 1: Topic sentence: "Paula Murphy is known as the fastest woman in the world." Sentence 3 should be deleted because it is irrelevant to the topic sentence.

Paragraph 2: "Your grandmother could probably tell you what it was like to run a house on coal." Paragraph is not sufficiently developed; it needs supporting details.

Paragraph 3: "I have never known a hotter July." Paragraph is well developed.

Paragraph 4: "The main advantage of the metric system is its simplicity." Paragraph is not sufficiently developed; it needs supporting facts and details.

Paragraph 5: "I think the park had something to do with it." Paragraph is well developed.

Individualizing the Lesson

Less-Advanced Students

Discuss each paragraph in the Exercise with the students. Have students pick out the topic sentence and tell whether each sentence in the paragraph relates to it. Also have them tell whether the paragraph has been thoroughly developed.

Advanced Students

After deciding which paragraphs in the Exercise lack unity or need further development, ask the students to revise them, correcting the faults. Brainstorm with the group, if necessary, to provide facts and details for the paragraphs that need development.

Optional Practice

Use the following topic sentence as the basis for a group paragraph.

Training a dog is easy if you know a few basic guidelines.

Write the paragraph on the chalkboard as students contribute sentences. Discuss whether each suggested sentence relates to the topic sentence. Have students decide when the paragraph has been adequately developed.

he describes the wolverine's fighting abilities. By doing so, he supports the main idea stated in the topic sentence.

In this example, and also in Example 1, all the sentences relate to one idea. They are tied together by that idea.

Example 3

Study the following example.

> Native Americans cultivated and developed many plants. Among them were white potatoes, sweet potatoes, corn, beans, tobacco, chocolate, peanuts, cotton, rubber, and gum. Native Americans were also expert builders and tanners. Plants were used for dyes, medicines, soap, clothes, shelter, and baskets.

The first sentence indicates that the paragraph will be about the cultivation and development of plants by Native Americans. However, sentence 3 refers to non-agricultural skills. This idea is not related to the main idea of the paragraph.

The problem is easily solved by removing the third sentence:

> Native Americans cultivated and developed many plants. Among them were white potatoes, sweet potatoes, corn, beans, tobacco, chocolate, peanuts, cotton, rubber, and gum. Plants were used for dyes, medicines, soap, clothes, shelter, and baskets.

Example 4

The following example has a different problem.

> Almost anyone would have treated me better than Uncle Eldon did. From the first day, he worked me like his slave.

This paragraph is incomplete. The reader is left with the question, "Exactly what did Uncle Eldon do to the writer?"

Sometimes a writer fails to explain thoroughly the idea stated in the topic sentence. The reader, therefore, does not get all the information needed to understand the idea completely.

The paragraph above needs specific detail, as in the revision on the next page.

Almost anyone would have treated me better than Uncle Eldon did. From the first day, he worked me like his slave. I cut down trees. I sawed the fallen trees into logs. I dragged the logs to the house and cut them into kindling. Whenever the kindling pile was high, I was sent to clean the drafty old barn.

By expanding the number of sentences, the writer has developed the topic into an interesting paragraph that explains the topic sentence and satisfies the reader. Every good paragraph must be developed just as thoroughly, with equal attention to detail.

Exercise Analyzing Paragraphs

Read each paragraph carefully. Some are good paragraphs; others are not. Some of the weak paragraphs contain sentences that are unrelated to the topic. Other paragraphs are not adequately developed. Identify the poor paragraphs. Be ready to discuss which sentences should be dropped, or the types of details that should be added.

Answers in Teacher Notes.

1   Paula Murphy is known as the fastest woman in the world. She has raced over Ontario Speedway and Bonneville Salt Flats fast enough to leave her competition far behind in the dust. She is slim, soft-spoken, and friendly. She has broken through speed records, broken down sex barriers, and broken her neck for racing. She is a female drag-strip racer.

2   Your grandmother could probably tell you what it was like to run a house on coal. Back then, she had a ton or so delivered down a chute into the basement.

3   I have never known a hotter July. There was a soft, hazy, constant heat that hung over everything and never let up—only seemed to turn dark with evening. In our garden the black earth dried and crumbled brown, shrinking away till the twisted tomato roots showed above the ground. Out in the country the fields were a parched patchwork and only the trees were still green against the dust-yellow roll of the hills.

4   The main advantage of the metric system is its simplicity. It uses three basic units of measurement.

Extending the Lesson

Type a three- or four-paragraph essay or article without the original paragraph indentations. Duplicate and distribute the article. Point out the comprehension problems and misunderstandings that may arise when reading a piece of writing which is not properly divided into paragraphs. Ask students to determine where the paragraph divisions should be and then to explain how they made their decisions. Students should mention topic sentences and unity of ideas.

I felt good. I think the park had something to do with it. Trees, grass, bushes—everything appeared in brand-new togs of shining green. The warm yellow sunlight sifted down through the trees, making my face feel alive and healthy and casting shadows on the paved walks and the unpaved walks and the wooden benches. Slight breezes tickled my nostrils, caressed my face, bringing with them a good, clean odor of things new and live and dripping with greenness.

Part 2 Paragraph Unity and Coherence

You have just learned that each sentence in a paragraph must relate to a single idea. The sentences either state the idea or contribute in some way to its development. When the sentences work together in this way, a paragraph is said to have **unity**.

Unity

The topic sentence of a paragraph plays a key role in establishing paragraph unity. The sentence is like a contract between writer and reader. The writer is saying, in effect, "I have an idea I want to explain to you." The reader is answering, "All right, explain it to me." For the writer to hold to the contract, he or she must explain the idea stated in the topic sentence.

Look at these three examples of topic sentences.

1. *The shell in my hand is deserted.*
2. *The King was a quiet man who did not like to speak overmuch.*
3. *The dodo was a very odd-looking bird.*

Writer 1 says she is going to explain something about a deserted shell. Writer 2 says she wants to explain something about the king's quietness. Writer 3 says he wants to explain something about the appearance of the dodo bird. Let's see how well each honors the contract implied by the topic sentence.

Part 2

Objective

To understand the concepts of unity and coherence in the paragraph

Presenting the Lesson

1. Read the introductory paragraph on page 130. Write the word *unity* on the chalkboard. Refer back to Examples 1 and 2 on page 127. Point out the quality of unity in paragraphs where each sentence is related to the main idea.

2. Read and discuss **Unity** on pages 130-131. Discuss the function of the topic sentence as a contract. Ask students what type of content each of the three sample topic sentences on page 130 promises. Then read the first two sample paragraphs on page 131, commenting on how the implied contract is honored in each case.

3. Read Paragraph 3 on page 131. Ask students what kinds of details would have been appropriate to support the topic sentence. (Dodo was covered with down instead of feathers; dodo could not fly; it was a large, clumsy bird with short legs; it had a hooked beak.)

1   *The shell in my hand is deserted*. It once housed a whelk, a snail-like creature. Then, after the death of the first occupant, it sheltered a little hermit crab, who has run away, leaving his tracks behind him like a delicate vine on the sand. He ran away and left me his shell. It was once a protection to him. I turn the shell in my hand, gazing into the wide open door from which he made his exit. Had it become a burden? Why did he run away? Did he hope to find a better home, a better mode of living?

The paragraph does give an explanation of the writer's opening statement, so the contract is complete.

2   *The King was a quiet man who did not like to speak over-much*. This was partly, no doubt, because he had a serious speech defect. He had inherited the long, heavy, out-of-balance jaw of the Hapsburg line, together with their round high forehead, golden hair, and blue eyes. Due to the configuration of his jaw, the King's teeth did not meet squarely; and when he spoke it was with a curious lisp. Besides, I believe that he was shy and that he had learned, in his years at court, that it was fatal to trust anyone with all your heart.

The remainder of the paragraph explains why the king was a quiet man. Again, the contract is complete.

3   *The dodo was a very odd-looking bird*. It was related to the solitaire and lived on the island of Mauritius in the Indian Ocean. Jacob Corneliszoon van Neck, a Dutch admiral, discovered the bird in 1598. Dutch settlers to the island, as well as the animals they brought, ate the dodo birds. The last dodo on Mauritius was eaten in 1681. By 1800, scientists were beginning to doubt whether the dodo bird had ever existed.

In this paragraph, the writer has not held to the contract. In his topic sentence, Writer 3 has promised to describe the dodo's appearance. By the end of the paragraph, you know other facts about the dodo, but you do not know a single specific detail concerning the dodo's unusual physical characteristics.

Be sure the class understands that it is not enough to have written sentences about the dodo. The topic sentence makes a contract to give details specifically about the dodo's appearance.

4. Read **Coherence**, pages 132–133, with the class. Point out that problems with coherence are often difficult to analyze simply because the writer's own ideas have not been properly organized and clarified. When the reader is confused by a paragraph or feels he or she is missing the point, it is often due to a lack of coherence in the paragraph. Discuss in detail the revision of the paragraph concerning the killing of whales.

5. Assign the Exercise on pages 134–135. Answers appear below.

Paragraph 1: Unified and coherent. The paragraph describes these two "men" who were the best of friends.

Paragraph 2: Lacks unity because sentences 2 & 3 are irrelevant; they should be deleted. The topic sentence needs further related development, such as a specific example.

Paragraph 3: Lacks unity and coherence. It is not possible to tell what point the writer wanted to make. Everything after "The house is dark" should be rewritten to support the topic sentence, "My father has a peculiar habit."

Paragraph 4: Unified and coherent.

Paragraph 5: Lacks unity because sentences 3 and 6 are unrelated to the topic sentence. Either they should be deleted, or the relevance of them to the rest of the paragraph should be made explicit.

Paragraph 6: Unified and coherent.

Paragraph 7: Lacks unity and coherence. The last sentence is irrelevant and should be deleted. Sentences 2 and 3 are not presented in logical order and should be reversed. Additional details should be added. *Paragraph 8:* Unified and coherent.

Individualizing the Lesson

Less-Advanced Students

Complete the Exercise on pages 134–135 orally with the students. Ask them to explain which paragraphs are well developed and which ones need to have sentences deleted, added, or rearranged.

Advanced Students

After eliminating those paragraphs in the Exercise that need no improvement, students may work individually on revising the remaining ones. Discuss the revisions in class.

Optional Practice

Use the following topic sentence as the basis for a group paragraph similar to the one suggested for Optional Practice in Part 1.

Noise pollution is a modern problem for which there are several causes.

Write the paragraph on the chalkboard as students contribute sentences. Have students use the words *unity* and *coherence* in discussing the development of the paragraph.

Extending the Lesson

To illustrate the concept of paragraph coherence, type in random order the sentences of a paragraph from a newspaper or magazine. Duplicate and distribute the incoherent paragraph and have students discuss how the sentences should be rearranged.

Coherence

Not only must all the sentences in a paragraph relate to one idea, but they must also logically relate to each other. When all of the sentences in a paragraph follow one another naturally, the paragraph has **coherence**.

The following paragraph has a problem with coherence.

Example

A whale, one of the largest animals in the world, is killed by Soviet and Japanese whale hunters every seventeen minutes. This makes some people angry. Someday, whales might be like the dinosaur and disappear forever. People are showing their anger in many ways. One Japanese businessman says, "Many Japanese could not live without whale meat." Some people are writing letters to the Japanese Prime Minister, and others are asking people not to buy Japanese products. If this hurts Japanese business enough, the Japanese government may stop the whale hunting.

Analysis

At first glance, all the sentences in the paragraph seem to relate to the killing of whales. However, it is hard to tell for sure because the ideas are so disorganized. They must be rearranged so that they relate to each other in a logical way.

If you were asked to revise this paragraph, you might begin by listing all the sentences that refer to whales.

1. A whale, one of the largest animals in the world, is killed by Soviet and Japanese whale hunters every seventeen minutes.
2. Someday, whales might be like the dinosaur and disappear forever.
3. One Japanese businessman says, "Many Japanese could not live without whale meat."

Next, list sentences that refer to the attitude of the people.

1. This makes some people angry.
2. People are showing their anger in many ways.

132

3. Some people are writing letters to the Japanese Prime Minister, and others are asking people not to buy Japanese products.
4. If this hurts Japanese business enough, the Japanese government may stop the whale hunting.

The first two sentences about whales are closely related. Sentence 1 is about the killing of whales. Sentence 2 suggests that if the killings continue, whales might someday disappear. The two sentences could be tied together even more closely with the addition of the clause "if this killing continues" to sentence 2.

A whale, one of the largest animals in the world, is killed by Soviet and Japanese whale hunters every seventeen minutes. Someday, if this killing continues, whales might be like the dinosaur and disappear forever.

The third sentence, about the Japanese businessman, does not relate to sentences 1 and 2. That sentence should be removed. Then the four sentences about the attitude of the people should be added, making the following six-sentence paragraph.

A whale, one of the largest animals in the world, is killed by Soviet and Japanese whale hunters every seventeen minutes. Someday, if this killing continues, whales might be like the dinosaur and disappear forever. This makes some people angry. People are showing their anger in several ways. Some people are writing letters to the Japanese Prime Minister, and others are asking people not to buy Japanese products. If this hurts Japanese business enough, the Japanese government may stop the whale hunting.

All the ideas in the paragraph are now presented in a logical way. Two sentences, however, contain a weak repetition of ideas.

1. This makes some people angry.
2. People are showing their anger in several ways.

The sentences can be combined.

This makes some people angry, and they are showing their anger in several ways.

Exercise Checking for Unity and Coherence in Paragraphs

Study the following groups of sentences. Some are good paragraphs. Others lack either unity or coherence in their presentation. Identify the groups of sentences that are not good paragraphs. Revise them by dropping sentences, by rearranging sentences, or by making other changes. Answers in Teacher Notes.

1   There lived in the Land of Oz two men who were the best of friends. One was a Scarecrow. That means he was a suit of blue Munchkin clothes, stuffed with straw, on top of which was fastened a round cloth head, filled with bran to hold it in shape. On the head were painted two eyes, two ears, a nose, and a mouth. The Scarecrow had never been much of a success in scaring crows; but he prided himself on being a superior man because he could feel no pain, was never tired, and did not have to eat or drink. His brains were sharp, for the Wizard of Oz had put pins and needles in the Scarecrow's brains. The other man was made all of tin, and his arms and legs and head were cleverly jointed so that he could move them freely. He was known as the Tin Woodman, having at one time been a wood-chopper. Everyone loved him because the Wizard had given him an excellent heart of red plush.

2   If parents show an interest in the programs their teenagers watch on television, useful discussions will often result. Few things are more important to fourteen-year-olds than having their opinions listened to and respected. The types of things teenagers watch on television will change with age. Values and situations shown on television can be the basis for lively exchanges of ideas.

3   My father has a peculiar habit. He is fond of sitting in the dark, alone. Sometimes I come home very late. The house is dark. I let myself in quietly because I do not want to disturb my mother. She is a light sleeper and has to get up early to go to work. I tiptoe into my room and undress in the dark. I go downstairs to the kitchen for a drink of water. My bare feet make no noise.

4   The rainy season came to the forest, as it must come every year. At night the water fell with a roar like thunder. In the morning it beat against the branches of the trees and tore their leaves from them. It pounded against the thatched roofs of the villages and rushed about the footpaths. Little girls set pots under the sky to catch the water, and ran back slipping and sliding. The small, friendly rivers became deep and wide, and covered the sides of their banks. During the darkness the people fastened their doors and did not even look outside, for they could hear nothing but rain, rain, rain.

5   When my little dog died, I was very sad. It happened on Valentine's Day. My birthday is on February 22, eight days after Valentine's Day. I cried a lot, but it didn't bring my dog back. My Dad and I buried him in a vacant lot, and put a tombstone on the grave. On my birthday, I got new roller skates.

6   People have trouble identifying my heritage. Indians mistake me for one of their own. In Chinatown they give me a menu written in Chinese, and once a Japanese boy asked me if I was Korean. My ancestors are full-blooded Japanese, but I have had to get used to people thinking I'm something else.

7   The needs of our country have changed since its beginnings. The first settlers had to work very hard. Now the majority of American workers do not do hard physical labor. The Pilgrims were able to increase their food supply and build shelters from the cold. In Japan, too, industry is highly mechanized.

8   I grew up on the island of Puerto Rico in an atmosphere of natural story-tellers. I had a father whose occupation took him all over the island; a grandmother whose stories always ended with a nonsense rhyme or song, setting feet to jump, skip or dance; elder sisters who still remembered tales told by a mother; and finally, a stepmother whose literary taste was universal. I never ever went to bed without a round of stories told. The characters of my favorite ones became part of my everyday life: I traveled to strange lands of shepherds, princesses and princes, Kings and Queens; I laughed at the cunning of the animals and suffered with the punished ones.

Objective

To choose and narrow a topic and write a suitable topic sentence

Presenting the Lesson

1. Read and discuss **Deciding on a Topic**, page 136. Refer back to Chapter 7, pages 112–113 for review of techniques for selecting and limiting a topic.

2. Read **The Topic Sentence**, pages 136–138. Show students how a good topic sentence not only announces the subject, but arouses interest and suggests what specific details or further explanation will follow as well. Point out that sample Paragraph 1 fulfills the contract of the topic sentence with specific examples. Paragraph 2 fulfills the contract of its topic sentence with further explanation.

3. Complete Exercise A, page 138 orally. Read each paragraph and its *Hint*. Students should then write their topic sentences. Select volunteers to read theirs aloud to the class. Have other students comment on the effectiveness of each one.

4. Assign Exercise B on page 140. You may wish to have students who chose the same topic sentences work together to combine their lists of details.

5. Read and discuss **The Function of the Topic Sentence**, pages 140–141. Emphasize that the function of the topic sentence is to control and limit the content of the paragraph. Just as the title of a paper announces and limits the subject of the paper, so the topic sentence an-

Part 3 Pre-Writing: Deciding on a Topic

You are now ready to begin writing effective paragraphs of your own. The first step, of course, is to choose a topic. Remember that you yourself are a good source for interesting topics. Survey your own interests, knowledge, and concerns. Choose a subject that appeals to you, and limit it to a size suitable for a paragraph. A little background reading or observation might help you in this task. Determining your audience and purpose will also provide some guidelines.

Careful attention to this part of the process can result in many interesting topic possibilities. Describing the crucial play of a football game for someone who did not see the game, giving reasons why soccer is a better sport than football to someone who is deciding which sport to play, and explaining the history of the National Football League to someone who is very familiar with the game are three possible paragraph topics involving football. Yet, each would include very different material based on considerations of purpose and audience.

Once you have decided on a topic, audience, and purpose, writing a topic sentence will help you to clarify what you want to accomplish with your paragraph. The topic sentence provides an "umbrella statement" that helps to shape the rest of your paragraph.

The Topic Sentence

A topic sentence makes a general statement that is wider in its scope than the rest of the sentences in the paragraph. A good topic sentence is broad enough to be developed by specific details.

To clarify this point, let's look at two good topic sentences:

1. *The English language spoken in the United States owes much to Spanish importation.*

2. *A person must be quite courageous to be an individual.*

These sentences contain very little specific information. They are well written and interesting, but the information contained in them is only enough to arouse curiosity. After reading them, you might find yourself saying "Don't stop there. How did the Spanish language influence English? Why does it take courage for one to be an individual? Tell me more."

A good writer will satisfy your curiosity by giving specific details in the rest of the paragraph. The details will explain the general statement in the topic sentence.

Let's see how the writers of the two topic sentences explained their general statements.

1   *The English language spoken in the United States owes much to Spanish importation.*

The English language spoken in the United States owes much to Spanish importation. Such Spanish words as *desperado, sombrero, mesa, sierra, arroyo, cañon, chaparral, mesquite, adobe, ramada, cabaña, hacienda, patio, plaza, coyote, jaguar, serape, machete, mañana* are used all the time. Also, a long list of Spanish words has become so thoroughly "naturalized" that people have forgotten they were ever Spanish — words like *vigilante, filibuster, barbecue, corral, tobacco, vanilla, hammock, tornado, cigar,* and *banana.* More than two thousand cities and towns in the United States have Spanish names. At least four hundred of them are in California, with two hundred and fifty each in Texas and New Mexico, and more than a hundred in both Colorado and Arizona. Spanish place names can be found all over the West and, in fact, in every state in the Union.—JOHN TEBBEL AND RAMÓN EDUARDO RUIZ

The writers of this paragraph first make the general statement, "The English language spoken in the United States owes much to Spanish importation." Then, to develop this idea, they give three supporting details for their statement: Spanish words are used often; Spanish words have been "naturalized" into English; and the United States has thousands of Spanish place names. Notice that each of the three supporting details is further developed through the use of specific examples.

nounces and limits the subject of a paragraph.

6. Use Exercise A on pages 141–142 to illustrate the need to limit a topic sentence. Students should be able to see in each case which sentence is more specific and could, therefore, be used to control a single paragraph.

7. Do the first five sentences in Exercise B, page 142, orally. For Sentence 1 explain that at least two words in the sentence, *automobile* and *safe,* can be made more specific. Let the class experiment with various revisions for Sentence 1. Repeat the process for the next four sentences. Have students complete the rest of the exercise individually.

8. Assign Exercise C on page 143. Discuss several of your students' answers in class.

Individualizing the Lesson

Less-Advanced Students

1. Work on Exercise B, page 140, as a group. After listing details for two or three of the topic sentences on the board, ask students to pick one other to be completed individually. Then call on volunteers to read their details to the class.

2. Have students work in pairs to complete the second half of Exercise B on page 142. After completing the work, the teams may read their revisions to the group.

Advanced Students

1. For Exercise B on page 140, ask students to select one set of details and write the paragraph.

2. After students complete the second half of Exercise B on page

142, ask them to choose one sentence in the Exercise and write a paragraph with the original topic sentence and another with the revised topic sentence. Then ask them to discuss the ease and manageability of each task.

Optional Practice

Show the class several slides or photographs of interesting people, places, animals, or things. Have students write limited topic sentences for paragraphs based on each picture.

Extending the Lesson

Ask students to look in their history books, science books, and other texts for examples of suitable topic sentences that control and limit the content of the paragraph that follows. Have them read the best examples, along with the paragraphs, to the class.

2 *A person must be quite courageous to be an individual.*

A person must be quite courageous to be an individual. How much easier it is to blend in with a crowd, to accept generally held beliefs and adopt the popular lifestyles. How difficult it is, though, to listen to sneers when your ideas differ. How frustrating and frightening it can be when a unique action leads to suspicion from others. Yet a person of courage knows that daring to be an individual is the only way to achieve a truly good life, and that is worth the struggle.

This writer also makes a general statement, "A person must be quite courageous to be an individual." However, instead of giving supporting details, he develops, or expands, his idea. He explains *why* being an individual takes courage: one must listen to the criticisms of others. Then he states why having courage is important: it is the only true means of having a satisfying life.

Exercises Pre-Writing: Composing Topic Sentences

A. In the following paragraphs, the topic sentences have been removed, leaving only the specific details. Read the paragraphs. Study the hint given after each. Then write an interesting topic sentence for each paragraph. Be sure your topic sentence is broader than the details in the rest of the paragraph. Answers will vary. Sample answers are provided.

1   It was already hot, and the grasshoppers began to fill the air. Still, it was early in the morning, and the birds sang out of the shadows. The long, yellow grass on the mountain shone in the bright light, and a scissortail hied above the land.

Hint: The topic sentence might include the idea of a person waking up on a summer morning. The day began with the sounds and sights of summer.

2   Take a lesson from the cat, who so well represents potential energy. As he moves, stretches, relaxes, he looks almost lazy. He wastes no energy. Let a mouse run by, though, and the cat pounces with one swift, forceful movement.

Hint: The topic sentence should present the idea that human beings can learn from animals about the conservation of energy.
Learn to conserve your body's energy.

3 At first his feet slipped but then they took hold. He charged low and hard with mouth opened up like a steam shovel. The lower jaw and the big teeth flashed as he crossed the pit bottom. The wildcat fell back from the heavy charge and rolled under the dog. In that second he raked his claws into the dog's stomach.

Hint: The topic sentence should describe the start of the attack.

Fighting for his life, the dog attacked the wildcat.

4 One group of Indians caught big Southern catfish by diving into the water with any available red object for bait. They grabbed the fish as it approached and dragged it to shore. Inspired by their example, the explorers in Lewis and Clark's party invented new ways to catch fish. Once, using only bayonets, they caught enough salmon to feed themselves. Another time, an explorer killed a sturgeon with an ax.

Hint: The topic sentence should include the information that long ago, people fished without having what is now called "fishing equipment."

The inhabitants and settlers of the American wilderness did not need bait, tackle, reels, and other fishing gear.

5 The largest complexes, like Vail and Aspen, have plenty of rooms, and also plenty of people to fill them. Christmas week and much of February and March are especially hectic there and at all resorts. Many lodges take reservations for these periods as early as July. Most resorts advise that, no matter the time of year, visitors should call ahead for reservations well in advance of their intended trips.

Hint: The topic sentence should indicate that reservations at ski resorts can be a problem.

Reservations at popular ski resorts can be a problem.

6 According to folklore experts, *light elves* are masters at shape-changing and can travel through four dimensions. They are good-natured but seldom seen by humans. *Dark elves* make their homes in the earth and their skin reflects its colors: grey, brown, red, and black. These elves prefer to roam late at night. *Dusky elves* are the most numerous. They are bound by laws of time, space, and place, and are easily recognized by humans.

Hint: The topic sentence should introduce the idea that there are three classifications of the old folklore creatures, elves.

There are three distinct classifications of the folklore creatures called elves.

B. Following is a list of topic sentences, each of which makes a general statement. Choose at least two of these sentences. For each, make a list of three or four specific details that support or develop the topic sentence. Answers will vary.

1. Autumn was advancing, and the sky was full of luminous clouds.
2. The Rolling Stones are a successful rock group.
3. Mr. Nolan's grocery store had closed for the last time.
4. Sometimes I feel as though I'm a half-dozen different people.
5. A TV addict is a person who can't turn off a television set.
6. Today people talk about "the good old days."
7. Television advertisers are masters of persuasion.
8. Why does my tongue always freeze at the wrong time?
9. The car wheezed, coughed, and sputtered, fouling the air with dirty black smoke.
10. In the world of make-believe, I can be anything I wish.
11. Shabbiness and neglect marked the apartment building.
12. Pets-a-Plenty is the noisiest store in the shopping center.

The Function of the Topic Sentence

In your earlier study of the paragraph, you saw how the topic sentence operates as a type of contract. With it, you promise your audience that you are going to explain something about your topic. The topic sentence states the main idea, and *all the other sentences must be related to this topic sentence.* Therefore, the topic sentence, written with a specific audience and purpose in mind, *controls* the content of the paragraph.

In *limiting* what can be discussed in the paragraph, the topic sentence functions in a slightly different way.

The topic sentence makes a general statement, a statement that is broader in scope than the rest of the paragraph. However, if the topic sentence is too general, the remainder of the paragraph will have to be either extremely long in order to give an adequate explanation of the idea, or it will have to contain nothing but more general statements.

The following is an example of a paragraph with a topic sentence that is too general.

> Winter is a cold season, but it is also beautiful. The white, glistening snow on the ground, trees, and houses is an eye-catching scene.

"Winter is a cold season, but it is also beautiful" is much too broad a topic sentence to be adequately supported in a paragraph. You could write an entire composition on that subject. Because it is so broad, all the writer can do is give another general statement about the snow.

To limit the topic sentence so that the idea can be developed in a paragraph, the writer first had to narrow the subject. She narrowed it to a specific winter's morning and wrote the following topic sentence: "The winter morning was cold and still." Then she added specific details to develop the idea, as follows:

> The winter morning was cold and still. The crust of the snow was like fragile glass and shattered with a loud noise as my feet broke through it. The icy air froze my nostrils and numbed my hands. Except for my footsteps, the world was silent, frozen to attention by winter's command.

The writer now has described a cold, still winter morning, using many specific details that help the reader to visualize the scene.

Exercises Working with Topic Sentences

A. Below is a series of sentence pairs. In each pair, one topic sentence is too general; the other is limited in its scope. Decide which one is too broad and which one has been sufficiently limited to be covered in a paragraph.

1. a. Basketball is an interesting game. broad
   b. Basketball demands quick thinking and split-second timing. limited

2. a. James failed history because he spent too much time in dramatics. limited
   b. Extra-curricular activities are time-consuming. broad

3. a. Several old buildings on Mason Street should be torn down because of their bad condition. limited
   b. Old buildings should be torn down. broad

4. a. Mountains are beautiful. broad
   b. The Blue Ridge Mountains stretched before us like a scene from a movie. limited

5. a. Pets can be a nuisance. broad
   b. My cat, Siggy, is constantly getting into mischief. limited

6. a. Because he bought the cheapest one he could find, Joe's bicycle didn't last very long. limited
   b. Economy doesn't always pay. broad

7. a. Graduation from high school is very important. broad
   b. Without a high school diploma, it is almost impossible to get a good job. limited

8. a. People of all ages read comic books. broad
   b. My grandmother likes to read my *Super Comics*. limited

9. a. Reckless driving is a serious problem. broad
   b. Statistics show that most automobile accidents are caused by reckless driving. limited

10. a. Works of art are difficult to create. broad
    b. Oil painting takes time, effort, and patience. limited

B. Following is a list of broad topic sentences. Rewrite each one, limiting its scope. Answers will vary.

1. Automobiles are not as safe as they could be.
2. Travel is becoming faster—and noisier—all the time.
3. Pedestrians should be careful.
4. The Presidency of the United States is a difficult job.
5. You couldn't find a more interesting neighborhood than the one I live in.
6. Smoking is dangerous to a person's health.
7. Cats are interesting animals.
8. Growing vegetables is educational.
9. Most television programs are alike.
10. I wear different clothes for different occasions.

C. Study the following list of subjects. Write a limited topic sentence for each subject. Answers will vary.

1. Things I Fear
2. Radio Shows
3. Human Rights
4. Cities
5. The Future
6. Unpleasant People
7. Photography
8. Television Commentators
9. Popular Dances
10. Lonely Feelings
11. Records
12. The Game of Monopoly
13. Vacations
14. School Sports
15. Unfinished Projects

Part 4   Pre-Writing: Gathering Ideas

Once you have decided upon your topic and topic sentence, the next step is to develop your main idea into a well-organized paragraph. Remember that you have many resources available for gathering information. Use the pre-writing techniques discussed in Chapter 7, and keep these points in mind as you plan your paragraph.

1. Don't overlook yourself. What information do you know about the topic? What ideas do you have? What can you observe about it?

2. Use other people as sources. What information can be obtained through discussion with others? through interviewing others? through observing others?

3. Use printed material to develop your idea. What books, articles, and pamphlets are available on your topic?

The types of details you gather about your topic can be classified in four ways.

1. Sensory details
2. Facts or statistics
3. Specific examples
4. Incidents and anecdotes

Part 4

Objective

To use different types of details to develop paragraphs

Presenting the Lesson

1. List on the chalkboard the four kinds of details used to support a topic sentence: sensory details, facts or statistics, specific examples, incidents and anecdotes. Read and discuss **Gathering Ideas** on page 143. Point out that sensory anecdotes are most likely to be derived from personal experience or from the experiences of other people. Facts or statistics, on the other hand, often come from printed sources. Specific examples may come from any of the three sources.

2. Read and discuss **Using Sensory Details**, page 144. Remind the students of the sensory word lists in Chapter 4, pages 62–77. Review these lists with the class before assigning the Exercise on page 145.

3. Have students make worksheets that list all of the senses in preparation for the Exercise. As they visit their chosen observation area, students should record their impressions in the appropriate categories on the worksheet. Tell students to use vivid, specific, adjectives, nouns, and verbs in their notes. Point out that, depending on the scene, one sense may predominate over the others.

4. Read and discuss **Using Facts or Statistics**, page 145. Tell students that a fact is a statement that can be proven true. A statistic is a fact that uses numbers and often requires research.

5. Complete Exercise A, page 146 orally. Have students identify the facts and statistics in each paragraph as you list them on the board. Note that the topic sentence in three of the paragraphs is a fact or statistic.

6. Assign Exercise B on page 146. Tell students that narrowing the topic somewhat before researching it will make the assignment easier. For example, "mass transportation in New York" is easier to research than "mass transportation." Call students' attention to the direction that says "write a limited topic sentence that can be developed into a paragraph." Even though they will have limited the topic once in order to do research, they may have to limit it further in order to write an appropriate topic sentence.

7. Read **Using Specific Examples** on page 147. Point out that the examples in the second sample paragraph are also facts.

8. Assign the Exercise on page 148. To help students make sure that they are using examples and not some other type of supporting detail, tell them to test each detail

Using Sensory Details

Vivid, descriptive words are essential to the development of an effective paragraph. They can make the difference between dull writing and lively, precise ideas. Through careful observation and the skillful use of your senses, you can find details that will help you re-create a scene or experience on paper.

Sensory details give your reader a feeling of participation, the opportunity to experience what you felt. They allow the reader to picture a scene and "hear" the sounds. Sensory details can even communicate ideas of touch, taste, and smell. Let's look at the following example.

Biting my pencil eraser, staring at my paper, and trying to think of a topic on which to write, I sit here in the library and listen to the sounds of silence. Soft whispers come from a table across the room. Someone giggles and I stop thinking for a moment. I glance up from my work, and the sudden shift in my concentration changes the people and their clothes into a blur of color. Now someone clumps along the floor, stops, and then whirrs the pencil sharpener over his pencil. Satisfied, he walks away. I hear a jingle and I turn around to see the janitor with a huge ring of keys fastened to his belt. Picking up papers as he goes along, he adds a rustle to the silence. Now I hear the sound, somewhat like a zipper, of someone tearing a sheet of paper from her spiral notebook. The background buzz of the flourescent lights overhead ties the other sounds together. The hum of the bell reminds me that I must leave. Study period is over.

The writer has chosen to appeal primarily to the sense of hearing in this paragraph because she has been struck by all of the noises she can identify in the "silence" of the school library. How many separate sounds has she identified? Notice the vivid, specific words she has used to help re-create the sounds she has heard. The boy doesn't "walk" along the floor; he "clumps." This writer has also used a comparison. To what does she compare the sound of tearing spiral paper from a notebook? Why is this comparison effective?

Exercise Pre-Writing: Developing a Paragraph with Sensory Details

Go to a specific place in your school, such as one of the areas listed below. Spend at least five minutes there and jot down exactly what you see, feel, hear, and smell. What vivid, specific words best describe these sensory details? Write a topic sentence for a paragraph that would describe this place. Then list your sensory details below the sentence. Save your work for use later in this chapter.

1. the hall during passing period
2. the hall after school
3. study hall
4. a locker room
5. homeroom before school
6. the auditorium
7. the front entrance
8. the cafeteria
9. your locker
10. the gymnasium

Using Facts or Statistics

To understand how topic sentences may be developed by the use of facts or statistics, let's look at the following example.

> The abacus, probably the earliest calculating tool, was invented by the Chinese so long ago that no one even knows for certain when it was. It is a framework of wires with beads mounted on them. Each bead on the bottom part of the frame, below the crossbar, represents one unit; each bead above the bar represents five. The beads that touch the bar are counted to make up a number, and by moving the beads on different rows, or places, any number can be recorded. The beads can be manipulated to do addition, subtraction, multiplication, or division. Using an abacus, an expert can do addition or subtraction even faster than an electric calculator can. It was many centuries before any other civilization invented a calculating tool so fast and efficient.—LINDA O'BRIEN

The writer begins with a topic sentence that identifies the abacus as an early calculating tool. She next gives facts about the abacus, facts related to its construction and use. Then in her final two sentences, she gives facts about the speed and efficiency of the abacus.

by mentally preceding it with the phrase, "for example." Remind them that it is all right for the example to be a fact or statistic.

9. Read and discuss **Using an Incident or an Anecdote** on pages 148–149. Point out the similarity between this kind of development and the act of telling a story.

10. Assign the Exercise on page 149. Point out that an incident or anecdote is essentially an extended example which makes the writer's point more effectively then several briefer examples would. Tell students that an anecdote often, although not necessarily, comes from personal experience.

Individualizing the Lesson

Less-Advanced Students

1. After students have completed the exercise **Developing a Paragraph by Using Sensory Detail** on page 145, ask for volunteers to write their lists of details on the chalkboard. Have the class help these students make the details more vivid and to create a dominant impression in the description.

2. Before assigning **Developing a Paragraph by Using Facts or Statistics**, discuss possible reference materials for a few sample topics. Point out, for example, that the encyclopedia would be a useful reference for "breeds of dogs," but that "cable television" would require more up-to-date information best found in *The Readers' Guide to Periodical Literature*.

Advanced Students

Write the following general statement on the chalkboard, pointing out that with slight modifications it could serve as the topic sentence for a paragraph developed by any one of the four methods discussed in this chapter.

> The Brooklyn Bridge is one of our nation's most interesting landmarks.

If students do not know anything about the Brooklyn Bridge, let them substitute another landmark (St. Louis's stainless steel arch, San Francisco's Golden Gate Bridge, Niagara Falls, etc.). Ask students to list the details they would use to develop the paragraph in each of the four different ways.

Optional Practice

Ask students to select a topic from the Exercise on page 149, which covers anecdotes and incidents. See if they can develop the topic using one of the other kinds of details. Then ask students to share the results of their efforts.

Extending the Lesson

Have students find and bring to class examples from magazines or newspapers of each kind of paragraph development studied in this section.

Exercises Pre-Writing: Developing a Paragraph with Facts or Statistics

A. Following is a series of paragraphs that were developed with facts or statistics. For each paragraph, list the facts or statistics given.

1   By 1963, almost 130,000 Czechs had migrated to this country. They had settled on rural homesteads and in farming communities. They also had formed enclaves in cities, principally in Chicago, Cleveland, and New York.

2   There are sixty million homes in the United States and over ninety-five percent of them are equipped with a television set. In the average home, the set is turned on for five hours and forty-five minutes a day. Average viewers watch television for a total of over 3,000 entire days — roughly nine full years.

3   Oysters provide valuable products. In addition to providing food, oysters can be induced to grow pearls inside their shells. The process is begun when workers place single grains of sand inside the shells of young oysters. Pearls grow around these grains.

4   The Great Wall of China is the largest fortification ever built. It meanders for 1,500 miles across northern China. At its base, the Great Wall is from 15 to 20 feet thick. At the top, 25 feet above the base, the wall narrows to 15 feet. Every 200 to 300 yards, towers project from 35 to 40 feet into the air.

B. Following is a list of general topics, that lend themselves to paragraph development through the use of facts or statistics. Choose two topics or make up two of your own. Research the topics; then write a limited topic sentence that can be developed in a paragraph. List the facts and/or statistics you would use to develop your topic sentence. Save your work for future use.

1. Television violence	6. Ocean pollution
2. Cable television	7. Mass transportation
3. Computers	8. Microsurgery
4. Solar heating	9. Cars
5. U.S. agriculture	10. Breeds of dogs

Using Specific Examples

Sometimes a topic sentence will be a general idea that is best supported with specific examples. Look at this paragraph.

> Life was hard for young Stevie Wonder. No matter how developed his sense of touch became, there were some things he could never understand through touch. He could never touch the sun, or the horizon. He could never touch a mountain. Some things were too fragile, like snowflakes and live butterflies. It would be too dangerous to try to understand burning or boiling through touch. No matter how developed his ability to measure "sound shadows" became, he would only be able to measure the width and bulk of a large building, not its height. He could learn that the sky is blue and the grass green, but he would never *see* blue or green. He could not *watch* television. —JAMES HASKINS

The writer begins with a general statement: "Life was hard for young Stevie Wonder." He goes on to explain that there were many things the boy couldn't understand through touch. In the next seven sentences he gives specific examples of these things.

The following paragraph uses a similar technique.

> Enterprising inventors have made American life richer, safer, and more comfortable. Gail Borden invented condensed milk, a healthy, safe product, in a time (1859) when fresh milk was often dangerous. In 1902 Willis Carrier invented something he called "air conditioning." Clarence Birdseye developed frozen foods, and Aaron Montgomery Ward brought the department store to the most isolated farm through the distribution of a mail order catalog. —K.S. KNODT

This writer also states a general idea: "Enterprising inventors have made American life richer, safer, and more comfortable." He then supports that statement with examples.

1. Gail Borden's invention of condensed milk
2. Willis Carrier's invention of air conditioning
3. Clarence Birdseye's development of frozen foods
4. Ward's distribution of a mail order catalog

Exercise Pre-Writing: Developing a Paragraph with Specific Examples

Here is a list of general topic sentences. Choose three of them or write your own. Then list at least three specific examples for each of them. Save your work for use later in the chapter.

1. Yesterday's science fiction is today's reality.
2. Even great leaders can fail in something.
3. Animals are often surprisingly intelligent.
4. Some comic strips are more serious than funny.
5. Winners have sometimes overcome severe handicaps.
6. Some common houseplants are poisonous.
7. Disaster movies are popular entertainment.
8. Fast food restaurants line the main street of our town.
9. Some people are experts at everything.
10. Americans are a generous people.

Using an Incident or an Anecdote

The incident or anecdote can add a personal touch to almost any form of writing. In this type of development, the writer explains or clarifies a general idea by relating an amusing story or describing an interesting event. The selection may be from personal experience or from the experiences of others. The strength of this type of development lies in the fact that an incident or anecdote, if well chosen, can imprint an idea clearly on the reader's mind. Read the following example.

> Children have taught me much of what I know about love. To them love is nothing fancy, but very real—a feeling to be taken seriously. "If you love somebody," a six-year-old boy named Charlie once told me, "you help him put his boots on when they get stuck."—LESLIE KENTON

The writer could have developed the topic sentence with the addition of several more impersonal statements, but instead she includes a simple personal experience that makes the paragraph "come alive." Notice how the writer of the following paragraph has used a wonderful childhood experience to explain an idea.

I think that one of the reasons I became a writer was because once, when I was driving home with my parents, they let me keep a date with a rainbow. There had been a heavy summer storm, when suddenly I screamed, "Stop the car! I must write a poem about that beautiful rainbow!" My father pulled up at the side of the road and off I went into the drizzle and the sunshine, while they waited. It was one of those special moments that change you, make you more than you've been. It is an experience in saying "Yes!" to life — and that's really what spontaneity and joy are all about. —EDA LeSHAN

Here again, the writer could have explained her topic sentence with facts or examples. Instead, she used one simple anecdote to clarify her reasons for becoming a writer.

Exercise Pre-Writing: Developing a Paragraph with an Incident or an Anecdote

Here is a list of topic sentences, each one of which may be developed by an incident or an anecdote. Choose two of the sentences or write sentences of your own. For each, make a list of details related to a specific incident or anecdote that develops the topic. Save your work for use later in this chapter.

1. A kind friend can help you forget your troubles.
2. Sometimes a bad experience can turn out to be funny.
3. An angry word can ruin your day.
4. It usually pays to be on time.
5. Experience is sometimes a tough teacher.
6. You don't have to travel to find adventure.
7. Sometimes you have to learn to say "No!"
8. Baby-sitting is not the world's easiest job.
9. There are some things you can't learn from books.
10. A good laugh can sometimes be "good medicine."
11. A pet can teach you how to love.
12. You don't have to join a team to learn sportsmanship.
13. Repairing a _____ can teach you patience.
14. Hero-worship sometimes pays off.
15. There are times when you have to forgive.

Part 5

Objective

To organize the ideas in a paragraph using the following methods:

1. chronological order
2. spatial order
3. order from least to most important idea
4. order from most to least familiar idea
5. order by comparison and contrast

Presenting the Lesson

1. Read the introductory paragraphs on page 150. List on the chalkboard the five methods of organization. Briefly define each type. Then explain that certain methods of organization best fit certain types of development. Ask students which of the five methods would be most effective for organizing a paragraph that

describes a neighbor's kitchen (spatial order)

shows how two brothers are alike, or different (comparison and contrast)

presents a new idea to the reader (most to least familiar)

tells about an experience the writer has had (chronological)

presents several reasons why air pollution is a health hazard (least to most important)

If students have difficulty, repeat the exercise at the end of the lesson.

2. Read and discuss **Chronological Order** on pages 150–151. Explain that this is the natural order for telling stories or anecdotes, and that it may also be useful for organizing facts or examples if you want to emphasize historical development.

Once you have gathered information and ideas for your paragraph, it is important to decide on a good order for presenting them. An orderly and logical presentation is helpful to your readers. It enables them to understand how your ideas are related to each other.

In selecting a method of organization, consider both the purpose and type of development you have decided on for your paragraph. Then ask yourself questions such as the following:

1. How does this idea relate to my other details?
2. Does one piece of information logically precede another in time or in degree of importance?
3. Is one idea more familiar to my readers than another?

When you make decisions based on these questions, you are taking the first steps toward coherence in your writing.

There are five main methods of organization:

1. Chronological order, or time sequence
2. Spatial order
3. Order of importance
4. Order of familiarity
5. Order by comparison and contrast

Chronological Order

When you use chronological order, or time sequence, you arrange your details in the order in which they happened. This method of organization is particularly useful for paragraphs developed by anecdote or incident, as in the following example.

Over the years, a number of major league baseball players have developed odd mental blocks. Mike Ivie, an outstanding catching prospect, was signed as a teenager by the San Diego Padres in 1970. In his first workout with the Padres, Ivie threw the ball too low to the pitcher and hit the screen used to protect pitchers during batting practice. A fellow catcher joked about it, and Ivie developed a block about throwing the ball back to the pitcher. Ivie switched to first base and, after a mediocre career with two other teams, is now a journeyman player for the Detroit Tigers. —TIME

The topic sentence in this paragraph promises to tell about the mental blocks that some baseball players develop. The incident that develops this promise begins with information about a promising rookie, Mike Ivie. The paragraph continues by describing, in the order in which they occurred, the problems that led to this player's mental block. The paragraph ends with a statement about Ivie's situation today.

Spatial Order

With spatial order, details are presented in a sequence that duplicates the order in which a viewer might notice them. Such an organization might proceed from side to side, from top to bottom (or the reverse), or from near to far (or the reverse). This method is useful in organizing sensory details, primarily visual ones. Read the following description of a canyon. Be aware of how the writer shares his impression of the scene by presenting the details in the order he himself probably noticed them.

> On one side, beginning at the very lip of the pool, was a tiny meadow, a cool surface of green that extended to the base of the frowning wall. Beyond the pool a gentle slope of earth ran up and up to meet the opposing wall. Fine grass covered the slope—grass that was spangled with flowers, with here and there patches of color, orange and purple and golden. Below, the canyon was shut in. There was no view. The walls leaned together abruptly and the canyon ended in a chaos of rocks, moss-covered and hidden by a green screen of vines and creepers and boughs of trees. Up the canyon rose far hills and peaks, the big foothills, pine-covered and remote. And far beyond, like clouds upon the border of the sky, towered minarets of white, where the Sierra's eternal snows flashed austerely the blazes of the sun.—JACK LONDON

3. Read and discuss **Spatial Order** on page 151. Explain that this is often a logical organization for descriptive writing.

4. Read and discuss **Order of Importance** on page 152. Explain that this is a useful order for informative or persuasive writing when there is an especially strong or important example or fact to emphasize. Remind students that the information presented last often stays with a reader longest.

5. Read and discuss **Order of Familiarity** on pages 152–153. Explain how the readers' understanding is aided by presenting familiar facts first and new information last.

6. Read and discuss **Comparisons or Contrasts** on pages 153–154. Point out how comparison is used to focus on the similarities between the bicycles. Have students read the second sample paragraph. Point out contrast is used to focus on the differences between Henry Chatillon and Tête Rouge.

7. Assign the Exercise on page 154. Have students write at the top of their papers the method of organization they choose. Emphasize that this is an important step in the pre-writing process: unnecessary ideas are deleted, helpful details are added, and details are arranged in their most effective order.

Individualizing the Lesson

Less-Advanced Students

Work with individuals to help them decide on a method of organization for the set of pre-writing notes they have decided to develop. Try to make students understand the logic behind the selection.

Order of Importance

This method of organization is appropriate for organizing facts and statistics, or for arranging specific examples. Judge the specific statements you wish to use according to the impact you think that they will have on your readers. Then organize them, beginning with the least important idea and ending with the strongest.

Space has been called the last frontier, and eager adventurers are already seeking to tame it. Yet, unlike the Old West, space is one unknown that we can never hope to explore or understand completely. Where once an explorer could muster an expedition with several thousand dollars and a few volunteers, now billions must be spent to develop equipment and armies of personnel are required. Despite these numbers, each journey results in only a small increase in our understanding of the stars and planets that whirl around us. Most daunting, however, is the fact that no matter how much of the universe we explore, an infinite amount will remain unknown.

The writer began with the general idea that space is an unconquerable frontier. The first reasons he gave concerned basic restrictions of money and distance. The final, most powerful statement notes the impossibility of exploring the endless regions of space.

Order of Familiarity

This is another good method for organizing facts and statistics or specific examples. You move from ideas that are familiar to your reader to those that are not. In this way, you can prepare your reader for new concepts by providing familiar background.

There may be a revolution going on in the audio industry. Despite improvements in quality, the basic technology of sound reproduction—the needle and groove—hasn't changed since Thomas Edison's phonograph in 1877. Now, however, the audio industry has come up with something that may turn the stereo turntable and record albums into quaint antiques. It is the compact digital audio disk player. Known as the CD player, this stereo sound system is considered revolutionary because music is represented by a digital code that is embedded under the surface of a 4.5-inch disk. When it is played, the information is "read" by a low-power laser beam, which erases background noise and the hiss found on conventional records.

Here the writer begins with the familiar historical beginnings of the phonograph. She introduces the basic technology, and then mentions a new technological concept, the CD player.

Comparisons or Contrasts

This approach can be used to organize facts, examples, and incidents. This method helps to highlight the similarities or differences between two or more things.

A paragraph that compares persons, things, or events emphasizes the similarities between the subjects.

> A five-speed bike combines the worst of a three-speed and a ten-speed. The typical five-speed is built on the same heavy frame as the three-speed, often has the same wide saddle and upright handlebars, but has the five-speed gear cluster and changer bolted on in back. For two extra gears of questionable value, you pay almost as much as you would for a low-priced ten-speed.—S. MARSHALL

By comparing the five-speed bike with three-speed and ten-speed bikes, the writer is able to bring out the disadvantages of the five-speed. He has noted the similarities that illustrate his purpose and left out all irrelevant points of comparison.

A paragraph that contrasts persons, things, or events emphasizes differences. The following paragraph is an example.

> Although Henry Chatillon and Tête Rouge were the same age, that is, about thirty, they were very different. Henry was twice as large, and fully six times as strong as Tête Rouge. Henry's face was roughened by winds and storms; Tête Rouge's was softened by idle living. Henry had led a life of hardship and privation; Tête Rouge never had a whim which he did not gratify the first moment he was able.—FRANCIS PARKMAN

153

Part 6

Objective

To write a first draft of a paragraph and revise it

Presenting the Lesson

1. Read and discuss **First Draft and Revision** on pages 154–155. Review with the class **Writing a First Draft** on page 117 of Chapter 7. Once again, direct students to concentrate at this stage on expressing their ideas in sentences and not on correcting mechanical errors.

2. Assign Exercise A on page 155. Remind students that they should still be expanding on the ideas discovered in the pre-writing stage.

3. Review the discussion of revision on pages 119 and 120 of Chapter 7 and the checklists for revising and proofreading on pages 122 and 123. Discuss the sample revision on page 155. Ask students to remark on specific changes and additions made at this stage.

4. Have students exchange papers and make suggestions for revisions in each other's paragraphs. Then assign Exercise B on page 155.

Individualizing the Lesson

Less-Advanced Students

Read both the original version and the improved version of each sentence in the sample revised first draft. Discuss why and how each change was made. Suggest that students review their own work this carefully, sentence by sentence, for the most effective revision. You

When an idea is presented side-by-side with its opposite, both become more striking because of the contrast. The personalities of the two men in the paragraph on the preceding page become clearer and more vivid because of this method of organization.

Exercise Pre-Writing: Organizing Details

Select one of the sets of pre-writing notes that you developed in the earlier exercises on paragraph development. Decide what method of organization would best fit your purpose. Then, number your specific details in the order in which you would present them. Delete or add details if necessary.

Part 6   First Draft and Revision

After carefully following all the steps of the pre-writing stage, you are ready to write your first draft. Remember that the first draft is simply your initial attempt to get your ideas on paper. Do not worry about spelling and punctuation at this point. You are still in the process of discovering, expanding, and refining.

At the revision stage, however, you must work thoughtfully. Review the discussion of revision in Chapter 7, "The Process of Writing." Refresh your memory about what you should be considering and asking yourself at this point.

All good writers go through this stage, as the example on the next page illustrates. This is a revised rough draft of the paragraph on page 144 which is developed through sensory details.

Notice the many different types of revisions this writer made. Of course, there are some corrections of errors in grammar, usage, and mechanics. The writer has also improved her word choice and expanded some of her ideas. Problems of coherence were solved when the writer moved sentences from the middle of her paragraph to the beginning. She has also reorganized details so that the details that broke her concentration are grouped together at the beginning. Finally, she omitted the statement, "I'll never get my homework done!" While this might be a real concern, it interrupts the unity of her development.

Biting my pencil eraser, staring at my paper, and /on which\ sit here in the
~~As I sit here~~ trying to think of a topic to write, ~~I can hear~~ library and
~~ten to~~ silence. Soft whispers come from a table across the room.
~~he sounds of the library. I can hear the sounds of whisper-~~
glance from my work, and the sudden shift in my concentration
~~ng people.~~ I look up and ~~I can see many colors of clothes.~~ changes the
clumps   and   people and their
~~low~~ someone ~~walks~~ along the floor, then ~~that same person~~ clothes into a
                                                               blur of color.
irrs
~~urns~~ the pencil sharpener over his pencil. Satisfied, he walks
        jingle   with a huge ring of
~~way.~~ I hear a ~~noise~~ and I turn around to see the janitor ~~be-~~ keys fastened
        he adds a rustle to the silence.   to his belt.
~~ind me~~ picking up papers as he goes along. Someone gig-
~~els~~ and I stop thinking for a moment. ~~The buzzing sound~~
~~bove is bugging me. I'll never get my homework done!~~ Now

The background
buzz of the
fluorescent
lights overhead
ties the other
sounds together.

hear the sound, somewhat like a zipper, of someone tear-
ng a sheet of paper from their spiral notebook. The hum of
                    that
he bell reminds me I must leave. ~~I rush up the stairs and~~
tudy period is over.

Exercises Writing and Revising the Rough Draft

A. Use the pre-writing notes that you developed in the previous
parts to write a rough draft of a paragrah.

B. Revise the rough draft of the paragraph that you wrote for Exercise A. Work on improvements in unity, coherence, and word
choice.

Go over the summary with
the class. Make sure they understand that the concepts
covered in this chapter will be
of great importance in every
piece of writing they do.

Encourage students to use
this summary for review or as
part of the **SQ3R** method of
study (See Chapter 15). Remind them, though, that more
specific points can only be reviewed by skimming the chapter itself.

Applications in Other Subject Areas

When the students have
written their paragraphs for
the History activity, ask them
to read the paragraphs aloud
to the class. Then have them
explain which type of development they used (sensory
details, facts and statistics,
specific examples, incident or
anecdote). Also ask students
to explain which type of paragraph organization they used
(chronological, spatial, familiarity, importance, compari-
son/contrast). If a student's
paragraph lacks unity or coherence, make suggestions
for revisions and have the student write another draft.

SUMMARY AND APPLICATIONS

1. A paragraph is a group of sentences dealing with a single topic.

2. The topic sentence of a paragraph is a general statement of what
    the paragraph will be about.

3. When all of the sentences in a paragraph develop the topic sen-
    tence and relate logically to each other, the paragraph has **unity**
    and **coherence**. Remember that unity and coherence are impor-
    tant to any clear expression of ideas.

4. Paragraphs can be developed with sensory details, facts, statis-
    tics, examples, incidents, or anecdotes.

5. Ways of organizing paragraphs include the following five meth-
    ods: chronological order, spatial order, order of importance,
    order of familiarity, and comparison-contrast. Whenever you
    are given a writing assignment in one of your classes, choose the
    most appropriate organizational method for your presentation.

Applications in Other Subject Areas

History. Using news magazines or a United States history textbook,
choose one recent event (since 1960) that you believe greatly affects
life today. Write a paragraph that supports your view. Your topic
sentence should tell which event you have chosen and how it affects
people now. The remainder of the paragraph should support your
idea with specific evidence.

History / Science. In your history or science textbook, find examples
of each of the following:

    a. a paragraph developed with facts or statistics
    b. a paragraph developed with specific examples
    c. a paragraph organized in chronological order

Copy the topic sentence in each paragraph. List the supporting
details and any connective words or transitions.

Chapter 9

Types of Paragraphs

You have studied four different ways of developing paragraphs—with sensory details, with facts or statistics, with specific examples, or with an incident or anecdote. You have also learned several different methods of organizing your ideas. You are now ready to apply what you have learned to composing specific types of paragraphs:

> Narrative paragraphs
> Descriptive paragraphs
> Explanatory paragraphs

Each type of paragraph has special characteristics and is used for a particular purpose. Your strategies for the development and organization of each kind will vary. The wide range of options available to you will help you develop paragraphs that are uniquely suited to the ideas you want to express.

Chapter Objectives

1. To write a narrative paragraph using specific details arranged in chronological order

2. To write a descriptive paragraph using sensory details organized according to spatial order

3. To write four types of explanatory paragraphs: the paragraph that explains a process, the paragraph that defines, the paragraph that gives reasons, and the paragraph that persuades

Preparing the Students

Read page 157 and write on the chalkboard the three types of paragraphs to be studied. Briefly define each type. Help students understand the purposes of the three types by pointing out that spoken communication of ideas can be categorized in a similar manner. For example, ask students what type of communication is being used when they tell a friend what happened on vacation last summer (narration), when they discuss the clothes to wear to a party (description), when they give the steps of a recipe (process) or tell why they missed the school bus (reasons).

Additional Resources

Mastery Test — See pages 25–26 in the test booklet

Skills Practice Book — pages 46–51

Duplicating Masters — pages 47–52

Special Populations — See special section at the front of this Teacher's Edition

Objective

To write a narrative paragraph using specific details arranged in chronological order

Presenting the Lesson

1. Read and discuss the introduction to **The Narrative Paragraph** on page 158. Point out that jokes, anecdotes, or the simple telling of an event are all types of narratives.

2. Ask students how they can recognize first-person writing (the use of the pronoun *I*) and third-person writing (the absence of *I* and the use of the pronouns *he, she, they,* and *it*). Read the two sample paragraphs on page 158. Point out how the first person narrative allows the reader to feel more a part of the narrator's experience, while the third person narrative has a more objective quality.

3. Read **Pre-Writing Steps** on pages 159–160. Discuss the first pre-writing step for a narrative paragraph: gathering details. Point out that, as in any type of writing, gathering details for a narrative involves choosing the most important and effective details.

4. Discuss the second pre-writing step for a narrative: organizing the details in chronological order. Remind students that chronological order is sometimes called "time order because it presents events in the order in which they happened."

5. Call attention to the list of time words and phrases on page 160,

Part 1   The Narrative Paragraph

The purpose of the narrative paragraph is to relate an event. "Once upon a time…"; "Last night while I was watching television…" are phrases that signal the beginning of a narrative.

The narrative paragraph is a simple, natural form of writing with many variations. It may be based on fact, on imagination, or on a combination of both. The narrowed topic of a narrative paragraph may recall a personal experience or an event observed by, told to, or thought up by the writer. Narrative paragraphs may be written in the first or in the third person.

FIRST PERSON

When I woke, the sun was low. Looking down from where I lay, I saw a dog sitting on his haunches. His tongue was hanging out of his mouth; he looked as if he were laughing. He was a big dog, with a gray-brown coat, as big as a wolf. I sprang up and shouted at him but he did not move—he just sat there. I did not like that. When I reached for a stone to throw, he moved swiftly out of the way of the stone. He was not afraid of me; he looked at me as if I were meat. No doubt I could have killed him with an arrow, but I did not know if there were others. Moreover, night was falling.—STEPHEN VINCENT BENÉT

THIRD PERSON

Leaning on his cane, Mr. Mendelsohn stood up and walked out of the kitchen and down the long hallway into the living room. It was empty. He went over to a large armchair by the window. The sun shone through the window, covering the entire armchair and Mr. Mendelsohn. A canary cage was also by the window, and two tiny yellow birds chirped and hopped back and forth energetically. Mr. Mendelsohn felt drowsy; he shut his eyes. So many aches and pains, he thought. It was hard to sleep at night, but here, well…the birds began to chirp in unison and the old man opened one eye, glancing at them, and smiled. Then he shut his eyes once more and fell fast asleep.

—NICHOLASA MOHR

Pre-Writing Steps

Selecting Details for a Narrative Paragraph. It is not difficult to gather the information needed for a narrative paragraph. This simply consists of recalling or developing all of the details needed to re-create the story for the reader. A writer should, however, be careful not to stray from the main story line or include details that interrupt the flow of the narrative. The writer should also attempt to make the story as interesting as possible by choosing sharp, precise words to develop the ideas. This will help the resulting story to be vivid and extremely effective.

Organizing a Narrative Paragraph. The events or actions described in a narrative paragraph are usually told in **chronological order**, the order in which they occurred in time. In some paragraphs, such as the following narrative about a fisherman, the chronological order is clear and direct from beginning to end.

> A fisherman walked along a beach on a moonlit night, searching for firewood. Above the reaches of the high tide, he saw a gnarled branch, polished by the rough sand and entwined in seaweed. In the eerie silver light and sudden shadows, the branch seemed almost alive. The fisherman lifted it cautiously and shook off the sand. As he turned it in his hand and the moonlight gleamed on its polished surface, he saw the subtle outline that had caused him to mistake the branch for a living creature. The fisherman took his knife from his pocket and quickly cut away the protruding twigs. Then he carefully cut, shaped, and smoothed the ancient wood. Finally he held in his hand a graceful wood sculpture—the perfect, almost living form of an undersea serpent!—BARBARA BRUNO

Many narrative paragraphs indicate the order of time and the passing of time by using words and phrases such as those listed in the chart on the following page. These words and phrases are called **transitional devices.** They help to unify your paragraph by providing signals to your reader about how your details are related to each other.

pointing out that these transitional devices are always helpful and sometimes necessary to make the order of events clear. Point out the transitional words in the paragraph on page 159 ("then" and "finally" in the last two sentences). Then have students close their books. Read the sample paragraph on page 160 to them, omitting the underlined transitional words and phrases. Have students note the difficulty in understanding the action described. Then have students open their books and read the actual paragraph. Discuss the difference the transitional devices make.

6. Read the first sample paragraph under **The Topic Sentence**, page 161, pointing out that the lack of a topic sentence in the paragraph does not detract from its interest or clarity. Read the next two sample paragraphs on pages 161–162, pointing out the use of topic sentences. Have students note how the topic sentences describe generally the action which is then narrated in greater detail.

7. Assign the Exercise on page 162. List the following possible topics on the chalkboard:

   a. learning to swim
   b. a trick that backfired
   c. the night I cooked dinner
   d. a frightening experience
   e. meeting an extra-terrestrial
   f. a trip to a dream
   g. a night alone
   h. a memorable meal
   i. caught in a storm
   j. meeting a famous person

8. Remind the students to follow each step in the writing process as described on page 162. Emphasize the pre-writing process by holding a class brainstorming session on one sample topic. Help the students narrow the topic and formulate a topic sentence. For example, the general topic "A Memorable Meal" might yield the topic sentence "I will never forget the night my grandfather and I dined and danced at a Hungarian restaurant." List on the board possible details for this paragraph, urging students to be imaginative. Then have students number the details in chronological order. For their own paragraphs, remind students of the choices to be made at this stage: Will the narrative be in first person or third person? Will the narrative be true or imaginary or a combination of the two?

Emphasize the use of transitional words in writing the first draft from the pre-writing notes. Also remind the students of the importance of revision. For a narrative paragraph, students should make sure that their details are strong and vivid, that there are no unnecessary details, and that the chronological order is clear, supported by transitional words and phrases.

Individualizing the Lesson

Less-Advanced Students

1. Ask students to re-read the sample paragraphs on pages 159, 160, and 161 and tell whether they are written in the first or third person. Be sure students understand that a person's name is a third person reference, as well as the pronouns *he, she, they*, and *it*.

2. When students are ready to revise their first drafts, emphasize the

Time Words and Phrases

A POINT IN TIME

one month	next year	at midnight
two days	yesterday	tonight
tomorrow	last week	at this moment

ORDER OF TIME

next	soon	immediately
then	instantly	the next day
later	finally	the following Friday

PERIODS OF TIME

for a moment	during the day	for a long time
for an hour	after a week	during the winter

ACTIONS REPEATED IN TIME

seldom	occasionally	once
sometimes	frequently	twice

A BREAK IN TIME

meanwhile	before this	at the same time

When chronological order is clear as in the paragraph about the fisherman, time words merely reinforce the flow of the narrative. However, in paragraphs where the passage of time is uneven, time words are essential to understanding the events.

Soon the biggest of the boys poised himself, shot down into the water, and did not come up. The others stood about, watching. *After a long time* the boy came up on the other side of a big, dark rock, letting the air out of his lungs in a sputtering gasp and a shout of triumph. *Immediately,* the rest of them dived in. *One moment,* the morning seemed full of chattering boys; *the next,* the air and the surface of the water were empty, but through the heavy blue, dark shapes could be seen moving and groping.—DORIS LESSING

The Topic Sentence

Because narrative paragraphs tell a story rather than develop a single idea, they do not always have a topic sentence. In the following paragraph, for example, the writer begins telling her story without making a preliminary controlling statement.

Paul was cutting trees one morning up in Minnesota. He had to get them to the sawmill which was in New Orleans, and he decided that the best way to do it would be by river—but there was no river. So Paul had a light lunch of 19 pounds of sausage, 6 hams, 8 loaves of bread, and 231 flapjacks, and each flapjack was slathered with a pound of butter and a quart of maple syrup. It was a skimpy lunch for Paul, but he figured on eating a hearty supper to make up for it. Paul dug his river that afternoon and he called it the Mississippi, which as far as I know, is what it is called to this day.—BARBARA EMBERLEY

Although this type of paragraph is common, you should practice writing narrative paragraphs *with* topic sentences:

1. *I spent the day wandering aimlessly through the bright streets.* The noisy penny arcades with the gaggle-giggle of sailors and children and the games of chance were tempting. After walking through one of them, though, it was obvious that I could only win more chances and no money. I went to the library and used a part of my day reading science fiction.—MAYA ANGELOU

2. *One day a strange thing happened.* It was spring, and for some reason I had been hot and irritable all morning. It was a beautiful spring. I could feel it as I played barefoot in the backyard. Blossoms hung up from the thorny, black locust trees like clusters of fragrant, white grapes. Butterflies flickered in the sunlight above the short, new dew-wet grass. I had gone into the house for bread and butter, and coming out I heard a steady, unfamiliar drone. It was unlike anything I had ever heard before. I tried to place the sound. It was no use. It was like a sensation I had when searching for my father's watch, heard ticking unseen in a room. It made me feel as though I had forgotten to perform some task that my mother had ordered. Then I lo-

use of a wide variety of transitional words and phrases. Have students use in their paragraphs a minimum of three different transitions from the chart on page 160, if possible. This will help students resist over-reliance on "then" and "and then" to create narrative continuity. When students have finished their rough drafts, have them underline the transitions they used.

Advanced Students

Explain that chronological order does not always start at the beginning of an event and move progressively forward to the end. Ask students for examples of movies or books that start in the middle or at the end of the action and move backward in time (or *flashback*) to previous events. Ask these students to experiment with the form.

Optional Practice

1. Discuss the importance of using strong, vivid verbs in writing narratives. Point out how the repetition of dull, general verbs can weaken a narrative paragraph. Have students think of more vivid synonyms for the following common verbs:

walk, talk, eat, think

2. Type several student narrative paragraphs with the sentences in random order. Distribute the paragraphs and have students arrange the paragraphs in correct chronological order. Suggest that they add transitional devices to clarify the order.

cated it, overhead. In the sky, flying quite low and about a hundred yards off was a plane! It was a little plane, flying no higher than the eaves of our roof. Seeing it come steadily forward, I felt the world grow warm with promise. I would catch the plane as it came over and swing down fast and run into the house before anyone could see me. Then no one could come to claim the plane. It droned nearer. Then, when it hung like a silver cross in the blue directly above me, I stretched out my hand and grabbed. It was like sticking my finger through a soap bubble. The plane flew on, as though I had simply blown my breath after it.—RALPH ELLISON

Exercise Writing Narrative Paragraphs

Choose an interesting incident to write about. The incident may be real or imaginary. Write a narrative paragraph about this incident. Complete the following steps.

Pre-Writing: After selecting your general topic, narrow it by identifying the peak point or points of the experience. Decide how the experience made you or your main character feel. Also decide on the impression you want your readers to have when they have finished reading.

Write a topic sentence that identifies your narrowed topic and the impression you want to give your readers. Select details that help re-create the experience as vividly as possible. Organize the details, using chronological order.

First Draft: Referring to your pre-writing notes, get your ideas down on paper. Remember to use transitional words and phrases to help you re-create the flow of events.

Revision: Go over your rough draft several times. Are the details organized logically? Do any details need to be added or deleted? Have you included vivid words and details that will make your story come alive for your readers? Refer to the Guidelines for the Process of Writing on page 122 for further help with revision. When you are satisfied with your content, use the Checklist on page 123 to help you check sentence structure, spelling, capitalization, and punctuation.

Part 2   The Descriptive Paragraph

A descriptive paragraph paints a word picture that appeals to a reader's senses. The clarity of the word picture depends on carefully selected words and precise details. The writer's purpose and the impression he or she wants to create for an audience guide the selection of those words and details.

Pre-Writing Steps

Selecting Details for a Descriptive Paragraph. In the following example, the writer selected details that appeal to the reader's visual sense.

> The village was a fairly typical one. It consisted of small shacks with walls built out of the jagged offcuts from the sawmill, and whitewashed. Each stood in its own little patch of ground, surrounded by a bamboo fence. The gardens around the shacks were sometimes filled with a strange variety of old tins, kettles, and broken barrels, each brimming over with flowers. Wide ditches full of muddy water separated these "gardens" from the road. The ditches were spanned at each front gate by a small, rickety bridge of roughly nailed branches.—GERALD DURRELL

The writer's purpose was to describe the village so that his audience could clearly visualize it. During the pre-writing stage, he had to decide exactly what he wanted his readers to see. By focusing on the houses and gardens, he narrowed his topic. Then he carefully selected precise details that helped to create a vivid impression of the scene. Follow a similar line of thought as you plan your own paragraphs.

Organizing a Descriptive Paragraph. The details, particularly in visual descriptions, are usually organized in **spatial order.** You will recall that in spatial order, the writer presents details from top to bottom, from side to side, or from near to far. Other methods of organization are possible, however, provided that the order is clear to the readers.

Part 2

Objective

To write a descriptive paragraph using sensory details organized according to spatial order

Presenting the Lesson

1. Read and discuss pages 163–164. Emphasize the importance of choosing details that create a specific impression. Also discuss the necessity of strong transitional devices in this type of paragraph. After going over the chart of **Space Words and Phrases** on page 164, have students read the paragraph by Jack London on page 151 of the previous chapter. Have students point out the most vivid of the details in the paragraph. Then ask them to identify all of the words and phrases that help the reader visualize the spatial relationships in the scene. (On one side, beginning at the very lip, extended to the base, Beyond the pool, ran up and up, here and there, Below, ended, Up the canyon, far, remote, far beyond)

2. Read and discuss the four sample paragraphs on pages 165 and 166. Then ask the students to read the paragraphs by Edward Abbey on page 80. Ask them to describe the spatial organization of Abbey's description. (top, halfway down, top, bottom) Point out that an effective paragraph organization can be a variation on one of the patterns listed on page 165, just as Abbey's paragraphs are a variation on the top-to-bottom organization.

3. Assign Exercise A on page 168. Read the directions with the students to be sure they understand the steps.

4. Read and discuss **Describing a Person**, pages 166–167. Point out that a well-written description usually uses physical details to suggest the psychological and personality traits of the subject.

Have the students read the description of Wheldon on page 167 two or three times. Ask them what kinds of things the author suggests about Wheldon's character that go beyond the physical description. (His paleness, underdevelopment, briefcase, and spectacles suggest a boy who has spent more time on intellectual development than physical. His clothes and hair suggest that his tastes are dominated by an overbearing parent rather than by his peers. His cheerfulness suggests potential for friendship in spite of his unusual appearance.)

5. Assign Exercise B on page 168. Go over the directions with students to be sure they understand the necessary steps in writing a description of a person.

6. Read and discuss **Appealing to the Senses**, pages 169–170. Remind the class that Chapter 4 gives an introduction, examples, and word lists for using the senses in writing.

7. Read through the Exercise on pages 170–171 with the class. Ask each student to write one paragraph from A–E and another paragraph for F. The paragraph they write for F should not emphasize the same sense as the one they stress in the other paragraph. Have students read their paragraphs aloud to a small group for revision suggestions before they write their final draft.

When a writer needs to clarify the order, he or she uses the types of transitional devices shown in the chart below. These space words and phrases follow the description from one place or thing to another.

Transitions relating to space fall into three general categories: those indicating direction, those specifying distance, and those identifying area.

Space Words and Phrases

DIRECTIONS

left	through	around
right	into	between
above	ahead	among
below	behind	in front of
center	across	in back of
up	toward	forward
down	away from	backward
past	against	parallel

DISTANCE

foreground	on the edge of	close to
background	in the center of	next to
first	approximately	leading to
last	twenty feet	far
halfway	about ten miles	near
beyond	twenty kilometers	long
distant	remote	short

AREA OF SPACE

outside	field	hall
inside	plain	stairway
interior	hillside	stage
exterior	acre	alley
lawn	hut	street
garden	villa	road
courtyard	mansion	narrow
park	closet	wide

Following are four descriptive paragraphs. Three have common methods of organization. In the fourth, the writer has followed a unique order. As you read the paragraphs, notice how space words lead you from one place or thing to another.

1. FROM SIDE TO SIDE

The set is magnificent. The left half of the stage depicts a hillside in cherryblossom time with, in the foreground, a garden and thatched entrance gateway. The gateway is freestanding—the fence omitted as superfluous. On the right-hand side is a villa raised off the ground.—WIM SWANN

Notice the use of the space words *left, foreground,* and *right*—all of which lead the reader from one side of the stage to the other. Notice also the many space words that indicate area.

2. FROM TOP TO BOTTOM (OR THE REVERSE)

Ruiz had come to our town about a month before from Seville, in Spain. He was tall, and his shoulders were so wide and powerful that they seemed to be armored in steel instead of muscle. His hair, which was gold-colored, grew thick on his head like a helmet. He had blue eyes, so blue and handsome that anyone would have envied them. His face was handsome, too, except that around his mouth there always lurked the shadow of a sneer.—SCOTT O'DELL

After introducing Ruiz, the writer makes a general statement about his size, emphasizing the man's shoulders. He then leads you down from hair, to eyes, to face, to mouth. This writer does not need to use space words, as the order is clear without them.

3. FROM NEAR TO FAR (OR THE REVERSE)

We drove past a barbed-wire fence, through a gate, and into an open space. There, trunks and sacks and packages had been dumped from the baggage trucks that drove out ahead of us. I could see a few tents set up, the first rows of black barracks, and beyond them, blurred by sand, rows of barracks that seemed to spread for miles across this plain.

—JEANNE WAKATSUKI HOUSTON AND JAMES D. HOUSTON

Less-Advanced Students

1. Before asking students to do Exercise A on page 168, work through one of the topics with the class on the board. Then ask for suggestions on how the other topics might be organized.

2. Before assigning Exercise B on page 168, work through one of the topics with the class on the board. Ask for suggestions for physical details that might indicate aspects of the person's personality. (For example, if a grandfather always dresses in a suit and tie, even for casual occasions, it might suggest that he is rigid in his habits or old-fashioned and out of touch with contemporary customs. On the other hand, if a grandfather wears jeans and jogging shoes it might suggest an extremely youthful outlook.)

3. Before assigning the Exercise on pages 170–171, work through one of each of the topics on the board. Ask students for suggestions of specific details and sense words to make each description come alive.

Advanced Students

Have students take three of the paragraphs they have written for this section—a place, a person, and a sense or description—and work them into one single story. The results may be a little unusual, or comical in some cases. Have them read their stories to the class.

Optional Practice

Remind students of the comparisons in the descriptive paragraphs in this section: "rubbery flesh," "the mountain of her brow," "as white as a sheet in a TV ad," "more delicious than the butter from the gussak store," "seemed to be armored in steel instead of muscle."

Encourage students to use imaginative comparisons in their own writing. Have students complete each comparison below for practice. Have several volunteers read their comparisons to the class.

fresher than a _____
as tired as _____
her hands were like _____
a voice that was louder than _____
as brilliant as _____
as cuddly as _____
not as small as _____

Extending the Lesson

Have the class read the following paragraphs by Eudora Welty and discuss them. Which of the techniques covered in this section does each one illustrate?

It was quiet in the waiting room of the remote little station, except for the night sounds of insects. You could hear their embroidering movements in the weeds outside, which somehow gave the effect of some tenuous voice in the night, telling a story. Or you could listen to the fat thudding of the light bugs and the hoarse rushing of their big wings against the wooden ceiling. Some of the bugs were clinging heavily to the yellow globe, like idiot bees to a senseless smell. (Sensory description—sound)

That's Mr. Marblehall. He has short white bangs, and a bit of snapdragon in his lapel. He walks with a big polished stick, a present, That's what people think of him. Everybody says to his face, "So well preserved!" Behind

The writers begin with a description of the scene nearest them. They then draw your attention to "a few tents," to "the first rows of black barracks," to "rows of barracks that seemed to spread for miles across this plain," using space words such as *past, through, into, first,* and *beyond.*

4. UNIQUE ORDER

Our first camp in Glen Canyon is almost unimaginably beautiful. The site is a sandstone ledge below two arched caves. Clear cliffs soar up behind the caves. Just below the camp is the masked entrance of Hidden Passage Canyon. Its outthrust masking wall throws a strong shadow against the cliffs. Beyond this masking wall is the kind of canyon that is almost commonplace here, but that anywhere else would be a wonder.

—WALLACE STEGNER

The writer first explains that the camp is located below two caves, behind which are cliffs. He next describes the scene below the camp. His description moves back to the cliffs, then down again to the scene below. The writer uses space words and phrases to eliminate any confusion from these changes in direction.

Describing a Person

Describing a person is different from describing a place or a thing. The writer's purpose is to capture the essence of a person by going beyond physical characteristics.

Example 1

The writer of the following description, for example, selects words and details that reveal much about the inner reality of the woman being described.

She was a big, awkward woman, with big bones and hard, rubbery flesh. Her short arms ended in ham hands, and her neck was a squat roll of fat that protruded behind her head as a big bump. Her skin was rough and puffy, with plump, mole-like freckles down her cheeks. Her eyes glowered from under the mountain of her brow and were circled with expensive mauve shadow. They were nervous and quick when she was flustered and darted about at nothing in particular while she was dressing hair or talking to people.—ALICE WALKER

With phrases such as "rubbery flesh," "ham hands," and "squat roll," the writer creates an overall impression of ugliness. She notes the woman's "expensive mauve shadow," which hints at vanity. She uses words such as *glowered, nervous, quick,* and *darted* to imply suspicion and insecurity.

The writer makes the woman come alive for the reader. She paints a picture of an interesting, complex human being.

Example 2

Here is another description, this time of a young boy. Try to determine how the writer has made his description so colorful.

> When Wheldon first arrived at our school, he was carrying a natty little briefcase and wore a pink spotted tie and short trousers. His long, thin face was as white as a sheet in a TV ad, and his eyes were so watery behind his huge spectacles that gazing into them was like looking out of the portholes of a sinking ship. He had collapsed shoulders almost meeting under his chin, and his hair looked as if each separate strand had been carefully glued into place, ready for church. He reminded me of a cheerful but undernourished sheep.
>
> —PETER JONES

The writer has used descriptive words such as *natty, pink spotted, watery,* and *collapsed.* He has also incorporated several direct and indirect comparisons into the description:

He compares the color of the boy's face to a sheet in a TV ad.
He equates gazing into the boy's eyes with looking out of the portholes of a sinking ship.
He compares the boy to an undernourished sheep.

Like the writer of the previous description, this writer has presented a physical description that reveals inner qualities as well. Can you describe in your own words some of these qualities?

his back they say cheerfully, "One foot in the grave." He has on his thick, beautiful glowing coat—tweed, but he looks as gratified as an animal in its own tingling fur. You see, even in summer he wears it, because he is cold all the time. He looks quaintly secretive and prepared for anything, out walking very luxuriously on Catherine Street. (Description of a person with internal characteristics emphasized through external details)

Across the end of the road, crumbling under her eyes, was a two-story building with a remnant of gallery, and that was Jenny's destination. The store and the post office were in the one used room. Across the tin awning hung the moss icicles with which the postmaster had decorated for Christmas. Over the door was the shriveled mistletoe, and the gun that had shot it down still standing in the corner. Tipped back against the front wall sat five old men in their chairs, with one holding the white cat. On the step, Son Alford was playing his mandolin that had been Jenny's mother's and given away. He was singing his fast song. (Spatial organization)

Exercises Writing Descriptive Paragraphs

A. Choose a topic from the box or make up one of your own. Write a descriptive paragraph. Complete each of the steps below.

Possible Topics
1. An interesting building in your home town
2. The waiting area in an airport or train station
3. A machine shop or car repair garage
4. The check-out counter of a store
5. A doctor's or dentist's office
6. An interesting piece of art

Pre-Writing: Narrow your topic by selecting a specific place or thing to describe. What impression do you want to create? What details will reinforce this impression? What organization will you use?

First Draft: Use your pre-writing notes to get your ideas down on paper. Use vivid words that will help your reader "see" your subject.

Revision: Go over your rough draft several times. Can you add space words and phrases to help with unity? Can you add more precise words and phrases to make your description more vivid? When you are satisfied with the content, check sentence structure, spelling, and mechanics. Refer to the Guidelines on pages 122 and 180.

B. Choose a topic from the box or make one up. Write a paragraph describing a person. Complete the steps on the next page.

Possible Topics
1. An interesting person you have known
2. A character in a movie
3. A grandparent
4. An unusual individual you noticed on the street
5. A singer
6. The host on a TV game show

Pre-Writing: Narrow the topic by selecting a *specific* person. Decide exactly what qualities you wish to reveal about the person. What details will help communicate these qualities? What would be the best organization for these details?

First Draft: Use your pre-writing notes to get your ideas down on paper.

Revision: Go over your rough draft several times. Does every detail reinforce what you wish to reveal about the character? Can you add other details that will tell even more about the physical appearance or personality of the character? Check for spelling, punctuation, and capitalization errors. Refer to the Guidelines on pages 122 and 180.

Appealing to the Senses

Thus far, the examples of description have appealed only to the sense of sight. Descriptive paragraphs may also appeal to the other senses, either individually or in combination. Following are five paragraphs, four of which appeal to a single sense and one of which appeals to two senses. As you read, pay particular attention to the vivid language each writer uses.

SOUND

Through the window next to her chair she heard the household noises as sounds on a distant stage. There was Father's pipe clacking against the ashtray, and the rustle of his newspaper. There was a small boy throwing books onto a chair, and the cookie jar thudding onto tile.—ROSEMARIE BODENHEIMER

TASTE

Gradually the peat glowed, the water boiled, and an hour later Miyax had a pot of caribou stew. On it floated great chunks of golden grease, more delicious than the butter from the gussak store. She put a savory bite into her mouth, sucked the juices, then chewed a long time before she swallowed.

—JEAN CRAIGHEAD GEORGE

TOUCH

A few months ago, on her sixteenth birthday, Mr. Dale had given Muffin a new, wide suede watchband. Lately, she found herself rubbing the velvety leather, letting her fingers smooth the fine, sleek texture, but then suddenly dragging her fingers backward against the grain, feeling the bits of leather recoil.

—SHARON BELL MATHIS

SMELL

The filthy streets are seldom cleaned. The inaccessible alleys and rear yards are never touched, and in the hot summer months the stench of rotting things will mark these places. Here and there an unwitting newcomer tries the disastrous experiment of keeping a goat, adding thereby to the distinctive flavor of the neighborhood.

COMBINATION

Early morning is a time of magic in Cannery Row. In the gray time after the light has come and before the sun has risen, the Row seems to hang suspended out of time in a silvery light. The street lights go out, and the weeds are a brilliant green. The corrugated iron of the canneries glows with the pearly lucence of platinum or old pewter. No automobiles are running then. The street is silent of progress and business. The rush and drag of the waves can be heard as they splash in among the piles of the canneries. It is a time of great peace, a deserted time, a little era of rest. —JOHN STEINBECK

Exercises Using the Senses in Describing

A. Write a paragraph describing the *sound* of an item below. (For all the exercises in this section, remember to follow all of the steps of the process of writing.)

1. A jet landing	5. A ticking clock
2. Eating potato chips	6. A crying baby
3. A cricket	7. Traffic on a city street
4. A police siren	8. A musical group

B. Write a paragraph describing the *taste* of an item below.

1. A hot pepper
2. Root beer
3. An apple
4. A lemon
5. A pickle
6. Peanut butter
7. Fresh mushrooms
8. Vanilla ice cream

C. Write a paragraph describing the *feeling* of an item below.

1. Walking barefoot
2. Snow down your back
3. Sandpaper
4. A foot falling asleep
5. An electric shock
6. Burning your finger
7. Petting a dog or cat
8. Drinking ice water

D. Write a paragraph describing the *smell* of an item below.

1. A barbecue
2. A bouquet
3. A dentist's office
4. A stale garbage can
5. Frying hamburgers
6. A school gymnasium
7. A laundromat
8. A crowded room

E. Write a paragraph in which you use a *combination of senses* to describe an item below.

1. A cut finger
2. Eating a raw carrot
3. A rainy afternoon
4. A football game
5. A classroom
6. A child crying
7. Riding a bicycle
8. A forest trail

F. Select one of the following statements as the topic sentence for a paragraph. Write a short description in which you create a single sensory impression.

1. The scene before me was one of total dreariness.
2. The room was bright with color.
3. The street was a carnival of activity.
4. The delicious smells made my mouth water.
5. The outfit was as crazy as the wearer.
6. I had never seen him so angry.
7. He was trying to make lunch for the children.
8. The room was an absolute mess.

Objective

To write four types of explanatory paragraphs: the paragraph that explains a process, the paragraph that defines, the paragraph that gives reasons, and the paragraph that persuades

Presenting the Lesson

1. Read the introduction and **The Paragraph That Explains a Process** on pages 172–173. Ask the students if they would be able to grow bean sprouts after reading the sample paragraph. Mention that this is a good test for an effective explanation of a process. Apply the same test to the first paragraph on page 173. Ask students if they would know how to open a hallway door during a fire. Point out that the second paragraph on page 173 is not meant to be used as instructions. It is written to convey information only.

2. Assign the Exercise on page 174. Emphasize the importance of a logical, step-by-step sequence in writing an effective explanation of a process.

3. Read and discuss **The Paragraph That Defines**. The use of the term *definition* as a paragraph type may be new to most students. Have them imagine situations in which defining a term at length is useful or necessary.

Point out that formal definitions place a word in a general category and then differentiate the word from other members of the category. Informal definitions, on the other

Part 3 The Explanatory Paragraph

A friend asks how to write up a science experiment, and you give instructions. A foreign exchange student wants to know what Thanksgiving is, and you define it. Your parents want to know why you want to join the soccer team, and you give them reasons. Although your purposes are somewhat different, in each of these situations you are being asked to do the same thing—explain something.

Explanations are often oral. However, they can also be written. When a written explanation takes the form of a paragraph, it is called an explanatory, or expository, paragraph. There are three main types of explanatory paragraphs:

those that explain a process
those that define
those that give reasons

The Paragraph That Explains a Process

In its simplest form, the explanatory paragraph is used to explain a process. It may tell how something is done or how something works. The following paragraph, for example, gives clear, accurate instructions on how to grow bean sprouts.

Here's a quick and easy way to grow bean sprouts. Put about two tablespoons of bean seeds into a wide-mouthed jar and cover with at least three-quarters of a cup of warm water. Let the seeds soak overnight. In the morning, drain the water off the swollen seeds and rinse them with warm water. Drain well and return to the jar. Cover the jar with two layers of cheesecloth held in place with a rubber band. Keep the jar in a dark place. Rinse the seeds with warm water morning and night. The sprouts will be about one inch long in two to three days. When they are one to two inches long, place them in the refrigerator to stop growth. You can eat the entire sprout—root, seed, and if there are some, the tiny leaves. —BARBARA AND D.X. FENTEN

When you are composing a paragraph that explains a process, your pre-writing notes should list all of the facts necessary for the successful completion or understanding of the process. Since most paragraphs that explain a process are organized in chronological order, the next pre-writing step would be to number your facts using this method. As you write the first draft, include transitional words and phrases to make the order of the ideas even more definite. Notice the clear order of the following two paragraphs.

1   During a fire, opening a hallway door to attempt an escape can be dangerous. To minimize the risks, take these simple precautions. First, touch the door. A hot door means danger. Do not open it. If the door is not hot, brace your foot against the bottom and carefully open the door about an inch. If you feel pressure against the door or an in-rush of heat and fire, close the door at once. If there is no pressure or heat, open the door wide enough to look into the hall. An absence of fire and extreme heat means that the hallway is safe. You can proceed rapidly through it to the outside.

2   Video cassette recorders are becoming increasingly popular in American homes, yet few people understand how they work. Actually, the basic principles are quite simple. A television program is made up of sound and light patterns. These patterns are transmitted by converting them into electric waves. The waves can then be channeled into the video recorder. There, they magnetize the recording head of the machine which, in turn, transfers the pattern to a special magnetic tape. This tape, a thin plastic ribbon coated on one side with iron oxide or some other easily magnetized material, records the magnetic pattern from the recording head. When the process is reversed, the patterns are converted back into electric waves. The electric waves are then turned back into the sound and light of the television program.

In these paragraphs, the steps of the process are presented in the order in which they should be followed or the order in which they occur.

hand, simply give the writer's personal views on the meaning of a word. For example, the word "love" or "friendship" cannot be strictly defined. Each person has his or her own personal definition.

4. Ask students whether the paragraph on jai alai is a formal or an informal definition. (It is formal because it places the word in a large category, "games," and then lists characteristics that distinguish it from other games.)

5. Assign the Exercise on page 175–176. Ask students which of the topics in the box could not be answered with a formal definition. (a good friend) Which of the topics could be answered with a formal definition or an informal definition? (a grandparent)

6. Read and discuss **The Paragraph That Gives Reasons**, pages 176–177. Emphasize the importance of a strong topic sentence and solid supporting details. You may wish to refer students to Chapter 13, "Critical Thinking," for more discussion on supporting ideas and opinions.

7. Assign the Exercise on page 177. Tell students that, in writing their first drafts, they should remain open to new reasons which occur to them. In revising their paragraphs, they should check for coherence by mentally inserting "because" before each supporting statement.

8. Read and discuss **The Paragraph That Persuades**, pages 178–179. Explain that the difference between this type of paragraph and other paragraphs that give reasons is that a persuasive paragraph attempts to sway readers who may not agree with the writer's ideas. It does this by presenting a definite stand on an issue and offering logical support for that stance. Emphasize that harsh or unreasonable language is *not* a good means of support.

9. Assign the Exercise on page 179.

Individualizing the Lesson

Less-Advanced Students

1. Emphasize that clarity is the most important quality of a paragraph that explains a process. Have each student check for clarity by exchanging first drafts with a classmate and imagining that he or she must follow the steps outlined in the paragraph. Advise students to correct any confusion by making sure that they have included all important steps and have used clear chronological order and appropriate transitions.

2. Before assigning the Exercises on pages 175, 177, or 179, work through one of the topics on the chalkboard with the students. Be sure they understand how to proceed in narrowing a topic and writing the various drafts of the paragraph.

Advanced Students

1. Have students write one paragraph to explain a process for a reader to follow for informational purposes only. Write the following additional topics, which may require some research, on the board.

  a. Explain how the Dewey Decimal system of cataloging books works. (You may refer students to Chapter 14.)

Exercise Writing To Explain a Process

Choose a topic from the box or make up your own. Write a paragraph explaining a process. Complete each of the steps below.

Possible Topics

1. Explain how to find information in the Yellow Pages of the telephone directory.
2. Tell how to adjust a television set.
3. Explain how to repair a flat bicycle tire.
4. Describe how a pencil sharpener or some other simple machine works.
5. Choose a park, a building, a shopping center, or an historical site in your area. Write a paragraph telling how to get there from your house.
6. Explain how a three-speed bicycle works.

Pre-Writing: Narrow your subject and write a topic sentence that indicates your specific topic, purpose, and audience. What are the steps of the process? In what order should they be presented?

First Draft: Use your pre-writing notes to get your ideas down on paper. Include all the details your reader would need to understand the process completely.

Revision: Go over your rough draft several times. Are your instructions or descriptions clear? Has anything been left out? Are there any errors in spelling, usage, or mechanics?

The Paragraph That Defines

Clear definitions help a person to understand new words, things, and ideas. Expanding upon the short "dictionary definition," a paragraph of definition first places the term to be defined in a general category, and then identifies several distinguishing characteristics of the term. These characteristics help to separate the term being defined from others closely related to it.

To explain Thanksgiving to a foreign exchange student, for example, you might begin by identifying it as an American holiday. Next you would give identifying characteristics of this holiday, such as its origin, its traditions, its purpose, and its date of observance. These details would differentiate Thanksgiving from other holidays such as Labor Day or Independence Day.

Generally, the details in a paragraph of definition are organized from most general to most specific:

> Jai alai is a fast-paced game that closely resembles handball. It is popular in many parts of Latin America and in Florida. Jai alai is played with a small, hard ball, called a *pelota,* and a basketlike container, called a *cesta,* which is strapped to the player's arm. The game is played on a court that has high walls on three sides. The server hits the ball against the wall by hurling it from the curved end of the *cesta.* The opponent must catch the ball in his or her *cesta* either before it hits the floor or on the first bounce. The opponent then hurls the ball back against the wall, and the server must try to catch it. Play continues until one player misses the ball.

This paragraph begins by placing jai alai in a larger category, games. The sentences that follow give specific characteristics that distinguish jai alai from other games. Often, defining paragraphs include a physical description as well as an explanation of the term's function, purpose, or use.

Exercise Writing a Definition

Choose a topic from the box or make up your own. Write a paragraph of definition. Complete each of the steps on the next page.

Possible Topics

1. An unusual animal
2. A grandparent
3. A good friend
4. A sand dune
5. Jazz
6. A dirt bike
7. A hologram
8. A board game

---

b. Explain how hail or snow is formed.
c. Explain how the British game of cricket is played.
d. Explain how to change the tire of a car.
e. Explain how a battery works.

2. After students have written their persuasive paragraphs, ask them to list any arguments they can think of on the opposite side of the issue. Ask them to consider whether their paragraph takes into account the other side's point of view honestly and fairly. They direct them to write another paragraph arguing the opposite position from the one they took in their first paragraphs.

Optional Practice

1. To make sure students understand the process of defining a term, write the following topics on the board. Have students put each item into its general category and then list distinguishing characteristics.

sofa
train
measles
skyscraper

2. Tell students that the following sentences appeared in persuasion paragraphs. Ask them whether sentences like these strengthen or weaken the author's argument.

a. I think everyone should vote for Barbara Farley because anyone who doesn't is obviously stupid and prejudiced.
b. Fellini is the best movie director ever to have lived. All of his movies are timeless masterpieces that are flawlessly directed and will endure forever.
c. Only old people who are too feeble to enjoy rock think that classical music is entertaining.

d. Cats are the best housepets for apartment dwellers. Birds are boring, fish are even more boring, and dogs always cause problems with barking and disturbing the neighbors.

(All of the statements are biased and overstated. They would weaken the writer's argument.)

3. Have the student write a persuasive letter to the local newspaper or to a local politician. Students should choose issues about which they have strong feelings. They should support their opinions with logical, carefully thought-out reasons.

Extending the Lesson

Remind students that one most familiar source for paragraphs that describe processes is a cookbook. Have students criticize the following recipe and rewrite it so that the reader can follow the directions easily.

Chocolate Chip Cookies

Drop the batter from a teaspoon onto a cookie sheet and bake the cookies in the oven until they are brown.

You need ½ cup of chocolate chips if you are making 4 dozen cookies. You also should add ½ cup of chopped walnuts.

The oven needs to be preheated to 375° for 10 minutes before you put the cookies in to bake.

Also, the cookie sheet must be buttered before you drop the batter onto it and the cookies have to be at least 2 inches apart because that is how big the cookies will be.

To make the batter, mix brown sugar and white sugar in even proportions so you have a total of 1 cup. Mix

Pre-Writing: Decide whether the term to be defined is specific enough to be explained in one paragraph, or whether it needs to be narrowed further. To what general class does your subject belong? What are its identifying features? What is the best method of organization?

First Draft: Use your pre-writing notes to get your ideas on paper. Use precise words to present your subject's characteristics clearly.

Revision: Go over your rough draft several times. Did you state a general category for your term? Do the characteristics you chose help to distinguish your term from closely related ones? Do your facts or examples illustrate your characteristics? When your definition is complete, carefully check your paper for mechanical correctness.

The Paragraph That Gives Reasons

Whenever you try to explain why something is, or why something should be, you are composing an explanatory paragraph that gives reasons. You say that something happens *because* something else occurred first, or that an action or idea is right *because* certain facts or reasons logically support it.

For this type of writing, it is especially important to design a good topic sentence that clearly states your topic and reflects your purpose. Often, the topic sentence of this type of paragraph is a statement of opinion: It presents your personal view on a subject. Such a statement needs strong reasons to support it.

Many types of details can be used to develop a paragraph that gives reasons. You may use facts, statistics, examples, or anecdotes. Choose these details carefully. They should provide logical support for your topic sentence. They then become evidence of the truth of your topic sentence.

In a paragraph that gives reasons, organization is closely related to both the purpose and the type of development.

In spite of claims of a "fitness boom," most Americans do not get enough exercise to be considered physically fit. A recent U.S. Department of Health and Human Services study supports this claim. It reports that nearly two-thirds of American adults did not engage in enough regular exercise to achieve fitness. Our lifestyle is a major cause of this lack of physical activity. Given a choice, we often prefer to watch television rather than play an active sport, and we are more likely to take an elevator than to climb the stairs. Secondly, a majority of American adults are only "weekend exercisers." They engage in physical activity only when it does not conflict with the daily routine of work or school. Finally, even those Americans who do participate in sports may achieve only partial fitness. For instance, sports such as bowling or softball are more for socializing than they are for fitness. Even conditioning sports such as basketball and tennis are stop-and-go activities. They are less helpful in achieving overall fitness than sustained aerobic exercises such as swimming or jogging.

In the topic sentence, the writer states that most Americans are physically unfit. She then gives three reasons which support this statement. Her last reason is her strongest because it explains how even people who participate in sports may not be totally fit.

Exercise Giving Reasons

Choose a topic from the box or make up your own. Write a paragraph giving reasons. Complete each step on the next page.

Possible Topics

1. A new wrist watch you have had for only a few days has already stopped running three times. You have decided to send the watch back to the company for a refund. Write a one-paragraph letter to the company, explaining why you are returning the watch.

2. You have just read a help-wanted ad for a job that interests you. Write a one-paragraph letter to the company, explaining why you are qualified for the job.

3. In a paragraph, explain something you like or don't like.

4. Think of a book, movie, or song that you enjoyed. Write a "review," telling why you thought it was good.

---

the sugar into butter with the back of a large spoon. You need $\frac{1}{2}$ cup of softened butter.

Beat 1 egg and $\frac{1}{2}$ teaspoon of vanilla into the sugar and butter, but beat the egg first. Then mix in a cup of flour, $\frac{1}{2}$ teaspoon of salt and $\frac{1}{2}$ teaspoon of baking powder. Sift all of the dry ingredients before you mix them in. Then add the chocolate chips and walnuts, and bake.

The cookies should be brown in about 10 minutes.

(Answers will vary, but the revised version should be something like the following:

Chocolate Chip Cookies

Makes 4 dozen 2-inch cookies

$\frac{1}{2}$ cup	softened butter
$\frac{1}{2}$ cup	brown sugar
$\frac{1}{2}$ cup	white sugar
1 egg	beaten
$\frac{1}{2}$ tsp.	vanilla
1 cup	flour
$\frac{1}{2}$ tsp.	salt
$\frac{1}{2}$ tsp.	baking powder
$\frac{1}{2}$ cup	chocolate chips
$\frac{1}{2}$ cup	chopped walnuts

Preheat the oven to 375° for at least 10 minutes.

Blend the sugars into the softened butter with the back of a large spoon; then beat in the egg and vanilla. Sift the flour, salt and baking powder, and mix into the other ingredients. Add the chocolate chips and chopped nuts.

Butter the cookie sheets and drop the batter in teaspoonfuls at least two inches apart on the sheets. Bake for about 10 minutes until brown.)

Point out to the students how much easier it is to follow directions when they are organized into logical, step-by-step order.

Pre-Writing: Write a topic sentence that states an idea or opinion that needs to be supported by reasons. The sentence should also reflect your narrowed topic, your purpose, and your audience. What reasons could be used to support your topic? What details can help develop these reasons? What method of organization would be most effective?

First Draft: Using your pre-writing notes, get your ideas down on paper. You may think of better supporting reasons as you write. Include them.

Revision: Go over your rough draft several times. Check for coherence by imagining a "because" in front of every piece of evidence you use. If you can logically link each piece of evidence to your topic sentence with a "because," your paragraph has coherence. Then check further. Are your reasons fully explained? Are your reasons organized to have the best effect on the reader? Remember to do a final check for errors in grammar, usage, and mechanics.

The Paragraph That Persuades

A paragraph of persuasion is a special type of paragraph that gives reasons. A paragraph of persuasion usually contains a signal of its purpose in the topic sentence. The sentence will be worded so that a definite opinion is given on an issue that has two or more sides. It may also contain words such as *should* or *ought to*, or words that express a judgment about a thing or idea.

The reasons in a persuasive paragraph must be chosen and organized carefully because your purpose is to persuade others who may not agree with the idea you are expressing. Facts and statistics provide strong support, but examples and incidents may also be used effectively. The reasons in a persuasive paragraph are often organized from the least important to the most important. This helps to build strong support for the opinion, and leaves your reader with your strongest reason freshly in mind.

When you write a persuasive paragraph, use reasonable language. Do not make unfair remarks or use harsh, slanted language. Let your reasons make your point. See Chapter 13, "Critical Thinking," for a discussion on logical argument.

"The first black mayor." "The first woman astronaut." Such phrases are common on TV, in newspapers and magazines, and in casual conversation. It is time we made them obsolete. First of all, a person's race, sex, or religion has nothing to do with whether he or she is qualified for a certain position. What does matter is whether the individual has mastered the skills and knowledge necessary to perform the job well. If this is the case, labels such as the ones mentioned only make the qualifications seem less important. Moreover, our society should be beyond the point where such distinctions are something that we even notice. If a police chief is a Latino, or a senator a Jew, these facts should be as unimportant as hair color or height. Only when we stop pointing out these characteristics will we be close to the time when we are no longer aware of them.

Exercise Writing To Persuade

Choose one of the topics from the box or make up one of your own. Write a persuasive paragraph. Complete the steps below.

Possible Topics

1. _____ music is _____.
2. TV has a beneficial/harmful effect on young children.
3. _____ is a good/bad book because _____.
4. The news media are/are not effective in reporting events.
5. The driving age should be raised/lowered.
6. Air pollution is/is not a serious issue.

Pre-Writing: Narrow your topic to a specific issue and write a topic sentence that identifies your opinion. What reasons support your opinion? Which of these are most effective?

First Draft: Use your pre-writing notes to get your ideas down on paper. Use well thought-out reasons and reasonable language.

Revision: Go over your rough draft several times. Is your opinion clearly stated? Do all your reasons logically support your opinion? Have you included specific details to support your claims? Have you arranged your reasons in the most effective order?

Guidelines for Writing and Revising Paragraphs

These Guidelines will help to remind you of the qualities necessary for good paragraphs. However, your writing procedure should also include the steps in Guidelines for the Process of Writing on page 122.

1. Does the paragraph deal with only one main idea?

2. Does the topic sentence state the main idea?

3. Does the topic sentence control and limit the ideas that are discussed in the rest of the paragraph?

4. Does the paragraph have unity and coherence?

5. Are there enough details — facts, statistics, examples, incidents, or anecdotes — to develop the paragraph fully?

6. If it is a narrative paragraph, is it developed in chronological order? Does it use time words and phrases?

7. If it is a descriptive paragraph, does it use vivid sensory details? Does it present these details in a logical order? Does it use space words and phrases? If the paragraph describes a person, does it try to capture the essence of the person? Does it appeal to the senses?

8. If it is an explanatory paragraph, does it clearly explain a process? give reasons? define? Is the supporting material presented in an effective order? Is the purpose of the paragraph clear to the reader?

SUMMARY AND APPLICATIONS

CHAPTER 9

1. There are three main types of paragraphs: narrative, descriptive, and explanatory.

2. Narrative paragraphs relate events. They can be written in the first or third person, and are generally organized in chronological order.

3. Descriptive paragraphs create word pictures through the use of sensory details. These details are usually organized in spatial order.

4. Explanatory, or expository, paragraphs can explain a process, give definitions, or offer reasons to support an idea. The most common methods of organization for this type of writing are most familiar to least familiar idea, and least important to most important idea.

5. Different topics require different types of paragraphs. Whenever you are writing for any of your classes, choose types of paragraphs that are appropriate to your material.

Applications in Other Subject Areas

Science. Explanatory paragraphs are extremely common in scientific writing. Using a science textbook or an encyclopedia, collect information on one of the following terms. Then, write a paragraph that explains or defines it.

Photosynthesis   The Doppler Effect   Oxidation

Fine Arts. Choose an area of the fine arts—drama, music, dance, or art—and write three paragraphs about that general topic, as follows:

a. Describe an exciting or embarrassing incident connected with the subject (your first recital, for example).
b. Describe an effective example of that art (a striking sculpture, a haunting melody).
c. Explain how to perform an activity in that area (a dance step, a dramatic monologue).

Math. Choose a difficult problem in your math book. Write a paragraph explaining how the problem could be solved.

181

Summary and Applications

Discuss this summary with the class. Point out the importance of selecting the right type of paragraph to suit a specific purpose.

Encourage students to use this summary for review, or as part of the SQ3R method of study (see Chapter 15). Remind them, though, that more specific points can only be reviewed by skimming the chapter itself.

Applications in Other Subject Areas

1. Read and discuss the **Science** activity. Add the following terms for the students to consider:

a. Astigmatism
b. Titration
c. Solar eclipse

2. Allow the students to substitute another general area for the **Fine Arts** activity. They may work the three types of paragraph for one of the topics below

a. an historical event
b. a biographical sketch
c. a new type of automobile

3. For the **Mathematics** activity tell the students to imagine that they are explaining the problem, or a specific technique, to someone who was absent when the material was discussed in class.

Chapter 10

Writing a Composition

From your work in Chapters 8 and 9, you know that paragraphs may be developed in several ways. Despite these variations, you may have felt limited as to what you could accomplish in the space of a single paragraph. For this reason, the different types of paragraphs are seldom used alone. Instead, they are usually combined in larger pieces of writing called **compositions**.

A composition provides you with the opportunity to explore many different aspects of an idea. Before you can do so, however, you must have a good understanding of how a composition works. In this Chapter, you will study the different parts of a composition. You will also learn how you can apply your knowledge of the writing process to take advantage of the possibilities this type of writing offers.

Part 1   Defining a Composition

The definition of a composition is only slightly different from that of a paragraph.

A paragraph is a group of sentences dealing with a single topic or idea. Usually, one sentence, called the topic sentence, states the main idea. All the other sentences are related to this topic sentence. They further explain or support the main idea.

A **composition** is a group of paragraphs dealing with a single topic or idea. Usually, one paragraph, called the introductory paragraph, states the main idea of the composition. All the other paragraphs are related to the introductory paragraph. They further explain or support the main idea.

A composition has three main parts: the introductory paragraph, the body, and the conclusion.

The **introductory paragraph** is similar to the topic sentence of a paragraph. It presents the main idea of the composition.

The **body**, or middle paragraphs, support the main idea.

The **conclusion**, or final paragraph, may perform one or more of the following tasks: It may restate the main idea. It may summarize the information that has been presented in the preceding paragraphs. It may also make a final comment on the information that has been given. The three parts all work together to develop a single topic or idea, the subject of the composition.

Here is an example of a composition.

Television

We sometimes find it difficult to think of our television sets as mere pieces of machinery. They greet us with news and music in the morning, entertain us in the evening, and soothe us to sleep at night. They are an important part of the world in which we live.

Television has had great influence on the feelings and beliefs of contemporary Americans. It has affected our feelings about politics by bringing us face to face with the candidates. It has affected our feelings about violence in our cities by giv-

Part 1

Objective

To understand the characteristics of a composition

Presenting the Lesson

1. Read the definition of a composition on page 183. Discuss the functions of the three main parts of a composition.

2. Read the sample composition, "Television." Point out that the introductory paragraph states a topic that could not have been satisfactorily developed in one paragraph. Have students discuss how each subsequent paragraph further develops the main idea of the introductory paragraph, that television is an important part of our world.

Individualizing the Lesson

Less-Advanced Students

Make sure students understand the similarities between the paragraph, with which they are familiar, and the composition. Suggest that they restrict themselves to writing five-paragraph compositions for your class. This allows for sufficient development of a topic, but is a more manageable length for a beginning writer.

Advanced Students

Have students review two or three paragraphs that they have written for previous chapters and decide whether the topics they developed could be expanded in a composition. Emphasize the greater freedom and latitude that the longer form offers to a writer. Do not restrict these students to a five-paragraph format. Allow them to develop ideas as thoroughly as they wish.

Optional Practice

Have the students point out the topic sentence of each paragraph in the essay "Television." (These will be the first sentence in each paragraph.) Discuss unity and coherence in each paragraph. Then have students discuss how each paragraph relates to the introductory paragraph of the composition, and discuss the concepts of unity and coherence in the composition.

Extending the Lesson

Have each student bring to class an article from a magazine or newspaper of at least five paragraphs. Divide the class into small groups to exchange and read the articles. Then lead a discussion on the differences (content, purpose, intended audience) and similarities (introduction, body, conclusion, unity, coherence) in these professional "compositions."

ing us close-up views of the disorders. Finally, it has affected our feelings about war by bringing the ugliness and the pain of the battlefields into our living rooms.

Television has increased our general level of education through news coverage, special reports, and talk shows, as well as with educational programming. Teachers, acknowledging the importance of television, have brought both public and closed circuit broadcasts into many classrooms.

Television has greatly affected the popular arts. Despite some of its poor drama, television has actually encouraged the production of several good plays. By offering entertainment that competes with movie theaters and by showing movies, television has stimulated the movie industry to produce films that are destined for the home screen. Television has also affected the book publishing industry. By raising the general level of public knowledge, TV encourages people to buy books. On the other hand, it lures some people away from books by providing a competitive source of entertainment and escape.

The inferiority of so many television programs stems from the economic forces that control the industry. Most broadcasting in this country is commercial; it is paid for by advertisers. Programs are selected and retained, not for their quality but for the number of viewers they can reach and convert into customers. This practice of programming for immediate financial advantage has, thus far, prevented television from realizing its full educational and cultural potential.

—RISSOVER AND BIRCH

The introductory paragraph tells you that the composition is going to be about television in our lives. The next three paragraphs explain this idea by giving the following information.

1. The political and social influence of television
2. The impact of television on education
3. The effect of television on the popular arts

The final paragraph comments on the economic factors that have limited television's potential influence on the political, social, educational, and artistic aspects of American life. Each paragraph develops in some way the main idea of the composition.

Part 2 Pre-Writing: Deciding on a Subject

The first step in writing a composition is to choose a subject. When you are doing so, keep these three guidelines in mind:

1. *Choose a subject that interests you.* This is important. Without interest on your part, you will have a difficult time creating interest on the part of your readers.
2. *Choose a subject that is familiar to you.* You will then be able to write with confidence about your subject.
3. *Choose a subject that has value for you.* You will then communicate something of value to your readers.

Your best source of subjects that are interesting, familiar, and valuable is your own feelings, ideas, knowledge, and memories. Your journal is a good source for this type of subject. Brainstorming is another way to search your mind for ideas. Of course, you should not overlook other people as a source of subjects for writing. Discussion and interviews with others can yield a rich store of subject ideas for your composition. In general, these personal subjects fall into two groups.

1. Subjects based on first-hand experiences and knowledge
2. Subjects based on imagination

Subjects Based on First-Hand Experiences

You are an individual. No one else in the world is exactly like you. No one has lived the same life as you. No one has had the same experiences or the same feelings. Your experiences, therefore, are a good source for unique composition subjects. They can also lead to many different types of writing.

Subjects based on things that have happened to you are likely to meet the three guidelines for choosing subjects. They are interesting because they are drawn from your own life. They are familiar because they are part of you. They are valuable because your experiences and feelings help to make you the person you are, and thus may help others understand you better.

Part 2

Objective

To use first-hand experiences and/or imagination to discover a subject for a composition

Presenting the Lesson

1. Read **Deciding on a Subject**, page 185. Discuss the three guidelines for choosing a subject for a composition (interest, familiarity, value). Emphasize that an exciting topic is likely to lead to an interesting and worthwhile composition. Review the pre-writing techniques listed on page 122 in Chapter 6, reminding students that journals and brainstorming are especially good sources for ideas.

2. Read **Subjects Based on First-Hand Experiences**, pages 185–186. Discuss the advantages of using one's own experiences in finding subjects to write about. Discuss the sample essay on page 186. Point out that the writer tells the story not only because it is interesting in itself but because it makes a valuable point.

3. Read **Subjects Based on Imagination**, pages 187–188. Discuss writing about subjects drawn from one's imagination. Then have the class read the essay on pages 187–188. Ask students what kind of details are used (descriptive) and what the purpose of the essay is (to inform and/or persuade). Be sure that students understand that Carson's fable has a serious message. Ask them what has caused the "silent spring." (insecticides)

185

4. Assign Exercise A on page 188. Make sure students think of at least ten subjects of their own before they add any of the sample topics to their lists. Assign Exercise B on page 188. Encourage the choice of an interesting, challenging topic.

Individualizing the Lesson

Less-Advanced Students

1. Hold a class brainstorming session to help students generate writing topics. Start with several general subjects based on the list in Exercise A. Some possible general subjects are "embarrassing moments," "my family," "meaningful experiences," "the first day of high school." Have students think of progressively more specific topics for one of these general subjects. Instruct students to perform the same process in thinking of their own subject.

2. You might guide these students toward more realistic, concrete topics. Such topics will make the task of generating details easier during later stages of the writing process.

Advanced Students

1. Emphasize the usefulness of a journal in assembling a list of writing topics. If students have previously been assigned journals, discuss how interesting writing topics can be found in students' daily descriptions of ideas, opinions, feelings, and activities.

2. Challenge these students to attempt some writing based on imagination. More experienced or creative writers can often stretch their abilities in this manner.

The writer of the following composition has drawn from his personal experiences to communicate his thoughts and feelings about his upbringing and its importance to his career as a pilot and astronaut.

Words To Grow on

So far as I can remember, my training to become a command pilot of the space shuttle *Columbia* began when I was an eight-year-old boy writing a letter to my favorite aunt.

After finishing the letter, I showed it to my parents, expecting a pat on the back. To my surprise, they were not enthusiastic. "I see you've misspelled a few words and scratched out some things, Jack," my father said. "Better make a clean copy." My mother nodded in firm assent and told me to *"Do it right or not at all."* That was the first time I'd heard that old cliché, but it sure wasn't the last. Those words were a caution to take the time and care to do a job correctly — and my parents applied them to everything I did.

In March 1982, I had special reason to be grateful that my parents insisted on excellence in performance. After I'd spent six years as an astronaut and 1,000 hours training in a computerized flight simulator, I rocketed into space with my co-pilot, Colonel C. Gordon Fullerton. It was the *Columbia*'s third mission, an eight-day marathon of tests and experiments.

But nothing we did in outer space was more crucial than the last moments of the mission: setting the ship safely down on planet Earth. Our instructions were to take over the 110-ton Columbia from the automatic system and land it manually. Our airspeed would be 230 miles an hour. Our target for landing at this blinding speed: a scant three miles of runway. Talk about putting a camel through the eye of a needle!

In a fraction of a minute, all the hours I'd put into doing the job right in the simulator came into play — for real. So, when our wheels kissed the ground and *Columbia* was home, I paused for a moment of thanks. And I thanked my mother and father for setting the standard that helped me react to pressure with confidence.—COLONEL JACK R. LOUSMA

Subjects Based on Imagination

Some of the most interesting subjects are drawn from imagination. These subjects often are developed into narrative compositions. However, they can also be developed into other types of compositions, as illustrated in the following description.

A Fable for Tomorrow

There was once a town in the heart of America where all life seemed to live in harmony with its surroundings. The town lay in the midst of a checkerboard of prosperous farms, with fields of grain and hillsides of orchards where, in spring, white clouds of bloom drifted above the green fields. In autumn, oak and maple and birch set up a blaze of color that flamed and flickered across a backdrop of pines. Foxes barked in the hills and deer silently crossed the fields, half hidden in the mists of the fall mornings.

Then a strange blight crept over the area and everything began to change. Some evil spell had settled on the community: mysterious maladies swept the flocks of chickens; the cattle and sheep sickened and died. Everywhere was a shadow of death. The farmers spoke of much illness among their families. In the town the doctors had become more and more puzzled by new kinds of sickness appearing among their patients. There had been several sudden and unexplained deaths, not only among adults but even among children, who would be stricken suddenly while at play and die within a few hours.

There was a strange stillness. The birds, for example—where had they gone? Many people spoke of them, puzzled and disturbed. The feeding stations in the backyards were deserted. The few birds seen anywhere were moribund. They trembled violently and could not fly. It was a spring without voices. On the mornings that had once throbbed with the dawn chorus of robins, catbirds, doves, jays, wrens, and scores of other bird voices there was now no sound. Only silence lay over the fields and woods and marsh.

On the farms the hens brooded, but no chickens hatched.

The farmers complained that they were unable to raise any pigs—the litters were small and the young survived only a few days. The apple trees were coming into bloom, but no bees droned among the blossoms, so there was no pollination and there would be no fruit. The fields browned and withered as though swept by fire. These, too, were silent, deserted by all living things.

No witchcraft, no enemy action had silenced the rebirth of new life in this stricken world. The people had done it themselves.—RACHEL CARSON

Exercises Pre-Writing: Choosing a Subject

A. The following subjects are meant to stimulate your thinking about possible topics for compositions. Study them. Then, begin to brainstorm. Drawing from your own experiences, knowledge, and imagination, make a list of at least ten subjects. If any of the subjects listed here interest you, add them to your list.

1. I Am Owned by a Cat/Dog
2. Violent Storms
3. Growing Up Bilingual
4. A Strange Noise in the Night
5. Being a Friend
6. Thank Goodness, No Bones Were Broken
7. Getting in Shape for _____
8. I Shouldn't Have Said It
9. The Day I Grew Up
10. Rural Life
11. The Uniqueness of My Parents
12. I Wish I Were _____
13. The Art of Following Directions
14. How I Have Changed in the Past Year
15. Family Rituals

B. Study your list of subjects carefully. Select the one that interests you the most. This will be the first pre-writing step in the Process of Writing.

Part 3 Pre-Writing: Narrowing the Subject

In your study of the paragraph, you learned that an idea must be narrow enough to be developed adequately within the limits of the paragraph. The same holds true for the composition. The topic must be narrow enough to be covered in a few paragraphs.

Sometimes a subject based on first-hand experience does not need to be narrowed if a writer has a specific incident in mind. On the other hand, a subject in which you have a general interest or knowledge may be too broad for a composition. Your hobby may be collecting butterflies, but, unfocused, this subject would be too broad for a short composition. Brainstorming might help you to identify possible composition topics within this subject:

> Identifying Butterflies
> Capturing and Mounting Butterflies
> Catching a Monarch
> The Joys of Butterfly Collecting

The subject "Video Games" is also too broad for a composition. Again, the writer must decide on a specific topic. Some possibilities include the time spent on video games, the money spent on video games, the types of video games, or the writer's favorite video game. By choosing one of these specific topics, you could cover the material in a few paragraphs, as did the writer of the following composition.

Too Much Money!

Almost anyone could use an extra $100. This is the amount a person would spend in a year by playing video games at the rate of $2.00 a week. If the player regularly spends more than that amount, as many do, the total can skyrocket. Although many people like the games, some are also worried that they are spending too much money on them. They also wonder *why* they spend so much. Actually, there are several simple reasons why players spend more than they should on video games.

Part 3

Objective

To narrow a general subject for a composition

Presenting the Lesson

1. Read and discuss **Narrowing the Subject**, pages 189–190. Emphasize that although a composition can develop a topic more thoroughly than a paragraph, a composition still requires a specific topic that can be handled in the assigned length of the paper.

2. Discuss the sample essay on pages 189–190. Emphasize that the writer of the essay has narrowed his or her general topic, "video games," to a topic that is specific enough to be discussed thoroughly and interestingly in a five-paragraph composition.

3. Assign the Exercise on page 190. Have students work in pairs to discuss and evaluate their stated topics. Let students help each other to determine whether they have chosen sufficiently narrow topics.

Individualizing the Lesson

Less-Advanced Students

Work with students individually to make sure they have chosen a sufficiently narrow topic for a five-paragraph composition.

Advanced Students

Before assigning the Exercise on page 190, have the students analyze in detail the sample essay. Discuss the promises made in the introductory paragraph, the function of each paragraph in the body, and the summarizing quality of the conclusion.

Optional Practice

Have students formulate five topics narrow enough for a five-paragraph composition from the list of topics on page 188.

Extending the Lesson

Have students think of narrow topics for five of the general topics they found in newspapers in **Extending the Lesson**, Part 2, on page 187 of this Teacher's Edition.

First of all, most players think the games are entertaining and exciting. The games are not only fun, they are also challenging and stimulating to players' imaginations. This sense of excitement can cause problems. Because players are having so much fun, they don't realize how much they're spending.

Second, a single game is fairly inexpensive. Each time a person plays, he or she thinks, "It's only a quarter." Yet all those quarters add up, and it is easy to overspend. If people had to pay for all their games *before* entering a game room, they might think twice about whether an hour in front of some machines is worth the price.

A third reason people spend more than they should is that video games are addictive. Many people have admitted, "Once I start, I can't stop." There is always the challenge of beating your own score, or of reaching the highest score ever achieved on a particular machine. People play over and over and put in dozens of quarters with the hope of achieving that elusive top score. They always think it will be "next time!"

Just imagine a one-hundred-dollar bill disappearing like an enemy spaceship on a video screen. Video games may be exciting, challenging, and inexpensive, but the money certainly does add up!

Notice how thoroughly the writer of this composition was able to develop the main idea after the subject was narrowed. Three reasons for video "addiction" were identified, and each one was solidly supported with different types of details. If, on the other hand, the writer had not narrowed the subject, the composition would have been merely a collection of unsupported and uninteresting generalizations. Careful limitation of the topic, therefore, can make the difference between a strong and a weak composition.

Exercise Pre-Writing: Narrowing the Subject

In your last assignment, you chose a subject for a composition. Think about that subject and decide whether it is narrow enough to be covered in a five-paragraph composition. If it is not, list several specific topics within the general subject and choose one as the topic for your composition.

Part 4   Pre-Writing: Deciding on the Audience and the Purpose

Before you begin to develop a plan for your composition, you must answer two questions.

1. For whom are you writing the composition?
2. What is your purpose for writing?

Your Audience. You should know two things about your readers. First, you should know their approximate age. The need for this information is clear. If, for example, your readers will be very young, you must use simple words, avoid difficult ideas, and explain your ideas very carefully.

Second, you should know the readers' familiarity with your subject. This will influence the amount and difficulty of the information you can include. It will also determine the number and types of explanations and definitions that you must give.

Your Purpose. Before developing a plan for your composition, decide whether you want to tell a story; to describe an object, place, or person; or to explain something. You must decide whether you want your readers to laugh, to cry, or to think seriously about an idea.

A one-sentence **statement of purpose** might help you to clarify your topic and goal. This statement is for your own guidance only. It will not be included in your composition. Here are three examples of such statements:

1. In my composition I will *explain* why it is important to take part in extracurricular activities.
2. In my composition I will *describe* the three most beautiful areas of Yellowstone Park.
3. In my composition I will *tell a story about* a humorous incident that happened on my first day of high school.

Later, when you write the introduction for your composition, you may wish to include a more formal version of this statement. It will then become the **thesis statement** of your composition.

191

Part 4

Objective

To consider the audience and purpose before writing a composition

Presenting the Lesson

1. Read and discuss **Deciding on the Audience and the Purpose**, pages 191–192.

2. Discuss the two points, age and familiarity with subject matter, that students should consider when identifying their audience. Point out the importance of knowing these things about the audience.

3. Discuss the importance of deciding on one's purpose in writing when planning a composition. Define "statement of purpose" and read the three sample statements of purpose.

4. Read the two sample paragraphs on page 192 aloud. Discuss the differences that purpose and audience made between the two paragraphs.

5. Assign the Exercise on page 192. You may wish to have your students write for an audience of their peers in your English class, or you may wish to specify an older or younger audience, students in another class, or you yourself. Review the sample statements of purpose on page 191, reminding students that the statement is for their own use.

Individualizing the Lesson

Less-Advanced Students

Use analogies to spoken communication to clarify the concept of adapting one's writing for a particular audience. Ask students, for example, how they would explain the causes of the American Revolution to an elementary school child and to their history teacher.

Advanced Students

Have students write three different possible statements of purpose for their compositions. Have several students read their statements aloud, and discuss how these differing purposes would affect the composition.

Optional Practice

1. Have students list the kinds of words they would use to write on the subjects given below for each of the audiences in parentheses. List the words in pairs.

Examples: climate / weather moisture / water

a. changing the oil in an automobile (auto club, English classmates)
b. keeping physically fit (football team, senior citizens' group)

2. Have students discuss the different kinds of details and examples they would use to write on the following subjects.

a. volunteer work in a hospital (to tell a story, to explain)
b. riding a bicycle from New York to California (to describe, to tell a story)

Extending the Lesson

Have each student find a short magazine article and bring it to class. Encourage students to look in magazines aimed at a specific audience (teens, puzzle enthusiasts). Ask students to read their articles aloud and have classmates try to determine the intended audience and purpose.

Sample Paragraphs. The two paragraphs that follow are both written on the same general subject, sickness. However, they are written with different audiences and purposes in mind.

1   Finding the cause of a sore throat calls for some detective work. Your doctor will ask you questions, give you an examination, and maybe do some tests. Doctors do this to get clues. The doctor will ask how you feel, how long you have been sick, and if anything else hurts. When you tell the doctor how you feel, you are telling your symptoms. The doctor will examine you to look for other clues, called signs. Some signs that doctors look for are fever, rash, swollen tonsils, and swollen lymph nodes, small lumps under the skin on the sides of the neck.

—DONAHUE AND CAPELLARO

2   Snooks, under a pile of faded quilts, made a small, gravelike mound in the bed. His head was like a ball of black putty wedged between the thin covers and the dingy yellow pillow. His little eyes were partly open, as if he were peeping out of his hard, wasted skull at the chilly room. The forceful pulse of his breathing caused a faint rustling in the sheets near his mouth, like the wind pushing damp papers in a shallow ditch.

—ALICE WALKER

Paragraph 1 is explanatory. It explains the detective work needed to find the cause of a sore throat. Most of the words are simple; two of the harder words, *symptoms* and *lymph nodes*, are defined within the paragraph. The writer presents simple information, easily understood by most young readers.

Paragraph 2 is a narrative paragraph. It paints a grim picture of a very sick child. In contrast to Paragraph 1, it contains difficult words; longer, more complicated sentences; and complex language. The writer of this paragraph had a much older, more experienced audience in mind than the writer of Paragraph 1.

Exercise   Pre-Writing: Deciding on the Audience and the Purpose

Decide on the audience for your composition. Then write a one-sentence statement of purpose.

Part 5 Pre-Writing: Planning the Composition

Before you begin writing, you will need to develop a writing plan. This will allow you to work with your ideas before you write your first draft. A writing plan has two main steps:

1. Putting down ideas
2. Organizing the ideas.

Putting Down Ideas

As you begin to plan your composition, you probably have ideas about what you want to include. Write these ideas on a sheet of paper or on 3″ x 5″ cards, keeping in mind your audience and your purpose for writing. As you think more about your topic, additional ideas will come to you. Jot them down also. Make no attempt at this time to write the ideas in any particular order.

One writer chose the universal appeal of music as her topic. Her purpose was to give several reasons why everyone seems to enjoy music. She made the following list of ideas.

Music: The Universal Language

everyone involved ← touches our feelings
different age groups respond to
everyone can create

cultural exchanges	blues
Mendelssohn	popular artists
Bach	Latin music
Handel	elation of boogie
high school choirs, bands	jam sessions
festivals	rhythm bands
ethnic music	campfire sing-alongs
concerts	toddlers dancing, responding
jazz	everyone has contributed

Part 5

Objective

To use pre-writing to plan a composition

Presenting the Lesson

1. Name and list the three steps in the pre-writing stage of writing a composition: putting down ideas, identifying main ideas, and organizing ideas.

2. Read and discuss **Putting Down Ideas** pages 193–194. Call attention to the writer's random listing of the ideas related to her topic. Point out that the more ideas a writer lists at this stage, the more he or she has to choose from at a later stage of writing. Also mention that one idea often leads to another, so a lengthy brainstorming session can produce previously unthought of ideas. Caution students, however, to keep their idea selection focused through a constant reference to topic and purpose.

3. Assign the Exercise on page 194. Tell students simply to list as many ideas as possible at this stage, reminding them that they will add, delete, and organize ideas in a later stage of pre-writing.

4. Read and discuss **Organizing the Ideas** pages 194–195. Point out that at this stage writers must examine their informal lists carefully to see how their ideas fit together. Emphasize that there is no single right way to organize a particular group of ideas. Different approaches may work equally well.

Discuss the process by which the writer of the composition "Music:

The Universal Language" groups her ideas, deletes some ideas, and adds some ideas to focus and balance her three main headings. Ask students to name ideas that were added under each main idea ("folk tunes" to round out her first heading, "work companion" and "triggers memories in old people" under her second heading, and specific emotions under her third heading).

5. Assign Exercise A on page 195. This exercise shows students one way that the ideas for a descriptive composition about camping could be organized. Point out that other methods of organization (sights, sounds, smells, for example) would also be possible.

6. Assign Exercise B on pages 195–196. This exercise helps students choose main ideas under which other ideas can be grouped.

7. Assign Exercise C on page 196. Tell students to study their prewriting lists carefully. Remind students that their three general headings may be included in their list of ideas, as in Exercise B on pages 195–196. On the other hand, students may need to formulate one or more new, more general ideas under which the other ideas can be grouped. Remind students that they may need to add or delete ideas at this stage, as did the writer of the sample pre-writing notes for the composition "Music: The Universal Language."

8. Tell students that the next pre-writing step is to arrange their ideas in a logical order. Read **Completing Your Writing Plan**, pages 196–197. Review chronological order, order of importance, order of familiarity, spatial order, and comparison and

The purpose of this first step is to get down as many ideas as possible. Many of these will become details in the writer's composition, but the list is not final. As the writer works through the writing process, she will continue to delete unrelated ideas and to add better ones. Note that the list has no real organization. The sorting and organizing take place in the next step.

Exercise Pre-Writing: Writing Down Ideas

Make a list of ideas related to your composition topic. Keep in mind your audience and your purpose for writing.

Organizing the Ideas

Your next step in planning is to organize your ideas in relation to each other; that is, to group similar ideas together.

The writer of "Music: The Universal Language" studied her list of ideas. She decided that they fell into three groups. She then listed the related ideas under each heading.

1. People of many times and cultures have contributed to music.
   –Bach } old masters
   –Handel
   –jazz } Black America
   –blues
   –Latin music
   –folk tunes

2. All ages respond to music.
   –rhythm bands
   –triggers memories in older people
   –toddlers
   –work companion
   –campfire sing-alongs
   –jam sessions

3. People respond emotionally to music.
   –Mendelssohn—sadness
   –Jump Shout Boogie—elation
   –popular artists—love

After grouping your ideas, you may have a few "extra" ideas that do not seem to fit under any of your headings. The writer of the sample composition had several such ideas. These were deleted so that they would not disturb the unity of the individual paragraphs. On the other hand, the writer added other details so that the three general groups became more focused. For instance, under the group, "All ages respond to music," the writer decided that all age groups should be mentioned. Many of her original ideas related only to teenagers. She deleted some of those so she could include details pertaining to other age groups, too. Can you find additional details that were added?

Exercises Pre-Writing: Grouping Ideas

A. Following is a list of ideas related to the topic "Camping in a Cabin." They can be grouped under two general headings.

> I. Six A.M.
> II. Midnight

Write each idea under the appropriate heading.

> II. 1. Sounds: a scratching, a rustling, then silence
> I. 2. Sights: sunlight in the cabin
> II. 3. Sights: stars, blackness
> II. 4. Sights: moonlight through the window
> I. 5. Smells: coffee, bacon
> I. 6. Sounds: friends laughing and talking
> I. 7. Sounds: fire crackling, bacon sizzling
> II. 8. Smells: lingering trace of smoke

B. Two of the following ideas can be used as general headings. Find them. Then group the remaining ideas under the appropriate headings.

> B 1. provide adequate street lighting
> A 2. pedestrians injure themselves main head
> A 3. they cross streets diagonally
> A 4. they cross streets in the middle of the block
> A 5. they walk with their backs to traffic on the highway

9. Read the sample writing plan on page 197 for the composition "Music: The Universal Language." Have students discuss why the writer might have decided on an order of familiarity for her ideas. Then help students discover the logic behind the writer's organization of ideas within paragraphs. Point out that the writer's first group of ideas was arranged from the youngest age group to the oldest age group, a type of chronological order. The second paragraph was organized from least to most pleasant emotion. The third paragraph was again organized chronologically.

10. Assign the Exercise on page 198. Remind students to organize not only the main groups of ideas, but also the ideas within each group.

Individualizing the Lesson

Less-Advanced Students

1. Encourage students to think freely when jotting down ideas. To ensure that students have enough ideas to work with, conduct a timed writing in class: have students list any ideas which occur to them on their topic, writing continuously for a set time period of ten or fifteen minutes. Remind students that they can add or delete ideas later, but that the objective at this stage is to have plenty of material with which to work.

2. Do Exercise A on page 195 orally. Help students see that the sensory details for the descriptive essay are being arranged chronologically.

3. For Exercise B on pages 195–196 have students identify orally the two main headings ("pedestrians injure themselves," and "pedestrian lives can be saved"). Have students do the remainder of the exercise individually.

4. For Exercise C, page 196, work with individuals as much as possible in grouping and organizing ideas. Have students work in pairs to help one another see the overall patterns formed by their pre-writing lists. Encourage students to re-create carefully the process performed by the writer of the sample pre-writing notes.

Advanced Students

1. Point out that the technique for organizing ideas presented in this Chapter results in a plan that is much like an outline. Refer students to pages 251–254 in Chapter 12 for more information on outlines.

2. As suggested earlier, do not restrict these students to a five paragraph composition. Allow them to develop more grouping if they wish.

Optional Practice

Have students list ideas for a second topic on their list of possible subjects. Students may find that they are more successful in discovering ideas for their second topic and choose to develop that topic in their composition.

Extending the Lesson

Point out that the organization technique studied in this lesson is a

B 6. pedestrian lives can be saved main head
A 7. they step into traffic from parked cars
B 8. provide traffic lights for pedestrians
A 9. they step from behind parked cars
B 10. give traffic tickets to pedestrians
A 11. they cross against lights
A 12. they don't watch for traffic

C. Study the ideas for your own composition. Decide on three general headings that seem to cover most of them. Then list each idea under the appropriate heading.

Completing Your Writing Plan

After gathering and grouping your ideas, you are ready to organize them into a final writing plan. This involves two steps:

1. Arranging groups of related ideas into logical order
2. Organizing the ideas within each group.

Logical Order. Logical order is an order that is appropriate to the content of the composition and is, therefore, easy for a reader to follow. Just as paragraphs use different orders, so do compositions. As a writer, you must find the order that best suits the ideas you want to express.

Some compositions are organized in **chronological order**; that is, in the order of time. Most narratives and some explanatory compositions are developed in this way.

Some compositions are organized in **order of importance**; that is, from the least important to the most important, according to the writer's way of thinking. When order of importance cannot be established, a writer might arrange groups of ideas in **order of familiarity**, from the most familiar to the least familiar.

A fourth way to organize compositions is in **spatial order**; that is, in the order in which a writer wishes the reader to picture a place, object, or person. For example, a writer might decide to describe a room from near to far. The group of details that describes the nearest part of the room would be first. The group of details that describes the farthest part of the room would be last.

Comparison and contrast organization is a useful method of organization when the writer is explaining the similarities or differences between two or more things. In this type of organization, the writer first discusses a characteristic of one subject. He or she then presents the corresponding detail of the other subject, pointing out how the two are alike or different. Another way of handling this type of organization is to discuss all the characteristics of one subject before going on to the characteristics of the other.

Look at the following writing plan for the composition on music. Notice the order in which the writer has organized both the main ideas of the composition and the details that support those main ideas.

process of division and classification. Discuss with the class other situations where ideas or things are grouped and classified. Examples are plants and animals in science, library books, and school classes.

Music: The Universal Language

1. All ages respond to music.
   –toddlers dancing
   –rhythm bands in elementary school
   –campfire sing-alongs
   –jam sessions (teenagers)
   –companion for work (teenagers/adults)
   –triggers memories in older people

2. People respond emotionally to music.
   –Mendelssohn causes sorrow.
   –Jump Shout Boogie causes a feeling of elation.
   –Other music strengthens feelings of love.

3. People of many times and cultures have contributed to music.
   –folk music
   –old masters like Bach and Handel
   –Latin music
   –jazz and blues of Black America

The writer rearranged not only her groups of ideas, but also the ideas within each group. The main groups of ideas were organized in order of familiarity. Within paragraphs, other methods of organization were used. Can you identify the order for each paragraph?

To write the introduction, body, and conclusion of a composition

Presenting the Lesson

1. Read and discuss **The Introductory Paragraph**, pages 198–199. Emphasize the two functions of an introductory paragraph: to give the main idea of the composition and to catch the reader's attention.

2. Read the examples of poor opening sentences on page 198. Have students discuss why each sentence is inadequate. Read the four sample introductory paragraphs, pointing out how the specific details attract a reader's attention. Point out also that a good introduction does *not* include an explicit statement of the writer's purpose.

3. Assign Exercise A on page 200. Help students discover that sentences 1, 2, 5, 8, 9, 12, 16, 17, 18, and 20 motivate the reader to continue reading by offering enough detail to create suspense or curiosity, while sentences 3, 4, 6, 7, 10, 11, 13, 14, 15, and 19 are too general, trite, or obvious to capture the reader's attention.

4. Assign Exercise B on page 200. Have students make sure that their paragraphs perform both functions of a good introductory paragraph.

Exercise Pre-Writing: Making a Writing Plan

Make a writing plan by organizing the three groups of ideas for your own composition in a logical order. If necessary, rearrange the ideas within each group so that they are presented more effectively.

Part 6   First Draft: Writing the Composition

Your pre-writing stage is now finished. Your topic has been selected, your audience and purpose identified, and your ideas organized into an outline. You are now ready to write the first draft of your composition.

The Introductory Paragraph

The introductory paragraph of a composition serves two important functions.

1. It gives the main idea of the composition.
2. It catches the reader's attention.

The opening sentence of an introductory paragraph sets the tone for the entire paragraph. A good writer, therefore, avoids dull and uninteresting opening sentences such as these.

1. In this paper, I am going to describe someone who died.
2. Families can be fun.
3. I am going to explain something about being an American.
4. Music is enjoyed by everyone.

Each of these sentences indicates, in a general way, the main idea of the composition. However, the sentences lack the specific details that would catch the interest of a reader.

The four introductory paragraphs on the next page begin with good opening sentences. The paragraphs are based on the same subjects as the poor topic sentences above. Notice how each paragraph now gives the main idea of a composition in a way that makes you want to read further.

1   Charley Lockjaw died last summer on the reservation. He was very old — a hundred years, he had claimed. He still wore his hair in braids, as only the older men do in his tribe, and the braids were thin and white. His fierce old face was like a withered apple. He was bent and frail and trembling, and his voice was like a wailing of the wind across the prairie grass.

—DOROTHY JOHNSON

2   There were seldom fewer than fifteen men, women, and children at our Sunday get-together. On the Sundays when it rained, there would be as many as thirty. It was obvious that no one else in Mount Allegro had as many relatives as I did. It was also true that no one else's relatives seemed to seek one another's company as much as mine did. Sundays or weekdays, they were as gregarious as ants but had a far more pleasant time. There were always relatives and friends present or about to arrive. When they finally left for the night, they occasionally came back for a surprise visit which they called a *sirinata*. —JERRE MANGIONE

3   "We, the people" is an eloquent beginning. However, when the Constitution of the United States was completed on the seventeenth of September in 1787, I was not included in that "We, the people." I felt for many years that somehow George Washington and Alexander Hamilton just left me out by mistake. Through the process of amendment, interpretation, and court decisions I have finally been included in "We, the people." —BARBARA JORDAN

4   Every person is a unique collection of opinions, tastes, ideas, and beliefs. No two people like exactly the same things or feel precisely the same way about an issue. Yet there is one thing that all people enjoy, and which is an important part of almost everyone's life — music. Music is a universal art that ignores boundaries of age, culture, and time.

The last paragraph is the final version of the introduction for "Music: The Universal Language." Read it again and decide whether it has the requirements necessary for a good opening paragraph.

199

5. Read and discuss **The Body**, page 201. Refer students to the author's writing plan on page 197 and the first draft of the introductory paragraph on page 201. Ask students what changes and additions were made in writing the first draft from the pre-writing notes. (Barry Manilow is added as well as specific mention of tango and rhumba under Latin music.) Point out that errors in spelling, punctuation, and capitalization inevitably occur in a first draft.

6. Read and discuss **Achieving Unity and Coherence**, pages 202–204. Refer students to the discussion of unity and coherence in paragraphs in Chapter 8, pages 130–135. Tell students that a composition has unity when each paragraph of the body relates to the introductory paragraph and each sentence within the paragraphs relates to its topic sentence. A composition has coherence when the paragraphs are logically tied together.

7. Discuss the six basic types of transitional devices. Read the sample paragraphs, calling attention to the transitional devices in each.

8. Assign and discuss Exercise A on pages 204–206. Then assign Exercise B on page 206. Remind students to concentrate at this stage on getting their ideas down in sentence form. Tell students to base the drafts on their pre-writing plans but to feel free to add new ideas or experiment with order. Remind them of the importance of transitional devices to show the connections among the paragraphs. Also remind them that errors in grammar and mechanics will probably occur at this stage. These errors may be corrected during revision.

9. Read and discuss **The Conclusion**, pages 206–207. Emphasize the fact that this paragraph must be as interesting as the introduction.

10. Assign Exercises A and B on page 207. Tell students that a title is a necessary part of any composition; however, it is not necessary to use the "working title." Often the title is the last part of a composition to be written.

Individualizing the Lesson

Less-Advanced Students

1. Emphasize the importance of an interesting introductory paragraph. Discuss in detail Exercise A on page 200. Focus on avoiding sentences such as 3, 7, 11, and 15, which offer an obvious and unappealing statement of purpose. Have students compare sentences 14 and 5. Help them to see that sentence 14 offers one general description, "old," while sentence 5 helps the reader imagine a specific scene.

2. In discussing the six basic transitional devices, be sure to define "synonym" and "pronoun" in items 5 and 6. Remind students that transitional devices are useful to writers in making clear to themselves the connections between ideas in the pre-writing plan.

3. Emphasize the importance of the conclusion in letting the reader know that the composition is finished. Point out that the ending must also be satisfying to the reader. Tell students that if they simply end on their final detail or example, or with the last action of a story, the reader is likely to feel that the writer has simply gotten tired and stopped writing.

Exercises Writing the Introductory Paragraph

A. Read the following opening sentences for introductory paragraphs. Decide which ones have definite reader appeal. Be ready to explain why the others do not catch your attention.

Answers in Teacher Notes.

1. By the time the saber-toothed tiger had slunk into oblivion, and the mastodon was only a memory, the human being had developed two brains.

2. In skiing and skating and riding a bicycle, the beginner is faced with one overwhelming problem.

3. This composition is about learning to meditate.

4. My horse is a good animal.

5. As I rounded the curve of the mountain, I saw the tiny village far below me.

6. I spent a nice week at the Mardi Gras in New Orleans.

7. First of all, I want to introduce myself.

8. I'm glad I'm a woman!

9. I'm glad I'm a man!

10. Once we lived in my grandfather's house.

11. Well, this young girl I'm going to tell you about was named Angela.

12. The strange young boy had the type of otherwordly appearance that made you notice him immediately.

13. My mother had a happy childhood.

14. Most zoos are old.

15. My teacher has asked me to write a paper about mythology.

16. I was prepared to dislike Max even before I knew him.

17. Imagine, if you can, a small room, hexagonal in shape, like the cell of a bee.

18. The little fellow was lying on the bare hospital cot, arms rigidly straight and teeth clenched tightly together.

19. I remember my first pet.

20. His name was Frank X. Farrell and I guess the X stood for "Excuse me."

B. Write the introductory paragraph for your composition. Be sure that it gives the main idea of your composition and that it will catch your readers' attention.

The Body

The body is the second major part of a composition. In the body paragraphs, the main idea of the composition, which was presented in the introductory paragraph, is supported or explained.

The writer of "Music: The Universal Language" used her writing plan to get her ideas down in a first draft of her body paragraph. In doing so, she not only recorded the details she had already thought of, but she also discovered some new ideas. These were included where they were appropriate and where they did not upset the unity of a paragraph.

Even if you're not a famous composer, and even if you don't like orchestra concerts, music is still a part of you. Almost as soon as they are steady on their feet, toddlers begin "dancing" by moving in time to the rhythm of music. As these babys get older, there will be rhythm bands in school campfire sing-alongs or jam sessions with friends. Music on the radio or stereo will become a companion for work around the house or for travel. Finally, for old folks, the strains of certain tunes will recall memories of times gone by.

Music touches us all because it evokes a lot of feeling. One person may be touched by a sorrowful selection of mendelssohn. Another person may get the same feeling when Barry Manilow sings This Song's for you. Music can also bring joy. Who can resist feeling good when a rythmic tune like Jump Shout Boogie bounces across the air waves? And of course, music can affect love. Music edifies the soul!

Not only do we all like music, we all take part in it's creation. Some of us can do no more than hum off key, but we have still made a contribution. So have other poeple. Folk melodies remain with us from a long time ago. Back and Handel sent us music from Europe. South Americans gave us the tango and rhumba. Black Americans gave us jazz and the blues.

The writer has already made some changes and additions from her writing plan to her rough draft. Remember that changes at this stage are still likely, and usually desirable. You need only keep your audience, purpose, and main idea in mind as you work.

201

Advanced Students

1. Have students analyze the first two sentences in Exercise A, page 200, to see why they are particularly attention-getting. For example, students should note that in sentence 1, details on prehistoric animals stimulate the reader's imagination and the mention of two brains stimulates his or her curiosity. Sentence 2 creates curiosity about the single "overwhelming" problem that three simple, enjoyable sports share. Challenge students to come up with five to ten excellent lead-in sentences of their own.

2. Refer students to the chart on page 372 for other interesting ways to develop an introduction. Challenge them to use one of these methods in their own composition. Have students discuss the types of transitional devices appropriate to certain types of composition organizations. For example, point out that words indicating time are natural to stories and that words showing an opposite point of view are useful with organization by comparison or contrast.

Optional Practice

1. Provide short magazine articles with the introductory paragraphs deleted. Challenge students to supply these paragraphs. Then show them the originals. See if any of the student-generated paragraphs are actually an improvement.

2. Have students work in small groups on developing the bodies of their compositions. After students have written first drafts of their body paragraphs, have them exchange papers with two or three other students. Instruct students to read the paragraphs specifically for development of improvement details. Tell them to point out any instances where a writer could add details for improved clarity or vividness.

3. Have students discuss the function of a title in attracting readers' attention and in giving them an idea about the subject of a composition. Have students find at least five excellent titles in a magazine or in a literature book. Have them explain why each title appeals to them.

Extending the Lesson

Read to the class a few famous introductions and conclusions from well-known novels. Examples are the opening sentences of *Anna Karenina* and *Pride and Prejudice* and the concluding sentence of *The Great Gatsby*. Ask the students to think about why these particular introductions and conclusions are famous. How do they capture a reader's attention?

Achieving Unity and Coherence

Unity. When writing a first draft, a good writer tries to keep the ideas unified. As you write, check to see that each body paragraph directly relates to the introductory paragraph. Then make sure that the supporting details in each paragraph relate directly to the topic sentence. If you keep these things in mind, your composition will be unified by the main idea that is presented in the opening paragraph.

Coherence. To reinforce the unity of idea, a writer may repeat key words and phrases throughout a composition. For example, the writer of the sample composition repeated the word *music* in the introductory paragraph and in each body paragraph.

A writer may also make use of transitional devices. These words and phrases tie the paragraphs of a composition together by referring both to the idea that precedes and the idea that follows.

There are six basic transitional devices.

1. **Using a Word That Indicates Time.** These words include:

first	before	meanwhile
next	after	until
then	afterwards	later
finally	today	hundreds of years ago

EXAMPLE

A special type of Japanese wrestling is called *sumo.* Sumo is probably Japan's oldest sport. It began hundreds of years ago as part of a Shinto religious ceremony. Some Shinto shrines had special buildings built for sumo matches, held to honor the gods. In the year 858, it is said, the two sons of the emperor wrestled to see who would succeed to the throne.

Today sumo is so popular that tournaments are held every year in the large cities. Thousands go to the huge stadiums to watch the matches. Others view them on television. The sumo wrestlers are tall and heavy, sometimes weighing 300 pounds. Each wrestler wears only a ring about his waist and a loincloth. The place where they perform is a circle that measures fifteen feet across. —LEE W. FARNSWORTH

2. Using a Word That Shows the Relationship Between Ideas. Such words include the following:

and	because	therefore	moreover	unless
also	since	besides	similarly	

EXAMPLE

For the individual American, the main advantage of the metric system is its simplicity. Instead of the fifty-five measurement units of the English system, the metric system has only three: meters, grams, and liters. They all are made up of units of ten.

Because all multiples are powers of ten, calculations are simpler. To multiply, you simply move the decimal point.

3. Using a Word That Shows an Opposite Point of View. Such words include the following:

but	while	on the other hand
however	although	in contrast

EXAMPLE

Over the years, oil and natural gas gradually replaced coal as the major fuels for homes and industry. Gas and oil were cheaper. They were also more convenient.

Today, however, America is faced with an energy dilemma. The demand for gas and oil has outstripped domestic supplies. Now, America must rely heavily on foreign imports. Gas and oil are no longer cheap or convenient.

4. Using a Word That Repeats a Word Used Earlier.

EXAMPLE

Almost everybody daydreams. What do such dreams indicate about a person? How do one person's dreams differ from another person's?

Science is just beginning to probe the deeper meanings of daydreams, yet it has come up with some startling preliminary findings. —DOROTHY BRANT WARWICK

5. Using a Synonym for a Word Used Earlier.

EXAMPLE

A tornado blew through Arcadia, Nebraska, last week, and the next day in a town seventy-five miles east, somebody picked up a canceled check that had been in an Arcadia business-man's desk drawer. Impressed by this news, I turned to Roger Welsch, who teaches folklore at the university and keeps up with which way the Nebraska wind blows, to ask him if storms like that are common here.

Roger said that after one of these Nebraska cyclones, a sleeping man found himself still in bed, but the bed was in the kitchen. The only damage done was that his underclothes were on upside down and buttoned in the back. —CHARLES KURALT

6. Using a Pronoun That Refers to a Word Used Earlier.

EXAMPLE

Along the cool morning dew, along the cool forest floor crept a spider, a shabby little thing of a spider, looking for a place to spin a silken line or two.

Over speckled fishlike skins of leaves he crept, over earth-soft mossy pads, over turtle still adream, earth-anchored in its shell, over bogs of stones and crackling twigs he crept, crept on and on, seeking a place to spin a silken line or two.

—GEORGE MENDOZA

Exercises Studying and Writing Body Paragraphs

A. Study the following pairs of paragraphs carefully. Identify the transitional device, or devices, that each writer has used to tie the paragraphs together.

1 The coach, noting Sarah's unusual stamina and fluid motion, had convinced her that long-distance events were her best, and Sarah had trained long and hard for them.

Henry's coach on the other hand, had permitted Henry to play basketball even though he knew that he lacked peripheral vision. —*Woman's Day* Repetition of word *coach*; use of *on the other hand* to show opposite point of view.

2 I was standing in the driveway, alone, stock still, but shivering. Someone had given the polyphemus moth his freedom, and he was walking away.

He heaved himself down the asphalt driveway by infinite degrees, unwavering. His hideous, crumpled wings lay glued and rucked on his back, perfectly still now, like a collapsed tent.

Repetition of word *driveway*; use of *he* and *his* to refer to *polyphemus moth*.   —ANNIE DILLARD

3 They came, silently, dark-bellied clouds drifting up from the south, and the wind, increasing, swept in the heavy scent of the approaching storm. Lightning flashed over the low, distant hills, and the clouds closed quietly around the moon. The thunder rumbled and the heavy drops began to fall, slowly at first, then irregularly, then increasing to a rhythmic rush of noise as the gusts of wind forced the rain in vertical waves across the shingled roof.

Much later, when the rain had moved ahead and the water began to drip from the roof and the countless leaves, the boy slipped out of his worn denim pants and took off his shirt and lay down. —DURANGO MENDOZA Repetition of word *rain*; use of similar words *waves* and *water*; use of time phrase *much later*.

4 Paul loved his father "like no one in all the world," although as a young man he would later regret that his childhood was so programmed. "If I had had time ... that wasn't blocked out and filled in for me, I think my imagination would have been more developed. As it is, I've almost none. All my time was crowded with lessons to learn, games to play, books to read, chores to do. I never can remember having had hours in which I had nothing to do, and had actually to entertain myself out of my own mind."

Nevertheless, he always looked forward to the summer, when his sister and brothers would come home on vacations. He would play football with Ben, who would show him how to throw a pass, how to block and tackle. Bill, the brain of the family, taught him how to question what he read, how to draw his own conclusions, and how to defend them. Then there was Marion, who intended to become a teacher like her mother. Strong-willed but cheerful, she always brought laughter to the household.

Use of *he* and *his* to refer to *Paul*; use of *nevertheless* to show relationship between ideas   —DOROTHY BUTLER GILLIAM

5   We were in the marsh now, moving, on our way to say good-bye to Bald Head Island.

Bald Head sits at the southeastern tip of North Carolina, where the Cape Fear River flows into the Atlantic Ocean, and the best access is by boat, across four miles of relatively tranquil water from the shrimp and fishing village of Southport.

Repetition of name *Bald Head* —WILLIAM McILWAIN

6   They circled a square and slipped into a quiet, narrow street overlooking a park, stopping before the tallest of the apartment houses in the single commanding row.

Alighting, Miss Cynthie gave this imposing structure one sidewise, upward glance, and said, "You live like bees in a hive, don't you?" —RUDOLPH FISHER Use of *imposing structure* to refer to *tallest of the apartment houses*; (or *structure* used as synonym for *apartment house*.)

7   I walk on past brown unpainted houses, chipped sidewalks. Home is near and I want to get there and feed my hungry stomach. I see a plain brick house and run towards its broken wooden gate. I smile at the smell of stewing beans. I enter and sit at a table made of Hunt's tomato boxes. My mother silently brings me a plate of cooked beans with sliced onions and chile and a half-dozen tortillas.

She sits next to me and watches me eat. I dip a large spoon into the beans, bring it up to my mouth and, slurping, swallow the stuff on it. A rolled tortilla follows, and munching sounds come from me. —RUDY GALLARDO use of *She* and *me* to refer to *mother* and *I*

B. Write a draft for the body of your composition. Use your writing plan as a guide. Add new ideas that occur to you as you write. If necessary, change your organization as your ideas develop.

The Conclusion

After you have finished writing the body of your composition, your final step is to write the conclusion. The concluding paragraph indicates to the reader that the composition is finished. It can restate the main idea of the composition, summarize the ideas that have been presented in the body paragraphs, or make a comment about the information that has been given. The conclusion is the final idea that your readers will take from your work. Therefore, it should be as interesting as the introduction.

The writer of the following conclusion summarizes his feelings toward his subject, mountain rivers.

> By such a river it is impossible to believe that one will ever be tired or old. Every sense applauds it. Taste it, feel its chill on the teeth: it is purity absolute. Watch its racing current, its steady renewal of force. It is transient and eternal. Listen again to its symphony of sounds hiss and splash and gurgle, the small talk of side channels, the whisper of blown and scattered spray gathering itself and beginning to flow again, secret and irresistible, among the wet rocks. —WALLACE STEGNER

The following writer ends his composition with a moving statement on the death of his dog.

> That afternoon I drove Shamrock's body back to the gorge in the hills and buried him there. The bear cubs will tell the others that the little white lion has come home at last. When winter comes, the deer will step high in the snowdrifts in that green glade, over the place where lies my little friend, the one I can never forget. —FREDERICK A. BIRMINGHAM

The writer of "Music: The Universal Language" wrote this conclusion. Does it meet the requirements of a good conclusion?

> Music is a universal language. It springs from every country and affects each individual. It will exist as long as there are people to listen.

The first sentence in this conclusion restates the main idea of the composition. The conclusion also ties in to the title.

Exercises Finishing the Composition

A. Write the concluding paragraph of your composition. Be sure that it ties in well with the rest of your paper.

B. Write the title for your composition. You can take the title from your writing plan, or you can write a new one.

Objective

To revise the first draft of a composition

Presenting the Lesson

   1. Read **Revising the Composition**, page 208. Suggest to students that a multi-step revision will allow them to focus carefully on individual elements such as word choice, organization, unity, and coherence.
   2. Have students study the revisions made in "Music: The Universal Language." Read the itemized revisions on page 208. Ask students to find additional examples of each type of revision.
   3. Have students perform a multi-step revision of their compositions, referring to the revision of the sample essay. Remind students to proofread their drafts for errors in grammar and mechanics after they have revised for content and organization.
   4. Instruct students to make a final copy. Call attention to the final copy of the sample composition, on pages 210–211.

Individualizing the Lesson

Less-Advanced Students

   1. Lead the students step-by-step through the revision process. For example, briefly discuss word choice, reminding students to use vivid language and to keep their audience and purpose in mind. Then give students time to consider the use of words in their writing and ask questions if necessary. Continue in

Part 7   Revising the Composition

This is the stage of the writing process where you are concerned with getting everything just right! At this point, you want to select the most vivid word or phrase, strengthen your organization, and check the unity and coherence.

To keep your concentration focused during this stage, you may find that the best solution is a many-part revision process. Since you will want to check and revise your ideas, word choice, unity, coherence, and level of language, try looking over your draft several times. Correct problems in just one or two areas at a time.

Chapter 7, "The Process of Writing" and the Guidelines for Writing and Revising Compositions on page 212 will help you focus your revisions and do a thorough job.

The writer of "Music: The Universal Language" made many revisions in her rough draft, as shown on the next page.

Analysis of the Revision

The changes that the writer made in her revised draft improved her composition in many ways.

1. Vivid, specific words have been added or have replaced weaker language. For instance, the writer has added "distinctive wails" to modify jazz and "torchy strains" to modify blues.

2. More formal language has replaced informal language. For instance, the writer deleted all uses of "you" in her paper. She also deleted the term "old folks" in paragraph two.

3. Unity has been strengthened. For instance, the word "universal" now appears in the title, the introduction, and the conclusion. The addition of "reflecting all time periods and cultures," to the topic sentence in the third body paragraph ties it more closely to the introduction, too.

4. Coherence is strengthened by adding transitional words and phrases such as "still later in life" in the first body paragraph.

5. Many errors in grammar and mechanics were spotted. For instance, the writer corrected the misspelling of "babies." She also inserted commas where they were needed in a series.

Music: The Universal Language

is a unique collection of

Every person ~~has special~~ opinions, tastes, ideas, and beliefs.
exactly *precisely* *about an issue*
No two people like the same things or feel the same way. Yet

there is one thing that all people enjoy — music. Music is an
universal *boundaries of* *(and which is an important part of almost everyone's life)*
~~universal~~ art that ignores age, culture, and time.
everyone is
~~Even if you're~~ not a famous composer, ~~and even if you don't~~
or an *buff, yet* *important to each one of us, no*
~~like~~ orchestra concerts, music is still ~~a part of you.~~ Almost as *matter what our age*

soon as they are steady on their feet, toddlers begin "dancing" *ie*
they take part in
by moving in time to the rhythm of music. As these babys get

older, ~~there will be~~ rhythm bands in school, campfire sing-
Still later in life,
alongs, or jam sessions with friends. Music on the radio or ste-

reo ~~will~~ becomes a companion for work around the house or
It provides entertainment at parties and background for dancing.
for travel. Finally, ~~for old folks,~~ the strains of certain tunes
as more time passes
~~will~~ recall memories of times gone by.

multitude *s*
Music touches us all because it evokes a ~~lot~~ of feeling. One
deeply affected
person may be ~~touched~~ by a sorrowful selection of mendels-

sohn. Another person may get that same feeling when Barry
dolefully
Manilow sings This Song's for you. Music can also bring joy.
Few people *elated* *h* *,spirited*
~~Who~~ can resist feeling ~~good~~ when a rythmic tune like Jump

Shout Boogie bounces across the air waves? And of course,
enhance *How many times has a special song made one*
music can affect love. ~~Music edifies the soul!~~ *person long for another.*
can *enjoy* *but* *can also*
Not only ~~do~~ we all ~~like~~ music, we ~~all~~ take part in it's creation.
little
Some of us can do ~~no~~ more than hum off key, but we have still
of all time periods and cultures
made a contribution. So have ~~other people.~~ Folk melodies re-
centuries *h* *The* *of simple people*
main with us from ~~a long time~~ ago. Back and Handel sent us
the graceful, complex *Composers such as*
music ~~from~~ Europe. South Americans ~~gave us~~ the tango and
of *contributed* *enticing rhythms*
rhumba. Black Americans ~~gave us~~ jazz and the blues. *of the*
the distinctive wails of *torchy strains of the*

this manner for the five items in the discussion of the revision on page 208.

2. Allow time for individual conferences. Help students work out any revision problems they might have.

Advanced Students

1. Encourage students to read their compositions aloud during revision, either at home or in small groups in class. Explain that hearing one's own writing often brings to light any problems with coherence, awkwardness in sentence structure, or vague or inappropriate language.

2. Set up peer-editing groups. Be sure to make yourself available, however, to help resolve any problems.

Optional Practice

Before looking at the sample revised draft on page 209, have students list items that need revision. Then have students compare their suggestions and the actual revision, discussing any differences between the two.

Extending the Lesson

Share stories of famous writers' revision practices. Examples are Ernest Hemingway, who is said to have revised the last page of *A Farewell to Arms* thirty-nine times; and Leo Tolstoy, who said, "I scarcely ever reread my published writings. If by chance I come across a page, it always strikes me: all this must be rewritten; this is how I should have written it."

Proofreading

Many errors in grammar, capitalization, punctuation, and spelling will be corrected during revision. However, you must still proofread your revised draft specifically for these types of errors. Use the proofreading symbols on page 124 as the writer of the sample composition did. The following paragraph shows some of the errors the writer found during this final check.

Music touches us all because it evokes a ~~lot~~ multitude of feeling. One person may be ~~touched~~ deeply affected by a sorrowful selection of mendels-sohn. Another person may get that same feeling when Barry Manilow sings "This Song's for you." dolefully Music can also bring joy. ~~Who~~ Few people can resist feeling ~~good~~ elated when a rythmic, spirited tune like "Jump Shout Boogie" bounces across the air waves. And of course, music can ~~affect~~ enhance love. ~~Music edifies the soul!~~ How many times has a special song made one person long for another.

When you are satisfied with your composition, make a final, neat copy. Use whatever heading your teacher directs. Below is the final version of the composition on music.

Music: The Universal Language

Every person is a unique collection of opinions, tastes, ideas, and beliefs. No two people like exactly the same things or feel precisely the same way about an issue. Yet there is one thing that all people enjoy, and which is an important part of almost everyone's life—music. Music is a universal art that ignores boundaries of age, culture, and time.

Not everyone is a famous composer or an orchestra concert buff, yet music is still important to each one of us, no matter what our age. Almost as soon as they are steady on their feet, toddlers begin "dancing" by moving in time to the rhythm of the music. As these babies get older, they take part in bands in school, campfire sing-alongs, or jam sessions with friends. Still later in life, music on the radio and stereo becomes a companion for work around the house or for travel. It provides entertainment at parties and background for dancing. Finally, as more time passes, the strains of certain tunes recall memories of days gone by.

Music touches us all because it evokes a multitude of feelings, no matter what one's taste in music is. One person may be deeply affected by a sorrowful selection of Mendelssohn. Another person may get that same feeling when Barry Manilow dolefully sings "This One's For You." Music can also bring joy. Few can resist feeling elated when a spirited, rhythmic tune like "Jump Shout Boogie" bounces across the air waves. Of course, music can also enhance love. How many times has a special song made one person long for another?

Not only can we all enjoy music, but we can also take part in its creation. Some of us can do little more than hum off key, but we have still made our contribution. So have people of all time periods and cultures. The folk melodies of simple people remain with us from centuries ago. Composers such as Bach and Handel sent us the graceful, complex music of Europe. South Americans added the enticing rhythms of the tango and rhumba. Black Americans contributed the distinctive wails of jazz and the torchy strains of the blues.

Music is a universal language. It springs from every country and affects each individual. It will exist as long as there are people to listen.

Exercise Completing the Composition

Revise and proofread the rough draft of your composition. When you have completed your revision, make a neat, final copy.

Guidelines for Writing and Revising Compositions

As you write a composition, follow the steps in Guidelines for the Process of Writing on page 122. Use the following Guidelines as you revise your first draft.

1. Has the subject been narrowed to a topic that can be covered in a few paragraphs?
2. Does the composition deal with a single topic or idea?
3. Does it have an introduction, a body, and a conclusion?
4. Does the introduction present the main idea? Does it catch the reader's interest?
5. Does the body explain or support the main idea?
6. Does the conclusion restate the main idea, summarize the information, or comment upon it?
7. Do the paragraphs work together to develop a single topic or idea that is the subject of the composition?
8. Is the composition appropriate for the audience for which it is intended? Is the purpose clear?
9. Are the ideas presented in a clear, logical order?
10. Does the composition have unity? Are the supporting ideas in each paragraph related to the topic sentence? Is each paragraph directly related to the main idea in the introductory paragraph?
11. Does the composition have coherence? Are there transitional devices that tie the paragraphs together?
12. Is the title meaningful and interesting?

Additional Guidelines

If it is a narrative composition, are the events told in the order in which they happen?

If it is a descriptive composition, does it use specific sensory details to paint a word-picture? Are the sight details presented in spatial order?

If it is an explanatory composition, does it explain how something is done or why something is believed to be so? If the composition gives instructions, are the steps organized in time sequence? In a composition that supports an idea with reasons, are the reasons organized logically? Are the reasons convincing?

SUMMARY AND APPLICATIONS

CHAPTER 10

1. Compositions are groups of paragraphs that develop a single idea.
2. The introductory paragraph of a composition tells what the composition will be about. The body paragraphs develop this idea. The final paragraph, or conclusion, summarizes the information and says "the end" to the reader.
3. Narrow the subject of the composition to an idea that can be covered within the specified limits of the paper.
4. Organize information for a composition by taking notes, identifying main ideas, grouping details under these main ideas, and putting the material in logical order.
5. As you write rough drafts, remember that change and new ideas are expected, even desirable, at this point.
6. Revise for content, unity, and coherence. Proofread your material when the content changes are complete.
7. Follow these steps when you write compositions for all subjects and purposes.

Applications in Other Subject Areas

Literature/All Subjects. In an essay, a writer explains or analyzes something in a personal way. An essay may be humorous or serious. In your school library, find a book of essays. These may be from any subject area. Read two or three essays. Attempt to identify the purpose, audience, and main idea of each one.

All Subjects. Pretend that you are working on a student-written handbook for next year's freshman class. Write a brief composition entitled "How To Succeed in (name of a subject)." Follow the guidelines given in this chapter.

Chapter Objectives

1. To write a narrative composition

2. To write a descriptive composition

3. To write the three types of explanatory compositions: the composition that explains a process, the composition that defines, and the composition that gives reasons (including the composition that persuades)

Preparing the Students

Read and discuss page 214. Bring to class several magazine articles that have different purposes (to tell a story, to describe, to explain, and to persuade. Explain that this chapter will teach students to match their topic and purpose to particular types of compositions.

Additional Resources

Mastery Test — See pages 29–30 in the test booklet

Skills Practice Book — pages 60–65

Duplicating Masters — pages 61–66

Special Populations — See special section at the front of this Teacher's Edition

Chapter 11

Types of Compositions

Skim the pages of a magazine or newspaper. Look at the different kinds of articles you find. Each type has its own particular purpose and special characteristics. Some articles are written to inform, some to entertain, some to explain, and some to persuade. Each writer has carefully matched what he or she wanted to say and accomplish with a particular type of writing.

As you write your own compositions, you must go through a similar process. You must match your topic and purpose to the type of composition that will most effectively communicate those ideas. In this chapter you will learn how to apply the process of writing to different types of compositions.

Part 1   The Narrative Composition

Pre-Writing: Planning the Narrative

The narrative paragraph describes an event or tells a story. The narrative composition has the same purpose. In the longer narrative composition, however, elements such as character, setting, point of view, and conflict are more thoroughly developed. During the pre-writing stage of the composition, each area must be explored.

Character refers to the people (or animals) in the narrative. Each character should have a distinct personality. This personality may be described directly or revealed through the action or speech of the characters. In thinking about the characters in a narrative composition, ask these questions: Who are the characters? What are they like? What do they do? What do they want? How do they feel about themselves and their situation?

Setting refers to the time and place of the story. It tells where the action develops. To develop your setting, you might ask these questions: Where is the action taking place? What does the area look like? Does it have any effect on the characters?

Point of view refers to the "angle" from which the narrative is told. It helps determine the kind of information that the narrative includes.

Sometimes the narrator, or person telling the story, takes part in the action. Then the narrative is written from the **first-person point of view.** Stories written from the first-person point of view use pronouns such as "I" or "we." You are limited in this type of narrative to what you (or the imaginary character who is telling the story) personally know, see, observe, think, or feel.

At other times, the narrator is outside the action of the story. The narrative itself tells about what happened to others. This type of composition is written from the **third-person point of view**. Personal pronouns such as "he," "she," and "they" are used. Using the third-person point of view, the writer has two choices. He or she may present a strictly factual account, or enter the minds of various characters and tell what they think, feel, see, or hear.

Objective

To write a narrative composition

Presenting the Lesson

1. Read **Planning the Narrative**, pages 215–216. Write on the board the following topics for discussion: character, setting, point of view, and conflict.

2. Name the two ways in which the distinctive personality of a character can be revealed through narrative: 1) through description by an observer or the narrator or 2) through the character's own speech and actions. Refer students to Chapter 9, pages 166–167, to review how to make a character come alive through description.

3. Refer back to Chapter 9, pages 165–166, in discussing setting.

4. Ask the class if they can think of a story they have read that was written using the first-person or third-person point of view. If they cannot, point out that often the reader is unaware of the kinds of decisions an author must make in writing a narrative.

5. Discuss the four kinds of conflict presented on page 216. Ask students to provide composition ideas that might exemplify each type of conflict.

6. Discuss "Rascal" in terms of the four topics on the board. Be sure students know that it is written from the point of view of a first-person narrator. Ask them whether character or setting is more important in this narrative. Point out that the conflict is used to reveal aspects of the animals' characters. Also mention that the conflict in the narrative is an extension of the first kind of conflict presented in the chart. It is told as the struggle between two individuals—even though the individuals are not people.

7. Read and discuss **Unity, Coherence, and Emphasis**, page 218. Remind students that they have already learned about unity and coherence in paragraphs (Chapter 8, pages 130–133) and in compositions (Chapter 10, pages 202–204).

8. Assign the Exercise on page 219.

Individualizing the Lesson

Less-Advanced Students

Students may be confused about the meaning of "point of view." They may observe that there are more third-person pronouns in "Rascal" than first-person pronouns. Tell them that if a narrative is written by a narrator who uses the words "I," "me," "my," or "mine," then it is a first-person narrative. Otherwise, it is third person. Use the two narratives on pages 186 and 187 as examples of first- and third-person narratives.

Advanced Students

1. Have students write their narratives for the Exercise, choosing a particular point of view. Then, ask them to write the same narrative using a different point of view. Which version is more effective for their particular narrative? Why? Have the

Conflict refers to the struggle or problem in which the characters become involved. Conflict usually arises because of something the character wants. There are four types of conflict.

Types of Conflict

THE INDIVIDUAL AGAINST SOCIETY: the struggle against such problems as injustice, prejudice, and loss of individual freedom. This also includes the struggle of one person against another.

THE INDIVIDUAL AGAINST SELF: the struggle within the mind of an individual as he or she tries to make a personal decision.

THE INDIVIDUAL AGAINST A SUPERNATURAL FORCE: the struggle against God, or the gods (as in the ancient myths and legends). Also, the struggle against the devil or evil forces.

THE INDIVIDUAL AGAINST NATURE: the struggle to survive natural catastrophes, such as floods, earthquakes, and hurricanes. This would also include the struggle against animals, and, in some cases, against plants.

Following is an example of a narrative composition. As you read it, keep in mind the definitions of character, setting, point of view, and conflict.

Rascal

All raccoons are attracted by shining objects, and Rascal was no exception. He was fascinated by brass doorknobs, glass marbles, my broken watch, and small coins. I gave him three bright, new pennies which he hoarded with the happiness of a little miser. He felt them carefully, smelled them, tasted them, and then hid them in a dark corner with some of his other treasures.

One day Rascal decided to carry one of his pennies to the

back porch. Poe-the-Crow was perched on the porch rail teasing the cats, but keeping just beyond their reach. This raucous old bird, who cawed and cussed in crow language, was arching his wings and strutting like a poolroom bully as Rascal pushed open the screen and trundled into the sunlight, his penny shining like newly minted gold.

Poe and Rascal had taken an instant dislike to each other when first they met. Crows, like most other birds, know that raccoons steal birds' eggs and sometimes eat fledglings. In addition Poe was jealous. He had seen me petting and pampering my small raccoon. However, Rascal was large enough now to pull a few tail feathers from the big, black bird during their noisy squabbles. And Poe, who was no fool, was taking few chances.

The penny, however, was so tempting that the crow threw caution to the winds and made a dive for the bright object (for crows are as insatiably attracted by glittering trinkets as are raccoons and in addition are inveterate thieves). Rascal was carrying the penny in his mouth, and when Poe swooped to conquer, his beak closed not only on the penny but upon half a dozen of Rascal's coarse, strong whiskers. When the black thief tried to make his fast getaway he found himself attached to the raccoon, who with a high scream of fury began fighting for his property and his life. Such a tangle of shining, black feathers and furious fur you have seldom seen as Rascal and Poe wrestled and struggled. I arrived to untangle them, and both were angry with me. Rascal nipped me slightly for the first time, and Poe made several ungracious comments.

The penny, meanwhile, had rolled from the porch into the grass below, where the crow promptly spotted it, seized it once again, and took wing. I gave the incident no more thought, pacified Rascal with another penny, and resumed work on my canoe in the living room.—STERLING NORTH

There are three *characters* in this narrative. The major characters are Rascal, a pet raccoon, and Poe-the-Crow, an ill-tempered old bird. The minor character is the narrator. The *setting* is the back porch of the narrator's house. It is on the porch that the *conflict* between Rascal and Poe-the-Crow takes place, a

students discuss the different problems involved in using a first-person point of view and a third-person point of view.

2. Have students write detailed "biographies" for one or two imaginary characters. Explain that the more detailed a character is in their own minds, the more effectively they will be able to create the character for their readers.

Optional Practice

Have students, as a class, brainstorm all of the elements for a narrative based on an imaginary incident. Encourage the development of in-depth characters and a detailed setting.

Extending the Lesson

Read the class the opening lines from several stories by Edgar Allan Poe such as the ones that follow.

"True!—nervous—very, very dreadfully nervous I had been and am; but why *will* you say that I am mad? The disease had sharpened my senses— not destroyed—not dulled them." ("The Tell-Tale Heart")

"During the whole of a dull, dark, and soundless day in the autumn of the year, when the clouds hung oppressively low in the heavens, I had been passing alone, on horseback, through a singularly dreary tract of country, and at length found myself, as the shades of the evening drew on, within view of the melancholy House of Usher." ("The Fall of the House of Usher") struggle between two individuals over possession of a bright penny. In describing this struggle, the author uses the *first-person point of view*.

Unity, Coherence, and Emphasis

Like any good piece of writing, a narrative composition must show unity and coherence.

Unity is achieved when every sentence in the composition relates to one main idea. The writer of the narrative about Rascal achieves unity by developing the idea presented in the introductory paragraph: he explains what happens because of Rascal's attraction to shining objects. He makes use of two other unifying techniques as well. He uses colorful, interesting details throughout the narrative, and he ties together ideas with these transitional devices:

1. Repeating the names *Rascal* and *Poe*
2. Repeating the words *crow, raccoon*, and *penny*
3. Using synonyms for the word *shining*
4. Using the word *however* to show opposite points of view
5. Using the words *and* and *in addition* to show the relationships between ideas
6. Using *one day, now, when*, and *meanwhile* to indicate time.

Coherence is the logical arrangement of ideas. The writer achieves coherence in this narrative by organizing the ideas into chronological order. With the exception of one flashback in which he recalls the dislike between Rascal and Poe, the writer describes the incident as it happened.

Emphasis is achieved (1) by selecting a central idea, then grouping details around that idea; and (2) by stressing those details that are important in relation to the central idea. The writer of "Rascal" achieves emphasis by focusing on one central idea in the narrative—the fight between Rascal and Poe-the-Crow over the penny. All the details relate to that central idea. These details include those that he gives about Rascal's attraction to shining objects, about Poe's character, and about the animals' dislike for each other.

218

Exercise   Writing a Narrative Composition

Check your writing journal for possible subjects for a narrative composition. They can be based on events in which you participated or on events that were observed by you. They can even be based on events that were described to you by someone else. They can be based on fact, on imagination, or on a combination of both.

List some possible subjects. Then complete the following steps:

Pre-Writing: Select and narrow your topic. Who are the characters? What is the setting? What is the conflict? Choose details to develop each of these elements. Then concentrate on some finer points. What point of view will you use? What order will be the most effective for your material?

First Draft: Use your pre-writing notes to get your ideas down on paper. Give some thought to unity and coherence. Add new details as they occur to you.

Revision: Go over your rough draft several times. Are your characters well developed? Is the conflict clear? Is the same point of view used throughout? Do you need to include other details? Refer to the Guidelines for Writing and Revising Compositions on page 212. Also review the two sets of guidelines at the end of Chapter 7.

Part 2   The Descriptive Composition

Description is seldom the basis for an entire composition. Instead, it is usually used along with other types of writing. However, there may be times when you are particularly moved by a place, a scene, or a person and want to express your feelings in writing. The descriptive composition is one way of doing so.

Before you begin a descriptive composition, you need to understand unity, coherence, and emphasis as they apply to this type of writing. You also need a better understanding of point of view, which affects the other three characteristics.

Part 2

Objective

To write a descriptive composition

Presenting the Lesson

1. Read and discuss **The Descriptive Composition**, pages 219–223. To illustrate the idea of physical point of view, ask half the class to make a list of sensory details— sights, sounds, smells, etc.—that they imagine they might see from the basement window of a forty-story building on a city street. Have the other half of the class write sensory details as if they were standing on the roof of the building. Then compare the lists. Point out that a writer should describe a scene from a consistent perspective.

To illustrate mood, have half of the class write details for a scene in which they wake up in the country on a snowy winter morning. Tell them that the scene makes them feel isolated and depressed. Have the other half of the class write details for waking up in the same situation, but to a feeling of peace and wonder. Then have the two groups compare lists.

2. Point out that unity, coherence, and emphasis in descriptive compositions are achieved through the use of carefully selected details, effective transitional devices and a consistent perspective. Show students how the author of "November Afternoon" re-creates a vividly remembered scene by describing it from a consistent perspective both in space and in mood. The focus on "light" provides the necessary emphasis. The author has also used transitional devices to guide the reader through the chronological order of the composition.

3. Assign the Exercise on page 224. Remind the students that there are lists of sense words in Chapter 4 that might be useful in writing their descriptive compositions.

Individualizing the Lesson

Less-Advanced Students

Help students understand the idea of mood in a composition by

Point of View

Physical Point of View. In your study of the descriptive paragraph, you learned to put details into a logical order. You learned to describe things from side to side, from top to bottom (or the reverse), and from near to far (or the reverse). You also learned to use other methods of organization, along with key words that show a change in direction.

What you learned about organizing paragraphs also applies to compositions. You can arrange the details in a descriptive composition in any order, as long as it is logical and fits your subject. No matter what plan you choose, though, you must have a physical point of view. This is the place from which you choose to view the object of your description.

Once you have decided on a physical point of view, your description should include only those details that can be observed from that point. For example, if you choose a high cliff overlooking a mountain valley as your physical point of view, you will describe only the things that you can hear, see, touch, taste, and smell from that location. A physical point of view provides a sense of realism to your composition. Your readers will "see" in their mind only what they would see if they were actually looking at the scene you are describing.

Mood, or Mental Point of View. The mood of a piece of writing is the overall feeling the writer wishes to create. In a description, mood changes according to the individual and the situation. For example, imagine that you are looking at a mountain valley. The sky is dark; heavy, black clouds are forming on the horizon; the wind is moaning faintly through the pines; and thunder crashes over the distant peaks. The sight may make you feel sad and depressed. This is your mood at the moment, and you will want to re-create this feeling in your composition. Choose details and descriptive words that convey this mood to your reader.

Now imagine that you visit the valley on another day. The morning sun is shining; the sky is a cloudless blue; a woodpecker is clattering rhythmically in the distance; and a hint of pine scents the air. You may feel happy, carefree, even excited. This is the mood that you want to communicate in your composition.

Unity

When you write a descriptive composition, you are trying to create a single, unified impression for your reader. You can achieve this if you do the following:

1. Maintain a definite physical point of view and mood.
2. Choose details carefully.
3. Make sure that the sentences in each paragraph relate to the topic sentence. Also make certain that each paragraph relates back to the introductory paragraph.
4. Use transitional devices that tie ideas together.

Choosing Details To Achieve Unity. Choosing details carefully means selecting those details that add to the impression you wish to create. It also means describing the details with precise words that create a strong image for the reader.

For an example of precise writing, contrast the following:

1. The bird sang in the tree.
2. The mourning dove grieved in the old pine.

The first sentence is vague and imprecise. The second sentence carefully identifies the bird, the tree, and the action being performed.

Here is another example:

1. The elephant moved down the ramp.
2. The huge elephant lumbered down the wooden ramp.

The second sentence includes specific adjectives and a strong, precise verb. It creates a much clearer image than does the first sentence.

Coherence

Coherence, or clarity, is achieved through the logical arrangement of ideas. Several logical orders were mentioned in the discussion of physical point of view. Another order is chronological, or time, order. It is used occasionally in description, but more

reading several paragraphs that illustrate various moods. The paragraphs on page 69, page 79, page 130, and page 141 provide suitable examples.

Advanced Students

Point out that the physical point of view and the mood of a composition are generally not stated explicitly. Rather, they are implied by the details that the writer provides. After the students have written their descriptive compositions, ask them to read them aloud and have other students comment on the author's physical point of view and mood. If these aspects are not clearly implied in the composition, have the author revise according to the class's suggestions.

Optional Practice

To reinforce the idea of physical point of view, have the class list details for three descriptive compositions about a traffic jam. The lists should reflect the point of view as experienced by the following participants: a pedestrian, a motorist, a traffic reporter in a heliocopter.

Extending the Lesson

Tell students that descriptive compositions are most likely to be found in travel literature, diaries, and journals. Read aloud the following excerpts from *The Travels of William Bartram* (1791). (You may want to preface the reading with an explanation that the slightly odd language and sentence structure are due to the journal format and the time period during which the excerpt was written.) Ask the class to comment on physical point of view, mood, and specific sense words used to create the mood.

"The morning pleasant, we decamped early, proceeding on, rising gently for several miles, over sandy, gravelly ridges, we find ourselves in an elevated, high, open, airy region, somewhat rocky, on the backs of the ridges, and present to view on every side the most dreary, solitary, desert waste I had ever beheld; groups of bare rocks emerging out of the naked gravel and drifts of white sand; the grass thinly scattered and but few trees; the pines; oaks, olives and sideroxilons, poor, misshapen and tattered; scarce an animal to be seen or noise heard, save the symphony of the western breeze, through the bristly pine leaves, or solitary sand crickets screech, or at best the more social converse of the frogs, in solemn chorus with the swift breezes, brought from distant fens and forests."

often in explanatory and narrative compositions. Whatever order you use, transitional words and phrases—such as those listed on pages 160 and 164—help to tie your ideas together and make them clear to your reader.

Emphasis

Emphasis may seem easy to achieve in a descriptive composition. After all, you have already chosen one specific scene or particular object as the subject of your description. However, an even more precise focus may help to strengthen your descriptive composition even more.

In describing a scene, for example, the writer often chooses a center of interest. This may be an unusual mountain, a unique building, or an interesting play of light or color. All other details are then grouped around this point of focus. The central image dominates the scene; the other details are described in relation to it.

Studying a Descriptive Composition

The following composition, which describes a fall afternoon, illustrates the concepts presented thus far in Part 2. As you read, try to determine the author's point of view. Also look for ways in which the writer achieves unity and coherence.

November Afternoon

It is not yet 4:30, and the sun is nearing the low ridge to the west. Soon the brightness of the late autumn afternoon will yield to twilight, to dusk, and to dark.

The sun begins to set behind the ridge. The last, long light climbs from the valley's frosted pasture grass up the gray trunks of the naked maples and seems to pause on the hilltops to the east. Then it is gone. Twilight, the glow of November evening, possesses the day.

At first there is the bright, shadowless light, a sunless daylight in which the growing moon, halfway up the eastern sky, is only a ghost. Then the glow comes, a rosy suffusion so subtle it could be a reflection of the maple leaves at the roadside or the bronze-red grass in the neglected meadow. The air seems to thin and brighten, and the chill diminishes distances. The world comes close, the familiar world of this place called home.

The glow fades. Dusk creeps in, unhurried but insistent, and the clarity of vision dims. In its place is a deceptive clarity of hearing. The farm dog barking just down the road sounds no closer than a truck shifting gears on a hill a mile away. The rustle of leathery leaves in an oak not ten feet away seems as far off as the hooting of the barred owl across the valley. And time somehow has lost its dimensions. It is evening and it is autumn, and the moon has begun to glow. The scuffle of leaves at the roadside just ahead could be a noontime cat or a midnight fox or the evening breeze.

Sunset, twilight, dusk, darkness, all by six o'clock on a mid-November evening, is late autumn's summary of serenity.

—*The New York Times*

The physical point of view is a spot within a valley. The mood is one of peace. The single, unified impression is that of serenity. Unity is achieved through a stable point of view and the choice of precise details. Carefully chosen words, such as "The last, long light climbs from the valley's frosted pasture grass" and "Dusk creeps in, unhurried, but insistent" strengthen the feeling of serenity.

Each paragraph relates to the introductory paragraph by telling something about the late autumn afternoon. The paragraphs, and the ideas within the paragraphs, are tied together by the use of the word *light*. The repeated use of synonyms for light— for example, *brightness, glow,* and *rosy*—also ties ideas together in the composition.

Coherence is achieved through the logical arrangement of ideas into chronological order. The writer describes sunset, twilight, dusk, and darkness in the order in which they happen.

Emphasis is achieved by grouping the details in relation to *light*. The changing light, reflecting the oncoming night, is the central image in the composition. All other objects are seen and heard through this light.

Exercise Writing a Description

Following the techniques described in Chapter 10, "Writing a Composition," write a descriptive composition of five paragraphs. Begin by choosing a subject based on personal experience. Check your journal for possibilities, or try brainstorming for ideas. Once you have a topic, complete the following steps:

Pre-Writing: Narrow your subject. Decide on your audience and your purpose. Decide on your physical point of view and mood. Gather, group, and organize your ideas in a writing plan.

First Draft: Write a rough draft, using your writing plan as a guide. Try to use vivid, precise words in your description.

Revision: Check to make sure that all ideas are related to each other and to the introductory paragraph. Does your composition have unity, coherence, and emphasis? Did you use strong verbs, precise nouns, and vivid descriptive words and phrases? Refer to the Guidelines for Writing and Revising Compositions on page 212. Also review the two charts at the end of Chapter 7.

Part 3   The Explanatory Composition

There are three main types of explanatory compositions. An explanatory composition, sometimes called an expository composition, can explain a process, define, or give reasons. Like all compositions, an explanatory composition opens with an introductory paragraph that catches the reader's attention and gives an indication of what will follow. The body paragraphs explain or support the ideas presented in the opening paragraph. A concluding paragraph signals the end of the composition.

The well written explanatory composition is characterized by unity, coherence, and emphasis. These three qualities are achieved in much the same way as they are achieved in descriptive compositions. Unity is created by a structure in which all the parts

Part 3

Objectives

1. To understand and be able to write the three types of explanatory compositions: the composition that explains a process, the composition that defines, and the composition that gives reasons
2. To understand and write a composition that persuades

Presenting the Lesson

1. Read the introduction to **The Explanatory Composition**, pages 224–225. Point out to students that they have already studied paragraphs work together, by precise details, and by transitional devices. Coherence is created by the logical arrangement of ideas. In some compositions, especially those that give instructions and those that include incidents or anecdotes, logical order means chronological order. In others, logical order fits the special content of the composition. The third quality, emphasis, is achieved by selecting a central idea that dominates the other ideas presented in the composition.

The Composition That Explains a Process

A composition that explains a process tells how to do something or how something works. The writer's purpose is to explain the process so that it may be easily done or understood by the reader. Therefore, the composition is usually written in a direct, straightforward style. A composition of this type is most often developed through facts or examples that are presented in chronological order.

Following is an example of an explanatory composition that explains a process. See if you can identify the specific methods used by the writer to achieve unity, coherence, and emphasis.

How To Read Faster

When I was a kid in Philadelphia, I must have read every comic book ever published. I zipped through all of them in a couple of days, then reread the good ones until the next issues arrived. As I got older, though, my eyeballs must have slowed down. I mean, comic books started to pile up faster than my brother Russell and I could read them. It wasn't until much later, when I was getting my doctorate, that I realized it wasn't my eyeballs that were to blame. The problem is that there is too much to read these days, and too little time to read every word of it. That's when I started to look around for common-sense, practical ways to help me read faster. I found three that are especially good. And if I can learn them, so can you—and you can put them to use immediately.

The first way is previewing. It is especially useful for getting

that explain a process, define, give reasons, and persuade in Chapter 9, pages 172–179. Emphasize that explanatory compositions are written for subjects that are too complex to be covered in a single paragraph.

2. Read and discuss **The Composition that Explains a Process**, pages 225–227. Point out that clarity is one of the most important qualities of a composition that explains a process, and that it is achieved by including all important steps, grouping similar ideas together, and organizing the groups into a logical order.

3. Discuss the sample composition "How to Read Faster," pointing out that the author has created interest by including amusing personal details as well as by explaining the points he wants to make in a clear and organized fashion.

4. Assign the Exercise on pages 227–228.

5. Read and discuss **The Composition That Defines**, pages 228–229. Review the process of defining a term by writing a simple word such as "hammer" on the board. Have students put the word into its general category, "tools," then list characteristics which distinguish it from other members of the category. Explain that a composition that defines a term includes the basic definition plus further explanatory facts or examples.

6. Discuss "Lasers" with the class. Ask students to find the general category into which the laser is placed (light form). Then ask them to tell where in the composition the definition of laser appears (second paragraph). The analysis after the composition will help them see how each paragraph contributes to the definition.

7. Assign the Exercise on page 230.

8. Read and discuss **The Composition That Gives Reasons**, pages 230–232. Point out that, although the title of the sample composition is "Pets Are Better Than Medicine," the author actually gives reasons that show the emotional and psychologicial benefits of pets as well.

9. Assign the Exercise on page 232. Remind students to look at the list of words in Chapter 10, page 203, that show the relationshp between ideas.

10. Read and discuss **The Composition That Persuades**, pages 233–234. Ask students if they can imagine anyone disagreeing with the ideas in the composition "The Computer as Friend." They are no doubt aware that some people think of computers as mechanical monsters that are taking over our lives; in fact, the author of the composition even mentions the view that is opposite to his. Point out that the sign of a persuasive composition is that it addresses a controversial subject— that is, a subject that has more than one reasonable side—and attempts to persuade the readers to feel the same way the writer does, about the subject. To convince the audience, the writer tries to select strong, unarguable reasons. Ask the class if the composition makes any points that they had never previously thought of.

11. Assign the Exercise on page 235. When students are choosing their topics, tell them to be sure to select a point of view that someone could reasonably disagree with. Stress the importance of consider-

a general idea of heavy reading like long magazine or newspaper articles and nonfiction books. To preview, read the entire first two paragraphs of whatever you've chosen. Next read only the first sentence of each successive paragraph. Then read the entire last two paragraphs. This will give you a quick, overall view of the long, unfamiliar material. It will keep you from spending time on things you don't really want—or need—to read.

The second way to read faster is skimming. It is a good way to get a general idea of light reading like popular magazines or the sports and entertainment sections of the paper. It is also a good way to review material you've read before. To skim, think of your eyes as magnets. Force them to move fast. Sweep them across each and every line of type. Pick up only a few key words in each line. You will end up reading about half the words in *less* than half the time it would take to read every word.

The third way to increase your reading speed is clustering. Clustering trains you to look at groups of words rather than one at a time. For example, instead of reading a line like this: My—brother—Russell—thinks—monsters, you would read it like this:

$$\left(\text{My brother Russell}\right) \quad \left(\text{thinks monsters}\right)$$

For most of us, clustering takes constant practice because it's a totally different way of seeing what we read. To practice clustering, begin with something easy to read. Read it as fast as you can. Concentrate on seeing three to four words at once rather than one word at a time. Then reread the piece at your normal speed to see what you missed the first time. Practice fifteen minutes every day until you can read clusters without missing much the first time.

So now you have three ways to help you read faster: previewing to cut down on unnecessary heavy reading; skimming to get a quick, general idea of light reading; and clustering to increase your speed and comprehension. With enough practice, you'll be able to handle more reading at school and at home in less time. You should even have enough time to read your favorite comic books!—BILL COSBY

The introductory paragraph explains that the composition is about three ways to help you read faster. The three body paragraphs develop this idea. The sentences in each paragraph relate directly to the topic sentence. Following the body is a conclusion which summarizes the ideas in the composition and which relates back to the introductory paragraph. This carefully thought out structure contributes to the unity of the composition.

Another way that this composition is unified is by the repetition of the words *read* and *way* throughout the five paragraphs.

Coherence is achieved by the logical arrangement of ideas throughout the composition and within each paragraph. The opening paragraph introduces the idea of three ways to read. The next three paragraphs each explain one way. Each paragraph is structured so that it first names the way, next tells a little more about it, then gives specific directions for applying the method.

Emphasis is achieved by grouping all the ideas around the central idea of reading faster. Details about why it is important to read faster, about what kind of materials can and should be read faster, and about the ways to increase reading speed are all related to the central idea.

Exercise Writing a Composition That Explains a Process

Choose one of the topics from the box or make up one of your own. Then complete the steps that follow.

Possible Topics

1. How to get a part-time job
2. How to study for a test
3. How to tune a bicycle
4. How to train a dog

5. How to build a model
6. How a rocket works
7. How a telephone works
8. How a camera works

Pre-Writing: Narrow your topic and identify your purpose and audience. What facts and examples are necessary to explain the process clearly? What are the main steps? How should your material be organized so that the reader can follow the steps easily?

ing the audience when selecting supporting details.

Individualizing the Lesson
Less-Advanced Students

1. In a group, develop a pre-writing plan for a composition that explains a process. Have students brainstorm for a simple topic, such as how to prepare a simple meal or how to play checkers. Have the students list the steps in the process, make sure the order of steps is logical, and list possible transitional words and phrases to connect the steps. Have students discuss possible details and examples for the introduction, body, and conclusion of a composition based on the pre-writing plan.

2. Provide students with several topics that lend themselves to relatively simple definitions. Choose subjects that they would be both familiar and comfortable with, such as a type of music, or style of clothing. A class brainstorming session might prove helpful.

3. Hold a group brainstorming session to help students discover topics for a persuasive composition. Start with general topics such as world events, local or national elections, education, environment, and fads, and write on the chalkboard students' ideas for more specific topics. Emphasize that the purpose of a persuasive composition is to convince other people to accept an idea, and not simply to state an opinion. Work with students individually to help them avoid circular reasoning ("Our rivers should be cleaned up because our rivers are very polluted.") and other fallacies in logic.

After students have written their compositions that persuade, have them write another composition that takes the opposite side of the issue. See if they can come up with reasonable arguments on both sides.

Optional Practice

To emphasize the use of reasonable language in a persuasive composition, have students complete the following assignment:

Imagine that you bought a new pocket calculator. After using it for two weeks, it stopped working, so you returned it to the dealer for repairs. After two more weeks it was finally fixed, but promptly stopped working again. Write a letter to the manufacturer stating why you are returning the calculator for a full refund. Explain what is wrong with the calculator, being sure to use reasonable, persuasive language.

Extending the Lesson

Have each student find and bring to class an editorial from a magazine or newspaper. Have students analyze the editorial by determining its intended audience and purpose, the writer's viewpoint, and the reasons given to support that viewpoint. Tell students to underline transitional words and phrases and to circle any uses of harsh or overly emotional language.

First Draft: Using your pre-writing notes, get your ideas down on paper. Concentrate on thorough explanation and clear transitions.

Revision: Go over your rough draft several times. Is your explanation broken down into simple steps? Is it easy to understand? Have any steps been left out? Refer to the Guidelines for Writing and Revising Compositions. Also review the two sets of Guidelines at the end of Chapter 7.

The Composition That Defines

A composition that defines includes the same main parts as the paragraph that defines. It states

1. the term to be defined
2. the general category to which the term belongs
3. the unique characteristics that separate the term from similar members of the general category.

The remainder of the composition builds on that basic definition. It may further explain the unique characteristics of the subject. It may also identify the term's various parts, types, or uses. The facts or examples that develop the composition are usually presented from least important to most important. Another common order is most familiar idea to least familiar idea. This order helps the reader by building on knowledge he or she already has.

The following composition defines a sophisticated term that could not be thoroughly explained in a single paragraph.

Lasers

Compared to other light forms, laser light is definitely "the new kid on the block." Lasers were developed less than twenty-five years ago, but they are already used in such widely different areas as medicine, manufacturing, and the military.

A laser is an electronic device that emits an intense, highly concentrated beam of energy in the form of light rays. It does this by amplifying an existing light. In fact, the word *laser* itself is an acronym standing for **l**ight **a**mplification by **s**timulated **e**mission of **r**adiation. Laser light differs from ordinary light forms in two ways. First, a laser light is a single, pure color. Secondly, laser light is highly directional. Where regular light travels in all directions, a laser light travels in a narrow beam and thus has high intensity.

Lasers are divided into three types based on their light-amplifying substance. The most widely used is the *solid laser*. Its light is amplified by a crystal, glass, or semi-conductor. *Gas lasers* use gas or a mixture of gases to amplify light. They produce a continuous beam of light, and are especially useful in communications and in measuring. A third type of laser is the *liquid laser* which uses a dye dissolved in a special liquid. It can produce either bursts of light or continuous light.

More and more uses are being found for lasers all the time. In manufacturing, lasers are used for a source of intense heat. They can weld a variety of metals, cut hard materials, and drill minute holes. In medicine, the laser substitutes for the surgeon's scalpel. Its heat seals off blood vessels during operations, resulting in so-called "bloodless surgery." Lasers even have a use in national defense! The military can bounce lasers off moving targets and determine their distance and speed.

Lasers produce the most powerful light beam known today. They may be new, but they've already proven their worth.

The first paragraph introduces a very general definition of a laser as a light form. It also makes a statement about the value of lasers. The second paragraph contains the full definition of the term as well as its unique characteristics. The third paragraph divides the term into various types and briefly identifies each of these. Finally, the last body paragraph presents various uses of the laser. The conclusion refers back to the introduction by restating the laser's general category and value.

This structure and the repetition of the term *laser* help create unity. Coherence is achieved by presenting the material in a logical order, least to most important. That is, although the definition and description of the laser are necessary to the reader's understanding, the most important thing for the reader to understand is how the laser is important to his or her life.

Exercise Writing a Composition That Defines

Imagine that you have been asked to write an article for your school newspaper. This article should define an organization to which you belong or a subject about which you have special knowledge. Once you have identified and narrowed a topic, complete the following steps:

Pre-Writing: Consider your audience. What do they know about your topic? What details will they need? Next consider your subject itself. To what general category does your term belong? What are its identifying characteristics? Can it be divided into types or parts? What is its function? Finally, select and organize your details. Which order would work best? Least to most important? Most to least familiar?

First Draft: Use your pre-writing plan to get your ideas down on paper. Remember to begin with a general definition. Then work toward a more specific definition.

Revision: Have you clearly explained your term? Can it easily be distinguished from other closely related terms? Are your supporting paragraphs developed with enough detail? Refer to the Guidelines for Writing and Revising Compositions on page 212. Also review the two sets of Guidelines at the end of Chapter 7.

The Composition That Gives Reasons

Compositions of this type give reasons why a fact or an opinion is so. In the introductory paragraph, you clearly state a fact or present an opinion. The paragraphs that follow give reasons that support the fact or opinion in this type of composition.

The reasons may be additional facts, statistics, examples, or anecdotes. They must be carefully chosen, though, if they are to provide good support for your initial statement or opinion. Generally, you present your reasons either in their order of importance or in order of familiarity. Make this decision based on the material itself and on your knowledge of your audience.

Pets Are Better Than Medicine

Pets are usually thought of as pleasant, amusing little animals that stroll through the house or patiently swim around in a bowl. Their purpose is simply to provide companionship and simple amusement for their owners. Yet animals can be much more than friendly housepets. When used by knowledgeable therapists, they can actually be powerful weapons against disease and mental illness. It is this function of pets that we must recognize and take better advantage of.

In a very basic way, animals can improve everyone's health. Recent studies show that the simple pastime of watching a tank full of fish can actually *lower* a person's blood pressure. Also, even though blood pressure will rise when people talk to other people, there is no rise in people's blood pressure when they talk to their pets. This may be because animal companionship is uncritical and non-judgmental. Whatever the reason, pets seem to provide a safe, non-threatening outlet for our emotions and concerns.

In medicine, animals are being used increasingly in physical therapy. For instance, riding horseback can have several advantages for physically disabled children. It can give them confidence and help them improve their balance. Riding also stimulates muscles that can't develop in wheelchairs. People with cerebral palsy, for example, suffer from tightness of the thigh muscles. Sitting on a horse stretches those muscles.

Pets can also be used to reach people who are withdrawn and lonely, or who are severely depressed. In several cities, the Anti-Cruelty Society takes puppies around to centers for the elderly. In one case, an elderly woman who had suffered a stroke was very withdrawn. At first she responded only to the dog, but on later visits she began to show the puppy to other patients and to interact with them. Pets are used as therapy in hospitals for the mentally ill, too. Social workers feel that animals help to establish bonds of trust and communication.

For all these reasons, the therapeutic value of animals should be recognized. Pets may be friendly, lovable, or cuddly; but they can also be powerful medicine.

In the introductory paragraph, the writer states her position that animals should be thought of as valuable aids to good health. She achieves unity by developing three reasons why this is so:

1. Animals are beneficial to general well-being.
2. Animals are used in physical therapy.
3. Animals are used in mental and emotional therapy.

Each reason ties into the initial statement about pets and is developed with specific examples. Phrases such as "for instance," "for example," and "finally" also provide unity. The reasons are organized so that the most widely understood appears first. From this familiar idea, the writer moves to the more unfamiliar uses of animal therapy. This order helps provide a coherent structure.

Exercise Writing a Composition That Gives Reasons

Choose one of the topics from the box or make up one of your own. Then complete the steps below.

Possible Topics

1. Favorite movies
2. My best quality/my worst quality
3. Why study history?
4. It is the best of times/it is the worst of times
5. The advantages of newspaper/television news

Pre-Writing: Narrow your topic and identify your purpose and audience. What idea or opinion do you want to express? What details develop these reasons? How can they best be presented?

First Draft: Use your writing plan to get your ideas down on paper. Try to present your reasons clearly and logically.

Revision: Have you stated your position clearly? Are your reasons logical? fully developed? Refer to the Guidelines for Writing and Revising Compositions on page 212. Also use the two sets of Guidelines at the end of Chapter 7.

The Composition That Persuades

A special type of composition that gives reasons is the composition that persuades. The first step in writing this type of composition is to find an issue with two or more sides. Next, you must decide which side you will take. Identifying your audience in the pre-writing stage is a crucial matter. For this type of paper, your audience will be those people who have not made up their minds about the issue, or those who disagree with your opinion. Your purpose, then, is to persuade this audience that you are right.

To persuade this audience, select the strongest and most convincing reasons possible. Also, select reasons that will have the most impact on your particular group of readers. The same reasons may not be equally effective with different age groups or types of people.

As with paragraphs of this type, your reasons and supporting details may include statistics, facts, examples, or anecdotes. The order you present your ideas in is usually from least important to most important. In this way, you build a case that leaves a strong impression in your reader's mind.

The Computer as Friend

The growing influence of computers has many people ill at ease. They fear the way these machines are creeping into businesses, homes, and even such familiar places as libraries and stores. Yet these individuals shouldn't be so concerned. Despite their forbidding aspects, computers really have a great deal going for them. Each of us must set aside our misconceptions and prejudices, and see computers for the fantastic resources they are.

Computers, if you're not afraid of them, can be marvelous companions. First of all, they are an endless source of stimulation and fun. They can tease you, play games with you, and stretch your creative powers. Also, in contrast to TV which does not interact with viewers, computers force users to keep their minds alert. In addition, computers can help you with your work (something even your best friends might be reluctant to do).

Uncomplainingly, a computer will plan your budget, reorganize a report, or draw a graph. It will do its best to make you look good.

Computers also provide their users with a sense of achievement. The day you finally understand computer techniques, you feel as you did the day you learned to ride a bicycle. You also finally realize that computers will not one day rule the world. You rule the computer. It is yours to direct.

Finally, computers provide a chance to prepare for the future. Like it or not, these devices are here to stay. In a few years, the ability to use a computer may be a standard requirement for high school graduation. Ignorance of computers will hinder an individual in all phases of his or her life. Those people who establish early friendships with computers will enjoy a head start in the race toward the twenty-first century.

Computers can be a treasure chest of wonders, if only we're not afraid to look inside. They can also be powerful friends. It's time to put aside our distrust and welcome them into our lives as wonderful new companions.

Notice that the writer has identified his audience, those who feel ill at ease with computers, in his introduction. His opinion is that computers "have a great deal going for them." His purpose is to convince his audience that it is time to put aside fears and learn what computers have to offer.

The emphasis in the composition is placed on the positive, nonthreatening aspect of computers. This mood is reinforced with words such as "marvelous," "fun," "achievement," and "friendships." The writer's reasons for championing the computer become increasingly more serious. His first reason points out the fun of computers while his last reason emphasizes the computer's link to future success. Finally, the writer achieves unity by repeating the word "computer" and by clearly stating his reasons so that they relate to his opinion.

Finally, notice the writer's use of reasonable language. He lets his reasons do his arguing for him, and he does not resort to undue criticism of others or harsh language. All good persuasive compositions follow this strategy.

Exercise Writing a Composition That Persuades

Consult your writing journal, look through a newspaper, or brainstorm for topics that require persuasion. Choose a topic and then complete the following steps:

Pre-Writing: Narrow your topic. What is your opinion? Who is your audience? What reasons support your opinion? What details will best develop those reasons? What would be the most effective order for presenting your reasons?

First Draft: Use your pre-writing plan to get your ideas down on paper. Use unbiased, reasonable language to present your material.

Revision: Have you clearly stated your opinion? Does the emphasis of your composition reflect your audience's concerns? Does your paper have unity and coherence? Refer to the Guidelines for Writing and Revising Compositions on page 212. Also use the two sets of Guidelines at the end of Chapter 7.

Discuss this summary with
the students. Emphasize that
understanding the different
types of compositions can
help a writer make effective
choices for presenting ideas.

Encourage students to use
this summary for review, or as
part of the SQ3R method of
study (see Chapter 15). Remind them, though, that more
specific points can only be reviewed by skimming the chapter itself.

Applications in Other Subject Areas

Read and discuss **Home Economics/Industrial Education**
on page 236. After students
have written a composition
that explains a process that
they have learned in Home
Economics or Industrial Arts
class, have them think of a
technical term, such as *selvage, blanch,* or *bevelled* that
they have learned in these
classes. Ask students to write
a paragraph or composition
that defines the term.

SUMMARY AND APPLICATIONS   CHAPTER 11

1. Narrative, descriptive, and explanatory compositions each have
   specific purposes and characteristics. All well-written compositions, however, incorporate unity, coherence, and emphasis.

2. Narrative compositions are used to relate events or incidents. They
   include the elements of character, setting, conflict, and point
   of view.

3. Descriptive compositions are used to "paint a word picture" of
   places, scenes or people. Such compositions emphasize sensory
   details.

4. Explanatory, or expository, compositions can be used to explain
   a process, define a term or idea, or provide reasons for a statement or opinion. A special type of composition that gives reasons
   is the composition that persuades.

Applications in Other Subject Areas

Home Economics / Industrial Arts. Write down several projects that you
have completed this year, such as making an item of clothing or tuning up an engine. Write a composition that would explain one aspect of the project to someone who has just transferred into the class.
The composition should be clear enough that the student would be
able to complete the project after reading the composition.

Mass Media / Social Studies. A newspaper includes many different types
of items. Choose one of the following ideas and write a short article
that could be turned in to an editor.

    a. A human interest story about a special moment in the life
       of an individual.

    b. A special feature story describing a local event such as a
       school carnival, art fair, concert, canoe race, or marathon.

    c. An editorial giving reasons for or against taking some action
       in your school or community.

Chapter 12

Writing a Report

Chapter Objectives

1. To choose and narrow a subject for a report

2. To prepeare to research a report by identifying purpose and audience, learning the difference between fact and opinion, and making a list of questions to be answered in the report

3. To prepare a working bibliography and take notes for a report

4. To organize the facts for a report and prepare an outline

5. To write a first draft of a report

6. To revise a report

7. To prepare a bibliography for a report

Preparing the Students

Ask the students where they would find the details for a composition on the migration of the Monarch butterfly, the history of the piano, or how to amend the Constitution. Point out that none of these topics can be developed from their own first-hand, personal experiences. Each one requires research in outside sources. Then read and discuss the introductory paragraphs to Chapter 12 on page 237.

Additional Resources

Mastery Test — See pages 31–32 in the test booklet.

Skills Practice Book — page 66–71.

Duplicating Masters — pages 67–72.

Special Populations — See special section at the front of this Teacher's Edition.

You are asked to report on different types of painting styles for your art class. Your science teacher assigns a paper on the development of a chicken embyro. A history project is due, and you decide to write about the causes of the Industrial Revolution. In each of these cases, you may know something about the subject, but not enough to write a fully developed composition.

When the material for a composition must come from outside sources, rather than from your own knowledge or experience, the composition is called a **report.** The main purpose of writing a report is to gather information from a number of sources and then to present the material clearly and accurately. Preparing a report involves the same stages of pre-writing, development, and revision as any other composition.

Part 1

To choose and narrow a subject for a report

Presenting the Lesson

1. Read Choosing a Subject page 238. Stress the enormous amount of guidance students can receive through reference to a book or encyclopedia. Ask students if they can think of any other suitably narrow topics under the general topics "Japanese Culture" or "The Rodeo." Point out that it will be much easier to do research for a paper if the topic is narrowed from the beginning.

2. Assign Exercise A on page 239. Do the first two orally with the class, writing their suggestions for narrowed topics on the board. If the topics they suggest are still too broad, (for example, "famous American architects,") help them limit the topic even further ("Frank Lloyd Wright").

3. Assign Exercise B, page 239. Tell the class to spend time choosing their topics because they will write on one of the topics from this list later on in the chapter.

Individualizing the Lesson

Less-Advanced Students

Explain that some of the ways of limiting a general topic are to choose a specific example (Native Americans—Sitting Bull), to pick a particular time period (the British monarchy in 1603), or to pick a particular place (acupuncture at St. Luke's Hospital).

Part 1 Pre-Writing: Choosing a Subject

When you are not assigned a specific topic for a report, your first step is to choose a subject. Make a list of subjects that interest you and that would be interesting to your readers. Remember that the subject you select should not have *you* as the main source of information.

Subjects based on learned information may need to be narrowed. In limiting your subject, keep two things in mind:

1. the amount of information available on the subject
2. the length of your report

At this stage, it is sometimes helpful to consult a general encyclopedia article on your subject or the index of a book dealing with your subject. Checking either of these may provide possibilities for limited subjects.

Consider, for example, the subject "Japanese Culture." It is so broad that to develop it would take an entire book at least. Even if the subject were narrowed to "Japanese Culture in the Twentieth Century," it would still be too broad for a short, five-paragraph report.

The general topic "Japanese Culture" does, however, contain a number of possible report topics. Examination of a book or article on Japan might yield the following ideas:

Japanese Family Relationships	A Japanese Garden
The Japanese New Year Celebration	Koto Music of Japan
Residential Architecture in Japan	Japanese *No* Theater

Many more topics could be added to the list. Each could be developed adequately in a short report.

Another example of a subject that is too broad for a short report is "The Rodeo." A little research, however, could provide these topic possibilities:

The Ropers	Steer Wrestling
Bronc Riding	The Bull Ride
Barrel Racing	History of the Rodeo

Exercises Choosing and Limiting a Report Topic

A. The following topics are too general to be covered in a short report. Choose ten of the topics and limit each one so that it is suitable for a five-paragraph paper. You may have to do some research.

1. famous architects
2. Native Americans
3. acupuncture
4. mythology
5. the British monarchy
6. folk music
7. oceanography
8. early explorers
9. photography
10. railroads
11. weather
12. pollution
13. YMCA
14. metric system
15. earthquakes
16. space flight
17. extinct species
18. Franklin Roosevelt
19. the ocean
20. hang gliders

B. From the list of topics you made in Exercise A, choose five topics for which you might like to gather more information. Then add five more topics of your own. Be sure to limit each one so that it is appropriate for a five-paragraph report. Keep this list.

Part 2 Pre-Writing: Preparing To Do Research

Once you have narrowed your topic, you may be tempted to check out an armload of books and begin reading. However, a little thought and preparation at this point could save you hours of unnecessary research time later.

Identifying Your Purpose

A subject can be approached in several different ways depending on the purpose of the report. Identifying the purpose will help you to focus your thinking and research.

For most reports, your purpose will be to **inform** your readers about your topic. Look for material that will give your readers

Advanced Students

After the students have worked on Exercises A and B, ask them to articulate some of the principles for narrowing a topic, such as the ones given above under **Less-Advanced Students**. Have them share their specific techniques with their classmates.

Optional Practice

Ask students to develop five different narrowed topics for each of the following general topics.

a. popular dances
b. the African nations
c. legendary sports figures

Allow them to use the library, if necessary

Extending the Lesson

Have students develop five topics based on other courses they are taking in school. Refer to the examples in the introduction to this chapter; also indicate that fascinating and unusual topics may be suggested by foreign language, physical education, and mathematics courses.

Part 2

Objective

To prepare to research a report by identifying purpose and audience, learning the difference between fact and opinion, and making a list of questions to be answered in the report

1. Read and discuss **Preparing To Do Research**, pages 239–241. Review with students what they have learned about the importance of identifying the purpose and audience when writing paragraphs and compositions. Discuss the difference each element could make in a report.

2. Ask students which of the following statements is a fact and which is an opinion:

Joseph Conrad is the greatest English prose stylist of the modern era. (opinion)

English was not Joseph Conrad's first language. (fact)

Remind students that it is necessary to be on guard against using opinions—their own or someone else's—in a factual report. Refer students to Chapter 13, "Critical Thinking," for more information on facts and opinions.

3. Do the Exercise on pages 241–242 with the class. Be sure that the distinction between fact and opinion is clear to all students.

4. Read and discuss **Making a List of Questions**, page 242. Point out that the list of questions for the topic "Snake Venom" indicates that the author has already done some preliminary research and knows something about the subject.

5. Assign the Exercise on page 242. Have students read their lists of questions to the class. Then let the class suggest additional questions that they might want answered.

the facts and details they need to understand your subject. For instance, if your topic were "Frank Lloyd Wright's Prairie Style," you would have to find facts defining this style of architecture.

On the other hand, your purpose might be to **compare and contrast** Wright's style of architecture with that of another architect. If this were your purpose, you would begin by reading about each style separately. Then, you would look for details that the two styles share or ways in which they are directly opposite.

Finally, your purpose might also be to **analyze** your topic. For example, you might decide to write on "The Effect of Wright's Prairie Style on Modern Architecture." In this case, you would need to present facts that would help your readers draw conclusions about the topic.

At this point, you may wish to clarify your topic by writing a **statement of purpose.** This statement, sometimes called a **thesis statement,** may be used in the introduction to your report.

Identifying Your Audience

Identifying your audience is an important task. The audience's knowledge of your subject will determine the amount of background material you will have to present. It will also help you to know how technical you can get in the body of your report.

Suppose, for example, that your topic is the use of home computers. Your audience is your classmates, who have just finished a home computer unit in math. In this case, you would not need to define a home computer in your report. You would, however, be able to use terms from that specialized area that a less-informed audience might not understand.

Understanding Fact and Opinion

As you begin to do your research, you should know how to identify useful information. One important skill that will help you is the ability to separate fact from opinion. A report is composed of facts. A **fact** is a piece of information that is verifiable; that is, a fact can be shown to be true. "Frank Lloyd Wright was born on June 8, 1867," is a statement of fact. To verify it, you could read a biography or an encyclopedia article about Wright. You could also go right to the source by traveling to his birth place and searching out the old birth records.

An **opinion,** on the other hand, is not verifiable. It cannot be proven true. An opinion is often signaled by judgment words, such as *best, worst, valuable,* and *terrible*. An opinion may also be signaled by such phrases as *should* or *ought to*. You may agree with an opinion, but that does not make it a fact that is appropriate for a report. "*Great Expectations* was written by Charles Dickens" is a usable fact. "*Great Expectations* is a good book" is an opinion. You may agree with it, but you should not use it for your report.

In gathering material for your report, be sure to record only facts. You must also make sure these facts are from a source that is up-to-date, reliable, and unbiased. See Chapter 13, "Critical Thinking," for more information on facts and opinions.

Exercise Learning To Work with Facts

Assume that you are writing a report called "Bronc Riding." The purpose is to inform people of your age who are unfamiliar with the topic. Look at the following statements. Keeping your subject, purpose, and audience in mind, find five statements that are not appropriate for your report. Write them and be ready to tell why you would not use them. Remember that opinions should not be used.

1. The broncbuster supplied ranchers, the U.S. Army Calvary, the stage lines, and Wells Fargo wagons with fresh supplies of horses.
2. Broncbusters were the toughest men in the West.
3. Bronc riding should be outlawed because it is a form of cruelty to animals.
4. The rider must keep one hand free and away from the horse.
5. Bronc riders developed from the early professional horse trainers.
6. Each animal is fitted with two belts in the chute.
7. Bronc riding is usually the opening activity at a rodeo.
8. Bronc riding is too dangerous to be enjoyable as a sport.
9. Twisting and jumping broncs bound out of the chute.
10. Bareback bronc contests are limited to eight seconds.

Extending the Lesson

Have each student bring to class a short factual article from a magazine or newspaper. Have students determine the article's intended audience and purpose and then identify five questions that the article answers.

11. There are very specific rules for bronc riding.
12. Bronc riding has a fascinating history.
13. The bronc's strongest bucks come during the first two or three seconds.
14. Bronc riding is a more interesting event than calf roping.
15. The rider must spur the horse above the point of the shoulders during the first jump out of the chute.

Making a List of Questions

Identifying your purpose and learning to recognize facts are two ways to focus your research. Another method is to make a list of questions that you or your audience might want answered about your subject. With these questions in mind, you will be sidetracked less easily. You will also know that you have done adequate preliminary research when you have answers to all your questions.

After a little preliminary reading, a writer who decided on "Snake Venom" as a topic made a list of the following questions to guide her research:

1. How is snake bite treated?
2. Do poisonous snakes provide any benefit for people?
3. What is antivenin?
4. How is antivenin made?
5. How is venom extracted?

As you continue research for your report, other questions may occur to you, and you may find and record facts that do not fit in as answers to your original questions. It is all right to use this new information if it seems consistent with your audience and purpose.

Exercise Preparing To Do Research

Choose a topic from the list you made in Part 1. This will be the topic of your report. Identify your purpose and audience. Then write five to ten questions about your topic that you can use to guide your reading.

Part 3 Pre-Writing: Gathering Information

After doing some preliminary work on your topic, your time in the library will be well spent. Begin by reading a general encyclopedia article for an overview of your topic. Then use the *Readers' Guide to Periodical Literature* and the card catalog to find articles and books on your subject. You may also want to use specialized reference books. See Chapter 14 for help in using the library.

Making a Working Bibliography

As you use the *Readers' Guide* and the card catalog, record on 3″ x 5″ note cards the sources that you find. Write only one source on each card. Organize these cards in alphabetical order, and write an identifying number on the upper right-hand corner of each card. This list of sources, recorded in this manner, is your **working bibliography**. Even after you have found your sources, keep your bibliography cards; they will be useful later.

Guidelines for Bibliography Cards

1. **Books.** Give the author, last name first; the title of the book; and the year of publication. Put the library call number in the upper left-hand corner of your card.

2. **Magazines.** Give the author, last name first (unless the article is unsigned); the title of the article; the name of the magazine; the date of the magazine; and the page numbers of the article.

3. **Encyclopedias.** Give the title of the entry; the name of the encyclopedia set; and the year of the edition.

4. **Other reference works.** Give the title of the article or entry; the name of the book or set; the volume number of the entry; the page numbers of the entry; and the year of publication.

---

5. Assign Exercise B, page 247. After students have written their practice note cards, ask them if they have any questions about how they should be done. Then check the cards, or create student groups to do so. After any confusion has been cleared up, assign Exercise C.

6. Read and discuss **Using Graphic Aids** and **Interviewing** on page 248. Emphasize the wealth of information these two types of sources can yield. Do Exercise A, page 249 orally with the class. Tell them the purpose of the exercise is to translate the diagram into words on note cards.

7. Complete Exercise B orally with the class on a sample topic. Help students phrase interview questions that will elicit full responses, not merely a "yes" or a "no." Then have them complete the exercise independently, devising questions based on their own topics.

Individualizing the Lesson

Less-Advanced Students

1. Ask students which types of reference sources (magazine articles, books, dictionaries, encyclopedias, almanacs, atlases, biographical references) would be most useful in gathering information on the following topics:

   a. cable televison
   b. phobias
   c. John F. Kennedy
   d. Mt. St. Helens
   e. the country of Chad

2. Give students additional practice in paraphrasing material by selecting passages from this or another textbook and having students rewrite the material in their

The writer of a paper on robots had the following cards in her working bibliography.

Book

> RD
> 130
> .B47   Berger, Melvin.
>   Bionics.
>   1978.
>
>   School Library ①

Magazine

> Friedrich, Otto. ②
> "The Robot Revolution,"
> Time,
> Dec. 8 1980,
> pp. 72-83. Public Library

Encyclopedia

> "Robot." ③
> Collier's Encyclopedia.
> 1984 ed.
>   School Library

You may not use all of the sources you record. Some may not be available, and others will not have the right information. Delete or add cards, as necessary.

Exercise Making a Working Bibliography

Make a working bibliography for your report. Use 3″ x 5″ cards to record your information. Follow the guidelines given in this lesson for recording sources. Save your cards for later use.

Taking Notes

As you find information on your topic, use 3″ x 5″ note card to record your facts. Be sure to write only one item on each card. This will allow you to organize your information easily, either as you are doing research or later on, during the actual organization process. Also include the number of the bibliography card that identifies the source of the information, and the page numbers on which the information can be found.

Rewording Information. When you are taking notes for your report, be sure to record the information in your own words. This will ensure that your report is an original one. It will also help you avoid **plagiarism**—the uncredited use of another person's material. Notice how the writer of the note card below transferred information from her source to her notes.

Now that robots have proved efficient and economical, the main effort is to create "smart" robots and thus give them an ability to make decisions. To become smarter, robots are learning to "see" and "touch," and report to their computer brains what their new senses tell them.

*Robots that can "see" and "touch" ②
are now being designed. These
new capabilities will make
robots "smarter" and capable
of making decisions.
                        page 72*

If a university library or other major research library is conveniently located, take students on a guided tour of it so they can see the vast resources available to scholars and researchers.

Quoting a Source Directly. Sometimes an author will say something so well that you will want to use an exact quote. In this case, accurately copy the passage you want to quote. Put quotation marks around it on your note card. Give credit for the quote in your report by mentioning the author's name.

The writer of the report on robots also had the following cards.

> ①
> The simplest industrial robot is a mechanical arm that brings raw material to a machine to be processed and then takes the processed item away.
> page 76

> ④
> Robots with rudimentary "vision" are able to inspect glowing diodes that light numbers in pocket calculators. Humans could do this work accurately for only a short time.
> page 76

> ③
> An android is a robot that resembles a human in both appearance and activity.
> page 114

Exercises Taking Notes

A. Rewrite the following information in your own words.

A fairly sure sign of possible volcanic eruption is a series of earthquakes near a volcano. These, with tilting of the ground, indicate that sections of the earth's crust are shifting. New channels may be opening up for magma, and underground pressures are perhaps increasing. Wells in the area may go dry–indicating that cracks underground are allowing the water to leak deeper into the earth. Water reaching hot rocks, far down, may turn to steam and boost the pressures that are causing the quakes. A volcanic eruption may also be hinted at by changes in the earth's magnetism. —*The Story of Geology*

B. Assume that you are writing a report on the Mohawk Indians. Write five note cards on this article from page 48 of *The Indian Book*. Assume you have assigned this book source number "2."

The Mohawk lived in what is now upper New York State and a bit of Canada. Their villages stood in clearings in the forest that covered the land. They had large houses, called longhouses, in which a number of families lived. The men hunted, fished, and made war. The women grew corn, beans, and squash outside the village.

Four other tribes, the Oneida, Onondaga, Cayuga, and Seneca, lived near the Mohawk. All five tribes spoke the same basic language and lived in much the same way. Long ago, these five tribes had joined together to form a strong group. They called their group by a name meaning, "we are of the longhouse."

Their enemies, the Algonquin Indians, called all the people of the longhouse by a name meaning "poisonous snakes." To French explorers, the Algonquin word sounded like Iroquois (IHR uh kwoy). We still know them by this name.

C. Take notes for your own report on 3″ x 5″ cards. Follow the guidelines in this lesson for recording sources and information.

Using Graphic Aids

"A picture is worth a thousand words" is an old cliché, but there is some truth in it. Often such graphic aids as pictures, illustrations, sketches, diagrams, maps, tables, and charts will accompany the text of a book or article. Don't overlook them. They contain facts that could be used in your report. Information from graphic aids can be summarized and put on your note cards, too. As with written text, you must interpret the material accurately and carefully. See Chapter 15, "Study and Research Skills," for more information on graphic aids.

Interviewing

Even though a report cannot have you as a main source of information, it could have someone else as a source. Interviewing experts or authorities is another means of gaining facts for your report. Authorities and experts are people with specialized knowledge in a field. They can often give more current information on subjects than you can find in books.

If you do ask an expert for an interview, be sure to make the most of your opportunity by following these guidelines:

Guidelines for Conducting an Interview

1. Arrange a specific time and place for the interview.
2. Do background work on your topic before the interview.
3. Prepare a list of questions to ask during the interview.
4. Leave space under each question to take notes on the answers that the interviewee gives.
5. Be prompt for the interview.
6. Be prepared with pens, paper, and/or a tape recorder.
7. Phrase your questions so that they cannot be answered with a simple "yes" or "no."
8. Ask follow-up questions.
9. Be courteous.

Exercises Using Additional Sources

A. Study the following diagram from page 471 of *A Proud Nation*, by Ernest R. May. The diagram illustrates the structure of a corporation from the stockholders, or investors, to the actual employees of the company. Make note cards summarizing the information given in the diagram.

CORPORATION STRUCTURE

B. Consider the topic of your report. Assume that you will use an authority or expert as a source of information. Describe the credentials of the person you plan to interview. Then prepare ten precise interview questions that you could ask such an expert. Remember to phrase your questions in a manner that calls for a full answer, not merely a "yes" or "no."

1. To organize the facts for a report

2. To prepare an outline

Presenting the Lesson

1. Read and discuss **Organizing a Report,** pages 250–251. Point out that the author of "Venom" has organized each paragraph in logical order but has not yet established the order of the composition as a whole.

2. Read and discuss **The Order of Information**, pages 251–252. Tell students that it is important to achieve unity and coherence in each individual paragraph and also to achieve unity and coherence in the composition as a whole.

Discuss in detail the "thoughts" of the writer as discussed on page 252. Point out that the process of organizing a piece of writing is not based so much on any formula as it is a logic and common sense.

3. Read **Making an Outline**, pages 252–254. Point out the various features of the outline: main headings are next to Roman numerals, subheadings in decending order of importance are placed next to capital letters, Arabic numbers, small letters. Tell students that a well-constructed outline is a great aid in writing the first draft of a report. It prevents the writer from digressing into an unnecessary or irrelevant point.

4. Assign Exercises A and B on page 254. Remind students that the

Part 4 Pre-Writing: Organizing a Report

Once you have gathered all your information, you are ready to organize your notes. At this point, the reason for putting a single fact on each note card will become clear. Find a big table and begin arranging your note cards by ideas. Which facts seem to be related? What term or key idea describes each grouping? The note cards allow you to try out various groupings and to delete, rearrange, and add to your ideas as you refine them.

The writer of the report on snake venom had note cards with these facts:

–Venom cannot be extracted by machine
–Drug from Russell's viper for clotting of blood
–The large snake fangs are grooved or hollow
–Venom is stored in a freezer
–Small amount of venom injected into horses
–Blood from immune horses collected and processed
–Venom used to make snakebite serum
–Venom used in some unusual ways
–Herpetologist uses sterile container
–People with snakebite are given horse serum; lives saved
–Horses become immune gradually
–The snake bites the covering of the container
–Drug from Egyptian cobra is not perfected yet but could be used to fight organ transplant rejection
–Collections of snakes maintained for extracting venom
–*Cobroxin* from cobras is a painkilling drug; no addiction
–Death from snakebite is a rarity
–The venom collects in the vial until the snake's supply is gone

After experimenting with a few arrangements, the writer found that her notes seemed to fall into four main groups. They were:

Valuable Product
Unusual Uses
Venom Extraction
Snakebite Serum

Once the writer had determined the four main ideas, she organized her note cards under those ideas, as follows:

VALUABLE PRODUCT
1. Collections of snakes maintained for extracting venom
2. Venom used to make snakebite serum
3. Venom used in some unusual ways

UNUSUAL USES
1. *Cobroxin* from cobras is a painkilling drug; no addiction
2. Drug from Russell's viper for clotting of blood
3. Drug from Egyptian cobra is not perfected yet but could be used to fight organ transplant rejection

VENOM EXTRACTION
1. Venom cannot be extracted by machine
2. Herpetologist uses sterile container
3. The snake bites the covering of the container
4. The venom collects in the vial until the snake's supply is gone
5. Venom is stored in a freezer

SNAKEBITE SERUM
1. Small amount of venom injected into horses
2. Horses become immune gradually
3. Blood from immune horses collected and processed
4. People with snakebite are given horse serum; lives saved

Notice that the writer was not able to use two of her facts:

–Death from snakebite is a rarity
–The large snake fangs are grooved or hollow

These facts did not fit under any of her main ideas, so she deleted them from her report.

The Order of Information

As with other types of compositions, the method you use for organizing your report will depend on your subject and your purpose. Reports are often organized from least important idea

organization process is no different than that of any other type of composition.

Individualizing the Lesson

Less-Advanced Students

For many students, organizing ideas into logically ordered groups is the most difficult part of writing a report. Give each student individual attention at this stage of the report to be sure he or she is developing a satisfactory writing plan. Individual conferences would be most helpful. If this cannot be arranged, have students present their plans to a small group and have other students offer suggestions for improved organization. You might also pair a student who has problems with one who has an easier time with organization.

Advanced Students

Before students write their own outlines, have them outline "Lasers," p. 228, for practice.

Optional Practice

1. Have students outline "The Computer as Friend," page 233–234.

2. Provide students with an unorganized list of ideas that you have gathered from a short magazine article. Ask students to put these ideas into related groups.

Extending the Lesson

Have students prepare an outline for the information from the interview conducted in Optional Practice, page 245.

to most important idea, or from most familiar concept to least familiar concept. Comparison and contrast is a useful order for a topic such as "Farming Before and After Machines." For still other subjects, spatial order and chronological order will be the best method of organization. Sometimes, the facts themselves will determine the order.

The writer of "Venom" may have had the following thoughts as she chose an order for her groups of ideas:

1. The audience is not likely to know much about snake venom or its uses. They may also find the subject unattractive. Therefore, the idea group that gives some basic information about snake venom and emphasizes its value should come first.

2. The idea groups on how venom is extracted and how serum is produced from venom are two parts of a process. They should be presented in chronological order.

3. The remaining group of ideas is on unusual uses of venom. These ideas help the audience understand just how important the products of venom may someday be in their own lives. This group works well as a final body paragraph.

Your own planning and organization should be similarly thought out. Also remember to organize the ideas within each group in a logical order.

Making an Outline

Some writers like to compose their rough drafts working directly from their organized note cards. Others prefer to prepare an outline first. An outline gives you a structured framework from which to work in writing your paper. It is easier to refer to than a stack of cards. It also formalizes the organizational work that you started with your note cards.

Each group of note cards becomes a major division in an outline. The key idea of the group becomes the division's main heading. It is labeled with a Roman numeral. The individual facts on the note cards become major points underneath the heading. They are labeled with capital letters. Refer to Section 17 for more detailed information on outlining.

The writer of "Venom" made the following outline.

Venom

I. Valuable product
   A. Obtained from snakes
   B. Used to make serum
   C. Used in unusual ways

II. Venom extraction
   A. Cannot be done by machine
   B. Must be done by herpetologist using
      a sterile container
      1. Forces snake to bite covering of container
      2. Pumps venom into container until snake's
         supply is gone
      3. Stores venom in freezer

III. Production of snakebite serum
   A. Venom injected into horses
   B. Horses develop immunity
   C. Blood collected and processed

IV. Unusual uses of venom
   A. *Cobroxin*
      1. Is obtained from cobras
      2. Is a non-addicting painkiller
   B. Drug from the Russell's viper venom
      1. Used by dentists
      2. Aids blood clotting
   C. Drug from Egyptian cobra venom
      1. Still being developed
      2. Will be used to fight organ transplant
         rejection

Notice that the writer used chronological order in developing her individual paragraphs on venom extraction and snakebite serum. She arranged her ideas in the last paragraph from most to least familiar or common. She mentioned the major use of venom before she mentioned some lesser known uses.

As you work, you may find that you need to return to the library to gather more facts to develop one or more divisions of your outline. You may also want to try several organizational methods in your outline before settling on the one that best fits your purpose, audience, and topic.

Exercises Organizing Your Report

A. Divide the note cards you prepared in Part 3 into three or four related groups. Put the groups and the ideas within them into a logical order.

B. Working from your note cards, prepare an outline for your report.

Part 5   The First Draft

The report, like other types of compositions, has three main divisions: the introduction, the body, and the conclusion.

The Introduction

In the introduction of a report, you want both to introduce your topic and to catch your audience's attention.

The following paragraphs are possible introductions for the report on venom.

1. I am going to report on venom. Although it is poisonous, venom can be useful.
2. The most valuable product provided by snakes comes from their greatly feared venom. Some collections of poisonous snakes are maintained for the specific purpose of extracting venom. Once removed from the snakes, venom is used in making snakebite serum and also in some surprising other ways.

Part 5

Objective

To write a first draft of a report

Presenting the Lesson

1. Read and discuss **The Introduction**, pages 254–255. Refer students to the material on pages 198–200 to review ideas about how to write interesting introductions. You might also refer them to the chart on page 372 of Chapter 17, "Preparing a Talk."

2. Assign the Exercise on page 255.

3. Read and discuss **The Body**, pages 255–256. Refer students to the material on body paragraphs on pages 201–206 to review ideas on how to write a unified and coherent composition. Remind students of

The first paragraph does introduce the topic, but it is dull and lifeless. It does nothing to catch the reader's attention or to maintain the reader's interest. On the other hand, the second introductory paragraph introduces the topic in a more lively way. By stating that something valuable comes from something greatly feared, the writer suggests an irony that catches the reader's attention. Cleverly, the writer introduces some interesting factual material from her outline, but she also leaves her reader wondering, "What are these other surprising uses for snake venom?" Leaving a question planted in the reader's mind is often a good technique for sustaining interest in your report.

Some writers believe that the introduction is the hardest part of a report to produce. If you are one of those writers, you may want to work on the body of the report first. This often helps you feel more secure about your subject.

Exercise Writing an Introduction

Write an introduction for your report. Either use Section I from your outline or begin with an entirely new idea.

The Body

You are now ready to write the body paragraphs of your report. In a sense, you are filling in the details on the framework of your outline.

Each body paragraph will cover the information listed under one of your outline headings. The key idea of each heading will be used to write the topic sentence for each paragraph. The sentences that follow develop the key idea. Of course, if you have done a careful, thoughtful job in constructing your outline, your body paragraphs will take shape more easily.

The writer of "Venom" used Section I on her outline for her introduction. She then developed the remaining divisions.

II. Venom extraction
III. Snakebite serum
IV. Unusual uses

the experimental nature of the rough draft.

4. Assign the Exercise on page 256.

5. Read **The Conclusion**, pages 256–257. Refer students to the material on pages 206–207 to review ideas on the writing of conclusions.

6. Assign the Exercise on page 257.

Individualizing the Lesson

Less-Advanced Students

After students have written first drafts of their introductions, have them share their drafts in small groups. Have classmates tell whether the introductions catch their attention and let the reader know what the report is going to be about. Also have them offer to aid in the revision process.

Advanced Students

Have students analyze the language of the sample report on pages 256–257. For what kind of audience is the report intended? Is the language consistent with the audience and purpose? Have students list the sensory words in paragraph 2 of the sample report. Emphasize the use of vivid details to avoid making a report simply a bare recitation of facts.

Optional Practice

Have students list the transitional devices used in the sample report. Some of the devices are repetition of the words "snake" and "venom," synonyms such as "precious golden fluid" and "poison" for "venom," and transitional words indicating time in the second and third paragraphs, which describe processes.

Extending the Lesson

Have students analyze the articles that they brought to class for **Extending the Lesson** on page 242 by checking for interesting introductions and conclusions, logical transitions, and strong facts supported by vivid language and interesting, specific details.

As this writer worked on her rough drafts, she revised the content of her report several times. Sometimes she reorganized details. Often, she added or deleted information. Finally, she checked for precise word usage and errors in mechanics.

As you work on the drafts of your own report, remember that it is not too late to add, delete, or rearrange ideas. In fact, such work is expected since revision is a natural part of writing.

Exercise Writing the Body Paragraphs of a Report

Using your outline, write the three body paragraphs of your report. Add, delete, and rearrange your material as long as you are careful to maintain the unity of your composition.

The Conclusion

Like any composition, the report should end with a short conclusion in which you restate your main point or briefly summarize your facts. The conclusion should also leave your readers with a sense of closure, a feeling of "the end."

The writer of "Venom" dramatically underscores the main idea of her report, the value of venom, in her conclusion. In doing so, she also adds to the unity of the paper.

> Ounce for ounce, venom has a greater dollar value than gold. However, its medical value to people cannot be measured in terms of money.

Now look at the final report on "Venom." Notice how the three body paragraphs fit together to form a unified whole. Remember that this is the final copy. It is the result of several drafts.

Venom

The most valuable product provided by snakes comes from their greatly feared venom. Some collections of poisonous snakes are maintained for the specific purpose of extracting venom. Once removed from the snakes, venom is used in making snakebite serum and also in some surprising other ways.

No machines have been invented that can carry out the dangerous task of extracting venom. To obtain the precious golden fluid, a trained herpetologist carries a venomous snake to a special table to which a sterile collecting vial is fastened. As the herpetologist holds the snake, the serpent sinks its fangs into the fleshlike, rubberized covering of the container. The fluid from the snake's fangs trickles down the inside of the collecting vial until the venom supply is used up. The snake's fangs are then lifted from the collecting glass, and the poison is stored in a freezer.

To produce snakebite serum, small quantities of snake venom are injected into "donor horses." These horses are kept under special care for many months. Eventually the injections of poison cease to have an effect on the horses. As each horse becomes immune to the snake venom, a quantity of its blood is collected. In a medical laboratory the horse blood is processed into snakebite serum, which is distributed to hospitals and doctors. When a person bitten by a poisonous snake is injected with the horse serum, or antivenin, the snake poison in the victim's body is made ineffective.

Medical researchers have developed many drugs from snake venom. One is *cobroxin,* an astonishing, painkilling drug made from cobra venom that does not cause addiction as narcotic painkillers often do. Another is a blood-clotting medication containing venom from the Russell's viper. This drug is administered by dentists to stop bleeding after a tooth has been pulled. Researchers are working on a drug made from the poison of the Egyptian cobra that someday may be used to overcome the body's rejection of transplanted organs and tissues.

Ounce for ounce, venom has a greater dollar value than gold. However, its medical value to people cannot be measured in terms of money—J.M. ROEVER

Exercise   Writing Conclusions

Write the conclusion to your report. Make sure that it ties the report together, restates your main idea, and provides the report with a definite finish.

Objective

To revise a report

Presenting the Lesson

1. Read and discuss **Revising Your Report**, page 258. Ask students why checking facts for accuracy is so important.

2. Assign the Exercise on page 258.

Individualizing the Lesson

Less-Advanced Students

In individual conferences, check students' corrections before they make the final copy. If possible, let students spot-check each others' facts for accuracy.

Advanced Students

Have students work in pairs to check final corrections before they make their final copies.

Part 7

Objective

To prepare a bibliography for a report

Presenting the Lesson

1. Read and discuss **Preparing a Bibliography**, pages 258–259. Emphasize that these are *modifed* guidelines, and that more formal research papers require more extensive bibliograhies.

2. Assign the Exercise on page 259. Be sure each student has at

Part 6   Revising Your Report

As with other types of compositions, revisions of your notes, outlines, and rough drafts have been an ongoing part of the writing process. After you complete your final draft, however, revision is again important. Use the Guidelines on pages 122 and 212 to improve your writing.

In a report, there is also an extra step in the revision process. This involves checking all your facts for accuracy. Check the spelling of names and terms, the accuracy of dates, and the correct relationship of the ideas and procedures mentioned.

When all your revisions are complete, make a clean copy of your report. Follow your teacher's directions for preparing the final copy.

Proofread for errors in mechanics one more time. Use the checklist on page 123 to guide your revision.

Exercise Revising a Report

Read, revise, and proofread your report. Make a final copy.

Part 7   Preparing a Bibliography

After you have completed your actual report, there is still one more part you need to prepare. This is the bibliography.

The **bibliography** is a list of the sources you consulted in gathering facts for your report. This list appears at the end of your report.

To prepare your bibliography, look back over the cards from your working bibliography. Discard any that you did not consult or use in writing your final report. Your bibliography should consist of only those references from which you directly obtained information.

Next, alphabetize your list by the author's last name, or by the title of the source if no author is given. Copy the source information from your bibliography cards.

Look at the following bibliography. The first entry is for a magazine article, the second for a book, and the third for an encyclopedia article. Use this form in your own bibliography.

Bibliography

Hecht, Annabelle. "Snake Venom — A Medicine?" *FDA Consumer,* Sept. 1981, pp. 18-20.
Minton, Sherman A., Jr. *Venomous Reptiles.* 1980.
"Snake." *World Book Encyclopedia.* 1984 ed.

Notice that periods follow the author's name and the end of the entry. In addition, a period follows a book title. Finally, if an entry runs to more than one line, all lines after the first line of an entry are indented.

Exercise Preparing a Bibliography

Using your bibliography cards, make a bibliography for your report. Follow the form and procedure that was discussed in the lesson. Depending on your teacher's directions, place your bibliography directly after your conclusion or on a separate sheet of paper. Now proofread the final copy of your report one last time. Correct any remaining errors.

least three entries in his or her bibliography.

Individualizing the Lesson

Less-Advanced Students

Have students work on preparing their bibliographies during classtime. Use examples from students' working bibliographies to put sample entries on the board for magazine articles, encyclopedia articles, and books.

Advanced Students

Point out that bibliographies at the ends of books and articles are often valuable sources for researchers. Often one book will not have specific information that will help a researcher, but the bibliography may contain useful material.

Optional Practice

Have students arrange each group of items below into a formal bibliography entry and then put the entries in correct alphabetical order.

Lawrance Thompson, *Robert Frost: The Early Years, 1874–1915,* 1966 (Book)
Archibald MacLeish, "Robert Frost and New England," *National Geographic,* April 1976, pp. 438–444 (Magazine)
Richard Poirier, *Robert Frost: The Work of Knowing,* 1977 (Book)

Extending the Lesson

Bring to class sample bibliographies from an encyclopedia, a magazine article, and a book. Call attention to information in these bibliographies not found in student report bibliographies.

Discuss this summary with the class. Encourage students to use it for review, or as part of the SQ3R method of study (see Chapter 15). Remind them, though, that more specific points can only be reviewed by skimming the chapter itself.

Applications in Other Subject Areas

1. For the **Science** activity, read and discuss the suggested research subjects. Allow the students to suggest other topics that they are currently studying in science. You may wish to coordinate this activity with the science teachers in your school so that the student can produce a piece of writing that will help in another class.

2. Read and discuss the **Computer Science** activity. In addition to computer magazines, other magazines and newspapers have made comparative studies of the home computer. Tell the students to use the **Readers' Guide** to find these articles for their research. Suggest that these reports could be made available in the school library for other interested students or faculty.

SUMMARY AND APPLICATIONS   CHAPTER 12

1. A report is a piece of writing in which information is gathered from outside sources and presented clearly and accurately. Writers compose reports for school, in newspapers, in business situations, and for many other purposes.

2. Reports can inform the reader, compare or contrast subjects, or analyze a topic. The topic and purpose of the report determine the kind of research needed.

3. A working bibliography should be prepared on 3″ x 5″ note cards. Research information should also be put on 3″ x 5″ cards. Be sure to record facts, not opinions. Also record information in your own words.

4. A special part of any report is the bibliography. A bibliography is the list of outside sources used in the report.

5. When you are writing a report, be sure to complete every stage in the process of writing.

Applications in Other Subject Areas

Science. Choose one of the following subjects, research it, and write an explanatory report concerning it:

a. the stages of sleep
b. the space shuttle
c. the structure of a cell
d. the social organization of a bee, termite, or baboon colony
e. the creation of a mountain, volcano, or glacier.

Computer Science. There are hundreds of home computers on the market today. Visit a computer store, or read some issues of a computer magazine. Gather information on two of the top-selling units. Write a short report aimed at the typical confused consumer. Compare the strengths and weaknesses of the two brands.

Chapter 13

Critical Thinking

Chapter Objectives

1. To differentiate between statements of fact and statements of opinion and to recognize judgment words

2. To evaluate statements of fact

3. To evaluate statements of opinion

4. To recognize errors in reasoning

Preparing the Students

Read the introduction to Chapter 13 on page 261. Discuss with students the types of persuasive messages they are confronted with every day—on television, in magazines and newspapers, on highway billboards, and from other people. Ask them how they decide which messages to believe and which to reject. Explain that this chapter will help them learn to evaluate the accuracy of the information with which they are bombarded. Then, they will also be able to apply those techniques to their own speaking, listening, and writing.

Additonal Resources

Mastering Test — See pages 33–34 in test booklet.

Skills Practice Book — pages 72–74

Duplicating Masters — pages 73–75.

Special Populations — See special section at the front of this Teacher's Edition.

The U.S. Library of Congress contains over 535 miles of bookshelves. The U.S. Government Printing Office produces millions of books and pamphlets every year. A single big city newspaper contains more printed information than most people of two hundred years ago read in their entire lives.

You live in an age of information. Every day you read or hear hundreds of facts and opinions. Some come from television, books, newspapers, or magazines. Some come from other people. To make the best use of all this information, you must know how to analyze and evaluate it. In other words, you need to learn the principles of critical thinking.

To differentiate between statements of fact and statements of opinion and to recognize judgment words

Presenting the Lesson

1. Read the introduction to **Facts and Opinions** on page 262. Discuss the basic difference between a fact and an opinion. Make two columns on the chalkboard, and ask the students to think of ten facts and ten opinions. Put each in the proper column.

2. Read **Facts** on page 262. Discuss the two ways facts may be true—by definition or by observation. Refer back to the column of facts on the chalkboard. Ask the students to determine which are true by definition and which are true by observation.

3. Read **Opinions** on page 263. Discuss how opinions cannot be proved through observation. Discuss judgment words and how they appeal to feelings rather than to facts. Refer to the column of opinions on the chalkboard. Have the students identify all the judgment words.

4. Assign and discuss Exercises A and B on page 264. Exercise C may be optional.

Individualizing the Lesson

Less-Advanced Students

Before assigning Exercises A and B do the **Optional Practice** for this part orally with the students.

Part 1   Facts and Opinions

Most information comes to us as statements about the people, things, and events around us. Statements can be as simple as the sentence "This is a hot day" or as complicated as a long mathematical equation. Some statements can be proven true. They are called **facts**. Other statements cannot be proven true or false. Such statements are called **opinions**.

Facts

There are two kinds of facts: **definitions** and **observations.**

Definitions. The following statements are definitions:

> An *isthmus* is a narrow strip of land having water at each side and connecting two larger bodies of land.

> *Cytoplasm* is the living matter of all animal or plant cells.

Such statements of fact do not have to be proved. They are true because people have agreed upon the meanings of the words that they contain. In other words, they are *true by definition.*

Observations. All other statements of fact are observations. Consider the following examples:

> Adult blue whales are larger than adult humans.

> The precise geographical center of the North American continent is in a town called Rugby, North Dakota.

> There are more people in New York City than in the entire country of Ireland.

These statements are all facts because they can be shown to be true by at least one of the following methods:

1. Making personal observations
2. Asking experts who have made personal observations
3. Referring to a work in which other people have recorded their personal observations.

Opinions

An opinion is a statement that cannot be shown to be true or untrue. Consider the following statements:

STATEMENT OF FACT: The works of Beethoven are considered classical music.

STATEMENT OF OPINION: Classical music is more enjoyable than rock and roll music.

By referring to an encyclopedia or consulting a music expert, you can prove whether or not the first statement is true. Therefore, it is a statement of fact. However, no amount of observation can prove the second statement. People can and do disagree about what type of music is more enjoyable. Because the second statement cannot be proved, it is an opinion. The following statements are also opinions:

Detective fiction is more interesting than science fiction.

There is life on other planets.

The first statement is an opinion because people disagree about it and cannot settle their differences by making observations. The second statement is also an opinion because there is no way to make observations to prove whether it is true or false. If someday it becomes possible to prove the second statement, then it will become fact.

Many opinions can be recognized by their use of judgment words. These are words that tell how someone feels about a subject. The following judgment words are often found in opinions:

good, better, best   excellent, wonderful, magnificent
bad, worse, worst   terrible, awful, worthless
ugly, beautiful   stupid, clever, intelligent
valuable, worthless

Many other opinions contain words that express desires, such as *should* or *ought to: People should be more considerate; the committee ought to rethink its decision.*

Exercises Facts and Opinions

A. Tell whether the following facts are true by definition or true by observation. If the statement is true by observation, tell what observation you would have to make to prove that it is true.

1. Some horses are easily frightened. observation
2. Appaloosa horses have black and white markings. observation
3. The Greek thinker Thales believed that the world was made entirely of water. observation
4. Water and H_2O are the same thing. definition
5. An abacus is a kind of calculating machine. definition
6. Few people in America use the abacus for calculations. observation
7. A cheetah can run up to seventy miles an hour. observation
8. Offside plays are among the most common hockey violations. observation
9. The appestat is the appetite control center of the brain. definition
10. Origami is the Japanese art of paper folding. definition

B. Tell whether the following are statements of fact or statements of opinion. If the statement is an opinion, identify any <u>judgment words</u> that it contains.

1. This senator would make an <u>excellent</u> President. opinion
2. Life was much <u>better</u> in the <u>good</u> old days. opinion
3. Astrological forecasts are <u>poor</u> reasons for decisions. opinion
4. Jupiter is the largest planet in our solar system. fact
5. Popsicles taste <u>wonderful</u> on a hot summer's day. opinion
6. Thousands of popsicles are sold on hot summer days. fact
7. There are only about one hundred whooping cranes left in existence. fact
8. The Mississippi is the longest North American river. fact
9. Autumn is the <u>best</u> of the four seasons. opinion
10. Today's music is <u>not as interesting</u> as that of the last two decades. opinion

C. Keep a notebook of facts and opinions for three days. Every day, write down five facts and five opinions that you hear or read. Put a star beside facts that are true by definition.

Part 2 Evaluating Statements of Fact

Often, you will have to act upon information provided by some other source. Because everyone can make mistakes, some of this information will be false. To avoid accepting false statements as facts, it is important for you to learn how to evaluate factual information. As mentioned earlier, facts can be evaluated in one of three ways: by making personal observations, by asking an authority, or by consulting a reference work.

Evaluating Facts Through Personal Observation

Whenever possible, check the facts yourself. If someone tells you that there is a kangaroo in your yard, take a look. If an advertiser claims that his or her prices are cheaper than anyone else's, contact competitors and compare the results. Personal observation is not always convenient or even possible, but it is by far the most reliable method for evaluating statements of fact.

Evaluating Facts Through Reference to Authority

Much of the information that we act upon every day comes from other people. We may receive this information through direct contact or through such media as books, newspapers, or television programs. The following are some helpful guidelines for evaluating these statements:

1. Is the statement provable? Suppose that you read a statement like "Life was much more exciting in the 1920's." The first step in evaluating this statement is to decide whether it is indeed a statement of fact. Ask yourself whether observations can be made that will prove the statement true or false. If the answer is "no," the statement is not a fact. It is an opinion.

Part 2

Objective

To evaluate statements of fact

Presenting the Lesson

1. Read and discuss pages 265–266. Discuss with the students the types of information we encounter every day and assume to be true, such as the information in newspapers, magazines, books, and on television. Point out that the fact that information is in print does not necessarily make it true.

2. Review the five guidelines for evaluating information. Have the students decide which guideline is relevant to each of the following examples:

a. Lee Iaccoca insists that a Chrysler is the best-built car.
b. A nineteenth century medical textbook states that the average height for women is five feet two inches tall.
c. A movie star writes an exercise book and says that jogging is bad for you.
d. A journalist states that there is intelligent life on the planet Jupiter.
e. A car's speedometer reads 30 m.p.h., yet the driver passes a line of cars on the highway and is stopped for speeding in a 55 m.p.h. zone.

3. Assign the Exercises on pages 266–267. Discuss some of the students' statements for Exercise C in class.

Individualizing the Lesson

Less-Advanced Students

1. Provide other examples for each of the guidelines on pages

265–266. Make sure students understand each one.

2. Do Exercise A on page 266 orally. Revise each statement so that it is factual.

3. Have the students check each statement in Exercise B in two sources. Discuss which was the better source.

Advanced Students

Have the students suggest as many sources as possible to check the following statements:

a. The United States was being pulled into World War II long before Pearl Harbor.
b. Brushing with flouride toothpaste helps prevent cavities.
c. Shakespeare's Globe Theatre sat approximately 2,000 people.
d. Most Americans favor a freeze on nuclear arms production.
e. Wilt Chamberlain was named best player in the N.B.A.

Optional Practice

Have each student find three statements of fact in a newspaper article. These facts should relate to some current event. Have students check each fact in another source and evaluate the reliability of that source.

Extending the Lesson

Discuss how newspaper reporters must confirm their information with at least two sources before printing it. Ask students why such precautions are important. What types of negative situations could result if information were *not* confirmed?

2. **Is the information up-to-date?** A history textbook written before 1959 will say that there are forty-eight states in the United States. Many scientific articles written before 1887 will tell you that space is filled with an invisible substance called ether. Today, both of these statements would be considered false. When you use an authoritative source, you use the most recent one available.

3. **Is the statement consistent with other known facts?** Suppose the clock on your wall says 12:00, but a sunrise can be seen through your window. Since the time indicated by the clock contradicts, or *is inconsistent with,* other known facts, the clock must be wrong. Whenever you evaluate a fact, check to see that it is consistent with other facts that you already know.

4. **Is the source of the information reliable?** If your source is a person, does this person speak from expertise or personal experience? If your source is other than a person, is the source well regarded? For example, a doctor would be a reliable source on the treatment of headaches. However, a television commercial would not be a reliable source on the same subject. Television commercials are written by people with no special training.

5. **Is the source of the information unbiased?** Always make sure that your source does not have any personal prejudices that would lead to inaccurate statements. For example, a salesperson for one company is unlikely to be an unbiased source on the quality of a competing company's products. Such a salesperson would be biased by loyalty to his or her company and product.

Exercises Evaluating Facts

A. None of the following statements are true. Identify each statement as out-of-date, inconsistent with other known facts, or both.

1. Most news about world events is received by word of mouth. out-of-date
2. Use "he" when referring to professional people because women do not usually hold professional jobs. both
3. Objects that are heavier than air always fall. inconsistent with other facts
4. Ninety percent of Americans live on farms. out-of-date
5. It is possible for objects to burn without oxygen.
inconsistent with other facts

B. List two possible kinds of sources for answers to the following questions. The sources may be specific reference works, authorities, or your own experience and knowledge. Which of your sources is the most reliable in each case? Be specific in your answers, and be prepared to defend these answers in class. Answers will vary.

1. Who has the best batting average in the major leagues?
2. Are dogs and wolves related?
3. You discover a rash on your skin. What is its cause?
4. Where was Thomas Jefferson born?
5. How do you keep a bicycle in perfect working order?

C. Make a list of six facts that you know to be true. Two of these facts should come from personal observation. Two should come from an acknowledged expert. Two should come from a respected written source. Make sure that you gather facts, not opinions. Be prepared to defend in class the reliability of these facts and of your sources.

Part 3 Evaluating Statements of Opinion

Many people believe that "one opinion is as good as another." This is untrue. For example, in Christopher Columbus's day, only a few people believed that the earth was round. This belief was considered an opinion because people of the time had no way to prove that it was true. However, there *was* evidence to support this opinion: When a ship sailed out to sea, the top of the sails could still be seen after the rest of the ship had disappeared over the horizon. Good opinions are those that can be supported by *evidence,* which is another name for facts.

Recognizing Weak Opinions

Weak opinions are those that have few or no facts to support them. The opinions on the following page are all weak.

Part 3

Objective

To evaluate statements of opinion

Presenting the Lesson

1. Read and discuss **Evaluating Statements of Opinion**, pages 267–269. Discuss the importance of supporting opinions with proven statements of fact. Also point out that different individuals can have opposing but equally valid opinions.

2. Ask students to give examples from their own experience of the use of overstatement, "snarl" words, "purr" words, and undefined terms.

3. Have students volunteer opinions about various aspects of school, such as the cafeteria, school spirit, and intramural athletics. (You may substitute another subject, if you wish.) Write these opinions on the chalkboard. Have students support each statement with several facts. Then evaluate with the class each of the facts to determine whether it meets the following criteria:

a. reliable
b. unbiased
c. up-to-date
d. consistent with known facts

4. Complete Exercise A, page 269, with the class. Discuss why statements like sentences 3, 4, 6, and 7 will always be matters of personal opinion or personal preference.

5. Assign Exercise B, page 270.

6. Discuss Exercise C as a class. Be sure students have noticed that the discussion is about a matter of personal taste that can never be proved right or wrong. The speakers use overstatement and undefined words, such as "great," "everything," "most." They also use "snarl" words, such as "noise," and "garbage."

Individualizing the Lesson

Less-Advanced Students

Before assigning Exercise B on page 270, go back to the list of opinions you have written on the chalkboard about school. Identify with the students any use of overstatement, "snarl" words, "purr" words, or undefined words. Be sure students understand these concepts before they begin the exercise. Go over students' answers to the exercise in class.

Advanced Students

Have students write out dialogues similar to that presented in Exercise

Women are more emotional than men.
He's hot-tempered because he's a redhead.
Very few people really care about one another.
Politicians are all dishonest.

When evaluating an opinion, apply what you have learned about evaluating statements of fact. See if observations can be made to support the opinion. Make sure that the source of the opinion is reliable, unbiased, and up-to-date. Make certain that the opinion agrees with presently known facts.

Weak opinions often contain the following errors:

1. Overstatement. Weak opinions often contain words such as *all, every, always, everyone, never, no one, none,* and *most*. Better opinions often use words such as *many, few, some, several, often, occasionally,* and *frequently*.

WEAK OPINION: Everyone should attend college.

ANALYSIS: College is important for success in many careers. It can be valuable in other ways as well. However, for some people, attending a vocational school, getting a job, or serving an apprenticeship may be better.

BETTER OPINION: Some students should attend college.

2. Use of "snarl words" and "purr words." These are words that are used to create negative or positive reactions in others. They express emotion not information. Included among "snarl words" are many terms that are used in "name calling" such as *crook* or *bum*. Included among "purr words" are such expressions of approval as *lovely, good,* and *sweet*.

WEAK OPINION: *Decent* citizens will support this program.

ANALYSIS: The word *decent*, offers no facts about the program or the citizens who support it. The term merely creates a positive feeling that is then associated with the program.

BETTER OPINION: This program will cause a decrease in the crime rate.

3. Use of undefined or unclear terms. Sometimes a word has no one, clear definition. Its meaning may vary depending on the speaker or the situation. Such words should be avoided unless they are clearly defined. Many snarl words and purr words fall into this category.

> WEAK OPINION: Libraries should carry only the *right* kind of books.
>
> ANALYSIS: *Right* in what sense? *Right* for whom? *Right* in what circumstance? Because the meaning of the word *right* is not clear in the context of this sentence, the statement itself has little or no meaning.

In matters of personal taste, everyone is entitled to his or her opinion. Some people like comedies; some people like dramas. Some people like solitude; some people like being in groups. When expressing personal tastes, it is permissible to use snarl words, purr words, and vague, undefined judgment words like *wonderful* or *beautiful*. However, it is important to remember that personal tastes are not facts. You cannot expect other people to share them.

Exercises Evaluating Opinions

A. All of the following statements are opinions. Identify those opinions that can never become facts and those opinions that may eventually become facts.

1. Scientists can find a cure for cancer. might
2. Every home needs a computer. might
3. Algebra is much easier than geometry. never
4. Lilacs smell better than roses. never
5. Solar energy is the most efficient and practical energy source to use. might
6. Abraham Lincoln was as great a President as Thomas Jefferson. never
7. Visiting New York City is more interesting than visiting Washington, D.C. never
8. There is life on other planets. might

C. Ask several students to perform their dialogues with a partner, and have the rest of the class analyze the weaknesses of the arguments.

Optional Practice

Ask the students to rewrite the opinions in Exercise B, eliminating overstatements, "snarl" and "purr" words, and undefined or unclear terms.

Extending the Lesson

Have students write dialogue for conversations they remember that included a difference of opinion. You may also want to tape such conversations from a TV show. Discuss the dialogues, tell whether the opinions were presented as facts or expressions of personal taste.

B. The following statements of opinion contain overstatements, snarl words, purr words, and words that are undefined or unclear. Identify the problem or problems in each sentence.

1. At the time of Columbus's arrival, North America was populated by savages. <small>snarl word</small>
2. He created the most beautiful sculpture the world will ever see. <small>purr word</small>
3. Nobody goes to discos anymore. <small>overstatement</small>
4. Only proper clothing and behavior are suitable for attending an important event. <small>undefined</small>
5. Personal freedom is the most important goal for people to strive for. <small>purr word, undefined</small>
6. Fabulous Zip laundry detergent cleans and brightens your clothes until they are wonderfully fresh, blindingly clean, and bursting with the fragrant scent of roses. <small>purr words; overstatement</small>
7. Everyone should participate in a team sport. <small>overstatement</small>
8. That is the most idiotic statement I've ever heard. <small>snarl word</small>

C. Study the following dialogue. What are the two people arguing about? Why can they never come to an agreement about the subject of their argument? Why are they failing to communicate? What overstatements, snarl words, and purr words are used by the speakers?

MONICA: Why don't we go to the *Men at Work* concert next month?

MAURICE: You're kidding.

MONICA: What do you mean, "You're kidding"? They're great.

MAURICE: Great what? Certainly not musicians. I don't know how you can listen to that noise. It gives me a headache.

MONICA: They happen to be one of the most popular groups around these days.

MAURICE: I tell you, some people enjoy every piece of garbage that comes along.

MONICA: Well, you're certainly not one of them, because I can't think of anything that *you* enjoy. You've got a negative attitude about everything.

Part 4 Discovering Errors in Reasoning

Reasoning is the process of drawing a conclusion from known information. Poor opinions often result from errors in reasoning. Such errors are called **fallacies.** The following fallacies are among the most common:

Circular Reasoning

Occasionally someone attempts to prove a statement by simply repeating that statement in other words. This is called **circular reasoning.** The statement "team sports are better than individual sports because it's better to play with a team," is an example of circular reasoning. The speaker has not provided any evidence to support the argument. Instead, the initial statement has just been repeated in different words.

The Cause and Effect Fallacy

When one event happens after another event, people sometimes assume that the first event caused the second. They make this conclusion even though there is no direct evidence proving that the two events are related. This error is a **fallacy of cause and effect.** Many superstitions are based upon just such reasoning. For example, a person who breaks a mirror and then has bad luck might conclude that breaking mirrors causes bad luck. However, the two events would actually be unrelated.

The Either/Or Fallacy

When someone claims that there are only two alternatives when there are actually more, this is called the **either/or fallacy.** One common example of this fallacy is the remark "You're either with us or against us." This remark leaves out several possibilities. The person being spoken to might not have taken any side, or perhaps the person sees good points on both sides.

Objective

To recognize errors in reasoning

Presenting the Lesson

1. Read and discuss **Discovering Errors in Reasoning**, pages 271–272. Tell students that the fallacies presented in this section are not the only kinds of false reasoning, but they are kinds with which students are probably very familiar. Ask students to provide examples of the various kinds of fallacies from their own experiences.

2. Ask students which of the fallacies is contained in each of the following statements:

a. Teenagers are destructive and irresponsible. (stereotyping)
b. Getting wet causes warts. My Uncle Fred got wet last week and he discovered warts this week. (cause and effect)
c. Tennis is a better sport than bowling because it is more fun to play tennis. (circular)
d. You are either in favor of war or you are a coward. (either/or)
e. I should be able to wear my hair this way because all the other kids do. (bandwagon)
f. Jeffrey wasn't a good player, but he says he was cut from the team because Coach Bader has a grudge against his family. (rationalizing)
g. Women are smarter than men. (over generalization)

3. Assign the Exercises on page 273. Have students read their own examples of fallacies to the class after they have written them for Exercise B. See if the rest of the class can identify the fallacies.

Individualizing the Lesson

Less-Advanced Students

Be sure students understand the difference among the various fallacies. Provide them with as many examples as they need to understand each concept. Do Exercise A orally with the students to check their understanding. Then complete Exercise B as a group. Have the group think of one or two examples of each kind of fallacy.

Advanced Students

Introduce students to two other frequently encountered fallacies.

a. The use of *transfer*. This is arguing by associating one object with another that creates a strong positive or negative emotion: "Eat at Country Chicken; as American as apple pie."
b. Arguing *ad hominem*, which attacks the person instead of his opinion: "How can you support for my opponent, who is a completely untrustworthy individual?"

Have students make up several examples of their own.

Optional Practice

Have the students discuss the reasons they give their parents for why they should be allowed to do things, such as stay out late, buy new things, or get an increase in allowance. List the reasons on the chalkboard, then evaluate each of them for logical fallacies.

Extending the Lesson

Have students recall as many details as possible from advertisements they have seen on television, heard on radio, or read in magazines and newspapers. Discuss the

Overgeneralization

A statement that refers to several people, places, things, or events is a **generalization:** *Many people study best in the afternoon.* When a generalization is so broad that it covers people, places, things, or events that it should not cover, then it is an **overgeneralization:** *All people study best in the afternoon.*

Stereotype

One type of overgeneralization is the **stereotype.** Stereotyping occurs when an entire group is said to have the characteristics of a few individual members of the group. For example, you might meet a discourteous salesperson in a local store and decide that "All salespeople in this store are discourteous." This would be an unfair stereotype of the other salespeople in the store.

Rationalizing

Sometimes a person or a group justifies an action by giving a reason that is believable, but which is not the real reason. This is called **rationalizing.** For example, suppose that a community council decides to spend money on a cable TV system rather than a little league program. The council cancels its youth program stating, "We feel that Little League creates an unhealthy, overly competitive atmosphere for our youngsters." The council has attempted to justify its action with an explanation that is believable, but which is not the real reason.

Bandwagon/Snob Appeal

When someone tells you that a particular idea is right simply because others believe that it is, this is called the **bandwagon fallacy.** If someone says that you ought to like certain things because everyone else does, you are being asked to "hop on a bandwagon." One form of the bandwagon fallacy is **snob appeal.** This is used to make people feel that taking a certain action will make them part of an elite group. Snob appeal is common in advertising: *People with style wear our styles.*

272

Exercises Discovering Fallacies

A. Identify the logical fallacies in the statements given below. Each fallacy is used only once.

    a. circular reasoning   e. stereotyping
    b. the cause and effect fallacy   f. rationalizing
    c. the either/or fallacy   g. bandwagon/snob
    d. overgeneralization   appeal

b. 1. Drinking milk is really good for a cold. I drank a quart of milk, and I was much better in just a couple of days.

g. 2. Wear Action jeans. Or be the only one who isn't.

a. 3. These guitars are the best made because they are so well constructed.

c. 4. Come on, make up your mind. You liked the movie, or you didn't. It's that simple.

f. 5. I need to watch my diet, but if I eat this one little piece of chocolate, it will give me lots of energy for my exam next period.

d. 6. Nobody believes in palm reading anymore.

e. 7. The people on that team are unfair. I heard one of them say he would gladly move the ball while the referee wasn't looking.

B. Write your own example of each of the logical fallacies listed above.

logical fallacies the commercials contain.

Emphasize that some of the fallacies are *implied* rather than directly stated. For example:

If you drink a certain brand of soft drink, you will be thin and beautiful and have lots of friends and dates.

Discuss this summary with the class. Stress the importance of actively evaluating information instead of passively accepting every piece of information one is exposed to.

Applications in Other Subject Areas

1. Before assigning the **Science** activity, tell the students to bring their science textbooks to class. Choose an experiment and have the students evaluate the hypothesis together. What facts or information will be used to prove the hypothesis?

2. For the **History** activity, bring several news magazines to class. Use them to identify two statements of fact and two statements of opinion. Discuss these with the class concentrating especially on how well the opinions are supported. Have students complete the rest of the assignment using either their history textbooks or news magazines.

3. Read and discuss **Mass Media**. Tell each student to select three commercials for analysis. Ask them to choose one to rewrite without the fallacies. Tell them to notice the effect of the message and whether or not it is different in the rewritten version.

SUMMARY AND APPLICATIONS   CHAPTER 13

1. Logical thinking is necessary for clear writing and speaking. It is also essential to help you evaluate what you read and hear.

2. Facts are statements that can be proved through observation or by referring to authorities.

3. Opinions cannot be proved through observation. Sound opinions can be supported by factual evidence.

4. A factual statement must be evaluated before it can be used. Make sure that observations can be made to prove the statement. If direct observation is impossible, check your source. Be sure that the information is up-to-date, consistent with other known facts, and taken from a reliable, unbiased source.

5. To evaluate an opinion, apply the same process used for evaluating facts. Make sure the opinion is supported by factual evidence. Also check the opinion for overstatements, snarl words, purr words, and undefined or unclear terms.

6. Be alert to logical fallacies in your own writing and speaking and in the writing and speaking of others.

Applications in Other Subject Areas

Science. A scientific hypothesis is a type of opinion. Read about a scientific experiment in your science textbook or in a scientific magazine. Identify the hypothesis or opinion being evaluated. Then discover the method used by scientists to support or disprove the hypothesis.

History. Find a history textbook and identify two statements of fact and two statements of opinion. Determine what facts are used to support the two statements of opinion that you discover.

Mass Media. Listen to several commercials on TV or radio. List the fallacies and poorly supported ideas that you hear.

Chapter 14

Using the Library

Learning to use library resources efficiently and quickly will be of great practical value not only for your work in English but for all your studies. In high school you will do research in literature, history, science, and other subjects. You will find the library an indispensable tool.

Before you can make efficient use of the library, however, you will have to know how books are classified and arranged on the shelves. You will have to know how to use the card catalog to find books. You should also be familiar with a wide variety of reference works, so that you will be able to find the best available information on any subject.

Suppose, for example, that you were asked to write a brief biographical sketch of Mark Twain. Would you read a short biography, or read entries on Twain in *Twentieth Century Authors* and in a large encyclopedia? What other sources could you use? If you know what resources the library has, you will be able to answer these questions immediately.

This chapter will give you the basic information you need to make the best use of the library.

Part 1

Objective

To understand how books are classified and arranged in school and community libraries

Presenting the Lesson

1. Read the introduction and **Fiction** under **The Classification of Books** on page 276. Point out that many libraries show the first three letters of the author's last name on the spine of the book to make alphabetizing easier: i.e., for Steinbeck you would see STE.

Remind the students that when there is more than one book by the same author, the books are alphabetized by title: i.e., Steinbeck, *Of Mice and Men* would come before Steinbeck, *The Pearl.*

2. Read **Nonfiction** on pages 276–277. Discuss the ten major categories of the Dewey Decimal System. Use the Literature subdivisions at the bottom of page 277 to emphasize that every category is similarly subdivided.

3. Read and discuss **Arrangement of Books on the Shelves** on page 278. Remind the students that nonfiction books are arranged first numerically, then by author except for biographies. Explain that biography is not literature, but part of history. Collected biographies are 920, arranged by the author's last name, and individual biographies are 921, arranged by the subject's last name.

4. Assign Exercises A and B on pages 278 and 279.

Part 1 How Books Are Classified and Arranged

It is important for you to understand the classification and arrangement of books in a library. All libraries, no matter what their size or purpose, arrange materials according to the same basic system. Understanding this system will enable you to find any book you need.

The Classification of Books

Fiction. Novels and short-story collections are usually arranged in alphabetical order by author. For example, if you want to read the American classic *The Pearl*, by John Steinbeck, you would first look for the section in the library that has shelves marked FICTION. Then you would look for books that have authors whose last names begin with *S* and find the book in its alphabetical position. If the book is not there, someone else has borrowed it, or a browser has carelessly returned it to the wrong position. You would be wise to check part of the shelf to see if the book has been returned out of alphabetical order. If you do not find the book and you need it soon, fill out a reserve card (a postcard mailed to you when the book has been returned to the library) that the librarian will give you.

Nonfiction. Most libraries classify nonfiction books according to the Dewey Decimal System. This system, which is named for its originator, the American librarian Melvil Dewey, classifies all books by number in ten major categories:

000–099	**General Works**	(encyclopedias, handbooks, almanacs, etc.)
100–199	**Philosophy**	(includes psychology, ethics, etc.)
200–299	**Religion**	(the Bible, theology, mythology)

300–399	**Social Science**	(sociology, economics, government, education, law, folklore)
400–499	**Language**	(languages, grammars, dictionaries)
500–599	**Science**	(mathematics, chemistry, physics, biology, etc.)
600–699	**Useful Arts**	(farming, cooking, sewing, nursing, engineering, radio, television, gardening, industries, inventions)
700–799	**Fine Arts**	(music, painting, drawing, acting, photography, games, sports, amusements)
800–899	**Literature**	(poetry, plays, essays)
900–999	**History**	(biography, travel, geography)

As you can see from the major categories of the Dewey Decimal System, each field has a classification number. For example, all science books have a number between 500 and 599, and all history books have a number between 900 and 999. The system becomes more detailed as each of these major groups is subdivided. The table below shows how the subdividing works in the literature category (800–899).

800–899 Literature	**810–819 Literature Subdivided**
810 American literature	810 American literature
820 English literature	811 Poetry
830 German literature	812 Drama
840 French literature	813 Fiction
850 Italian literature	814 Essays
860 Spanish literature	815 Speeches
870 Latin literature (classic)	816 Letters
880 Greek literature (classic)	817 Satire and Humor
890 Other literatures	818 Miscellany
	819 Canadian-English Literature

6. *Quasars, Pulsars and Black Stars*, by Frederic Golden. (500)
7. *The Loch Ness Monster*, by Ellen Rabinowich. (300)
8. *Early Pennsylvania Settlers*, by Emma C. Dowling and Anna A. Rapp. (900)
9. *Old Testament Stories*, by E. O. Grover. (200)
10. *American Words*, by Mitford M. Mathews. (400)

2. Have the students arrange these fiction books in proper shelf order:

The Invisible Man, by H. G. Wells. (9)
For Whom the Bell Tolls, by Ernest Hemingway. (4)
Ordinary People, by Judith Guest. (2)
Lord of the Flies, by William Golding. (1)
The Once and Future King, by T. H. White.
Gone with the Wind by Margaret Mitchell. (5)
A Farewell to Arms, by Ernest Hemingway. (3)
Slaughterhouse Five, by Kurt Vonnegut. (8)
Them, by Joyce Carol Oates. (6)
Dinner at the Homesick Restaurant, by Anne Tyler. (7)

Extending the Lesson

1. Arrange to have the class visit the library. Ask the librarian to show the students the location of fiction and nonfiction materials, including biographies, the vertical file, films, records, and various indices.
2. Ask the students to make a map or diagram of the school library.
3. After their visit to the library, ask the students to find out where records are kept, and what kinds of records the library owns. Also ask them to find out what microfilm is, and how it is used.

Arrangement of Books on the Shelves

You will see at a glance that books are arranged on the shelves numerically in order of classification. Most libraries mark their shelves prominently with the numbers indicating the books to be found in each particular section. Within each classification except biography, books are arranged alphabetically by authors' last names. Biographies are arranged alphabetically by the last name of the person the book is about.

Biography. The Dewey Decimal System division for Biography is 920. However, large libraries will often place biographies in a separate section because of the large number of these books. In this case they will have a "B" or a "920" on the spine of the book and on the catalog card. If you are looking for a particular biography and are unable to find it, ask the librarian for assistance.

Reference Books. Reference books of particular types or on specific subjects are also shelved together, often with the letter *R* above the classification number.

Exercises How Books Are Classified and Arranged

A. In which major division would the following information be located?

1. Plays for high school productions 700, 800
2. How to plant a vegetable garden 600
3. A comparison of Greek and Roman gods 200
4. "Killer" bees 500
5. Motocross racing 600, 700
6. Recessions and depressions in the United States 300, 900
7. Macramé 700
8. Rules for playing lacrosse 700
9. How to say "no" in any country 400
10. Operating a CB radio 600

B. Using the Dewey Decimal System listed in this chapter on pages 276 and 277, assign the correct classification number to each of the following books:

1. *Voices of the Rainbow: Contemporary Poetry by American Indians,* ed. Kenneth Rosen 811
2. *Great Religions of the World,* ed. Merle Severy 200
3. *America,* by Alistair Cooke 900
4. *Metric Power,* by Richard Deming 500, 300
5. *A History of American Painting,* by Ian Bennett 700
6. *Dolphins,* by Jacques Cousteau and P. Diolé 500
7. *Planning the Perfect Garden,* ed. *Good Housekeeping* 600
8. *Afro-American Folklore,* ed. Harold Courlander 300
9. *The Art of Printmaking,* by E. Rhein 700
10. *Clarence Darrow: A One-Man Play,* by David W. Rintels 812

Part 2   Using the Card Catalog

To determine whether the library has a book you want and where to find it, use the **card catalog**. The card catalog is a cabinet of small drawers or file trays containing alphabetically arranged cards. Each card bears the title of a book that the library has on its shelves. The card also carries the classification number, or as librarians say, **call number**, in the upper left-hand corner. (See the illustration on the next page.)

To find your book, write down the call number on a slip of paper. If it is a literature book—for example, *Selected Poems* by Langston Hughes—the call number will be in the 800 range. Specifically, American poetry will be found in 811.

Go to the section of shelves marked 811, and you will find your book alphabetically placed among those authors' last names that begin with *H*. The same call number you originally found on the catalog card will be imprinted on the spine of the book near the bottom.

There are usually three cards for the same book in the card catalog: the *author card*, the *title card*, and the *subject card*.

cates the category of the book, is always the first item on the card. Discuss the location of the title on each card. Point out that the title is not in italics or capitalized, and therefore may be hard to find on the author and subject cards.

3. Read **Card Information** on pages 281 and 282. Have the students refer to the sample cards on pages 280 and 281 and compare the information on each card. Discuss the various kinds of information found on the cards in addition to title, author and call number. Note, for example, the subtitle, the name of the co-author, and the author's birthdate (on the author card).

4. Read and discuss **Cross-Reference Cards** on page 282. Explain that **See** and **See also** references refer to subject cards, not to specific titles or authors.

5. Read about **Guide Cards** on page 283. Explain that guide cards are like the guide words in a dictionary: only the author names, subjects and titles that come alphabetically between the two guide cards will be found in that section of the drawer.

6. Have students complete Exercises A and C on pages 283–284 in class. For Exercise C, explain that students may have to look under several possible subjects before they find the information they want.

Exercises B and D must be completed independently in the library. Make sure to allow students sufficient time to complete these projects.

Individualizing the Lesson

Less-Advanced Students

1. Before assigning the exercises on 283–284, discuss the alphabetization of the card catalog. Tell the

The Author Card. Perhaps you are writing a paper about a modern-day sports figure, or you are simply interested in reading about sports. Sports conditioning is the topic of a book by Frank O'Neill. The author card in the card catalog looks like this:

Author cards for all books by one author will be filed together alphabetically according to title. Notice also that books *about* the author are filed *behind* his or her author cards.

The Title Card. Suppose you do not know the author's name, but do know the title of the book about sports conditioning. Look in the card catalog for a card bearing the title at the top as follows:

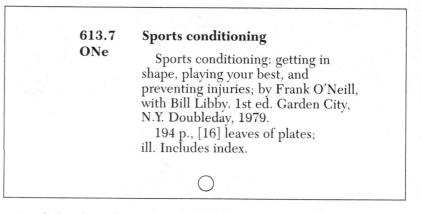

Look for the title card under the first letter of the first word in the title. (*A, An,* and *The* do not count as first words.)

The Subject Card. You may not know whether a book has been written about sports conditioning. To check, you examine the cards cataloged under the general subject *Sports*. There, you will find the following card:

```
613.7     SPORTS
ONe
              Sports conditioning: getting in
          shape, playing your best, and
          preventing injuries; by Frank O'Neill,
          with Bill Libby. 1st ed. Garden City,
          N.Y. Doubleday, 1979.
              194 p., [16] leaves of plates;
          ill. Includes index.

                        ○
```

Subject cards are most useful when you want information on a specific topic from a variety of sources. Cards for all books on a particular subject are cataloged together. The subject card may also indicate whether a book has chapters on a single aspect of the topic you are interested in. The publication date on the card will help you find the most up-to-date book on your subject. Note that the heading is printed in capital letters. This will help you distinguish a subject card from an author or title card.

Card Information

Notice that all three types of catalog cards (author, title, subject) give the same information.

1. The call number
2. The title, author, publisher, and date of publication
3. The number of pages, and a notation on whether the book has illustrations, maps, tables, or other features

Often the catalog card will provide more information.

4. A brief description of the nature and scope of the book
5. A listing of other catalog cards for the book

students that author cards are alphabetized according to the author's last name, and that titles are arranged according to the first important word in the title, ignoring the articles **a, an,** and **the**. For example, *A Wizard of Earthsea* would be found under *W* and *The Chocolate War* would be found under *C*.

2. For Exercise C on page 281 go over the first two or three items with the students. Explain that they should always have several possible subject areas in mind: if a topic is not mentioned under one subject, it may be under another. Have the students complete the exercise independently. Discuss their answers in class.

3. Read Exercise D on page 284. Assign only one person for each student to research. Stress the importance of always recording the information accurately.

Advanced Students

1. Do Exercise C on page 281 orally. Assign two topics for each student to look up in the card catalog. Have them give the number of cards they find for each topic. Ask them to list any *See* or *See also* cards they find.

2. Have the students follow the directions for Exercise D on page 284, adding two more people of their own choosing. Explain that listing sources is an important step in the research process. They must record the information accurately in order to use it for research and, later, in a bibliography.

Optional Practice

1. Duplicate the following list of books or write it on the chalkboard.

Have the students select one title and make three cards for it: a title card, a subject card, and an author card. Ask them to use index cards or 3″ x 5″ boxes drawn on paper. They may need to use the detailed Dewey Decimal charts in the library to find the correct call number.

A History of Western Music, by Donald Jay Grout, New York, W. W. Norton, 1980. (780.9 Gro)

Abraham Lincoln, The Prairie Years and the War Years, by Carl Sandburg, New York, Harcourt 1970, illustrated edition, 640 pages. (921 Lin)

Your Adolescent: An Owner's Manual, by Carol Eisen Rizzler. Drawings by Devera Ehrenberg. New York, Atheneum, 1981, 107 pages. (136.73 Rin)

The Stars, by H. A. Rey, Boston, Houghton Mifflin, 1966, 160 pages. Illustrated. (523.8 Rey)

The Teenage Chef, by Jonathan Jackson, New York, Frederick Warne, 1983, 86 pages. (641.5 Jac)

2. Bring a nonfiction book to class. On the chalkboard write a sample author card for the book. Number the parts of the card and have the students write labels for these parts on a piece of paper. Discuss their answers, relating them to the actual book. Include these parts:

1. Call number
2. Author
3. Dates of birth and death
4. Title
5. Subtitle
6. Place of publication
7. Publisher
8. Publication date
9. Illustrator
10. Number of pages
11. Maps, bibliographies, or indices

Cross-Reference Cards

Sometimes you will find a card that reads *See* or *See also*. A "See" card refers you to another subject heading in the catalog that will give you the information you want. Look at this card for the subject "television commercials":

```
Television commercials
          see
Television advertising
```

This card means that the library catalogs all books on television commercials under the heading of television advertising.

The "See also" card refers you to other subjects closely related to the one you are interested in.

```
Biology

   see also
Natural history
Physiology
Psychobiology
Variation (Biology)
Vitalism
Zoology

   See also headings Biological
```

Guide Cards

Besides the catalog cards, you will find guide cards in the cabinet trays. These are blank except for the guide word on a tab that projects above the other cards. Guide cards aid you in finding other catalog cards quickly. For example, if you want books on cartooning, you will find them easily by means of alphabetically arranged guide cards such as the following:

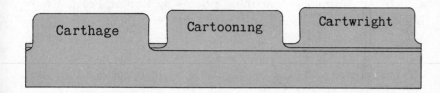

Exercises Using the Card Catalog

A. The drawing below represents the first six trays of a card catalog. The items at the right name authors, titles, and subjects that would be filed in these trays. Copy the list at the right on a separate sheet of paper, and write 1, 2, 3, 4, 5, or 6 in the blanks to show in which trays you would find the items listed. Remember that *A, An,* and *The* do not count as first words in a title.

Tray	Guide words
1—	A—Boat
2—	Bog—Cist
3—	City—Deep
4—	Den—Ebony
5—	Eco—Fed
6—	Fil—From

4 *A Doll's House*
4 Charles Dickens
2 *The Call of the Wild*
1 *The Art of Walt Disney*
1 Backgammon
3 E. E. Cummings
6 Frisbees
1 *The Bermuda Triangle Mystery—Solved*
1 Backpacking
2 *A Christmas Carol*
1 Nathaniel Benchley
5 *Famous Ghost Stories*

Extending the Lesson

Have each student choose a subject heading using the card catalog in the school or community library. Assign the following questions, based on information in the card catalog:

a. What is the subject?
b. How many titles are listed under that subject heading?
c. Name the oldest book under that subject heading.
d. Name the most recent book.
e. List any cross-reference cards.

B. Use the card catalog in your public library to find the title, author, call number, and publication date of the following books. Number your paper from 1 to 10 and write the answers.

Answers will vary.

1. A book by Ray Bradbury
2. A book about Harry S. Truman
3. A book on consumerism
4. A book on Renaissance art
5. A book by Agatha Christie
6. An anthology containing poems by Robert Frost, Emily Dickinson, and Carl Sandburg
7. A book with information and statistics on immigration to the United States
8. A book with plays by Eugene O'Neill, Tennessee Williams, and Thornton Wilder
9. A book by Harper Lee
10. A book about cross-country skiing

C. What subject cards would direct you to books about the following topics? Discuss your answers in class. Answers may vary.

1. "Peanuts" cartoons Cartoons
2. Repairing minibikes Bicycles, Repair
3. Developing photographs Photography
4. Stamp collecting Collecting, Stamps
5. How films are made Film Production
6. The origin of the Olympics Olympic Games
7. The first astronauts Space Flight, Astronauts
8. Popular music Music, Popular
9. Fashions of today's youth Fashions
10. The first television program Television

D. Using the card catalog in your school or public library, list the title, author, call number, and publication date of all books about two of the following people: Answers will vary.

1. Eleanor Roosevelt
2. Henry Kissinger
3. Mark Twain
4. Gwendolyn Brooks
5. Pablo Picasso
6. Billie Jean King
7. James Baldwin
8. Walt Whitman
9. Beverly Sills
10. Ernest Hemingway

Part 3 Using Reference Works

One of the best ways to get information is to consult a reference work. Suppose your teacher asked you to write a brief biographical sketch of the American writer John Steinbeck. One good source would be *Twentieth Century Authors*, by Kunitz and Haycraft. It may be found in the reference room of most libraries. Know the various types of reference works and where they are kept in your school and public library.

Reference works are tools, and like tools, should be used in definite ways. Information may be arranged in any of various ways within a reference work. It may be alphabetical, chronological, or under major subject headings. Most reference works have prefaces that describe how information is arranged, show sample entries, and explain the symbols and abbreviations used in the book. Before using any reference work for the first time, you would be wise to skim the preface.

Nine basic types of reference works are described in this part.

1. Dictionaries. The most widely used reference books in the library are the general dictionaries. They may be classified in three major types. The first is the unabridged (complete) dictionary containing more than 500,000 words. Second, there are abridged (shorter) editions, commonly called "desk" or "collegiate" dictionaries. The third group are pocket-sized; they are convenient for checking the spelling of ordinary words, but too limited for high school and college use.

Here is a list of reliable dictionaries for your use.

GENERAL DICTIONARIES

The American Heritage Dictionary of the English Language
The Macmillan Dictionary
The Random House Dictionary of the English Language
Thorndike-Barnhart Dictionary
Webster's New World Dictionary of the American Language
*Webster's Third New International Dictionary of the English
    Language*

Part 3

Objective

To become familiar with the content and organization of nine types of reference works

Presenting the Lesson

1. Read and discuss the introduction to Part 3 on page 285. Explain to students that a knowledge of the various types of reference works will help them not only in their English class, but in many other classes. Writing reports for classes such as social studies, science, and foreign languages will be easier when they have learned the sources available to them.

Make sure that students are familiar with the various parts of a book. This information will enable them to locate specific material quickly and easily. Tell students that while every book will not contain every part, they should be familiar with the following:

a. title page—gives complete title, author's name, publisher, and place of publication
b. copyright page—gives copyright dates, copyright holders, dates of editions or printings, and Library of Congress catalog card number.
c. table of contents—gives summary of book's contents
d. text—contains body of the book
e. appendices—provide additional information, often in the form of maps, charts, etc.
f. notes—contains footnotes to works cited in text
g. bibliography—lists sources used in writing the book
h. glossary—gives definitions of unusual or technical terms
i. index—provides alphabetical list of subjects in the book and their page numbers.

2. Read **Dictionaries** on pages 285–286. Discuss the uses of dictionaries for finding information other than definitions and syllabification. Refer students to Chapter 2 for more information on this subject. Using a dictionary, show the students sections that might include the following information:

    a. signs and symbols
    b. biographical names
    c. weights and measures
    d. given names
    e. abbreviations
    f. populations
    g. colleges and universities

Also discuss the specialized information that might be found in the dictionaries listed on page 286. You may need the help of a librarian for this discussion.

3. Read and discuss **Encyclopedias**, pages 286–288. Tell the students that the encyclopedia is an important first source for many research projects because it supplies the reader with general information on a subject. The cross reference and list of related materials at the end of each entry are also valuable guides to more specific information. Remind students to avoid plagiarism by recording information in their own words as much as possible. Only material they wish to quote directly should be copied word for word.

4. Read and discuss **Almanacs and Yearbooks** on page 288. Explain that due to their popularity, these books are often not found on the regular shelves, but are kept behind the main or reference desk. You might want to bring several of these books to class, and read several odd or interesting bits of information from each one.

Another group of dictionaries are those dealing with certain aspects of the English language: synonyms and antonyms, rhymes, slang, Americanisms, etymology (word history), and so forth. Finally, there are special-purpose dictionaries that deal exclusively with music, medicine, biography, and many other subjects. The list below is by no means complete, but it provides good source material for you. You may check your school and community library as to the availability of specific-subject dictionaries.

DICTIONARIES ON SPECIFIC SUBJECTS

Abbreviations Dictionary (Abbreviations, Acronyms, Contractions, Signs, and Symbols Defined)
Acronyms, Initialisms, and Abbreviations Dictionary
Brewer's Dictionary of Phrase and Fable
Comprehensive Dictionary of Psychological and Psychoanalytical Terms: A Guide to Usage
Compton's Illustrated Science Dictionary
Dictionary of Biology
Dictionary of Economics
Dictionary of Literary Terms
Dictionary of Science and Technology
A Dictionary of Slang and Unconventional English
A Dictionary of Word and Phrase Origins (3 volumes)
Gregg Shorthand Dictionary
Grove's Dictionary of Music and Musicians (10 volumes)
Harper's Dictionary of Contemporary Usage
Harvard Dictionary of Music
Mathews' Dictionary of Americanisms
The New Roget's Thesaurus in Dictionary Form
The Oxford Dictionary of English Etymology
Roget's International Thesaurus
Webster's Biographical Dictionary
Wood's Unabridged Rhyming Dictionary

2. Encyclopedias. These are collections of articles, alphabetically arranged, on many subjects. Guide letters on the spine of each volume and guide words at the top of the pages aid you in finding information. It is best, however, to check the general index first when looking for information. It may list several good sources. For up-to-date information on a topic, check the yearbook that many encyclopedias issue. (A word of caution: When you write essays and reports, you must put all material taken verbatim from encyclopedias and all other sources in quotation marks or separate it from the rest of your paper by indention and single-spacing.) The following are some of the most reliable encyclopedias:

GENERAL ENCYCLOPEDIAS

Collier's Encyclopedia (24 volumes)
Compton's Encyclopedia (26 volumes)
Encyclopaedia Britannica (30 volumes)
Encyclopedia Americana (30 volumes)
World Book Encyclopedia (22 volumes)

The library has many special-purpose encyclopedias dealing with a wide variety of subjects. These encyclopedias are located in the library's reference room or area.

ENCYCLOPEDIAS ON SPECIFIC SUBJECTS

The Baseball Encyclopedia
The Concise Encyclopedia of Archaeology
The Concise Encyclopedia of English and American Poets and Poetry
The Concise Encyclopedia of Modern Drama
The Encyclopedia of American Facts and Dates
Encyclopedia of Animal Care
Encyclopedia of Auto Racing Greats
Encyclopedia of Careers and Vocational Guidance
The Encyclopedia of Chemistry
Encyclopedia of Gardening
Encyclopedia of Occultism
Encyclopedia of Religion
Encyclopedia of World Art (15 volumes)
Grzimek's Animal Life Encyclopedia (13 volumes)
The Illustrated Encyclopedia of Aviation and Space
The Illustrated Encyclopedia of World Coins
The International Encyclopedia of Cooking

5. Read **Biographical References** on page 288. Explain that these reference books contain more detailed information on individuals than dictionaries or encyclopedias might.

6. Read **Books About Authors** on page 289. Point out that these books will be especially useful for assignments in English class, giving students the background of a particular author as well as information on his or her beliefs, techniques, and style.

7. Read **Literary Reference Books** on page 289. Discuss the usefulness of some of these sources for finding quotations for use in the introductions and conclusions of both written and oral reports. Also point out the value of these books in defining and explaining unfamiliar literary terms.

8. Read and discuss **Pamphlets, Handbooks, and Catalogs** on page 289. Tell the class that the vertical file is a valuable source for information on a very recent or limited subject, when they cannot find enough information in books alone. The material is arranged alphabetically by subject.

9. Read **Atlases** on page 290. Emphasize that atlases are not merely collections of maps, but books that contain important information about weather, economics, history, and other statistics. Explain that gazeteers, like atlases, deal with geography and are comprised of alphabetical lists of countries, cities, mountains, rivers and lakes, including the correct pronunciations. Many dictionaries contain brief gazeteers.

10. Read **Magazines**, pages 290–291. Before discussing the excerpt on page 291, review with the stu-

287

dents the location of the *Readers' Guide* in the library. Tell the class to always determine which periodicals the library subscribes to before beginning their research, since not all of the periodicals listed in the *Readers' Guide* are found in all libraries. Also remind the students to check the dates on the cover of each magazine. Tell them to use the latest *Guide* first to find the most recent article.

Discuss the excerpt. Point out a) that the page numbers are as important to note as the title and date of a magazine to find the article quickly, and b) the use of cross references with the *See* and *See also* listings.

11. Assign Exercises A, B, C, D, E on pages 292–294. These exercises must be completed in the library. Schedule class time for these assignments so that you will be available to help students with their work.

Individualizing the Lesson

Less-Advanced Students

1. Read Exercise A on page 292 aloud. Instruct the students to use two encyclopedias instead of three. Have them limit their reports to one paragraph. (Help them narrow the topics, if necessary.) Remind them to put the information in their own words.

2. Divide students into three groups. Have each of the groups answer only five of the questions in Exercise B on page 292. Use a similar technique for Exercises C and E.

3. Have a volume of the *Readers' Guide* available to do step 1 in Exercise D on page 293 in class. For step 2 have the students list the titles of three articles on one subject.

International Encyclopedia of Social Sciences (17 volumes)
LaRousse Encyclopedia of Mythology
McGraw-Hill Encyclopedia of World Biography (12 volumes)
McGraw-Hill Encyclopedia of World Drama (4 volumes)
The Mammals of America
The New Columbia Encyclopedia
The Pictorial Encyclopedia of Birds
Universal Encyclopedia of Mathematics

3. Almanacs and Yearbooks. Published annually, almanacs and yearbooks are the most useful sources of facts and statistics on current events, as well as matters of historical record in government, economics, population, sports, and other fields.

Guinness Book of World Records
Information Please Almanac, Atlas and Yearbook
Statesman's Yearbook
Statistical Abstract of the United States
Women's Rights Almanac
World Almanac and Book of Facts

4. Biographical References. There are brief biographical notations in dictionaries and longer biographical articles in encyclopedias. Often, however, a better source is one of these specialized works:

American Men and Women of Science
The Book of Presidents
Current Biography
Dictionary of American Biography
Dictionary of National Biography
The International Who's Who
Twentieth Century Authors
Who's Who
Who's Who in America
Who's Who in American Women
Who's Who in the East (and Eastern Canada)
Who's Who in the Midwest
Who's Who in the South and Southwest
Who's Who in the West

5. Books About Authors. Six good reference works are the following:

> *American Authors 1600–1900*
> *British Authors of the Nineteenth Century*
> *Contemporary Authors*
> *Twentieth Century Authors*
> *Twentieth Century Authors: First Supplement*
> *Writers at Work*

6. Literary Reference Books. The following are valuable reference books on the history of literature, on quotations and proverbs, for locating poems and stories, and for finding information about writers:

> *Bartlett's Familiar Quotations*
> *Contemporary Poets*
> *Cyclopedia of Literary Characters*
> *A Dictionary of Literature in the English Language*
> *Encyclopedia of World Drama*
> *Granger's Index to Poetry*
> *A Literary History of England*
> *A Literary History of the United States*
> Mencken's *A New Dictionary of Quotations*
> *The Oxford Companion to American Literature*
> *The Oxford Companion to English Literature*
> *The Oxford Companion to the Theater*
> *Poetry Handbook*
> *Twentieth Century Authors*
> *World Authors*

7. Pamphlets, Handbooks, and Catalogs. Many libraries have pamphlets, handbooks, booklets, and clippings on a variety of subjects, including vocations, travel, census data, and program schedules. They also have a collection of college catalogs. All of these are kept in a set of file cabinets called the **vertical file**. One important feature about the vertical file is that the information in it is kept current. This file can be an invaluable source to you when writing a report on a contemporary topic, seeking current statistics, or looking for information on careers.

Have them complete step 3 independently.

Advanced Students

1. Instruct each student to select two subjects in Exercise A on page 292.

2. After completing Exercise B on page 292, have each student give the origin and definition of these words:

glich	featherbedding
taboo	junta
cadence	vinaigrette

3. When the students have completed Exercise C on page 293, have them choose a subject to write up as it would appear in the *World Almanac*. For example, the number of lunches sold in the school cafeteria for five years, the number of students in the school, the athletic record of a particular school team, or the number of students taking a foreign language.

4. Have the students use the *Readers' Guide* to list all the titles of books reviewed in a particular month.

5. Add the following activity to Exercise E on pages 293–294.

> 11. Find two quotations that you could use in an essay on *courage*. Name the author, reference work, and the page number.

Optional Practice

1. Instruct the students to use an unabridged dictionary to explain the meaning and *use* of these words.

1. hoofer	(slang)
2. faitor	(obsolete)
3. tote	(dialect)
4. affright	(archaic)
5. fiddle	(informal or colloquial)

2. Assign the students, individually or in groups, to research the first nine biographical dictionaries listed on page 288. Have them write a report describing the type of information given, as well as the arrangement of this information. Allow time for the students to share their information in class.

3. Ask the students to find the populations of the following countries based on the last available census: France, Egypt, China, the United States, and the U.S.S.R. Tell them to list the names and page numbers of the reference materials used.

Extending the Lesson

1. Have the students select five magazines available in the school library and rate them from 1 to 5, with 5 being the highest score, on each of these questions.

a. How useful are the articles in the magazine for typical class assignments? (You may also ask students to specify particular subject areas that these magazines would be most useful for.)

b. Are the articles written in an interesting style?

c. Is the magazine easy to use? Are special sections clearly indicated?

d. Are the form and design attractive?

e. Does the magazine contain useful illustrations, charts, or other graphic aids?

2. Duplicate these *Readers' Guide* entries or write them on the chalkboard. Have the students explain all the parts of each entry.

SCHAEFFER, Dirk L.
  Naming of the President, 1980.
  Psychol Today 13:96+ Ap '80

8. Atlases. We usually think of an atlas mainly as a book of maps, but it contains interesting data on a number of subjects. The excellent *National Geographic Atlas of the World*, for example, lists some of the following topics in its table of contents: "Great Moments in Geography," "Global Statistics," and sections on population, temperatures, oceans, and place names. Following is a list of other widely used atlases.

Atlas of World Cultures
Atlas of World History
Atlas of World Wildlife
The Britannica Atlas
Collier's World Atlas and Gazetteer
Goode's World Atlas
Grosset World Atlas
Hammond Contemporary World Atlas
Hayden's Atlas of the Classical World
The International World Atlas from Rand McNally
The Times Atlas of the World
Webster's Atlas with ZIP Code Directory

9. Magazines. When you are writing about a current topic, magazines are an important resource. They often contain the latest information on a subject. Most libraries subscribe to many magazines and journals. Recent issues are generally kept on open racks, while back issues are stored in bound volumes or on microfilm. The librarian can tell you what periodicals your library collects and how to go about requesting the issue you need for your research.

The *Readers' Guide to Periodical Literature* is an invaluable aid when you are looking for articles on a particular topic. It is an index that lists the titles of articles, stories, and poems published during the preceding month in more than one hundred leading magazines. It is issued twice a month from September through June and once a month in July and August. An entire year's issues are bound in one hardcover volume at the end of the year. Articles are listed alphabetically under *subject* and *author* (and *titles* when necessary).

The following excerpt from the *Readers' Guide* illustrates how articles are listed:

Excerpt from the *Readers' Guide*

PARISH management. See Church management ———— **"see" cross reference**
PARK CITY, Utah
  Park City Utah. C. Pepper. Trav/Holiday 151:31 F '79
PARKER, Ann, and Neal, Avon
  Molas: dazzling folk art of the Cuna Indians. il Horizon ——— **title of article**
  22:60-4 Mr '79
PARKER, Dave
  Loudmouth and his loud bat. R. Blount. il por Sports Illus ——— **name of magazine**
  50:42-5 Ap 9 '79 *
PARKER, David M.
  Thoughts on wind wanes; excerpt from Ocean voyaging.
    Motor B & S 143:60+ Ap '79
PARKER, Olivia ——————— **volume number**
  Clear Yankee eye. O. Edwards. il Sat R 6:46-7 Mr 3 '79 * ——— **page reference**
PARKER, Sanford S. and others
  Business roundup. See issues of Fortune
PARKER, Stewart
  Spokesong. Reviews
    N Y 12:85 Ap 2 '79 •
    New Yorker 55:53 Mr 26 '79 • ——————— **date of magazine**
PARKER, Thomas Wendell
  Topographical and marine paintings in the Bostonian Society.
    il Antiques 115:522-33 Mr '79
PARKER, Tracey
  She sets sights on the Olympics. il pors Ebony 34:47-8+ F '79 * ——— **illustrated article**
PARKER-SPARROW, Bradley
  Public monies a solution to this musician's job needs. por
    Down Beat 46:10 Mr 22 '79
PARKER Pen Company. See Pens—Manufacture
PARKES, Joseph P.
  Ireland after England leaves. America 140:210-12 Mr 17 '79
PARKING meters ——————— **subject entry**
  Is it such a sin to put another nickel in? P. Carlyle-Gordge.
    il Macleans 92:4 Ja 15 '79
PARKINSON, C. Northcote ——————— **author entry**
  To the tables down at Guernsey. Sat R 6:57-8 Mr 31 '79
PARKINSON'S disease
  Parkinson's disease: search for better therapies. J. L. Marx.
    il Science 203:737-8 F 23 '79
PARKS, Lillian (Rogers)
  Her tales of White House life head for TV. G. Clifford. il
    pors People 11:26-7 Ja 29 '79 *
PARKS
  See also
  National parks and reserves
  Playgrounds ——————— **"see also" cross reference**

NATIONAL conventions, Democratic
  11h Scenario [delegate binding rule] J. Maslow. Nation 230:580 My 17 '80
  Squalls among the Democrats [delegate binding rule] il por Time 115:25 My 19 '80

Note that the second article in the second entry has no author.

Exercises Using Reference Works

A. Find information on one of the following subjects by using the general index of three different encyclopedias available in your school or public libraries. You may need to look under more than one subject heading. Write a brief report on the topic. At the end of your report tell which of the three encyclopedias was most useful. Give reasons for your choice. Answers will vary.

The Middle Ages	Greek Mythology
The Globe Theatre	Aberdeen Angus Cattle
Ellis Island	The Metric System
The Roaring Twenties	The Structure of a Cell
The Opera	Great American Humorists
Television Networks	The Olympic Games
Volcanoes	Impressionist Painting

B. Using the dictionaries available in your library, write answers to the following questions. After each answer, write the title of the dictionary you used. If possible, try not to use the same dictionary more than once. Answers will vary.

1. Define the word *crepuscular* and use it in a sentence.
2. What is the origin of the American word *gerrymander*?
3. List four synonyms for the word *product*.
4. List three antonyms for the word *delightful*.
5. List fifteen words that rhyme with *kind*.
6. Define the word *antediluvian*. Discuss its origin and use it in a sentence.
7. List three synonyms for the word *devote*. Define each one.
8. Define the word *nepotism* and use it in a sentence.
9. Give three different meanings for the word *mute*.
10. What is *Bushido*? Who uses it?
11. Define the slang term *skedaddle*. During what historical period did it become popular?
12. What is a synonym for the word *vortex*?
13. Define *discophile* and tell whether or not you are one.
14. Define the word *plover* and give its origins.
15. List three synonyms for the word *banish*. Define each one.

C. Use the current *World Almanac* to answer these questions:

1. When was the Smithsonian Institution established? 1846
2. What is the principal form of religion in Japan? Buddhism
3. What happened on May 4, 1886, in Chicago?   Haymarket Riot
4. What team won the Stanley Cup in hockey last year? (answer depends on year)
5. Where are the following national parks located?

Bryce Canyon Utah   Rocky Mountain Colorado

Everglades Florida   Mammoth Cave Kentucky

Yosemite California   Acadia Maine

6. What is the capital of Ethiopia? What is the country's official language? Addis Ababa, Amharic

7. Give the name and location of the world's highest waterfall. Angel Falls, Venezuela

8. In the election of 1844, Henry Clay was a candidate of what political party? How many electoral votes did he receive? Whig Party, 105 votes

9. Which American magazine has the largest circulation? Reader's Digest

10. Who won the Academy Award for Best Actor in 1963? Sidney Poitier

D. Use the *Readers' Guide* to answer the following:

1. Turn to the "Key to Abbreviations" in the *Readers' Guide* and write the meaning of the following symbols: Answers in margin.

bibliog	v	Je	Mr	pub	abr	Jl
O	il	rev	no	bi-m	ed	Ja

2. List the titles of three articles on each of three subjects of current international importance. (List titles, authors, magazines, page numbers, and dates.)

3. Following the directions above, make a list of articles about a prominent person who interests you.

E. Using the special-purpose dictionaries, encyclopedias, and biographical and literary reference works noted in this chapter, find answers to the following questions. Write the name of the reference work you used after each answer. Reference works will vary.

1. Who are the authors of the following four passages and from what works are they taken? Carl Sandburg "Chicago"

"Hog butcher for the world, Tool maker, stacker of wheat,
Player with railroads and the nation's freighthandler;…"

Exercise D

1. "Key to Abbreviations" in *Readers' Guide*
   bibliog—bibliography
   O—October
   v—volume
   il—illustrated, illustration, illustrator
   Je—June
   rev—revised
   Mr—March
   no—number
   pub—publisher, published, publishing
   bi-m—bi-monthly
   abr—abridged
   ed—edited, edition, editor
   Jl—July
   Ja—January

"I'm Nobody! Who are you?
Are you—Nobody—Too?" Emily Dickinson
"I'm Nobody! Who are you?"

"Before I built a wall I'd ask to know
What I was walling in or walling out." Robert Frost "Mending Wall"

"I must go down to the seas again to the lonely sea and sky,
And all I ask is a tall ship and a star to steer her by."
John Masefield "Sea Fever"

2. What reference works contain information on the following? Answers will vary.

Susan B. Anthony	William Shakespeare
Carl Sandburg	Gerald R. Ford
Helen Keller	Clarence Darrow

3. What literary reference work includes a discussion of *Tom Sawyer?* Answers will vary.

4. What are pelagic animals? those that live in the open sea.

5. Name four works by the conductor-composer Leonard Bernstein. *West Side Story, Candide, Jeremiah, Wonderful Town, Mass*

6. In what year did the Russian author, Alexander I. Solzhenitsyn, win the Nobel Prize? 1970

7. Who was Crispus Attucks, and what did he do? A black patriot leader who died in the Boston Massacre

8. What great American President lived at Monticello, and where is it located? Thomas Jefferson— Virginia

9. What is the longest river in your state? Answer depends on state

10. Name the three goddesses known as The Fates in Greek mythology. Clotho, Lachesis, Atropos

SUMMARY AND APPLICATIONS

1. Libraries contain different materials and sources of information on every subject area. Learning to use the library properly is particularly important for research. It can also provide you with many enjoyable opportunities in reading.

2. Fiction books are arranged on the library shelves in alphabetical order, according to the author's last name.

3. Nonfiction books are shelved in categories and subcategories according to the Dewey Decimal System.

4. The card catalog holds alphabetically organized cards for every book in the library. A book may be listed on author, title, and subject cards.

5. Reference books are generally marked with an "R" and kept in a special section of the library. They include dictionaries, encyclopedias, almanacs, yearbooks, biographical and literary reference works, pamphlets, atlases, and magazines.

Applications in Other Subject Areas

Math. The following is a list of famous people in the history of mathematics:

Euclid   Archimedes
Pythagoras   Sir Isaac Newton

Go to the library and find at least five sources of information on the people in this list. Only one of your sources may be an encyclopedia article.

Computer Science. Many libraries, especially city and university libraries, are being equipped with computers. These computers help the library visitor locate books and other sources quickly. They may also provide information about the local community. Write to or visit a library that has such a system. Find out what information a visitor has access to. If you can, find out something about the program the library uses to store information.

Summary and Applications

Discuss this summary with the class. Encourage students to use this summary for review, or as part of the SQ3R method of study (see Chapter 15). Remind them, though, that more specific points can only be reviewed by skimming the chapter itself.

Stress once more the importance of viewing the library not only as a center of research, but as a source for finding hours of interesting and enjoyable activities.

Applications in Other Subject Areas

1. Divide the class into four groups for the **Mathematics** activity. Assign one of the famous mathematicians to each group. Have the students complete the assignment independently. Discuss with the math teachers of your school the possibility of giving the students credit for these activities in their math class.

2. Read and discuss the **Computer Science** activity. If your community does not have a computerized library system, provide the students with a list of libraries that do. Check with the school guidance counselor for the names and addresses of universities that have such libraries. Have students write for information and share their findings with the rest of the class.

Study and Research Skills

Chapter Objectives

1. To learn to follow directions and keep a clear record of assignments
2. To find a study area and organize study time
3. To understand and use the SQ3R study method
4. To learn how to take notes
5. To learn when and how to adjust reading rate
6. To understand and use graphic aids
7. To learn how to prepare for tests

Preparing the Students

Ask students to imagine that it is Monday morning and that they have a history test on Tuesday, a math test on Wednesday, a drama club meeting Wednesday afternoon, a science project due on Thursday, and an English composition due on Friday. How will they get everything done well on schedule?

Read the introductory paragraphs to Chapter 15 on page 296. Explain that this chapter will help them make the most efficient use of their time. Mention that this ability to manage their time will help them not only in school but in other areas of life as well.

Additional Resources

Mastery Test — See pages 37–38 in the test booklet.

Skills Practice Book — pages 78–81.

Duplicating Masters — pages 76–78.

Special Populations — See special section at the front of this Teacher's Edition.

In your high school classes, you will be asked to perform many varied and complex tasks. Tests, quizzes, reports, projects, exercises, compositions, experiments, speeches, research papers—all of these and more will be required of you. In addition, you may begin to have many outside interests and responsibilities that will take up a great deal of your time.

If you are to meet the demands of your high school years, it is important that you understand how to manage your time well. This includes learning how to study efficiently and productively, how to prepare for examinations, and how to balance the demands of school and outside activities. This chapter will help you to master these and many other skills.

Part 1 Understanding and Remembering Assignments

Following Directions

Before you begin an assignment, be sure you understand exactly what needs to be done. These guidelines will help.

How To Follow Directions

1. Pay careful attention to the assignment instructions.

2. If your directions are written, read all of them through carefully *before* beginning the assignment.

3. If your instructions are oral, listen carefully and take notes. List the steps involved in their required order.

4. Associate each step in the assignment with a key word that describes what you must do. The following key words often appear in assignment directions:

answer	memorize	research
construct	organize	review
edit	present	take notes
learn	read	write

5. Examine any diagrams, illustrations, or other materials that are included in the directions.

6. Know exactly what should be handed in and when. Make sure that you know *all* of the following:

   The form the assignment should take (a written paper, a booklet, a model)

   The due date of the assignment

   Any other requirements related to the assignment (type of paper, use of pencil or ink)

7. Ask questions if you need more information.

Part 1

Objective

To learn how to follow directions and keep a clear record of assignments

Presenting the Lesson

1. Read and discuss **Following Directions**, page 297. Ask students for examples of directions, other than schoolwork, that they encounter in the course of a day. Emphasize the importance of reading or listening to *all* directions before beginning an assignment.

2. Read and discuss **Keeping an Assignment Notebook**, page 298. Tell students that oral instructions, as well as written ones, should be noted in the assignment notebook.

3. Assign Exercise A on pages 298–299.
Read step 9 out loud. Then draw the following chart on the board. Tell them that their charts should be similar.

Student's Name

Class

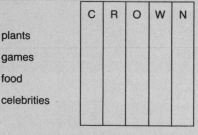

	C	R	O	W	N
plants					
games					
food					
celebrities					

4. Assign Exercise B, page 299.

Have students record all their assignments for one day on a piece of paper. The next day, have students trade papers to see if they can follow each others' directions.

Advanced Students

Have students work in pairs. One student in each pair will give detailed directions on how to get to his or her house from school while the other student takes notes. Then the student can read back the directions to check his or her notes for accuracy.

Optional Practice

Have students pick out the key words and instructions in each assignment below and discuss the kinds of work that each assignment would entail.

a. **Take notes** on *Chapter 3* in your Science book.
b. **Review** the material from today's class discussion on Abraham Lincoln for a quiz on Friday.
c. **Memorize** the formulas for the areas of a triangle, a square, and a circle.
d. **Construct** a graph showing the shift in U.S. population from the country to the city since 1945.
e. **Present** to the class a French dialogue about introducing a friend.

Extending the Lesson

To emphasize the importance of good listening, give the following instructions orally. Tell students that you will give each instruction only twice.

Keeping an Assignment Notebook

Record each assignment in an assignment notebook. The pages of the notebook should resemble the one shown in the sample below. Include in the notebook the directions and due dates for every assignment. Make sure to copy down all oral instructions or suggestions.

	Class	Assignment	Date Assigned	Date Due
○	Algebra	1. Read chapter 9	12/3	12/4
		2. Do even-numbered problems on p. 56		
		3. Use pencil		
	English	Write personal essay	12/1	12/5
		a. Write controlling idea and outline	—	12/1
		b. Gather materials	—	
		c. Write rough draft	—	12/3
		d. Revise rough draft	—	12/4
		e. Proofread revision	—	12/4
○				

Exercises Understanding and Remembering Assignments

A. Complete the following assignment:

1. Find an 8½" x 11" piece of unlined, white paper.
2. Write your name and class period in the upper left-hand corner of the paper.
3. Draw five vertical columns on the paper.
4. Choose any five-letter word.
5. Write the letters of the word at the top of your paper, one letter in each column.
6. On the left-hand side of the paper, make a list of any four categories of objects; these may be books, animals, games, or whatever you wish.

7. Think of two words that begin with each of the letters at the top of the page. The two words must also be examples of the categories listed on the left-hand side of the page. Example: *chrysanthemum* and *catnip* are the names of two plants that begin with the letter "c."

8. Write your answers in the appropriate spaces on the chart you made on your paper.

9. Do not complete steps 7 and 8.

10. Use pencil.

B. Start keeping an assignment notebook to record your school work. Follow the directions given in this chapter. Use the illustration on page 298 as a guide.

Part 2   Organizing Your Studies

Choosing a Study Area

Football should be played on a playing field. A show should be performed on a stage. Sculpting is best done in an art studio. In fact, any activity is more successful when carried out in the proper setting. Studying should also occur in an appropriate place: at school, at home, or in a public library. Whatever place you choose as your study area, make sure that it meets the following requirements:

1. It must be **quiet**. Distractions such as television, radio, or telephones should not interrupt your study sessions or interfere with your concentration.
2. It must be **well lighted**. Studying in poorly-lighted areas can strain your eyes and give you headaches.
3. It must be **cleared** and **neat**. You should have room in which to work with supplies in order. Clutter can be as much of a distraction as noise.
4. It must be **properly equipped**. Tools such as pencils, pens, paper, and a dictionary should always be close by so that you do not have to waste time searching for them.

a. On the top line at the left side of your paper, to the right of the red rule, write the heading "School" in capital letters.

b. Skip one line beneath the heading. Then write down each class that you take, skipping two lines between each item.

c. Beneath the name of each class, write down the approximate number of hours you must study for the course outside of class each week.

d. On the top line at the right side of your paper, write the heading "Other Activities" in capital letters.

e. Beneath the heading, write down other obligations such as school clubs, church or community activities, or part-time jobs. Skip two lines between each item.

f. Beneath the name of each extra-curricular activity, write down how much time you devote to the activity, for example, two hours once every two weeks.

g. Save this exercise. It may help you when planning a study calendar.

Part 2

Objective

To find a study area and organize study time

Presenting the Lesson

1. Read and discuss **Choosing a Study Area**, page 299. Ask students to identify their personal study places at home, at school, and at the library. Then ask them to evaluate how well this area meets the criteria outlined on page 299.

2. Read and discuss **Setting Goals**, page 300. Complete Exercise A, page 301, orally with the class. Make sure the students understand how to break down a larger assignment.

3. Read and discuss **Keeping a Calendar**, pages 300–301. Then go over the study techniques on page 301. See if students have any additional techniques to add to the chart.

4. Assign Exercise B, page 301.

Individualizing the Lesson

Less-Advanced Students

In working on Exercise A, page 301, help students see how they could break down the long-term assignments into manageable tasks. For example, to write the analysis of a character in a short story, they could first read the story and list characters, then re-read the story looking for significant details and character traits, choose the subject for the analysis, organize ideas into an outline, write a first draft, revise the first draft, prepare a final copy, and finally proofread and correct the final copy. Go through several hypothetical assignments in this manner. Also discuss how much time would be needed for each step.

Advanced Students

Have students prepare a weekly calendar like the one on page 300, using the notes made in **Extending the Lesson**, pages 298–299. Then instruct students to list short-term and long-term assignments for this week on the calendar, breaking the long-term assignments up into manageable tasks.

Optional Practice

Have students record each of the following assignments as if in an as-

Setting Goals

Usually you receive assignments that are due in one or two days. These are called **short-term** assignments. Other assignments may be due after several days, weeks, or even months. These are called **long-term** assignments. To complete each type of assignment by its due date, you must set goals. For a short-term assignment, simply decide at what time you will sit down and do the assignment completely. To set goals for a long-term assignment, you must first break the assignment down into manageable steps. Then plan time for completing each step. Look again at the sample page from an assignment notebook on page 298. Notice how the long-term assignment to write a personal essay has been broken down.

Keeping a Calendar

In addition to keeping an assignment notebook, it is a good idea to keep a calendar on which you record all of your outside activities and obligations. At the end of every school day, look over your assignment notebook. At this time, enter on your calendar all the work that you are required to do. Make sure that you avoid any conflicts with previously made commitments. For example, if you have a paper to revise for Friday and a family trip planned for Thursday evening, it would probably be a good idea to schedule your revision for Wednesday night. Keeping a study calendar will help you avoid conflicts and get your work done on time.

Monday	Tuesday	Wednesday	Thursday	Friday	Saturday	Sunday
Go to library Begin research	Staff meeting for yearbook	Research	Write article for yearbook	Pep rally and football game	Finish research	Organize notes
Begin rough draft	Rough draft	Study for Spanish test	Revise	Pizza at Sandburg's	Jazz fest all day	Make final copy

Here are some additional guidelines for organizing your studies:

Study Techniques

1. Try to allot two 20- to 40-minute study sessions per day, with at least a 15-minute break between sessions.
2. Set aside some study time each day for each class. If there is no homework one day, the time can be used for review or for a long-term project.
3. Tackle the hardest assignment first, while you are fresh.
4. Review all material within twenty-four hours of the time you first learn it. This will help you to remember what you've learned.
5. Try to learn even more about the material than what is required by the assignment. Know it so well that you can automatically recall and recite it.

Exercises Organizing Your Studies

A. Label each of the following as short-term or long-term assignments. Then break down each of the long-term assignments into short, manageable tasks.

1. Completing twenty problems from your math book, due for class tomorrow short term
2. Writing an analysis of a character in a short story, due in one week long term
3. Memorizing a French dialogue for tomorrow short term
4. Presenting a five-minute oral report on a topic of your choice, due in three days long term
5. Collecting a variety of local insects, displaying them, labeling them, and preparing an accompanying chart telling where each was caught. Due in two weeks. long term

B. Prepare an assignment notebook like the one shown on page 298. Then, enter the assignments in Exercise A in the notebook following the directions given in this chapter.

signment notebook. Then, have them identify the steps involved in each assignment and record each step on a study calendar. Tell them to assume these assignments were given on a Monday.

a. Read an article on symbiosis in an encyclopedia. Write a one-page summary of the article to present to the class. Due Friday.
b. Find three poems by three different poets on one of the following topics: childhood, work, war. Memorize your favorite and be ready to recite it for class next Monday.
c. Read Chapters 16 and 17 in your social studies book. Write out the answers to the questions at the end of each chapter for Wednesday. There will be a test on the material on Friday.

Extending the Lesson

1. Have the students make lists of all the distractions they encounter during one day of studying. Discuss ways in which these distractions can be reduced or eliminated.
2. Ask students how some of the techniques described in this chapter could be applied in non-school situations. For example, what other uses would an activity calendar have?

Part 3   The SQ3R Study Method

Have you ever read a chapter in a textbook, closed the book, and then forgotten most of what you'd just read? If so, you need a more effective approach to studying written material.

One way to get the most from what you read is to use the **SQ3R** method of study. This method consists of five steps: **S**urvey, **Q**uestion, **R**ead, **R**ecite, and **R**eview.

Objective

To understand the SQ3R method of study

Presenting the Lesson

1. Read and discuss page 302.
2. Assign the Exercise on page 302.

Individualizing the Lesson

Less-Advanced Students

Complete the Exercise orally. During the survey, direct students' attention to headings, the underlined words, and the charts. Then complete the question stage. Here are some of the questions students might formulate: Why take notes? When should I take notes? How should I take notes? What are some useful abbreviations? What should I do with my notes after I have taken them? After they formulate these questions, have students read Part 4 carefully. Ask them to recite the answers to the questions and review the material to impress it on their memories.

Advanced Students

After students have used the SQ3R method of study for Part 4, give them a quiz on the material to dramatize the effectiveness of the method.

Extending the Lesson

Have students write an explanatory composition that explains the process involved in the SQ3R method for an audience of junior high students.

Using SQ3R

Survey the material. Look over the entire article or selection to get a general idea of what you will be reading. Read the introduction and also the summary, if there is one. Check the titles and headings and look at any illustrations.

Question. Prepare a set of questions. Decide what questions you should be able to answer at the end of your reading. Use any study questions presented in the book or provided by your teacher. You can also make up your own questions by turning each title and heading into a question. Pictures, maps, or charts can also be used to make up questions.

Read the selection. Look for the answers to the questions as you read. Also identify the central thoughts in each section.

Recite the answers. After you finish your reading, recite in your own words the answers to your prepared questions. Make notes on the answers. Also make sure you have grasped any other important points of the selection and record those, too.

Review the selection. Quickly read over your notes and look over the main points in the book to impress them on your memory. Look up the answers to any questions you are still not sure of.

Exercise   Applying the SQ3R Method

Apply the SQ3R method to Part 4 of this chapter, "Taking Notes." Be sure to complete all five steps.

Part 4　Taking Notes

Few people can remember all that they read and hear. Taking notes is one method of remedying this problem. Notes are useful as memory aids and as references or study guides for review.

When To Take Notes

Take notes on all important information that you encounter as a student. In class, take notes on material presented by the teacher, on useful comments or presentations made by other students, and on lab work or in-class reading. Do not try to copy down every word that is said in class. Instead, record only essential information. Note main ideas and important details such as definitions, dates, and the names of people, places, and events.

Listen for clues that indicate which points are most important. Such clues include key words and phrases such as *most importantly, for these reasons, first, for example,* and *to review.* Vocal signals, such as slowing down, repetition, or pausing for emphasis can also be indicators. Finally, the speaker's use of a blackboard or transparency almost always signals an important concept.

Outside of class, take notes on reading for all classes, and on all special projects, including interviews and other research work. Before taking notes on written material, skim the selection so that you will know which points are the most important and why. Take notes on these important points. Also record the answers to any questions that you prepared during SQ3R.

How To Take Notes

Use a separate notebook for each class, or a single, large notebook divided into class sections. Make sure that your name, the subject, and the date appear on each page.

When you take notes, do not worry about writing in complete sentences. Short phrases are perfectly acceptable, as long as you can make sense of them later. You might also want to take notes using a modified outline form, as shown on the next page.

Part 4

Objective

To learn how to take notes

Presenting the Lesson

1. Students will have already read Part 4 very carefully in fulfillment of the Exercise on page 302. Discuss note-taking, emphasize its importance in recording oral presentations, summarizing important points in written material, and completing research.

Tell students that skill in note-taking improves with practice. Remind them that information should be recorded as briefly as possible, but that relationships among facts and ideas must be clear. The modified outline form helps clarify these relationships by indicating main headings and supporting details.

2. Assign Exercises A and B on page 304.

Individualizing the Lesson

Less-Advanced Students

For Exercise A on page 304, outline the first page or so of Part 2 on the chalkboard. Help students find the main ideas ("A study area should meet certain requirements" and "There are two kinds of assignments") and list supporting details for each in brief form.

Advanced Students

Have students consult their notes from other classes and list often-used abbreviations. A list of abbreviations similar to the one on page 304 can be compiled on the chalkboard and then reproduced for the class's use. Point out that special abbreviations can be invented for use on specific lectures. For example, if an entire lecture is going to be on Shakespeare's plays, you could use the abbreviation "Sh." throughout those notes.

Optional Practice

Have students prepare a modified outline of a magazine article that they find interesting. Then, ask each student to make an oral presentation of the information from the article, using the outline as notes.

Extending the Lesson

Have the students watch an educational program on television, such as *Nova* or a National Geographic Special. Direct them to take notes on the content. The next day, discuss the program to see how much the students remember. Allow them to use their notes for the discussion.

Notes in Modified Outline Form

○	The Middle Ages
	Time period — approximately 1,000 years
	— Began at end of Roman Empire
	— Ended in the 1500's
	Social classes
	— Clergy (priests, monks, etc.)
	— Nobility (princes, dukes, earls, etc.)
	— Peasants (common people)

Notice that main ideas are placed to the left. Supporting or related details are indented beneath the main ideas to which they refer and are introduced by dashes. As with all notes, write in phrases, not in complete sentences.

If your notes are to be complete, you must be able to record information quickly. Develop a set of abbreviations and symbols to save time. The following chart offers some possibilities:

Possible Abbreviations and Symbols for Note-Taking			
w/	with	info.	information
w/o	without	def.	definition
+	and	*	important
bef.	before	amer.	American
tho.	though	hist.	history

Exercises Taking Notes

A. Make a modified outline of Part 2 of this chapter, using abbreviations where appropriate.

B. Interview a friend or family member concerning some event or experience. Use a modified outline form and abbreviations.

Part 5 Adjusting Your Reading To Suit Your Purpose

You don't walk at the same pace all of the time. Sometimes you run, sometimes you walk briskly, and sometimes you stroll. Reading has similar paces. The way you read changes with the type of material and with your purpose for reading.

In-Depth Reading

When you need to absorb all of the material in a book, read it slowly and carefully, following the SQ3R method. It isn't enough to read every word; you must also understand what you read and be able to relate details to main ideas. Do this by looking for definitions, key words, headings or subheadings, and topic sentences. These are all sources for main ideas. Once you have identified a main idea, look for supporting details in the text.

Fast Reading

There are two kinds of fast reading, each with its own method and purpose. These are **skimming** and **scanning**.

Skimming involves moving your eyes quickly over a whole page or selection. Note titles, topic sentences, chapter headings, and highlighted words or phrases. Also examine the table of contents, the index, and any pictures or other graphic aids. Skim whenever you want to get a general idea of a book's content. For example, skim to decide whether a book might be a useful reference source. Also skim when you begin the SQ3R method.

Scanning involves moving your eyes quickly across a line or down a page to locate particular information. To train yourself to scan, choose a textbook that you use in one of your classes, place a folded paper or a card over the first line, and move the paper quickly down the page. Look for key words and phrases that indicate you are close to the information you need. When you locate such a clue, stop scanning and read slowly.

Part 5

Objective

To learn when and how to adjust reading rate

Presenting the Lesson

1. Read and discuss **Adjusting Your Reading**, page 305. Ask students to name some situations in which it is important to read every word. Point out that it is necessary to read material in-depth in order to understand the exact relationships among ideas. Be sure students understand the difference between skimming and scanning. Skimming surveys a whole work to get an idea of its over-all content. Scanning, on the other hand, is a method for locating a specific piece of information in a text.

2. Assign the Exercise on page 306.

Individualizing the Lesson

Less-Advanced Students

Go over each step of the Exercise with students. After students have skimmed the article ask them what the topic is and what clues (the title, subtitles, and italicized words) helped them determine the topic. After an in-depth reading of the article, ask students to discuss the main ideas of the article. Before students scan the article, read the study questions and suggest the clues to seek in scanning the material for answers.

Advanced Students

Have students practice their skimming and scanning skills by finding answers to the following questions in biographical references in the library.

a. For what movie is Orson Welles chiefly known?
b. For his work in what field is B. F. Skinner chiefly known?
c. In what year did Sandra Day O'Connor become a Supreme Court judge?
d. What is the title of John Updike's first published novel?
e. Who is Margaret Atwood, and from what country does she come?

Optional Practice

Have students use three kinds of reading when you assign Part 6 of this chapter. After students have skimmed the material and read it in depth, ask them to scan it for answers to the following questions:

a. What is the purpose of maps?
b. What kind of information do tables usually present?
c. Why are subjects in a table called variables?
d. What are four major types of graphs?

Extending the Lesson

Explain that most of our information about the world comes from newspapers and magazines. Point out that due to the volume of material, we have to be selective about what we read and the way in which we read it. Ask students to bring a newspaper to class and complete the following activities:

a. Skim the classified ads to see what types of ads are contained there.
b. Scan the sports pages and list the day's winning teams.
c. Read in-depth a national news story. Then prepare a brief summary to present to the class.

Exercise Adjusting Your Reading Rate

Follow these directions, one at a time. Do not read all of the directions first.

1. Skim the paragraph below to see what the topic is.
2. Read the paragraph in depth.
3. Scan to find the answers to the following questions:

According to the ancients, what human activities were guided by Mars? farming, fertility, war

In what country was Mars originally worshiped? Rome

Who were Romulus and Remus? the founders of Rome

Who was the Greek god of war? Ares

What is the meaning of the word *martial*? warlike

The Roman God Mars

Mars was the god of war in Roman mythology. The ancient Romans gave Mars special importance because they considered him the father of Romulus and Remus, the legendary founders of Rome.

Origin. Originally, Mars was a god of farmland and fertility. The month of March, the beginning of the Roman growing season, was named for him. Since ancient times, the area enclosed by a bend in the Tiber River in Rome has been called the Field of Mars. The early Romans dedicated this section of land to Mars because of its fertility.

Mars, God of War. Mars became the god of war after the Romans came into contact with Greek culture. They gave him many characteristics of the Greek god of war, **Ares**. In time, the Romans associated Mars principally with war. Before going into battle, Roman troops offered sacrifices to him. After a victory, they gave Mars a share of their spoils. The word *martial*, which means *warlike*, is based on his name. The planet Mars is named for him.

—*World Book Encyclopedia*

Part 6 Using Graphic Aids

Sometimes information is presented in the form of pictures, charts, tables, diagrams, maps, and graphs. Such materials are called **graphic aids**. The following chart lists the most common graphic aids and presents guidelines for studying them.

Common Graphic Aids		
Type	**Purpose**	**Study Tips**
Pictures Sketches Diagrams	To illustrate text To show the parts or functions of the subject	Read caption or title Relate picture, sketch, or diagram to text Pay attention to labels of parts
Maps	To display geographical areas or geographical distribution	Read caption or title to determine the purpose of the map Look for the *legend* or *key* (list of symbols and abbreviations; indication of *scale*)
Tables Charts	To list information To compare information	Read caption or title Check key, if there is one, to determine how information is organized
Graphs	To show relationships between groups or sets To show development over time	Read caption or title Read all labels of parts of the graph Determine what relationship is being shown between what groups or sets

Part 6

Objective

To understand and use graphic aids

Presenting the Lesson

1. Read and discuss **Using Graphic Aids**, page 307. Go over the types of graphic aids and the purposes for which each is used. Try to have several examples of each available, or ask students to look for each type in their textbooks as you discuss it.

2. Read and discuss **Reading Tables and Charts** on page 308. Make sure students understand the term *variable*. Then ask students to study the statistical chart and answer the following questions.

  a. How many males graduated in 1930? (74,000)
  b. What was the increase in female graduates between 1970 and 1980? (130,000)
  c. What was the total increase in graduates between 1920 and 1940? (138,000)

Have student volunteers make up other questions to ask the class.

3. Read and discuss **Reading Graphs**, page 308–311. Be sure students understand the differences between circle, bar, picture, and lines graphs. Have them use the graphs given on pages 309–311 to answer the following questions.

  a. How much does the artist get from the sale of 100 records? ($100)
  b. How much did the largest recorded pineapple weigh? (17 lbs.)
  c. How many Africans populate two square miles? (88)
  d. In 1975, what percentage of women worked? (48 per cent)

Have student volunteers make up other questions to ask the class based on the graphs to ask the class.

4. Assign Exercises A, B, and C on pages 312–313.

Individualizing the Lesson

Less-Advanced Students

1. Do Exercises A and B on pages 311–312 in class. Have students answer each question orally and explain how they arrived at the answers.

2. Before assigning Exercise C, review the examples of the four major types of graphs. Construct on the chalkboard a picture graph for the information. Instruct students to use a bar graph to complete the assignment independently. Point out why a circle graph or a line graph would not be suitable. (A circle graph must be based on 100% of something. A line graph shows a trend or time period.)

Advanced Students

Have students select a topic in which they have a particular interest. Have them find or construct four different types of graphic aids on the subject, referring to the categories listed on page 307.

Optional Practice

1. Divide the class into four groups and assign one of the following topics to each group. The groups should then gather the necessary information and construct a graph on the material to present to the rest of the class.

   a. the number of male and female students involved in five school athletic activities

Reading Tables and Charts

Tables and **charts** provide a simple way of presenting large amounts of information. Most tables present information in numerical form and are called **statistical tables**. Study the chart shown below. What information does it provide?

American College Graduates 1900 — 1980

Year	Total (in thousands)	Male (in thousands)	Female (in thousands)
1980	999	526	473
1970	827	484	343
1960	389	253	136
1950	432	329	103
1940	187	110	77
1930	122	74	49
1920	49	32	17
1910	37	29	8
1900	27	22	5

(Figures include bachelor's and first professional degrees. Because of rounding, details may not add up to totals. Source: U.S. Department of Education.)

Every table presents information about one or more subjects called **variables**. These subjects are called variables because the numbers associated with them vary. The variables in the above table include *year, total, male,* and *female.* Whenever you read a table, make sure that you identify the variables presented. Then, determine what information is being presented about them.

Reading Graphs

Graphs are used to show relationships between sets of variables. To understand a graph, read the title and the key to symbols and abbreviations. Then, determine what variables are being presented by the graph and how these are related.

There are four major types of graphs: circle graphs, bar graphs, picture graphs, and line graphs.

Circle graphs use the circle shape to show relationships. The circle itself represents 100%, or the whole, of something. The sections within the circle graph represent parts of the whole.

A Circle Graph

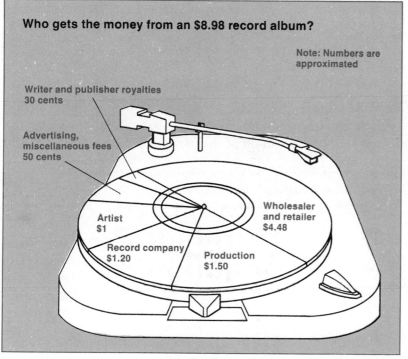

Who gets the money from an $8.98 record album?

Note: Numbers are approximated

Writer and publisher royalties
30 cents

Advertising, miscellaneous fees
50 cents

Artist
$1

Record company
$1.20

Production
$1.50

Wholesaler and retailer
$4.48

Source: *Chicago Tribune* and "Making It With Music" by Kenny Rogers and Len Epand

Bar graphs show a relationship between two variables. One variable is usually expressed in numbers. The other variable is usually expressed in words. One of the variables is listed horizontally, and the other is listed vertically. A bar extends from the variable that is expressed in words. By drawing an imaginary line along the side of the bar, you can determine the amount of the variable that is expressed in words. Look at the bar graph example at the top of the next page.

b. the number of books purchased for the school library for each of the last five years

c. the number of lunches served in the school cafeteria each month for the past school year

d. the number of students taking each foreign language available during the current school year

2. Have students construct graphs based on local weather information. Tell students to use information from newspapers such as temperature, rainfall, snowfall, or amount of sunshine for a period of time such as a week, a month, or a year. The information can then be presented on the type of graph of the student's choice. Emphasize that students must choose limited, specific information to present graphically.

Extending the Lesson

Have students gather at least ten graphic aids from their reading of newspapers and magazines for two weeks. Ask each student to present a brief written summary of the material in one of these graphic aids. (You may wish to ask them specifically *not* to include pictures.)

Largest Recorded Fruits

Fruit	Pounds
Apple	
Grapefruit	
Lemon	
Orange	
Pear	
Pineapple	

Pounds   3   5   7   9   11   13   15   17

Picture graphs are similar to bar graphs except that they use symbols to represent information instead of bars. Normally, the key explains the meaning of the pictured symbols.

Population Density of the Continents*
Estimated number of persons on each continent in 1983

= 10 people per square mile

Asia
166 per sq. mi. (64 per km²)

Europe
166 per sq. mi. (64 per km²)

Africa
44 per sq. mi. (17 per km²)

North America
41 per sq. mi. (16 per km²)

South America
36 per sq. mi. (14 per km²)

Australia
5 per sq. mi. (2 per km²)

*Antarctica has no permanent population.   Source: UN Statistical Office.

Line graphs are also used to show how two variables are related. Such graphs show a relationship over a period of time or a trend in a certain direction. By following the direction of the line, you can determine a pattern of change. By drawing imaginary lines horizontally and vertically from a particular point on the line, you can find out specific information.

Percentage of Working Women 16 Years and Over

Source: U.S. Statistical Abstracts

Exercises Using Graphic Aids

A. Answer the following questions by referring to the preceding graphic aids.

1. How many women graduated from college in America in the year 1980? 473,000

2. Between what two dates did the number of college graduates *decrease*? 1950-1960

3. How much of the cost of an average album is earned by the recording artist? $1.00

wholesaler and retailer

4. Who gets the most money from the sale of a record album?

5. Approximately how heavy was the heaviest lemon ever grown? 6 pounds

fruits and pounds

6. What are the two variables shown on the bar graph? 10 people

7. What does the symbol 👤 represent in the picture graph? per sq. mile

8. Which continents have the most people per square mile? What continent has the fewest? Antarctica

Asia, Europe

9. What was the approximate increase in the percentage of working women between the years 1960 and 1970? 7 percent

10. What decade showed the slowest rise in the percentage of working women? 1950-1960

B. Study the weather map given below. It provides a summary of the present weather situation and allows the reader to make predictions. After you familiarize yourself with the symbols, answer the questions that follow.

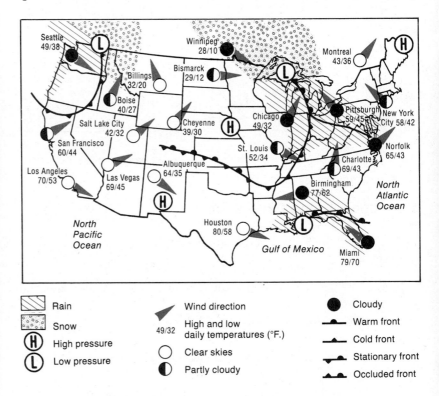

	Rain		Wind direction		Cloudy
	Snow	49/32	High and low daily temperatures (°F.)		Warm front
(H)	High pressure				Cold front
(L)	Low pressure		Clear skies		Stationary front
			Partly cloudy		Occluded front

1. What western city is experiencing completely cloudy skies? Seattle

2. Is Birmingham, Alabama, likely to become warmer or colder in the next day or two? warmer

3. In what direction is the wind blowing in Bismarck, North Dakota? east

4. What American cities on the map are experiencing rain? Seattle, Chicago, Pittsburgh, Norfolk, Birmingham, Miami

5. In what Canadian city shown on the map is it snowing? Winnipeg

C. Construct a graph to display the following information. You may choose any type of graph you wish.

Of the eight major religions of the world, Christianity is the largest, with approximately 950,000,000 members. Islam has approximately 538,000,000 adherents, followed closely by Hinduism, with 519,000,000. In addition, the following religions all have members numbering in the millions: Buddhism (245,000,000), Confucianism (176,000,000), Shinto (61,000,000), Taoism (29,000,000) and Judaism (15,000,000). These numbers are rounded to the nearest million.

Part 7   Taking Tests

Because tests are one of the primary tools employed by teachers for evaluation and grading, students are often nervous about taking them. To combat this nervousness and to increase your test scores, adopt the attitude that tests are really just another type of assignment that you can learn to prepare yourself for. Then complete the following three steps:

1. Learn how to prepare yourself mentally and physically for taking tests.
2. Learn how to study for tests.
3. Learn strategies for taking tests.

Preparing Yourself for Tests

Always get a good night's sleep and eat properly before tests. Your study plans should allow sufficient time for review so that you can avoid last-minute, late-night cramming. Just prior to taking a test, put yourself in a confident and relaxed state of mind. Remember that once you actually begin taking a test, it is no longer possible for you to prepare more thoroughly or do more studying. Worry about insufficient preparation will only detract from your concentration on the test questions and decrease your chances of doing well.

Presenting the Lesson

1. Read and discuss the introductory paragraph and **Preparing Yourself for Tests** on page 313. Remind students of the role that good study habits and a well-planned schedule, as discussed in Part 2, can play in preparing for tests. Stress the importance of mental attitude in preparation. You may wish to have students discuss how anxiety or insecurity has affected them in the past.

2. Read the chart **How To Study for a Tests** on page 314. Explain that individuals have different learning styles: some students learn best by hearing, some by seeing, and some by writing. Ask students which type of learner they feel they are. Point out that they should modify their study techniques to suit their learning style. For example, a visual learner might read over material several times, while a student who learns by writing might recopy notes.

3. Read **Taking the Test** on pages 314–315. Emphasize that these simple strategies can greatly improve students' chances for successful completion of a test.

4. Read **Applying Test-Taking Strategies**, pages 315–318. Discuss the types of tests: objective, short answer, and essay. Go over the chart on pages 316 and 317 for the various types of objective tests and the strategies for answering each kind of question. Emphasize the advantages of guessing when there is no penalty for incorrect answers. Caution students, however, that on many standardized tests there is often a penalty for guessing.

5. Assign Exercise A, page 319.

6. Stress the importance of writing in complete sentences for short-answer and essay tests. Point out that the three steps in the process of writing (pre-writing, writing, and revision) should be used in writing essay tests. Mention that an abbreviated revision step is all that is possible usually because of time constraints.

7. Assign Exercise B, page 319.

Individualizing the Lesson

Less-Advanced Students

1. Emphasize the importance of identifying key instructional words in essay test questions. Before students do Exercise B on page 319, ask them to name the key word (explaining) that tells them how to answer the question. Then have students pick out the key instructional word in each sample essay question below and tell how it controls

Studying for Tests

The following guidelines will help you study for tests:

How To Study for a Test

1. Know precisely what information will be covered by the test. If you have questions, ask your teacher.
2. Allow yourself sufficient time to study for the test.
3. Review your notes, recopying, underlining, or highlighting important material.
4. Skim any reading covered by the test.
5. Answer any study questions provided by your teacher. Review the questions that you devised using the SQ3R method.
6. Make separate lists of important names, dates, definitions, events, or formulas.
7. If the test requires a great deal of memorization, use flash cards or have someone quiz you.
8. Go over materials more than once.

Taking the Test

How you take a test is just as important as how you prepare for it. The following techniques will help you use your time wisely.

1. Survey the test. Look it over completely to see what types of questions are included and how long the test is.

2. Plan your time. Read all of the directions and decide in what order you will begin answering questions. Also decide how much time you will need for each portion of the test. Allow more time for sections that require planning, such as essay questions.

3. Read each test item carefully. Make sure you understand the questions and directions completely. If there are several essay questions, read all of them before you begin so that you don't repeat yourself in several answers. Also make sure you are following the directions. For example, are you supposed to answer only one of the essay questions or all of them? Where answers are provided, read through all the choices before deciding on the correct one.

4. Save time at the end to review the test. Scan to make sure you have not accidentally omitted any answers. Try to answer those questions you skipped. Reread any answers you are unsure of. Do not change answers too often, however. Your first ideas are usually the correct ones.

The following pages contain more specific strategies for different types of test questions.

Applying Test-Taking Strategies

There are two main types of tests. One type requires you to identify correct answers or fill in blanks in statements that are given on the test. Tests of this type are called **objective examinations** and may consist of true/false, multiple choice, matching, or completion questions. The second type requires answers in complete sentences. Such tests include short answer and essay tests.

Objective Examinations

When taking objective tests, begin by answering all of the questions that you know readily. Mark difficult questions and return to them when you have finished the rest of the test. Watch for information supplied in one question that suggests the answer to another. If a question is very difficult, restate it in your own words before answering. If you cannot determine the correct answer, go ahead and guess. If you have already eliminated most of the answers provided, your chances of guessing the correct answer are greatly increased.

The following chart describes some specific types of objective tests. Read each description and study the guidelines for approaching each type.

the way they would answer the question:

   a. *Describe* the steps by which a caterpillar becomes a butterfly.
   b. *Discuss* in detail our government's system of checks and balances.
   c. *Interpret* the poem "I'm Nobody! Who Are You?" by Emily Dickinson.
   d. *Summarize* the theories explaining the extinction of dinosaurs.

2. Encourage students to try to answer questions that they think they don't know. Explain that the act of writing often stimulates thinking.

Advanced Students

Emphasize step 2 in pre-writing for essay tests: "Know precisely what information the essay should cover." Discourage students from giving additional information or different information than the teacher requests on essay tests. Discuss the difference between developing an answer in detail and "padding" an answer with irrelevant details.

Optional Practice

Have students make up a test on a popular movie, television show, or singing group. The test should include at least five objective questions and one essay question on the information in Part 4 of this chapter.

Extending the Lesson

1. Hold a class discussion about combatting test anxiety. Point out that almost everyone suffers some degree of test anxiety, but successful test takers have developed ways to overcome their nervousness. Remind students that time spent on panic detracts from time that could be used in answering test questions. Point out, also, that the ability to combat anxiety will help them in many situations outside of tests.

2. Obtain from some local businesses tests that employers use to determine an applicant's suitability for a job. These include tests of figure aptitude and verbal ability. Reproduce these for your students. Discuss how the techniques of mental preparation would aid them in these tests, too. Also go over the types of test questions that are involved.

Objective Examinations

Description	Strategies
TRUE/FALSE The student is given a statement and asked to tell whether the statement is true or false.	1. Remember that, if any part of a statement is false, the whole statement is false. 2. Words like *all, always, only,* and *never,* often appear in false statements. 3. Words like *generally, probably, some, usually, often,* and *most* often appear in true statements.
MATCHING The student is asked to match items in one column with corresponding items in a second column.	1. Check the directions to see if each item is used only once and if some are not used. 2. Read all items in both columns before starting. 3. Match those you know first. 4. Cross out items as you use them.
MULTIPLE CHOICE The student is asked to choose the *best* answer among a group of answers provided on the test.	1. Read all choices before answering. 2. Eliminate incorrect answers first. 3. Choose the answer that is most complete or accurate. 4. Pay particular attention to choices such as *none of the above* or *all of the above.*
COMPLETION The student is asked to fill in a gap in a statement provided on the exam.	1. Make sure that your answer fits grammatically into the space provided. 2. If several words are needed to make logical sense, write in all of them. 3. Write legibly, using proper spelling, grammar, punctuation, and capitalization.
ANALOGIES The student is given a related pair of words and is asked to select a second pair of words that expresses a similar relationship.	1. Determine the exact relationship between the first two words. 2. State this relationship as clearly as you can to yourself. 3. Create a sentence, using the first two words, that shows the relationship between these words. 4. Insert the paired answers into your sentence. 5. Choose the paired answer that best fits your sentence.

Amphibians live only in water. _____*false*_____

Newts are amphibians. _____*true*_____

1. simile   A. I'm so happy I could cry.
2. personification B. I'm as hungry as a horse.
3. metaphor   C. The sun smiled down on us all.
4. paradox   D. The road was a ribbon of moonlight.

Mark Twain was born
    a. on the banks of the Mississippi   (c.) in Florida, Missouri
    b. in Hannibal, Missouri   d. none of the above

INCORRECT: When a ball is hit parallel to the ground, this hit is called _____*Line Drive*_____.

CORRECT: When a ball is hit parallel to the ground, this hit is called _____*a line drive*_____.

COLT: HORSE : : **(a)** dachshund : dog
(b) herd : buffalo   **(c)** fawn : deer

A *dachshund* is a young _____*dog*_____.

A _____*herd*_____ is a young _____*buffalo*_____.

✳ A _____*fawn*_____ is a young _____*deer*_____.

Short Answer Examinations

Always respond to short answer questions in complete sentences. Write legibly, paying close attention to grammar, spelling, punctuation, and capitalization.

When, where, and by whom was paper invented?

Paper was invented in China by Ts'ai Lun in A.D. 105.

Essay Examinations

Whenever you write an essay follow these guidelines:

Writing Essay Tests

Pre-Writing

1. Read the question carefully. Circle informational verbs such as *compare, prove, explain, interpret*, or *summarize*.
2. Know precisely what information the essay should cover.
3. If the essay question is divided into parts, organize your essay into corresponding sections.
4. Make an outline of major points and supporting details.
5. Write a statement of the main idea that includes a brief restatement of the essay question, and place this in the first paragraph.

Writing

Pay attention to all aspects of good writing, including topic sentences, transitions, and concluding sentences.

Revision

Normally, one does not have time to do complete revisions of essay exams. However, make sure that you leave yourself enough time to proofread thoroughly.

Exercises Taking Tests

A. Answer the following questions:

1. In addition to studying and applying test strategies, students who prepare well for tests __sleep__ and __eat__ properly before tests.

2. Which of the following is not a type of objective test?
   a. multiple choice
   b. matching
   c. completion
   d. true/false
   <u>e. none of the above</u>

3. Match the following types of objective tests with their corresponding strategies:

   ₃ A. True/False

   ₄ B. Multiple Choice

   ₁ C. Completion

   ₂ D. Matching

   1. Make sure your answer fits grammatically into the space provided.
   2. Read all items in both columns before starting.
   3. Remember that, if any part of a statement is not true, the entire statement is not true.
   4. Choose the most complete or accurate of the answers provided.

B. Write a one-paragraph essay explaining the importance of providing wheelchair ramps in all public buildings. Be sure to use your own words, give reasons or examples to support your topic sentence, and follow the strategies outlined in this section. Allow yourself exactly 20 minutes to write this paragraph.

Go over this summary with your students. Emphasize that a logical, well-planned approach to any task increases an individual's chances of success.

Encourage students to use this summary for review, or a part of the SQ3R method of study (see Chapter 15). Remind them, though, that more specific points can only be reviewed by skimming the chapter itself.

Applications in Other Subject Areas

Before assigning the **Speech/All Subjects** activity, explain the idea of "generalization" to the students. Ask them what generalizations or trends they can observe in the graphs on pages 308 and 311.

SUMMARY AND APPLICATIONS   CHAPTER 15

1. Learning good study techniques can help you approach any type of task in a logical, organized manner.

2. When you are given an assignment, record directions and other important information carefully. Schedule a time to complete the assignment and follow directions precisely.

3. When studying printed materials, use the SQ3R Method of study (**S**urvey, **Q**uestion, **R**ead, **R**ecite, **R**eview). Take notes using short phrases or a modified outline.

4. Adjust your reading speed to the materials you are studying and to the purpose for which you are reading.

5. Graphic aids include pictures, sketches, diagrams, maps, tables, charts, and graphs. Know how to interpret them.

6. Prepare yourself physically and mentally for every test. Always review the test-taking strategies described in this chapter.

Applications in Other Subject Areas

Speech / All Subjects. Collect three graphs from textbooks in other classes. Attach each one to a separate piece of lined notebook paper. Under each graph, state the following:

a. The variables that are listed by the graph.
b. A generalization or trend illustrated by the graph.

Prepare a short talk explaining the graph to your class.

All Subjects. Pick a class you are now taking in which you must regularly take notes. Open your notebook from that class to the most recent unit of study and skim over the last two or three pages of notes. Copy these over, using a modified outline form. Use abbreviations for commonly occurring words.

Chapter 16

Letters, Forms, and Applications

Chapter Objectives

1. To learn the correct form for addressing envelopes

2. To use proper style and form for informal notes

3. To use proper style and form for friendly letters

4. To use proper style and form for three types of business letters

5. To learn the correct method for completing forms

6. To use skills to find a part-time job

Preparing the Students

Tell students to think of the last three letters they have written. Ask them whether these letters were informal notes, business letters, or letters to friends. Then ask if they are ever uncertain about the proper form for these various kinds of letters.

Tell students that this chapter will give instructions and examples and serve as a reference to which they may turn when in doubt. It will also show them how to apply these and other business skills to the practical situation of obtaining a part-time job.

Additional Resources

Skills Practice Book — pages 82–86.
Duplicating Masters — pages 83–87.
Special Populations — See special section at the front of this Teacher's Edition.

Every day, over two hundred million pieces of first-class mail are handled by the post office. People are mailing friendly notes, invitations, cards, business letters, and many other kinds of communication. In addition, they are reading and filling out hundreds of thousands of forms as they apply for jobs, request library cards, complete questionnaires, and order from catalogs. Clearly, writing has its uses outside of reports and homework assignments!

Because writing letters and completing forms are such common, everyday tasks, you probably give them little thought. Yet each requires special skills and knowledge that are important to understand. Such skills may even determine whether or not you get a particular job or are accepted at a college. This chapter will provide you with some guidelines for these special types of writing, and will show you how to apply your skills in getting a part-time job.

Part 1

Objective

To learn the correct form for addressing envelopes

Presenting the Lesson

1. Read and discuss pages 322–324. Point out that the envelopes in the examples are addressed in "box" style, that is, with the lines of the addresses lined up evenly at the left. Another acceptable style is to indent each line a few spaces more than the previous line. Tell students that, if the indented style is used for the address, it must also be used for the return address.

2. Have students examine carefully the list of abbreviations on page 324. Tell them that these two-letter, all capital abbreviations are approved for addresses only. They should not be used in other contexts.

3. Explain that the ZIP code is a summary of the last two or three items in numerical code that makes sorting easier at the post office.

4. Assign Exercise A on page 325 to be completed in class. Be sure students understand the correct order of information and punctuation for addresses. Assign Exercise B to be completed at home with a telephone directory.

Individualizing the Lesson

Less-Advanced Students

Explain that the order of information in an address is from the most specific to the most general. In a business letter, for example, they would begin the address with the

Let's start with the simplest part of letter-writing first—the envelope. Probably the worst thing that could happen to a letter you have painstakingly written is that it is not delivered. Hundreds of thousands of letters end up in the Dead Letter Office in Washington, D.C. The usual problem is an incorrect address, which can be easily avoided. Double-check to be certain you have not transposed any numbers in the address. Do not forget the ZIP code. This is a five-digit code that identifies a small area within a city or state, and enables the post office to sort mail much more efficiently and rapidly. The ZIP should immediately follow the state in addresses. If you do not know the ZIP, and cannot find it in your telephone directory, call your post office. They have a complete ZIP code listing for every community in the United States and will be happy to help you.

Always put your return address on the envelope.

Ms. Betty Sergeant
1429 Oakridge Road
Ft. Worth TX 76135

Mr. Larry Spenser
341 Queen Avenue
Yakima WA 98902

Envelopes come in many different sizes and colors. The two most-used sizes are 9½″ x 4″ and 6½″ x 3½″. When sending a business letter, you should always use a white 9½″ x 4″ envelope.

If you are writing a specific person or department within a large company, you will use four lines for the address.

Ms. Betty Sergeant
1429 Oakridge Road
Ft. Worth TX 76135

            Mr. Larry Spenser
            A + G Electronics Company
            341 Queen Avenue
            Yakima WA 98902

When addressing the small, square envelope that is usually included with invitations or note cards, you may put your return address on the flap on the back of the envelope, with the receiver's name and address centered on the front.

        Mr. Larry Spenser
        341 Queen Avenue
        Yakima WA 98902

        Ms. Betty Sergeant
        1429 Oakridge Road
        Ft. Worth TX
            76135

Caution: Be sure to check the back on any envelope before addressing it. You may have it upside down.

name of a specific person, then put the department in which he or she works, then the name of the company, the street the company is on, the city, and the state.

Advanced Students

Have students do research to learn what all the numbers in the ZIP codes stand for.

Optional Practice

Have students put the following addresses in the proper form.

a. waltham MA six overlook road 02154 ms. marina marshal
b. 07043 stuart pembroke 153 watchung avenue president pembroke furs montclair new jersey
c. 44 high street repairs department clara's auto hospital peterborough new hampshire 03458

Extending the Lesson

Have students find the addresses of their state senators and representatives. Tell them to write these addresses in proper form on a piece of paper. They should keep this handily as a reference material for times when they wish to express an opinion in writing concerning local or national issues.

Did you notice the abbreviations of the names of states on the examples? These may be used in addressing envelopes, but you *must* use the ZIP code with them. When you use these abbreviations, you do not need to separate the city and state with a comma. However, if you do not use these abbreviations, you must place a comma between the city and state.

Mr. Larry Spenser
341 Queen Avenue
Yakima WA 98902

Mr. Larry Spenser
341 Queen Avenue
Yakima, Washington 98902

Abbreviations of State Names

State	Abbr.	State	Abbr.
Alabama	AL	Montana	MT
Alaska	AK	Nebraska	NE
Arizona	AZ	Nevada	NV
Arkansas	AR	New Hampshire	NH
American Samoa	AS	New Jersey	NJ
California	CA	New Mexico	NM
Canal Zone	CZ	New York	NY
Colorado	CO	North Carolina	NC
Connecticut	CT	North Dakota	ND
Delaware	DE	Ohio	OH
District of Columbia	DC	Oklahoma	OK
Florida	FL	Oregon	OR
Georgia	GA	Pennsylvania	PA
Guam	GU	Puerto Rico	PR
Hawaii	HI	Rhode Island	RI
Idaho	ID	South Carolina	SC
Illinois	IL	South Dakota	SD
Indiana	IN	Tennessee	TN
Iowa	IA	Trust Territories	TT
Kansas	KS	Texas	TX
Kentucky	KY	Utah	UT
Louisiana	LA	Vermont	VT
Maine	ME	Virginia	VA
Maryland	MD	Virgin Islands	VI
Massachusetts	MA	Washington	WA
Michigan	MI	West Virginia	WV
Minnesota	MN	Wisconsin	WI
Mississippi	MS	Wyoming	WY
Missouri	MO		

Exercises Addressing Envelopes

A. Put each of the addresses below in proper three or four-line form as it should appear on an envelope. Capitalize, abbreviate, and punctuate correctly.   Answers in margin.

1. 462 zane avenue philadelphia pennsylvania 19111 mrs. jill erikson

2. washington d c 20013 national geographic society melvin m payne post office box 2895

3. 111 west washington street chicago illinois 60602 chicago title insurance company

4. salt lake city utah 84104 appliance department 1133 glendale drive gibson's discount center

5. mr. john johnson oklahoma city oklahoma 1462 longridge road 73115

B. Draw four "envelopes" on plain paper. Three of the envelopes should measure 9½″ × 4″, and one should measure 5″ × 5″. Now pick three of the choices below and with the aid of a telephone directory, write the addresses correctly on the envelopes. Address the 5″ × 5″ envelope to your best friend. Do not forget to include your return address.

1. Anyone whose last name is Smith

2. The service department of an automobile agency

3. Your favorite disc jockey

4. An employment agency

5. The sportswear department of a department store

6. A television station

Now that you are familiar with addressing envelopes, you are ready to study the different types of letters to put inside them. The form for an envelope does not change; it is the same for any letter.

Exercise A

1. Mrs. Jill Erikson
    462 Zane Avenue
    Philadelphia, Pennsylvania 19111 (or
    Philadelphia PA 19111)
2. Melvin M. Payne
    National Geographic Society
    Post Office Box 2895
    Washington, D.C. 20013 (or Washington
    DC 20013)
3. Chicago Title Insurance Company
    111 West Washington Street
    Chicago, Illinois 60602 (or Chicago IL
    60602)
4. Appliance Department
    Gibson's Discount Center
    1133 Glendale Drive
    Salt Lake City, Utah 84104 (or Salt Lake
    City UT 84104)
5. Mr. John Johnson
    1462 Longridge Road
    Oklahoma City, Oklahoma 73115 (or
    Oklahoma City OK 73115)

Part 2

Objective

To use proper style and form for informal notes

Presenting the Lesson

1. Read and discuss pages 326–328. Tell students that courtesy notes thanking people for hospitality or gifts are sometimes called "bread-and-butter" notes. Be sure students realize that it is customary to send such courtesy notes.

2. Have students write one of the notes for the Exercise on page 329. Then tell students to exchange papers and comment on the form and the message of each others' notes. Assign the second note to be completed independently at home.

Individualizing the Lesson

Less-Advanced Students

Go over the five basic parts of all informal notes. Tell them that closings should be somewhat dignified. Such closings as *Fondly*, *Affectionately*, and *Your friend* are acceptable; however, "cute" closings, such as "Luv Ya," or "Love and Lollipops" are not.

Advanced Students

Have students think of real-life situations in which an informal courtesy note would have been appropriate. Then have students write the note for practice. Point out that these notes are usually very easy and quick to write and are greatly appreciated by the receivers.

Whenever you have written a short letter thanking a relative for a gift or expressing your appreciation for a weekend visit, you have used a form of letter known as an **informal note**.

These notes all have one thing in common. They are short. They could be referred to as "people-pleasers" because they definitely impress the receiver. You might have been less than completely delighted with the complete dental-care kit your aunt and uncle sent you for Christmas, but they will be pleased to receive your letter of thanks.

Informal notes have a definite form:

Date
August 30, 1985

Salutation

Dear Uncle Fred and Aunt Fran,

You never told me you had ESP- how else could you have known I've been craving that particular album? It's great! I've played it at least twenty times, and Mom says that next time you send an album to me, she'd appreciate your enclosing a pair of earplugs for her.

Body

Thanks so much for the perfect gift. I hope you can visit sometime and hear it for yourselves- before I wear it out!

Closing *Love,*
Signature *Jennie*

The first part of the form of an informal note is the **date**. Remember to leave a margin between the end of the date and the right side of the paper.

The second item is the **salutation**. This simply addresses the person to whom you are writing. Always use a comma after the salutation. Next is the **body** of the letter, or the message. The **closing** can be one of many, depending on the relationship. *Sincerely, Affectionately, Lovingly, Happily*, or *Good luck* are some of the choices. If the closing is more than one word, capitalize only the first word. Always use a comma after the closing.

As you can see, a casual language style is fine. Write naturally, the way you would normally speak to the person to whom you are writing.

There are other varieties of the informal note. Apologies, congratulations, invitations, and R.S.V.P.'s are the most common. Of these, only the R.S.V.P. might require some explanation.

> July 27, 1985
>
> Dear Jim,
>   You are invited to attend my birthday dinner on August 16. It will be held at the Sundance Room of the Hotel Towers at 7:30 p.m.
>   I'm looking forward to seeing you.
>
>   Sincerely,
>   Mary Barnes
>
> R.S.V.P.

R.S.V.P. is an abbreviation for a French phrase meaning "please respond." It is necessary for the sender to have an exact count of the attending guests before the party. Unless you want to appear "uninformed," you must reply. You write a brief note stating your intention to attend or not.

August 1, 1985

Dear Mary,

I would love to attend your birthday dinner, but will be unable to as we are planning a vacation and will be out of town on August 16.

Have a very happy birthday!

Sincerely,
Jim Harris

August 1, 1985

Dear Mary,

Thank you so much for the invitation to your birthday dinner. I'd be delighted to attend.

Sincerely,
Jim Harris

Exercise Writing Informal Notes

Choose two of the following and write the appropriate notes on plain paper. On the back draw an envelope for each and address it correctly.

1. Write a note thanking a friend for the fantastic party he gave last Saturday.

2. Write to your friend's parents, apologizing for dropping a full bowl of punch on their new white carpet.

3. Write a note of congratulation to a friend who has moved from your neighborhood. You have just learned that he or she has won a cash prize in a contest. You determine the contest.

4. Write a note thanking a relative for something. The only problem is that you have no idea what the item is.

5. Write an invitation to a party, using R.S.V.P. Exchange your invitation with another student and write a reply.

6. Write a note to a friend's mother or father for something very nice the person did for you. You decide the reason.

7. Write a note to a cheerleader at your school, apologizing for tackling her during the last game.

8. Write a note congratulating your dog for passing obedience school.

Part 3 Writing Friendly Letters

These letters seem to be going down in popularity while long-distance telephone bills are going up. Haven't you tearfully said goodbye to a friend, promising to write, and then put it off until you didn't know what to write or where to start? It happens to everyone, and it's too bad. Through this type of letter, friendships endure over many years and more miles. This should be an easy letter to write, as you're communicating with someone you know very well—someone who has shared many experiences with you. Just keep sharing experiences—only now through letters. The language is informal, just as you would speak to the person.

Part 3

Objective

To use proper style and form for friendly letters

Presenting the Lesson

1. Read and discuss pages 329–332. Throughout the discussion, stress the value of written communication among friends. Since letter writing has declined since the invention of the telephone, remind students of the fun of receiving let-

ters and of the pleasure that letter writing can provide the writer.

2. Discuss in detail the difference between the dull letter on page 331 and the enjoyable, interesting letter on 332. What makes the second letter such a pleasure to read?

3. Assign the Exercise on page 333. Encourage the students to write real letters that can be mailed to friends who have moved to other cities or distant neighborhoods. Remind them of the importance of detail.

Individualizing the Lesson

Less-Advanced Students

Point out the differences in form and style between an informal courtesy note and a friendly letter. The friendly letter has a heading, whereas the informal note has only the date. The content of a friendly letter is more personal and "newsy" while an informal note usually centers around a single idea, such as an invitation or gratitude for a gift.

Advanced Students

Letters written in the past by ordinary people can provide valuable insights and clues to the way life was lived in earlier times. Ask students to locate, either in their family records or in textbooks, old letters that tell about the history of our country—even if that history is only a few decades ago. Make sure that you allow time for these letters to be presented to the class.

Optional Practice

Contact a pen pal service and provide students with an opportunity to correspond with a person from another section of the United States or from another country.

There is a little more involved in the form of a friendly letter than in informal notes. Below is an example. Once you learn the parts of a friendly letter, you'll have to concentrate only on writing the body of the letter itself.

The **heading** is written in three lines. The first line consists of your street address. The second line contains the city, state and ZIP. The third line is the date of the letter. Don't abbreviate on the date line.

The **salutation** can be casual in a friendly letter. The only two rules are to capitalize the first word and any proper nouns, and to use a comma following the salutation.

Dear Sue,   *Hi Slim,*
Howdy Pete,   *Hello Mark,*

The **closing** is usually kept simple: *Love, Sincerely, Always,* etc. The first word is the only one capitalized. You can use your originality and the closeness of the friendship for something more appropriate for the particular person to whom you are writing.

Lovingly yours,   *Still waiting,*
Always here,   *Frustrated,*

The most important part of any letter is the **body**. Let's hope you haven't received or been guilty of sending such an empty letter as the following:

---

162 New Road
Raleigh NC 27608
July 16, 1985

Dear Jess,

    Your letter arrived yesterday and I'm happy to hear about all the great things you've been doing.

    As usual, things around here aren't very exciting. The weather's been hot for so long I can't remember what "cool" means.

    Everyone here says to say "hi."

    There's not much more to write. Wish you were here so we could have a good talk. Write soon.

        Love,

        Jill

Extending the Lesson

1. Letters written by famous people are often published in book form. Explain to the students that these personal letters offer fascinating insights into the letter-writer's personal life. Have students look for such collections in the library and bring them to class for group discussion.

2. Students may be interested in writing letters to authors of books they have enjoyed, recording artists, or film stars. Offer assistance in obtaining the addresses. Replies could be used for an interesting display.

All that is needed to turn dull paragraphs into interesting ones is detail. If the person to whom you are writing were with you, what would you say? Here are a few points to remember when writing a friendly letter:

1. Make comments on the letter you have received.
2. Avoid the constant use of *I*.
3. Write one or two detailed paragraphs regarding events and people. They will be much more interesting than a series of one-sentence statements.
4. Ask questions. Then the person has something to write to you about.

With a little more time and thought, Jill might have written two opening paragraphs like this:

> Maybe this letter should be written in special ink so you can read it underwater—don't you ever get waterlogged? From the sound of things you're either in training for the Olympics or trying to get a role in the next "Jaws." You're way out of my class now—unless they've started giving medals for floating in a tube. Couldn't you manage to compete in a meet around here?

> Things here are not too exciting—and that's an understatement! It's been so hot for so long that everyone's dragging. I've been lying around the yard or the house most of the time. But you know my Mom—if I'm not "doing something," I can't possibly be happy. So she keeps finding things for me to "do." Clean out your closet. Water the lawn. Straighten your dresser. Water the lawn! Run to the store. Water the lawn! I'm beginning to feel as if I've got a hose growing out of my right arm! The lawn's so soaked now we could grow rice! Next summer a job is a necessity—only with my luck it would probably be watering lawns.

Detail, along with conversational writing, can make a letter come to life. Choose one of the statements in Jill's letter on page 331 and rewrite it in a detailed paragraph. Make it interesting. Be prepared to exchange your paragraph with a classmate, or read it aloud to the class.

Exercise Writing Friendly Letters

One of your best friends has moved out of the city. Write a friendly letter detailing three events that have taken place since he or she left. You can use events that have actually happened or choose from the list below.

1. Your school team lost a close game for the state basketball championship.

2. A good friend gave you a surprise birthday party.

3. You are certain that someone tried to break into your house when your parents were out.

4. Your new puppy is methodically eating his way through the house—couch, chairs, carpets, shoes.

5. You tried waterskiing (or another sport) for the first time. The results were hilarious.

6. Your class wants to go to Washington, D.C. You are on a committee to raise funds for the trip.

Part 4   Writing Business Letters

Over ten thousand business letters are processed for each friendly letter or informal note that is written. With odds like that, the business letter has to be an important letter to master. The term *business* means that the letters have a definite purpose to accomplish, not that they are written only by and for business firms.

There are two main skills you need to master in order to write an effective business letter: (1) Use the proper form. (2) Be brief and specific.

Using the Proper Form

There are two basic forms for business letters: **block form** and **modified block form**.

Presenting the Lesson

1. Read the introductory paragraphs to Part 4 and **Using the Proper Form**, pages 333–337. Tell the students that business letters are usually written to get results of some kind. Letter-writers increase their chances of getting the desired results if their business letters are written in standard, accepted form. Such letters are more likely to get the respect and attention of the recipient than those that are sloppy or that imply indifference on the part of the writer.

2. Complete Exercise A, page 338, with the class, Be sure students understand all the parts and the correct punctuation for a business letter. Then assign Exercise B, page 338, to be completed independently.

3. Read **Being Brief and Specific**, pages 339–340. Point out that the recipients of business letters do not have the time to wade through unnecessary information.

Assign the Exercise on page 340. After students have written their sample letters, have them exchange letters and comment on each others' work. Do the letters get right to the point? Do they include all necessary information?

4. Read and discuss **Types of Business Letters**, pages 341–344. Read the sample request for information and letter of complaint aloud. Point out that the letter of complaint has a mature, fair-minded tone that is more apt to get favorable results than an angry and insulting letter would.

5. Assign the Exercises on pages 342 and 345.

6. Read and discuss **Knowing Where and to Whom to Write**, pages 345–346.

Tell students that a letter that is not addressed to a specific person sometimes gets lost in the paper shuffle of a large company. Point out that it is often a good idea to make a phone call and get the name and title of a specific person to whom to write the letter—especially if it is a letter of complaint. Often, if a particular person is targeted, he or she will assume the necessary responsibility to get results.

Block Form   (used only when the letter is typewritten)

Heading

416 Paxton Road
Rochester, New York 14617
April 23, 1985

Inside Address

Sales Department
Stereophonics, Inc.
231 Garrison
Boston, Massachusetts 02116

Salutation

Ladies and Gentlemen:

_____
_____
_____ Body
_____
_____
_____

Sincerely,   Closing

José Martinez

José Martinez   Signature

Note: Always use plain white 8½″ x 11″ paper for business letters, whether you handwrite or type them.

Modified Block Form

Heading

416 Paxton Road
Rochester, New York 14617
April 23, 1985

Inside Address

Sales Department
Stereophonics, Inc.
231 Garrison
Boston, Massachusetts 02116

Salutation

Dear Sir or Madam:

_____

_____

_____ — Body

_____

_____

_____

Sincerely,   Closing

José Martinez

José Martinez   Signature

You are already familiar with the heading of a letter. It is the same as that used for writing friendly letters.

sentence has an insulting word, "stupid," that is apt to aggravate whoever reads the letter.)

Extending the Lesson

Point out that businesses seldom receive letters complimenting their services, but that such letters are extremely satisfying to recieve. They can also be instrumental in helping a good employee get some recognition.

Discuss with the class occasions when they have been particularly satisfied with a service or product. Have them compose business letters stating their satisfaction and mail them to the companies concerned.

The one section that has been added is the **inside address**. It is important to have the name and address of the person or department to whom you are writing on the face of the letter. Occasionally a letter is opened by mistake and the envelope misplaced; if this happens, the name and address are still clearly visible. The inside address is usually four lines on a business letter, as you will be writing to a specific person or department within a company. Leave a space between the inside address and the salutation.

The salutation varies, depending upon the first line of the inside address. If you are writing to a company or department within a company, use one of the following:

```
Dear Sir or Madam:
Ladies and Gentlemen:
```

If you are writing to a particular person, but do not know his or her name (such as the Personnel Manager, president, or General Manager), you should use *Dear Sir or Madam*.

The form for someone whose name you know is quite simple:

```
Dear Mr. Brown:
Dear Ms. Allred:
Dear Miss Allred:
Dear Mrs. Allred:
```

Capitalize only the first word and any proper nouns in the salutation, and always follow the salutation with a colon. Leave a space between the salutation and the body of the letter and between the body of the letter and the closing. Capitalize only the first word of the closing, and always follow the closing with a comma.

```
Sincerely,
Very truly yours,
Respectfully yours,
```

Type or print your name four spaces below the closing, and write your signature in the space between. Typing or printing your name makes it legible if you have a fancy but illegible signature.

Make a Copy. Whenever you write a business letter, make a carbon copy or photocopy for yourself. Then you will know just what you wrote or ordered in case you do not receive an immediate reply. If you use carbon paper, first place a piece of plain paper on your desk. Then place a sheet of carbon paper on top of it. The "shiny" or carbon side of the paper should be face down. Now place another piece of plain paper on top and you are ready to write. To avoid slippage, you can use a paper clip to hold the three pieces together. When you write, be certain you use the type of carbon paper that is made for pen or pencil. Typewriter keys exert much more pressure on the carbon paper than a person's hand.

Fold the Letter Correctly. Folding a business letter correctly is sometimes a problem. You want only two folds in your paper when using a standard 9½″ x 4″ envelope. Starting at the bottom of the paper, fold it into thirds toward the top. Usually you will find that after the first fold is completed, only the inside address and heading will be visible to you. When properly folded, the letter will easily fit into the envelope, and can readily be taken out by the receiver.

First Fold	Second Fold	Complete

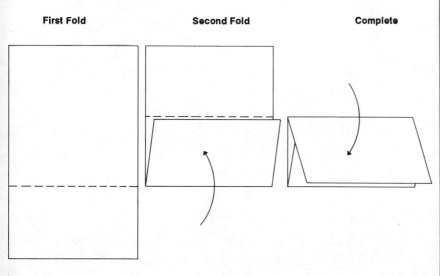

Exercises Using the Proper Form

A. Below is an example of a business letter in modified block form. There are errors in capitalization, punctuation, and spacing. Correct the errors by rewriting the letter on a plain sheet of paper.

_{January}
~~Jan~~. 14, 1985
1452 Balboa Drive
Pensacola, Florida/ 32506

^S
General supply Company
_{Sales Manager}
~~sales mgr~~.
462 ᴬacacia ᴬavenue
Palo Alto, ~~Calif~~. 94306
_{California}

Dear Sir or Madam/:

    Regarding the order I placed with you on
December 15, _____

_____

_____

_____

_____

_____

Very ᵗTruly ʸYours,

Thomas A. O'Leary } ⟶

Thomas A. O'Leary

B. Using correct form, write a letter of your own with a local company as the addressee. You do not have to write the body of the letter.

Being Brief and Specific

When you write a business letter you include only what is absolutely necessary. State the purpose of the letter and then stop. Use only those details that are vital to accomplish your purpose.

1942 Griffin Road
Indianapolis, Indiana 46227
June 14, 1985

West Hills Pro Shop
571 Moon Clinton Road
Coraopolis, Pennsylvania 15108

Dear Sir or Madam:

Please send me the following items which appeared in your advertisement in the June issue of <u>Travel</u> and <u>Leisure</u>.

1 pr.	Foot-Joy Golf Shoes	Size 11D	Black	$ 48.00
2	Canvas Sunday Bags		@$19.00	38.00
1	Model M-20 Lynx Putter			25.00
			Total	$111.00

Enclosed is a money order for $111.00. The advertisement states that prices include postage and insurance.

Yours truly,

Scott Andersen

Scott Andersen

Whenever you place an order, be sure you have a complete description or a model number. Include sizes, colors, and the number of items desired. Check the charge for postage. In some instances the buyer will pay for postage and this amount must be included with the order. Also check instructions about sales tax. Any errors on your part will result in a delay in delivery, or in receiving unwanted merchandise. It is much easier to double-check an order than to return merchandise. Keep a carbon copy in case any mix-ups occur.

Exercise Being Brief and Specific

Clip an advertisement from a magazine, or choose one of the groups below and write an order letter. Total the order and add any postage that is necessary. On the back of the order draw an envelope and address it correctly.

1. Columbia House, 1400 North Fruitridge Ave., Terre Haute, Indiana 47808

> 1 8-track cartridge No. JCA34860 *Chicago XI* $7.98
> 1 record No. RS-2-4200 *BeeGees Greatest* $6.98
> 1 two-record set No. 2HS3350 *Tusk* $15.98
> Postage $.75

2. Walter Drake & Sons, 4085 Drake Building, Colorado Springs, Colorado 80940—Advertisement in August issue of *Better Homes and Gardens*

> No. S717—two sets of 1,000 name labels @ $1.00 per set
> No. S854—one set of personalized pencils @ $.89 per set
> No. S6066—two full-page magnifiers @ $1.98 each
> Postage and handling—$.40

3. Sea Horses, Box 342096, Coral Gables, Florida 33134—Advertisement in July issue of *Boy's Life*

> 3 live sea horse kits @ $ 2.98
> 2 custom aquariums @ $ 5.98
> 1 deluxe aquarium $10.95
>
> Air mail postage paid by advertiser—live delivery guaranteed

Types of Business Letters

1. Requests for Information. Perhaps you have been thinking about buying some stereo equipment. You could write a business letter requesting information regarding additional speakers.

2. Letters of Order. You would order your stereo equipment through a business letter if you were unable to purchase it locally. See the sample letter on page 339.

3. Letters of Complaint. If your speaker did not operate when you received it, you would write a business letter to complain. The ability to write this type of letter is invaluable.

Requests for Information. Letters that request information must be as specific as possible. They should also be polite.

1315 Summer Road
Trenton, New Jersey 08618
May 15, 1985

Chamber of Commerce
Zuni
New Mexico 87327

Dear Sir or Madam:

As a class assignment, I am working on a paper dealing with the Indians of New Mexico, and particularly the Zuni tribe. Any information or addresses you could provide would be appreciated.

I am particularly interested in the culture of the Zuni Indians today as compared with the culture of the 1800's.

Very truly yours,
Susan Campbell

Special Note for Typists: If any of your business letters are extremely short, you may double-space for the sake of appearance. If you do double-space, be consistent with the prescribed form.

Exercises Writing a Request for Information

A. Write a letter to a chamber of commerce asking for information about their city. Be specific as to why you need this information: you are planning to move to that city; you are interested in vacationing there; or you have been given that particular area to research as a class assignment.

B. Write to a college or university requesting information regarding tuition costs. State your major field of interest: law, medicine, computer science, etc.

C. Write to a company in your area asking for information about summer employment. Let them know your age, qualifications, and previous experience.

D. In groups, plan the "ideal" vacation to an exotic spot. Write the various letters necessary for transportation, hotels, and tours. Then plan the vacation with the information you receive.

Letters of Complaint. Have you ever purchased something that fell apart, did not work, or was a disappointment? Write a letter of complaint. This is not a "gripe" letter; it is written to let a store or company know that there is a problem and you would like to have it taken care of. Most companies are interested in hearing from you. If you are not happy with a purchase, you probably will not buy that brand again, or maybe you will shop at a different store. This is of great concern to the seller. After all, he or she wants you to keep buying that particular product or coming to the store. Do not merely sit around and tell your friends how upset you are; let the proper people know you are unhappy. You will be surprised at their response.

Avoid the temptation to be sarcastic, angry, or vulgar. This will not accomplish your purpose; it will merely make you look bad. Let the store or company know when and where you purchased the item and exactly what is wrong with it. Volunteer to mail the item if they would like to inspect it. Manufacturers can rapidly tell if the problem was their fault or yours.

631 Inca Lane
St. Paul, Minnesota 55112
October 6, 1985

Public Relations Department
Woolcraft, Inc.
1300 West Fremont Place
St. Louis, Missouri 63142

Gentlemen:

    In September I purchased one of your new "Ski-Sno" sweaters from a local department store. After wearing it twice, I washed it according to the directions on the label. While it is still soft and the colors are as bright as when it was brand-new, it is now several sizes smaller. Needless to say, I am very disappointed.

    I would be happy to send the sweater directly to you, as there has obviously been some oversight in your washing instructions. I would appreciate an explanation.

        Sincerely,
        Elsa Johnson

Perhaps your problem is closer to home than Elsa's. After many futile phone calls to a local company, you might find it easier to state your problem in a letter.

123 La Clede Avenue
Memphis, Tennessee 38126
August 31, 1985

General Manager
Sutton's Department Store
432 Oak Street
Memphis, Tennessee 38142

Dear Sir:

In June I purchased a pair of water skis in your Sporting Goods Department. These skis are model no. 143 and the price was $26.95, on sale. I used my parents' charge account, number 47727, for this purchase. Enclosed is a copy of the sales receipt.

The July statement which we received shows a charge in the amount of $269.50. Upon calling the Billing Department, I was informed that this was a computer error and would be corrected. The August statement has a past-due charge of $2,695.00. Is there some way you can communicate with the computer and correct this error?

Your earliest attention to this problem would be greatly appreciated.

Very truly yours,
Benjamin Erickson

Exercise Writing a Letter of Complaint

Write a letter of complaint regarding one of the following problems:

1. The new jeans you purchased fell apart after three wearings. (Write to the manufacturing company.)

2. You ordered a CB antenna through the mail, but received an aquarium. (Write to a hobby shop.)

3. The records you ordered from your club were warped when delivered. (Write to a record club.)

4. The live sea horses you ordered through the mail weren't. (Write to a pet shop.)

5. Four weeks ago you ordered $28.70 in supplies for a science project. You have not received them, and it is now too late to complete your project. Explain the problem and ask for a refund. (Write to a hobby shop.)

Knowing Where and to Whom To Write

You can spend a great deal of time writing the "perfect" letter, addressing it correctly, and still not receive a response. It is frustrating, but curable. The usual problem is that you have not directed the letter to a specific person or department. There are many different departments within each large company which have different purposes. A request for employment would go one place and a complaint another. There are special sections to handle orders, service calls, parts, etc. If the address on your letter is simply to the company, it might take a week or more for it to find its way to the person qualified to respond.

If your particular problem is one that originated with the manufacturer and not the store where you made the purchase, you should write directly to the manufacturer. The address is usually on the label attached to the product. If not, you can obtain the necessary information through your local store. There is a special department that will pay particular attention to your letter and is interested in hearing from you. This department is referred to as Public Relations. They would like to hear from you because they want to keep you happy. One important thing to bear in mind is that you do not have to have a complaint to write a business letter. If you have been thoroughly happy with one particular product, let the manufacturer know. After all, we all appreciate a nice comment now and then.

Exercises Knowing Where and to Whom To Write

A. Using the list provided, where would you send a letter dealing with each of the numbered problems below?

Personnel Department   Sportswear Department
Accounting Department   Service Department
Parts Department

1. Employment information personnel
2. Ordering parts Parts (possibly Service)   Service
3. Requesting information regarding the operation of a product
4. Asking if a store carries a specific brand of swimwear Sportswear
5. Being charged twice for the same item Accounting

B. How many different departments does a large store in your area contain? Can you list the different departments within a large corporation such as the telephone company? Write down as many as you can; then look in a telephone directory to see how close you are.

Part 5 Filling Out Forms

Forms fulfill many needs and perform many different functions. Their primary purpose is to obtain specific information in a particular order. An employer reads an application form to determine your qualifications for a job. A bank teller uses a savings account deposit form to keep a record of your money.

You probably have been faced with filling out at least one form in your lifetime. Most likely, you will fill out hundreds more of them as you continue through school and begin looking for employment.

Part 5

Objective

To learn the correct method for completing forms

Presenting the Lesson

1. Read and discuss **Filling Out Forms**, pages 346–347. Ask students if they have had any experience filling out forms, possibly for bank accounts, social security

The following guidelines may be helpful to you as you complete various types of forms:

Completing Forms

1. Read all directions carefully and *skim* the entire form before making any marks on it. Notice any special requirements indicated in the directions. Then, gather all information that you need such as your social security number, mother's maiden name, parents' birthdates, references' names and addresses, etc.

2. Assemble your writing tools. Use a good pen or a typewriter and an eraser. Do not use pencil unless specifically requested to do so.

3. Begin filling out the form *line by line*, rereading all directions. Directions for procedures as simple as filling in your name may vary from form to form.

4. When the form is finished, check it for accuracy, spelling, and completeness. Proofread carefully.

5. If references are required, remember to obtain permission from the people whose names you plan to use. Find out their job titles, the correct spellings of their names, and their complete addresses, including ZIP codes. You will also want to provide their telephone numbers.

Keep in mind that you usually will have only one copy of a form. Take time to complete this copy correctly.

Exercises Completing Forms

A. You are organizing a school newspaper staff. Design a form for students who want to apply for a position on the newspaper. Be sure that the form provides you with any information that you might need, such as the student's year in school, the position the applicant is interested in, previous experience, grade point average, and how the student can be contacted.

cards, or applications for camps or special school programs. Ask if there were any unforeseen difficulties in filling out the forms.

2. Go over the guidelines in the chart on page 347, carefully pointing out the importance of each one.

3. Assign Exercises A and B on pages 348–349. You may wish to do Exercise B orally.

Individualizing the Lesson
Less-Advanced Students

Tell students that it is often a good idea to make a xerox copy of a form when only one copy has been provided. The student can use the xerox as a "working copy" and fill in the blanks with necessary information for practice before writing in ink on the original form.

Advanced Students

Ask each student to obtain a real form from a library, police station, catalog house, business, or other source. Ask students to read and fill out the form, and to note on a separate piece of paper any interesting or unusual requirements.

Optional Practice

Have students work in groups to design forms for imaginative purposes, such as an application for becoming an astronaut, an application for President of the United States, or an order for extravagant items like chocolate Scrabble sets and mink-lined bedroom slippers. You may want to bring in an unusual catalog, such as the Neiman-Marcus Christmas catalog, to use as a source.

Bring in a variety of real forms for students to fill in. Discuss the purpose of each, the information that is requested, and any unfamiliar terminology.

B. Below is a sample order form from a catalog house. Examine it carefully. Then tell whether each of the following statements is true or false.

1. Information may be printed or cursive.   False
2. Charge cards are not acceptable for payment. False
3. Sporting goods should be listed on the same form as other items being purchased. False
4. Items may be returned within two weeks after purchase.   False
5. The narrow column after the catalog number should not be completed by the customer. True

InstaBuy Warehouse
TO PURCHASE MERCHANDISE FROM SHOWROOM OR CATALOG, COMPLETE THIS FORM AND PRESENT IT TO THE INFORMATION DESK.   PLEASE PRINT

1679115

FOR PROMPT SERVICE ON SPECIALTY ITEMS
JEWELRY • PHOTOGRAPHIC • SPORTING GOODS
PLACE YOUR ORDER ON A SEPARATE ORDER BLANK AND PRESENT IT TO THE CASHIER IN THAT DEPARTMENT.

NAME

ADDRESS

CITY   STATE   ZIP

PHONE   ORDER TO BE PAID FOR BY: ☐ CHECK ☐ BANKCARD ☐ CASH

COMPLETE CATALOG NUMBER FROM CATALOG OR SAMPLE TAGS	WHSE USE ONLY	QTY.	ITEM DESCRIPTION SPECIFY COLOR, SIZE, ETC.	YOUR COST EACH
1 2 0 5 L E (example)		1	ATTACHÉ CASE 5 INCH BLACK	9 77

ALL RETURNS MUST BE ACCOMPANIED BY SALES RECEIPT AND IN THEIR ORIGINAL CARTON AND PACKING. (NO RETURNS AFTER 10 DAYS)

Part 6

Objective

To use skills to find a part-time job

Presenting the Lesson

1. Read and discuss **Making an Activities Schedule** and **Assessing Your Skills**, pages 349–350. Stress the importance of not taking on a job if it would interfere with more important obligations at school or at home.

Part 6   Using Your Skills To Find a Part-Time Job

Roughly nine million teenagers, approximately half of America's teenage population, work in part-time jobs. Teenagers work for many reasons: to help with family expenses, to earn money for college, or simply to gain job experience that will be useful in later life. If you decide to look for a part-time job yourself, there are some particular guidelines that you can follow to make your job search successful.

Making an Activities Schedule

School is your full-time job, and nothing should interfere with it. Before beginning a job hunt, ask yourself, "Can I work part-time and also fulfill my school, family, and other obligations?" If the answer is yes, design an **activities schedule** by recording your daily activities, hour by hour, for one week. Examine this weekly activities schedule and determine how many hours you can realistically devote to a part-time job. Discuss this schedule with a parent or with your guidance counselor.

Activities Schedule	Mon.	Tues.	Wed.	Thurs.	Fri.	Sat.	Sun.
3:00 – 4:00	Speech team		Speech team			Mowed lawn	
4:00 – 5:00						Revised English paper	Youth group meeting
5:00 – 6:00	←		Band practice		→		
6:00 – 7:00	←		Dinner		→		
7:00 – 8:00	Homework	Wrote English paper	←	Homework	→	Movie	
8:00 – 9:00							
9:00 – 10:00							
10:00 –							

Note: Federal and state laws protect teens from overwork and dangerous working conditions. Under Federal law, if you are fourteen or fifteen years old, you may work a maximum of three hours on a school day and up to eighteen hours per week. (Hours are extended during the summer.) State laws vary and supersede Federal laws. Check with your guidance counselor about your state's child labor laws.

Assessing Your Skills

Take a good look at yourself, at the things you like to do and do well. Do you enjoy helping people? repairing bikes or small appliances? training pets? working outside? Interests often translate into job skills. For example, a talent for fixing appliances could lead to a job in a repair shop. Learning to type in school could result in an office job.

Ask students to talk about job experiences they have already had. This might include baby-sitting, taking care of neighbors' plants and pets while they are away, working in a family business, or mowing lawns. Ask students to relate how they have gotten these jobs, any unforeseen difficulties they had in carrying out responsibilities, how much they were paid, and other aspects that might be helpful or interesting to classmates.

2. Allow students time in class to write down a list of their interests and skills. Then have them write down several possible jobs that would be related to these personal strengths.

3. Assign Exercise A on page 350. Have students complete Exercise B in class and take some time to discuss their experiences.

4. Read and discuss **Contacting Employers**, **Job Application Forms**, **Interviewing for a Job**, and **Obtaining Other Job-Related Forms**, pages 351–355. Have students discuss in class experiences they have had interviewing for jobs. You may wish to share your experience, too. Remind students that it is important to find out from a prospective employer exactly what duties and hours are connected with the job. Tell them not to accept employment until there is a clear understanding about what the job entails, and what the employer expects from them in terms of time commitment.

5. Refer students back to Part 5 for more information on filling out forms. Stress the importance of completing a job application neatly and carefully.

6. Many teens tend to look for jobs or attend interviews wearing jeans or other casual clothing. They may also speak to the employer in either an informal or monosyllabic style. Point out to your students that the employer is often looking for someone who can interact well with the public as well as with other employees. Therefore the image they present in an interview may determine whether or not they get a job.

7. Assign Exercises A and B on page 356. Review with students the proper style and form for business letters and the correct form for addressing envelopes.

Individualizing the Lesson

Less-Advanced Students

Sometimes these students have a low level of confidence that would interfere with their presenting themselves well to an employer. Discuss the importance of identifying and concentrating on personal strengths, not weakness. Point out that everyone is good at something whether it's working with people, caring for animals, or organizing materials. Stress that a positive mental attitude is important at all times, not only in job-seeking.

Advanced Students

Have students research the qualifications for a career in which they are interested. As part of their research, they may wish to interview a person who works in that field. Then have them list part-time jobs they could hold now that would enable them to learn more about their chosen career and obtain valuable on-the-job experience.

The following chart will give you some idea of the opportunities that exist for part-time employment:

Common Occupations Among Teenagers	
Self-Employment	**Employment by Others**
washing and waxing cars	newspaper route
pet sitting	clerical jobs (typist, filer, receptionist)
child care	
delivery	shoeshine stand
answering service	cashier
housework/cleaning garages or basements	retail sales (grocery stores, departments stores, etc.)
handicrafts	sales clerk
repairs	food service (waiter/waitress/cook/dishwasher)
mowing lawns/gardening	
farm work	

Exercises Preparing To Look for a Job

A. Make up an activities schedule that includes all of your commitments for a week. From this schedule, determine how many days and hours you could realistically devote to a part-time job.

B. Choose at least five words from the following list that describe activities you have done. Then, add details telling what you have done, when, and where.

> EXAMPLE: *Organized* a baseball team in my neighborhood during the summer of 1983.

performed	repaired	assisted	won
operated	cared for	participated in	scheduled
handcrafted	taught/trained	organized	served
supervised	prepared	sold	designed
typed	wrote	earned	built

Contacting Employers

How do you actually find a job? If you are going to be self-employed, speak to friends and neighbors whom you think might be interested in your services. Make up flyers and distribute them in your neighborhood. Post notices in supermarkets. You might even consider placing an ad in your local paper.

If you are looking for outside employment, the procedure becomes more complex. First, ask your school guidance counselor if he or she knows of job openings. Then, check the want ads section of your local newspaper for part-time positions. Job ads are usually carefully written to indicate requirements for the job. Look for jobs that match your skills, age, and experience.

You may also want to contact businesses in your area that hire teens. Avoid dropping in unannounced. Call, or write a letter, requesting a job application and an interview. When you call a prospective employer, give your name and ask if the business has any openings. Be sure to identify the type of job you are looking for, and briefly state the qualifications you have. Speak clearly and politely and obtain the information quickly. Keep in mind that you may be disrupting a busy work day for the person on the other end of the line.

Remember the following points when speaking with a prospective employer:

Speaking to Prospective Employers

1. Be polite. Use *please* and *thank you*.
2. Learn the employer's last name and use it along with *Mr.*, *Ms.*, or *Mrs.* Write down the employer's name for future reference.
3. Briefly provide all information requested.
4. Briefly present your qualifications, skills, and experience.
5. Write down any essential information that you learn during the call, such as the employer's address or the time that he or she wants you to come for an interview.

Optional Practice

1. Let the students practice for job interviews by role-playing in class. Stress the importance of introductions and conclusions to the interview as well as speaking clearly and responding to questions with confidence. The teacher should play the role of the prospective employer. Try to take on a variety of personality types to prepare students for the possibility of being interviewed by someone who is friendly and supportive, someone who is hurried and indifferent, or someone who is distrustful and unpleasant. Be sure that students ask about the terms of employement (duties, hours, salary) before the interview is ended.

2. Bring a telephone into class and have students enact phone inquiries for part-time jobs they have found listed in the classified section of the newspapers.

Extending the Lesson

1. Have students mail the letters they wrote for Exercise A on page 356. Responses may be organized into a class career file.

2. Invite a personnel manager to class to discuss interview techniques.

3. Divide the class into groups of four to six students. Give each group a major career division and have them research job opportunities within their division. Possible divisions are Communications, Science, Education, and Entertainment. Groups can also design information brochures on the careers, or design bulletin board displays.

Job Application Forms

The next step in getting a job is obtaining and completing application forms. You may obtain application forms either by asking prospective employers to send them to you or by asking permission to drop by the place of business to pick one up.

Remember that the job application form is the first sample of your work that an employer sees. A neat, accurate, legible application will greatly increase your chances of being hired.

Read over the entire job application before filling in any spaces. This will tell you what kind of information must be provided and in what order.

Most application forms require the following information:

Job Application Forms	
Personal Data	name, address, phone, date of birth, social security number
Schools Attended	names, cities and states, dates of attendance, subjects studied, activities
Employment History	names, places, supervisors, dates, job titles, duties
Skills and Achievements	job-related skills, honors or awards, volunteer positions (Examples: *type 60 wpm, speak Spanish fluently, science lab assistant*)
References	names, titles, addresses, relationship to you

It is a good idea to prepare a list of such information that you can carry with you for easy reference.

Complete the application neatly and legibly, using a typewriter or a pen. Follow all of the guidelines given in Part 5 for completing forms.

Interviewing for a Job

The interview is the final and most crucial step in getting a job. Employers will ask about your skills and background to get a complete picture of you as a prospective employee. In an interview, employers usually observe and consider the following:

What an Employer Looks for in an Interview	
Appearance	neatness, cleanliness, posture, good grooming
Courtesy	tact, politeness, maturity of manner, friendliness
Communication Skills	listening skills, ability to answer questions, articulation of words, correct grammar, vocal quality
Job Qualifications	experience, abilities, skills, enthusiasm, eagerness to learn
Availability	other commitments, such as hours at school or special activities

A polite handshake and "Hello, my name is _____ " will begin the interview on a positive note. Listen carefully and answer all questions completely. Speak in a more formal manner than you might use in more casual conversation. Sloppy language might indicate to the employer that you would not present a good image to his or her customers.

As you answer questions, be honest about your skills and availability. Ask the interviewer about the duties you will be expected to perform. Do not accept a job you will be unable to do well.

When the interview is ended, thank the interviewer.

OPENING: Hello, Ms. White. I'm glad to meet you.

CLOSING: Thank you, Ms. White, for your time. I hope to hear from you soon.

Obtaining Other Job-Related Forms

Once you have accepted a job, there are several forms that you will have to present to your employer. The following forms are commonly required:

Work Permits. Most states require that teens obtain work permits and present these to their employers before beginning to work. To obtain an application for a permit, see your employer or your school guidance counselor. To apply for the permit, you will need a birth certificate and, in some states, a physician's statement of health.

A Sample Work Permit

	STATE OF ILLINOIS	BILLIE ANN PILLING
	DEPARTMENT OF LABOR	SUPERINTENDENT
STATE OF_____	DIVISION OF LABOR STANDARDS	DUPLICATE—FOR DEPT. OF LABOR
COUNTY OF_____	910 SO. MICHIGAN AVE., CHICAGO, ILLINOIS 60605 Certificate of Age for Minors 16 yrs. of Age and Over	CERTIFICATE NO._____
CITY OF_____	(ACCEPTED AS PROOF OF AGE UNDER THE U.S. FAIR LABOR STANDARDS ACT OF 1938)	DATE OF ISSUE_____

ISSUED FOR_____ 2. _____ 3. AGE_____
(NAME OF MINOR) (SEX) (YEARS) (MONTHS)

4. THIS IS TO CERTIFY THAT THE FOLLOWING EVIDENCE OF AGE OR A TRANSCRIPT THEREOF HAS BEEN FILED IN THIS OFFICE FOR THE ABOVE-NAMED MINOR. CHECK EVIDENCE ACCEPTED.

5. DATE OF BIRTH_____
   MONTH   DAY   YEAR

6. PLACE OF BIRTH _____
   TOWN

   COUNTY   STATE

7. PARENT OR GUARDIAN_____
   NAME   ADDRESS

8. THE ABOVE-NAMED MINOR IS TO BE EMPLOYED BY:
   FIRM'S NAME
   FIRM'S ADDRESS

   INDUSTRY   OCCUPATION

EVIDENCE OF AGE:
1. BIRTH CERTIFICATE OR TRANSCRIPT THEREOF_____
2. OTHER DOCUMENTARY EVIDENCE, SUCH AS:
   BAPTISMAL CERTIFICATE_____
   PASSPORT_____
   BIBLE RECORD_____
   INSURANCE POLICY_____
   OTHER (SPECIFY)_____
3. PHYSICIAN'S CERTIFICATE OF AGE ACCOMPANIED BY SCHOOL RECORD OF AGE, AND PARENT'S AFFIDAVIT OF AGE _____

9. SIGNATURE OF MINOR _____
10. ADDRESS OF MINOR _____
11. _____ 12. _____ 13. _____
    SIGNATURE OF ISSUING OFFICER   TITLE   NAME OF SCHOOL

NOTE: IN CASE OF A MINOR UNDER 18 YEARS OF AGE THIS CERTIFICATE IS TO BE RETURNED BY THE EMPLOYER TO THE ISSUING OFFICER UPON THE TERMINATION OF THE MINOR'S EMPLOYMENT. (SEE OTHER SIDE).

W-4 Forms. These are used for tax purposes. Obtain one of these from your employer after accepting a position.

Health Permits. For certain jobs, especially jobs in food service, you must have a permit certifying your state of health. If your employer does not have the appropriate application form, he or she will be able to tell you where to obtain one.

Social Security Cards. Workers in jobs covered by social security (about 90 percent of the U.S. work force) must have a social security card. You apply for a card by filling out an application form. These forms are available at any social security office.

A Sample Social Security Application Form

DEPARTMENT OF HEALTH AND HUMAN SERVICES
SOCIAL SECURITY ADMINISTRATION

Form Approved
OMB No. 0960-0066

FORM SS-5 – APPLICATION FOR A
SOCIAL SECURITY NUMBER CARD
(Original, Replacement or Correction)

MICROFILM REF. NO. (SSA USE ONLY)

Unless the requested information is provided, we may not be able to issue a Social Security Number (20 CFR 422.103(b).)

INSTRUCTIONS TO APPLICANT ▶ Before completing this form, please read the instructions on the opposite page. You can type or print, using pen with dark blue or black ink. Do not use pencil.

NAA	NAME TO BE SHOWN ON CARD	First / Middle / Last	
1 NAB	FULL NAME AT BIRTH (IF OTHER THAN ABOVE)	First / Middle / Last	
ONA	OTHER NAME(S) USED		
2 STT	MAILING ADDRESS	(Street Apt. No., P.O. Box, Rural Route No.)	
CTY STE ZIP	CITY	STATE	ZIP CODE

3 CSP CITIZENSHIP (Check one only)
☐ a. U.S. citizen   ☐ c. Legal alien not allowed to work
☐ b. Legal alien allowed to work   ☐ d. Other (See instructions on Page 2)

4 SEX   SEX   ☐ Male   ☐ Female

5 DOS DATE OF BIRTH ▶	MONTH DAY YEAR	**6** AGE PRESENT AGE **7** PLB PLACE OF BIRTH ▶ CITY STATE OR FOREIGN COUNTRY
8 MNA	MOTHER'S NAME AT HER BIRTH	First / Middle / Last (her maiden name)
FNA	FATHER'S NAME	First / Middle / Last

9 PNO a. Have you or someone on your behalf applied for a social security number before?
☐ No   ☐ Don't Know   ☐ Yes
If you checked "Yes", complete items "b" through "e" below; otherwise go to item 11.

SSN PNS PNY b. Enter social security number
c. In what State did you apply?   What year?

NLC d. Enter the name shown on your most recent social security card
e. If the birth date you used was different from the date shown in item 5, enter it here.   MONTH DAY YEAR

10 DON TODAY'S DATE ▶ MONTH DAY YEAR
11 Telephone number where we can reach you during the day ▶ HOME OTHER

ASD **WARNING: Deliberately providing false information on this application is punishable by a fine of $1,000 or one year in jail, or both.**

12 YOUR SIGNATURE

13 YOUR RELATIONSHIP TO PERSON IN ITEM 1
☐ Self   ☐ Other _____ (Specify)

WITNESS (Needed only if signed by mark "X")   WITNESS (Needed only if signed by mark "X")

DO NOT WRITE BELOW THIS LINE (FOR SSA USE ONLY)   DTC SSA RECEIPT DATE _____

☐ SUPPORTING DOCUMENT-
☐ EXPEDITE CASE
DUP ISSUED SSN ASSIGNED OR VERIFIED
SSN
NPN
BIC SIGNATURE AND TITLE OF EMPLOYEE(S) REVIEWING EVIDENCE AND/OR CONDUCTING INTERVIEW.
DOC NTC CAN
TYPE(S) OF EVIDENCE SUBMITTED
☐ MANDATORY IN PERSON INTERVIEW CONDUCTED DATE
DATE
IDN ITV DCL

Form **SS-5** (2-81)

Exercises Finding a Part-Time Job

A. Select a business in your area that employs teens. Write a letter to the owner or manager expressing interest in employment opportunities and requesting a job application. Remember to give some background about yourself and your skills.

B. Look at the social security form on page 355. Write out the information you would provide for sections 1, 2, 8, and 9. What would you write in the box at the bottom of the form labeled "Types of Evidence Submitted"?

Be sure to read the application carefully.

SUMMARY AND APPLICATIONS

1. Proper form in writing is important to all forms of written communication. Your letters can make as strong an impression as your style of dress or manner of speaking.

2. The form of any letter includes the date, salutation, body, closing, and signature. Formal letters also include a heading and an inside address.

3. Business letters should be brief and specific. Types of business letters include letters of order, letters of complaint, letters of application, and requests for information.

4. When completing forms and applications, read all directions before beginning. Fill out the form carefully.

5. To find a job, begin by evaluating your time commitments and assessing your skills.

6. Possible employers should first be contacted by phone or letter.

7. Remember that the way you complete an application form and the way you present yourself during an interview may determine whether or not you are hired.

Applications in Other Subject Areas

Current Events. Write a letter to your state representative. Express your opinions on some important current issues. Remember to keep the tone of the letter polite.

All Subjects. Choose your favorite from among the following subject areas. Do some research to find out what careers are open to people who are interested in this area. Your guidance counselor may be able to provide you with sources of information or addresses to which you can write.

History	Mathematics	Home Economics
English	Fine Arts	Industrial Arts
Science	Physical Education	

Summary and Applications

Discuss this summary with the class. Brainstorm for situations in which the skills they have learned about would be useful.

Encourage students to use this summary for review, or as part of the SQ3R method of study (see Chapter 15). Remind them, though, that more specific points can only be reviewed by skimming the chapter itself.

Applications in Other Subject Areas

1. Read the **Current Events** activity on page 357. Remind students that they listed the names and addresses of their state representatives in **Extending the Lesson**, Part 1.

Discuss current issues which could be possible subjects. Then have students use stationery or plain white paper to compose their letters. Explain that in addition to politeness, neatness and legibility are important if they want their letters to be taken seriously.

2. Read and discuss the **All Subjects** activity on page 357. Have the students suggest possible careers available in each field. Tell the students to compose a letter to someone in the field they choose, requesting further information or job descriptions.

Chapter Objectives

1. To prepare informal talks
2. To prepare formal speeches
3. To learn how to deliver informal and formal speeches effectively
4. To listen to and evaluate informal and formal speeches accurately and fairly

Preparing the Students

Ask for a student volunteer to explain to the class how to do the proper heading for an English paper. The student may also demonstrate on the chalkboard. Then, ask another volunteer to inform the class about an upcoming school or community event. Finally, have a third volunteer tell the class why they should study hard in high school.

Tell the class that they have just heard brief versions of three different kinds of informal talks. Ask the students to determine the purpose of each one.

Have the students tell about their own speaking experiences. Ask them to discuss the positive and negative aspects of those situation.

Read the introduction to Chapter 17 on page 358, and explain that this chapter will help the students learn to prepare and deliver effective informal and formal speeches.

Additional Resources

Skills Practice Book — page 87–88.

Duplicating Masters — page 88.

Special Populations — See special section at the front of this Teacher's Edition.

Chapter 17

Giving a Talk

There is one assignment that strikes fear into the hearts of most students, turning the biggest and bravest into a mass of quivering bones and quavering voices. That assignment is, "Next week you will present an oral report to the class." Fear of speaking before groups can be overwhelming, but it can also be overcome. By acquiring the skills needed to deliver an effective speech, you can learn to speak knowledgeably and confidently to any group. You may still shake inside, but, with a little practice, no one else will even notice.

Part 1 Informal Talks

Often during your school years, you will be required to make some sort of informal oral presentation. You might be asked to introduce the speaker at an all-school assembly, to make an announcement for your club, or to issue directions at an athletic event. Your informal presentations might also include demonstrations. This part of the chapter will prepare you for giving such informal speeches.

Preparing an Informal Talk

While the amount of preparation involved in an informal talk is not great, you must do some background work. Know what you are going to say, and be sure your information is accurate and complete.

In most instances, you will not be speaking for more than a minute or two, so it is easy to write out the talk. For brief announcements, you will find that notes are adequate, but make sure that you practice reading aloud from the notes. Practicing aloud helps you to realize that what looks good on paper is sometimes difficult to read aloud.

Types of Informal Talks

Making Introductions

The chances are good that at some time you will be asked to introduce someone to a class, a club, an organization, or other group with which you are involved. Such an introduction will require more than, "This is Anita Rivera, president of the ninth grade." First, you must get some background information on the person to give to the audience. Who is she? What has she done? Why is she here? If possible, try to find some interesting or amusing anecdote to lighten your introduction. Be careful, though. While everyone should be amused, no one must ever be embarrassed.

Objective

To prepare informal talks for the following purposes:

a. making introductions
b. making announcements
c. giving directions
d. presenting a demonstration
e. persuading an audience

Presenting the Lesson

1. Read and discuss **Informal Talks** and **Preparing an Informal Talk** on page 359. List on the board the five kinds of informal talks students will be working on in this Part: introductions, announcements, directions, demonstrations, and persuasive talks.

2. Read **Making Introductions**, under **Types of Informal Talks**, page 359. Have the students tell about introductions they have made or heard. You might tell about your own experiences with this type of speech, as well.

3. Have the students name talk show hosts with whom they are familiar. Discuss each host's style, mannerisms, and any noticeable characteristics of their introductions. Then assign Exercises A and B on page 360.

4. Assign and discuss Exercise C on page 360. Have the students work in pairs. You may wish to assign Exercise D as an alternative to Exercise B.

5. Read and discuss **Making Announcements** on page 360. Point out the speaker's responsibility to include all important information and the audience's responsibility to listen carefully.

359

6. Assign Exercises A and B on page 361.

7. Read and discuss **Giving Directions** on page 361. Stress the importance of clear, complete details. (You may wish to refer students to pages 172–173 under Explanatory Paragraphs.) Complete Exercises A and B on page 362 in class.

8. Read and discuss **Giving a Demonstration Talk** on page 362. Discuss the importance of props and visual aids. Then assign the Exercise on page 363. Explain to the students that the presenter of a demonstration talk should

a. choose a subject he or she knows well
b. organize the information in logical step-by-step order
c. gather all necessary props and make sure the equipment works properly
d. compose an effective opening statement.

The students might make check sheets for themselves listing the four steps.

9. Read and discuss the first paragraph of **Persuading an Audience** on page 363. Have the students describe situations from their own experience that involved persuasive speaking.

Read aloud the second paragraph, emphasizing careful preparation and effective organization of material. You might also refer students to the composition sections on persuasive writing on pages 233–234.

10. Assign exercises A and B on page 364. For Exercise C have the students suggest ideas for this talk and identify an audience for each idea.

Exercises Making Introductions

A. You are the host of a nationally syndicated talk show and will be introducing a well known author, actor, or public figure. Write an introduction that could have been used at some time in his or her life, or one that could be used today.

B. Choose a character from a book, movie, or television series and introduce him or her to the class.

C. Introduce one of your classmates. You will need to find out some information beforehand. Interview him or her, asking about hobbies, favorite subjects, jobs, favorite reading material, taste in music, and what he or she does after school.

D. Choose a famous historical figure, perhaps someone you have studied this year. Introduce this person to your class. You decide on the occasion and the circumstances for the introduction. Be sure to include any important historical facts.

Making Announcements

"Today is October 16, and here are today's announcements." You may listen to words just like these every day over your school's public address system. This is the simplest kind of informal talk, but even when delivering a speech as short and simple as a daily announcement, you must remember to include answers to the following questions:

What is happening?
Where is it happening?
When is it happening?
Why should the listeners be interested?

Always repeat *where* and *when*. Your audience may have a short attention span or may not even realize that they are interested in the announcement until you are about halfway through. They will need to hear *where* and *when* repeated at the conclusion of the speech. Speak distinctly and clearly. Do not rush. Emphasize the important information. Above all, keep the announcement short and simple.

Exercises Making Announcements

A. Pretend that you are organizing a new club, one that your school does not have. Name your club and make an announcement to the class that (1) tells the name and functions of the club, (2) tells where and when the first meeting will take place, and (3) will attract members.

B. Make an announcement to the class regarding one of the events below, or announce something else that is going on at your school or in your community. After three or four announcements have been given, see how many *what's*, *where's*, *when's*, and *why's* the class can remember.

an athletic event	an awards assembly
school elections	tryouts for cheerleaders
a field trip	college representative visits

Giving Directions

Have you ever stopped someone on the first day of school to ask the location of a classroom? If so, you know how few people can really help. The reply is usually similar to the one below.

> Just go down this hall and then turn by the water fountain (there are three) and then keep going past the typing room (you have no idea where the typing room is) and then turn at the next corner (which way?) and you'll find it.

Think your directions through before presenting them. Use accurate details, give the directions step by step, and be as clear as possible. Never back up to correct yourself. Instead, start over again, and be sure that your listener understands.

> Go down this hall towards the front of the building. Turn right at the second water fountain. At the next corner turn left, and the room will be the third one on your left.

This is still complicated for a new student, but at least the directions are accurate. Of course, if you ask for directions, you have to be a good listener.

Individualizing the Lesson

Less-Advanced Students

1. For Exercise A in **Making Introductions**, present your own sample introduction to the class. you might "introduce" an author the students are currently reading. If your students are uncertain of what to say, you might have them do Exercise C first and then A and B.

2. For Exercise B have the students select a character and, as a group, compose a sample introduction. You may wish to allow the introductions to be humorous in order to lessen the anxiety that students associate with public speaking.

3. For Exercise C, duplicate an interview form for the students. List the important categories of information and leave space for the students to take notes.

Ask for two student volunteers to demonstrate the interview in front of the class. Transfer the interviewer's notes to the chalkboard, and have the class compose a sample introduction. Students should then work in pairs to do the Exercise.

4. You may wish to modify Exercise A in **Giving Directions** by having each student make a list of directions for a partner to use in locating a certain place or object in the classroom. The directions should begin at the door of the classroom.

5. For the Exercise in **Giving a Demonstration**, the students may need help with organizing the information and the props for their talks. Some demonstrations cannot be done in the classroom ("build a campfire" "groom a pet"); however, students can use "dummy" props as if they were the real thing.

6. Discuss Exercise A in **Persuading an Audience** with the class. Then have students model their own commercial for Exercise B on one of their ads from Exercise A.

7. Exercise C may be difficult for these students to do effectively. Give them a check sheet that will structure their planning. Include the following:

a. What change are you recommending?
b. Who is your audience?
c. What are three good reasons for the proposed change?
d. How can you best organize the reasons?

Advanced Students

1. For Exercise A in **Making Introductions**, have the speakers not name their subjects. Challenge the speakers to present such clear, important, and interesting information that the rest of the class can guess who is being introduced and supply the name.

2. For Exercise C, give the students time limits for their interviews (5–10 minutes), do the interview in class, and begin making the introductions during the same class period.

3. If possible, for **Giving Directions**, have the students work in teams to set up treasure hunts within the school. The "treasures" to be found might be such items as a painting in the hallway, an art object in a display case, a trophy or plaque. Each team should list five treasures and write directions for finding them. They should not name the object directly.

4. After the students have completed Exercises A and B in **Persuading an Audience**, have them do

Exercises Giving Directions

A. Choose a specific place with which your classmates are familiar. It can be in the school building or in your community. Without identifying the place, give specific directions for getting there from your classroom. Then see who can identify the exact place.

B. Give your classmates directions on how to draw some object. You may not name the actual subject of the drawing. You may only use words for geometrical shapes such as *line, circle, square,* or *triangle;* words for drawing utensils such as *pen, paper,* or *pencil;* words for relationships such as *inside, below, next to,* or *between;* and commands such as *Place, Move, Draw,* or *Sketch.*

The other students cannot ask questions as they try to follow the directions you are giving. You will know if they understand by the expressions on their faces. When you have finished, see how many students actually drew the figure. Was the problem in the directions? Was it that those who did not draw the correct figure were not listening closely? Try to analyze the problem.

Giving a Demonstration Talk

Have you ever tried to teach a child how to catch a ball without demonstrating the procedure with your hands? It seems impossible to do. Try sitting on your hands and telling a friend how to make a paper airplane or how to do a simple physical exercise. Doing one of these things makes one realize that there are some instances when it is absolutely necessary to demonstrate what you mean. In a demonstration talk, you tell how something is done while demonstrating the action at the same time.

A demonstration talk must be extremely well organized. Begin by gathering all the materials that you will need for your demonstration. Then, write your speech, making sure that you cover every part of the procedure, explaining each step precisely and thoroughly. Carefully coordinate the physical aspects of the demonstration with your speech and practice using your props. When you deliver the speech, stop occasionally to see if your listeners have understood you up to that point. Remember, what seems easy to you can be sheer frustration to someone else.

Exercise Giving a Demonstration Talk

Give a demonstration talk to the class. Remember to come prepared with all necessary props. You might show how to do one of the following:

swing a golf club	bake a cake or pie
repot a plant	groom a dog
work with macrame	change a bicycle tire
plant a terrarium	build a bird house
hook a rug	handle a rod and reel
make a candle	arrange flowers
make a collage	throw a Frisbee
catch a football	prepare a special salad
strum a guitar	build a campfire

Persuading an Audience

Does a future as a salesperson appeal to you? Whether you know it or not, you are a salesperson and will be one for the rest of your life. You may not have any experience selling products to the public, but you probably have a great deal of experience "selling" your ideas to teachers, friends, and employers. Many occasions arise for this kind of persuasive speaking. You might want to persuade your parents to take a particular family vacation, or convince the school administration to allow a particular field trip for your club or organization. Whatever the occasion for persuasion may be, to win your point you must be well prepared, sincere, and, above all, enthusiastic.

Organize a persuasive talk much as you would any piece of persuasive writing. First, be sure you understand your purpose. Know exactly what it is you want to accomplish. Next, consider the audience to whom you will be speaking and select several good reasons or arguments that you think will persuade them to accept your ideas. Finally, organize those reasons so that you build up to your strongest point. Present your reasons to your audience using a sincere, pleasant tone and reasonable language. Remember, a positive attitude and a genuine interest in your subject may be your strongest assets.

in-depth analyses of at least three television commercials. They should consider the actual words used, the organization of the information, and the hidden appeals intended to persuade.

5. For Exercise C the students should select real issues on which they have strong feelings. If possible, arrange for the students to present their talks to the intended audience.

Optional Practice

1. If possible, arrange for the students to read your school's daily announcements, in home rooms or over the public address system.

2. Have the students work in groups of five to put together a newscast or talk show that includes all five kinds of informal talks covered in Part 1.

Extending the Lesson

1. Record several radio and television editorials. Identify the issue in each and analyze the organization of material. Bring in some newspaper editorials for comparison with the spoken ones. Discuss the advantages and disadvantages of presenting a persuasive message orally, rather than in print.

2. Show a videotape of a television demonstration show (cooking, sports, home renovation, for example). Have the students list the steps in the process being demonstrated. Then, discuss the effectiveness of the speaker's organization and use of equipment.

3. Ask each student to choose a person, real or fictional, living or dead, who has said or done something with which the student disagrees. Then have the students prepare short talks designed to persuade the class that the person was wrong. Remind them to explain the circumstances of their person's beliefs or actions before presenting the persuasive talk.

Exercises Persuading an Audience

A. Find a commercial on TV that appeals to you and list at least three things that made you like it. Do the same for a commercial that did not appeal to you, listing three things that made you dislike it. Do you think everyone would respond to these commercials as you did?

B. Ads use hidden appeals to persuade consumers, such as humor or the association of products with patriotic feelings, happy families, or famous people. Using one of these appeals, sell a fictitious or real product to your class in a one-minute commercial. Time yourself to keep your remarks brief and to-the-point.

C. Prepare a persuasive talk in which you try to convince your audience to make some sort of change. The audience may be your classmates, a school board, or your parents.

Part 2

Objective

To prepare formal speeches

Presenting the Lesson

1. Read the introduction to Part 2 on pages 364–365. Have the students discuss their own experiences with formal speaking. Ask them what was most difficult and most enjoyable about delivering a formal speech.

2. Read aloud **Formal Speeches: Pre-Writing** on page 365. Emphasize that students should follow the same steps as in writing a composition or report, beginning by first choosing the topic and identifying the main idea. Throughout this Part, stress the parallels with the Process of Writing and refer students to Chapter 7.

Part 2 Formal Speeches

You don't have to be the President of the United States addressing the nation or an athlete accepting a place in the hall of fame to need to know how to speak formally in front of a group. As a student, you may find yourself giving a formal talk or report in biology class, presenting a project to a committee, or making a speech at an assembly.

A formal speech is one delivered on a specific topic to a specific audience, for a specific purpose. It is lengthier than an informal talk and requires more thought, time, and preparation. Formal talks should be organized completely on paper, in a manner similar to that used to organize a composition. However, unlike compositions, speeches must be rehearsed out loud after they are written. Effective speakers do not just "read" their notes or papers. They also add expression and gestures and use good eye contact. To do this, however, they must be thoroughly familiar with their material. Practice will provide you with this familiarity. It will also help you to spot sections of your speech that seem fine on paper but become dry or dull when read aloud.

The steps required before the actual writing of a formal speech are identical to the pre-writing stage of the process of writing.

Formal Speeches: Pre-Writing

DEVELOPING YOUR TOPIC AND MAIN IDEA

1. Select and narrow your topic.
2. Define your purpose.
3. Identify your audience.
4. Develop a statement of your main idea.

RESEARCHING YOUR TOPIC

1. Gather information.
   a. from personal experience
   b. from other people (interviews)
   c. from reference materials
2. Take notes.

ORGANIZING YOUR MATERIAL

1. Group similar ideas.
2. Arrange ideas in a logical order.

Selecting a Topic

Choose a topic that will interest both you and your audience. Be aware of the following:

Unusual subjects appeal to everyone.

The familiar topic has value, but be sure to provide a fresh angle or new point of view or your speech will be dull.

Remember one thing: if you are really interested in the topic, your interest will be contagious.

As you choose your topic, remember that most speeches have time limitations. Narrow the scope of your subject to fit whatever time has been allotted, but be careful not to limit your topic too much. There is nothing worse than running out of material.

3. Read and discuss **Selecting a Topic** on page 365. Assign the Exercise on page 366. Discuss the students' responses in terms of appropriateness, interest, and probable length of time.

4. Read and discuss **Defining Your Purpose** on pages 366–367. Ask students to give examples of speeches they have heard that fit each of the three categories. Complete Exercise A on page 367 orally.

5. Assign and discuss Exercise B on page 367. Remind students that formal talks might include campaign speeches, sermons, lectures, committee reports, or assembly speakers.

6. Read and discuss **Identifying Your Audience** and **Determining Your Main Idea** on page 368. Tell students that the main idea of a speech or essay is sometimes called a "thesis." Complete Exercise A, page 369 with the class.

7. Assign and discuss Exercise B, page 369. Help students select and narrow topics that are interesting and appropriate. Tell them this assignment will extend into several more steps and should therefore center on a subject that is of genuine interest.

8. Read and discuss **Researching Your Topic**, pages 369–370. Refer students to Parts 3, 4, and 5 of Chapter 12 for detailed information on note-taking and organization.

9. Assign the Exercise on page 371, allowing students time to do research and assisting them in finding source materials. Tell students to bring their completed note cards to class for evaluation.

10. Read and discuss **Organizing Note Cards**, page 371, and **The Intro-**

duction, **The Body**, and **The Conclusion**, pages 371–373. Tell students it is often wise to write the body of the speech before deciding on the right anecdote, statistic, quotation, etc., for the introduction. Also mention reference sources (See Chapter 12) that might provide the type of attention-getting device they need.

11. Assign the Exercise on page 373. When students have completed their preliminary outlines, have them read the outlines to a small group for helpful ideas and suggestions.

12. Read and discuss **Writing Your Speech**, page 374, and assign the Exercise on page 374. Tell students that they will have an opportunity to present their speeches in later sections of this chapter.

Individualizing the Lesson

Less-Advanced Students

1. For the Exercise in **Selecting and Narrowing a Topic** on page 366, do all ten items orally.

2. For Exercise B on page 367 have each student focus on just one speech and tell the following: occasion, topic, audience, purpose, most effective aspects, least effective aspects. Have them summarize in one sentence why the speaker did or did not accomplish his or her purpose.

3. For Exercise B on page 369, work with the students individually to make sure each chooses a promising topic for a five-minute speech. Then help the students locate good sources for their material, go over note-taking procedure, and assign the Exercise in **Gathering Your Material** on page 371. Check the students' note cards frequently.

Exercise Selecting and Narrowing a Topic

Choose three of the following occasions and decide on one appropriate topic for each. Assume that your speech is to be between ten and fifteen minutes long. Remember to keep your audience in mind as you select and narrow your topic.

1. You are a class officer and must prepare a talk for the opening assembly.

2. Your teen group (scout troop, 4-H Club, church group) has asked you to deliver a talk at the awards banquet.

3. You have been chosen by your classmates to deliver a talk to a group of senior citizens.

4. You are giving a talk to the school board concerning an issue of importance to the students.

5. You are to give a talk to your social science class about some other part of the United States.

6. You have been asked to talk about a custom associated with some particular holiday.

7. You are the captain of a team and have to give a talk after your final game.

8. You have been asked to talk to a group of eighth graders about high school.

9. You have been asked to give a campaign speech in support of a classmate who is running for student council president.

10. You are an exhibitor at a hobby fair. The fair organizers have asked you to explain your hobby to a group of reporters.

Defining Your Purpose

Almost any speech that you will be asked to give will have one of the following purposes: *to inform, to persuade,* or *to entertain.* You must decide which of these three your speech involves.

The **informative speech** is the type you are most often asked to give. Most class reports are informative. You simply want your audience to understand or to appreciate what you are telling them. Speeches that inform might describe the advantages of belonging to a school club, explain the brake system of a car, or report on a book.

The **persuasive speech** attempts to lead to some change in the listener's point of view, attitude, or course of action. Speeches that appeal for the election of a candidate, encourage support for a school or charitable activity, or argue against an unwise course of action are all examples of persuasion.

In the **entertainment speech** you simply want your audience to enjoy what you say. A speech meant to entertain might be an after-dinner speech or a between-the-acts speech by a master of ceremonies.

Of course, any one of these speeches does not exclude aspects of the others. An informative speech, for example, should also be interesting and entertaining. A persuasive speech should also contain information to support its points.

Exercises Defining Your Purpose

A. Decide whether the purpose of each of the following speeches would be primarily to inform, to persuade, or to entertain. Explain your choice.

1. How to register to vote.
2. The voting age should be raised to age 21.
3. How to get hired for a summer job.
4. Machines are out to get me.
5. The minimum wage should be raised.
6. Cats are people, too!
7. Every household needs a computer.
8. My winter vacation, or how to do absolutely nothing for two glorious weeks.
9. Our town could benefit from a public swimming pool.
10. Magic tricks that everyone can do.
11. How to survive life with an older sister.
12. Students should attend high school all year.

B. How many formal talks have you listened to recently? Write down the occasions, the topics, the audience, and the purposes of the talks. Were they effective? If not, briefly state why you think the speaker failed in his or her purpose. You may limit yourself to five different talks.

4. Before assigning the Exercise on **Organizing Your Material** on page 373, review how to determine main ideas and construct an outline. You may want to use a student volunteer's completed note cards for this demonstration. You may also wish to create a "demonstration set" of notes on pieces of poster board and physically show the grouping and organization process.

5. Allow class time for the students to start the Exercise on **Writing Your Speech** on page 374. Provide assistance as necessary.

Advanced Students

These students should have little difficulty in writing a speech once they realize that the process is no different than that of writing a composition. Therefore, insist that each student choose a challenging topic, a more difficult purpose, and an unfamiliar audience. Also, work with students on developing more sophisticated speeches with interesting introductions (see page 372) and well-researched content.

Optional Practice

1. Have the students select at least two appropriate topics for the following occasions.

  a. You are going to tell a group of foreign students about American traditions.
  b. You are going to speak to a group of fifth graders about safety.

2. Have each student choose one topic that could be the basis for all three kinds of speeches—informative, persuasive, and entertaining—and write appropriate opening statements for each.

1. Invite a person with public speaking experience to talk to the students about planning speeches. Many parents, administrators, and others in the school community have addressed different kinds of audiences. A parent who is a docent at a local museum, for example, may speak to groups of children, adults, and senior citizens. Such a speaker could tell how content and organization of material are adjusted to suit each group.

2. Many libraries subscribe to *Vital Speeches*, a bi-weekly magazine that includes the texts of current important speeches. This resource can provide you with any number of speeches for students to analyze for purpose, content, organization, and style. Libraries also have anthologies of speeches (*Treasury of The World's Greatest Speeches* edited by Houston Peterson, for example.)

Identifying Your Audience

Before you begin to deal with preparation of the actual talk, you must be aware of the audience. Consider your audience's average age, background, economic level, and education. Determine the amount of knowledge or background they have on the material you will be presenting. Be aware of what brings them together to listen to a speech. All of these factors can contribute to the way you develop and present your material.

Remember that your audience must be able to relate to what you are saying on an individual level. You will adjust your tone and level of language to suit the people to whom you are speaking. For example, a talk given to young children would differ considerably from a speech given to the school faculty.

Exercise Identifying Your Audience

What would you title each of the following talks if you were asked to present it to (1) your class, (2) a group of parents, (3) a sixth-grade class, and (4) a club or organization to which you belong?

robotics	a fourth of July celebration
teenage drivers	summer camp
school drop-outs	making compromises

Determining Your Main Idea

Begin the actual preparation of a speech by developing a statement of the main idea that you want to communicate to your audience. This idea can usually be stated in one sentence. It may express an opinion or a general fact about your topic.

Violent crimes are increasing rapidly in our community.
LucasFilms is one of the world's most successful companies.
Unless we act now, the panda will soon perish.

The statement of your main idea is the key to your entire speech. It communicates the point of your speech to your audience, and helps you to keep your ideas unified.

Exercises Determining Your Main Idea

A. Choose three of the following topics and write a sentence that could be used to state the main idea of a speech.

the movie rating system Halloween
year-round school   fantasy games
rumors   computer technology

B. Using your class as an audience, select a topic for a speech that you will prepare and give. Decide on the purpose and state the main idea. Do no more with it at the present time.

Researching Your Topic

In gathering material for a speech, look for ideas, details, illustrations, facts, figures, and quotations related to your topic. Possible sources include personal experience, interviews, and reference materials.

Personal experience can add a great deal of interest to a speech. It is much more fascinating to listen to someone who has actually been on a survival trip than to someone who has merely researched it. You can expand on your personal experience through reading and talking to others, but your speech will bear more weight if you can speak from actual observation and experiences.

Gathering material through interviews involves finding and questioning people who have personal experience or knowledge of your topic. When you go to an interview, be prepared. Have questions written ahead of time. Avoid any questions that can be answered "yes" or "no." Be a good listener. The person you are interviewing should do most of the talking.

When you obtain information from books or other reference materials, you must be careful. Here are some guidelines:

1. Read for specific purposes. Gather only those facts, details, and illustrations that develop your main idea.

2. Read for the main points. Do not get lost in the forest of words. Use the skimming and scanning methods studied in Chapter 15.

3. Evaluate the material. Do not accept ideas just because they are in print. Is the material up-to-date? authoritative? Is a particular piece of information a fact or an opinion? (See Chapter 13 for further discussion of fact and opinion.)

4. Make the material your own. Except for direct quotations, summarize what you want to use. Remember: put all information in your own words. Word-for-word copying is plagiarism, for which you could be penalized.

5. Make use of a variety of reference works. Your library will be an indispensable asset in gathering your material. In addition to encyclopedias and books, remember to refer to the vertical files and the *Readers' Guide to Periodical Literature.*

6. Take notes. Notes are the backbone of any good talk, so take notes on all research that you do, including interviews.

Notes should be taken on 3″ x 5″ cards. Write only one idea per card and write only on one side. In the top left corner of each card, write a one or two word summary of what the card contains. This will be helpful when you organize your notes. In the top right corner, indicate the source of the information and, if appropriate, the page number.

Sample Note Card

Capabilities of New Telescope   *Max Behring Interview*

"With this new telescope, we should be able to see to the edge of the known universe and — because it takes time for light to travel — almost to the beginning of time."

Exercise Gathering Your Material

Using 3″ x 5″ cards, take notes on everything you might include in your speech on the topic you have chosen. Remember to write only one note per card.

Organizing and Writing Your Speech

Organizing Note Cards

The first step in preparing to write your speech is the organization of your material. Do this according to the following guidelines:

> ### Organizing Your Notes
> 1. Scan the subject headings of your note cards.
> 2. Based upon these subject headings, make a separate list of main ideas.
> 3. Divide your note cards into separate groups, one group for each main idea.
> 4. You should have several notes providing supporting details for each main idea. If you do not, you may have to eliminate some of your main idea groups or do further research.

After you have organized your notes, make a modified outline of your speech. This outline should include, in shortened form, the material you will include in the three major parts of the speech: the **introduction, body,** and **conclusion**. In order to proceed with this organization, it will help you to know what the purpose of each main part is.

The Introduction. The introduction is used to gain your audience's attention. It should be forceful and interesting. It must set the tone of the speech and be appropriate for the occasion. Somewhere in the introduction, usually at the beginning or end of it, you must state your topic or controlling idea.

The chart below lists some ways to start introductions:

TYPE OF INTRODUCTION	EXAMPLE
An anecdote is an interesting short story that involves your audience in your talk.	A 29-year-old mother, with the help of paramedics, gave birth to a son on a moving subway train during rush hour last week. It was the woman's fifth child, but the subway system's first.
A quotation is simply a repetition of someone else's words. A humorous or inspiring quotation can be an effective introduction.	Abraham Lincoln said, "Wanting to work is so rare a merit, it should be encouraged." This statement holds true today for those teenagers who hope to find part-time employment.
A thought-provoking question or series of questions can be an excellent way to get your audience thinking about your subject.	What if you came to school one day, and everyone but you was wearing animal hides and speaking Tibetan?
An analogy is a comparison of a difficult idea or a complicated process to an idea or process your listener already knows.	If you can teach a youngster to tie a shoe, then you can program many of the "user-friendly" computers on the market today.
Startling or interesting facts surprise your audience or make them curious. Such statements can be effective attention-getters.	In the middle of the recent recession, it was revealed that six *million* U.S. homes already had video recorders. That seems to demonstrate that no matter what the situation, television and its related accessories are a high priority in the lives of most Americans.

The Body. The body of the speech is the longest and most important part. In the body, you must inform, entertain, or persuade your audience, giving them facts and information to support your main idea. The body of your speech should take at least twice as much time as the introduction and conclusion combined.

Here are some guidelines for organizing the body of your talk:

1. **Determine your major points.** Choose main ideas from the list that you made based upon the topic headings of your note cards. These main ideas will become the major headings in your outline.

2. **Arrange your main ideas in a logical order.** Your talk should build toward a climax. Sometimes, you will want to present your ideas in order of their importance. In other cases, you will have to present your ideas in a time sequence.

3. **Develop your main ideas.** After you have decided exactly what main ideas you are going to cover, use the information from your notes as supporting details listed under each main idea in your outline.

The Conclusion. The conclusion is a summary of the main points of your speech or a strong statement that signals the end of the presentation to the listener. In a persuasive speech, you might conclude with an appeal or challenge to the audience. An informative speech might end with an appropriate quotation or illustration. At some point during the conclusion of your speech, you should draw attention once again to your main idea. Remember that your conclusion may determine the final impression an audience carries away from your talk. Make sure it is as strong and interesting as the introduction.

Exercise Organizing Your Material

Organize the note cards that you made for the exercise on page 371. Follow the guidelines on the same page. Then make a list of main ideas, using the subject headings of your note cards. Based upon this list of main ideas, make a modified outline with an introduction, body, and conclusion.

Writing Your Speech

Once the outline has been written, the next step is to write the speech itself, developing the introduction, body, and conclusion so that they are both thorough and interesting. Any broad statements or opinions that are made in the speech should be backed up by specific details or references to recognized authorities. The written speech should follow all of the rules of good writing, including directness, unity, and clarity. A good speech, like any good piece of writing, requires thoughtful revision.

Exercise Writing Your Speech

Following your outline, write your speech as you expect to deliver it. You may want to refer to the Guidelines for Writing and Revising Compositions on page 212.

Part 3 Delivering a Speech

The effective presentation of any speech, whether formal or informal, is no easy task. It is possible, however, to appear relaxed and experienced if you are aware of the following three guidelines:

1. **Rehearse your speech aloud many times.** Try practicing in front of a mirror or for a friend or relative. Try to develop variety in facial and vocal expression. Don't be afraid to make corrections as you rehearse. Ask your listeners for suggestions. Eventually, the speech will flow easily.

2. **Take advantage of a tape recorder to listen to your delivery.** Be critical. If something does not sound right, try it again with emphasis on a different word or phrase. Rework your ideas into smoother sentences. If a point seems unclear or awkward, revise your sentences so that they say exactly what you want them to say. If some ideas seem out of place, do not hesitate to rearrange them so that each idea logically follows the one preceding it.

Part 3

Objective

To learn how to deliver formal and informal speeches effectively

Presenting the Lesson

1. Read **Delivering a Speech**, pages 374–376. Have students demonstrate items in the charts for Non-verbal and Verbal Communication. Ask them to give both ineffective and effective portrayals of each point.
2. Complete Exercise A, page 376, with the class. Ask each student in turn to stand up and recite one or two lines clearly, as if they were giving a speech. Some students will be nervous. Point out that they will be nervous in actual speech-giving situations, and that they should therefore not use their

3. **Choose a method of delivery that is comfortable for you.** If you prefer to memorize the entire talk, do so. If you feel more comfortable referring to notes, practice using them. You may even wish to have the entire talk written out in front of you. In either of the last two cases, however, do not merely read the speech. If you do, you will be so engrossed in your notes that an essential part of your presentation, personal contact with the audience, will be lost.

Creating an Effective Impression

Whenever you talk to other people, you should be aware of both nonverbal and verbal communication. The following guidelines will help you:

Keys to Effective Speaking

NONVERBAL COMMUNICATION
Dress and Grooming. Dress and groom yourself in a way that will not draw attention away from your speech. Make sure that your clothing is appropriate to the audience and to the occasion.
Eye Contact. Eye contact with your audience will make them more receptive and attentive. Scan the entire audience with your eyes. Do not look solely at any one person. If you find it difficult to look your audience in the eyes, try looking at the tops of their heads.
Poise and Posture. Do not pose; just stand comfortably. Try to appear relaxed and confident. Putting one foot slightly ahead of the other or adopting a wider stance than usual will help you to maintain your balance. Move about, if possible. Do not lean on a lectern or desk except to emphasize a point. Do not slouch.
Gestures and Facial Expressions. These can be very effective to emphasize particular points. A look of concern, for example, can communicate the seriousness of an idea. Avoid planned gestures and expressions. Instead, let these develop naturally from the emotions that you feel with regard to your subject.

anxiety as an excuse for not participating. You may, however, want to add or substitute tongue twisters to relieve the tension.

The sixth sick sheik's sixth sheep's silk.

She sells sea shells by the sea shore.

3. Assign Exercise B to be completed as homework. Discuss the findings in class. Have students use the speeches they wrote for Part 2 to complete Exercise C.

Individualizing the Lesson

Less-Advanced Students

1. Tell students that inexperienced public speakers often speak too rapidly because they are nervous or because they secretly wish to finish quickly. Have students practice speaking slowly and deliberately by memorizing the introduction to the speeches they wrote in Part 2 and reciting them clearly to the class.

2. Some students may have to battle low self-esteem as they deliver their speeches. Insist that the entire class dress well on "speech-days." Often, the physical change will have a positive effect on the class as a whole, and the speaker in particular.

Advanced Students

Have students compare two newscasters from competing television stations who appear on similar segments of the news (sports, weather, editorials) and compare their effectiveness as public speakers. Tell students to use the criteria given in this section to evaluate the speakers' verbal and nonverbal effectiveness.

Optional Practice

1. Have students memorize portions of well-known speeches, such as Lincoln's Gettysburg Address, and deliver them to the class.

2. Arrange to videotape the students' speeches or practice sessions. Students may view these tapes privately, in order to improve presentation, or in groups, for analysis. Be careful to guide criticism so that no one is embarrassed or hurt.

Extending the Lesson

1. Have students bring in newspaper and magazine photos of people giving speeches. Discuss the messages conveyed through facial expression and gestures.

2. Stress the importance of verbal and non-verbal communication in all situations. Discuss how following or not following the guidelines presented in this Part could affect the following situations:

   a. interviewing for a job
   b. participating in a discussion
   c. asking for a date
   d. auditioning for a play
   e. meeting new people
   f. speaking on the phone

VERBAL COMMUNICATION
Volume. Speak loudly enough for your audience to hear you without difficulty, but not so loudly that they become uncomfortable. Vary your volume for emphasis.
Articulation. Speak a little more precisely than you do in ordinary conversation. Pronounce every syllable of your words clearly and distinctly. Be careful to pronounce final consonants. Do not clip vowel sounds or hold s sounds.
Pace. Speak a little more slowly than is common in ordinary conversation. Speak at a steady rate, with some variation for emphasis.
Pitch. Avoid speech that is too high and thin or that is artificially low. Avoid monotony by varying your pitch, slightly exaggerating the natural pitch variations that occur in ordinary conversation.
Pauses. Pause before important points for dramatic effect.

Exercises Delivering a Speech

A. Pronounce the following sentences, articulating every syllable. Be careful to pronounce final consonant sounds. Avoid clipping vowel sounds or holding s sounds.

   1. In the mists and fiercest frosts we went in winter weather.
   2. Which width, thick or thin, best suits the situation?
   3. Naturally, I couldn't, wouldn't, and didn't do it.
   4. Earl heard his bird's nervous words.
   5. Manny insisted that Otto utter many mutters and murmurs.

B. Listen to a newscast. List two things about the anchorperson's appearance, volume, articulation, pace, pitch, and use of pauses.

C. Deliver a speech to friends or relatives, or tape a practice session and play it for them. Ask for suggestions for improvement in your volume, pitch, rate, and articulation.

Part 4   Listening to and Evaluating Speeches

There are many occasions in which you will find it necessary or important to listen to speeches by other people. Some of these speeches will be informal such as lectures or instructions from a coach or employer. Some may be formal such as campaign speeches or church sermons. Whatever the occasion there are a few guidelines for good listening that you should always follow:

Listening Courteously

1. Do not speak when someone else is speaking.
2. Sit upright and direct your attention to the speaker.
3. Give the speaker positive feedback by using appropriate facial expressions and maintaining eye contact.
4. Take notes if appropriate.

Listening for Content

In order to get the most out of a speech, you must learn to recognize important points that a speaker is making. Listen for key words or phrases that signal the introduction of a major idea. Such signals are often similar to the transitional words used in a composition:

first	another	most importantly
next	similarly	in addition

If you are taking notes on the speech, jot down these main points. Then focus on how the speaker supports or develops each idea. This may help you to draw certain conclusions about the material. A strong, well-documented development, for example, may indicate a valid point or an idea worth accepting. A weak development that uses poor methods of argument or support may indicate that you should examine the ideas much more closely.

Part 4

Objective

To listen to and evaluate informal and formal speeches accurately and fairly

Presenting the Lesson

1. Read and discuss the introduction on page 377. Emphasize the role of the listener, especially in this kind of classroom situation with students who are all beginning speakers. Point out that it is very important for the audience to be supportive of the speaker. The novice speaker will be sensitive to any signs of inattention, and may tend to interpret any inappropriate facial expressions or posture as derision.

2. Read **Listening for Content** on page 377. If necessary, refer to the discussion of note-taking, Chapter 15, pages 303–304.

3. Read and discuss **Listening to Evaluate**, page 378, and the chart for **Evaluating Speeches**. Emphasize the importance of careful listening and of identifying the positive aspects of the speech. Sometimes students assume that critical evaluation means mentioning only the weak points.

4. Read and discuss the sample checklist on page 379. Ask the class if they want to add, delete, or rephrase any items. Revise the checklist, if necessary.

5. Assign the Exercise on page 379. Have students deliver the speeches they wrote for Part 2. Before *beginning* this round of speeches, ask each student to evaluate his or her own material by using the checklist on page 379. Explain that this might help them identify areas that need improvement.

Individualizing the Lesson

Less-Advanced Students

1. To give the students additional practice in listening, play a tape of a speech or read it aloud in class. Have the students identify main ideas and listen for both the strong and weak points of the delivery.

2. As a group, derive an outline from a well-written speech. Tie the parts of the speech into the content evaluation checklist on page 379. Have students point out what verbal clues alerted them to main ideas.

Advanced Students

Have the students prepare a second speech on the same subject as the one they prepared for Part 2. For the second speech, have students identify a different audience, such as third-grade students or a senior citizens' group. Emphasize that "knowing your audience" is an important factor in determining presentation style.

Optional Practice

1. Give students more practice in evaluating presentation by reading a good speech (see *Treasury of the World's Greatest Speeches*) in an ineffective manner. Have students suggest ways to improve verbal and nonverbal communication.

2. Have students memorize part of a speech that is well known, such as Martin Luther King's "I Have A Dream" or J. F. Kennedy's inaugural address. Have them present what they have memorized to the class, emphasizing the elements of presentation and style.

Listening To Evaluate

In some classes, you may be asked to help another student improve his or her communications skills. To do this, you must be able to point out the strong and weak points of a speech. When you are asked to make such comments on another student's speech, avoid brief, useless generalizations such as "It was good" or "I didn't like it." You will find the following guidelines helpful:

Evaluating Speeches

Be constructive, not destructive.
Always offer suggestions for improvement with your criticism. This way you will be building the confidence as well as the communication skills of a classmate.

Never criticize people, only behavior.
"You're fun" and "You're unclear" do not help the speaker to improve. Be more specific and relate your comments directly to the speech. Statements such as "The opening joke warmed your audience" or "The third example was hard to follow" are clearer and more to the point.

Limit your criticisms.
Be selective in the points you wish to criticize. Too many will confuse or exasperate the speaker and do little to improve the speech.

Comment on specific aspects of content or delivery.
Mention specific instances or examples of good or poor eye contact, poise, posture, gestures, facial expression, volume, articulation, pace, pitch, or pausing. Look for instances or examples of particularly strong or weak organization, word choice, or support of main ideas.

Use a checklist similar to the one on the following page to help you in evaluating speeches. For points not covered on the list, you may want to add a section labeled "Other Comments."

Checklist for Evaluating Speeches

CONTENT	
Introduction	_____ gets audience's attention _____ is brief and to the point _____ is appropriate to the topic
Body	_____ supports the main idea _____ contains no irrelevant material _____ states supporting ideas clearly _____ develops supporting ideas completely
Conclusion	_____ is brief _____ provides a summary of major points or _____ draws attention back to main idea

PRESENTATION	
Nonverbal	_____ speaker has good posture _____ speaker is relaxed and confident _____ speaker has good eye contact _____ gestures and facial expressions are natural and appropriate
Verbal	_____ speaker is not too quiet or too loud _____ speaker's articulation is clear _____ speaker's pace is not too slow or too rapid _____ speaker's pitch is not too high or too low _____ speaker varies volume, pace, and pitch _____ speaker uses pauses effectively

Exercise Evaluating Speeches

Use the checklist above to critique a round of speeches in your class. Be sure your comments are specific and constructive.

Extending the Lesson

1. Obtain records or tapes of famous speeches from the library. Have the students discuss the speeches and evaluate them for content and verbal communication.

2. Have students dress in appropriate costume and deliver speeches from different periods of history (Cicero, Elizabeth I, Daniel Webster, etc.). Videotape the presentations, if possible. Ask the class to evaluate the effectiveness of each speaker.

Summary and Applications

Go over the summary with the class. Discuss ways in which the skills covered in this lesson can be applied to several different areas of communication.

Encourage students to use this summary for review, or as part of the SQ3R method of study (see Chapter 15). Remind them, though, that more specific points can only be reviewed by skimming the chapter itself.

Applications in Other Subject Areas

1. Before assigning the **Social Studies/Mass Media** activity, look through the TV listings for an appropriate program for the students to evaluate. If there are several, divide the class into groups, assigning each group to a different program.

2. For the second activity, point out that the range and intensity of emotion is often greater in literature, drama, and poetry than in formal talks. Have one student read Poe's "The Tell-Tale Heart" as an illustration. Here, the narrator is an insane murderer. Seldom would an orator want to create a similar impression! Also discuss the task of a performer to create a complete mood and atmosphere with only voice, expression, gestures, and body language.

1. All speeches, formal or informal, require preparation and should be rehearsed.

2. Informal talks include introductions, announcements, demonstration talks, and persuasive talks.

3. Formal speeches are delivered on specific topics, to specific audiences, for specific purposes. A formal speech may inform, persuade, or entertain.

4. In preparing a formal speech, follow these pre-writing steps:

    a. Select and narrow a topic.
    b. Identify your audience.
    c. Define your purpose.
    d. Research and organize supporting material.

5. Whenever you speak to others, be aware of the following elements. They can influence how well others accept what you say.

    proper dress and grooming
    poise and posture
    volume and articulation
    eye contact
    gestures and facial expressions
    pace, pitch, and pauses.

6. Always listen courteously to other speakers and be specific in your responses or evaluations. Learn to recognize the key points of the material that is presented.

Applications in Other Subject Areas

Social Studies / Mass Media. Watch a TV editorial, the next Presidential address, or a lecture on an educational channel. Evaluate the speaker's presentation. What aspects of the speech are effective? Which are distracting or irritating to you as a viewer?

Speech / Drama. Prepare a dramatic reading of a poem, short story, or play to deliver to your class. What different or additional points concerning voice and gestures must you consider for this type of presentation?

Grammar and Usage

The Mechanics of Writing

A detailed Table of Contents appears in the front of this book.

Grammar, Usage, and Mechanics

The following seventeen sections of this text deal with grammar, usage, and the mechanics of writing (capitalization, punctuation, spelling, the correct form for writing, and outlining).

Each of the sections is divided into parts. Each part explains a topic or concept fully and gives specific examples. Definitions appear in boldface type. There are numerous exercises in each part to test your understanding of the concepts explained. There is also a variety of additional exercises provided at the end of each section.

As you study each section, try to apply what you have learned to your own writing and speaking.

Section 1

The Sentence and Its Parts

Section Objectives

1. To distinguish between sentences and sentence fragments
2. To recognize the four kinds of sentences
3. To recognize subjects and predicates
4. To identify verbs and their simple subjects
5. To identify main verbs and helping verbs
6. To identify subjects and verbs in sentences with unusual order
7. To recognize direct and indirect objects and transitive and intransitive verbs
8. To recognize linking verbs and predicate words
9. To understand and recognize compound sentence parts
10. To recognize and form sentences using the five basic sentence patterns

Preparing the Students

Have the students read the introduction. Stress that the ability to express thoughts clearly is essential to effective communication.

Additional Resources

Diagnostic Test — See page 1 in the test booklet. Recommended for use before teaching the section.

Mastery Test — See page 39 in the test booklet. Recommended for use after teaching the section.

Additional Exercises — See pages 414–420 in the student text.

Skills Practice Book—pages 91–103.

Duplicating Masters—pages 91–103.

Special Populations — See special section at the front of this Teacher's Edition.

You may not think of yourself as a mechanic. However, speaking and writing English is somewhat like building an engine. Like a mechanic working on an engine, a good writer carefully combines parts to build the driving force of English, the sentence.

An engine is composed of pistons, shafts, and cylinders. In a similar way, a sentence is made from its separate parts—subjects, verbs, modifiers, and complements. When the parts of a motor are put together properly, it runs smoothly. A well put-together sentence is also smooth and efficient.

This section will introduce the parts of a sentence and how they work together. Following sections will teach you about each sentence part in detail.

To distinguish between sentences and sentence fragments

Presenting the Lesson

1. Read and discuss pages 386–387. Read the fragments at the end of the Part 1, letting your voice indicate incompleteness in fragments. Have students suggest other ways to complete these fragments.

2. Complete and discuss Exercises A and B on pages 385–387.

Individualizing the Lesson

Less-Advanced Students

If students have trouble identifying the fragments and sentences in the exercises, read each exercise problem aloud. Emphasize the incompleteness of the fragments with your voice. Help students to see what information is missing from the fragments.

Advanced Students

Have the students write complete sentences using the fragments in Exercise A. You might also hand out copies of a paragraph containing fragments. Have students identify the fragments and rewrite the paragraph correctly.

Reinforcement Exercise

Assign and discuss Exercise A on page 414.

Optional Practice

Write the following word groups on the chalkboard. Have students identify the fragments and rewrite them as complete sentences.

Part 1   The Complete Sentence

Sometimes in conversation we use only parts of sentences. For example, we might reply to a question with a word or two, or with a few words that do not make a complete sentence.

Not now.   That one.   Yes.   Over that hill.

In standard written English, however, complete sentences are important. With them, we can express our ideas more clearly.

A sentence is a group of words that expresses a complete thought.

The following groups of words are sentences:

Tom agreed to the plan.
That red car is blocking the alley.
The alarm at the bank sounded late last night.

When part of an idea is missing from a sentence, the group of words is a sentence fragment. A **sentence fragment** is a group of words that does not express a complete thought.

Agreed to the plan. (Who agreed?)
That red car. (What about the car?)
Late last night. (What happened?)

Exercise A: Number your paper from 1 to 10. For each group of words that is a sentence, write **S**. For each sentence fragment, write **F**.

F 1. Lost fifteen pounds in three months.
S 2. A giant towered above the trees.
F 3. The final score of the tennis match.
F 4. On the river bluff near Dubuque.
F 5. A photo of the family reunion last August.
S 6. This gas station is open twenty-four hours a day.
S 7. Val planned the route.
F 8. The hot dog vendors at the ballpark.
S 9. Where was your cousin's wedding held?
S 10. A monster named Nessie lives in Loch Ness.

Exercise B: Writing For each group of words that is a sentence, write **S**. Rewrite each fragment to express a complete thought.

Rewritten fragments will vary.

s 1. There were only sand and sagebrush for miles.
s 2. Who is this disc jockey?
f 3. Used to live in Iowa.
s 4. A downpour stalled the game.
f 5. Appeared on the video screen.
f 6. Our coach, Mr. Esposito.
s 7. The data processor made a mistake.
f 8. A possible new source of energy.
s 9. Kim raised tomatoes and pumpkins last summer.
f 10. Thick black smoke from the blaze.

Part 2 Kinds of Sentences

Sentences can be grouped into a few basic categories, depending on their purpose. No matter what you want to say or write, there is a particular kind of sentence to communicate your ideas. Using these different kinds of sentences, you can ask questions, issue commands, or express strong feelings.

A **declarative sentence** is used to make a statement. It ends with a period (.).

A float plane landed in the harbor.
One day Charles will be King of England.

An **interrogative sentence** asks a question. It ends with a question mark (?).

Do you enjoy volleyball?   What time is it?

An **imperative sentence** gives a command. It usually ends with a period.

Wait for the signal.   Save me a seat, please.

387

1. A winning touchdown
2. Fell off the counter
3. Fixed her bike
4. The afternoon ferry
5. The sun faded

Extending the Lesson

Magazine advertisements often use fragments and single words to capture the attention of potential buyers. Have each student bring in two such ads. In class, identify the fragments and rewrite each as a complete sentence. Discuss why advertisements take the liberty of using fragments.

Part 2

Objective

To recognize the four kinds of sentences

Presenting the Lesson

1. Read and discuss pages 387–388. Help the class become comfortable with the terms by using the terms throughout the discussion. Have students suggest additional examples of each kind of sentence. Stress the importance of using the proper end punctuation.
2. Complete Exercises A and B on page 388.

Individualizing the Lesson

Less-Advanced Students

Write several examples of each of the four kinds of sentences on the board. Ask students to identify the types of sentences and add the proper end punctuation. Allow students to work in pairs or small groups to complete Exercise B.

Advanced Students

Prepare a worksheet including several examples of each of the four kinds of sentences. Have students identify each sentence type, and then rewrite it as indicated by a term in parentheses.

Example — Will you please stand? (imperative)

Reinforcement Exercise

Assign and discuss Exercise B on page 414.

Extending the Lesson

Select a few passages from a short story that contains dialogue. Try to make sure that each of the four kinds of sentences is represented. Pass out copies of the passages to the students. Have them identify each sentence according to type. Discuss how the different kinds of sentences add excitement and variety to writing.

An **exclamatory sentence** expresses strong emotion. It ends with an exclamation point (!).

I won first prize!   What a day this has been!

Exercise A: For each of the following sentences, write *Declarative, Interrogative, Imperative,* or *Exclamatory* to show what kind each is. Add the proper punctuation mark.

1. Are you taking the subway or a bus ? interrogative
2. Turn off the lights when you leave the lab . imperative
3. My friend Antonio lives on the thirteenth floor of our apartment building . declarative
4. Do the elevators work ? interrogative
5. All his life, Gary wanted to be an Olympic competitor in gymnastics . declarative
6. Watch out ! exclamatory or imperative
7. Come out and see all the fireflies . imperative
8. Did Mrs. Henderson cover any new material in algebra class today ? interrogative
9. Pick a card . imperative
10. Thomas Jefferson enjoyed science more than his involvement in politics . declarative

Exercise B: Writing Identify each sentence by its type. Add the correct punctuation mark. Then write a sentence of your own that is the same type. Try to make your sentences interesting.

Sentences will vary.

1. When is the next game ? interrogative
2. Try this potato salad . imperative
3. I was born in Mobile, Alabama . declarative
4. Are you and Gretchen on the same team ? interrogative
5. What a view this is ! exclamatory
6. Tell Pedro to meet us here . imperative
7. Where do you go to school ? interrogative
8. That's fantastic ! exclamatory
9. Which is larger, Iceland or Greenland ? interrogative
10. I read a book about the Vikings . declarative

Part 3　The Subject and the Predicate

Every complete sentence is made up of two basic parts: the subject and the predicate. The **subject** tells *who* or *what* the sentence is about. The **predicate** is the idea expressed about the subject. It usually tells what the subject *is*, what the subject *did,* or *what happened to* the subject.

SUBJECT	PREDICATE
(*Who or what*)	(*The idea expressed about the subject*)
The volcano	erupted again.
A reporter from the paper	relayed the news.
My cousin	became a graphic artist.
The subway riders	raced for the doors.

Each of these sentences expresses a complete thought about a person, place, or thing. There is a simple method of identifying the parts of a sentence. Think of the sentence as telling who did something or what happened. The subject tells *who* or *what*. The predicate tells *is*, *did*, or *happened*.

WHO OR WHAT	IS, DID, OR HAPPENED
The soft mud under my feet	cushioned my toes.
Our lead-off hitter	got a stand-up double.
All four tires	need air.
The first contestant	is confident.

The subject of the sentence tells *who* or *what* the sentence is about.

The predicate of the sentence is the idea expressed about the subject.

389

Objective

To identify subjects and predicates

Presenting the Lesson

1. Read and discuss page 389. Review the two parts of the sentence. Stress that the subject tells *who* or *what* and that the *predicate* tells what *is*, *did*, or *happened*. Suggest that students look for the predicate first, then ask *who* or *what* to locate the subject.

2. Complete and discuss Exercise A and B on page 390.

Individualizing the Lesson

Less-Advanced Students

To reinforce the lesson, ask students to tell whether each of the following phrases is more likely to be a subject or a predicate. Have them explain why.

1. ate the last apricot
2. a dusty trunk in the attic
3. two Koala bears
4. completed her assignment
5. forgot the words

For Exercise A, suggest that students create a chart similar to that on page 389. Work with them to fill in the chart for the first two exercise questions. For Exercise B, allow students to work in pairs.

Advanced Students

Instruct students to observe what is going on in the classroom. Have them write five complete sentences describing the scene. Then ask them to identify the subject and predicate of each one.

Optional Practice

Write these sentences on the board. Instruct students to first read through all the sentences and then rewrite them, matching the subjects with the appropriate predicates.

1. The court jester shopped for the groceries.
2. Dad sutured the wound.
3. The emergency room physician leaped through the air.
4. The postmaster juggled five balls.
5. A gymnast cancelled the letters.

Extending the Lesson

Have the students create stories in the following manner. Direct the first student in each row to write the subject of a sentence. The second student should complete the subject with a predicate. The next student should then begin a new sentence that builds on the idea expressed by the first. Continue the papers around the classroom until the stories are complete. Then select students to read the stories aloud. Have the class check to see that each sentence is complete.

Exercise A: Head two columns *Subject* and *Predicate*. Write the proper words from each sentence in the columns.

EXAMPLE: My cousin needs a part-time job.

SUBJECT	PREDICATE
My cousin	needs a part-time job.

1. A line of motorcycles|zoomed down the freeway.
2. Charlene|won the bike-a-thon this year.
3. Ron|carried his radio to the beach.
4. The long silver train|streaked by us.
5. Our career counselor|has a great deal of information on summer jobs.
6. The new P.E. wing|contains two gyms.
7. This year's harvest of soybeans|is the biggest ever.
8. Those jeans|have been washed many times.
9. I|need fifty cents for the bus.
10. Tickets for the Men at Work concert|sold out after only two hours.

Exercise B: Writing Add a subject or predicate to each word group to make it into a sentence. Tell which part you are adding.

Sentences will vary.

EXAMPLE: goes to the day care center

My younger sister goes to the day care center. (Subject)

1. Cara's three brothers predicate
2. shrieked all night subject
3. the lean timber wolf predicate
4. our basketball team predicate
5. careened off the edge of the cliff subject
6. a bank of dark cumulus clouds predicate
7. the ancient, bearded wizard predicate
8. is going to take a ceramics class subject
9. is Rob's favorite pastime subject
10. suddenly emerged from the cave subject

Part 4 Simple Subjects and Verbs

In every sentence certain words are more important than others. These essential words are the basic framework of the sentence. Look at these examples:

SUBJECT	PREDICATE
The **volcano**	**erupted** again.
A **reporter** from the paper	**relayed** the news.
My **cousin**	**became** a graphic artist.
The subway **riders**	**raced** for the doors.

All the words in the subject part of the sentence are called the **complete subject**. Within the complete subject is a key word, the **simple subject**. In the last example above, *the subway riders* is the complete subject. *Riders* is the simple subject. Hereafter we will refer to this key word as the **subject**.

The **complete predicate** is all the words that express an idea about the subject. The key word within the complete predicate is called the **simple predicate**, or **verb**. In the sentence about the subway riders, the complete predicate is *raced for the doors*. The key word, or verb, is *raced*.

The key word in the subject of a sentence is called the simple subject. We refer to it as the **subject**.

The key word in the predicate is the simple predicate. Hereafter we will refer to the simple predicate as the **verb**.

Types of Verbs

You can more easily identify verbs if you realize that verbs can be grouped into two basic types. One type expresses action, so it is called an **action verb**. The following sentences contain action verbs:

We *skated* on Dreamland Lake.
Uncle Joe *built* a cabin last summer.

Part 4

Objective

To identify verbs and their simple subjects

Presenting the Lesson

1. Read page 391. Emphasize the difference between the complete subject and the simple subject, and between the complete predicate and the simple predicate, or verb. On the board, write *Fish swim*. Suggest ways to turn this simple subject and verb into a more detailed subject and predicate.

2. Discuss **Types of Verbs** on pages 391–392. Students will have more difficulty with the concept of state-of-being verbs, so put several examples of sentences containing such verbs on the board.

3. Read **Finding the Verb and the Subject** on page 392. Remind students to identify the verb of a sentence first, and then to ask *who* or *what* to locate the subject. Repeat the procedure shown on the middle of page 392 using sentences suggested by the students.

4. Introduce sentence diagraming. Explain that a diagram is a sort of "map" of a sentence, and that it is useful for showing how the parts of a sentence are related to each other. You may want to consider reserving the challenge of diagraming for the more advanced students. During class discussion, however, diagrams are useful teacher aids for sentence analyses.

5. Assign Exercises A and B on page 393. Caution students that intervening phrases, such as *of the city* in sentence 3, do not contain the subject.

391

1. Place the following sentences on a worksheet. Have students identify the simple subject and verb.

1. The rope broke under the weight.
2. A red arrow indicated the way.
3. The star is Lori Singer.
4. Damp wood makes a smoky campfire.
5. Ralph left the lights on.
6. Our canoe almost tipped over.
7. Sound carries easily over water.

Discuss their answers as a class.

2. Allow students to work in pairs or small groups on Exercise B.

Advanced Students

Have students write ten new sentences using *either* the subject or the predicate from each of the sentences in Exercise A.

Direct them to identify the new simple subject or verb in each sentence.

Reinforcement Exercise

Assign and discuss Exercise D on page 415.

Optional Practice

Have students identify the verb and simple subject for each sentence they write in Exercise B.

Extending the Lesson

Provide students with ten pairs of nouns and verbs. Have them construct sentences that use these words in detailed subjects and predicates. Point out that adding details to simple subjects and predicates adds to the interest of the sentence. Encourage them to expand sentences in this way whenever they write.

The other main type of verb expresses the existence or condition of something. It is called a **state-of-being verb**. These sentences contain state-of-being verbs.

Ramon *is* an expert swimmer.
The frog *became* a prince.

Finding the Verb and the Subject

In any sentence, the verb and the subject are the most important words. The other words only tell more about these key words.

To find these key words in any sentence, first find the verb. Remember that it expresses action or a state of being. Once you find the verb, form a question by placing *who* or *what* in front of the verb. The answer will give you the subject of the verb.

An attendant at the station checked the oil.

Verb: checked
Who checked? attendant
The subject is *attendant*.

The plane is on the runway.

Verb: is
What is? plane
The subject is *plane*.

Diagraming Subjects and Verbs

A sentence diagram is a drawing of the parts of a sentence. It is a visual representation of how the parts fit together.

A sentence diagram demonstrates the importance of the subject and the verb. These key parts are placed on a horizontal main line. They are separated by a vertical line that crosses the main line. No matter where the subject appears in the sentence, in a diagram it always appears before the verb. Later you will learn how every other word in the sentence has a particular position in the diagram, too.

In diagraming, only words capitalized in the sentence are capitalized in the diagram. No punctuation is used.

Adam spoke quietly.

Adam	spoke

Janelle writes poetry.

Janelle	writes

Exercise A: Label two columns *Verb* and *Subject*. Number your paper from 1 to 10. For each sentence, write the verb and its subject.

1. Jack works at the hospital each Saturday.
2. Ten students are in the play.
3. This map of the city indicates bus routes.
4. The huge trawler fished the rough, stormy Antarctic.
5. The network canceled that show after only two episodes.
6. Dana's sister sets high goals for herself.
7. Six different ingredients topped the pizza.
8. A professional stunt man performed the fall.
9. The annual carnival attracted large crowds.
10. An emu is a flightless bird.

Exercise B: Writing Complete these sentences by adding subjects, predicates, or both. Tell which part you are adding. Then identify the verb in each sentence as an *action* verb or a *state-of-being* verb. Answers will vary.

1. many of the best songs today
2. arrived in four days by pony express
3. Spielberg's latest movie
4. the vast expanse of desert
5. revved their powerful engines
6. two strange beings, with three eyes apiece
7. Marty and Jack
8. is on this side of the river
9. an elephant with a broken tusk
10. our upstairs neighbor

Objective

To identify main verbs and helping verbs

Presenting the Lesson

1. Read and discuss pages 394–395. Emphasize that verbs may be composed of a single word or several words. Also point out that some words may be used as either a main verb or a helping verb, as in *I am helping Susan* and *I am* late. Stress that the simple predicate, or verb, is the key element in the predicate of the sentence.

2. Make certain that students understand the concept of the separated parts of verbs. Caution them never to assume that one word is the complete verb simply because no helping verb appears directly next to it.

3. Do Exercises A and B on page 395. Remind students to watch for *n't* and other negatives.

Individualizing the Lesson

Less-Advanced Students

To sharpen students' awareness of what helping verbs are, write pairs of sentences, such as the following, on the board. Have students identify the ones that contain helping verbs.

Terry was late.
Ruth was collecting the tickets.

I have the list of names.
They have written to everyone.

Advanced Students

1. Put the following verbs on the chalkboard. Have students write a

Part 5   The Parts of a Verb

A verb may consist of one word, or of several words. It may be composed of a **main verb** and one or more **helping verbs**, also called **auxiliary verbs**.

HELPING VERBS	+ MAIN VERB	= VERB
will	return	will return
would	expect	would expect
is	leaving	is leaving
must have	shown	must have shown

To name the verb in any sentence, you must include all the words that make up the verb.

These words are frequently used as helping verbs:

am	are	have	will	may
is	be	do	would	might
was	has	does	can	shall
were	had	did	could	should

Most of these words can also be used as main verbs.

Mike *has played* guitar for years (helping verb)
Mike *has* a new guitar. (main verb)

Separated Parts of a Verb

At times you will find words inserted between the parts of a verb. These words are not included in the verb. Study the following sentences. The parts of the verb are in bold print.

Cassie **had** never **driven** a tractor.
My friends **could** not **offer** any advice.
The artist **will** gladly **show** you her work.

Some verbs are joined with other words to make contractions. In naming verbs that appear in contractions, pick out only the verb. The word *not* and its contraction *n't* are adverbs. They are never verb parts.

> Vernon **did**n't **notice** the car. (*Did notice* is the verb.)
> The carpenter **had**n't **measured** exactly. (*Had measured* is the verb.)

In Section 5 you will learn more about verbs and verb usage.

Exercise A: Number your paper from 1 to 10. List the <u>verbs</u> in the following sentences.

1. Bluegrass musicians <u>were gathering</u> for the festival.
2. You <u>haven't</u> ever <u>needed</u> any help before.
3. We <u>could</u> often <u>read</u> his mood.
4. David <u>has</u> never <u>seen</u> an ice hockey game.
5. You <u>should try</u> that new roller coaster.
6. The umpire <u>didn't respond</u> to the catcalls.
7. The conservation bill <u>hasn't passed</u> yet.
8. This year I <u>will</u> probably <u>get</u> a paper route.
9. The price <u>does</u> not <u>include</u> delivery.
10. We <u>have</u> never <u>called</u> ourselves experts.

Exercise B: On your paper make two columns headed *Helping Verbs* and *Main Verbs*. Write the verbs in each sentence in the appropriate columns. Not all sentences contain helping verbs.

1. Summer vacation doesn't begin until Tuesday.
2. A relief pitcher will sometimes finish the game.
3. My sister has already taken her driver's test.
4. A good job will usually require two coats of paint.
5. Michelle wrapped her father's present in glossy red plaid paper.
6. Someone must have cut the telephone line.
7. Your ideas will certainly help.
8. Lincoln's ghost doesn't walk until midnight.
9. The new clinic on Long Street will soon open.
10. Most of the team's new players have already signed their contracts.

sentence using each one. Direct them to circle any intruding contractions.

1. must have been planning
2. shouldn't be leaving
3. was
4. has been fixing
5. doesn't know

2. Have students suggest vivid alternative verbs for some of the sentences in the Exercises. Point out that lively verbs make lively writing.

Optional Practice

Have students replace the helping verbs in the sentences from Exercise A. Point out how much these auxiliaries affect the meaning of the sentences. This exercise can be a simple introduction to tenses.

Extending the Lesson

Have students find ten sentences in their textbooks that contain helping verbs. Require that at least three of these verbs be separated from the main verbs. Have students exchange papers and identify the parts of the verb.

Part 6 Subjects in Unusual Positions

Objective

To identify the subject and verb in sentences with unusual order

Presenting the Lesson

1. Read and discuss pages 396–399. Continue to stress that the subject is always found by first locating the verb and then forming a question by placing *who* or *what* before it.

2. To differentiate between the two functions of *there*, it may be useful to put these sentences on the chalkboard:

1. There is my coach.
2. There was a severe thunderstorm last night.
3. There can be no exceptions to the rule.
4. There is your seat.

Explain that when *there* provides direction, as in examples one and four, it is telling about the verb and is diagramed below the verb. Work with students to rewrite these four sentences in usual subject-verb order. Point out that when clarity is not retained after rewriting, *there* is serving simply as an introductory word and should be diagramed with the subject.

3. Do Exercise on page 397 orally.

4. Read and discuss pages 397–399. Discuss all examples carefully. Remind students that parts of the verb may be separated in sentences with unusual order. If the verb in a question is more than one word, for example, the subject of the sentence often separates it into parts.

Part 6 Subjects in Unusual Positions

The subject of a sentence usually comes before the verb. Sometimes, however, the structure of the sentence departs from this order. This may happen when the sentence is written to perform a special function. It may also occur if the writer is trying to add variety to his or her sentences. In these sentences, part or all of the verb may come before the subject.

To find the subject in any sentence, first find the verb. Then form a question by putting *who* or *what* in front of the verb. The answer will be the subject.

Sentences Beginning with *There*

In sentences beginning with *There*, the verb often comes before the subject.

There is used in two different ways. It may be used to modify the verb by telling *where* something is or happens.

> There are the Petersons. (*Petersons* is the subject; *are* is the verb. *There* tells where the Petersons are.)
> There is the exit. (*Exit* is the subject; *is* is the verb. *There* tells where the exit is.)

Sometimes *There* is used simply as an introductory word to help get the sentence started.

> There is a statue of Twain in the park. (*Statue* is the subject; *is* is the verb.)
> There are two drummers in the band. (*Drummers* is the subject; *are* is the verb.)

To diagram sentences beginning with *There*, you must determine whether *There* tells *where* or is an introductory word. If *There* tells *where*, it belongs on a slanted line below the verb. If *There* is an introductory word, it belongs on a horizontal line above the subject.

There stood the manager of the store.

There has been a mistake.

Exercise: Write the <u>subject</u> and the <u>verb</u> in each sentence. Tell whether *there* is used to tell *where* or as an introductory word.

1. There <u>is</u> our <u>canoe</u>.   tells where
2. There <u>will be</u> a Halloween <u>party</u> on Saturday.   Introductory word
3. There <u>were</u> some <u>questions</u> about the new schedule.   Introductory word
4. There <u>is</u> no <u>ferry</u> after ten o'clock.   Introductory word
5. There <u>is</u> the exchange <u>student</u> from Finland.   tells where
6. There <u>has been</u> a <u>change</u> of plans.   Introductory word
7. There <u>is</u> the city's civic <u>center</u>.   tells where
8. There <u>are</u> the <u>boxes</u> of job applications.   tells where
9. There <u>is</u> the kazoo marching <u>band</u>.   tells where
10. There <u>have been</u> many <u>advances</u> in computer technology.   Introductory word

Sentences Beginning with *Here*

In sentences beginning with *Here,* the subject often follows the verb.

Here comes the parade. Here is your wallet.

Unlike *there*, the word *here* always tells *where* about the verb. On a diagram it is placed on a slanted line below the verb.

Questions

In questions, subjects usually come between parts of the verb.

Have you finished? (*You* is the subject; *have finished* is the verb.)
Will Kate join us? (*Kate* is the subject; *will join* is the verb.)

397

Have students diagram the subject and verb of each sentence in Exercise A.

Ask students to listen to the commercials carefully the next time they are watching TV or listening to the radio. Direct them to write down ten examples of sentences with unusual order. (Sentences such as "here's your chance to . . ." should be plentiful.) Discuss the sentences in class, identifying the subjects and verbs.

Sentences Starting with Phrases or Other Words

Phrases are groups of words that do not make a complete sentence. Phrases are often used to modify other words in a sentence. When a sentence begins with a phrase or a single word modifier, the subject may come after the verb.

Around the curve raced the runners. (*Runners* is the subject; *raced* is the verb.)
Slowly came her reply. (*Reply* is the subject; *came* is the verb.)

To find the subject in any sentence with unusual word order, first find the verb. Then place *who* or *what* before the verb to form a question.

Here are the scripts.
Verb: are
Who or what are? scripts
Subject: scripts

Unusual word order in a sentence does not change the sentence diagram. The verb and the subject are still placed on the horizontal main line with the subject first and then the verb.

Under the rock slithered the snake.

snake	slithered

Imperative Sentences

You remember that imperative sentences give commands or state requests. In imperative sentences, the subject is usually not stated. Since commands are always given to the person spoken to, the subject is *you*. Because *you* is not stated, we say that it is *understood*.

Draw a straight line. (*You* is the subject of *draw*.)
Please repeat the question. (*You* is the subject of *repeat*.)

To diagram a sentence giving a command, place the subject *you* in parentheses.

Try again.

Exercise A: Label two columns *Subject* and *Verb*. Number your paper from 1 to 10. Write the subject and verb for each sentence.

(You) 1. Tell another joke.
2. Here is clear evidence of his guilt.
3. Have the plants been watered?
4. Quickly came his curt reply.
(You) 5. See Mammoth Cave on your trip to Kentucky.
6. Will you save a seat for me?
(You) 7. Enter through the side door.
8. Into the spotlight danced Marisa.
9. Did the psychic use tarot cards?
10. Underneath my foot lay a dollar bill.

Exercise B: Writing Rewrite these sentences using the directions in parentheses. Label the subject and verb in each new sentence.

Answers in margin.

1. A pod of whales swam in the distance.
   (Begin sentence with *In the distance*.)
2. Another space mission is planned for the near future.
   (Change this to a question.)
3. The brutal gales swept across the island.
   (Begin the sentence with *Across the island*.)
4. Snow is always on Mount Rainier.
   (Begin the sentence with *There*.)
5. The location of the buried treasure is here.
   (Begin the sentence with *Here*.)
6. You can try this one for size.
   (Make the sentence imperative.)
7. I need a flashlight and compass for the campout.
   (Change the sentence to a question.)

Exercise B

1. In the distance swam a pod of whales.
2. Is another space mission planned for the near future?
3. Across the island swept the brutal gales.
4. There is always snow on Mount Ranier.
5. Here is the buried treasure.
6. You try this one for size.
7. Do I need a flashlight and compass for the campout?
8. In the marsh stood a solitary blue heron.
9. Here is the new micro-computer.
10. You take a patch kit along on your bike trip.

399

8. A solitary blue <u>heron</u> <u>stood</u> on one leg in the marsh.
   (Begin the sentence with *In the marsh*.)
9. The new <u>micro-computer</u> <u>is</u> here.
   (Begin the sentence with *Here*.)
10. <u>You</u> <u>should take</u> a patch kit along on your bike trip.
    (Make the sentence imperative.)

Part 7 Objects of Verbs

Some verbs do not need other words to complete their meaning in a sentence. The action they describe is complete.

The players *rested*.   The rain finally *stopped*.
Nathan *was worrying*.   The T-shirt *will fade*.

Some verbs, though, do not express a complete meaning by themselves. They need other words to complete the meaning of a sentence. We call words that complete the meaning of a sentence **complements**.

Tony reserved _____ . (Reserved what?)
The campers brought _____ . (Brought what?)

Two kinds of complements are **direct objects** and **indirect objects**.

Direct Objects

One kind of verb complement is called the **direct object**. A direct object receives the action of the verb. In the sentences below, *space* receives or tells the result of the action of *reserved*. *Firewood* receives the action of *brought*.

Tony reserved a *space*.
The campers brought *firewood*.

To find the direct object, first find the verb. Then place *whom* or *what* after the verb to form a question. *Note*: other words may follow the direct object, as in the second example on the following page.

Part 7

Objectives

1. To understand the functions of direct and indirect objects
2. To recognize transitive and intransitive verbs

Presenting the Lesson

1. Read and discuss pages 400–402. Use these additional examples to emphasize that sometimes a subject and verb alone are not enough to express a complete thought.

Maria prepared _____ .
Greg wanted _____ .
The worker lifted _____ .

Make sure students understand the relationship between verbs and direct objects. Stress that a direct object answers the question *what?* or *whom?* after the verb.

2. Spend some time discussing the meanings of the words *transitive* and *intransitive*. Stress that some verbs may be transitive or intransitive, depending upon their context. Also caution students to avoid mistaking words in when, where, and *how* phrases for direct objects. When you are sure they understand the concepts, ask students to come up with more intransitive/transitive sentence pairs such as the one in the middle of page 401.

Steve invited six friends.

> *Verb*: invited
> *Invited whom?*: friends
> *Direct object*: friends

Ann repaired the motorcycle yesterday.

> *Verb*: repaired
> *Repaired what?*: motorcycle
> *Direct object*: motorcycle

Once you understand what a direct object is, you can learn to distinguish between two types of action verbs. A verb that has a direct object is called a **transitive verb**. A verb that does not have a direct object is called an **intransitive verb**. Notice the difference in these sentences:

> Our teacher *gave* a lecture. (*Gave* is transitive.
> It has a direct object, *lecture*.)
> The sun *was shining*. (*Was shining* is intransitive.
> It has no direct object.)

Some verbs may be transitive in one sentence and intransitive in another. Look at the way the verb *called* is used in the following examples.

> INTRANSITIVE: Your sister called.
> TRANSITIVE: Your sister called a taxi.

Transitive or Intransitive?

Look at the following sentences. Are the verbs transitive or intransitive?

> Louise *left* quickly.
> Louise *left* in the afternoon.
> Louise *left* the room.

In the first two examples, the verb *left* has no direct object. In those sentences, *left* is intransitive. However, in the third sentence, if you place *whom* or *what* after the verb to form a ques-

3. Assign and discuss Exercises A and B on page 402. Remind students that only transitive verbs have direct objects.

4. Read and discuss page 403. To help students understand indirect objects, write these three guidelines on the board:

> a. Indirect objects only appear in sentences that have direct objects.
> b. Indirect objects stand between the verb and the direct object.
> c. Indirect objects are not found after the words *to* or *for*.

4. Assign Exercises A and B on page 404.

Individualizing the Lesson

Less Advanced Students

1. For Exercise B on page 402, do the first two problems orally. Ask students to explain why the first *visited* is intransitive and the second transitive. Caution them not to be misled by modifiers, such as *yesterday*, that tell *when, how,* or *where*.

2. For Exercise A on page 404, direct students to use a three-step process for each sentence. First, have them find the verb and its subject in each sentence. Next, have them identify the direct objects. Finally have them ask *for whom?* or *for what?* or *to whom?* or *to what?* after the verb and the direct object to find the indirect object.

3. Do Exercise B orally, or allow students to work in pairs. The exercise directions are somewhat complex, and may require explanation.

Advanced Students

1. Have students devise sentence pairs where the same word is both a transitive and intransitive verb.

Jeffrey sang softly.
Jeffrey sang an old folk song.

2. Have students diagram the subjects, verbs, and objects for the sentences in Exercise A.

Reinforcement Exercise

Assign and discuss Exercise F on page 416.

Optional Practice

Have students find any objects in the two exercises on page 395.

Extending the Lesson

Label three columns on the chalkboard: *Verb, Indirect Object,* and *Direct Object.* Have students come up and fill in words. Then direct the class to devise sentences using the key words on the board. The sentences may be serious or humorous. Allow adequate time for sharing the various sentences.

tion, you find that *room* is the direct object. In that sentence, *left* is a transitive verb.

> Louise left the room.
> *Verb*: left
> *Left what?*: room
> *Direct object*: room

Remember, if the words following the verb tell *when, how,* or *where* the action took place, they are not direct objects.

Exercise A: Number your paper from 1 to 10. For each sentence, write the <u>direct object</u> of the verb.

1. The actors studied their <u>lines</u>.
2. Mr. Mendez has opened a new <u>business</u>.
3. The ship finally reached <u>Malaysia</u>.
4. In the morning, the workers will finish the <u>project</u>.
5. Please return my <u>notebook</u>.
6. We picked <u>blackberries</u> at Aunt Mae's.
7. The Canadian Prime Minister wore a red <u>rose</u> in his lapel.
8. Sara quickly smothered the <u>flames</u>.
9. The bus driver had nearly missed the <u>exit</u> to Tucson.
10. On Saturdays, Keith washes <u>cars</u> at his uncle's car wash.

Exercise B: Find the verb in each sentence. Tell whether it is *Transitive* or *Intransitive*.

1. My cousins <u>visited</u> yesterday. intransitive
2. She <u>visited</u> her friends. transitive
3. Amy's dad <u>leads</u> tours for the National Park Service. transitive
4. The general <u>led</u> with courage and decisiveness. intransitive
5. Some hedges <u>grow</u> quickly. intransitive
6. Constantine <u>grows</u> herbs in a window box. transitive
7. A new worker <u>joined</u> the crew. transitive
8. Some members <u>joined</u> late. intransitive
9. The supervisor <u>issued</u> several orders at once. transitive
10. This blood donor <u>gives</u> frequently. intransitive

402

Indirect Objects

Another type of complement is an **indirect object**. Indirect objects sometimes tell *to whom* or *to what* about the verb. At other times they tell *for whom* or *for what* about the verb. The words *to* and *for* are not used in the actual sentences, however.

> Jeff told **Marla** the *news*. (told *to* Marla)
> The clerk sold **us** the wrong *battery*. (sold *to* us)
> Carlos made **us** a Mexican *dinner*. (made *for* us)

In the sentences above, the words in bold type are the indirect objects. The words in italics are the direct objects. Indirect objects appear only in sentences with direct objects. Indirect objects are found between the verb and direct object.

> Andrew handed the *teller* his deposit. (*Teller* is the indirect object of *handed*.)
> Andrew handed his deposit to the *teller*. (*Teller* is not an indirect object.)

In a diagram, place a direct object on the main line after the verb. The vertical line between the verb and object does not extend below the main line.

> Lana bought a poster.

Lana	bought	poster

The indirect object belongs on a horizontal line attached below the verb.

> Lana bought her brother a poster.

403

Exercise A: Number your paper from 1 to 10. Label three columns *Verb, Indirect Object,* and *Direct Object*. For each sentence below, write down those parts. Not all sentences will have all three parts.

EXAMPLE: We brought Wendy a gift.

VERB	INDIRECT OBJECT	DIRECT OBJECT
brought	Wendy	gift

1. Jonah hurriedly handed Sarah her ticket.
2. The florist arranged the roses in a blue vase.
3. A survivor told the reporters her story.
4. Does this store give customers a discount?
5. Jim passed Willie the ball.
6. The neighbors are repairing their porch this weekend.
7. Joe left the genial waitress a tip.
8. Many waitresses earn generous tips.
9. This restaurant serves terrific chili.
10. Our gym teacher taught us a new dance today.

Exercise B: Writing Some of the following sentences contain direct objects. If a sentence has no direct object, add one. If a sentence has a direct object already, add an indirect object.

Answers will vary.

EXAMPLE: Austin typed on the word processor. (Sentence without direct object.)

Austin typed his report on the word processor. (Direct object added to sentence.)

1. The glee club sang.
2. Michelle told the history of Valentine's Day.
3. General MacArthur gave the orders.
4. Southern restaurants serve grits for breakfast.
5. Don't shove.
6. My grandparents left this afternoon.
7. Our neighbor bought a piano.
8. Ken finally called last night.
9. After football practice we ate.
10. Mrs. Graziano brought a beautiful basket of fresh blueberries and strawberries.

Part 8 Linking Verbs and Predicate Words

You learned earlier that some verbs do not express action. Instead, they tell that something *is* or *exists*. Such verbs are called **state-of-being** verbs.

Often, this type of verb links the subject of a sentence with a word or group of words in the predicate. When this occurs, we call the verb a **linking verb**.

> Jessica *is* a soprano. Thomas *must be* angry.
> We *are* the winners. The typists *were* busy.

The verb *to be* is the most commonly used linking verb. *To be* can have many forms. This list will help you to become familiar with them:

be	been	is	was
being	am	are	were

The verbs *be*, *being*, and *been* can also be used with helping verbs. These are examples:

should be	were being	had been
may be	was being	could have been
will be	is being	might have been

The word linked to the subject by a linking verb is called a **predicate word**. The three kinds of predicate words are **predicate nouns, predicate pronouns,** and **predicate adjectives.** All of them tell something about the subject.

Brad is a *plumber*. (predicate noun)

That was *he*. (predicate pronoun)

Carlotta is *tall*. (predicate adjective)

In the above sentences, the subjects and predicate words are joined by the linking verbs *is* and *was*.

405

Part 8

Objective

To recognize linking verbs and predicate words

Presenting the Lesson

1. Read and discuss pages 405–406. Stress that the predicate word renames or describes the subject. To demonstrate the relationship between subjects and predicate words, suggest that students imagine linking verbs as equal signs. For example, in the sentence *The soup tastes warm; soup = warm.*

2. Emphasize that direct objects appear only with action verbs and that predicate words are used only with linking verbs. Students will most often have difficulty with this concept when the verb used in the sentence can function as either an action verb or a linking verb. Go over several examples in which verbs such as the following function in both ways:

tasted	felt
looked	sound
smelled	grew

Point out that one must decide whether the complement is *receiving action* or *renaming the subject* in order to identify the type of verb.

3. Review helping verbs and separated parts of a verb. Remind students that linking verbs may have more than one part.

4. Assign and discuss Exercises A, B, and C on pages 407–408.

Individualizing the Lesson

Less-Advanced Students

1. Write ten verbs on the board. Point to each one in turn and direct students to write a sentence using that verb. Tell them whether the verb is to be used as an action verb or a linking verb (include some that could be either. For each verb, have several students read their sentences. Discuss the answers.

2. Allow students to work on Exercise C in pairs or small groups.

Advanced Students

Have students write a descriptive paragraph using each of the following linking verbs. They might, for example, write about a restaurant or a lunar landscape. Direct them to circle the predicate words.

1. are becoming
2. is
3. tasted
4. are
5. will be
6. would have been
7. appears
8. felt
9. seemed
10. has been

Reinforcement Exercise

Assign and discuss Exercise G on pages 416–417.

Optional Practice

Ask students to compose a set of sentences about someone they admire. Use Exercise B as an example. Require them to use at least four predicate words in their sentences.

Extending the Lesson

Have students find a picture of an interesting scene or individual in a newspaper or magazine. Have them write descriptive sentences about the picture using several linking verbs and predicate words. Encourage the use of vivid, specific adjectives.

Here are some other common linking verbs.

appear	seem	sound	grow
feel	look	taste	become

Like *be*, these linking verbs have various forms (*grow, grew,* or *grown,* for instance). They can be used with helping verbs, as in *will become, can seem,* or *might have sounded.*

The lake *looked* choppy.

Bruce *has become* an excellent gymnast.

In a sentence diagram, place the predicate word on the main line after the verb. A slanted line above the main line separates the verb from the predicate word. That line, like the predicate word, points back toward the subject.

Ms. Freeman is the new advisor.

Ms. Freeman	is \	advisor

That tire looks flat.

tire	looks \	flat

Direct Object or Predicate Word?

A verb may be completed in one of two ways. It may have a direct object, or it may have a predicate word. How can you tell whether a complement is a predicate word or a direct object?

The verb is the key word. If the verb is an action verb, the word following it that tells *whom* or *what* is a direct object.

The nurse comforted the patient. (*Comforted* is an action verb. *Patient* is its direct object.)

The ambulance rounded the corner. (*Rounded* is an action verb. *Corner* is its direct object.)

If the verb is a linking verb, the word following it that tells about the subject is a predicate word.

> David Brenner is a *comedian*. (*Is* is a linking verb. *Comedian* is a predicate word linked to *David Brenner*.)
>
> These French fries seem *soggy*. (*Seem* is a linking verb. *Soggy* is a predicate word linked to *fries*.)

Sometimes, however, it is difficult to tell whether the verb is an action verb or a linking verb. When you are not sure, ask yourself how the complement is functioning in the sentence. Is it *describing or renaming the subject*, or is it *receiving the action* of the verb? Look at the following sentences:

> Jenny tasted the *sherbet*.
>
> The sherbet tasted *tart*.

In the first sentence, *sherbet* receives the action of the verb. Therefore it is a direct object. In the second sentence, *tart* describes the subject. Therefore, it is a predicate word.

Exercise A: Label three columns *Subject*, *Linking Verb*, and *Predicate Word*. Find these parts and place them in the proper columns.

1. My uncle is a zookeeper.
2. The band sounded great.
3. One endangered species is the Siberian tiger.
4. John looked upset by the news.
5. This curry smells delicious.
6. The sky appeared pink at sunset.
7. Kim must feel miserable.
8. The producer is she.
9. Jesse will become an architect.
10. Roller skates are once again popular.

Exercise B: Label four columns *Subject*, <u>Verb</u>, *Direct Object*, and *Predicate Word*. Put these parts in the right columns. Remember, no sentence can contain a direct object *and* a predicate word.

1. <u>Sally Ride</u> <u>was</u> the first female astronaut in the U.S.
2. Her <u>home</u> <u>is</u> California.

3. In her childhood, Sally played football.

DO
4. Sally earned a doctorate in astrophysics.

DO
5. She married another astronaut.

DO
6. Sally flew her own plane to their wedding.

DO
7. Ride shared her assignment with Fabian, Crippen, Hauck, and Thagard.

DO
8. She gave the press many interviews before and after her famous ride.

DO
9. Sally Ride became a heroine to many young women.

PW
10. Can you tell me the name of her spaceship?

DO

Exercise C: Writing Write ten sentences about a famous person, past or present. Label each subject *S*, each verb *V*, each direct object *DO*, and each predicate word *PW*. Answers will vary.

Part 9

Objective

To understand and recognize compound sentence parts

Presenting the Lesson

1. Read and discuss pages 408–410. Review with students the sentence parts covered thus far: subject, verb, direct object, indirect object, and predicate word. Make sure that students understand that *conjunctions* are used to form *compounds*. Write the following sample sentences on the board before continuing with the text.

  Mom and Dad left for work. (subject)
  The birds chirped and warbled all night. (verb)
  Joe ordered tacos, a tamale, and a burrito. (direct object)
  Mr. Downs offered Ryan and me a job. (indirect object)

Part 9 Compound Parts of a Sentence

The word *compound* means "having two or more parts."

Each of the sentence parts described so far in this section can be compound—subjects, verbs, and complements.

Two parts in a compound construction are joined by a conjunction (*and, or, but*). In a compound construction of three or more parts, the conjunction usually comes between the last two parts.

The rival leaders were Jack *and* Ralph.
The boys swam, explored, *or* ate berries most of the day.

Diagraming Compound Subjects

To diagram compound subjects, split the subject line into as many levels as there are subjects. Place the conjunction on a dotted line connecting the subjects.

Sheep, goats, and wild horses roam the foothills.

Diagraming Compound Verbs

To diagram compound verbs, split the verb line.

The freighter tossed, pitched, and rolled.

Diagraming Compound Objects

To diagram compound direct objects or indirect objects, split the object line.

Gonzales hit a homer and two singles. (compound direct object)

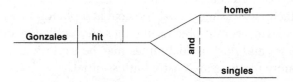

The director gave Brendon and Sandra lead roles. (compound indirect object)

Mike looks tall and very mature in his new suit. (predicate word)

2. Assign Exercise A on page 410. You may wish to have students come to the board and diagram the sentences.

3. Assign and discuss Exercise B on page 410.

Individualizing the Lesson

Less-Advanced Students

For Exercise A on page 410, remind students to look for a conjunction to help them find the compound parts. For Exercise B, do the first two sentences orally. Direct students to first locate the required sentence part that already exists in the sentence.

Advanced Students

1. Ask students to write two sentences containing each of these compound parts.

1. compound subject
2. compound verb
3. compound direct object
4. compound indirect object
5. compound predicate word

2. Direct students to diagram the sentences in Exercise A.

Reinforcement Exercise

Assign and discuss Exercise H on page 417.

Optional Practice

Ask each student to write ten sentences containing subjects, verbs, and objects or predicate words. Then have students exchange papers. Direct them to identify the previously mentioned parts in each sentence. Then have them rewrite each sentence, making at least one sentence part compound.

Diagraming Compound Predicate Words

To diagram compound predicate words, split the predicate word line.

The new coaches are Brock and Rudolph. (compound predicate word)

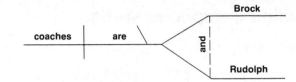

Exercise A: As your teacher directs, show the compound parts in the following sentences. Tell whether they are compound subjects, verbs, objects, or predicate words.

1. The Soviet Union and the United States produce most of the world's coal. compound subject
2. Coal is plentiful and relatively inexpensive. compound predicate word
3. In strip mines, machines remove earth and rock. compound object
4. In other mines, workers and equipment dig coal underground. compound su
5. Miners cut, drill, and blast through the rock. compound verb
6. Cars or belts carry the coal to the surface. compound subject
7. Machines wash and sort the coal at a plant. compound verb
8. Two dangerous problems in mines are ventilation and support. compound predic
9. Gases and dust in coal mines may be explosive. compound subject
10. Safety features are costly but essential. compound predicate word

Exercise B: Writing For each of the sentences, make the part noted in parentheses compound. Write the new sentences. Answers will vary.

> EXAMPLE: The baby scooted across the floor. (*verb*)
> The baby scooted and wriggled across the floor.

1. At the clambake we devoured lobster. (*direct object*)
2. The audience watched carefully. (*verb*)

3. The pie had been eaten. (*subject*)
4. The Coast Guard patrols the lakes. (*direct object*)
5. The alert camera crew ran to the scene of the burning building. (*subject*)
6. Our car sputtered down the driveway. (*verb*)
7. Their creative Halloween costumes were colorful. (*predicate word*)
8. The music told a story about growing up in Harlem. (*subject*)
9. Mr. Boehm showed our class a great movie about stop-action animation. (*indirect object*)
10. The picnickers brought a barbecue grill to the beach. (*direct object*)

Part 10   Basic Sentence Patterns

You have seen that words can be organized into sentences in an endless number of ways. However, most sentences follow certain basic **sentence patterns**. The five patterns that follow are the most common ones.

Study each sentence pattern carefully. Try to think of an example of your own for each pattern.

Pattern One

This is the most basic type of sentence. It has a subject and a verb. The subject is usually a noun or pronoun. In this chart, *N* stands for the noun (or pronoun) in the complete subject. *V* stands for the verb in the complete predicate. Either the noun or the verb can be compound in a Pattern One sentence.

N	V
Fashions	change.
We	worked hard.
The goose and goslings	wandered down the path.
The white cat	yawned and stretched.

Part 10

Objective

To recognize and form sentences using the five basic sentence patterns

Presenting the Lesson

1. Read and discuss pages 411–412. As you discuss each pattern, have students suggest further examples of each. As students suggest sentences, place the words in the appropriate column of a pattern chart such as those in the text.

2. Assign and discuss Exercises A and B on page 412.

Individualizing the Lesson

Less-Advanced Students

Do Exercise A on page 413 orally, placing sentence parts in a chart on the board. For Exercise B, do not have students write sentences to match the patterns in parentheses. Instead, have them write sentences that follow the *same* patterns as the originals.

Advanced Students

Have students reread the explanatory paragraph under the heading **Pattern One.** Have them identify the pattern of each sentence in the paragraph. They should find these patterns in the order they appear here: N LV N, NVN, N LV N, NV, NV, N LV Adj.

Optional Practice

Ask students to identify the patterns for the following sentences. Then have them rewrite the sentence so that it follows a different pattern. Students should identify the patterns of the new sentences, also.

1. Jonas Salk developed the polio vaccine.
2. A volunteer is available.
3. My cousin knitted me a warm sweater.
4. We celebrated after the race.
5. Heavy rain and floods spoiled our vacation.
6. Close the window.

Extending the Lesson

Have students write "Pattern Poems." The lines in each poem should follow one pattern only. Below is an example of an NV poem.

The Race
Legs pound
Arms churn
Faces strain
One wins

Pattern Two

In this pattern, the noun (or pronoun) that follows the verb is a *direct object*.

N	V	N
The manager	opened	the store.
Police	have named	a suspect.
Our coach	helped	us after school.

Pattern Three

Two nouns follow the verb in this pattern. The first is an *indirect object*. The second is a *direct object*.

N	V	N	N
Steve	slipped	me	a note.
Nobody	could give	Pat and Ann	directions.
The mayor	told	reporters	his latest plans.

Pattern Four

The verb in this pattern is a *linking verb* (LV). The noun that follows it is a *predicate noun* (or predicate pronoun).

N	LV	N
The experiment	was	a success.
Nashville	is	the home of country music.
The mysterious caller	is	I.

Pattern Five

Here, a linking verb is followed by a *predicate adjective*.

N	LV	Adj.
The gears	seem	stiff.
Ice hockey	is	rough and fast.
This route to Omaha	should be	direct.

Exercise A: Tell which sentence pattern is the basis of each sentence.

1. Jobs were scarce during the recession. (N LV Adj.)
2. The steelworkers called a strike on Monday. (N V N)
3. Juan Lopez was the star of our show. (N LV N)
4. These salmon from Alaska are fresh. (N LV Adj.)
5. David and Amy work in their dad's store on Saturdays. (N V)
6. Rhoda finally gave Leslie and me a hint. (N V N N)
7. Eric photographed the skyline of San Francisco. (N V N)
8. Greylock is the highest mountain in this area. (N LV N)
9. That request seems unfair. (N LV Adj.)
10. A blizzard hit suddenly, without warning. (N V)

Exercise B: Writing Identify the pattern of each of the following sentences. Then change each sentence to match the pattern indicated in parentheses. You will have to add or change words. Try to make your sentences interesting. Answers will vary.

1. The game ended early. (N LV Adj) N V
2. That dessert looks rich. (N V N) N LV Adj.
3. Meredith delivers pizzas. (N LV N) N V N
4. Ramon sold us his tickets. (N V N) N V N N
5. Beth told Jim her worries. (N LV Adj) N V N N
6. The computers had the answer in less than a minute. (N V N N) N V N
7. Erica studied in the afternoon. (N V N) N V
8. Please give this note to the inspector. (N V N N) N V N
9. The doctor taped Jason's ankle. (N LV N) N V N
10. Dense fog is a hazard. (N V) N LV N

REINFORCEMENT EXERCISES

The Sentence and Its Parts

A. Identify sentences and sentence fragments. Number your paper from 1 to 10. Then tell whether each group of words is a *Sentence* or a *Fragment*. (Use after page 387.)

S 1. Musicians entered the studio
F 2. Whistling in the dark
S 3. Harinder grew up in New Delhi
S 4. Doesn't she have any sense of humor
F 5. Arranged them in alphabetical order
F 6. A jigsaw puzzle with hundreds of pieces
F 7. Sent postcards to her friends
S 8. Don't just follow the crowd
F 9. The top album on the stack
F 10. On the parallel bars

B. Identify kinds of sentences. Decide whether the following sentences are *Declarative, Interrogative, Imperative,* or *Exclamatory*. Write your answer on your paper. Also write what punctuation mark should be used. (Use after page 388.)

1. Show us the pictures from the party. imperative
2. Did you get a haircut? interrogative
3. Yesterday Canada and the United States signed a three-year fishing treaty. declarative
4. How vicious that piranha looks! exclamatory
5. Who won the tournament? interrogative
6. Call your brother to dinner. imperative
7. What does this code mean? interrogative
8. Look out! exclamatory or imperative
9. Send to the Egyptian embassy for more information about the pyramids. imperative
10. Americans spend more than 350 million dollars a year on useless cold remedies. declarative

414

C. Find the complete subjects and complete predicates. Head two columns *Complete Subject* and *Complete Predicate*. Write the proper words from each sentence in the columns. (Use after page 390.)

1. The stunt man|leaped from the horse.
2. Some gardeners|grow plants without soil.
3. The helicopter|hovered over the small field.
4. The downhill skiers|zipped through the course.
5. A large yellow van|pulled into the driveway.
6. Cranberries|grow best in peat bogs.
7. Truckers from all over|gathered at Mel's.
8. Jeffrey|led the scavenger hunt at Bonnie's birthday party.
9. Two debaters from our school|won district trophies.
10. Many celebrities|appear in commercials.

D. Find the verb and its simple subject. Label two columns *Subject* and *Verb*. Write the proper words from each sentence in the columns. (Use after page 393.)

1. Paxton scored the first goal.
2. The nervous actors prepared for the first act of the play.
3. Bright banners in the school colors decorated the homecoming floats.
4. Beth's cousin appeared on TV.
5. Talented students from the drama club make the elaborate sets for our shows.
6. Donna asked for a map of China and Southeast Asia.
7. Few stations in this city play music all night.
8. A local store always sponsors the annual marathon.
9. Most of the music at the outdoor concert was too loud for Jody.
10. Each new student at our school sees a counselor.

E. Find the verb parts. Number your paper from 1 to 10. Write all parts of the verb in each sentence. Then write the simple subject. Watch for unusual kinds of sentences. (Use after page 400.)

1. This bus is seldom late in the morning.
2. The pilot has already radioed the control tower for instructions.

3. There <u>is</u> a special about Antarctic penguins on TV tonight.
4. We <u>drifted</u> on rubber rafts down the Merced River.
5. Here <u>is</u> a secret compartment.
6. On the sidelines <u>stood</u> a man in a chicken costume.
7. We <u>should have reported</u> the incident to one of the officers.
8. Some streets <u>have</u> not <u>been plowed</u> yet.
(You) 9. <u>Layer</u> the lasagna noodles with sauce and cheese.
10. <u>Does</u> Randi <u>write</u> for the school newspaper?

F. Recognize objects. Number your paper from 1 to 10. Label three columns *Verb*, *Indirect Object*, and *Direct Object*. For each sentence, write the words in the proper columns. Not every sentence will have an indirect object. (Use after page 404.)

1. Neil composes songs on his guitar.
2. Linda sewed me a skirt in home economics class.
3. The union finally settled its contract.
4. Every spring the theater department produces a musical.
5. Barry scheduled another appointment with his orthodontist.
6. This Japanese restaurant offers its guests sushi.
7. In the moonlight Elliot saw a strange little creature.
8. Nicholas wrote the editor a letter about the festival.
9. Snoopy told Woodstock a story.
10. The audience gave the singer a standing ovation.

G. Find predicate words and objects. Label four columns *Subject*, *Verb*, *Direct Object*, and *Predicate Word*. When these parts appear in the sentences below, write them in the columns. Remember, no sentence can contain both a direct object *and* a predicate word. (Use after page 408.)

1. The blueberries <u>will be</u> ripe next month.
2. Su Ling <u>tightened</u> the spokes on her bicycle.
3. The history department <u>has added</u> two new courses.
4. These brownies <u>seem</u> very chewy.
5. Tony recently <u>sold</u> his trombone to Lisa.
6. The cathedral in Coventry, England, <u>is</u> a memorial to World War II.

7. Mindy <u>read</u> a newspaper on microfilm. ^{DO}
8. Terry <u>is</u> a volunteer at the hospital. ^{PW}
9. The <u>musicians</u> <u>were playing</u> Dixieland jazz. ^{DO}
10. That wax <u>statue</u> <u>is</u> a perfect likeness of Winston Churchill. ^{PW}

H. Find compound parts in a sentence. Write the compound parts in the following sentences. Tell whether they are compound subjects, verbs, objects, or predicate words. (Use after page 411.)

1. <u>Ted</u> and <u>Janeen</u> are figure-skating partners. compound subjects
2. Roald Dahl has written many <u>novels</u>, <u>plays</u>, and <u>stories</u>. compound objects
3. The pavement <u>buckled</u> and <u>broke</u> in the heat. compound verbs
4. Down jackets look <u>soft</u> and <u>warm</u>. compound predicate words
5. The parachutist <u>waited</u> and then <u>jumped</u>. compound verbs
6. The king cobra <u>spread</u> its hood and <u>hissed</u>. compound verbs
7. This gum is <u>sweet</u> but <u>sugarless</u>. compound predicate words
8. <u>Vicky</u> and her <u>friends</u> threw a farewell party for Roger. compound subjects
9. What main product do <u>Argentina</u> and <u>Uruguay</u> export? compound subjects
10. The rowboat <u>bounced</u> and <u>splashed</u> through the waves. compound verbs

Mixed Review

These exercises provide review of the concepts presented in this Section. Each exercise challenges the students to apply several of the skills they have acquired during previous study. Because the "mixed" feature of these activities makes them more difficult, the teacher may wish to have less-advanced students do them orally or in small groups.

MIXED REVIEW

The Sentence and Its Parts

A. Copy each sentence. Tell whether it is *Declarative, Interrogative, Imperative*, or *Exclamatory*. Then add the correct end mark. Underline the subject once and the verb twice in each sentence. If the subject is *you* understood, write *you* in parentheses.

(You) 1. Please take the dog for a walk after dinner . imperative declarative

2. There were at least fifteen pinball machines at the auction .

3. When will Coach Mendez announce next year's team ? interrogative

4. Karen could have joined the Navy or the Army . declarative

(You) 5. Watch out for that car ! exclamatory or imperative

6. That may have been the best play of the season . declarative

7. Have you ever been in a hot air balloon ? interrogative

8. Here are the parts for Tom's bike . declarative

(You) 9. Come and play *Trivial Pursuit* with us . imperative

10. How long can you hold your breath underwater ? interrogative

11. The first American football game was played in 1869 . declarative

12. The house is on fire ! exclamatory

13. Joan and Gina were there when the hurricane hit . declarative

(You) 14. Tell me the name of one President from Virginia . imperative

15. Native Americans introduced popcorn to the Pilgrims . declarative

16. Who could have predicted that avalanche ? interrogative

B. Draw five columns on your paper. Label them *Subject, Verb, Indirect Object, Direct Object*, and *Predicate Word*. Write the parts of each of the following sentences in the correct column. Some parts may be compound.

1. The concert was a complete sellout. (PW)

2. The coach and the owner had different strategies. (DO)

3. Most critics gave the film bad reviews. (IO) (DO)

4. Bob served his family tacos and enchiladas. (IO) (DO) (DO)

5. We played volleyball and soccer. (DO) (DO)

6. Lynn and Suzanne were close friends. (PW)

7. Is your masterpiece complete? `PW`
8. Tim ordered bacon and eggs. `DO` `DO`
9. We sent Mom and Dad some flowers. `IO` `IO` `DO`
10. There is my missing album!
11. The two cats soon became gentle. `PW`
12. Larry became a cameraman. `PW`
13. Nora's aunt loaned me a calculator. `IO` `DO`
14. I replaced the turntable, the receiver, and the speakers. `DO` `DO` `DO`
15. The Bermuda Triangle is a mysterious area between Florida `PW`
    and Puerto Rico.

C. Identify the pattern of each of the following sentences as *N V*, *N V N*, *N V N N*, *N LV N*, or *N LV Adj*. Then rewrite each sentence to match the pattern shown in parentheses. The meaning of the sentence may change. Answers will vary.

> EXAMPLE: I sent my sister a telegram. (N V N)
> — Pattern is now (N V N N).
> *New Pattern:* I sent a telegram last week.

1. Julio was the class president. (N LV Adj.) N LV N
2. The doctor felt helpless. (N V N) N LV Adj.
3. The winning pitcher flashed a smile. (N V N N) N V N
4. Bands play only original music at this club. (N V) N V N
5. The odd animal was extremely rare. (N LV N) N LV Adj.
6. The ranger looked at the burned campsite. (N LV Adj.) N V
7. Elvis Presley was The King of Rock and Roll. (N LV Adj.) N LV N
8. Jill is a jazz musician. (N V N) N LV N
9. Joe studied architecture. (N V) N V N
10. Marlene remained friendly. (N LV N) N LV Adj.

USING GRAMMAR IN WRITING

The Sentence and Its Parts

A. Imagine that a friend has written you a note. Before you have a chance to read it, however, your dog takes several bites out of it. You have only the piece shown below. Write what you think the note originally said. Use only complete sentences.

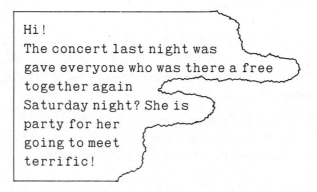

```
Hi!
The concert last night was
gave everyone who was there a free
together again
Saturday night? She is
party for her
going to meet
terrific!
```

B. "Urban belief tales" are a popular form of modern folklore. One well-known urban tale concerns alligators lurking in city sewers. Another tells about a hitchhiker who eerily appears on the road every twenty miles. Write the complete version of one of these tales, as you have heard it, or relate or invent some other similar story. In your narrative use all four kinds of sentences: declarative, imperative, interrogative, and exclamatory. Also try to vary the subject-verb order by using sentences that begin with phrases or other words.

C. Some people say that a dog is a person's best friend. Do you agree, or do you think that dogs are appealing only when they are attached to strong chains? Write a paragraph defending your opinion. Use sentences that include both predicate nouns and predicate adjectives. Also, try to use each of the five basic sentence patterns at least once. Underline the predicate words, and label each sentence according to its pattern type.

Section 2

Writing Complete Sentences

You now have a better understanding of the variety of fascinating ways sentences can be put together to express your thoughts. When sentences are written well, they communicate ideas clearly. If sentences are incorrectly written, however, they can cause confusion and misunderstandings.

Sometimes confusion is caused by leaving out part of a sentence. The remaining group of words is a **sentence fragment**. Another problem is created when two or more sentences are incorrectly written as one. Such a group of words is called a **run-on sentence**.

Both of these writing errors weaken communication. In this section you will learn how to avoid them.

Objective

To recognize and correct sentence fragments

Presenting the Lesson

1. Read and discuss pages 422–423. Remind students that every sentence must contain a subject and a verb. Have students suggest alternate ways to complete the fragments presented in the text.

2. As you discuss **Fragments Due to Incorrect Punctuation,** take extra time with the example about the baby whale. Point out that this is one of the most common types of fragments. It occurs when a descriptive phrase follows a complete sentence. Caution students to be especially conscious of this type of error.

3. Complete and discuss Exercises A and B on pages 423–424.

Individualizing the Lesson

Less-Advanced Students

Walk up to one of your students and say ". . . by tomorrow, okay?" Then, turn and walk back to the front of your class. Once this is done, ask the student what was wrong with your statement. After discussing complete ideas, give your students the following test for sentence fragments: If someone walked up to you and said this group of words, would you feel as though this person had finished the statement?

Advanced Students

Have students duplicate your introductory activity by tape recording

Part 1   What Is a Sentence Fragment?

A group of words that is only part of a sentence is called a **sentence fragment**. A sentence fragment does not express a complete thought.

A fragment is confusing because something is missing from the sentence. Sometimes the subject is left out, and the reader wonders *who* or *what* the sentence is about. At other times the verb is omitted. Then the reader wonders *what happened?* or *what about it?*

FRAGMENT: Shifted into a lower gear. (Who shifted? The subject is missing.)

SENTENCE: The trucker shifted into a lower gear.

FRAGMENT: The quarterback near the ten-yard line. (What happened? The verb is missing.)

SENTENCE: The quarterback fumbled near the ten-yard line.

Sometimes both the subject and verb are missing.

FRAGMENT: In the middle of the lake. (Who or what is in the middle of the lake? What is happening there?)

SENTENCE: A canoe tipped over in the middle of the lake.

Fragments Due to Incomplete Thoughts

When a writer is in a hurry, he or she sometimes jots down only bits of ideas. The writer's pen doesn't keep up with the flow of thoughts.

Often the writer understands these fragments of ideas. However, they will probably seem unclear to a reader because at least part of the subject or the predicate is missing.

Here is an example of a series of fragments:

Went to British Columbia. Canada's Pacific Province. Spectacular mountains! The ocean, too. Hiking and fishing the best.

These complete sentences show what the writer meant:

I went with my parents and brother to British Columbia. It is called Canada's Pacific Province. We saw spectacular mountains! We spent time along the ocean, too. For me, hiking and fishing were the best parts of our trip.

Fragments Due to Incorrect Punctuation

All sentences end with punctuation marks. The mark may be a period, a question mark, or an exclamation point. Sometimes a writer uses one of these punctuation marks too soon. Because the idea is incomplete, a sentence fragment results.

FRAGMENT: Cars with brake problems. Were recalled by the manufacturer.
SENTENCE: Cars with brake problems were recalled by the manufacturer.

FRAGMENT: Are you going? To the State Fair?
SENTENCE: Are you going to the State Fair?

FRAGMENT: A diver freed a baby whale. From a fishing net.
SENTENCE: A diver freed a baby whale from a fishing net.

Exercise A: For each group of words that is a sentence, write *S* on your paper. For each sentence fragment, write *F*. Then add words to change the fragments into sentences. Sentences will vary

S   1. A new series will begin this season
F   2. A TV show about police work
F   3. Will be seen on Monday evenings at 7 P.M.
F   4. Several young actors
S   5. The director offers advice
F   6. Scenery, props, and sound effects
F   7. In each episode a chase scene
S   8. A stunt person jumps from a building
S   9. Each scene is filmed several times
F 10. Usually ends with an arrest

a five-minute group discussion. Then, have them transcribe the discussion verbatim, noting the common occurrence of sentence fragments in speech. Ask them to rewrite each fragment as a complete sentence.

Reinforcement Exercise

Assign and discuss Exercise A on page 426.

Optional Practice

Prepare a worksheet of very long sentence fragments that include prepositional phrases. Point out to students that some fragments sometimes look like sentences because of their length. Then, have students complete each fragment and identify the reason that each one is incomplete (missing a subject or a verb **or** expressing an incomplete idea).

Extending the Lesson

Point out to students that writers of dialogue in novels, short stories, plays, and films often use sentence fragments to create the illusion of real speech. Have students compile a list of fragments from a dialogue excerpt in a novel or short story they are reading. Then, have them write their own short dialogues, underlining each sentence fragment used.

To recognize and correct run-on
sentences

Presenting the Lesson

1. Read and discuss pages 424–
425. Explain that, when people are
excited, they tend to speak quickly
and to run their words and sentences together. Point out that
something similar happens when
people write ideas down in a hurry:
separate ideas are sometimes run
together.

Emphasize that the key problem
in run-on sentences is one of punctuation. When the proper punctuation is missing, the reader lacks the
necessary guides for making sense
of the writer's idea.

2. Complete and discuss Exercises A and B on page 425.

Exercise B: Writing Identify the fragments in the following paragraph. Rewrite the paragraph, changing all fragments to sentences.
Sentences will vary.

We usually think of mazes as no more than amusing puzzles
Found in magazines or amusement parks. In the past, however, mazes were considered an art form. Also a means of protection or imprisonment. Palaces in Greece and Egypt were
designed as mazes. Protected the royal families. In Greek legend, a maze was built to house a horrible monster. The Min-
otaur. This maze was called the Labyrinth. In the 1700's, formal
gardens were designed to include hedge mazes. Very intricate.
The walls of these mazes are tall. Thick bushes. A person who
wandered in could become lost for hours. With no idea how to
get out.

Part 2 What Is a Run-on Sentence?

A **run-on sentence** is two or more sentences written incorrectly
as one.

A run-on confuses the reader because it does not show where
the first idea ends and the second one begins. The reader needs
a period or other end punctuation mark to signal the end of each
complete thought. Here are some examples:

RUN-ON: A motorcycle turned into the alley it skidded on the
gravel.

CORRECT: A motorcycle turned into the alley. It skidded on the
gravel.

RUN-ON: Tom likes country and western music does Carla like
New Wave?

CORRECT: Tom likes country and western music. Does Carla
like New Wave?

Sometimes writers make the mistake of using a comma instead
of a period. Again, the result is a run-on. Look at the examples
on the next page.

RUN-ON: The rookie running back carried the ball, he made a touchdown.

CORRECT: The rookie running back carried the ball. He made a touchdown.

RUN-ON: The floats were ready, the parade could begin.

CORRECT: The floats were ready. The parade could begin.

Exercise A: Correct the following run-on sentences.

1. Some radio stations have powerful signals/they can be heard in nearby states.
2. One disc jockey reads letters, he also jokes with callers.
3. Several stations hold contests/prizes are often albums.
4. Tanya won one contest/she named a song correctly.
5. The sound system is complex/few people could operate it.
6. The Reds won the pennant/they will play in the World Series.
7. Last summer we camped/it was the best vacation ever.
8. Tony has a set of barbells/he lifts weights every day.
9. We saw an old Hitchcock film/it was a classic thriller.
10. A raccoon visits our back porch every evening/we call him The Lone Ranger.

Exercise B: Writing Identify the run-on sentences in the following paragraph. Rewrite the paragraph correctly.

Glass is a common, inexpensive material that we take for granted. Yet long ago it was so rare and costly that it was used with gold and semi-precious stones in jewelry. Only wealthy women of ancient Egypt stored cosmetics and ointments in glass bottles. For centuries glass was used chiefly for ornaments, vases, mosaics, and tableware/some glass was used to make stained-glass church windows and to let light into houses. Glass was used for these relatively few purposes until the twelfth or thirteenth century. Even then glass was for the wealthy. When people moved, they took their valuable glass windows with them/they even handed them down to their children as heirlooms. In England a special luxury tax was imposed on owners of houses with more than ten windows.

425

Individualizing the Lesson

Less-Advanced Students

Have students work on the exercises in pairs, reading the sentences aloud to one another to test whether these express more than one idea.

Advanced Students

Discuss alternate ways of correcting run-ons. Use the following examples to show that run-ons need not always be broken into two separate parts.

Run-on: My uncle plays professional baseball he is not a well-known player.
Correct: My uncle plays professional baseball, but he is not a well-known player.

Run-on: We got new tires I never realized how bad the olds ones were.
Correct: Until we got new tires, I never realized how bad the old ones were.

Reinforcement Exercise

Assign and discuss Exercise B on page 426.

Optional Practice

Copy a paragraph from the students' literature text, removing all end punctuation. Have the students add punctuation.

Extending the Lesson

Have students do free association writings by giving them a topic and asking them to put on the paper whatever comes into their heads without pausing to reflect or to punctuate correctly. Give them a short time limit for filling an entire page. Then, have them go back over the paper, finding and correcting fragments and run-ons.

Reinforcement Exercises

These Reinforcement Exercises may be used for additional practice of the concepts presented in this Section. Each exercise focuses on a single concept, and should be used after the page number indicated in parentheses.

Review

If you have not assigned these Reinforcement Exercises before this time, you can also use them as an excellent Section Review.

REINFORCEMENT EXERCISES
Writing Complete Sentences

A. Recognize sentences and sentence fragments. Tell whether each group of words is a *Sentence* or a *Fragment*. Then add words to make each fragment into a complete sentence. Sentences will vary.
(Use after page 424.)

F 1. In our neighborhood
F 2. A nationally known cartoonist
F 3. Scampered up the oak tree in the front yard
F 4. The horoscope in the daily paper
S 5. A subway train sped past
S 6. The overturned truck blocked traffic
F 7. The inventor of the telephone
S 8. The totem pole was gray and weathered
S 9. Experience is a hard teacher
F 10. Draws with charcoal or ink

B. Recognize sentences and run-on sentences. For each group of words that is a sentence, write *S*. For each run-on sentence, write *R*. Then rewrite each run-on sentence correctly. (Use after page 425.)

R 1. Ray was a back-up singer. Now he sings lead.
R 2. Tony tried to skate backwards, he ended up with a badly sprained arm.
R 3. Burnett noticed the leaves of the bush, he realized it was a man-eating plant.
S 4. The peacock's tail feathers were iridescent in the early morning sunlight.
S 5. The German neighborhood celebrated Oktoberfest.
R 6. Larry was trained as a carpenter. He learned quickly.
R 7. A pipe burst. Water flooded the basement.
R 8. Eskimos prefer to be called *Inuit*, it means *native people*.
R 9. The school sponsors adult classes, many people attend.
S 10. Many of our impressions of the Civil War come from photographs by Mathew Brady.

426

MIXED REVIEW
Writing Complete Sentences

A. The following paragraphs contain both fragments and run-on sentences. Rewrite the paragraphs and correct these errors. Be sure to use proper capitalization and punctuation.

You may be familiar with Scotland Yard. From watching British mystery movies. However, it isn't in Scotland and it isn't a yard, it is a nickname. For the Metropolitan Police Force of London.

Scotland Yard got its name from a short street in London. This street was the site of a palace where visiting Scottish kings stayed. Between the 900's and the 1100's. In 1829, it became London's police center. In 1890, the Metropolitan Police moved into offices on the Thames Embankment, these offices were named New Scotland Yard. They retain this name to this day.

The force is now made up of beat policemen. And detectives. These detectives are part of the Criminal Investigation Department. That started with only eight officers. Part of their job was investigating the criminal underworld, it was very dangerous work. Today the department consists of hundreds of detectives, it is one of the most successful in the world. At solving crimes.

B. Use the following phrases to write a short paragraph. Avoid any sentence fragments or run-on sentences.

1. Pluto, planet ninth in distance from the sun
2. Discovered in 1930 by Clyde W. Tombaugh
3. Revolves around the sun once in about 248 years
4. Rotates every 6.4 earth days
5. Thought by some astronomers to have once been a satellite of Neptune.

USING GRAMMAR IN WRITING
Writing Complete Sentences

A. Write a twelve-month horoscope for one of the astrological signs by choosing adjectives, nouns, and verbs from the columns below. For example, the horoscope for one month might read: "Aquarius: A new relationship will bring unexpected information. Determination will bring about a valuable change." Use only complete sentences.

ADJECTIVES	NOUNS	VERBS
new	goal	gain
social	change	emphasize
creative	communications	increase
unexpected	vacation	focus
special	romance	win
valuable	sports	express
personal	response	attempt
probable	home	restore
immediate	environment	play
important	appearance	bring
sudden	information	select
foreign	problems	request
necessary	future	improve
reliable	popularity	detect
long-term	friend	realize
unusual	action	stress
secret	demands	share
financial	plans	expect
attractive	relationship	discuss
romantic	diet	join
favorable	opportunity	discover

B. Advertisers often use sentence fragments and run-ons to catch the attention of their readers. Find at least two examples of such ads in magazines or newspapers. Rewrite each one correctly.

Section 3

Using Nouns

Good, clear sentences are not accidents. They result from an understanding of how words work together.

The words used in sentences fall into certain classes, called the **parts of speech**. There are eight parts of speech:

nouns	verbs	adverbs	conjunctions
pronouns	adjectives	prepositions	interjections

You can speak and write without knowing these labels. However, skilled writers and speakers understand the different classes of words and the functions of each one.

In the next six Sections you will gain a greater understanding of the parts of speech. The first part of speech you will study is one of the most important: nouns.

To identify common nouns and proper nouns

Presenting the Lesson

1. Read and discuss pages 430–431. Make four columns on the chalkboard. Label these *people, places, things,* and *ideas.* Then, have students suggest nouns to put in each column. Ask students to explain why some nouns are capitalized and some are not.

2. Assign and discuss the Exercise on page 430. Students may overlook more abstract nouns, such as *popularity* and *idea.* Be sure that they understand why these are nouns.

3. Complete and discuss Exercises A and B on page 431. Have students put examples of their work for Exercise B on the chalkboard.

Individualizing the Lesson

Less-Advanced Students

1. Point out the following simple test for nouns: If *a, an,* or *the* can be placed before the word, it is a noun. (Note, however, that some proper nouns will not work with articles: the George Sanchez, for example.)

2. For each of the following common nouns, have students list three proper nouns.

1. athlete
2. river
3. newspaper
4. school
5. book

3. Encourage students to use a dictionary if they have questions about capitalization.

Part 1　What Are Nouns?

We use words to name the people, places, and things around us. We also have names for ideas, beliefs, and feelings — things we cannot see. Words that name are called **nouns**.

A noun is a word used to name a person, place, thing, or idea.

PERSONS:	landlord, Greg, Anne Murray, baby
PLACES:	kitchen, Savannah, hotel, West Virginia
THINGS:	blanket, mirror, lightning, *Challenger*
IDEAS:	freedom, joy, sincerity, democracy

Exercise: Make three columns on a sheet of paper. Label them *Names of Persons, Names of Places, Names of Things and Ideas.* Find the nouns in the following paragraph. List each one in the proper column.

Frisbees have been part of our recreation for over thirty years. The first Frisbees were plates made of tin that were tossed back and forth by workers at the Frisbee Baking Company in Connecticut. This game inspired one of the players with an idea. Soon, discs called Frisbees were being manufactured. Their popularity with both children and adults grew very quickly. The game has now become a competitive sport, with an international championship determined each year in Pasadena.

Proper Nouns and Common Nouns

How do these two italicized nouns differ?

One *sailor, George Ruiz,* jumped from the ship.

The word *sailor* is a general term that may refer to many people. This type of noun is called a **common noun**. A common noun is a general name.

The noun *George Ruiz,* on the other hand, refers to only one person. This type of noun is called a **proper noun**. A proper noun is a specific name.

A common noun is the name of a whole group of persons, places, things, or ideas.

A proper noun is the name of a particular person, place, thing, or idea.

Look at the following examples of common nouns and proper nouns. As you can see, some nouns are made up of more than one word. Note that proper nouns are always capitalized.

COMMON NOUNS	PROPER NOUNS
magazine	*Sports Illustrated*
mountain	Mount Everest
cartoonist	Jim Davis
game	Super Bowl
city	Burlington
mayor	Mayor Anderson
religion	Buddhism
author	Mark Twain

Exercise A: Make two columns on your paper. Label one column *Common Nouns* and the other *Proper Nouns*. Place each of the following nouns in the correct column. Capitalize all proper nouns.

1. holiday inn, motel, seabreeze motel, shores hotel
2. restaurant, diner, golden bear, cafeteria
3. singer, lou rawls, album, willie nelson, ballad
4. allentown, village, asheville, town, honolulu
5. court, judge, judge ellen rodriguez, jury
6. nation, new zealand, spain, country, canada
7. airlines, trans world airlines, airport, quantas airlines
8. los angeles county hospital, clinic, sheridan dental clinic
9. first national bank, bank, banker, mr. james black, continental bank
10. team, dallas cowboys, manager, cheerleader

Exercise B: Writing Write five sentences of your own, using at least one proper noun in each sentence. Then underline every noun in each sentence.

Have students choose one noun expressing an idea, one expressing a belief, and one expressing a feeling. Then, have them choose concrete nouns that they associate with these abstract nouns. Example: DEMOCRACY—flag, voting booth, Thomas Jefferson, Congress. At least one word in each list should be a proper noun.

Reinforcement Exercises

Assign and discuss Exercises A and B on page 438.

Optional Practice

Have students turn to a page in a textbook. Then, have them list at least ten of the common nouns and all of the proper nouns on the page.

Extending the Lesson

Give students an ancient fable, myth, or fairytale, with spaces provided in place of nouns. Have them insert nouns to complete the story. Ask students to update the story by inserting names for contemporary people, places, things, and ideas.

Objective

To understand the various functions of nouns in sentences

Presenting the Lesson

1. Read and discuss pages 432-433. Write the following sentences on the board. The same noun is used as a different part of speech in each sentence. Ask students to describe the relationship between this noun and the verb in each sentence.

The *actor* had a double for the dangerous scenes. (subject)

One fan asked the *actor* for his autograph. (direct object)

A speech coach gave the *actor* some help with his accent. (indirect object)

Harrison Ford is a popular *actor*. (predicate word)

2. Review the basic sentence patterns. Write these patterns on the board. Then, have students make up sentences corresponding to these patterns. After this is done, ask students to identify the functions of the nouns in these sentences.

Complete and discuss Exercises A, B, and C on pages 432–433.

Individualizing the Lesson

Less-Advanced Students

Break the process of discovering the function of a noun into steps. Have students begin by finding the verb and identifying it as an action verb or a state-of-being verb. Then, have students eliminate possible functions by checking the position of the noun before or after the verb.

Nouns can perform many different functions in a sentence. A noun may act as a subject, direct object, indirect object, or predicate word. Study the following examples:

Scientists can predict earthquakes. (The noun *scientists* is the subject of the verb *can predict*.)

The magician amazed the *audience*. (The noun *audience* is the direct object. It receives the action of the verb *amazed*.)

The coach showed the *quarterback* a new play. (The noun quarterback is the indirect object. It tells *to whom* about the verb *showed*.)

Gary became a carpenter's *assistant*. (The noun *assistant* is a predicate noun. It follows the linking verb *became*.)

Remember that any part of a sentence may be compound.

Exercise A: Tell whether the italicized noun in each sentence is functioning as a subject, direct object, indirect object, or predicate word.

1. A chemical *factory* dumps wastes into this river.
2. The shilling is a British *coin*.
3. The Prime Minister solemnly addressed *Parliament*.
4. Our catcher flashed the *pitcher* a secret signal.
5. The first contestant in the rodeo competition roped her *steer* in under thirty seconds.
6. Were Laurel and Hardy *actors* in silent films, too?
7. That *legend* has been told for centuries.
8. Into the hollow log slipped the frightened *fox*.
9. Dad and I made *pickles* from cucumbers.
10. The bored waiter handed each *diner* a menu.

Exercise B: Make four columns on your paper. Label them subject, indirect object, direct object, and predicate word. Write each of the nouns in the following sentences in the correct column.

1. The Olympic marathon covers twenty-six miles.
2. Police read the sullen suspect his rights.

3. The great "Satchmo" was Louis Armstrong. [S on Satchmo, PW on Armstrong]

4. Even small businesses can use computers. [S on businesses, DO on computers]

5. Did all three movies feature Mark Hamill, Carrie Fisher, and Harrison Ford? [S on movies, DO on Hamill, DO on Fisher, DO on Ford]

6. The old fisherman showed Ricardo his handmade nets and hooks. [S on fisherman, IO on Ricardo, DO on nets, DO on hooks]

7. The Steelers are tough defensive players. [S on Steelers, PW on players]

8. The persistent interviewer asked the President a complex question. [S on interviewer, IO on President, DO on question]

9. Leonardo da Vinci was both a scientist and an artist. [PW on scientist, PW on artist]

10. Television reporters and photographers recorded the devastating flood. [S on reporters, S on photographers, DO on flood]

Exercise C: Writing Complete each sentence by adding nouns. Make the sentences as interesting as possible. Then tell whether you have used your noun as a subject, indirect object, direct object, or predicate word. [S, IO, DO, PW labels in instructions]

1. ___S___ emerged slowly from the spacecraft.

2. King Kong knocked the ___DO___ and ___DO___ from the sky.

3. The animal trainer gave her ___IO___ a ___DO___ .

4. ___S___ and ___S___ are fascinating ___PW___ .

5. That house has a ___DO___ in the basement.

6. Many dancers are also excellent ___PW___ .

7. ___S___ tape-recorded the ___DO___ .

8. The wealthy woman left her ___IO___ only an old ___DO___ .

9. In the tree sat a ___S___ .

10. The ___S___ wore a ___DO___ on its head.

Part 3   The Plurals of Nouns

When a noun names one thing, it is singular. When a noun names more than one thing, it is plural.

Here are some rules for forming the plurals of nouns.

1. To form the plural of most nouns, just add -s:

prizes   dreams   circles   stations

433

Advanced Students

Challenge students to write a story using the following nouns in the ways indicated.

house (subject)
creature (subject)
machine (direct object)
hand (direct object)
family (indirect object)
reporter (predicate noun)
visitor (predicate noun)

Reinforcement Exercise

Assign and discuss Exercise C on page 439.

Optional Practice

Create a scrambled sentence worksheet. For each exercise item, provide a verb and one or more nouns, along with a description of the function of each noun. Have students combine these elements to produce sentences, as follows: *is + president* (predicate word) + *Randall* (subject) = *Randall is president.*

Extending the Lesson

Ask students to find sentences containing direct objects, indirect objects, and predicate words in a newspaper article.

Part 3

Objective

To understand how to form and use plural nouns

Presenting the Lesson

1. Read and discuss pages 433–435. Provide additional examples for each rule. When discussing the last rule, include examples of the plurals of hypenated nouns, such as *brothers-in-law*.

2. Make certain that students understand where the plural form would be located in a dictionary entry. Point out that often only the ending of the plural form is shown. Encourage students to use the dictionary if they are not sure of the spelling of any plural form.

3. Complete and discuss Exercises A and B on page 435.

Individualizing the Lesson

Less-Advanced Students

1. Have students prepare a set of flash cards with singular forms on one side and the corresponding plurals on the other side. Have students drill one another using these cards.

2. Give students a list of singular forms and have them look up the corresponding plurals in a dictionary.

Advanced Students

Have students play a quiz game in which they try to stump one another by giving singular forms that have to be made plural. Encourage them to find words that form plurals in unusual ways (hyphenated words, compound words, final *f* words, words from Greek and Latin).

Reinforcement Exercise

Assign and discuss Exercise D on page 439.

Optional Practice

Have students copy the following sentences, using the plural forms of the nouns in parentheses.

2. When the singular noun ends in *s*, *sh*, *ch*, *x*, or *z*, add -es:

waitresses   brushes   ditches   axes   buzzes

3. When the singular noun ends in *o*, add -s:

solos   halos   studios   photos   pianos

For a few words ending in *o*, add -*es:*

heroes   tomatoes   potatoes   echoes   cargoes

4. When a singular noun ends in *y* with a consonant before it, change the *y* to *i* and add -es:

army—armies   candy—candies   baby—babies

When a vowel (*a, e, i, o, u*) comes before the *y*, do not change the *y* to *i*. Just add -*s*:

boy—boys   way—ways   jockey—jockeys

5. For some nouns ending in *f*, add -s to make the plural:

roofs   chiefs   reefs   beliefs

For many nouns ending in *f* or *fe*, change the *f* to *v* and add -*s* or -*es*. Since there is no rule to follow, you will have to memorize such words. Here are some examples:

life—lives   calf—calves   knife—knives
thief—thieves   shelf—shelves   loaf—loaves

6. Some nouns have the same form for both singular and plural. They must be memorized.

deer   sheep   moose   salmon   trout

7. Some nouns form their plurals in special ways. They, too, must be memorized.

man—men   tooth—teeth   ox—oxen
woman—women   mouse—mice   foot—feet
goose—geese   child—children   louse—lice

Dictionaries show the plural of a word if it is formed in an unusual way. Here is a dictionary entry for the noun *duty*. The entry shows the plural, *duties*.

du·ty (dōōt′ē, dyōōt′ē) **n.,** *pl.* **-ties** [< Anglo-Fr. *dueté*, what is due: see DUE & -TY¹] **1.** obedience or respect that is due to parents, older people, etc. **2.** something that one ought to do because it is thought to be morally right or necessary *[the duty of a citizen to vote]* **3.** any action required by one's occupation or position *[her duties include writing the reports]* **4.** a sense of obligation *[duty calls]* **5.** service, esp. military service **6.** a payment due to the government, esp. a tax on imports, exports, etc. **7.** service or use: see HEAVY-DUTY — **on** (or **off**) **duty** at (or having time off from) one's work or duty

Use the dictionary if you have a question about plurals.

Exercise A: Number your paper from 1 to 20. Write the plural form of each of these nouns. Then use your dictionary to see if you have formed the plural correctly.

1. leaf leaves
2. year years
3. deer deer
4. holiday holidays
5. coach coaches
6. sky skies
7. knife knives
8. tooth teeth
9. radio radios
10. fox foxes
11. echo echoes
12. tomato tomatoes
13. bunch bunches
14. window windows
15. moose moose
16. spy spies
17. goose geese
18. hoof hooves
19. wish wishes
20. copy copies

Exercise B: Write each sentence. Correct any errors in plural forms of nouns.

1. The <u>childs</u> were told not to play ball in the alleys or ride their bikes in the street. children
2. The donkeys carried <u>pouchs</u> of gold. pouches
3. Several <u>tooths</u> from sharks were found on the <u>beachs</u> near the hotel. teeth, beaches
4. These forks and <u>knifes</u> are scratched. knives
5. Basketball hoops are ten <u>foots</u> from the floor. feet
6. Both armies crawled forward by <u>inchs.</u> inches
7. The <u>sheeps</u> and <u>calfs</u> are kept in separate <u>halfs</u> of the pasture. sheep, calves, halves
8. There are many types of <u>passs</u> and shots in the game. passes
9. Red tile <u>rooves</u> are common in the small towns and villages of southern Italy. roofs
10. Terry Fox is one of my <u>heros.</u> heroes

1. The (brush) at the carwash scratched our car.
2. Julia ate three (sandwich).
3. The (alto) and the (soprano) sang together.
4. Wash the (potato) and the (tomato) before slicing them.
5. Many of our (hero) are television and movie stars.
6. In the forest we saw (deer), but (moose) are rarely seen in this area.
7. Three (lady) bought the antique (piano) for the museum.
8. The (waitress) brought steak (knife) to the customers.
9. Dad got three (handkerchief) for Christmas.
10. The (shelf) with the (child) toys on them are loose.

Extending the Lesson

Have students write a short news report describing a grocery store that has been struck by a tornado. Instruct them to use plurals to describe the contents of the store.

435

To understand how to form and use possessive nouns

Presenting the Lesson

1. Read and discuss page 436. Discuss the meaning of the words *possession* and *ownership.* Point out that both spelling and punctuation are involved in the formation of possessive nouns. Have students provide additional examples for each of the three rules given.

2. Students should understand that in order to form a plural possessive, a noun must first be made plural and then possessive.

3. Complete and discuss Exercises A, B, and C on pages 436–437. Have students place answers on the chalkboard so that all may see the correct spelling and punctuation for each word.

4. Assign Exercise D. You may wish to have students select their favorite items to "donate" to a huge class rumamge sale. Ask each student to write his or her donations on the board. Check for misspellings.

Less-Advanced Students

Have students divide their papers into four columns, labeled *Singular, Plural, Singular Possessive,* and *Plural Possessive.* Students should copy the following nouns in the column labeled *Singular* and then fill in the other three columns for each word.

1. officer 6. girl
2. city 7. child
3. day 8. monkey
4. citizen 9. baby
5. lady 10. dancer

Part 4 The Possessives of Nouns

Nouns can indicate possession or ownership.

Mr. Lowe's car   a farmer's land   the lion's roar

Nouns can show that something is part of a person.

Meg's sense of humor   Harold's concern

Ownership is indicated by adding *'s* to a noun. Words like *farmer's, Meg's,* and *Harold's* are called **possessive nouns**.

Usually, only people and animals are considered able to possess items or qualities. Sometimes, however, things can also show possession. We speak of a *week's wages,* a *day's work,* or a *city's growth.*

Forming Possessives

There are three rules for forming the possessive of nouns.

1. If a noun is singular, add an apostrophe (') and s.

Amanda—Amanda's arm
Ross—Ross's desk

2. If a noun is plural and ends in s, add just the apostrophe.

artists—artists' studios   Spencers—Spencers' home

3. If a noun is plural but does not end in s, add an apostrophe and s.

women—women's discussion   people—people's choice

Exercise A: Write the possessive form of each of these singular nouns.

1. mayor's	6. ranch's	11. car's	16. admiral's
2. Meg's	7. child's	12. Charles's	17. Jenny's
3. country's	8. player's	13. runner's	18. salesperson's
4. senator's	9. Penny's	14. store's	19. boss's
5. today's	10. host's	15. secretary's	20. Linda's

Exercise B: Write the possessive form of each of these plural nouns.

1. people's	6. guests	11. mice's	16. families'
2. fans'	7. friends'	12. wives'	17. men's
3. brothers'	8. women's	13. workers'	18. clerks'
4. hours'	9. doctors'	14. sheep's	19. islands'
5. experts'	10. teachers'	15. Jacksons'	20. bodies'

Exercise C: Write the possessive form for each italicized word.

1. The *Bears* lineup looks strong. Bears'
2. *Jerry* car needs new shock absorbers. Jerry's
3. *Tuesday* game pits the Steelers against the Cowboys. Tuesday's
4. The *voters* choice is Ms. Marie Tonelli. voters'
5. Reynolds beat the other *racers* times. racers'
6. *Louis* favorite class is computer science. Louis's
7. The assistant *state* attorney met with the reporters. state's
8. The *children* zoo has baby animals. children's
9. A doctor measured the *astronauts* pulses. astronauts'
10. *Donna* neighborhood has a big barbecue every Fourth of July. Donna's

Exercise D: Writing List ten unusual items that might be collected for a rummage sale. Tell who donated each item by using the possessive form. Five items were donated by single individuals; five were given by groups of people. For example: Cecily's sequined ski boots, the babies' buggy bumpers.

Reinforcement Exercises

These Reinforcement Exercises may be used for additional practice of the concepts presented in this Section. Each exercise focuses on a single concept, and should be used after the page number indicated in parentheses.

Review

If you have not assigned these Reinforcement Exercises before this time, you can also use them as an excellent Section Review.

REINFORCEMENT EXERCISES
Using Nouns

A. Distinguish common and proper nouns. Head two columns *Common Nouns* and *Proper Nouns*. Place each noun in the proper column. Capitalize the proper nouns. (Use after page 431.)

> You don't have to visit antarctica to stroll past penguins and observe the icy blasts of winter. Instead you can go to sea world in san diego, california. On may 28, 1983, the popular park opened a new exhibit. Named penguin encounter by its proud creators, the display re-creates the frigid habitat of the comical birds. A separate exhibit features a tropical species of penguin—the humboldt—and other birds from the coasts of chile and peru. Travelers unable to join an expedition to south america or the antarctic will be delighted by this marvelous new world on the coast of the pacific ocean.

B. Find common and proper nouns. List the nouns in each of the following sentences. Be sure to capitalize each proper noun. Remember that proper nouns may contain more than one word. (Use after page 431.)

1. A strong wind blew the lamppost to the ground.
2. A ferry takes passengers to nantucket.
3. Charlene brought sandwiches and chips.
4. We ate lunch by the fountain at the metropolitan museum of art.
5. On tuesday our class visited the lincoln memorial and the washington monument.
6. The hurricane tore through cuba and haiti.
7. After we toured lake michigan, our ship docked in milwaukee.
8. Mr. rodriguez identified the thief from a photograph.
9. Our pet rabbit, named bugs, surprised us with a litter of five babies.
10. The firefighters and police went on strike last august.

C. Recognize nouns used in sentences. Decide how each italicized noun is used in these sentences. Write the word and label it *Subject*, *Direct Object*, *Indirect Object*, or *Predicate Noun*.

(Use after page 433.)

1. My first *attempt* at water skiing was a joke. subject
2. Indians inhabited *New Mexico* thousands of years before the Europeans. direct object
3. The difficult climb was a *challenge* to even the experienced campers. predicate noun
4. The challenge of climbing Mount McKinley captured Tom's *imagination*. direct object
5. Did Erin give *Elliot* my message? indirect object
6. Which artist painted *Starry Night*? direct object
7. The end of the movie was a *surprise*. predicate noun
8. Jessica showed *Kate* the shortcut. indirect object
9. The president assigned each *person* on the committee a task. indirect object
10. The *Pope* gave his annual Christmas greeting from the Vatican. subject

D. Form singular and plural nouns. Rewrite the following sentences, changing every singular noun to a plural noun and every plural noun to singular. (Use after page 435.)

1. The woman carried the box and package onto the bus. women, boxes, packages, buses
2. The athletes placed the trophies on the shelves of the display cases. athlete, trophy, shelf, case
3. The child loved the ox, the moose, the sheep, and the fox in the petting zoo. children, oxen, moose, sheep, foxes, zoos
4. The spies and thieves dreaded the arrival of the hero. spy, thief, arrivals, heroes
5. The man repaired the pier at the beach. men, piers, beaches
6. The cowboy crossed the county to reach the rodeo. cowboys, counties, rodeos
7. Will the waitress serve the potato with our steak? waitresses, potatoes, steaks
8. The clown smashed the old piano with the ax. clowns, pianos, axes
9. The chefs carefully placed the glazed strawberries on the pastries. chef, strawberry, pastry
10. The echo bounced off the side of the mountain and resounded through the valley. echoes, sides, mountains, valleys

E. Form the possessives of nouns. Write the possessive form for each italicized noun. (Use after page 437.)

1. *Nicholas* shirt doesn't match his pants. Nicholas's
2. *Jenny* family left for Cape Cod. Jenny's
3. Someone misplaced the *painters* ladder. painters'
4. Sarah carried *Josh* backpack after he twisted his ankle. Josh's
5. The emcee asked for the *contestant* answer. contestant's
6. *James* heroic act made the headlines. James's
7. The *Student Council* funds come from special projects. Student Council's
8. The *Johnsons* dog is a collie. Johnsons'
9. We saw slides of *Ms. Marsh* trip to the Galapagos Islands. Ms. Marsh's
10. The *children* theater produced a lively musical. children's
11. We heard the *gulls* cries as they whirled above us. gulls'
12. Socrates questioned his *students* answers. students'
13. *Men* clothing styles don't change much. Men's
14. The newspapers printed the *President* speech. President's
15. My *dad boss* house overlooks the lake. dad's, boss's

MIXED REVIEW
Using Nouns

A. Make four columns on your paper and label them *Singular Noun, Plural Noun, Singular Possessive*, and *Plural Possessive*. Next write each of the twenty-five nouns below in the correct column. Then complete the chart by writing the other forms of the noun in their proper columns. Answers in margin.

EXAMPLE:

Sing. Noun	Pl. Noun	Sing. Poss.	Pl. Poss.
hero	heroes	hero's	heroes'

1. boxes
2. city's
3. pianos'
4. bouquet
5. fish's
6. groups
7. fact
8. women's
9. flies
10. valleys
11. instructor's
12. deer
13. lioness
14. tomatoes
15. tax's
16. stereo
17. software
18. angles
19. masses
20. athlete
21. workmen
22. thieves
23. fox's
24. child
25. sea

B. Number your paper from 1 to 15. Tell whether the italicized nouns in the following paragraph are used as *Subjects, Direct Objects, Indirect Objects*, or *Predicate Nouns*. Then make a list of all of the other nouns in the paragraph. Remember to capitalize any proper nouns you find.

> The last *concert* at poplar stadium was the most popular musical *event* of the summer. There was a terrific *performance* by stevie wonder. I invited *nina*, my cousin, to come from washington. She is a devoted *fan* of stevie. My *brother* is a *promoter* for the stadium. He got our *tickets*. He also gave *nina money* for a souvenir. We packed a picnic *dinner*, took the *bus* to the stadium, gave the *usher* our *tickets*, and enjoyed a great *evening*!

other nouns: Poplar Stadium, summer, Stevie Wonder, I, cousin, Washington, She, Stevie, stadium, He, He, souvenir, We, stadium

441

Mixed Review

These exercises provide review of the concepts presented in this Section. Each exercise challenges the students to apply several of the skills they have acquired during previous study. Because the "mixed" feature of these activities makes them more difficult, the teacher may wish to have less-advanced students do them orally or in small groups.

Exercise A

1. box, boxes, box's, boxes'
2. city, cities, city's, cities'
3. piano, pianos, piano's, pianos'
4. bouquet, bouquets, bouquet's, bouquets'
5. fish, fishes, fish's, fishes'
6. group, groups, group's, groups'
7. fact, facts, fact's, facts'
8. woman, women, woman's, women's
9. fly, flies, fly's, flies'
10. valley, valleys, valley's, valleys'
11. instructor, instructors, instructor's, instructors'
12. deer, deer, deer's, deer's
13. lioness, lionesses, lioness's, lionesses'
14. tomato, tomatoes, tomato's, tomatoes'
15. tax, taxes, tax's, taxes'
16. stereo, stereos, stereo's, stereos'
17. software, software, software's, software's

18. angle, angles, angle's, angles'
19. mass, masses, mass's, masses'
20. athlete, athletes, athlete's, athletes'
21. workman, workmen, workman's, workmen's
22. thief, thieves, thief's, thieves'
23. fox, foxes, fox's, foxes'
24. child, children, child's, children's
25. sea, seas, sea's, seas'

C. Find the nouns in the following sentences. Then make two columns labeled *Common Nouns* and *Proper Nouns*. Write each of the nouns from the following sentences in the correct column. Capitalize each proper noun. Remember that proper nouns often contain more than one word.

1. Her sister barbara drove the children to michigan.
2. Our family went to canada for christmas.
3. The most popular program on sunday is *60 minutes*.
4. My favorite class is math, but mark prefers german.
5. The massachusetts transit authority provides transportation in boston.
6. Mayor marino promised that main street would be repaired next march.
7. My cousin and my brother fished on lake erie.
8. Mary always carries gum, change, keys, and a comb.
9. The world series is a major event in baseball.
10. My parents subscribe to several magazines, including *time* and *newsweek*.

USING GRAMMAR IN WRITING
Using Nouns

A. Look at the following excerpt from an old mail order catalog:

Write at least four descriptions of your own that could be included in this catalog. You might write about an article of clothing, a miracle cure, a new gadget that no household should be without, or some other item of your own choosing. Be sure to tell what each product does, and for whom it is intended. Include several plural nouns in your descriptions and at least two possessive nouns. When you have finished your descriptions, underline all nouns.

B. While on a dangerous expedition through a treacherous mountain range, you discover a valley that is unknown to the rest of the world. In the valley are a highly sophisticated civilization, a huge lake, and many previously undiscovered plants and animals. Write a report describing your discoveries. Include the names of the valley, the lake, the people, their language, and several of the plants and animals. When you have finished, circle all proper nouns and underline all common nouns. Then, label each noun according to its use in the sentence: S = Subject, DO = Direct Object, IO = Indirect Object, and PW = Predicate Word.

Objectives

1. To recognize singular and plural personal pronouns and to understand their functions

2. To use pronouns that agree in number with their antecedents

3. To recognize and correctly use the subject, object, and possessive forms of pronouns

4. To use correct pronoun forms in compound sentence parts

5. To use compound personal pronouns correctly

6. To use demonstrative pronouns correctly

7. To recognize interrogative pronouns

8. To recognize indefinite pronouns and use them correctly with possessive pronouns

9. To understand special problems in pronoun usage

Preparing the Students

Read and discuss the introduction on page 444. Stress the role of pronouns in making writing flow smoothly.

Additional Resources

Mastery Test — See page 47 in the test booklet. Recommended for use after teaching the chapter.

Additional Exercises — See pages 466–472 in the student text.

Skills Practice Book — pages 115–125.

Duplicating Masters — pages 115–125.

Special Populations — See special section at the front of this Teacher's Edition.

Using Pronouns

If you had only nouns to refer to people, places, and things, you would have to express an idea like this:

Andy strummed Andy's guitar and sang the lyrics that Andy had written.

Fortunately, you can avoid such awkward sentences. Instead of repeating some of the nouns, you can use **pronouns**. Then you can say:

Andy strummed *his* guitar and sang the lyrics that *he* had written.

Notice how the words *his* and *he* take the place of the noun *Andy*. These pronouns refer directly to the noun and convey the same meaning in a different way. Pronouns can be used to help sentences flow smoothly and to show clear relationships between words. In this section, you will learn how to use pronouns correctly.

Part 1 Personal Pronouns

A pronoun is a word used in place of a noun.

Pronouns help a speaker or writer present ideas clearly and efficiently. First of all, they help prevent unnecessary repetition. They can also be used as transitional devices to tie sentences or paragraphs together. In general, pronouns may be used in three ways:

1. They may refer to the person speaking. Such pronouns are called *first-person* pronouns.

   I pole-vault.   *We* played cards.
   That jacket is *mine*.   *Our* train leaves soon.

2. They may refer to the person spoken to. These words are called *second-person* pronouns.

   Did *you* bring *your* calculator?

3. They may refer to other people, places, or things. These pronouns are called *third-person* pronouns.

   She asked *him* a question.   *They* opened *their* mail.
   The horse tossed *its* mane.

The examples above show that a pronoun usually refers to a person. For that reason, the largest group of pronouns is called **personal pronouns**.

There are many variations of personal pronouns. Like nouns, personal pronouns may be singular or plural. In the following chart, see how personal pronouns change from the singular form to the plural form.

	FIRST PERSON	SECOND PERSON	THIRD PERSON
SINGULAR:	I, me	you, your	he, she, it
	my, mine	yours	him, her, its
PLURAL:	we, us	you, your	they, them
	our, ours	yours	their, theirs

Part 1

Objective

To recognize singular and plural personal pronouns and to understand their functions

Presenting the Lesson

1. Read and discuss pages 445–446. While personal pronouns are fairly familiar to students, the meanings and application of *first*, *second*, *third* person may not be clear. To help students understand these terms, bring a newspaper to class and read excerpts from interviews, columns, letters-to-the-editor, fiction, and straight news stories. Discuss how the use of first-, second-, and third-person pronouns affect what is being said in each excerpt.

2. Complete and discuss Exercises A and B on page 446.

Individualizing the Lesson

Less-Advanced Students

Prepare a worksheet of sentences and have students fill in the blanks with pronouns.

   The boys made pizza, but _____didn't bake _____long enough.

Point out how naturally they already use pronouns.

Advanced Students

Ask students to write the following:

1) a brief narrative in the first person
2) directions in the second person
3) a brief narrative in the third person

Discuss with them how their choice of pronouns affects their writing.

Assign and discuss Exercise A on page 466.

Optional Practice

Reproduce an excerpt from a novel or short story that contains a number of different types of pronouns. A selection that includes dialogue would work well. Have students circle each pronoun and label it as a first-, second-, or third-person pronoun.

Extending the Lesson

Explain that a writer often uses first-person pronouns to lend a sense of immediacy to a piece of writing. Third-person pronouns, on the other hand, are used to obtain a more objective mood.

Direct students to find a short newspaper story about some interesting event. Discuss the story's objective treatment of the subject. Then direct students to rewrite the story from the point of view of someone actually involved in the situation.

Pronouns can also be classified according to gender. Pronouns that refer to females are said to be in the *feminine gender.* Pronouns that refer to males are said to be in the *masculine gender.* Pronouns that refer to things (and often to animals) are in the *neuter gender.*

Exercise A: Number your paper from 1 to 10. Write the pronouns used in place of nouns in these sentences. After each pronoun, write the noun or nouns it stands for.

1. A crane lifted the boulder and loaded it onto a truck. boulder
2. Beth and George brought their own ice skates to the rink. Beth, George
3. The tiny hailstones bounced as they landed. hailstones
4. Itzak Perlman dazzled the audience with his violin playing. Itzak Perlman
5. "I was born in Vienna," Joanna said. Joanna
6. Marietta uses her hands when she talks. Marietta
7. Our language got many of its words from the ancient Greeks and Romans. language
8. The paramedics finally arrived. They immediately took charge. paramedics
9. The mirror shattered when it dropped. mirror
10. Susan, did you use the microwave oven earlier today? Susan

Exercise B: Writing Rewrite the following paragraph, replacing italicized words and phrases with the appropriate pronouns.

New York students with an interest in music, dance, or acting may attend the famous High School of the Performing Arts. At this school, *students* (they) take both academic classes and classes designed to improve *the students'* (their) performing talents. One girl, Shana, begins *Shana's* (her) day with a pre-school warm-up in the dance room. *Shana* (She) then studies math, English, and history, as well as classes in *Shana's* (her) chosen major of dance. Says Shana, "The school is difficult, but *Shana* (I) love *the school* (it). The teachers work hard to help *Shana* (me) reach *Shana's* (my) goal of becoming a dancer. *My friends and I* (We) all are grateful to the school, even when each of *my friends and me* (us) is exhausted from the work. *My friends and I* (We) feel that the school is truly *a school that belongs to each of us* (ours)."

Part 2 Pronouns and Antecedents

A pronoun is defined as a word used in place of a noun. This noun is called the pronoun's **antecedent**. A pronoun refers to its antecedent.

> Anna lost one of *her* contact lenses. (*Her* takes the place of the noun *Anna*. *Anna* is the antecedent.)
>
> The shop closed *its* doors. (*Its* refers to the noun *shop*. *Shop* is the antecedent.)

The antecedent usually appears before the pronoun. The antecedent may appear in the same sentence or in the preceding sentence, as in this example:

> The tractor pushed the stones and bricks. *It* cleared a path. (*It* stands for the antecedent *tractor*.)

Pronouns may be the antecedents of other pronouns.

> You missed *your* bus. (*You* is the antecedent of *your*.)

A pronoun must be like its antecedent in one important way. A pronoun must have the same *number* as its antecedent. If the antecedent is singular, the pronoun must be singular. If the antecedent is plural, then the pronoun must be plural.

A pronoun must agree with its antecedent in number.

> The photographers grabbed *their* cameras.
> (*Photographers* is plural; *their* is plural.)
>
> Roberto erased *his* error.
> (*Roberto* is singular; *his* is singular.)
>
> Five famous chefs prepared *their* favorite dinners.
> (*Chefs* is plural; *their* is plural.)

One important point should be made about the use of pronouns. In writing or speaking, the antecedent of a pronoun should always be very clear. There must be no confusion about what a pronoun refers to. Sometimes a pronoun must be replaced with a noun if there is no other way of making its meaning clear.

Advanced Students

Have each student write a paragraph describing a group activity in which he or she participated. Then, have students exchange papers. Direct them to copy down all pronouns in the papers and identify the antecedents of these pronouns.

Reinforcement Exercise

Assign and discuss Exercise B on page 466.

Optional Practice

Refer students to a page in their literature text. Have them copy down pronouns and their antecedents.

Extending the Lesson

Ask students to write a letter to an imaginary former student at your school. The letter should tell about the writer and about other students at the school. Have students circle all personal pronouns in their letters. Then, have them identify the antecedents of these pronouns.

CONFUSING: Melt the butter and chocolate, and let *it* cool. (Does *it* refer to the butter, the chocolate, or both?)

CLEAR: Melt the butter and chocolate, and let *the mixture* cool.

Exercise A: In these sentences the personal pronouns are italicized. Write each pronoun and its antecedent.

1. The window washers dangled from the harnesses that supported *them*. washers
2. Princess Diana looks stunning in *her* gown. Princess Diana
3. Jim looked at the shape of the package and knew *it* was an album. package
4. Don't wear those boots if *they* hurt. boots
5. Tony left the computer on so Jenny could use *it*. computer
6. John Travolta grinned at *his* fans outside the theater. John Travolta
7. The Petrakis family went to Phoenix, Arizona for *their* summer vacation. family
8. Frieda and Joe studied *their* menus in confusion. Frieda and Joe
9. The gymnast awkwardly regained *his* balance. gymnast
10. The trainer placed *her* hand on the killer whale's snout. trainer

Exercise B: Writing Rewrite each sentence, adding an appropriate pronoun. Underline the antecedent of each pronoun that you add. Be sure each pronoun agrees with its antecedent.

1. Some people hide __their__ feelings.
2. The ship veered from __its__ course.
3. I have decided on __my__ future career.
4. Peter played __his__ new Menudo album for me.
5. Gayle took off her backpack and placed __it__ on the ground.
6. The team members took the mascot with __them__ .
7. Lynne bought a flea collar for __her__ cat.
8. Rod and I split the cheesecake between the two of __us__ .
9. Would you lend us __your__ toboggan, please?
10. Adam didn't see the car behind __him__ .

Part 3 The Forms of Pronouns

Pronouns can perform all of the same functions that nouns can. Personal pronouns can be subjects, objects, predicate words, and possessives. Unlike a noun, however, a personal pronoun changes forms as its use in a sentence changes. Look at these sentences:

He pitched. (*He* is the subject.)
Riley tagged *him*. (*Him* is the direct object.)
His pitch was wild. (*His* shows possession.)

The three pronouns in these examples all refer to the same person. The forms, though, are different in each sentence.

The three forms of a personal pronoun are **subject form, object form,** and **possessive form**. Here are the three forms for all the personal pronouns:

	SUBJECT	OBJECT	POSSESSIVE
SINGULAR:	I	me	my, mine
	you	you	your, yours
	he, she, it	her, him, it	his, her, hers, its
PLURAL:	we	us	our, ours
	you	you	your, yours
	they	them	their, theirs

Exercise: The following sentences use different forms of pronouns correctly. Label each italicized word *subject form, object form*, or *possessive form*.

1. *We* reported the accident to the sheriff. subject form
2. A sudden, blinding blizzard halted *us* in *our* tracks. object form, possessive form
3. Did *she* bring *hers* or borrow *yours*? subject form, possessive form, possessive form
4. Wendy and *she* showed Tony *their* costumes for the skit. subject form, possessive form
5. The excellent editorial finally convinced *me* that a new community center is needed. object form
6. That was *he* in the plaid flannel shirt. subject form
7. *They* sent *us* a post card from Michigan. subject form, object form

449

Part 3

Objective

To recognize and correctly use the subject, object, and possessive forms of the personal pronouns

Presenting the Lesson

1. Read and discuss page 449. Review the ways in which nouns may be used in a sentence. Emphasize that, since pronouns may be used in place of nouns, they may be used in any way in which a noun is used.

2. Assign the Exercise on page 449.

3. Read **The Subject Form of Pronouns**. Explain that a predicate pronoun restates the subject and therefore takes the subject form. Ask students to create several sentences that include pronouns used as predicate words.

4. Review the definitions for direct objects and indirect objects and the procedures for identifying these. Then read **The Object Form of Pronouns** on page 451. Ask students to provide several more example sentences using pronouns as objects.

5. As you discuss pronouns used as the objects of prepositions, list prepositional phrases containing pronouns on the board. You may also wish to refer students to the list of prepositions on page 527.

6. Read **The Possessive Form of Pronouns**. Point out that some possessive pronouns have two forms, one that is used with a noun as a modifier (*my, their*), and one that is used alone (*mine, theirs*).

7. Complete and discuss Exercises A, B, and C on pages 452–453.

8. Assign Exercise D on page 453.

Individualizing the Lesson

Less-Advanced Students

Review each of the uses of subject pronouns (subject, predicate word) one at a time. Ask students to give examples of each usage. Then move on to the uses of object pronouns and possessive pronouns, again taking them one at a time.

Have students copy in their notecards the following chart of the uses of the three types of pronouns:

SUBJECT PRONOUNS

Used as subject

Used as predicate word

OBJECT PRONOUNS

Used as direct objects

Used as indirect objects

Used as objects of prepositions

POSSESSIVE PRONOUNS

All forms used to show possession

Some forms may be used as modifiers

Some forms may be used as nouns

Allow students to refer to this chart when doing exercises. Complete some of the exercises orally in class as examples.

Advanced Students

You may wish to introduce these students to the idea of clauses and show them how pronoun forms function within a clause. Refer to pages 592–593 for an introduction to clauses.

8. The camping gear and hiking boots are *his*. possessive form
9. *She* went fishing with Joe and *me*. subject form, object form
10. The space shuttle underwent a repair of *its* mechanical arm. possessive form
11. The Vice-President and *his* wife entertained the ambassador at *their* home. possessive forms
12. Sandy makes candles and sells *them*. object form
13. Are the ice skates *yours* or *his*? possessive forms
14. The calico cat with a bell on *its* collar is *mine*. possessive forms
15. Anthony sold *him* a book of raffle tickets. object form

The Subject Form of Pronouns

SUBJECT PRONOUNS

I	we
you	you
he, she, it	they

When a personal pronoun is used as the subject of a sentence, the subject form is used.

They laughed and sang.   *He* punted the ball.
She carried the boxes.   *I* drew a map.

Pronouns used as subjects usually cause few problems. Predicate pronouns, though, can be more troublesome. A predicate pronoun, you recall, is a pronoun that is linked with the subject. It follows a linking verb, just as a predicate noun does.

Look at these examples of predicate pronouns:

That must be *she*. (*she* is a predicate pronoun used after the linking verb *must be*.)
The caller was *he*. (*he* is a predicate pronoun used after the linking verb *was*.)

As you see, the subject forms of pronouns are also used for predicate pronouns. That form may not sound natural at first. If you are in doubt, try reversing the subject and the predicate pronoun. The sentence should still sound correct.

The singer was *she*.   *She* was the singer.

Here are more examples of the correct use of the subject form for predicate pronouns:

That was *he* on the phone.   The winner was *she*.
Was it *she* at the door?

Always use the subject form of a pronoun for subjects and predicate pronouns.

The Object Form of Pronouns

OBJECT PRONOUNS

me	us
you	you
him, her, it	them

When personal pronouns are used as objects, the object form is correct. Any pronoun that is not being used as a subject or a predicate pronoun is functioning as an object.

There are three kinds of objects: direct objects, indirect objects, and objects of prepositions.

In the following sentences, the object form of the pronoun is being used for direct objects.

Dennis introduced *them*.   The manager trained *me*.
Carla followed *us*.   The visitors surprised *her*.

These sentences use the object form for indirect objects:

Terry loaned *me* his pen.   Carol sent *them* gifts.
The height made *us* dizzy.   Mr. Lyle gave *her* some advice.

The third kind of object is the object of a preposition. **Prepositions** are short connecting words like *to, for, of, into,* and *with*. The pronouns that follow such words are the objects of the prepositions. For more explanation of prepositions, see Section 7.

These sentences use the object form for objects of prepositions:

We practiced with *him*.
My friends threw a party for *me*.
The director showed the costume designs to *us*.

Optional Practice

Have students practice writing sentences that include the different forms of pronouns. On the board, write directions such as the following:

I (direct object)
you (subject)
he (indirect object)

Tell students to write a sentence for each pronoun, using it in the position indicated. Caution them that they will have to change the forms of some pronouns to complete the task correctly.

Extending the Lesson

Have students search for sentences containing subject, object, and possessive pronouns in the school yearbook or newspaper. Ask them to copy these sentences and to label the pronouns according to their type and function.

The Possessive Form of Pronouns

POSSESSIVE PRONOUNS

my, mine	our, ours
your, yours	your, yours
his, her, hers, its	their, theirs

Possessive pronouns show belonging or ownership. Unlike possessive nouns, they are not formed with an apostrophe:

Her tape of the interview
Their version of the incident

Many times possessive pronouns are used by themselves: The suitcase is *his*. At other times, possessive pronouns are used with the nouns they refer to. Look at these sentences:

Phil trained *his* macaw to talk.
Each ethnic group has *its* customs.
The mountaineers celebrated *their* success.
Will you read *your* lines?

In such cases, the pronoun is functioning as a *modifier* of the noun.

Many times, however, possessive pronouns are used by themselves. Then, like a noun, a possessive pronoun functions as a subject, object, or predicate word. Look at these examples:

That suitcase is *his*. (predicate pronoun)
Hers is much heavier. (subject)
Paul and Maria are carrying *theirs*. (direct object)
Steve gave *his* a shove. (indirect object)
Put your suitcase with *mine*. (object of preposition)

Exercise A: The personal pronouns in the following sentences are in italics. Write each pronoun and label it *Subject Form, Object Form,* or *Possessive Form.*

1. Laura rehearsed the scene with *him*. object form
2. *She* loaded the film into the camera. subject form
3. The movie kept *us* on the edge of *our* seats for two hours. object form, possessive form
4. It is *they* who won the English sheep dog. subject form

5. Curt's older sister gave *him* a haircut. object form
6. Last week *I* got *my* first paycheck. subject form, possessive form
7. Jean and *her* dad went clam digging. possessive form
8. The best portrait is *his*. possessive form
9. In July *we* will leave for camp. subject form
10. Beth loaned *me* a sweatshirt. object form

Exercise B: Write the correct pronoun from the two given in parentheses. Then read the sentence to yourself.

1. The news shocked (he, <u>him</u>).
2. The waiter spilled spaghetti on (I, <u>me</u>).
3. (<u>They</u>, Them) moved to our neighborhood.
4. The artist sold (<u>her</u>, hers) work at a fair.
5. Was that (<u>he</u>, him) or his twin?
6. All of (we, <u>us</u>) are taller than our parents.
7. The idea was (my, <u>mine</u>).
8. The cashier gave (she, <u>her</u>) incorrect change.
9. The announcer is (<u>she</u>, her).
10. All of those novels were written by (he, <u>him</u>).

Exercise C: Follow the directions for Exercise B.

1. A pro team drafted (he, <u>him</u>).
2. Is (<u>he</u>, him) going to the game?
3. The center forward is (<u>she</u>, her).
4. (<u>He</u>, Him) cuts lawns in the summer.
5. Next year, (<u>we</u>, us) will be able to drive.
6. Wasn't it (<u>he</u>, him) at the door?
7. Garbage surrounded (they, <u>them</u>).
8. Aaron handed the earphones to (I, <u>me</u>).
9. King Arthur made (he, <u>him</u>) a knight.
10. Who is that sitting by (he, <u>him</u>)?

Exercise D: Writing Write a paragraph describing a classmate or relative. Do not use any personal pronouns. Then, rewrite the paragraph using personal pronouns wherever they seem appropriate. Notice how the use of pronouns helps to clarify your writing and make it flow more smoothly.

To use correct pronoun form in compound sentence parts

Presenting the Lesson

1. Read and discuss page 454. Put sentences on the board that have simple sentence parts. Then, ask students to add pronouns to these parts to make them compound. Suggest that students first identify the sentence part they are making compound. This will help them to use the correct pronoun.
2. Complete and discuss Exercises A and B on pages 454–455. Have students give reasons for their choices.

Individualizing the Lesson

Less-Advanced Students

1. Remind students to try each part of a compound construction separately to determine whether or not it is correct.
2. Have students write sentences using these phrases:

she and I   his and ours
him and me

Advanced Students

When students complete Exercises A and B on pages 454–455, have them identify the function of each compound pronoun in the sentence (subject, predicate word, direct object, indirect object, object of a preposition, or possessive).

Reinforcement Exercise

Assign and discuss Exercise C on page 467.

Part 4 Pronouns in Compound Constructions

You have already learned that any part of a sentence may be a compound construction. These compound sentence parts are usually joined by *and, or,* or *nor*, as in *Ben and me*. A pronoun may be one or both of these parts.

It is sometimes difficult to determine which pronoun form to use in a compound construction. Here are sentences with pronouns used correctly in compound parts:

> *Laura* and *I* learned a form of self-defense. (*Laura* and *I* are both subjects. The subject form of *I* is used.)

> Mr. Kim taught *her* and *me* judo. (*Her* and *me* are both indirect objects. The object forms are used.)

> Just between *you* and *me*, I'm tired. (*You* and *me* are objects of the preposition *between*. The object forms are used.)

The examples above demonstrate that compound constructions still must use the proper subject or object form. You can easily tell which form is correct if you think of each part separately. For instance, in the first example above, omit the words *Laura and*. Should the sentence read *I learned a form of self-defense* or *Me learned a form of self-defense*? The pronoun *I* is the correct choice.

Here is another example:

> Gail gave Dennis and (I, me) more watermelon.
> Gail gave *me* more watermelon.

Exercise A: Choose the right pronoun from the two given.

1. Tim and (she, her) have entered the dance contest.
2. Judy made banana milkshakes for Lori and (I, me).
3. The Lees invited Mom and (we, us) to their cabin.
4. The strange package was addressed to Miguel and (he, him).
5. The argument was between Jamie and (they, them).
6. The kitten was a Christmas present for Angela and (she, her).

7. The fastest runners are Chris and (he, <u>him</u>).
8. The electrical storm made the other campers and (we, <u>us</u>) nervous.
9. My dog Skipper runs along the beach with (she, <u>her</u>) and (I, <u>me</u>).
10. Just between you and (I, <u>me</u>), I'm scared.

Exercise B: Writing Rewrite each sentence. Replace the italicized word or words with a suitable pronoun. Be sure to use the correct subject or object form.

1. The shopkeeper ignored Meg and *Carol*. her
2. Katy and *David* met on a bus. he
3. That speeding car headed directly at John and *Elly*. her
4. It was *Marcia and her sister* who designed the maze. they
5. A child with a water pistol squirted Rick and *Mario*. him
6. Someone yelled at *Peter and Jim* and *Paula and me*. them, us
7. The Bogan team and *our team* will be riding on the same school bus. we
8. Tony and *Bill* may sign up for soccer. he
9. The best dancers are Marshall and *Judy*. she
10. Leave some chili for Marla and *Ted*. him

Part 5 Compound Personal Pronouns

A **compound personal pronoun** is a pronoun with -*self* or -*selves* added.

myself	ourselves
yourself	yourselves
himself, herself, itself	themselves

When a compound personal pronoun is used for emphasis, it is being used *intensively*.

Maggie *herself* opened the vault.
They called the police *themselves*.

Ask students to write sentences using the following:

Eric and I (as subjects)
Eric and I (as predicate words)
Eric and me (as direct objects)
Eric and me (as indirect objects)
Eric and me (as objects of a preposition)
Mine and Eric's (after *is* or *are*)

Extending the Lesson

Have students make a list of four other people with whom they have something in common. Then, ask them to write sentences about these shared interests using the names of these people and the pronouns *I*, *me*, and *mine* in compounds.

Using newspapers, have students find and copy three examples of pronouns used in compound sentence parts. Discuss how pronouns are used in these sentences.

Part 5

Objective

To use compound personal pronouns correctly

Presenting the Lesson

1. Read and discuss pages 455–456. Call attention to the difference in spelling between the singular forms and the plural forms of compound personal pronouns. Discuss the mistaken use of compound personal pronouns in sentences such as "Myself and a friend went to the movies," and "The winners were Jane and myself."

455

When a compound personal pronoun is used to indicate that the subject is acting on itself, it is being used *reflexively*.

Ella bought *herself* a digital watch.
We gave *ourselves* an hour to pack.

It is incorrect to use compound personal pronouns without antecedents.

INCORRECT: *Myself* knitted this sweater.
CORRECT: *I* knitted this sweater *myself*.

INCORRECT: You can come with Ann and *myself*.
CORRECT: You can come with Ann and *me*.

Exercise A: Number your paper from 1 to 10. Beside each number write the correct compound personal pronoun for each of the following sentences. After it, write its antecedent.

EXAMPLE: The actor thinks of (pronoun) as a star.
himself, actor

1. Dana and I wrote the lyrics (pronoun). (ourselves) Dana and I
2. Amy gave (pronoun) a permanent. (herself) Amy
3. The workers (pronoun) choose their hours. (themselves) workers
4. The governor (pronoun) pardoned the prisoner. (himself) governor
5. The members (pronoun) set the club rules. (themselves) members
6. I cooked this meal by (pronoun). (myself) I
7. The cheerleaders yelled (pronoun) hoarse during the last few minutes of the game. (themselves) cheerleaders
8. The special effects were good, but the movie (pronoun) was dull. (itself) movie
9. Are you going to Cheyenne by (pronoun), Emily? (yourself) you
10. We watched (pronoun) on TV. (ourselves) We

Exercise B: Follow the directions for Exercise A.

1. Sissy Spacek (pronoun) answered the letter. (herself) Sissy Spacek
2. Brian and Bob found (pronoun) in serious trouble. (themselves) Brian and Bob
3. The doctor (pronoun) became very sick during the epidemic. (himself) doctor

4. We built the canoes (pronoun). (ourselves) We
5. Give (pronoun) enough time, Debbie. (yourself) Debbie
6. JoAnn tuned the engine (pronoun). (herself) JoAnn
7. Carlos went camping by (pronoun). (himself) Carlos
8. The problem will work (pronoun) out. (itself) problem
9. I (pronoun) have never tried water-skiing. (myself) I
10. Vic and Tim made (pronoun) sick by eating too much candy. (themselves) Vic and Tim

Part 6   Demonstrative Pronouns

The pronouns *this, that, these,* and *those* point out people or things. They are called **demonstrative pronouns.**

This and *these* point to people or things that are near in space or time. *That* or *those* point to people or things that are farther away in space or time.

This makes a good dessert.   *These* are leather boots.
That was our first date.   *Those* were great times.

Exercise: Number your paper from 1 to 10. Write the correct demonstrative pronoun for the blank space in each of the following sentences.

1. __Those__ are your gloves, not these.
2. __These__ are spicier tacos than those Mom makes.
3. __This__ is a clearer tape than the one that Alexis recorded yesterday.
4. __That__ was a good concert last night.
5. __This__ is my bike, and that blue one in the garage is my brother's.
6. __That__ must be our bus over there.
7. __Those__ are the new computers, over there.
8. __This__ is the most humid day we've had.
9. __That__ is the edge of the canyon, just beyond those tall cacti.
10. __Those__ were Michelle's cousins from Rhode Island.

457

Part 6

Objective

To use demonstrative pronouns correctly

Presenting the Lesson

Read and discuss page 457. Explain to students that the words *this, these, that, those* stand alone in place of nouns. If these words accompany nouns, they are no longer demonstrative pronouns; they are modifiers. Add the word *cake* between *This* and *makes* in the example sentence to illustrate this point.

Individualizing the Lesson

Less-Advanced Students

Review with students the appropriate uses of *this* and *these* as opposed to *that* and *those*.

Advanced Students

Point out that demonstrative pronouns may have antecedents but that they frequently do not, especially when used in conversation and accompanied by a gesture or a glance. Ask them to give examples of each.

Optional Practice

Instruct students to visualize the cafeteria and to write sentences using demonstrative pronouns to describe the surroundings.

Extending the Lesson

Point out the usefulness of demonstrative pronouns in giving directions. Have each student write a set of instructions for a simple task. Encourage them to use as many demonstrative pronouns as possible.

Objective

To recognize interrogative pronouns

Presenting the Lesson

1. Read and discuss page 458. Remind the class that, like demonstrative pronouns, interrogative pronouns become modifiers when placed before nouns: *which record.*
2. Assign the Exercise.

Individualizing the Lesson

Less-Advanced Students

Have students write questions using interrogative pronouns. Then have them write answers using demonstrative pronouns.

Advanced Students

Have students prepare a set of questions to interview a person in the news.

Extending the Lesson

Hold a trivia contest. Ask students to find out little-known facts about their town. Then have them devise questions for each fact.

Part 8

Objectives

1. To differentiate between singular and plural indefinite pronouns
2. To use indefinite pronouns with possessive pronouns

Part 7 Interrogative Pronouns

Certain pronouns are used to ask questions. They are called **interrogative pronouns**. The interrogative pronouns are *who, whom, whose, which,* and *what*.

Who won an Emmy award?   *Which* is your favorite?
Whom did Gloria call?   *What* started the fire?
Whose is this parka?

Exercise: Number your paper from 1 to 10. Write all the <u>pronouns</u> in these sentences. After each pronoun, write *Demonstrative* or *Interrogative* to show what kind it is.

EXAMPLE: Is that the law?
                    that—demonstrative pronoun

1. <u>Who</u> knows how to determine the age of a tree? interrogative
2. <u>That</u> makes sense. demonstrative
3. <u>Which</u> is Carlos's suitcase? interrogative
4. <u>These</u> must arrive in Houston by tomorrow. demonstrative
5. Is <u>that</u> Rob's handwriting? demonstrative
6. <u>Whom</u> does Cal trust with the money? interrogative
7. Please store <u>these</u> in the equipment room. demonstrative
8. Are <u>those</u> the Green Mountains? demonstrative
9. <u>What</u> makes Ramona so lucky? interrogative
10. <u>Whose</u> are <u>these</u>? interrogative, demonstrative

Part 8 Indefinite Pronouns

Some pronouns do not refer to a definite person or thing. Such pronouns are called **indefinite pronouns.**
The following are indefinite pronouns. They are singular.

another	each	everything	one
anybody	either	neither	somebody
anyone	everybody	nobody	someone
anything	everyone	no one	

Since a pronoun must agree in number with its antecedent, the above singular pronouns are used with the singular possessive pronouns *his, her,* and *its.*

> *Each* of the stores has *its* own hours.
> *Somebody* forgot *his* ski cap.
> *Somebody* forgot *his or her* ski cap.

The final example uses the phrase *his or her* instead of simply *his.* That phrase may be used to show that the indefinite pronoun may refer to a male or female.

Although most indefinite pronouns are singular, some are plural. They refer to more than one person or thing, and are used with the plural possessive *their.* Study these examples.

> both   many   few   several

> *Both* of the swimmers timed *their* sprints.
> *Few* of the passengers left *their* seats.
> *Many* of our neighbors grow *their* own vegetables.
> *Several* of the racers overturned *their* cars.

A few indefinite pronouns can be either singular or plural, depending on their meaning in a sentence. Read these examples:

> all   none   some

> *All* of the water has chemicals in *it.*
> *All* of the drivers loaded *their* trucks.
> *None* of the medicine has lost *its* strength.
> *None* of these comedians use *their* own material.
> *Some* of the fire burned *itself* out.
> *Some* of the workers took *their* breaks.

Do not be confused by phrases that appear between the indefinite pronoun and the possessive pronoun. The two pronouns should always agree.

INCORRECT: One of the musicians left *their* instrument behind. (The possessive pronoun should agree with One, not *musicians.*)

CORRECT: One of the musicians left *her* instrument behind.

Presenting the Lesson

1. Read and discuss pages 458–459. First, study those indefinite pronouns that are always singular or always plural. Then, discuss the problem of agreement with these pronouns. Once students understand agreement with indefinite pronouns that are always singular or plural, proceed to discussion of indefinite pronouns that can be both.

2. Spend some time explaining the problem of the intervening prepositional phrase.

3. Complete Exercise A on page 460 orally. Then assign and discuss Exercises B and C. When you are sure the students understand the concepts, assign Exercise D.

Individualizing the Lesson

Less-Advanced Students

Students may have difficulty understanding that some indefinite pronouns are singular even though they are used in statements containing prepositional phrases that refer to groups. Explain that these pronouns refer to single people within a group. Demonstrate the difference between the commands "Talk to *each* of the students" and "Talk to *both* of the students" by acting out responses to each command.

Advanced Students

Explain that indefinite pronouns can be used as subject, object, or possessive pronouns. Demonstrate the change of form in indefinite pronouns used in the possessive case.

Reinforcement Exercises

Assign and discuss Exercises D and E on pages 467 and 468.

Optional Practice

Have students write sentence pairs using the words *all*, *none*, and *some* as both singular and plural pronouns.

Extending the Lesson

Have students devise questions for the purpose of conducting a classroom poll on a chosen topic. Instruct students to write up the results of the poll using indefinite pronouns. For example:

"Several of the students felt the movie was too violent."
"Another liked the chase scene."
"Few would see the movie again."

Exercise A: For each sentence write the indefinite pronoun.

1. None of us caught a fish during that whole, frustrating trip.
2. Did someone reserve a picnic table for us?
3. Anyone can win the sweepstakes.
4. What is everybody waiting for?
5. Only one of the headlights on that old car works.
6. Several of the soccer players signed long-term contracts.
7. Many of the leaves had already fallen.
8. I read both of the Agatha Christie mysteries.
9. Why is everyone cheering?
10. We have to learn all of the state capitals.

Exercise B: Write the indefinite pronoun in each sentence. Then choose the right pronoun from those given in parentheses.

1. One of the actresses missed (her, their) cue.
2. Many of the stores have lowered (its, their) prices.
3. Somebody left (his or her, their) checkbook here.
4. Some of the runners wore out (her, their) shoes.
5. If anyone calls, tell (him or her, them) I'll be right back.
6. Neither of our wrestlers pinned (his, their) opponent.
7. Everyone listed (his or her, their) address.
8. Each of these sundaes has (its, their) own special sauce.
9. All of the passengers in the boat wore (his or her, their) lifejackets.
10. Did anybody bring (his or her, their) own paintbrushes?

Exercise C: Follow the directions for Exercise B.

1. Nobody has received (his or her, their) tickets yet.
2. Has everyone checked (his, their) equipment?
3. Few of the actors needed (his or her, their) scripts.
4. Neither of the girls remembered (her, their) music.
5. One of the trees lost all of (its, their) leaves.
6. All of the candidates approved (his or her, their) staffs.
7. Each of the horses had (its, their) mane braided.
8. Some of the artists displayed (his or her, their) work.
9. Many of the winners wrote (his or her, their) own speeches.
10. Some of the food has lost (its, their) flavor.

Exercise D: Writing Write ten sentences of your own, using these indefinite pronouns as subjects. Each sentence should also have a possessive pronoun that agrees with its antecedent.

EXAMPLE: everything
Everything is in *its* place.

nobody	one	some
everyone	neither	many
few	each	both

Part 9   Special Problems with Pronouns

Possessive Pronouns and Contractions

Certain possessive pronouns are sometimes confused with contractions that sound the same. For example, *it's* and *its* are often confused in a sentence such as the following:

The seal balanced on (its, it's) flippers.

In this sentence, the possessive pronoun *its* is correct. Contractions are formed by joining two words and omitting one or more letters. An apostrophe shows where letters are left out.

it's = it + is *or* it + has	they're = they + are
you're = you + are	who's = who + is *or* who + has

The above contractions are sometimes confused with the possessive pronouns *its, your, their,* and *whose.* The words sound alike but are spelled differently. Remember, the possessive pronouns do not use an apostrophe.

INCORRECT: The plant lost *it's* leaves.
CORRECT: The plant lost *its* leaves.

INCORRECT: Is this *you're* radio?
CORRECT: Is this *your* radio?

461

Part 9

Objective

To correct special problems in pronoun usage

Presenting the Lesson

1. Review the use of the apostrophe in possessives and in contractions, using examples of possessive nouns and contracted verbs (wouldn't, couldn't).
2. Read and discuss the material on pages 461–462. Point out that apostrophes are never used with possessive pronouns; they are used in contractions to mark the place of the omitted letter or letters.
3. Assign and discuss Exercises A and B on page 462.
4. Review the uses of subject forms and object forms (Part 3).
5. Read and discuss page 463. Students should add examples to the sentences on page 463, particularly for *whom* used as a direct object.
6. Do Exercises A and B on pages 463–464, orally.
7. Read and discuss pages 464–465. The correct use of *we* and

us with accompanying nouns often sounds awkward to students. Remind them to omit nouns to make the correct choice.

Provide students with examples of *those* used as a demonstrative pronoun and as an adjective so students may compare the usage.

8. Assign and discuss Exercises A and B on page 465. Ask students to explain their choices. Then assign Exercise C.

Individualizing the Lesson

Less-Advanced Students

Review any pronouns that are causing difficulties and provide worksheets for completion and group discussion.

Advanced Students

1. Contrast indefinite pronouns, which form the possessive by using an apostrophe, with other pronouns, which do not.

2. Have students write sentences using the following phrases:

> it's easy
> their tennis shoes
> they're ready
> we boys
> from whom
> you're right

Reinforcement Exercise

Assign and discuss Exercise F on page 468.

Optional Practice

Have students write pairs of sentences that demonstrate their understanding of the special pronoun problems.

To decide which word is correct in a particular sentence, substitute the words the contraction stands for. If the sentence sounds right, then the contraction is correct. If it doesn't, a possessive pronoun is required.

> INCORRECT: *Who's* (who is) skates are these?
> CORRECT: *Whose* skates are these?

Exercise A: Choose the right word from the two in parentheses.

1. The movers parked (<u>their</u>, they're) van in front of the building.
2. (Your, <u>You're</u>) expecting a call, aren't you?
3. Someone forgot to replace the telephone receiver on (<u>its</u>, it's) hook.
4. (<u>Whose</u>, Who's) signature is this on the voucher?
5. Is that (<u>your</u>, you're) camera?
6. (Their, <u>They're</u>) trapped in the collapsed mine!
7. (Whose, <u>Who's</u>) taking the ball out of bounds?
8. When (its, <u>it's</u>) ten o'clock in Albuquerque, people are eating (they're, <u>their</u>) lunch in New York.
9. (Whose, <u>Who's</u>) the woman with the microphone?
10. (<u>Your</u>, You're) friends are waiting at the station.

Exercise B: If a sentence is incorrect, rewrite it correctly. Write *Correct* if a sentence does not contain an error.

1. They're going white water rafting in Colorado. correct
2. Ask if <u>its</u> too late to buy a ticket for the incline railway. it's
3. <u>Who's</u> house shall we meet at? Whose
4. Your subscription to *Seventeen* just expired. correct
5. The sign indicates that it's dangerous to travel through the mountains at night. correct
6. <u>They're</u> Dalmatian won a blue ribbon in the dog show. Their
7. Take <u>you're</u> time on the essay portion of the test. your
8. Do you know <u>whose</u> starring in the movie? who's
9. The troops grew concerned as their water supply diminished. correct
10. The bear scratched <u>it's</u> back on a tree. its

Who and Whom

Many people have trouble knowing when to use *who* and *whom*. *Who* is the subject form of the pronoun. It is used as the subject of a sentence.

> *Who* tuned the piano?　　*Who* is there?

Whom is the object form of the pronoun. Although it doesn't sound as natural as *who*, it should be used when the sentence requires an object.

> *Whom* did the Regans adopt?
> (direct object of the verb *did adopt*)
> With *whom* will you go to the party?
> (object of the preposition *with*)

Be especially alert to sentences that begin with the interrogative pronoun and end with a preposition. Such sentences also use *whom*.

> *Whom* was the message directed **to**?
> (object of the preposition *to*)
> *Whom* did the pianist play **for**?
> (object of the preposition *for*)

Exercise A: Choose the right pronoun from the two given in parentheses.

1. (Who, Whom) could possibly eat a whole pecan pie?
2. (Who, Whom) insulted your friend?
3. To (who, whom) should these roses be delivered?
4. (Who, Whom) were you watching on TV?
5. (Who, Whom) is the sportscaster that reports on high school games?
6. (Who, Whom) is our Secretary of State?
7. (Who, Whom) runs the drill press?
8. With (who, whom) will you stay in Tallahassee?
9. (Who, Whom) do these running shorts belong to?
10. When you went to St. Louis, (who, whom) did you visit?

Extending the Lesson

1. Ask students to listen for examples of incorrect pronoun usage in everyday conversations. Discuss the rule for each example and how to correct the errors.

2. Play a recording of Abbott and Costello's "Who's on First?" This is a classic routine that relies on the misuse of pronouns for humor.

3. Ask students to write a letter to an imaginary pen pal in another country. Have them use *we* or *us* with *students* to describe what a day in the life of an American student is like. Then have them ask questions of their pen pals using *who* and *whom*.

Exercise B: Follow the directions for Exercise A.

1. (<u>Who</u>, Whom) works the new, computerized switchboard at the hospital?
2. (Who, <u>Whom</u>) did the lifeguard call the ambulance for?
3. (Who, <u>Whom</u>) did the detective suspect?
4. (Who, <u>Whom</u>) is the telegram addressed to?
5. (Who, <u>Whom</u>) did your mother hire to do the filing?
6. (<u>Who</u>, Whom) used up all the hot water?
7. For (who, <u>whom</u>) was the school named?
8. (<u>Who</u>, Whom) founded Salt Lake City?
9. (Who, <u>Whom</u>) do you compete with at next week's swimming meet?
10. (<u>Who</u>, Whom) needs a yearly physical exam?

We and *Us* with Nouns

The pronouns *we* and *us* are often used with nouns, as in the phrases *we boys* or *us students*. Sometimes it is difficult to tell whether to use the subject form *we* or the object form *us*.

To decide whether to use *we* or *us*, omit the noun. Say the sentence with *we* and then with *us*. You will then probably be able to choose the correct pronoun.

    PROBLEM: (We, Us) linemen do the blocking.
    CORRECT: We do the blocking.
    CORRECT: We linemen do the blocking.

    PROBLEM: Nothing stops (we, us) campers.
    CORRECT: Nothing stops us.
    CORRECT: Nothing stops us campers.

Them and *Those*

Them and *Those* are sometimes confused. To use the words correctly, remember that *them* is always used as a pronoun. It is never used to modify a noun. *Those*, on the other hand, can be used as either a pronoun or a modifier. Look at the examples on the following page.

INCORRECT:	A search party found *them* hikers.
CORRECT:	A search party found *them*.
CORRECT:	A search party found *those* hikers.
CORRECT:	Hand me *those* tickets, please.
CORRECT:	Hand me *those*, please.

Exercise A: Choose the correct pronoun from the two given in parentheses.

1. (We, Us) girls hooked up the antenna.
2. (Them, Those) are the sweetest grapes I've ever tasted.
3. The foul ball nearly hit (we, us) spectators.
4. Can you take advantage of (them, those) new air fares?
5. (Them, Those) greeting cards are funny.
6. The Sunday paper ran a story about (we, us) Scouts.
7. (We, Us) athletes are often tense before games.
8. Micki King tried one of (them, those) difficult back dives.
9. When will (we, us) Americans host the Olympics again?
10. Did you see (them, those) state troopers?

Exercise B: Writing Pronouns are used incorrectly in some of the sentences below. Rewrite these sentences, correcting any errors. If there is no error, write *Correct*.

1. Fishing rights are important to us Native Americans. correct
2. Will them additives improve gas mileage? those
3. Us boys pushed the stalled car. We
4. Can any of them computers translate languages? those
5. Special facilities were provided for we handicapped students. us
6. There is a new club for us backgammon players. correct
7. Did you eat all of those blueberries? correct
8. Yesterday we campers hiked up Mount LeConte. correct
9. The hospital treats we patients well. us
10. Those stakes hold the tent in place. correct

Exercise C: Writing Write ten sentences. Use either *we, us, them,* or *those* at least once in each sentence.

Reinforcement Exercises

These Reinforcement Exercises may be used for additional practice of the concepts presented in this Section. Each exercise focuses on a single concept, and should be used after the page number indicated in parentheses.

Review

If you have not assigned these Reinforcement Exercises before this time, you can also use them as an excellent Section Review.

REINFORCEMENT EXERCISES
Using Pronouns

A. Find the pronouns. Number your paper from 1 to 10. Write the pronouns you find in each of the following sentences. (Use after page 446.)

1. He and I streaked down the toboggan slide on his new sled.
2. She held her breath for seventy seconds.
3. May I take it to him?
4. Luke Skywalker leaped onto his speeder bike and raced through the forest.
5. Ms. Duncan gave them an unusual project.
6. They turned off their TV for a month.
7. The dog retrieved your Frisbee from the lake, didn't he?
8. My uncle restored a Victorian house for a family on his street.
9. Jeff saved her a seat next to him.
10. Do you or your sister have allergies?

B. Find the antecedents of pronouns. Write each pronoun and its antecedent. (Use after page 448.)

1. Cheryl rode her horse into the meadow. Cheryl
2. The archer kept his left arm steady and took aim at the distant target. archer
3. Alison and Kate had their lunch in Thornwood Park. Alison and Kate
4. The sky divers released their parachutes at the last moment. sky divers
5. Laura had just hung up the telephone when it suddenly rang again. telephone
6. Yolanda is usually a guard, but today she is playing forward. Yolanda
7. The heartbeat and breathing of certain mammals and amphibians slow when they hibernate. mammals and amphibians
8. Mike, have you and Lee finished your tennis game? Mike, Mike and Lee
9. The Greeks built a huge wooden horse to fool their enemy. They hid soldiers inside. Greeks, Greeks
10. Will you sing the solo, Stephanie? Stephanie

C. Use subject and object forms of pronouns.

Choose the correct pronoun from the two given in parentheses. (Use after page 453.)

1. (She, Her) and Luther took the photos during the ceremony.
2. The reports about (they, them) and the new board members were biased.
3. The coach asked Suzanne and (I, me) for help.
4. Todd and (she, her) work in a sporting goods shop.
5. (Him, He) and (me, I) watched the gymnasts work out.
6. Greg and (he, him) learned a new dive.
7. It was (he, him), believe it or not, in the Rolls Royce.
8. Alec took Nancy and (I, me) to a roller derby.
9. Did Jill and (she, her) take archery in gym class?
10. Bill has sold the winning raffle ticket to (he, him) or (I, me).

D. Recognize different kinds of pronouns.

Number your paper from 1 to 10. Write the pronouns in these sentences. After each pronoun, write *Demonstrative, Interrogative*, or *Indefinite* to tell what kind it is. (Use after page 461.)

1. A computer could do this in a split-second. demonstrative
2. Which of the cars finished the race? interrogative
3. This is a replica of a clipper ship. demonstrative
4. Are those Sue's cousins from Nova Scotia? demonstrative
5. Anyone can learn to play a recorder. indefinite
6. Whom did the President assign to the task force? interrogative
7. What is the capital city of Belgium? interrogative
8. Nora had never heard that before. demonstrative
9. Everyone sensed a sudden change in the atmosphere. indefinite
10. Many of the witnesses refused to answer the district attorney's question. indefinite

E. Use indefinite pronouns correctly.

Choose the pronoun that agrees with the indefinite pronoun in each sentence. (Use after page 461.)

1. Neither of the runners slowed (her, their) pace.
2. Only one of the karate students had earned (his, their) black belt.

3. All of the teams brought (its, their) mascots to the state meet.
4. Both of the boys wore (his, their) hockey skates to the ice rink.
5. Every boat in the marina has (its, their) own name.
6. Most of the stores advertise (its, their) sales a week ahead of time.
7. Everyone should take (his or her, their) own camera.
8. Has anyone had (his or her, their) fortune told?
9. Some of the actors apply (her, their) make-up.
10. Each of the parking lots has (its, their) own rates.

F. Solve special pronoun problems. Choose the correct word from the two in parentheses.(Use after page 465.)

1. Have (your, you're) friends been waiting all this time?
2. (Who, Whom) did Mary Lou go to the concert with?
3. The president thanked (we, us) committee members.
4. (Who, Whom) received this year's Nobel Peace Prize?
5. (Them, Those) are Australia's hottest new singers.
6. (We, Us) students who ride the bus to school have to get up earlier.
7. (Whose, Who's) starring in that new comedy?
8. Have you tried one of (them, those) egg rolls?
9. The guide was very polite to (we, us) tourists.
10. The bikers loaded (their, they're) backpacks with food for the trip.

MIXED REVIEW
Using Pronouns

A. Complete each of the following sentences, using the type of pronoun given in parentheses. Answers may vary.

1. The actors <u>themselves</u> were distracted by some of the special
   effects. (compound personal)
2. <u>These</u> are the kinds of nails I need. (demonstrative)
3. <u>Who</u> won the Academy Award for best actor?
   (interrogative)
4. <u>That</u> was the best pizza I have ever tasted.
   (demonstrative)
5. In any friendship between two people, <u>one</u> should be
   able to trust the other. (indefinite)
6. Is that <u>your</u> bicycle or mine? (possessive)
7. Randy planned and prepared the entire dinner <u>himself</u> .
   (compound personal)
8. I cannot seem to get <u>that</u> out of my mind.
   (demonstrative)
9. <u>Some</u> of the students asked that the test be postponed.
   (indefinite)
10. With <u>whom</u> were you planning to play racquetball?
    (interrogative)

B. Number your paper from 1 to 15. Choose the correct pronoun
from the two given in parentheses.

1. (Who's, <u>Whose</u>) idea was it to tape this concert?
2. All of the orchestra members tuned (<u>their</u>, it's)
   instruments.
3. My friend told me that (your, <u>you're</u>) going sailing this
   weekend.
4. Tara could hardly wait to see the picture of (she, <u>her</u>) and
   (he, <u>him</u>).
5. (Who, <u>Whom</u>) did the class elect as representative to the
   student council?

469

6. (Who, Whom) won the Heisman Trophy last year?
7. The cooking instructor wondered (who's, whose) homemade bread would win the contest.
8. Have you ever seen one of (them, those) windsurfers?
9. (We, Us) citizens requested a better selection of books in the library.
10. The electrician demonstrated to (us, we) students how to repair a lamp.
11. The Johnsons found (themselves, theirselves) anxious to begin a new business after retirement.
12. Jim invited Mike and (he, him) to spend the weekend camping.
13. My grandfather and (she, her) taught (I, me) how to tune a piano.
14. Many people in the audience expressed (their, they're) appreciation by applauding.
15. Mrs. Lopez and (she, her) run a travel agency for senior citizens.

C. Rewrite the following sentences, changing all of the italicized words to personal pronouns. Then label each pronoun **S** for *Subject*, **O** for *Object*, or **P** for *Possessive*. Answers in margin.

> EXAMPLE: *Jane* bought *Jane's* silver bracelet in Mexico.
>   **S**   **P**
> She bought her silver bracelet in Mexico.

1. *Mary* read *Mary's* computer printout.
2. *Juan* admired the boxer for *the boxer's* agility.
3. Why isn't *Joan* wearing *Joan's* favorite dress to the homecoming dance?
4. Give *the dog the dog's* dinner.
5. *Mickey Rooney* and *Ann Miller* starred in the hit Broadway show.
6. *Kim and I* watched *Pat, Bill and Mario* swim the final laps.
7. *The mechanic* lost *the mechanic's* wrench under the hood.
8. *Supreme Court Justice Sandra Day O'Connor* is highly respected by the other members of the High Court.
9. *The reporter* refused to reveal *the reporter's* source.
10. The winter took *the winter's* toll on the crops.

D. Rewrite the following sentences correcting all pronoun errors. If there are no errors, write *Correct*.

1. <u>Us</u> band students decided that <u>them</u> green band uniforms were more attractive. We, those
2. <u>Who</u> does Nancy want for a homeroom teacher? Whom
3. Somebody turned in <u>their</u> homework late. his or her
4. A snake usually sheds <u>it's</u> skin once a year. Its
5. We players have great respect for our coach. correct
6. Were <u>them</u> boys at the hockey game? those
7. No one knew where <u>their</u> shoes had been hidden. his or her
8. <u>Who</u> did you skate with this afternoon? Whom
9. <u>Both</u> the Japanese and the Americans make reliable cars. correct
10. The plot of that movie doesn't make sense to me. correct
11. I listened to <u>she</u> and him on the radio. her
12. Someone left <u>their</u> ticket in this envelope. his or her
13. Its time for the zookeepers to feed <u>them</u> water buffaloes. It's, those
14. <u>Whom</u> did you say was playing center at the next game? Who
15. <u>Your</u> definitely the best reporter on the paper. You're

USING GRAMMAR IN WRITING
Using Pronouns

A. Imagine that you are a millionaire writing your will. You have some friends and relatives that you would like to reward for their kindness toward you. There are also a few strangers and some favorite pets that you would like to remember. Tell which of the objects from your great wealth you intend to give to particular individuals. Explain why each person is receiving his or her reward. Use as many different types of pronouns as possible. Underline them. Be ready to tell what type of pronoun each one is.

B. Sometimes a pronoun in one sentence refers to a noun in a preceding sentence:

> Antoine Becquerel discovered radioactivity.
> For *this*, *he* received a Nobel Prize.

The pronouns *this* and *he* help tie the two sentences together. Words that are used to tie sentences together in this way are called **transitional devices.** Write the following sentences in paragraph form. Substitute pronouns for some of the nouns in order to provide transitions.

> The miller was America's first industrial inventor.
>
> People of today might consider the miller just another merchant.
>
> People don't realize that the miller was banker, businessman, and host to the countryside.
>
> The miller also had a strenuous and dangerous job.
>
> The early mill that the miller worked in was massive and powerful.
>
> A mill had huge wheels and massive gears that could easily crush a person.
>
> "Killed in his mill" was a frequent epitaph of two hundred years ago.

472

Section 5

Using Verbs

An ancient jalopy *lurched* down the road.
The grass snake *slithered* through the weeds.

Look at the two sentences above. Each one creates a vivid image for the reader. The words *lurched* and *slithered,* in particular, bring the sentences to life. These two words are verbs. Skillful writers and speakers know that the verb is the key word in any sentence. Without a verb, no idea can be complete. In addition, the correct choice of verbs can make the difference between dull and lively writing.

You have already learned to identify this type of word. In this Section you will learn more about how verbs are used. You will also learn how the use of just the right verb can help make your writing more effective.

Objective

To recognize action and linking verbs and transitive and intransitive verbs

Presenting the Lesson

1. Read and discuss pages 474–475. Stress the importance of verbs by reading each example sentence given in the text aloud without its verb. Then, discuss what information the verb adds to the sentence. Ask students to add several examples of each type of verb to those given in the text.

2. Words that can be either linking verbs or action verbs are especially troublesome. Explain that linking verbs often act like equal signs in mathematics. The word that follows such a verb is a restatement or clarification of the subject.

3. Review the use of direct objects with action verbs. Stress that the presence or absence of the direct object makes the difference between a transitive and intransitive verb.

4. Assign and discuss Exercises A, B, and C on pages 475–476.

Individualizing the lesson

Less-Advanced Students

1. If the students have trouble recognizing verbs, review the material on subject and predicate in Section 1.

2. Have students memorize the list of linking verbs on page 474.

3. Have students identify the verbs in each of the following sentences, telling whether each is a

Part 1 What Is a Verb?

A verb expresses an action or a state of being.

Action Verbs

One kind of verb indicates action. The action may be visible or unseen.

> The storm *raged.*   Bill *expects* a raise.
> A plane *landed.*   Maria *has* great ambition.

An **action verb** tells that something is happening, has happened, or will happen.

Linking Verbs

Some verbs simply tell that something exists. Such verbs express a state of being rather than action.

> The election *is* Tuesday.   Spencer *was* our captain.
> Rita *seems* happy.   The cake *tastes* moist.

Most state-of-being verbs link the subject with a word or words in the predicate. These verbs are called **linking verbs.**

Here are the most common linking verbs:

be (am, are, is, was,	look	smell	seem
were, been, being)	appear	taste	sound
become	feel	grow	

Some linking verbs can also be used as action verbs.

LINKING VERB	ACTION VERB
The T-shirt *looked* dirty.	Kim *looked* at the painting.
The meal *grew* cold.	The gardener *grew* zinnias.

When you look at the verb in a sentence, notice how it is used. Decide whether it expresses action or simply links the subject with a word in the predicate.

Transitive and Intransitive Verbs

In many sentences an action verb expresses an idea by itself. In other sentences a direct object completes the action of the verb. The direct object, as you have learned, tells *who* or *what* receives the action of the verb.

Verbs that have direct objects are **transitive verbs.**

> Dave *met* the mayor.
> (The direct object *mayor* completes the meaning of the verb *met*.)

> The officer *wore* several medals.
> (The direct object *medals* completes the meaning of the verb *wore*.)

Verbs that do not have direct objects are called **intransitive verbs.**

> The winners *rejoiced*.
> Steve *rested* under a tree.

Notice that in the second sentence, the words following the verb modify it. They do not receive the action of the verb and are therefore not objects of the verb.

Some action verbs are always transitive or always intransitive. Other verbs may be transitive in one sentence and intransitive in another. Compare these examples. Direct objects are shown in boldface type.

TRANSITIVE VERB	INTRANSITIVE VERB
The girls *swam* a **mile.**	The girls *swam*.
The artist *sketched* the **model.**	The artist *sketched* by the sea.
Ella *sings* the **lead.**	Ella *sings* tonight.

Exercise A: Write the <u>verb</u> in each sentence. After each verb write *Action* or *Linking* to show what kind it is.

1. Jennifer and Marcia <u>portaged</u> the canoe. action
2. Who <u>won</u> this year's Nobel Prize in medicine? action
3. The Senator <u>campaigned</u> for reelection. action
4. That abandoned building <u>looks</u> spooky. linking

475

linking verb or action verb. For each action verb, have students tell whether the verb is transitive or intransitive. Direct objects should be indentified in sentences with transitive verbs.

1. Julie always sings melancholy songs.
2. The newscast was late.
3. I wrote a three-page report.
4. The caged animals looked restless.
5. Dana feels sorry for Lindsey.
6. The doctor checked Vera's pulse.
7. I have a pebble in my shoe.
8. Meryl Streep is a fine actress.

Advanced Students

Point out that excessive use of linking verbs leads to dull writing. Give students a list of sentences containing linking verbs followed by predicate adjectives (*The conductor was energetic*) and have students write replacement sentences using action verbs (*The conductor flailed the air with his baton*).

Reinforcement Exercises

Assign and discuss Exercises A and B on page 492.

Optional Practice

Give students a list of verbs that can be either linking verbs or action verbs. Have them write sentences using each verb in both ways.

Extending the Lesson

Have students write a paragraph describing how personality is revealed by the way in which a person walks. Ask them to use several vivid verbs to describe different kinds of walks (*skip, amble, lumber, tiptoe*). Ask them to use linking verbs to describe personalities (*Some people are extremely nervous*).

5. Diane programmed the computer. _{action}
6. The flight to Cleveland seemed very smooth. _{linking}
7. The ranch overlooks the Rockies. _{action}
8. Water became scarce during the summer. _{linking}
9. We saw an old-fashioned rodeo in Bishop, California. _{action}
10. Juan likes books about the American Civil War. _{action}

Exercise B: Follow the directions for Exercise A.

1. Judge Leonard Suchanek amazes most people. _{action}
2. At birth, Suchanek had only forty percent hearing. _{action}
3. At age five he became totally blind from an accident. _{linking}
4. He studied Braille for several years at a special school. _{action}
5. The young boy soon developed an important, positive attitude toward life. _{action}
6. From childhood, Suchanek constantly challenged the limits of his handicaps. _{action}
7. He was an excellent student in both high school and college. _{linking}
8. Eventually this man became a successful lawyer. _{linking}
9. Today Suchanek lives with his wife and son in our nation's capital, Washington, D.C. _{action}
10. He is a federal judge. _{linking}

Exercise C: Write the action verb in each sentence. After it write *Transitive* or *Intransitive* to show what kind it is. If a verb is transitive, write its (object.)

1. Those trucks have diesel engines. _{transitive (engines)}
2. The herd of elephants suddenly charged the hyenas. _{transitive (hyenas)}
3. Neon signs flashed in the dark. _{intransitive}
4. The spacecraft explored Saturn. _{transitive (Saturn)}
5. Mrs. LaPorte videotaped the final performance of our class play. _{transitive (performance)}
6. The train from Washington finally arrived. _{intransitive}
7. During the storm the airport closed. _{intransitive}
8. Tom often swims before school. _{intransitive}
9. Sarah reads horror stories and fantasies. _{transitive (stories and fantasies)}
10. Through the tangle of branches we saw luminous eyes. _{transitive (eyes)}

Part 2 The Parts of a Verb

Many verbs are made up of a **main verb** plus one or more **helping verbs.** Another name for helping verbs is **auxiliary verbs.**

The most common helping verbs are forms of *be, have,* and *do.* They may also be used as main verbs. Here are their forms:

BE—am, is, be, are, was, were, been
HAVE—has, have, had
DO—does, do, did

USED AS MAIN VERB	USED AS HELPING VERB
I *was* lucky.	I *was eating* lunch.
Jill *has* a cold.	Jill *has finished* her report.
We *did* our chores.	We *did like* the movie.

Here are other frequently used helping verbs:

can	will	shall	may	must
could	would	should	might	

Helping verbs combine with the main verb to become parts of the verb.

HELPING VERB(S) + MAIN VERB = VERB

am	going	am going
are	watching	are watching
will	stay	will stay
had	stayed	had stayed
should have	stayed	should have stayed
must	join	must join
has	joined·	has joined

Sometimes the parts of the verb are separated. The words that come between them are not part of the verb. Study these examples.

Chinese food *has* always *seemed* tasty.
The team *was* barely *paying* attention.
When *will* the President *hold* a press conference?
Did the press secretary *speak?*

Part 2

Objective

To recognize main verbs and helping verbs

Presenting the Lesson

1. Read and discuss page 477. Put sentences containing simple present tense verbs on the board. Ask students to suggest helping verbs that could be added to these sentences. Discuss ways in which adding helping verbs changes meaning. Also point out changes that must be made to the main verb.

2. Complete and discuss Exercises A and B on page 478.

Individualizing the Lesson

Less-Advanced Students

1. Before completing Exercises A and B on page 478, give students a list of helping verbs and a list of action verbs. Have students combine these to make their own sentences.

2. Have students memorize the helping verbs listed on page 477.

Advanced Students

1. Have students write sentences using the following verbs as indicated:

1. *crying* plus two helping verbs
2. *might have been* plus a main verb
3. *was* as a main verb
4. *was* as a helping verb
5. *could be* plus a main verb
6. *could* plus a main verb in a question
7. *been* plus a helping verb
8. *should be* plus a main verb
9. *enjoyed* plus a helping verb
10. *did* plus a main verb in a question

2. Have students rewrite the sentences in Exercise A, substituting different helping verbs and changing main verb endings as necessary.

Reinforcement Exercise

Assign and discuss Exercise C on page 492.

Optional Practice

Ask students to write sentences using the verbs listed on page 477 both as main verbs and as helping verbs.

Extending the Lesson

Have students bring in a magazine picture. Instruct them to write sentences describing the action in the picture. Underline helping verbs once and action verbs twice. Encourage them to use transitive and intransitive verbs, and to include separated verb parts in some of the sentences.

Exercise A: Make two columns. Label them *Helping Verb* (HV) and *Main Verb* (MV). Find the parts of the verb in each sentence. Write them in the proper columns.

1. A new snack shop has (HV) opened (MV).
2. The glider was (HV) soaring (MV) above the valley.
3. The express train does (HV) not stop (MV) at Webster Avenue.
4. A computer will (HV) prepare (MV) the class lists.
5. Has (HV) Bob been (HV) diving (MV) for scallops?
6. No fuel should (HV) be (HV) wasted (MV).
7. The roan stallion must (HV) have (HV) escaped (MV) from the corral.
8. No one had (HV) ever climbed (MV) that mountain.
9. Construction workers on a job site must (HV) always wear (MV) hardhats.
10. A smoke alarm would (HV) have (HV) alerted (MV) us to the fire.

Exercise B: The helping verbs have been omitted from the following sentences. Number your paper from 1 to 10. Write each sentence adding helping verbs to complete each one. Answers may vary.

1. The ice rink __will__ __be__ closed for repairs.
2. Greg __was__ expecting a call from Dad.
3. The lifeguard __had__ warned us several times.
4. __Did__ the Buckeyes receive the kickoff?
5. Jonas __should__ __have__ tried these clams.
6. __Will__ Melissa run for office?
7. The temperature __must__ __have__ climbed to 98°.
8. __Have__ the snowplows cleared the mountain pass?
9. Diaz __will__ surely pitch in Thursday's game.
10. Pilots of commercial jets __must__ pass rigorous requirements.

Exercise C: Writing Use the following helping verbs and main verbs to write sentences of your own.

1. may complete
2. would have followed
3. will record
4. might remember
5. must have meant
6. has believed
7. had been told
8. were nominated
9. should have brought
10. did agree

478

Part 3   Verb Tenses

In addition to expressing action or state of being, a verb can also tell *when* that action or state of being occurs. By changing form, verbs can indicate past time, present time, or future time.

These changes in form to indicate time are called **tenses**. The changes are usually made in one of these two ways:

1. Change in spelling

   run→ran   try→tried   close→closed

2. Use of helping verbs

   eat→had eaten   survive→will survive   climb→has climbed

In English there are three **simple tenses** and three **perfect tenses**. This list shows examples of the six main tenses for the verbs *paint* and *watch*.

PRESENT TENSE:	I paint.	She watches.
PAST TENSE:	I painted.	She watched.
FUTURE TENSE:	I will paint.	She will watch.
PRESENT PERFECT TENSE:	I have painted.	She has watched.
PAST PERFECT TENSE:	I had painted.	She had watched.
FUTURE PERFECT TENSE:	I will have painted.	She will have watched.

Simple Tenses

The **present tense** indicates time in the present. The present tense form is usually the same as the name of the verb. When verbs are used with most singular subjects, an *-s* is added to the end of verb.

   I *know*.   Cathy *knows*.   My mother *knows*.

The **past tense** shows past time. Most verbs form the past tense by adding *-d* or *-ed*.

   Ben *raced*.   Yvonne *called*.   I *laughed*.

are ones that use *to have* as a helping verb.

3. Have students identify the verbs in the following sentences and tell the tense of each.

1. Our dog, Coco, follows me everywhere.
2. The orchestra has begun its program.
3. Bert planted tomatoes near the fence.
4. The mayoral candidates will have a debate.
5. By next week, you will have learned all of the basic steps.
6. Before noon, the sun had disappeared behind the clouds.
7. Peter fell in the mud along the river bank.
8. The roses will be in bloom soon.
9. Wrens and robins gather around the fountain.
10. Dinner will be ready at 6:00.

Advanced Students

Have students write two original sentences for each of the six verb tenses. Some of the sentences should be written on the board for discussion.

Reinforcement Exercise

Assign and discuss Exercise D on page 493.

Optional Practice

Ask students to make charts of the six main tenses for the verbs *dance* and *work*. Then have them write a sentence to illustrate each tense.

Extending the Lesson

1. Ask students to write a series of predictions beginning with the phrase *By the year 2000.* Make

Some verbs form the past tense in irregular ways.

> They *rode.*   Sue *went* to the game.   Adam *swam.*

The **future tense** shows time in the future. In this tense, *shall* or *will* is used with the verb.

> Keith *will start.*   Donna *will guess.*   I *shall return.*

The three tenses just described are called the **simple tenses.**

Perfect Tenses

The **perfect tenses** are used when we have to speak of two different times, one earlier than the other. The perfect tenses are formed by using the helping verbs *has, have,* and *had.*

The **present perfect tense** tells of an action or state of being in some indefinite time before the present. The helping verb *has* or *have* is used.

> They *have arrived.*   The class *has elected*
> Dean *has sold* his stereo.   its officers.

The **past perfect tense** tells of an action or state of being that preceded some other past action or state of being. The helping verb *had* is used.

> They *had been* lonely until we *came.*
> Marie *had waited* for the bus for hours, but it never *arrived.*
> We *had* just *gone* into the house when the storm *hit.*

The **future perfect tense** tells of an action or state of being that will occur *before* some other future action or state of being.

> By this time tomorrow, *you will have met* the Governor.
> When the hike is over, *we will have walked* ten miles.

Exercise A: Write the <u>verbs</u> in the following sentences. Tell the tense of each.

1. Thunder <u>rumbled</u> in the distance. past
2. We <u>have lived</u> in Fort Collins for three years. present perfect

3. The Packers had already accepted the penalty. past perfect
4. Bernstein kicks most of the field goals. present
5. An overtime will decide the game. future
6. Helmets protect motorcycle riders. present
7. Each suspect will take a lie detector test. future
8. By noon the hikers will have reached the Alpine Meadows. future perfect
9. Police thoroughly searched the hideout. past
10. The mobsters had already fled through a hole in the roof. past perfect

Exercise B: Writing Write a sentence for each of the verbs below. Use the tense indicated. Sentences will vary.

1. judge (past) judged
2. deny (present perfect) has or have denied
3. notice (past perfect) had noticed
4. live (present) live or lives
5. flip (past) flipped
6. drive (present) drive or drives
7. explode (future) shall or will explode
8. prepare (future perfect) shall or will have prepared
9. work (present perfect) has or have worked
10. dance (future) shall or will dance

Part 4   The Progressive Forms

There is another way that a verb can show time. The **progressive form** of a verb indicates action which is ongoing. That action can be in the past, the present, or the future. Progressive forms are made by using the forms of *be* with the present participle:

Rosemary *is taking* mandolin lessons.
Craig *was thinking* about it.
We *will be marching* in the Labor Day parade.
Before you called, I *had been sleeping*.

Exercise: Identify the progressive forms in the following sentences. Write them on your paper.

1. They will be considering your application later this afternoon.
2. As the fog was rolling in, we were crossing the famous Golden Gate Bridge.
3. Will we be going to the movie with Jeremy?
4. The snow was piling up in huge drifts against the doors and windows.

481

them aware of the tenses they are using.

2. Ask students to look back over their years of schooling and to write a short summary of their most important learning experiences at each grade level, beginning each entry with the phrase "By grade ———, I . . ."

Part 4

Objective

To recognize and use the progressive forms of verbs

Presenting the Lesson

1. Read and discuss page 481. Review with students the forms of *to be*. Discuss spelling changes that occur when *-ing* is added to verbs.

2. Assign and discuss the Exercise on pages 481–482.

Individualizing the Lesson

Less-Advanced Students

Present the formation of progressives as a three-part process:

a. Determine the tense of the verb that is to be changed.

b. Choose a form of *to be* that is in the same tense and place this before the verb.

c. Add *-ing* to the original verb.

Assign and discuss Exercise E on pages 493–494.

Have students write instructions for how to run a three-legged race and then describe a specific race

Advanced Students

Discuss the usefulness of the progressive forms in describing present action.

Reinforcement Exercise

Assign and discuss Exercise E on pages 493–494.

Extending the Lesson

Have students write an imaginary live broadcast of a sports event. Action should be described as though the event were in progress.

Part 5

Objective

To recognize and form the principal parts of regular verbs

Presenting the Lesson

1. Read and discuss pages 482–483. Review the difference between simple and perfect tenses.

2. Assign Exercise on page 483.

Individualizing the Lesson

Less-Advanced Students

Write a regular verb on the board. Ask a student to use the verb in a sentence, orally. The student may add a helping verb and/or past tense ending. Then ask another student to say whether the verb part used is the present, past, or past participle.

Advanced Students

Have students write instructions for how to run a three-legged race and then describe a specific race

5. The band will soon be looking for a new lead singer.
6. After the storm, the clouds were moving slowly.
7. Marco will be waiting for you at the soccer field.
8. Mozart was already composing complicated music as a child.
9. Michael was telling the story about the haunted van.
10. We will be reading play scripts all evening.

Part 5 The Principal Parts of a Verb

The **principal parts** of a verb are its basic forms. The principal parts of a verb are the **present,** the **past,** and the **past participle.** By combining these forms with helping verbs, you can make all of the six main tenses.

Most verbs form the past and past participle by adding -*d* or -*ed* to the present form. These verbs are called **regular verbs** because they form the past and past participle by following a regular pattern.

PRESENT	PAST	PAST PARTICIPLE
trust	trusted	(have) trusted
want	wanted	(have) wanted
move	moved	(have) moved
change	changed	(have) changed

Note: Some regular verbs change their spelling when the -*d* or -*ed* is added. Study the examples that follow.

PRESENT	PAST	PAST PARTICIPLE
try	tried	(have) tried
trot	trotted	(have) trotted
say	said	(have) said
slip	slipped	(have) slipped

The past participle is used for all perfect tenses. It must be used with a helping verb.

They have changed.   We had tried.
Mark must have known.   Beth has slipped.

482

Exercise: Make three columns on your paper. Label them *Present*, *Past*, and *Past Participle*. List the principal parts of these regular verbs in the proper columns. Past tense and past participle are the same for these regular verbs.

1. cook cooked
2. marry married
3. seem seemed
4. belong belonged
5. pull pulled
6. copy copied
7. happen happened
8. lift lifted
9. act acted
10. toss tossed
11. follow followed
12. open opened
13. claim claimed
14. trip tripped
15. drag dragged

Part 6   Irregular Verbs

You have learned the principal parts for regular verbs. Many verbs, though, do not follow the regular pattern. That is, they do not add -*d* or -*ed* to form the past tense and past participle. Such verbs are called irregular verbs. Note the following examples.

PRESENT	PAST	PAST PARTICIPLE
throw	threw	(have) thrown
feel	felt	(have) felt
spring	sprang	(have) sprung
tell	told	(have) told
cut	cut	(have) cut

You will notice that some of the verbs have one or two different forms. Others, like the verbs *throw* and *spring*, have three different forms.

If you do not know the principal parts of a verb, look up the verb in a dictionary. If no parts are listed, the verb is regular. If the verb is irregular, the dictionary will list the irregular forms. It will give two forms if both the past and past participle are the same, as in *catch*, *caught*. It will give three forms if all principal parts are different, as in *ring, rang, rung*.

Some dictionaries will list a fourth principal part. It is called the **present participle.** The present participle of a verb is formed by adding -*ing* to the present form: *cook—cooking*. This participle is used to make the progressive forms of a verb.

483

they have seen. Tell them to use some of the verbs from the Exercise on page 483, using both the present and the past tenses.

Optional Practice

Provide a chart like the one below. Have the class fill in the missing parts. Use only regular verbs

Present	Past	Past Participle
	walked	
		(have) mixed
pry		

Extending the Lesson

Ask the class to invent imaginary regular verbs, such as *nork* and *glure*. Tell them to give the principal parts of their verbs and use each of the principal parts in a sentence.

Part 6

Objective

To recognize the principal parts of irregular verbs

Presenting the Lesson

1. Read and discuss page 483. To reinforce the difference between regular and irregular verbs, write several verbs on the board, such as *grab, put, write, skate,* and *run.* Call on students and have them give the principal parts of these verbs. Then ask another student whether each verb is regular or irregular. Point out for each of the irregular verbs whether it has one form, two forms, or three forms.

Call on students to form the pre-

2. Call on students to form the present participle of the verbs you have written on the board. Check the dictionaries in the classroom to see if they list the fourth principal part.

3. Give the class a list of irregular verbs. The list should include one verb from each of the five groups on pages 484–489: *cost, catch, freeze, swim, know.* Have the students look up these words and write down their principal parts. If only a few dictionaries are available, ask the students to work in groups. Point out that each of the verbs they looked up changed in a different way. Read and discuss pages 484–489. Point out that each of the five verbs they looked up in the dictionary belongs to a different group presented on these pages.

4. The A and B exercises on pages 485–489 may be started orally and completed individually. Assign each set after the verb type is discussed. Assign C exercises only after it is clear that students understand how to form the different parts of each type of irregular verb.

Individualizing the Lesson

Less-Advanced Students

1. Have students supply the correct form of the verb in parentheses for each of the following sentences. Do this exercise orally.

1. We have (know) about Mike's plans since May.
2. Bernie (cut) the ribbon to start the race.
3. The baby (drink) his milk this morning.
4. The game has (begin) already.
5. Dan (wear) his new jacket to school.
6. A thief (steal) Jan's bicycle.

Using Irregular Verbs

There are two ways to be sure of the forms of irregular verbs. One way is to look up the verbs in the dictionary. The other way is to learn the principal parts of commonly used irregular verbs.

Once you know the principal parts, keep the following ideas in mind. The past participle is always used with *have* or *be* helping verbs. The past participle is used for present perfect and past perfect tenses. The past form is not used with helping verbs.

The principal parts of irregular verbs can be confusing. They may seem simpler if you learn the following five patterns.

Group 1 Some irregular verbs keep the same form for all three principal parts. These are easy to remember.

PRESENT	PAST	PAST PARTICIPLE
burst	burst	(have) burst
cost	cost	(have) cost
cut	cut	(have) cut
let	let	(have) let
put	put	(have) put
set	set	(have) set

Here are some sentences using verbs from this group:

Those video games *cost* too much. (present)
I *put* my signature on the contract. (past)
Matt *has set* up the scenery. (past participle)

Group 2 Another group of irregular verbs changes form only once. The past and the past participle are the same.

PRESENT	PAST	PAST PARTICIPLE
bring	brought	(have) brought
catch	caught	(have) caught
lead	led	(have) led
lend	lent	(have) lent
lose	lost	(have) lost
say	said	(have) said
sit	sat	(have) sat

These sentences use irregular verbs from Group 2:

I *sit* in the lifeguard station. (present)
Tyrone *led* the league in R.B.I.'s. (past)
Garrett and Lynn *have caught* three salmon. (past participle)

Exercise A: Choose the correct form of the verb.

1. The convention (brang, brought) five thousand delegates to San Diego.
2. The infielder has (catched, caught) the foul ball.
3. These ice skates (costed, cost) twice as much as my old ones.
4. Estelle (put, putted) a videotape on the player.
5. Lauren (lent, lended) me a special wrench.
6. The stage crew (set, setted) up the props and scenery.
7. No one has ever (sayed, said) that before.
8. A hose in the engine (burst, bursted).
9. Duncan has (sat, sitted) on the bench all season.
10. Kris (leaded, led) in scoring for the Wildcats.

Exercise B: Follow the directions for Exercise A.

1. Somehow I (lost, losed) track of the time.
2. The reward for any helpful information was (setted, set) at $1,000.
3. Suddenly, Jane (burst, bursted) into the room.
4. Jim has (put, putted) more kerosene in the lamp.
5. Deena (caught, catched) the flu.
6. The fishermen had not (brang, brought) enough bait.
7. In 1978 gas (cost, costed) less than a dollar a gallon.
8. The exhausted soldiers (sat, sitted) wearily in their barracks.
9. Porter (led, leaded) by only a few thousand votes in the primary election.
10. The lawyer has (said, sayed) very little about the complicated case.

Exercise C: Writing Compose a paragraph that uses the present, past, and past participle forms of some of the Group 1 and 2 verbs.

7. The mayor has (speak) at five meetings.
8. parents (let) their children swim here.
9. The police have (catch) the vandals.
10. I have (say) all that I am going to.

2. Emphasize oral practice with each type of irregular verb. Complete an organized drill before assigning written practice.

Advanced Students

Have the students write a brief story about a personal adventure involving water. They must use as many verbs from Groups 3, 4, and 5 as possible. They should write the adventure in the past tense and be sure to use some past and present participles as well.

Reinforcement Exercise

Assign and discuss Exercise F on page 494.

Optional Practice

Point out that an intervening adverb or inverted order of the verb may make the choice of verb form difficult. Go over the following sentences with the students asking them to supply the correct form of the verb in parentheses.

1. I have already (drink) five glasses of milk.
2. Have you ever (swim) a mile?
3. The clown bravely (burst) the giant balloon.
4. Has the late bell (ring) yet?
5. Milton has probably (write) as much great poetry as any other English poet.
6. Have I (break) the school record yet?
7. Brett had already (wear) a hole in his shoe.

8. Have the girls ever (ride) a horse before?
9. Have you (grow) as many inches as your sister?
10. The rabbit fearfully (spring) away from the dog.

Extending the Lesson

Ask students to read a short article in the newspaper, listing all the verbs in the article in one of two columns: "Regular Verbs" and "Irregular Verbs." Point out the proportion of regular to irregular verbs in this randomly selected sample of the language.

Group 3 Verbs in this group add *-n* or *-en* to the past tense to form the past participle.

PRESENT	PAST	PAST PARTICIPLE
break	broke	(have) broken
choose	chose	(have) chosen
freeze	froze	(have) frozen
speak	spoke	(have) spoken
steal	stole	(have) stolen
wear	wore	(have) worn

Here are three sentences using Group 3 verbs:

Speak into the microphone. (present)
Everyone *wore* strange costumes. (past)
Joan and Bill *have chosen* their teams. (past participle)

Exercise A: Choose the correct form of the verb from the two forms given.

1. Ms. Gomez has (chose, chosen) a blue interior for her car.
2. The environmental group has (spoke, spoken) to the governor.
3. Money had been (stole, stolen) from the cash register.
4. The rock group (wore, worn) gold and glitter.
5. Evans (broke, broken) a land-speed record.
6. Tires squealed as the cars (tore, torn) around the track.
7. After an afternoon of ice skating, my feet were nearly (froze, frozen).
8. A rock has (broke, broken) the display window.
9. The country has (chose, chosen) a new leader.
10. Have you (wore, worn) the sweater your aunt bought you in Denmark?

Exercise B: Follow the directions for Exercise A.

1. A pickpocket (stole, stolen) Ken's wallet during the rally.
2. The sign read, "Spanish is (spoke, spoken) here."
3. The sailors (wore, worn) their dress uniforms.
4. The bickering lawyers have finally (chose, chosen) a jury.

5. Rain (froze, frozen) on the windshield.
6. Lori accidentally (tore, torn) up a dollar bill.
7. The relay team has (broke, broken) a world record.
8. The mourners have (wore, worn) black clothing.
9. Some top-secret papers have been (stole, stolen).
10. The social worker (spoke, spoken) about conflicts.

Group 4 The irregular verbs in this group change their final vowels. The vowel changes from *i* in the present tense to *a* in the past tense and *u* in the past participle.

PRESENT	PAST	PAST PARTICIPLE
begin	began	(have) begun
drink	drank	(have) drunk
ring	rang	(have) rung
sing	sang	(have) sung
swim	swam	(have) swum

Here are examples of irregular verbs from Group 4:

I usually *sing* off-key. (present)
The chimes *rang* softly. (past)
The police *have begun* a crackdown. (past participle)

Exercise A: Choose the correct verb form from the two given in parentheses.

1. Emily (began, begun) babysitting last year and now has many clients.
2. Someone must have (drank, drunk) all the lemonade.
3. Bill (rang, rung) for the flight attendant.
4. I wonder how many times the Beach Boys have (sang, sung) "California Girls."
5. The telephone had (rang, rung) all day.
6. When Paul Robeson (sang, sung) "Old Man River," the audience sat spellbound.
7. Our husky has (began, begun) his obedience school course.
8. Count Dracula (drank, drunk) the blood of his victims.
9. The hospital has (began, begun) a blood drive.
10. Stevie Wonder (sang, sung) his latest hit single.

Exercise B: Follow the directions for Exercise A.

1. The loud noises (<u>rang,</u> rung) in my ears.
2. Leslie (<u>swam,</u> swum) for an hour in the icy water of Lake Superior.
3. The team (<u>began,</u> begun) to rally in the fourth quarter.
4. Jeff (<u>drank,</u> drunk) a quart of milk at lunch.
5. A piranha (<u>swam,</u> swum) alone in the huge tank.
6. The candidates have (began, <u>begun</u>) to campaign.
7. After the wedding, bells (<u>rang,</u> rung).
8. Have you (drank, <u>drunk</u>) all the grape juice?
9. Many operas are (sang, <u>sung</u>) in Italian.
10. Had they (swam, <u>swum</u>) in the ocean before?

Exercise C: Writing Using Exercises A and B as a pattern, write ten of your own exercise sentences. Use verbs from Groups 3 and 4. Make a separate answer key for your exercise or, if possible, exchange exercises with a classmate.

Group 5 For some irregular verbs the past participle is formed from the present tense. The past participle looks more like the present tense than the past tense.

PRESENT	PAST	PAST PARTICIPLE
come	came	(have) come
do	did	(have) done
eat	ate	(have) eaten
fall	fell	(have) fallen
give	gave	(have) given
go	went	(have) gone
grow	grew	(have) grown
know	knew	(have) known
ride	rode	(have) ridden
rise	rose	(have) risen
run	ran	(have) run
see	saw	(have) seen
take	took	(have) taken
throw	threw	(have) thrown
write	wrote	(have) written

Here are sentences using Group 5 verbs:

    I usually *eat* in the cafeteria.
    Bob *ate* three helpings of spaghetti.
    My dog *has eaten* my homework.

    Marcy *knows* two movie stars.
    I once *knew* all the state capitals.
    Have you *known* him very long?

Exercise A: Choose the correct verb form from the two given.

1. Mr. Torres has (ran, run) his store for twenty years.
2. Cary (threw, thrown) a terrific party.
3. A passenger has (fell, fallen) overboard!
4. Vera (ate, eaten) raw fish at a Japanese restaurant.
5. Ken (grew, grown) four inches last year.
6. Charles Kuralt has (went, gone) to all corners of America.
7. Jory had (saw, seen) more horror films than any of us.
8. Paris is (knew, known) for its high fashion.
9. Sterling and Darrell (took, taken) a Greyhound bus to
   Flagstaff, Arizona.
10. Samantha has (rode, ridden) a bike across Nebraska and
    South Dakota.

Exercise B: Follow the directions for Exercise A.

1. The dictator has (fell, fallen) from power.
2. The job had (came, come) along just in time.
3. A gymnast (did, done) handsprings and back flips across
   the mat.
4. Since the 1930's, George Gallup has (took, taken) polls of
   public opinion.
5. Dennis (saw, seen) a strange object flying in the night sky.
6. Has everyone (gave, given) up on this project?
7. Anne (went, gone) to City Hall to see the mayor.
8. The candidate has (ran, run) her campaign honestly.
9. *The Outsiders* and *Rumble Fish* were (wrote, written) by
   S. E. Hinton.
10. The escaped prisoners were last (saw, seen) in an
    Oklahoma town.

Part 7

Objective

To distinguish between active and passive verbs

Presenting the Lesson

Emphasize the livelier language that results from the use of active verbs. Encourage students to limit their use of the passive voice to times when they do not know who performed the action, or when it is not important who performed the action.

1. Read and discuss page 490.

2. Review transitive and intransitive verbs. Point out that intransitive verbs and linking verbs cannot be expressed in the passive voice.

3. Distinguish between *voice* and *tense*. Go over the examples on page 490 pointing out that the change from active to passive does not affect the tense of the verb.

4. Ask a student to think of an active sentence with a transitive verb. Have a different student change the sentence to the passive voice. Discuss the difference.

5. Complete Exercise A on page 491 orally. Assign and discuss Exercise B.

Individualizing the Lesson

Less-Advanced Students

1. Ask the students to turn the following active sentences into passive sentences.

1. Gayle drew this picture.
2. Gabriel watered the plants.
3. A jackrabbit ate our vegetables.
4. Tom and Claire raked the leaves.
5. The operator placed the long-distance call.

Study the following two sentences:

> The committee proposed several possible solutions.
> Several possible solutions were proposed.

In the first sentence, the subject tells who performed the action. When the subject performs the action, the verb is said to be in the **active voice**.

In the second sentence, the subject tells what received the action of the verb. When the subject is the receiver or the result of the action, the verb is said to be in the **passive voice**. The word *passive* means "acted upon."

The use of active and passive voice can add variety to writing. However, a passive verb is usually not as strong as an active one. Most writers, therefore, prefer to use active verbs whenever possible to help make their writing more interesting and lively.

Forming the Passive

The passive voice is formed by using some form of *be* with the past participle. The receiver of the action precedes the verb.

ACTIVE	PASSIVE
Max *washed* the floor.	The floor *was washed* by Max.
Meg *has finished* the project.	The project *has been finished* by Meg.
The store *will add* the tax.	The tax *will be added* by the store.

Find the direct objects in the sentences in the first column above. In the sentences in the second column, the direct objects have become the subjects. Only verbs that have objects (transitive verbs) can be changed from active to passive.

A verb is active when its subject performs the action of the verb.

A verb is passive when its subject names the receiver or result of the action stated by the verb.

Exercise A: Write the verb in each sentence. After each, write *Active* or *Passive* to tell what kind it is.

1. One of the twins prefers country music. active
2. The weather service predicted a record snowfall. active
3. A meeting had been planned by the workers' union. passive
4. The local merchants held a street fair. active
5. Ms. O'Brien read the class an interesting article. active
6. A citizens' group patrolled the streets at night. active
7. Several sites were considered by the builder. passive
8. The Potter's Wheel also sells ceramic supplies. active
9. The S.W.A.T. unit was called to the scene. passive
10. Liz's plans were affected by inflation. passive

Exercise B: Writing Change the verbs in the following sentences from passive to active. Rewrite the sentences. You may have to add subjects. Sentences will vary. Correct verb form is given.

1. The rug was cleaned by Mr. Harvey. cleaned
2. The scores are given by the sportscaster. gives
3. A new comedian was introduced by Johnny Carson. introduced
4. New paintings were delivered to the museum. delivered
5. The trophy had been won by our team once before. had won
6. Five buildings were destroyed by the fire. destroyed
7. Mr. Walters is known by everybody on our block. knows
8. The African safari was led by Ms. Bernstein. led
9. The judge's decision will be appealed by the lawyer. will appeal
10. Letters had been sent to the President. had sent

Exercise C: Writing Write a paragraph that describes your favorite sport or activity. Use only the passive voice. Then, rewrite the paragraph changing the passive verbs to active verbs. Note the differences between the two paragraphs. Which is more effective?

2. Allow students to work in pairs to complete Exercise B.

Advanced Students

Have students complete a second set of paragraphs similar to those described in Exercise C. The topic should be a movie review.

Reinforcement Exercise

Assign and discuss Exercise G page 494.

Optional Practice

Point out that sometimes passive constructions are used to avoid naming the real performer of an action. Have students turn the following passive sentences into active ones, supplying a subject for the verb when necessary.

1. My brother was fired yesterday.
2. The decision was made unanimously.
3. The window was broken accidentally.
4. Several fires have been set recently.
5. The cut-backs will have been made by March.

Extending the Lesson

Have the students imagine that they have just witnessed a strange event involving a hot-air balloon and a radio tower. Ask them to write one or two paragraphs describing what they saw. Then have them check to see how many of the verbs are in the active form. Have them try to write all of their transitive verb sentences in passive form. Point out the effect of using too much passive voice.

REINFORCEMENT EXERCISES
Using Verbs

A. Identify action and linking verbs. Write the verb in each sentence. After it, write *Action* or *Linking* to tell what kind it is.

(Use after page 476.)

1. Michelangelo painted the ceiling of the Sistine Chapel. action
2. The sky appeared almost green before the storm. linking
3. The lineman ran out for the pass. action
4. That photo of the Grand Canyon is stunning. linking
5. Those stunt performers are real daredevils. linking
6. As a library aide, Susan shelves books. action
7. The evil troll gloated at the hero's dismay. action
8. Was Amy Russell the pinch hitter? linking
9. The sleepy cat folded his paws neatly under him. action
10. In the lobby, Superman looked for a phone booth. action

B. Recognize transitive and intransitive verbs. Write the verb in each sentence. After it, write *Transitive* or *Intransitive* to show what kind it is. (Use after page 476.)

1. Nicole pounded the last nail into the bookcase. transitive
2. My little brother and his friends pelted us with snowballs. transitive
3. I gasped at the news. intransitive
4. Keith's Frisbee landed on the telephone wires. intransitive
5. The timekeeper reset the clock for the next race. transitive
6. Lee calls Jessica almost every night. transitive
7. After a day on his cousin's sailboat, Anthony's skin glowed bright red. intransitive
8. Doug tightened the brakes on his bike. transitive
9. Which candidate won in that primary election? intransitive
10. The Mosses have lived in New Mexico and Wyoming. intransitive

C. Recognize verbs. Find the parts of the verb in each sentence. Put them in two columns labeled *Helping* Verb and *Main* Verb.

(Use after page 478.)

1. The carolers were singing "O Holy Night."
2. Lindbergh must be the most famous aviator in history.

492

3. My jeans have finally faded.
   HV — have, MV — faded

4. Won't you donate a can of food for the Thanksgiving baskets?
   HV — Won't, MV — donate

5. We will organize a softball league.
   HV — will, MV — organize

6. Jody's uncle has often ridden in rodeos.
   HV — has, MV — ridden

7. The passenger train will be passing through the tunnel in a few minutes.
   HV — will, HV — be, MV — passing

8. Will the parade start on time?
   HV — Will, MV — start

9. Nancy should be practicing for the talent show.
   HV — should, HV — be, MV — practicing

10. The pilot of the small plane could not see through the fog.
    HV — could, MV — see

D. Identify verb tenses. Write the verb in each sentence. Tell its tense: present, past, future, present perfect, past perfect, or future perfect tense. (Use after page 481.)

1. Lana is our camp counselor this summer. present
2. The actors' makeup will look strange. future
3. Tony has sold many of his paintings at art fairs. present perfect
4. We climbed over the rocks and driftwood along the shore. past
5. Are mouthpieces a necessary part of the football uniform? present
6. The monsoons will soon arrive in full force. future
7. Poisonous gases from that chemical factory had leaked into the air. past perfect
8. By tomorrow the fog will have cleared. future perfect
9. The divers have thoroughly searched the river. present perfect
10. Budapest was once two cities, Buda and Pest. past

E. Use progressive tenses of verbs. Rewrite each sentence, changing each verb to its progressive form. Present tense verbs should become present progressive. Future tense verbs should become future progressive. Past tense verbs should become past progressive. Remember to use appropriate helping verbs. (Use after page 482.)

1. The quail crouched invisibly in the tall grass. was crouching
2. The sailors slept soundly before the storm. were sleeping
3. My parakeet mimics the sounds my cat makes. is mimicking
4. The ushers will arrange the chairs for the recital. will be arranging
5. The bamboo grows very rapidly in the hothouse. is growing
6. You walked too fast for me, Sarah. were walking

7. We will make all the necessary travel arrangements. will be making
8. A bright comet streaks across the sky. is streaking
9. I will fly to Boston Friday to visit Dad. will be flying
10. The Haida chief carved a totem pole from a cedar tree. was carving

F. Use irregular verbs correctly. Write the correct verb form from the two given. (Use after page 489.)

1. Jon had (put, putted) the maps into the car.
2. Medical care has never (costed, cost) more.
3. The raft (brang, brought) us safely to the island.
4. The Celtics (lost, losed) by one point.
5. Someone (tore, torn) down the notice about the auction.
6. Has anyone (spoke, spoken) to the career counselor?
7. Stephanie has (broke, broken) her glasses again.
8. The actress had (began, begun) with only bit parts.
9. The hikers (drank, drunk) thirstily from the cool brook.
10. Eliza (saw, seen) the filming of a movie during her trip to San Antonio.

G. Recognize active and passive verb forms. Find the verb in each of the following sentences. Then tell whether it is *Active* or *Passive*. (Use after page 491.)

1. The Coast Guard patrols the shore. active
2. Lyle was removed from the game for the last four innings. passive
3. The koala eats only eucalyptus leaves. active
4. Residents have been informed of the danger. passive
5. The flight to Miami has been canceled. passive
6. The cast is holding its dress rehearsal. active
7. Inspector Grimm has searched every inch of the property. active
8. The pilot should have informed the crew. active
9. My allowance was spent too hastily on this album. passive
10. The rickety cart was reluctantly pulled by Dan's mule, Flossie. passive

MIXED REVIEW
Using Verbs

A. Find the <u>verb</u> in each sentence and tell whether it is *Action* or *Linking*. Then tell whether each action verb is *Transitive* or *Intransitive*.

1. Jogging <u>can be</u> good for you. linking
2. Earthquakes <u>are</u> common in California. linking
3. Underground movements <u>cause</u> earthquakes. action, transitive
4. *The Hound of the Baskervilles* <u>may be</u> the best of the Sherlock Holmes stories. linking
5. Colored grains of sand <u>formed</u> the picture. action, transitive
6. The term "doozy" <u>comes</u> from the Duesenberg auto. action, intr.
7. Light <u>travels</u> at the rate of 186,282 miles per second. action, intr.
8. The founder of the Islamic religion <u>was</u> Muhammad. linking
9. Earth <u>is</u> about four and one-half billion years old. linking
10. The children <u>will sleep</u> in their tent tonight. action, intransitive

B. Find the <u>verb</u> in each sentence. Identify the tense as *Present, Past, Future, Present Perfect, Past Perfect*, or *Future Perfect*. Then, rewrite each sentence, (changing the verb) to the tense or voice indicated in parentheses.

1. Chris <u>made</u> clocks in shop class. (present perfect tense) past, (has made)
2. Mary <u>has chosen</u> Jill for a running mate. (passive voice) present perfect, (has been chosen)
3. Some dinosaurs <u>may have been</u> intelligent. (past tense) present perfect, (were)
4. Susan <u>went</u> to law school. (present tense) past, (goes)
5. Aaron and Eva <u>study</u> modern dance. (past tense) present, (studied)
6. Mahavira <u>founded</u> Jainism, an Indian religion. (passive voice) past, (was founded)
7. We <u>have been waiting</u> for hours. (future perfect tense) present perfect, (will have been waiting)
8. John Creasey <u>wrote</u> twenty-two novels in one year. (passive voice) past, (were written)
9. Jerry Lewis <u>devotes</u> extraordinary amounts of time to the campaign. (present perfect tense) present, (has devoted)
10. After a brief introduction, Leontyne Price <u>sang</u> an aria. (future tense) past, (will sing)

495

Mixed Review

These exercises provide review of the concepts presented in this Section. Each exercise challenges the students to apply several of the skills they have acquired during previous study. Because the "mixed" feature of these activities makes them more difficult, the teacher may wish to have less-advanced students do them orally or in small groups.

Exercise C

1. sing–sang–sung
2. jog–jogged–jogged
3. camp–camped–camped
4. play–played–played
5. act–acted–acted
6. cheat–cheated–cheated
7. allow–allowed–allowed
8. describe–described–described
9. write–wrote–written
10. worship–worshiped–worshiped
11. start–started–started
12. dress–dressed–dressed
13. ride–rode–ridden
14. live–lived–lived
15. catch–caught–caught
16. eat–ate–eaten
17. love–loved–loved
18. create–created–created
19. coach–coached–coached
20. dance–danced–danced

Exercise E

During the Middle Ages (A.D. 400-1500), European peasants *composed* folktales. No one *wrote* down these stories. Instead, traveling minstrels and common people *circulated* them by word of mouth. In the mid-1800's, common people throughout Europe *were* still *telling* many of these folktales. To the delight of children everywhere, modern scholars *have collected* and *published* most of the surviving stories, which include "Cinderella" and the legends of Robin Hood.

C. Draw three columns on your paper. Label them *Present*, *Past*, and *Past Participle*. Write down the principal parts for the following twenty verbs in the proper columns. Then choose three of the verbs and write them in each of the six main tenses. Answers in margin

1. sing	6. cheat	11. start	16. eat
2. jog	7. allow	12. dress	17. love
3. camp	8. describe	13. ride	18. create
4. play	9. write	14. live	19. coach
5. act	10. worship	15. catch	20. dance

D. Choose the correct verb from the two given.

1. My father (freezed, <u>froze</u>) the leftovers.
2. Her hair was (<u>cut</u>, cutted) by a stylist at "Combing Attractions."
3. The balloon (<u>burst</u>, busted) in midair.
4. Alicia (<u>set</u>, sit) the keys on the table.
5. Larry (brang, <u>brought</u>) the records for the party.
6. We (<u>lost</u>, losed) the game by twenty points.
7. Gary was (chose, <u>chosen</u>) by the scholarship committee.
8. A coat was (lended, <u>lent</u>) to the older man.
9. Two twelve-year-old girls have (swam, <u>swum</u>) the English Channel.
10. Mystery writer Agatha Christie has (wrote, <u>written</u>) eighty-seven novels.

E. The following paragraph is weak because all of the verbs are in the passive voice. Replace the italicized passive verbs with active ones, changing the sentences as necessary. Answers in margin

During the Middle Ages (A.D. 400-1500), many folktales *were composed* by European peasants. These stories *were written* down by no one. Instead, they *were circulated* by word of mouth by traveling minstrels and by common people. In the mid-1800's, many of these folktales *were* still *being told* by common people throughout Europe. To the delight of children everywhere, most of the surviving stories, which include "Cinderella" and the legends of Robin Hood, *have been collected* and *published* by modern scholars.

USING GRAMMAR IN WRITING
Using Verbs

A. Imagine that you are a character in an old silent comedy. You are dangling from a flagpole that projects from the twentieth floor of a building. How did you get in this situation? How are you feeling now? How will you get down safely? Write down the thoughts that would be racing through your character's mind. Notice how the verbs change form as you switch from the past tense to present and future tenses.

B. Write out a humorous story that you have heard recently. First, write it in the past tense. Then, write it again in the present tense. Decide which version is funnier.

C. Lively verbs make lively writing. Rewrite the following ad for an amusement park. Make it come alive for the reader by replacing dull verbs with precise, vivid ones, and by changing passive verbs to active verbs. Some of the words that you might consider replacing or reworking are in italics.

> *Spend* a day at Adventure World. The park *can be visited* seven days a week, from 9:00 A.M. to midnight. *Ride* our new roller coaster, The Snake. It *will take* you to the top of a five-story hill, then *send* you down again. *Go* from The Snake to the Paratrooper. Your chair *will be lifted* high above the park and then *dropped*. A free fall *will be experienced* for several seconds before you *are stopped*. After you *get over* your ride on the Paratrooper, *walk* over to the Rapids. You *will sit* in a giant inner tube as it *goes* down a man-made river of churning waves and whirlpools. Finally, *go* to our Musical Review. There, our troupe of talented performers *will sing* and *dance* for you. *Come* out and *visit* us soon! Adventure World is an experience that *won't* soon *be forgotten*.

Section 6

Using Modifiers

How would you describe yourself so that someone could single you out in a crowd? How would you compare the ways two people walk, or describe the taste of pickles or popcorn?

If you had only nouns and verbs to communicate your thoughts, you would have difficulty describing anything clearly. You need other words to make your descriptions more specific. Such words are called **modifiers**.

Modifiers are words that change or limit the meaning of other words.

Notice the difference modifiers make in these two sentences:

A girl sat on a suitcase.
A slender girl with a large straw hat sat restlessly on her tattered suitcase.

Without modifiers, most writing and speech would be unclear and dull. Modifiers help you express your thoughts more precisely and vividly. In this section you will learn to identify and use modifiers.

498

Part 1   Using Adjectives

One kind of modifier is an **adjective**.

An adjective is a word that modifies a noun or pronoun.

Adjectives can tell three different kinds of things about nouns or pronouns.

WHICH ONE OR ONES?

this step, *that* hill, *these* fish, *those* cars

WHAT KIND?

purple line, *shiny* boots, *hilarious* mood, *narrow* alley

HOW MANY OR HOW MUCH?

three months, *several* visitors, *less* pain, *little* snow

Notice that in the first set of examples, demonstrative pronouns are being used as modifiers. Possessive nouns and pronouns can also be modifiers: the *dog's* leash, a *book's* pages, *her* comb, *their* boat.

Proper Adjectives

One special kind of adjective is the proper adjective.
A **proper adjective** is formed from a proper noun, and therefore refers to a specific person, place, or thing. This kind of adjective is always capitalized. Here are some examples:

Jan's skates   an Olympic medal
a British accent   a Pacific island
a Japanese car   Paul Newman's eyes
Mexican food   Victorian furniture

Predicate Adjectives

Another special kind of adjective is the **predicate adjective**. Although most adjectives come before the words they describe,

499

Objective

To recognize proper adjectives, predicate adjectives, and articles

Presenting the Lesson

1. Read and discuss pages 499–500. Go over the three questions that adjectives answer about nouns and pronouns.

2. In discussing proper adjectives, point out that the use of a word rather than its appearance determines its part of speech. Put the following sentences on the board: Italian is a beautiful language. Italian food is my favorite. Ask students to identify the subject and verb in each. Discuss how the word *Italian* functions in each sentence.

3. Review predicate words. Stress that **predicate adjectives** *follow* linking verbs.

4. As you discuss articles, emphasize that it is the *sound* of a word, not the spelling, that determines whether one uses *a* or *an*. Put examples on the board and ask students to say whether *a* or *an* is the appropriate indefinite article: only child; once-in-a-lifetime experience; honor, horror; NFL trophy; nation.

5. Read and discuss **Diagraming Adjectives** on page 501. Demonstrate by diagraming sentences that the students suggest to you.

6. Assign and discuss Exercises A and B on pages 501–502.

Individualizing the Lesson

Less-Advanced Students

1. Write the following sentences on the board. Call on students to add three adjectives to each.

the predicate adjective follows the word it modifies. **A predicate adjective** follows a linking verb and modifies the subject of the sentence.

> Nothing seemed *clear* anymore.
> (*Clear* modifies the subject, *Nothing*.)
>
> Her hair was *auburn*.
> (*Auburn* modifies the subject, *hair*.)

As you can see, *clear* and *auburn* are predicate adjectives. They follow the linking verbs *seemed* and *was*. Each one also modifies the subject of the sentence.

A predicate adjective can be compound, as can modifiers in any other part of the sentence. Look at the two examples that follow.

> The car was *rusty* and *dilapidated*.
>
> Angelo looked *tired* but *happy*.

Articles

The adjectives *a, an,* and *the* are called **articles**.
The is the **definite article**. It points out a specific person, place, or thing.

> Keep *the* ball in play. (a particular ball)

A and *an* are **indefinite articles**.

> Did you find *a* ball? (not a specific ball)
> I would like *an* ice cream cone. (no specific ice cream cone)

Notice that the indefinite article *a* is used before a consonant sound as in *a* rest, *a* school, *a* trip. The indefinite article *an* is used before a vowel sound, for example *an* elbow, *an* oboe, *an* urge.

Pay attention to the sound of the word, not the spelling. We say *a* helper, but *an* honor, for instance, since the *h* in *honor* is silent.

500

Diagraming Adjectives

In a sentence diagram, an adjective appears below the word it modifies. It is placed on a slanted line.

This team has a quick backfield.

Predicate adjectives are diagramed differently. Like predicate nouns and predicate pronouns, they are placed on the main line. A slanted line separates the verb and the predicate adjective.

These opponents are tough.

A compound predicate adjective appears on a split line.

The stereo sounds rich and full.

Exercise A: Write the adjectives in each sentence. After each adjective, write the word it modifies. Do not include articles.

1. The tiny shop sells old books and unusual games.
   tiny (shop); old (books); unusual (games)
2. The new suspension bridge is long and wide.
   new, suspension, long, wide (bridge)
3. Ellie spilled blue paint on her new white shirt.
   blue (paint); her, new, white (shirt)
4. The massive stalagmites in the cave felt cool and moist.
   massive, cool, moist (stalagmites)
5. Several foreign leaders had a private meeting with the President.
   Several, foreign (leaders); private (meeting)
6. Many soldiers were hot and tired after the long march.
   Many, hot, tired (soldiers); long (march)

7. Ten people rode in the back of the dirty, rusty truck. Ten (people); dirty, rusty (truck)
8. The baby giraffe has long, gangly legs. baby (giraffe); long, gangly (legs)
9. Janice drank several glasses of cold water with the salty fish. several (glasses); cold (water) salty (fis...
10. Even his marvelous voice sounded harsh and tinny through the defective microphone. his, marvelous, harsh, tinny (voice); defective, (microphone)

Exercise B: Writing Complete these sentences by adding adjectives. Underline each predicate adjective that you use. Answers will vary.

1. The _____ coach seems (_____) .
2. _____ cars are becoming (_____) .
3. The _____ team feels (_____) about the game.
4. The taste of the _____ _____ chicken was (_____) .
5. The gash looked (_____) and (_____) .
6. The _____ Ocean is (_____) and (_____) .
7. The sky appears (_____) in the evening.
8. A _____ bear lumbered toward our _____ campsite.
9. Sue Ann is a _____ and _____ musician.
10. The video screen displayed _____ images.

Part 2 Adjectives in Comparisons

You often learn about new things by comparing them with things you already know. You might describe a restaurant's food, for example, as "*better than* homemade food." Or you might explain that a cello is *larger than* a violin.

Adjectives can help you to make such comparisons.

The Comparative

Adjectives have special forms for making comparisons. When you compare or contrast one person or thing with another, you use the **comparative** form of an adjective. Here are some examples:

> Evans is a *stronger* pitcher than Richardson.
> Venus appears *brighter* than Saturn.
> Loretta is *less patient* than I am.

Part 2

Objective

To use adjectives correctly in comparisons

Presenting the Lesson

1. Read and discuss **The Comparative** and the **The Superlative** on pages 502–504. Point out that people often incorrectly use the superlative form to compare two things: Bill is the *nicest* of George's two older brothers. Remind them that the comparative is used for two and the superlative for more than two.

2. Read and discuss **Irregular Comparisons** on page 504. Go over the list in detail. Point out that the words *more*, *most*, *less*, and *least*

The comparative form is made in two ways:

1. Add *-er* to short adjectives like *big* and *bright*.

> big + er = bigger   fancy + er = fancier
> wide + er = wider   young + er = younger

Notice that the spelling of some adjectives changes in the comparative form.

2. Use *more* to compare longer adjectives like *unusual*.

> more energetic   more sensitive

Most adjectives ending in *-ful* or *-ous* form the comparative with *more*.

> more powerful   more courageous

The Superlative

When you compare a person or thing with more than two others in its class, you use the **superlative** form of the adjective. Here are some examples:

> Kevin has the *smallest* part in the play.
> Carmen is the *friendliest* person I know.
> He is the *most talented* drummer in the band.
> Of the three computers, this one is *fastest*.

The superlative form of an adjective is made by adding *-est* or by using *most*. If an adjective adds *-er* for the comparative, it adds *-est* for the superlative. If an adjective uses *more* for the comparative, it uses *most* for the superlative.

ADJECTIVE	COMPARATIVE	SUPERLATIVE
green	greener	greenest
smooth	smoother	smoothest
bright	brighter	brightest
helpful	more helpful	most helpful
difficult	more difficult	most difficult
capable	more capable	most capable

are not used with comparative and superlative words. Ask someone in the class to explain why a phrase such as "more better" is illogical.

3. Do Exercise A page 505, orally having students explain the corrections they make. Then ask the class to complete Exercise B on page 505 independently.

Individualizing the Lesson

Less-Advanced Students

Write the following list of adjectives on the board. For each one, have a student spell the comparative and superlative forms and then use them.

1. hot	6. bad
2. noisy	7. red
3. clean	8. many
4. careful	9. friendly
5. enjoyable	10. good

Advanced Students

Have students write a paragraph that compares or contrasts two movies, actors, muscians, etc. Emphasize the use of comparative and superlative adjectives.

Reinforcement Exercise

Assign and discuss Exercise C on pages 519–520.

Optional Practice

Ask the students to write commercials using the list of irregular comparisons from page 504. The ads may be serious or humorous.

Extending the Lesson

Have the students look for a book review or a movie review in which the reviewer compares the book subject to other works. Ask them to circle all comparative and superlative adjectives they find.

Remember these points about adjectives in comparison:

1. To compare two people or things, use the comparative. To compare more than two, use the superlative.

This old coin is *more valuable* than that one.
This coin is the *most valuable* one in the collection.

2. Use the word *other* when you compare something with everything else of its kind.

WRONG: Tim is faster than any runner.
          (This sentence says that Tim is not a runner.)
RIGHT: Tim is faster than any *other* runner.

WRONG: This chair is more solid than any piece of furniture.
          (This sentence implies that the chair is not a piece of furniture.)
RIGHT: This chair is more solid than any *other* piece of furniture.

3. Do not use *-er* with *more*, or *-est* with *most*.

WRONG: Sue is much more taller than her sister.
RIGHT: Sue is much *taller* than her sister.

WRONG: Newfoundlands are the most largest breed of dog.
RIGHT: Newfoundlands are the *largest* breed of dog.

Irregular Comparisons

Some comparatives and superlatives are formed in irregular ways. Study this list and learn to use each form correctly.

ADJECTIVE	COMPARATIVE	SUPERLATIVE
good	better	best
well	better	best
bad	worse	worst
little	less or lesser	least
much	more	most
many	more	most
far	farther	farthest

Exercise A: Writing Number your paper from 1 to 10. Only two of the following comparisons are correct. If a sentence is correct, write *Correct*. If it contains an <u>error</u>, rewrite the sentence correctly.

1. Knowledge about computers has become <u>importanter</u> to high school students. more important
2. Snow blowers are more expensive at this store than at our local store. correct
3. That sailboat is the ~~most~~ <u>biggest</u> in the harbor.
4. A basketball is <u>more big</u> than a soccer ball. bigger
5. The Flying Karamazov Brothers are the ~~most~~ best jugglers I've seen.
6. Bill swims ~~more~~ <u>faster</u> than any other boy on the team.
7. Chopsticks are <u>difficulter</u> for me to use than silverware. more difficult
8. Anna has the highest soprano voice of anyone in chorus. correct
9. The state of Maine is ~~more~~ <u>farther</u> from here than the state of North Dakota is.
10. Of the three tapes, this one is the <u>cheaper</u>. cheapest

Exercise B: Writing Follow the directions for Exercise A. Three of the comparisons are correct.

1. Which river is <u>longest</u>, the Amazon or the Volga? longer
2. Jack is taller than <u>any boy</u> at camp. any other boy
3. The raspberries this year are bigger than the ones we picked last year. correct
4. Who is the <u>most</u> popular cartoon animal, Snoopy or Garfield? more
5. This science fiction novel is the most fantastic book I have ever read. correct
6. Which of these six snakes is the <u>more deadlier</u>? most deadly
7. Who scored <u>the most</u> touchdowns during the first half, Sam or Nick? more
8. That television special on Sunday was the dullest program I have ever seen! correct
9. My sister says calculus is <u>difficulter</u> than geometry or trigonometry. more difficult
10. All of the performers in the piano recital were good, but Carol was <u>better</u>. best

To recognize and form adverbs and to understand their use

Presenting the Lesson

1. Read and discuss **Using Adverbs with Verbs** and **Using Adverbs with Adjectives**, pages 506–507. To help them distinguish between adjectives and adverbs, remind students that adjectives modify nouns and adverbs modify most other words. Review the three questions that adjectives may answer about nouns and the four questions an adverb may answer about the word it modifies.

2. Tell the class that adverbs may be compound (well-informed). Furthermore, a word may be modified by more than one adverb even when adverbs are not compound. Write the following series of sentences on the board to illustrate the various combinations of adverbs with a verb.

This computer works.
This computer works *accurately*.
This computer works *accurately* and *quickly*.
This computer *always* works *accurately* and *quickly*.

3. Read and discuss **Forming Adverbs** on pages 507–508. Point out that, although many adverbs are formed by adding *-ly*, not all words with this ending are adverbs. Words like *friendly, lovely,* and *costly* are adjectives.

4. Tell the class that most of the words that can be used as either adjectives or adverbs are one sylla-

Part 3   Using Adverbs

An **adverb** is another kind of modifier. Like adjectives, adverbs help you to express your ideas clearly and vividly. They tell *how, when, where,* or *to what extent* something is true.

Using Adverbs with Verbs

Adverbs frequently modify verbs. An adverb may appear either before or after the word it modifies.

Adverbs may be used with verbs to tell *how*:

Pat *proudly* displayed her sculpture.

This computer works *accurately*.

Adverbs can also tell *when* about verbs:

Small car sales have soared *recently*.

That old desk will collapse *soon*.

Adverbs can tell *where* about verbs:

Nearby was a white picket fence.

We sat *there* on the river bank for hours.

In addition, adverbs can tell *to what extent*:

Vanessa *nearly* choked on the soup.

The earthquake was *not* destructive.

Study the following list of adverbs:

HOW?	WHEN?	WHERE?	TO WHAT EXTENT?
quickly	now	here	never
furiously	then	there	often
quietly	yesterday	upstairs	not

Try using several adverbs in the following sentence to see how different adverbs can change or modify meaning:

Jimmy Connors responded to the reporter's questions.

Using Adverbs with Adjectives and Other Adverbs

Besides modifying verbs, adverbs also modify adjectives and other adverbs. Look at these sentences:

Our pet dog is *partially* blind.
(*Partially* tells to what extent. It is an adverb modifying the adjective *blind*.)

The assembly line moved *very* quickly.
(*Very* tells to what extent. It is an adverb modifying the adverb *quickly*.)

Here are other adverbs that often modify adjectives or other adverbs:

too	quite	rather	most	more	extremely
just	nearly	so	really	truly	somewhat

Adverbs that modify adjectives and other adverbs tell *to what extent* something is true.

Forming Adverbs

Many adverbs are formed by adding *-ly* to an adjective.

weak + ly = weakly   formal + ly = formally
obvious + ly = obviously   slight + ly = slightly

At times, the addition of *-ly* causes a spelling change in the adjective.

possible + ly = possibly   dull + ly = dully
happy + ly = happily

ble words. Ask the class to try to think of more examples besides *late* and *high*, given in the book. They must prove that their examples are correct by coming up with one sentence in which the word is an adjective and another in which it is an adverb. If they cannot think of any, suggest *fair, fast, loud, right, sharp.*

5. Read and discuss **Diagraming Adverbs** on pages 508–509. Put some of the sample sentences on pages 506–507 on the board and diagram them for the class. Ask the class to think of other sentences with adverbs to diagram.

6. Do Exercise A on page 509 orally with the class. Then ask them to complete Exercises B and C on pages 509–510.

Individualizing the Lesson

Less-Advanced Students

Have students form adverbs from the following adjectives and use each in a sentence.

1. sleepy	6. easy
2. glad	7. immediate
3. sudden	8. accurate
4. usual	9. perfect
5. angry	10. near

Advanced Students

Ask students to write three sentences: one with an adverb modifying a verb; one with an adverb modifying an adjective; and one with an adverb modifying another adverb. Then have the students diagram their sentences. If anyone has an example of a compound adverb, ask him or her to diagram it on the board.

Reinforcement Exercise

Assign and discuss Exercise D on page 520.

Optional Practice

Call the students' attention to the list of adverbs that often modify adjectives or other adverbs on page 507. Then ask them to write a description of the hottest or coldest day they can remember. Tell them to include at least three of the adverbs on the list.

Extending the Lesson

Ask one of the students to give a demonstration of some simple process for the class. Then have the class write a detailed description of how the procedure is done. Call on individual students to read their descriptions to the class. Observe the use of adverbs to create an accurate description. If necessary, suggest the use of more adverbs to make the description more precise.

Some adverbs are not formed from adjectives. *Quite, so, rather,* and *somewhat* are examples.

> The switchboard had never been *so* busy before.
> Suzanne did *rather* well on the Latin test.

Some words can be either adverbs or adjectives. *Late* and *high* are examples of such words.

The doctor arrived too *late*. (adverb)

Tony took a *late* bus. (adjective)

The glider soared *high* above the hills. (adverb)

The crew worked on a *high* tower. (adjective)

Diagraming Adverbs

In a diagram, an adverb is placed on a slanted line attached to the word it modifies. This diagram shows an adverb modifying a verb.

The fire spread rapidly.

Adverbs that modify adjectives or other adverbs are diagramed like this:

Too many jobs pay very poorly.

508

Exercise A: Number your paper from 1 to 10. Write the adverbs in these sentences. After each <u>adverb</u> write the (word it modifies.) Be ready to explain what the adverb tells about the word. A sentence may contain more than one adverb.

EXAMPLE: A new family moved here recently.

recently modifies *moved* (tells when)

here modifies *moved* (tells where)

1. We left <u>early</u> for the concert. early (left)
2. Laura stood <u>dangerously close</u> to the fire. dangerously (close); close (stood)
3. The tornado tore <u>fiendishly</u> across the town. fiendishly (tore)
4. The glider floated <u>gently</u> and <u>silently</u> over the airshow spectators. gently, silently (floated)
5. The pilot <u>very skillfully</u> controlled the fall. very (skillfully); skillfully (controlled)
6. Some spectators had become <u>extremely</u> nervous. extremely (nervous)
7. <u>Unfortunately</u>, you spoke <u>too soon</u>. Unfortunately, soon (spoke); too (soon)
8. A white angora cat sprawled <u>luxuriously</u> on the old Oriental rug. luxuriously (sprawled)
9. <u>Today</u> the great bell pealed <u>loudly</u>. Today, loudly (pealed)
10. The music stopped <u>quite unexpectedly</u>. quite (unexpectedly); unexpectedly (stopped)

Exercise B: Add appropriate adverbs that answer the questions in parentheses.   Answers will vary.

1. That Steven Spielberg movie was _____ advertised on TV. (when?)
2. The movie ads sounded _____ eerie. (to what extent?)
3. The movie itself was _____ scary. (how?)
4. We went to the theater _____ . (when?)
5. The film began _____ but soon improved. (how?)
6. _____ the action moved _____ _____ . (when, how?)
7. Stunt people _____ _____ replace the real actors. (to what extent, when?)
8. This theater _____ charges _____ low prices for tickets. (to what extent?)
9. Do you _____ go to movies? (how *or* to what extent?)
10. Adventure films _____ play _____ . (when, where?)

Exercise C: Writing Change these adjectives into adverbs by adding -*ly*. Then use each word in a sentence.

careless	forceful	natural	mischievous
hungry	joyful	noisy	terrible
proper	immediate	serious	tragic

Part 4 Adverbs in Comparisons

You can use adverbs to compare actions. For example, you might say, "This team wins often but that team wins *more often*." Or you might say, "Of all the players, Erica practices *hardest*." Such comparisons help you to convey ideas clearly. Like adjectives, adverbs have special forms for making comparisons.

The Comparative

The **comparative** form of an adverb compares one action with another. Look at this example:

This thunderstorm hit the town *harder* than the last one.

The comparative is made in two ways:

1. Add -*er* to short adverbs like *long* and *fast*.

   A computer does the job *faster* than a person could.

2. Use *more* with most adverbs ending in -*ly*.

   Some blockers tackle *more roughly* than is necessary.

The Superlative

The **superlative** form of an adverb compares one action with two or more others. Notice these examples.

This flight takes off *earliest* of all.
Of the three boys, Larry spoke the *most bitterly*.

Part 4

Objective

To use adverbs correctly in comparisons

Presenting the Lesson

1. Read and discuss **The Comparative** and **The Superlative** on pages 510–511. Review the formation of comparative and superlative adjectives and point out the similarities in the formation of comparative and superlative adverbs.

2. Read and discuss **Irregular Comparisons** on page 511. Write the adverbs *well, much, little, far* on the board. Call on students to give the comparative and superlative forms of these adverbs. Ask other students to think of sentences for each of the three forms.

3. Assign and discuss Exercises A and B on page 512. Have several students read their sentences out loud. Be alert for errors in adverb usage.

Individualizing the Lesson

Less-Advanced Students

Give students the following sentences and tell them to fill in the blanks with adverbs in either the comparative or the superlative form. Go over the sentences with them when they are finished.

To form the superlative, either add *-est* or use *most*. If an adverb adds *-er* for the comparative, it adds *-est* to form the superlative. If an adverb uses *more* for the comparative, it uses *most* to form the superlative.

ADVERB	COMPARATIVE	SUPERLATIVE
fast	faster	fastest
tightly	more tightly	most tightly

Remember these points about adverbs in comparisons:

1. To compare two actions, use the comparative. To compare more than two actions, use the superlative.

Air mail will arrive *sooner* than surface mail.
Special delivery mail will arrive *soonest* of all.

2. Use the word *other* when you compare with every other action of the same kind.

WRONG: A queen termite lives longer than any insect.
RIGHT: A queen termite lives longer than any *other* insect.

3. Do not use *-er* with *more*, or *-est* with *most*.

WRONG: Stars appear more brighter in the countryside.
RIGHT: Stars appear brighter in the countryside.

Irregular Comparisons

Some adverbs change completely in the comparative and superlative forms. These are examples:

ADVERB	COMPARATIVE	SUPERLATIVE
well	better	best
much	more	most
little	less	least
far	farther	farthest

This saw works well.
That new saw works better.
A table saw would work best of all.

1. This radio _____ than that one.
2. Yesterday I worked _____ than today.
3. Of all the babies, this one cries _____ .
4. The snow melted on the front walk _____ than in the alley.
5. I finished my homework _____ than my sister.

Advanced Students

Present the following sentences and call on students to explain why they are incorrect.

1. Jets will get you to your destination faster than any form of transportation.
2. Of the two candidates, Lonnie campaigned hardest.
3. Miriam swam more farther than Deena.
4. Who fought most bravely, Sherman or Lee?
5. Jacqueline Kennedy spoke Spanish more fluently than any first lady.

Reinforcement Exercise

Assign and discuss Exercise E on page 520.

Optional Practice

Have students write the comparative and superlative forms of the following adverbs and use each in a sentence.

1. easily
2. patiently
3. much
4. slowly
5. naturally
6. recently

Extending the Lesson

Ask students to choose a sports figure whom they admire and to write a description of him or her in action. Tell them to compare this person's style to some other athlete's. They should use the comparative and superlative form of adverbs in writing their paragraphs.

511

To distinguish adjectives and adverbs by their use

Presenting the Lesson

1. Read and discuss **Adjective or Adverb?** on page 512. Emphasize the importance of locating the word that is being modified in order to determine which type of modifier is appropriate. Present the sentences in Exercise A on page 513 orally. Call on students to identify each modifier and state what question it answers about the word it modifies. Then assign Exercise B.

Exercise A: Writing If a sentence is correct, write *Correct*. If there is an error in the comparison of adverbs, write the sentence correctly.

1. The gymnast performed smoothlier after practice. more smoothly
2. Foods cook more faster over an open fire. faster
3. We ate fish more often when we lived in Maine. correct
4. Some cars run better on unleaded gas. correct
5. Of all my friends, Helena speaks more openly. most openly
6. I awaken cheerfullest on Saturdays. most cheerfully
7. Gardner competes more vigorously than Reese. correct
8. These bananas ripened the most fastest. fastest
9. Of the four pitchers, James pitches more accurately. most accurately
10. Epoxy glue holds bestest of all. best

Exercise B: Writing Use the comparative and superlative forms of the following adverbs in sentences.

1. wildly	3. gradually	5. soon	7. generously
2. loosely	4. deeply	6. intelligently	8. early

Part 5　Adjective or Adverb?

It is not always easy to know when to use an adjective and when to use an adverb. Which of the following sentences is correct?

The blast came *sudden*.　　The blast came *suddenly*.

Sometimes you may have trouble deciding whether to use an adjective or an adverb. To decide, ask yourself:

1. *What kind of word does the modifier describe?*
If the word is an action verb, adjective, or adverb, use the adverb. If the word is a noun or pronoun, use the adjective.

2. *What does the modifier tell about the word it describes?*
If it tells *how, when, where,* or *to what extent*, use the adverb. If it tells *which one, what kind,* or *how many*, use the adjective.

If you applied both tests to the two sentences at the beginning of this part, you would determine that *came* requires an adverb.

An **ADJECTIVE** tells	An **ADVERB** tells
which one	how
what kind	when
how many	where
	to what extent
about a noun or pronoun	**about a verb, adjective or adverb**

Exercise A: Label two columns *Adjective* and *Adverb*. Put the modifiers you find in the appropriate column. After each adjective or adverb, write the word it modifies. Do not include articles.

Answers in margin

1. The three motorcycles swerved sharply.
2. Heavy tractors slowly pushed the deep snow aside.
3. Open that broken window very carefully.
4. Today Lauren walked her neighbor's two large dogs.
5. Most of these shows are too predictable.
6. Two of my favorite books are *Call of the Wild* and *My Side of the Mountain*.
7. Several series have somewhat similar plots.
8. The screen glows brightly in the dark room.
9. Julio spoke very patiently to his little sister.
10. The Swiss hikers walked rather quickly and sang folk songs.

Exercise B: Choose the correct modifier from the two in parentheses. Tell whether it is an adjective or an adverb.

1. We worked (furious, furiously) to halt the flooding. adv.
2. We'll make it to Milwaukee (easy, easily) by tonight. adv.
3. It was (terrible, terribly) hot driving across the desert. adv.
4. You look particularly (nice, nicely) this morning. adj.
5. The truckers drove (slow, slowly) down the steep grade. adv.
6. The new car gleamed (bright, brightly) in the sun. adv.
7. The team felt (awful, awfully) about the loss. adj.
8. An (extreme, extremely) upset man burst into the office. adv.
9. The two teams battled (fierce, fiercely) at the game. adv.
10. Beth's decision was very (quick, quickly). adj.

2. Read and discuss **Adverb or Predicate Adjective?** on page 514. Review the concept of linking verbs and predicate words. Go over the examples given on page 514 and show the class how they may test linking verbs by substituting forms of the verb *to be*.

3. Assign and discuss the Exercise on page 515.

Exercise A

1. three (motorcycles) adj.; sharply (swerved) adv.
2. Heavy (tractors) adj.; slowly (pushed) adv.; deep (snow) adj.; aside (pushed) adv.
3. that (window) adj.; broken (window) adj.; very (carefully) adv.; carefully (Open) adv.
4. Today (walked) adv.; her (neighbor's) adj.; neighbor's (dogs) adj.; two, large (dogs) adjs.
5. these (shows) adj.; too (predictable) adv.; predictable (shows) adj.
6. my, favorite (books) adjs.; *My* (*Side*) adj.
7. Several (series) adj.; somewhat (similar) adv.; similar (plots) adj.
8. brightly (glows) adv.; dark (room) adj.
9. very (patiently) adv.; patiently (spoke) adv.; his, little (sister) adjs.
10. Swiss (hikers) adj.; rather (quickly) adv.; quickly (walked) adv.; folk (songs) adj.

Individualizing the Lesson

Less-Advanced Students

Have students choose the correct modifier and tell whether it is an adjective or an adverb.

Adverb or Predicate Adjective?

You have learned that a predicate adjective follows a linking verb and modifies the subject. Besides forms of *be*, other linking verbs are *become, seem, appear, look, sound, feel, taste, smell* and *grow*.

This melon smells sweet. (*Sweet* modifies *melon*.)

The parking lot looks full. (*Full* modifies *lot*.)

The thunder grew louder. (*Louder* modifies *thunder*.)

Alex felt cold. (*Cold* modifies *Alex*.)

In the previous sentences, the verbs *smells, looks*, and *grew* function as linking verbs. Therefore, the words that follow them are adjectives. However, these same verbs can also be action verbs. So can *sound, appear, feel*, and *taste*. When these verbs are action verbs, they are followed by adverbs instead of predicate adjectives. As you recall, adverbs tell *how, when, where,* or *to what extent* about the action verbs.

Here are sentences using the same words as linking verbs and as action verbs.

LINKING VERBS WITH ADJECTIVES	ACTION VERBS WITH ADVERBS
The water *looked* clear.	Dave *looked* carefully.
The team *appeared* eager.	Clouds *appeared* suddenly.
The pizza *smells* delicious.	A bloodhound *smells* keenly.
This music *sounds* peaceful.	The fire alarm *sounds* often.

If you have trouble deciding whether to use an adverb or an adjective, ask yourself the following questions:

1. Can you substitute *is* or *was* for the verb? If so, the modifier is probably an adjective.
2. Does the modifier tell *how, when, where,* or *to what extent?* If so, the modifier is probably an adverb.

514

Exercise: Choose the right modifier for the following sentences.

1. Adam looked (angry, angrily) at Bill.
2. The trumpet sounded (loud, loudly) and shrill.
3. Stained glass looks (brilliant, brilliantly) in bright light.
4. A man in a cape appeared (sudden, suddenly).
5. During the overtime the crowd grew (tense, tensely).
6. The teller sounded the burglar alarm (immediate, immediately).
7. Aretha felt (nervous, nervously) before her recital.
8. The new father looked (proud, proudly) at his daughter.
9. I feel (bad, badly) about the mistake.
10. Those big dill pickles taste (sour, sourly).

Part 6   Troublesome Modifiers

Certain modifiers are frequently used incorrectly. By studying the following pages carefully, you can avoid these errors in your writing and speaking.

Those and *Them*

Those can be used as an adjective or a pronoun.

Where are the controls for *those* power saws? (adjective)
Those are the Jackson twins. (pronoun)

Them is never an adjective, and therefore cannot be used in place of *those*. *Them* should only be used as a pronoun.

WRONG: We framed *them* photos.
RIGHT: We framed *those* photos.
RIGHT: We framed *them*.

Note: The pronoun *them* should only be used as an object. Never use it as a subject.

WRONG: *Them* are the right keys.
RIGHT: The witness didn't recall *them*.

515

Part 6

Objective

To avoid common problems with modifiers

Presenting the Lesson

1. Read and discuss the pairs of troublesome modifiers presented on pages 515–516. Explain the distinctions for each pair.

2. Read and discuss **The Double Negative** on page 517. Ask students to name the negative words that should not be used with *not* and *-n't*. As they name the words, write them on the board.

3. Go over Exercise A on page 518 orally to be sure students understand the material.

4. Assign and discuss Exercises B and C on page 518.

Individualizing the Lesson

Less-Advanced Students

Present the following sentences and ask students to correct any errors in the use of modifiers.

1. There wasn't *hardly* any snow on the ground.
2. Emily felt well, but her voice sounded *scratchily*.
3. We do*n't never* eat dinner before 7:00.
4. Do you like *these kind* of jeans?
5. The chef uses *this here* kind of shortening.
6. Coolidge shot *good* from the free-throw line.
7. Have you ever had this kind of mushroom?
8. Where did you find *them* goggles?
9. *Them* boys don't have *no* right to be here.
10. Santee skated well in the competition.

Advanced Students

Ask students to write a short composition about what kinds of people would like a vacation in the back woods. Instruct them to use the modifiers *kind*, *sort*, *those*, and *them* in their papers.

Reinforcement Exercise

Assign and discuss Exercise G page 521.

Optional Practice

Have the students imagine that they are veterinarians called in to inspect the animals being held in the city pound. Ask them to write a report on two dogs, a cat, and a monkey that they examined. Tell them to be careful in the use of modifiers, especially *good* and *well*.

Extending the Lesson

Bring in a sample of American dialect (Mark Twain, Josh Billings, etc.) that makes colorful use of the nonstandard expressions presented in Part 6. Explain how these

Here and *There*

Sometimes people incorrectly say "this here jacket" or "that there room." "This here" and "that there" are repetitious phrases. The word *this* includes the idea of *here*. The word *that* includes the idea of *there*. Avoid "this here" and "that there."

WRONG: This here sandwich is stale.
RIGHT: *This* sandwich is stale.

Kind and *Sort*

Kind and *sort* are singular. *Kinds* and *sorts* are plural. These words are often combined with demonstrative pronouns, as in the phrases *this sort* or *those kinds*. In such phrases, the noun and pronoun must agree in number. No matter what words follow, use *this* or *that* with *kind* and *sort*. Use *these* and *those* with *kinds* and *sorts*.

This kind of boot is made of cowhide. (singular)
Those sorts of snacks are high in calories. (plural)

Good and *Well*

Good and *well* have similar meanings, but the words are not used in the same situations. You cannot always substitute one word for the other. Look at the differences in these sentences:

That is a *good* photo of you.
(The adjective *good* modifies the noun *photo*.)

You sing *well*.
(The adverb *well* modifies the verb *sing*.)

Good is almost always an adjective, modifying nouns and pronouns. It is never used as an adverb.

Well can be either an adjective or an adverb. In the sentence above, *well* is used as an adverb modifying an action verb. *Well* can also be used after a linking verb to mean "in good health."

Tara doesn't look *well*.
   (*Well* is a predicate adjective modifying *Tara*.)

Yvonne dances *well*.
   (*Well* is an adverb modifying the action verb *dances*.)

If you are describing an action or the state of someone's health, use *well*.

The Double Negative

Two negative words used together when only one is necessary is called a **double negative**. Avoid using double negatives.

WRONG: We didn't take no time-outs.
RIGHT: We did*n't* take *any* time-outs.

WRONG: My out-of-town friends never write no letters.
RIGHT: My out-of-town friends *never* write *any* letters.

WRONG: John couldn't eat nothing all day.
RIGHT: John could*n't* eat *anything* all day.

Contractions like *couldn't* contain a shortened form of the negative *not*. Do not use other negative words after them.

Some common negative words are *no, none, not, nothing*, and *never*. Instead of these words, use *any, anything*, or *ever* after negative contractions.

Rod has*n't ever* hit a grand-slam home run.
Michelle could*n't* find *any* bargains.
The new Senator did*n't* change *anything*.

Other negative words are *hardly, scarcely*, and *barely*. Don't use them with negative contractions like *hasn't* and *didn't*.

WRONG: Rick couldn't barely control the machine.
RIGHT: Rick could *barely* control the machine.

WRONG: The movers hadn't scarcely begun.
RIGHT: The movers had *scarcely* begun.

WRONG: Lightning hardly never strikes houses.
RIGHT: Lightning *hardly ever* strikes houses.

expressions may be used by authors to create a regional dialect that is effective and expressive. Point out that these expressions are not acceptable in formal writing or public speaking, however.

Exercise A: Choose the correct word from the two in parentheses.

1. (Them, <u>Those</u>) cheerleaders sound hoarse.
2. (<u>This</u>, This here) video recorder has remote control.
3. You did very (good, <u>well</u>) at the track meet, Jed.
4. These (sort, <u>sorts</u>) of gym shoes wear longer than those.
5. I don't care for (<u>any</u>, no) cheese on my hamburger.
6. The movie we saw last night was very (<u>good</u>, well).
7. There (<u>is</u>, isn't) nobody at the computer terminal now.
8. (<u>That</u>, That there) car is the one that ran into our fence.
9. Are (them, <u>those</u>) railroad cars headed for the coast?
10. (Those, <u>That</u>) kind of palm tree grows all over Florida.

Exercise B: Writing Rewrite the sentences that contain <u>errors</u>.

Answers may vary.

1. If you listen <u>good</u>, you can hear a whippoorwill. well
2. Barbara has not yet finished <u>none</u> of her homework. any
3. Is <u>that there</u> restaurant open on Mondays? that
4. The pilot <u>couldn't</u> barely see the runway through the fog. could
5. These kinds of boats are called catamarans. correct
6. Although he speaks <u>good</u>, Ed doesn't like to make speeches. well
7. Have you ever gone through <u>them</u> caves in Kentucky? those
8. These <u>sort</u> of problems are difficult for a jury to consider. sorts
9. The twins don't ever try to fool their friends. correct
10. Ella has taught <u>them</u> parrots to talk. those

Exercise C: Writing Rewrite all sentences that contain <u>double negatives</u>, correcting the errors. Two sentences are correct.

1. Jason hasn't seen <u>no</u> movies lately. any
2. Haven't you <u>never</u> been to a soccer match? ever
3. One runner <u>couldn't</u> barely clear the hurdles. could
4. During the test Amy couldn't remember <u>nothing</u>. anything
5. The elevator doesn't ever work. correct
6. This hot dog doesn't have <u>no</u> mustard on it. any
7. Pam hardly knows <u>nobody</u> in her French class. anybody
8. Ramon and Todd <u>haven't</u> <u>scarcely</u> talked to each other. have
9. Chris doesn't expect any reward for finding the purse. correct
10. The team <u>doesn't have no</u> returning players. any

REINFORCEMENT EXERCISES
Using Modifiers

A. Recognize adjectives. Write each adjective in these sentences. Tell which word it modifies. Do not include articles. (Use after page 502.) Answers in margin.

1. This special exhibit will travel to thirty museums.
2. That Italian sports car has a deluxe interior.
3. Dense, black smoke poured out of the rusty tailpipe.
4. Three mysterious strangers appeared at the door.
5. Several famous sculptors worked on that huge marble statue.
6. I ate one of the biggest red raspberries in the bowl.
7. Two dignified bronze lions guarded the gate.
8. Some Indian food is cooked in clay ovens.
9. The violent storm destroyed many large homes.
10. Tiny green buds dotted the forsythia branches.

B. Find predicate adjectives. Write the predicate adjective in each sentence. Tell which word it modifies. (Use after page 502.)

1. Rebecca seems quiet today. Rebecca
2. That odd melody somehow sounds very familiar. melody
3. This dead tree is hollow. tree
4. The bridge is usually slippery after a storm. bridge
5. Claire is very artistic. Claire
6. American consumers must become more aware of safety factors. consumers
7. Your jigsaw puzzle looks difficult. puzzle
8. The paths through the swamp were treacherous. paths
9. Many popular children's shows are also educational. shows
10. This beautiful roll-top desk is very old. desk

C. Use adjectives in comparison. Choose the correct adjective. (Use after page 505.)

1. Jori seems (more cheerful, cheerfuller) than usual.
2. These new shoestrings are (shorter, more shorter) than the ones that broke.

519

Reinforcement Exercises

These Reinforcement Exercises may be used for additional practice of the concepts presented in this Section. Each exercise focuses on a single concept, and should be used after the page number indicated in parentheses.

Review

If you have not assigned these Reinforcement Exercises before this time, you can also use them as an excellent Section Review.

Exercise A

1. special (exhibit); thirty (museums)
2. That, Italian, sports (car); deluxe (interior)
3. Dense, black (smoke); rusty (tailpipe)
4. Three, mysterious (strangers)
5. Several, famous (sculptors); that, huge, marble (statue)
6. biggest, red (raspberries)
7. Two, dignified, bronze (lions)
8. Some, Indian (food); clay (ovens)
9. violent (storm); many, large (homes)
10. Tiny, green (buds); forsythia (branches)

3. Of the three stories, which is (more factual, most factual)?
4. The budget for this film was the (most lowest, lowest) of the series.
5. The combat forces have become (stronger, more strong) in the past few years.
6. Have you ever tasted (more spicier, spicier) chili?
7. Who was the (younger, youngest) of all the Presidents?
8. This year the business was (more profitable, most profitable) than last year.
9. Jennifer looks (happier, more happier) than her friends.
10. Of all these paperbacks, this one is the (more humorous, most humorous) to read.

D. Recognize adverbs. Write each adverb and the word it modifies. Sentences may contain more than one adverb.

(Use after page 509.)   Answers in margin

1. A trap door in the floor slowly opened.
2. My grandparents arrived yesterday from Tulsa.
3. Cindy Nicholas swam the English Channel twice.
4. Carrie is too busy to answer the phone now.
5. The photographer carefully focused the camera.
6. Professional skaters practice here quite frequently.
7. Phil seemed extremely proud of his brother.
8. Currently, Congress is seriously considering other energy sources.
9. The fishing fleet always returns here in the evening.
10. Two helicopters hovered loudly overhead.

E. Use adverbs in comparison. Choose the correct adverb.

(Use after page 512.)

1. The sun shines (more intensely, most intensely) in California than in Alaska.
2. You will play (better, more better) if you warm up.
3. Of all the joggers, Al runs (farther, farthest).
4. She sang (more better, better) tonight than last night.
5. Brian eats (littler, less) than anyone else in the family.
6. The storm hit (hardest, most hard) in the tropics.
7. Randy can repair appliances (more skillfully, most skillfully) than his brother.

8. Of our group, Amanda lives (nearer, <u>nearest</u>) to the park.
9. Connors played (badder, <u>worse</u>, worst) than usual.
10. The flood waters receded (quicklier, <u>more quickly</u>) than expected.

F. Use modifiers correctly. Choose the correct word.

(Use after page 513.)

1. The fresh bread smelled (<u>wonderful</u>, wonderfully).
2. Their coach looks (<u>impatient</u>, impatiently).
3. The winners seemed (<u>proud</u>, proudly).
4. Black rolling clouds appeared (sudden, <u>suddenly</u>).
5. The judges tasted each contestant's pie (<u>careful</u>, carefully).
6. Tim's voice sounded (<u>groggy</u>, groggily).
7. That African nation has just become (<u>independent</u>, independently).
8. The veterans talked (honest, <u>honestly</u>) about their concerns.
9. The ice-cold watermelon tasted (<u>sweet</u>, sweetly).
10. Nicole looked (eager, <u>eagerly</u>) at the swimming pool.

G. Solve modifier problems. Eleven of the sentences below contain errors in the use of modifiers. Rewrite those sentences correctly. Write *Correct* if the sentence contains no error.

(Use after page 518.)   Some answers may vary.

1. Jeremy dances well. _{correct}
2. Take this here camera to Brad. _{this}
3. You didn't put no paste on the wallpaper. _{any}
4. Kathy couldn't find any patches to use on the tire. _{correct}
5. My brothers scarcely never fight. _{ever}
6. Those sort of music is called reggae. _{This or That}
7. Please pass me them potato pancakes. _{those}
8. Can them twigs be used as kindling for the fire? _{those or these}
9. Mr. Viner explained the lab procedure good. _{well}
10. These kinds of motorbikes use hardly no gasoline. _{any}
11. Phil bought a pair of those argyle socks. _{correct}
12. The stranded motorist couldn't get no help. _{any}
13. These sort of fish is good for frying. _{This or That}
14. Lemonade tastes good on a hot day. _{correct}
15. The audience couldn't barely hear the actors. _{could}

MIXED REVIEW
Using Modifiers

A. List all the modifiers in the following sentences. Identify them as adjectives or adverbs. Then list the word that each adjective or adverb modifies. Answers in margin.

1. The nervous man walked rapidly into the subway.
2. The fans screamed wildly as the talented quarterback threw a perfect pass.
3. The young violinist drew enthusiastic applause from the audience.
4. That old house stood silent and empty for years.
5. Angela's teeth chattered uncontrollably in the bitterly cold air.
6. Miners work underground under extremely dangerous conditions.
7. Sam and his friends arrived at the game too late for the first kickoff.
8. The famous technique of this artist is very unusual.
9. Expertly, he pressed the shining apples into sweet, clear cider.
10. My new bicycle was definitely my favorite gift.

B. List the modifiers in each sentence. Do not include articles. Tell whether each modifier is an adjective or an adverb. Then give the comparative and superlative forms of each modifier. Answers in margin.

> EXAMPLE: Angie promised to write soon.
>
> soon-sooner-soonest (adverb)

1. Has the family saved much money?
2. The tired, old sailor slept soundly in the tiny bunk.
3. A few little children raced wildly through the park.
4. The children in the community swim well.
5. We had a long and difficult hike because of the storm.
6. The tired announcer spoke slowly, but clearly.
7. Many people believed the honest salesperson.

8. Carol was given a pleasant assignment.
9. Sergio thought that the instructor was patient.
10. The engine in the new car was quiet.

C. All but two of the following sentences contain errors in the use of modifiers. Rewrite each sentence correctly. If a sentence contains no errors, write *Correct*.

1. Benjamin has always been <u>real</u> interested in mathematics. *really*
2. The team didn't have <u>no losses</u> after that game. *any*
3. Terry always dresses <u>well</u> for interviews. *correct*
4. Jan <u>couldn't</u> hardly wait for the mail to come. *could*
5. On the corner, a musician was playing sorrowfully on a tenor saxophone. *correct*
6. <u>These</u> kind of shoe can be extremely comfortable. *This*
7. I see my friends <u>oftener</u> than I see most of my relatives. *more often*
8. Is Lake Superior <u>more far</u> away than Lake Michigan? *farther*
9. The Angels played <u>worst</u> than usual today. *worse*
10. The band's early albums were <u>more better</u> than its recent ones. *better*

D. Tell whether each italicized word or phrase in the following sentences is *Correct* or *Incorrect*. Rewrite all incorrect sentences using modifiers correctly.

1. I would not cut *them* hedges if I were you. *those*
2. My grandparents love *that sort* of music and books. *correct*
3. My ankle still feels *tenderly* from the sprain. *tender*
4. I may look fine, but I don't feel very *good*. *well*
5. Be *carefuller* with *them* darts. *more careful, those*
6. Even those huge elephants are *fast* when they have to be. *correct*
7. I haven't seen *any* birds in this neighborhood for weeks. *correct*
8. Many people feel that boxing is the *most dangerous* of the two sports. *more dangerous*
9. Ted *couldn't barely* control his temper. *could barely*
10. *That there* game *hadn't scarcely* started when it began to rain. *That game, had scarcely*

3. few–fewer–fewest (adj.)
   little–littler–littlest (adj.)
   wildly–more wildly–most wildly (adv.)
4. well–better–best (adv.)
5. long–longer–longest (adj.)
   difficult–more difficult–most difficult (adj.)
6. tired–more tired–most tired (adj.)
   slowly–more slowly–most slowly (adv.)
   clearly–more clearly–most clearly (adv.)
7. Many–more–most (adj.)
   honest–more honest–most honest (adj.)
8. pleasant–more pleasant–most pleasant (adj.)
9. patient–more patient–most patient (adj.)
10. new–newer–newest (adj.)
    quiet–quieter–quietest (adj.)

These challenging and enjoyable activities allow the students to see how the concepts of grammar, usage, and mechanics may be applied in actual writing situations. Each exercise is designed to allow students practice in several of the skills they have acquired in this Section. The activities also provide opportunities for students to write creatively about a wide variety of interesting and unusual subjects.

USING GRAMMAR IN WRITING
Using Modifiers

A. If you had to choose, would you rather live the life of a house cat or that of an alley cat? Contrast the advantages of each, being sure to use both adjectives and adverbs in their comparative forms. For example, "A house cat may have a *softer* bed than an alley cat, but an alley cat can run *more freely* and roam through the town *more often.*"

B. Describe the best or worst place you have ever been. Was it a building? a place you visited on a trip? a run-down town? Be sure to involve all of your senses in describing the place. How did it smell? How did it look? How did it sound? How did it feel? If you had to eat something in this place, you might even include the sense of taste in your description.

C. The use of modifiers can change a dull piece of writing into one that is much more colorful and precise. Rewrite the following movie review. Add colorful, precise adjectives and adverbs. Replace overused or weak modifiers with strong ones.

> The best movie of this season has to be *Gold Fever,* director I. M. Speshul's box office smash. Based on a good book by Vera Bose, the movie re-creates the atmosphere of the Klondike gold rush in the 1890's. Against this background—captured well by the pretty, on-location photography of cameraman Len Shutter—an interesting story unfolds. The story tells of a couple torn between their love for each other and their love for that shiny metal. Ivan Ego, the strong and good-looking star of television's *Suds,* gives an okay performance as "Yukon Jim," but the really nice thing about the show is Hope Foran Oscar's portrayal of "Honey," Yukon's smart but unusual sidekick. This movie is certain to leave adult audiences pleased and happy and is also great entertainment for children.

Section 7

Using Prepositions and Conjunctions

Section Objectives

  1. To recognize prepositions and prepositional phrases

  2. To identify prepositional phrases as adjective or adverb phrases

  3. To recognize coordinating and correlative conjunctions

Preparing the Students

  Read and discuss page 525. Highlight the importance of prepositions and conjunctions for making relationships clear. Put the following words on the board:

  Jim my mother hid the presents the decorations the coat closet the couch the living room.

  Call on students to suggest how these words may be combined to make a meaningful sentence. The class will discover that there are many combinations of conjunctions and prepositions that may be used in this group of words.

Additional Resources

Diagnostic Test — See page 5 in the test booklet. Recommended for use before teaching the Section.

Mastery Test — See pages 57–58 in the test booklet. Recommended for use after teaching this Section.

Additional Exercises — See pages 536–540 in the student text.

Skills Practice Book — pages 144–148.

Duplicating Masters — pages 144–148.

Special Populations — See special section at the front of this Teacher's Edition.

Sometimes you can communicate ideas with short sentences like these:

    Beth raced.
    The class uses paints.

More often, though, you will want to provide more information to clarify your ideas. Modifiers are useful for that purpose.

    Beth raced yesterday.
    The art class uses acrylic paints.

At times, the ideas you want to express are even more complicated. Suppose you want to say where Beth raced. Suppose you want to add that the art class also uses clay. Then you will need words to show those relationships.

    Beth raced yesterday along the lake.
    The art class uses acrylic paints and clay.

Presenting the Lesson

1. Read and discuss **What Are Prepositions?**, pages 526–527. Give the students three minutes to study the list "Words Often Used as Prepositions." Then have them see how many they remember by writing the list without referring to the book. Emphasize that some of these words may be used as other parts of speech.

2. Complete Exercise A on page 527 orally. Ask students to identify the preposition, its object, and any modifiers for each prepositional phrase. Then assign Exercise B.

3. Read and discuss **Preposition or Adverb?** on page 528. Complete Exercise C, page 528 orally. Stress that prepositions show a relationship between words and do not appear alone. Assign Exercise D.

4. Assign Exercise B on page 529. Assign Exercise D and discuss several possible developments of each sentence.

Individualizing the Lesson

Less-Advanced Students

Ask students to complete each of the following sentences in three dif-

---

Relationships dealing with people, actions, and things are expressed by words that connect other words. In this section you will learn about two kinds of connecting words: **prepositions** and **conjunctions**.

Part 1   What Are Prepositions?

Words that join other words or word groups are called **connectives.** One important kind of connective is the **preposition.** Prepositions express a relationship between different parts of a sentence. Look at the relationships expressed in the following examples. Notice how changing the preposition can affect the meaning of the sentence as a whole.

> Sara leaped *off* her bike.
> Sara leaped *onto* her bike.
> Sara leaped *over* her bike.

The prepositions *off, onto,* and *over* show the relationship between *bike* and the verb *leaped.* In each of the above sentences, *bike* is the **object of the preposition.** Like all prepositions, *off, onto,* and *over* connect their objects to another part of the sentence.

Prepositions do not show relationships all by themselves. They begin a *phrase,* a group of words that do not have a subject or verb. The **prepositional phrase** consists of the preposition, its object, and any words that come between. In the sentences above, *off her bike, onto her bike,* and *over her bike* are prepositional phrases. Here are some other sentences that contain prepositional phrases:

> Zack politely asked *for a refund.*
> *In the spring,* Darrell returned *to school.*
> The box *of books* was too heavy.

A preposition is a word used with a noun or pronoun, called its *object,* to show the relationship between the noun or pronoun and some other word in the sentence.

A prepositional phrase consists of a preposition, its object, and any modifiers of the object.

The following list presents words often used as prepositions. Many of them, like *above, over, in,* and *beside,* help to show location. Others like *until, after,* and *before,* show a relationship of time. Still others show different kinds of relationships. Study these prepositions and try to determine the relationship each one suggests.

Words Often Used as Prepositions

about	behind	during	off	to
above	below	except	on	toward
across	beneath	for	onto	under
after	beside	from	out	until
against	between	in	outside	up
along	beyond	inside	over	upon
among	but (*except*)	into	past	with
around	by	like	since	within
at	concerning	near	through	without
before	down	of	throughout	

Exercise A: Number your paper from 1 to 10. Write the prepositional phrases in the following sentences.

EXAMPLE: Mac went to the game with Gwen.

to the game, with Gwen.

1. The first competitor vaulted easily over the high bar.
2. Ask the woman at the desk for an application.
3. I waited outside the office for Pam.
4. Marta works at the mall after school.
5. By all means, talk with Gene about your plans.
6. During this season, Franklin pitched three no-hitters.
7. At first, the bite of a black widow spider may not even be noticed.
8. The figures on a totem pole have special significance to the tribe.
9. Walter jumped over the fallen halfback.
10. Don't walk through that tunnel after dark.

ferent ways, using three different prepositional phrases.

1. The shirt _____ is torn and dirty.
2. The chipmunks lived _____.
3. The airplane flew _____.

Advanced Students

Discuss the prepositions that do not express time or space relationships, such as *for, except, concerning, like, of.* Get students to articulate the kinds of relationships these words express.

Reinforcement Exercises

Assign and discuss Exercises A and B on page 536.

Optional Practice

Have students use the following prepositional phrases in sentences.

1. on the radio
2. through the gym
3. between two trees
4. toward the Atlantic coast
5. along the path

Extending the Lesson

Students enjoy creating the longest reasonable sentence they can using prepositional phrases. Write a sentence such as "The moon shone" or "The runners dashed" on the board. Call on students to add prepositional phrases to both the subject and predicate of the sentence, using prepositions from the list and never repeating the same preposition. See how far you can go before the credibility of the sentence is gone. The sentence will no doubt be a caricature, but the usage of prepositional phrases will be clearly established.

Exercise B: Follow the directions for Exercise A.

1. The network heard nothing from its foreign correspondent for two weeks.
2. During the storm, everyone except Dee stayed inside the bus shelter.
3. Beyond a doubt, someone had been in that cellar before us.
4. There is no one else like you in the world.
5. Bright crepe paper was strung across the gym.
6. There is a pit of quicksand near the dead tree.
7. Since last week, Anthony has been under pressure.
8. Meryl Streep walked off the stage with her award.
9. With little trouble, the Cowboys broke through the Bears' defense.
10. For over a month, that rusty old car has been parked in the alley.

Preposition or Adverb?

Many words used as prepositions may also be used as adverbs. How can you tell if a word is a preposition or an adverb?

A preposition is never used alone. It is always followed by a noun or pronoun as part of a phrase. If the word is in a phrase, it is probably a preposition. If the word has no object, it is probably an adverb.

> The visitors walked *around the courtyard.* (preposition)
> The visitors walked *around.* (adverb)
> Can you jump *over that hurdle?* (preposition)
> Can you come *over* later? (adverb)

Exercise A: Decide whether the italicized words are adverbs or prepositions. Write *Adverb* or *Preposition* for each sentence.

1. Turn the water *on* now. adv.
2. Seagulls waited *on* the pier for handouts. prep.
3. The golf ball ricocheted *off* a tree trunk. prep.
4. Have you turned the oven *off* yet? adv.
5. The captives have not been seen *since* then. adv.

6. That was the Pirates' best game *since* last fall. prep.
7. They found a rich vein of silver *down* there. adv.
8. I have not seen Juanita *around* here. adv.
9. Kittle hit the ball *over* the fence. prep.
10. An old steam locomotive rumbled *down* the track. prep.

Exercise B: Follow the directions for Exercise A.

1. Suzy does not ride *without* headgear. prep.
2. What is going *on* here? adv.
3. *Without* a word, Sam handed her the letter. prep.
4. My aunt lives *on* San Juan Island. prep.
5. Has the boat come *in* yet? adv.
6. Tony put a quarter *into* the slot. prep.
7. Finally the ball fell *through* the hoop. prep.
8. A message to the stranded travelers got *through* on Monday. adv.
9. Do you mind if I go *along* too? adv.
10. Caroline inched *along* the narrow ledge. prep.

Exercise C: Writing Make the following sentences more interesting by adding prepositional phrases where indicated. Answers will vary.

1. A hungry panther stalked his prey (prep. phrase).
2. That map (prep. phrase) was printed over a century ago.
3. The Flying Karamazov Brothers performed (prep. phrase).
4. The bridge (prep. phrase) is closed for repairs.
5. Are you taking the ferry (prep. phrase)?
6. (Prep. phrase) there appeared a ghostly figure.
7. Tall fir trees grew (prep. phrase) (prep. phrase).
8. A girl (prep. phrase) walked slowly (prep. phrase).
9. Davis climbed (prep. phrase) (prep. phrase).
10. A pile (prep. phrase) lay (prep. phrase) (prep. phrase).

Exercise D: Writing Write two sentences for each of the words below. In the first sentence, use the word as a preposition. In the second sentence, use the word as an adverb.

across	inside	below	out
after	near	by	past

Objective

To identify prepositional phrases as adjective or adverb phrases

Presenting the Lesson

1. Review the uses of adjectives and adverbs as modifiers. Read and discuss pages 530–531. Use the sentences in Exercise A on page 532 to practice finding prepositional phrases and the words they modify. Call on students to tell whether each phrase is being used as an adjective or as an adverb. Have them tell which of the questions (*which one, what kind, how, when, where, to what extent*) each prepositional phrase answers.

2. Choose two or three of the sentences from Exercise A to diagram on the board. Be sure to select at least one where the prepositional phrase is used as an adjective and one where it is used as an adverb.

3. Assign and discuss Exercise B on page 532. Assign Exercise C. Emphasize how prepositional phrases make a piece of writing more lively and specific.

Individualizing the Lesson

Less-Advanced Students

Have students identify the prepositional phrases in each of the following sentences and say whether they are used as adjectives or adverbs.

1. Gloria put the vase on the shelf in her room.
2. Roses bloom throughout the year in Arizona.

Part 2 Prepositional Phrases as Modifiers

Modifiers, as you know, are often single words. However, groups of words may also function as modifiers. Prepositional phrases, for example, work the same way as single-word adjectives or adverbs to modify various parts of a sentence.

An adjective phrase is a prepositional phrase that modifies a noun or pronoun.

The phrase always includes the preposition, its object, and any modifiers of the object. Like adjectives, adjective phrases tell *which one* or *what kind.* Here are three examples.

The school needs a new coach *for the track team.*
(*For the track team* is an adjective phrase, modifying the noun *coach.* It tells *what kind* of coach.)

The door *on the left* is the emergency exit.
(*On the left* is an adjective phrase, modifying the noun *door.* It tells *which one.*).

All *of the bank tellers* wear matching uniforms.
(*Of the bank tellers* is an adjective phrase that modifies the pronoun *all.* It tells *what kind.*)

Adverb phrases are prepositional phrases that modify verbs.

Like single-word adverbs, an adverb phrase tells *how, when, where,* or *to what extent* something occurred.

The bottles are sealed *by a huge machine.*
(*By a huge machine* is an adverb phrase telling *how.* It modifies the verb *are sealed.*)

On Saturday the playoffs will begin.
(*On Saturday* is an adverb phrase. It tells *when* about the verb *will begin.*)

Hendricks sat *on the bench.*
(*On the bench* is an adverb phrase. It tells *where* about the verb *sat.*)

Sometimes one prepositional phrase follows another. Sometimes both phrases modify the same word. Frequently, however, the second phrase is an adjective phrase modifying the object in the first phrase.

> Cecily decided *on a name for her new dog.*
> (*On a name* is an adverb phrase modifying the verb *decided.*
> *For her new dog* is an adjective phrase modifying the noun *name.*)

> Jim topped the salad *with bits of cheese.*
> (The adverb phrase *with bits* tells *how* about the verb *topped.*
> *Of cheese* is an adjective phrase describing the noun *bits.*)

Diagraming Prepositional Phrases

To diagram a prepositional phrase, place it under the word it modifies.

The guests on the show talked about their new movies.

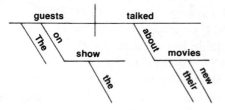

At times two or more nouns or pronouns may function as compound objects in the prepositional phrase.

On warm days we fished for trout and bass.

3. Stretch your arms above your head.
4. We parked in the lot behind the library.
5. Everyone sent cards to Louis on his birthday.
6. The key is under the mat near the door.
7. Adam went to the library after dinner.
8. The judge of the contest chose the winner.

Advanced Students

Have students write paragraphs about something that happened to them recently. Then direct them to revise their stories by adding prepositional phrases wherever they can be used to add interest to the story.

Reinforcement Exercise

Assign and discuss Exercise C page 537.

Optional Practice

Diagram sentences 4, 5, and 7 on the board. Ask students to diagram sentences 3, 6, and 8 individually.

Extending the Lesson

Ask each student to imagine his or her favorite place and to then write a series of prepositional phrases that will take him or her to that place. The result will be a Preposition Poem.

Example: Off my chair
Out the door
Into the street
Onto the bus
Off the bus
Over the lawns
Into my house
Toward the refrigerator.

Exercise A: Copy these sentences. Underline each prepositional phrase and draw an arrow from the phrase to the (word it modifies). Tell whether the phrase is an adjective phrase or an adverb phrase.

adj. (jacket)
1. Nicole bought a new red jacket with a deep hood.

adv. (walked); adv. (walked); adj. (cast)
2. Ted walked to school with a cast on his leg.

adv. (work); adv. (work)
3. Do you work for your mom after school?

adv. (were); adj. (hundreds)
4. The Navajos and Apaches were foes for hundreds of years.

adj. (center); adv. (was)
5. Sacramento was a center of activity during the gold rush.

adv. (most); adv. (spent)
6. We spent most of the day at the zoo.

adv. (was); adj. (top)
7. At the top of the hill was an abandoned farmhouse.

adv. (Out); adj. (man)
8. Out of nowhere rode a man with a black cape.

adv. (left); adv. (arrived)
9. We left after lunch and arrived before dinner.

adv. (fouled); adj. (four)
10. During the first half, four of our players fouled out.

Exercise B: Follow the directions for Exercise A.

adv. (lay)
1. A coiled black snake lay behind the rock.

adj. (store)
2. The store down the block sells tamales.

adv. (spread); adv. (spread)
3. The forest fire spread through the hills with incredible speed.

adj. (home); adv. (open)
4. The home of Abe Lincoln is open to the public.

adv. (fell); adv. (crashed)
5. The fixture fell from the ceiling and crashed onto the floor.

adj. (box); adj. (sweaters)
6. The box under the table has sweaters for the sale.

adv. (shall go); adv. (shall go)
7. After the game, shall we go to the dance?

adv. (tripped); adj. (rug)
8. Keith tripped over the rug on the stairs.

adv. (saw); adj. (hull)
9. At low tide we saw the submerged hull of an ancient ship.

adj. (beauty); adv. (overlooked)
10. The beauty of the desert is overlooked by many people.

Exercise C: Writing Rewrite the following paragraph, adding an adjective (adj.) phrase or adverb (adv.) phrase as indicated.
Answers will vary.

We gave my brother a surprise party _____ (adv.). It was held _____ (adv.) _____ (adj.). You should have seen the look of shock _____ (adj.) when we yelled "Surprise!" _____ (adv.) we cooked hot dogs and ate buckets _____ (adj.). My brother sat _____ (adv.), with sixteen helium balloons tied _____ (adv.). Then came the presents. The funniest gift was made _____ (adv.) and looked _____ (adv.). The party concluded back home, where we made gigantic ice cream sundaes _____ (adj.).

Part 3   Conjunctions

A conjunction is another part of speech that shows relationships between parts of a sentence.

A conjunction connects words or groups of words.

Kent wrote *and* narrated the skits.
My typing is fast *but* sloppy.
We will take the train *or* the bus.
The sculptor carves *either* wood *or* stone.
Hot oatmeal is *not only* nutritious, *but also* economical.

Conjunctions connect similar words or groups of words. There are three kinds of conjunctions — coordinating conjunctions, correlative conjunctions, and subordinate conjunctions. On the following pages you will learn about the first two types of conjunctions. In Section 11 of this book you will learn about subordinate conjunctions.

Coordinating Conjunctions

Coordinating conjunctions are used to connect single words or groups of words of the same kind. *And, but,* and *or* are the most common coordinating conjunctions. The words connected by coordinating conjunctions are compound constructions— compound subjects, compound direct objects, and compound verbs, for example.

Cars *and* trucks often have different speed limits. (compound subject)

The skater tripped *and* fell. (compound verb)

Sue looked at the tire *but* couldn't find the leak. (compound predicate)

The candidate appeared realistic *but* hopeful. (compound predicate words)

In June *or* July we will take our vacation. (compound objects of a preposition)

533

Part 3

Objective

To recognize coordinating and correlative conjunctions

Presenting the Lesson

1. Read and discuss pages 533–534. Review compound subjects, verbs, objects, and predicate words that were introduced in Section 1. Emphasize that conjunctions join sentence parts that express ideas of similarity or alternative.

2. Complete Exercise A on page 534 orally, identifying the compound elements in the sentences.

3. Assign and discuss Exercise B on page 534 to be completed independently.

4. At this time, you may want to teach Parts 1 and 2 of Chapter 5, "Sentence Combining," at the front of the student text.

Less-Advanced Students

Have students combine the ideas in the sentence pairs below using conjunctions. Point out how the use of conjunctions helps to eliminate choppy or repetitive sentences.

1. The nurse applied a bandage. The nurse applied antiseptic cream.
2. Bill goes fishing on his vacation. At other times, Bill goes golfing on vacation.
3. Many women attended the meeting. Many men attended the meeting.
4. The room was large. The room was stuffy.
5. Flowers bloomed in the garden. Flowers flourished in the garden.

Advanced Students

Have students complete Exercise C on page 535.

Optional Practice

Have students rewrite the following sentences making the parts given in parentheses compound. Tell them to vary the conjunctions they use.

1. The mirror fell with a splintering noise. (verb)
2. Parents should go to the meeting. (subject)
3. Give Juan the prize for first place. (indirect object)
4. The day was cloudy. (predicate word)
5. Lloyd grew up in Alabama. (object of the preposition)

Extending the Lesson

Ask the students to rewrite a paragraph from one of their favorite books leaving out all the coordinating and correlative conjunctions. Then have them write a sentence describing the effect of this change on the writing.

Correlative Conjunctions

Like coordinating conjunctions, **correlative conjunctions** join similar words or groups of words. However, these conjunctions are always used in pairs.

both...and   not only...but (also)
either...or   whether...or
neither...nor

Both oak *and* walnut are used for furniture.
We will go to *either* Cape Cod *or* Martha's Vineyard.
I am *neither* tired *nor* hungry.
The cafeteria serves *not only* lunch *but also* breakfast.
The team discussed *whether* to kick *or* to run.

Exercise A: Write the conjunctions in the following sentences, along with words or word groups that are connected by the conjunction. Put two lines under the conjunction.

EXAMPLE: The Honda skidded and swerved.

skidded and *swerved*

1. Pigeons and sparrows pecked at the bread crumbs on the frozen ground.
2. Alice darted quickly and nervously to the telephone on the hall table.
3. The blueprints for the community center were both clear and precise.
4. Simon overslept and missed soccer practice.
5. Would you rather be a singer or a dancer?
6. Does Tokyo, Mexico City, or Los Angeles have the largest population?
7. Barbara writes humorous slogans for T-shirts and bumper stickers.
8. Todd not only notices but also remembers.
9. Do you know whether the Italians or the Chinese invented pasta?
10. The team had neither an experienced coach nor a good relief pitcher.

534

Exercise B: Write each compound construction with its <u>conjunc-tion</u>. Then tell what kind of compound construction each one is.

1. Borg <u>crouched</u> <u>and</u> <u>waited</u> for the serve. compound verb
2. Dallas <u>called time-out</u> <u>but</u> <u>couldn't decide on a new strategy</u>. compound predicate
3. <u>Bobcats</u> <u>and</u> <u>bears</u> prowl the back woods. compound subject
4. A piston moves <u>up</u> <u>and</u> <u>down</u> in its cylinder. compound adverb
5. The wooden walkway was <u>narrow</u>, <u>shaky</u>, <u>and</u> <u>dangerous</u>. compound adjective
6. I'll telephone <u>either</u> <u>Jane's mother</u> <u>or</u> <u>her brother</u> immediately. compound direct object
7. Billie has <u>not only</u> <u>a sore throat</u> <u>but also</u> <u>a bad cough</u>. compound direct object
8. In January, is New Zealand <u>warm</u> <u>or</u> <u>cold</u>? compound adjective
9. <u>Both</u> the <u>length</u> <u>and</u> <u>width</u> of my skate blades need adjusting. compound subject
10. The restaurant specializes in <u>salads</u>, <u>fruit drinks</u>, <u>and</u> <u>felafel sandwiches</u>. compound object of preposition

Exercise C: Writing Write two sentences for each conjunction below. After each sentence, write the word or words that are joined by the conjunctions.

and	both...and
but	either...or
or	neither...nor

REINFORCEMENT EXERCISES
Using Prepositions and Conjunctions

A. Recognize prepositional phrases. Write the prepositional phrase or phrases in each sentence. (Use after page 528.)

1. During our vacation, we toured Mark Twain's home in Hartford, Connecticut.
2. Mary searched everywhere in the house for the old photograph album.
3. At the edge of the forest we saw a deer.
4. The Underground City in Montreal is the largest mall of its kind in the world.
5. Rick plays in a rock band after school, on weekends, and during the summer.
6. I have changed my mind about the party.
7. Have you looked for the article on microfilm?
8. The plane flew over the clusters of clouds.
9. At the base of the canyon is a winding stream.
10. We got off the cable car at Fisherman's Wharf in San Francisco.

B. Recognize prepositions and adverbs. Tell whether the italicized word in each sentence is a *Preposition* or an *Adverb*. If it is a preposition, write its (object.) (Use after page 529.)

1. Carla heard someone *within* the room. preposition (room)
2. Did you look *behind* the couch? preposition (couch)
3. We raced *inside* when the storm began. adverb
4. Has Marianne stopped *by* yet? adverb
5. Ken has never skated *before* now. adverb
6. Utter destruction lay *in* the hurricane's wake. preposition (wake)
7. Don't stand *near* those speakers when the band begins to play. preposition (speakers)
8. Turn the lights *off* to conserve energy. adverb
9. One runner lagged far *behind*. adverb
10. The restaurant is just *past* that sign. preposition (sign)

C. Identify prepositional phrases as modifiers. Write the prepositional phrases in each sentence. Label each phrase *Adjective* or *Adverb* and tell what word it modifies. (Use after page 532.)

1. The construction crew drove piles <u>into the riverbed</u>. adv. (drove)
2. Are you going <u>to camp</u> <u>in Wisconsin</u> this year? adv. (going); adj. (camp)
3. A movie <u>about the Kennedys</u> is <u>on TV</u>. adj. (movie); adv. (is)
4. <u>Around the castle</u> was a moat <u>with crocodiles</u> <u>in it</u>. adj. (crocodiles)
   adv. (was); adj. (moat)
5. This ski jacket is filled <u>with down</u>. adv. (filled)
6. The woman <u>with the briefcase</u> is Dr. Sanchez. adj. (woman)
7. A crowd <u>of eager fans</u> swarmed the stage <u>after the show</u>.
   adj. (crowd)   adv. (swarmed)
8. The young man <u>in the green jacket</u> is Jake Houston. adj. (man)
9. <u>To everyone's surprise</u>, the ball landed <u>in the bleachers</u>.
   adv. (landed)
10. Nobody <u>but Rachel</u> understood the point <u>of the story</u>.
    adj. (Nobody); adj. (point)

D. Recognize conjunctions. For each sentence write the conjunction. Then write the words or groups of words joined by the conjunction. (Use after page 535.)

1. The <u>Pirates</u> <u>and</u> the <u>Steelers</u> are Pittsburgh teams.
2. Father Hildalgo of Mexico was a <u>priest</u> <u>and</u> a political <u>leader</u>.
3. The soldier <u>saluted</u> <u>and</u> <u>turned</u> to leave.
4. The speaker's voice was <u>powerful</u> <u>and</u> <u>engaging</u>.
5. Andrew was <u>not only</u> hungry <u>but also</u> thirsty.
6. Can you tell whether a <u>computer</u> <u>or</u> a <u>person</u> made the mistake?
7. <u>Rugs</u>, <u>drapes</u>, <u>and</u> <u>pillows</u> muffle the noises in a room.
8. Somebody <u>called</u> for you <u>but</u> <u>left</u> no message.
9. In gym class, we'll play <u>either</u> volleyball <u>or</u> softball.
10. <u>Neither</u> Kelley <u>nor</u> Rivera caught the grounder to left field.

Mixed Review

These exercises provide review of the concepts presented in this Section. Each exercise challenges the students to apply several of the skills they have acquired during previous study. Because the "mixed" feature of these activities makes them more difficult, the teacher may wish to have less-advanced students do them orally or in small groups.

MIXED REVIEW
Using Prepositions and Conjunctions

A. Tell whether the italicized word in each sentence is a preposition or an adverb. If it is an adverb, copy the (word that it modifies.) If it is a preposition, copy the object of the preposition.

1. *Outside,* a heavy rain was falling. adv. (was falling)
2. Three children ran *past,* each with a candy apple in one hand and tickets for rides in the other. adv. (ran)
3. The Grand Old Opry is a country music hall located *in* Nashville, Tennessee. prep. (Nashville, Tennessee)
4. The garden is beautiful, but have you seen the view *beyond?* adv. (have seen)   prep. (noon)
5. *Around* noon, a band started to play on the grandstand.
6. The ice cream truck slowed *down* and stopped *nearby.* adv. (slowed
                                                           adv. (stoppe
7. Most of the birds have migrated, but these ducks have remained *behind.* adv. (remained)
8. Her cat goes *out* whenever it pleases. adv. (goes)
9. The archaeologist's assistant wouldn't wait *inside* the tomb alone. prep. (tomb)
10. The country bridge was so rotten that we were afraid of falling *through* it. prep. (it)

B. Write the prepositional phrases in the following sentences. Then tell whether they are used as adverb phrases or adjective phrases.

1. *Star Wars,* a film by Steven Spielberg, was the first in a series of three films. adj., adj., adj.
2. With a sheepish grin, the toddler removed his hand from the cookie jar. adv., adv.
3. The elaborate wig on the dancer's head was dyed a bright blue. adj.
                                                                  adv., adv.
4. After the play, Jack and Diane walked to the restaurant.
5. The security guard in the supermarket looked suspiciously at the customer. adj., adv.
6. *Nova* is a show on PBS that deals with unusual subjects of interest. adj., adv., adj.

7. The actors and actresses at the Academy Awards waited for the announcements with anticipation. adj., adv., adv.
8. The bride and groom walked toward the altar and stood under an arch during the ceremony. adv., adv., adv.   adj., adv., adj.
9. The school of fish wove through the coral of the huge reef.
10. The line outside the theater stretched around the corner and beyond the intersection. adj., adv., adv.

C. Complete the following phrases or sentences, using the type of conjunction called for in parentheses. Answers will vary.

1. __Both__ carrots __and__ celery are vegetables often used in salads. (correlative)
2. The runner tripped over the hurdle __and__ sprained his ankle. (coordinating)
3. Our new quarterback is small __but__ fast. (coordinating)
4. __Either__ Charles __or__ José went to interview the mayor. (correlative)
5. Karen designs __and__ fires her own pottery and clay sculpture. (coordinating)
6. Sheila is __not only__ class president __but also__ head cheerleader. (correlative)
7. Tina could not decide whether to tell her grandmother __or__ her grandfather the good news first. (coordinating)
8. Larry saw the tree, __but__ could not avoid skiing directly into it. (coordinating)
9. I was told that my stereo would be repaired by Friday __or__ Saturday. (coordinating)
10. Jana enjoys __both__ classical music __and__ reggae. (correlative)

Using Grammar in Writing

These challenging and enjoyable activities allow the students to see how the concepts of grammar, usage, and mechanics may be applied in actual writing situations. Each exercise is designed to allow students practice in several of the skills they have acquired in this Section. The activities also provide opportunities for students to write creatively about a wide variety of interesting and unusual subjects.

USING GRAMMAR IN WRITING
Using Prepositions and Conjunctions

A. Describe in detail how to perform some specific athletic activity like swinging a bat, catching a football, or serving a volleyball. Circle all of the prepositions that you use in your description. Notice that prepositions often express a change in position or a relationship between two objects. For example, "Pull the string *of* the bow *toward* your chin," or "Place your hands *near* the bottom *of* the bat."

B. Write a poem in which each line begins with a preposition. It is not necessary that the lines of the poem rhyme. Here is an example:

> *From* space a single twinkle came
> *Into* my eye from a distant star
> *Through* the atmosphere and endless time
> *Beyond* my dreams and all imagining.

C. Try to write another poem in which every other line begins with the conjunction *but*. Notice that the word *but* introduces a word or an idea that is contrary to expectation.

> I'd like to be swimming in moonlight,
> *But* I'm washing the dishes instead.
> I'd like to be dancing by starlight,
> *But* it's already past time for bed.

D. Write a paragraph comparing a hot fudge sundae to a banana split. Make your descriptions so vivid that someone who has never seen or tasted these treats will feel as if he or she had just done so. Use the conjunctions *and, or, but, either/or,* and *both/and* in your comparison.

Section 8

Review of Parts of Speech

Part 1 The Parts of Speech

In Section 3 you learned that there are eight **parts of speech.** A word is classified as one of these parts of speech according to its use in a sentence. Before continuing with this section, quickly review the names of the eight groups:

The Parts of Speech			
nouns	verbs	adverbs	conjunctions
pronouns	adjectives	prepositions	interjections

The last part of speech, **interjections,** is the only one you have not studied.

Section Objectives

1. To review the eight parts of speech and interjections

2. To determine the part of speech by identifying how a word is used in a sentence

Preparing the Students

List the following words on the board: *down, plant, produce, around, but, step, slow, those.* Ask the students to say what part of speech each of the words is. Write their responses on the board next to the words. If they give more than one part of speech for a word, write both parts of speech next to the word and ask for examples to support the designations. This will serve as a review of the various parts of speech and also bring to light the fact that the same word may be used in several different ways.

Additional Resources

Mastery Test — See pages 59–60 in the test booklet. Recommended for use after teaching this Section.

Additional Exercises — See pages 545–548 in the student text.

Skills Practice Book — pages 149–151.

Duplicating Masters — pages 149–159.

Special Populations — See special section at the front of this Teacher's Edition.

Part 1

Objective

To review the eight parts of speech and interjections

Presenting the Lesson

1. Read and discuss **The Parts of Speech** on page 541. Review with the class the use(s) of each of the parts of speech in sentences.

2. Read and discuss **What Is an Interjection?** on page 542. Tell the class that interjections have no grammatical relationship to the rest of the sentence.

3. Do Exercise A on page 542 with the class. Assign Exercise B to be completed independently.

Individualizing the Lesson

Less-Advanced Students

Write the following sentences on the board. Call on students to identify the part of speech of each word in the sentences.

1. Green plants require sunlight.
2. Bob and I make birchbark canoes in our spare time.
3. Wow! You ate that piece of pizza quickly.

Advanced Students

Discuss the etymologies of the names of the various parts of speech. Point out how the roots of the words from which the names were formed suggest the functions of the parts of speech in sentences.

Examples:

noun: "name"
interjection: "between" "throw"
conjunction: "with" "join"

Reinforcement Exercise

Assign and discuss Exercise A on page 545.

Optional Practice

Have students compile a list of interjections and write sentences that make use of the interjections.

What Is an Interjection?

An interjection is a word or group of words used to express strong feeling.

An interjection may be either a phrase or a word. It expresses strong feeling, such as joy, anger, terror, surprise, disgust, or sadness. Because it conveys strong emotions, an interjection is followed by an exclamation mark as in the following examples.

Wow! Look at those mountains.   *Oh!* You scared me.

You now have nearly all of the terms you need to identify and classify any word in the English language. You will learn the remaining few terms in Section 9.

Exercise A: Write each italicized word and its part of speech.

1. *Fantastic!* The agent likes Vicky's demonstration record. interjection
2. Philips *charged* frantically for the end zone. verb
3. Did *anybody* ever thank the Lone Ranger? pronoun
4. Anne hung a poster *inside* her locker. preposition
5. Is Portland *or* Salem the capital of Oregon? conjunction
6. Denise will *probably* become a lawyer. adverb
7. Your phone is always *busy*. adjective
8. With a *tremendous* roar the volcano erupted. adjective
9. The *stories* of O. Henry end with a surprise. noun
10. Lydia *remembered* the warmth of her old neighborhood. verb

Exercise B: Follow the directions for Exercise A.

1. The truck swerved and *avoided* a *collision*. verb noun
2. Country music *has influenced* both rock *and* soul music. verb conjunct
3. Many glaciers *in* Greenland are over a mile *thick*. preposition adjec
4. *Ugh!* I can't stand licorice. interjection
5. The steel mills in *Gary* reddened *the* sky. noun adjective
6. The explorers took a month's *supply* of food with *them*. noun pronoun
7. Leslie cleared the hurdles *easily*. adverb
8. The *polite* bus driver waited *for* the limping man. adjective preposit
9. The zoo director *recently* returned from *Panama*. adverb noun
10. Margaret Bourke-White *is* famous for her war photos. verb

Part 2 Using Words as Different Parts of Speech

Very often the same word can be used as different parts of speech. For example, a word might be used as a noun in one sentence and an adjective in another.

The only way to identify the part of speech of any word is to determine how that word is used in a sentence.

The artist folded *paper* into unusual shapes.
(*Paper* is used as a noun, the direct object of the verb *folded*.)

At the picnic, we ate on *paper* plates.
(*Paper* is used as an adjective, modifying *plates*.)

The five-dollar *bill* has a picture of Abraham Lincoln.
(*Bill* is used as a noun, the subject of the sentence.)

The store will *bill* us for our purchases.
(*Bill* is used as the main verb.)

What is your favorite song?
(*What* is used as a pronoun, the subject of the sentence.)

What shows are on TV now?
(*What* is used as an adjective, modifying the noun *shows*.)

A *low* wall surrounded the building.
(*Low* is used as an adjective, modifying the noun *wall*.)

A plane flew *low* over the beach.
(*Low* is used as an adverb, modifying the verb *flew*.)

After her speech, Sally sat *down*.
(*Down* is used as an adverb, modifying the verb *sat*.)

We rowed the boat *down* the river.
(*Down* is used as a preposition.)

Never! I won't try it again.
(*Never* is used as an interjection.)

Mr. Bailey *never* raises his voice.
(*Never* is used as an adverb, modifying the verb *raises*.)

543

Extending the Lesson

Ask students to try and label every word in the sentences in Exercises A and B on page 542. In preparation for Part 2, call attention to the use of the word *end* as an adjective in sentence 2 and as a verb in sentence 9 of Exercise A.

Part 2

Objective

To determine the part of speech by identifying how a word is used in a sentence

Presenting the Lesson

1. Read and discuss **Using Words as Different Parts of Speech** on page 543. Point out that the part of speech of many words can only be determined in context. Use the sentences in Exercise A on page 544 for oral practice.

2. Assign and discuss Exercises B and C on page 544.

Individualizing the Lesson

Less-Advanced Students

1. Have students identify the part of speech of the italicized word in each of the following sentences.

1. *Cotton* is a natural fiber.
2. Stacey ate *cotton* candy.
3. *Surprise!* You win the prize.
4. The play had a *surprise* ending.
5. Joey set a *record* in the 100-yard dash.
6. The score-keeper will *record* the time.
7. A *record* number of people signed up.
8. The weekend is *over*.
9. The eagle flew *over* the peak.
10. A chair fell *over*.

2. Allow students to work on Exercise C in pairs.

Advanced Students

Have students write a story using each word in Exercise C as specified in the parentheses.

Reinforcement Exercise

Assign and discuss Exercise B on page 546.

Optional Practice

Have students write pairs of sentences for each of the following words.

1. these (pronoun and adjective)
2. around (adverb and preposition)
3. British (proper noun and proper adjective)
4. loudest (adjective and adverb)
5. no (interjection and adjective)
6. off (preposition and adverb)
7. this (pronoun and adjective)
8. color (verb and noun)
9. but (conjunction and preposition)
10. drop (verb and adjective)

Extending the Lesson

Explain to the students that *homographs* are words identical in spelling but different in meaning and sometimes pronunciation.

How much should we *tip* the waiter?
Don't *tip* back in your chair.

The *wind* blew hard all day.
Please *wind* the clock before you go to bed.

Ask the class to come up with five more homographs. Write the words on the board and ask the students to think of sentences that illustrate all meanings of the words.

Exercise A: Write the italicized word. Next to it, write what part of speech it functions as in that sentence.

1. *Really!* Do you expect me to believe that? interjection
2. Mom *really* wants to see Paris. adverb
3. *Name* another famous player who was with the New York Yankees at the same time as Babe Ruth. verb
4. One *name* given to the Conestoga wagon by pioneers was "camel of the desert." noun
5. *Daydreams* can serve a useful purpose. noun
6. Paul *daydreams* about winning an Olympic medal. verb
7. Who lives in *this* houseboat? adjective
8. *This* is the corner where the accident happened. pronoun
9. *Fire* drills are scheduled every month. adjective
10. *Fire* at the target when I signal. verb

Exercise B: Follow the directions for Exercise A.

1. Don't turn *on* the television during an electrical storm. adverb
2. Her homework was lying *on* the table, under the newspaper. preposition
3. Our mail carrier *growls* back at dogs. verb
4. The *growls* were getting meaner and deeper. noun
5. *Park* your bike in those racks. verb
6. This *park* provides nature walks with Braille signs. noun
7. The youth center keeps an up-to-date job *file*. noun
8. Passengers usually *file* quietly down to the subway. verb
9. *That* was my idea. pronoun
10. Have you already seen *that* movie? adjective

Exercise C: Writing Write sentences using the following words as the parts of speech indicated in parentheses.

1. travel (verb)
2. travel (adjective)
3. right (noun)
4. right (adjective)
5. skate (verb)
6. guard (noun)
7. those (pronoun)
8. those (adjective)
9. fantastic (interjection)
10. fast (adverb)

REINFORCEMENT EXERCISES
Review of Parts of Speech

A. Recognize the parts of speech. Write the italicized word in each sentence and tell what part of speech it is. (Use after page 544.)

1. Did the reporter quote *you* accurately? pronoun
2. *Ouch!* That antiseptic really stings. interjection
3. *Canadians* celebrate their national independence on July first. noun
4. Jim talks too fast *and* too much. conjunction
5. The emergency room in Weiss Memorial Hospital is *always* crowded. adverb
6. The art class designed and *sold* hooked rugs. verb
7. Robert takes his *youngest* sister to a day-care center each morning. adjective
8. *Wow!* We got here just in time to see the kickoff! interjection
9. A squirrel looked down at us *from* a branch of the old maple tree. preposition
10. In North and South Dakota, winter begins *early* and ends late. adverb
11. *This* was Norman Rockwell's studio. pronoun
12. The detective examined the skid *marks* in an effort to trace the car. noun
13. It can rain *for* weeks in Seattle during the winter. preposition
14. Are you studying vertebrates in biology *now*? adverb
15. Mr. Diaz showed us his collection of *African* masks and sculpture. adjective
16. How did Indian summer get its *name*? noun
17. Did *anyone* see the No Swimming sign? pronoun
18. The oddly-shaped *leaves* of the ancient ginkgo tree look like small fans. noun
19. The Milwaukee Brewers won their first American League pennant *in* 1982. preposition
20. The Navajo woman carefully *wove* bright red yarn into the blanket's design. verb

These Reinforcement Exercises may be used for additional practice of the concepts presented in this Section. Each exercise focuses on a single concept, and should be used after the page number indicated in parentheses.

Review

If you have not assigned these Reinforcement Exercises before this time, you can also use them as an excellent Section Review.

B. Identify words used as different parts of speech. Write the italicized word in each sentence. Tell what part of speech it is in that sentence. (Use after page 544.)

1. The President tossed out the *game* ball. adjective
2. "Facts in Fives" is my family's favorite *game*. noun
3. The police officers looked for *signs* of forced entry. noun
4. Angelo *signs* his name with a flourish. verb
5. My grandad was born *in* Austria. preposition
6. We stayed *in* because of the tornado warning. adverb
7. *That* shop specialized in exotic pets. adjective
8. *That* was Robert Duvall's best role. pronoun
9. That man looks exactly *like* Lou Gossett, Jr. preposition
10. We *like* to explore caves and caverns. verb
11. During the *rush* hour, helicopters hover above the freeways. adjective
12. *Rush* the fallen skier to the emergency room! verb
13. That *picture* by Van Gogh sold for half a million dollars. noun
14. *Picture* yourself swimming in a cool, clear lake. verb
15. *This* is the third time I've run the program. pronoun
16. Can anyone read *this* message? adjective
17. Tom trailed *behind* the other hikers. preposition
18. We left many good friends *behind* in Indiana. adverb
19. The hot-air balloon sailed *high* into the sky. adverb
20. At *high* tide this area is under water. adjective

MIXED REVIEW
Review of Parts of Speech

A. Complete this short story by inserting the parts of speech asked for in parentheses. Answers will vary.

It (verb) a dark and (adjective) night. The (adjective) detectives, (proper noun) and (proper noun), were investigating a (noun) which took place (prepositional phrase).

"There definitely (verb) some kind (prepositional phrase) here," said (proper noun) to (proper noun). (Pronoun) crept (adverb) around the (noun) only to find (noun). Then the two detectives (verb) (prepositional phrase) and realized that (pronoun) was missing!

"(Pronoun) (verb) everything!" exclaimed (proper noun). "(Adverb) we'll have to (verb) back (prepositional phrase) (coordinating conjunction) try to (verb) this to our (noun)."

B. Write two sentences for ten of the following words. The word should be used as a different part of speech in each sentence. Tell what part of speech the word is used as in each of your sentences.

EXAMPLE: 1. Lynn and Carrie *feed* their pets each day. (verb)
2. The *feed* store closes at noon on Wednesday. (adjective)

picture	like	time	loose
rush	frame	sting	store
that	finish	throw	chase
signs	design	whistle	run
lead	wet	cut	close
watch	place	trade	open

Mixed Review

These exercises provide review of the concepts presented in this Section. Each exercise challenges the students to apply several of the skills they have acquired during previous study. Because the "mixed" feature of these activities makes them more difficult, the teacher may wish to have less-advanced students do them orally or in small groups.

USING GRAMMAR IN WRITING
Review of Parts of Speech

A. Try to imagine what it must feel like to go sky-diving for the first time. Record your feelings as you experience the sensation of free fall, the sudden catch of the chute in the wind, and the slow drift to earth. Use a few interjections to express your intense emotions as you plunge through the air and the ground rushes to meet you. Your paragraph should also include examples of each of the other parts of speech.

B. Imagine that you work for an advertising agency and that your supervisor has assigned you the task of writing an ad for a new means of transportation. The manufacturers of the product claim that it will make cars obsolete. Your boss says to you, "Make every word count! Give me powerful verbs! Dynamic nouns! Dazzling modifiers! Perfect pronouns and punchy interjections!" You have been given a limit of one hundred words to "Sell that product!" To top it off, you must underline ten verbs, ten nouns, five modifiers, and two interjections that you have used in the ad so that your boss can see at a glance how interesting it is.

C. Flip through a dictionary, magazine, or book and select sixteen words. Try to include two of each of the eight parts of speech. Now, try to use these words to write a story. The story must make sense, but it may be serious or humorous.

Section 9

Using Verbals

Section Objectives

1. To recognize gerunds and gerund phrases

2. To recognize participles and participial phrases

3. To recognize infinitives and infinitive phrases

4. To review verbals and verbal phrases

Preparing the Students

Put the following sayings on the board:

Seeing is *believing.*
A *rolling* stone gathers no moss.

Ask the students if they can identify the parts of speech of the underlined words. Tell them that the Section they are about to study will help them understand these words and how they function in sentences.

Additional Resources

Diagnostic Test — See page 6 in the test booklet. Recommended for use before teaching this Section.

Mastery Test — See page 63 in the test booklet. Recommended for use after teaching the Section.

Additional Exercises — See pages 61–62 in the student text.

Skills Practice Book — pages 152–155.

Duplicating Masters — pages 152–155.

Special Populations — See special section at the front of this Teacher's Edition.

In addition to the eight basic parts of speech, there are three other useful kinds of words. Because they are formed from verbs, these words are called **verbals.** The three verbals are **gerunds, participles,** and **infinitives.** Even though verbals are formed from verbs, they do not function as verbs in sentences. In this section you will learn to use verbals and verbal phrases.

549

A gerund is a verb form that functions as a noun.

A gerund ends in *-ing*. It may be used in any way that a noun is used — as a subject, a direct object, an object of a preposition, or as a predicate word.

> *Drawing* is Alissa's hobby. (subject)
> Debbie tried *surfing*. (direct object)
> The best place for *jogging* is the park. (object of a preposition)
> A major industry here is *mining*. (predicate word)

The Gerund Phrase

Often a gerund has a modifier or an object or both. Together they form a **gerund phrase.** The entire gerund phrase is used like a noun.

Because a gerund is formed from a verb, it can have an object.

> We won by *scoring a touchdown* in the last minute.
> (*Scoring* is a gerund; *touchdown* is the object of *scoring.* The phrase *scoring a touchdown* is the object of the preposition *by.*)

Because a gerund is formed from a verb, it can be modified by adverbs.

> Elliot started *laughing again*.
> (*Laughing* is a gerund; *again* is an adverb modifying *laughing*. The phrase *laughing again* is the object of the verb *started.*)

Because a gerund is used as a noun, it can be modified by adjectives.

> *Quick thinking* saved us.
> (*Thinking* is a gerund; *quick* is an adjective modifying *thinking.* The phrase *quick thinking* is the subject of the verb *saved.*)

Objective

To recognize gerunds and gerund phrases

Presenting the Lesson

1. Read and discuss **Gerunds** and **The Gerund Phrase** on pages 550–551. Remind the class that they learned about the present participle in Section 5 Part 6 on page 483. Point out that both the gerund and the present participle are verb forms that end in *-ing*. They can only tell that a verb form is a gerund by identifying its function in the sentence as that of a noun.

2. Do Exercise A on page 552 orally. Ask the students to point out any modifiers or direct objects that are related to the gerund.

3. Read and discuss **Diagraming Gerunds** on page 551. Diagram the four sample sentences on the top of page 550 on the board with the class.

4. Assign and discuss Exercise B on page 553.

Individualizing the Lesson

Less-Advanced Students

Have students fill in the blanks with a gerund made from the verb given in parentheses. Point out before they do that the part of speech called for in each sentence is a noun.

1. _____ is an expensive hobby. (ski)
2. My brother loves _____. (dance)
3. Seeing is _____. (believe)
4. John won a prize for _____. (sculpt)
5. _____ is good for your circulation. (run)

550

Gerunds can also be modified by prepositional phrases.

> *Sitting on these benches* is uncomfortable.
>> (*Sitting* is a gerund; *on these benches* is a prepositional phrase modifying *sitting*. The entire gerund phrase is the subject of *is*.)

In these examples *drawing, surfing, jogging, mining, scoring, laughing, thinking,* and *sitting* all look like verbs but are used as nouns. Therefore, they are gerunds. Along with the modifiers and objects that are used with them, they form gerund phrases.

Diagraming Gerunds

A gerund or gerund phrase used as a subject, direct object, or predicate word is diagramed on a line above the main line. The gerund belongs on a line drawn as a step. Its modifiers are placed on slanted lines below it. Its object is shown on the horizontal line following the gerund.

Telling jokes will cheer us up.

This job requires fast, accurate typing.

His hobby is painting miniatures.

A gerund or gerund phrase used as the object of a preposition is diagramed below the main line. The preposition belongs on a slanted line going down from the word modified. Again, the gerund appears on a stepped line.

We thanked Valerie for helping us.

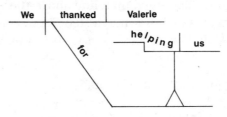

Exercise A: Write the gerunds or gerund phrases. Then tell how each one functions in the sentence.

1. Yelling at the umpire caused Joanne's laryngitis.subject
2. Faulty wiring started the disastrous fire in the apartment complex.subject
3. The big concern in this valley is flooding.predicate word
4. We were tired from running so far.object of preposition
5. Our vacation plans include a day of water skiing on Lake Michigan.object of preposition
6. Washing the windows of skyscrapers is hazardous.subject
7. Nearly everybody dislikes dieting.direct object
8. Wind surfing is one sport I'd like to try.subject
9. Logical thinking can be learned.subject
10. One worthwhile way to spend free time is volunteering at the health clinic. predicate word

Exercise B: Follow the directions for Exercise A.

1. Sharpening her tennis game is Jean's current goal. subject
2. Will writing to the editor have any effect? subject
3. My grandmother enjoys scuba diving. direct object
4. Moving to Boston stirred Ken's interest in history. subject
5. Painting a dragon on the van was Sonya's idea. subject
6. Mending nets took much of the old fisherman's time. subject
7. Winning the war cost many lives. subject
8. Is discus throwing an Olympic event? subject
9. How many calories does an hour of walking burn? object of preposition
10. The fire department warns against keeping the oven on for warmth. object of preposition

Part 2   Participles

A participle is a verb form that functions as an adjective.

You learned that the **past participle** is one of the principal parts of a verb. The past participle of a regular verb is formed by adding -d or -ed to the present tense, as in *dance — danced* or *dress — dressed*. The past participles of irregular verbs are formed differently and must be learned separately: *tear—torn, sing—sung*.

You also learned that there is another kind of participle besides the past participle, called the **present participle.** The present participle is always formed by adding -ing to the present tense: *dance—dancing, dress—dressing, tear—tearing, sing—singing*.

VERB	PAST PARTICIPLE	PRESENT PARTICIPLE
look	looked	looking
bring	brought	bringing
cry	cried	crying

Participles may be used as parts of verb phrases: *had danced, am going*. When used as verbals, however, both past and present participles always function as adjectives. A participle modifies either a noun or a pronoun.

Part 2

Objective

To recognize participles and participial phrases

Presenting the Lesson

1. Read and discuss **Participles** and **The Participial Phrase** on pages 553–554. Review the formation of regular and irregular past participles. Point out that the past participle and the simple past tense are often spelled alike. To determine whether a verb form is a simple past tense or a past participle, it is necessary to examine the sentence as a whole.

2. Point out that participles can change from present to past tense because they are verb forms. Emphasize that participles are used as adjectives to modify nouns, pronouns, and words acting as nouns. Go over the sentences in Exercise A on page 555 orally. Assign Exercise B.

3. Read and discuss **Diagraming Participles** on page 555. Diagram the sample sentences from page 554 on the board with the class.

4. Read and discuss **Gerund or Participle?** on page 556. Remind the class that in the last section they practiced recognizing the part of speech of a word by its use in a particular sentence. The same kind of analysis is necessary to decide if an *-ing* verb is a gerund or a participle.

5. Assign and discuss the Exercise on page 556.

Individualizing the Lesson

Less-Advanced Students

Have students identify the gerund phrases and participial phrases in the following sentences and tell how each functions.

1. The panther frightened everyone by *pacing about his cage*. (G)
2. *Pacing nervously*, the young man waited for some news. (P)
3. *Acting comically* comes naturally to Carol Burnett. (G)
4. The children were feeling ill, and their *worried* mother called the doctor. (P)
5. After *finishing lunch*, we walked to the theater. (G)
6. A *smiling* Anita accepted the award. (P)
7. The boys *driving the sports car* are my cousins. (P)
8. *Playing a trumpet* requires good breath control. (G)
9. The *leaping* dolphins performed tricks. (P)
10. *Warned by the alarm*, the police caught the thief. (P)

Advanced Students

Discuss the idea of parallel construction in writing. Tell students that

---

Exhausted, Martina sat down with a sigh.
  (*Exhausted* is a past participle modifying the noun *Martina.*)
Whistling, he made his way home through the snow.
  (*Whistling* is a present participle modifying the pronoun *he.*)
A *fallen* tree blocked the street.
  (*Fallen* is a past participle modifying the noun *tree.*)
The *flying* object had four headlights.
  (*Flying* is a present participle modifying the noun *object.*)

The Participial Phrase

A participle is not always used alone. Often a participle has a modifier or an object or both. Together, they form a **participial phrase.** The entire participial phrase is used as an adjective.

Because a participle is formed from a verb, it may have an object.

> The goat *chewing the shoe* belongs to Pete.
> (*Chewing the shoe* is a participial phrase modifying *goat. Shoe* is the object of the participle *chewing.*)

Because a participle comes from a verb, it may be modified by adverbs.

> *Racing madly,* Carla beat the throw to home plate.
> (*Racing madly* is a participial phrase modifying *Carla. Madly* is an adverb modifying the participle *racing.*)

A participle may also be modified by prepositional phrases.

> We heard the foghorn *moaning in the distance.*
> (*Moaning in the distance* is a participial phrase modifying *foghorn. In the distance* is a prepositional phrase modifying the participle *moaning.*)

In the examples on this page, *exhausted, whistling, fallen, flying, chewing, racing,* and *moaning* all look like verbs but are used as adjectives. Therefore, they are called participles. Modifiers and objects used with them form participial phrases.

Diagraming Participles

To diagram a participle, place it on an angled line below the noun or pronoun it modifies. Put modifiers of the participle on lines slanted down from it. An object follows the participle on a horizontal line.

Reading the fine print carefully, Erin studied the contract.

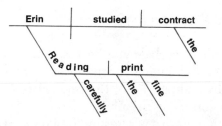

Exercise A: Write the <u>participles</u> or <u>participial phrases</u> in these sentences. Show which word the participle or phrase modifies.

> EXAMPLE: Raising her eyebrows, Regina stared at the conductor.
> *Raising her eyebrows* (modifies *Regina*)

1. <u>Working hard,</u> the firefighters controlled the blaze. firefighters
2. The <u>glittering</u> snow blinded him for a minute. snow
3. <u>Fried</u> chicken was heaped on the platters. chicken   .
4. Cheryl scraped the <u>peeling</u> paint from the rocker. paint
5. <u>Frightened by the odd noise,</u> I called the police.
6. Harris slipped on the <u>freshly waxed</u> floor. floor
7. Someone <u>wearing high heels</u> made these footprints. Someone
8. The pie <u>cooling on the table</u> is for dessert. pie
9. <u>Snapping her fingers,</u> Lynn set the rhythm. Lynn
10. The man <u>with the hat pulled down over his eyes</u> was once a baseball star. man

Exercise B: Follow the directions for Exercise A.

1. <u>Nodding her head,</u> Mrs. Chang accepted the salesman's final offer. Mrs. Chang
2. That is a <u>widely-known</u> fact. fact
3. There was no hope for a seat on the <u>packed</u> bus. bus

a series beginning with nouns must continue with nouns; one that begins with adjectives must continue with adjectives. Similarly the tense of participles should not shift in the middle of a series. Ask students how they would revise the following sentences.

Jorry was panting hard, sweating profusely, and looked exhausted.

My favorite outdoor activities are swimming, hiking, and to barbeque hamburgers.

Thinking clearly, organizing carefully, and good grammar are necessary to write well.

Reinforcement Exercise

Assign and discuss Exercise B on page 563.

Optional Practice

Have students use the following participial phrases in sentences.

1. wearing a blue jacket
2. taken by surprise
3. awakened by the alarm
4. torn to shreds
5. diving gracefully

Two of the above phrases could also be gerund phrases. Call on volunteers to think of sentences that use them as gerunds.

Extending the Lesson

Explain that participles and participial phrases can be used to add a feeling of action to a description. Ask students to find examples in a short story or other piece of writing.

4. <u>Opening the door</u>, Mark accidentally bumped Mr. Hays. ^{Mark}
5. Bits of <u>broken</u> glass in the street told the story. ^{glass}
6. Take gloves off <u>frostbitten</u> hands slowly and carefully. ^{hands}
7. <u>Falling softly on the roof</u>, the rain sounded peaceful. ^{rain}
8. Most of our <u>scattered</u> relatives got together for the reunion. ^{relatives}
9. I was trapped inside the <u>revolving</u> door for an hour. ^{door}
10. Payton, <u>leaping into the air</u>, caught the ball. ^{Payton}

Gerund or Participle?

The two kinds of verbals you have studied, gerunds and participles, often look the same. Gerunds and present participles are both formed by adding *-ing* to the present tense of verbs. How can you avoid confusing them?

To tell whether a word is a gerund or a present participle, look at how it is used. If it is used as a modifier, it is a participle. If it is used as a noun, it is a gerund.

Look at the following sentences.

> *Hiking along the nature trail* takes two hours.
> (The gerund phrase *hiking along the nature trail* is the subject of the verb *takes*.)

> *Hiking along the nature trail*, we saw several deer.
> (The participial phrase *hiking along the nature trail* modifies the pronoun *we*.)

Exercise: For each sentence, write the <u>gerund</u> or <u>participle</u> and say which each is. Be prepared to explain your answer.

1. <u>Diving from the high board</u> requires control. ^{gerund}
2. <u>Diving from the high board</u>, Jeff lost control. ^{participle}
3. <u>Tuning the old piano</u>, Hank listened carefully to each tone. ^{participle}
4. <u>Tuning the old piano</u> will improve its sound. ^{gerund}
5. We were <u>exhausted</u> after <u>climbing the hill</u>. ^{participle, gerund}
6. <u>Climbing the hill</u>, Sandy spotted a waterfall. ^{participle}
7. The police chief suggested <u>dusting for fingerprints</u>. ^{gerund}
8. <u>Using a newspaper</u>, Lynn chased the bee outside. ^{participle}
9. The people <u>sitting in the front row</u> get the best view. ^{participle}
10. Steve calmed the dog by <u>stroking it</u>. ^{gerund}

Part 3 Infinitives

An infinitive is a verb form that usually begins with the word *to*.

to write	to shout	to find	to forget
to say	to like	to join	to remind

You have learned that the word *to* is used as a preposition. *To* is a preposition when it is followed by a noun or pronoun as its object. However, when *to* is followed by a verb, it is called the **sign of the infinitive**. Compare these examples:

PREPOSITIONAL PHRASES	INFINITIVES
We went to the youth center.	We tried to remember.
Justin listened to the music.	Kristin wants to rollerskate.
A sign was nailed to the tree.	Evan wants to leave.

The Infinitive Phrase

Like gerunds and participles, infinitives are not always used alone. An infinitive can have modifiers and objects. The infinitive with its modifiers and objects forms an **infinitive phrase**.

Because an infinitive is formed from a verb, it may have an object.

> Megan planned *to have a party*.
> (*Party* is the direct object of the infinitive *to have*.)

> The coach wanted *to give the team a good workout*.
> (*Team* is the indirect object and *workout* is the direct object of the infinitive *to give*.)

Because an infinitive is formed from a verb, it may be modified by adverbs.

> The choir tried *to sing together*.
> (*Together* is an adverb modifying the infinitive *to sing*.)

> A tape recording asked me *to call again later*.
> (*Again* and *later* are adverbs modifying the infinitive *to call*.)

557

Part 3

Objective

To recognize infinitives and infinitive phrases

Presenting the Lesson

1. Read and discuss **Infinitives, The Infinitive Phrase**, and **Uses of the Infinitive Phrase** on pages 557–558. Put the following sentence on the board:

> The judges decided to give the prize to Jessica.

Point to the two *to*'s in the sentence and call on a student to explain the difference. Emphasize the point that infintives and infinitive phrases can serve as nouns, adjectives, and adverbs.

Complete Exercise A on page 560 orally with the class.

2. Read and discuss **The Split Infinitive** and **Diagraming Infinitives** on page 559. For additional examples of split infinitves, see Optional Practice. Diagram several of the sample sentences from page 558 on the board.

3. Assign and discuss Exercise B on page 560.

Individualizing the Lesson

Less-Advanced Students

Have students identify the infinitive phrases in the following sentences and tell how each is used.

1. I went to see the lastest Indiana Jones movie.
2. To earn his allowance, Adam mows the lawn.
3. To sing in the musical was Perry's goal.
4. My lock is hard to open.
5. Everyone likes to get presents.

Infinitives may also be modified by prepositional phrases.

> One customer demanded *to talk to the manager.*
> (*To the manager* is a prepositional phrase modifying the infinitive *to talk*.)

> Many people like *to picnic in the park.*
> (*In the park* is a prepositional phrase modifying the infinitive *to picnic*.)

Uses of the Infinitive Phrase

Unlike gerunds and participles, infinitives can be used as more than one part of speech. An infinitive or infinitive phrase can be used as a noun, an adjective, or an adverb.

Infinitives and infinitive phrases can be used in ways that nouns are used. As you know, nouns may be subjects or direct objects.

> SUBJECT: *To learn a new language* takes time.
> (*To learn a new language* is the subject.)
> DIRECT OBJECT: Diane forgot *to send the entry fee.*
> (*To send the entry fee* is the direct object.)

Infinitives and infinitive phrases can also be used as adjectives or adverbs. The infinitive or infinitive phrase is used as an adjective if it modifies a noun or pronoun. It is used as an adverb if it modifies a verb, adjective, or adverb.

> ADJECTIVE: These are the logs *to burn in the fireplace.*
> (*To burn in the fireplace* modifies the noun *logs*.)
> ADJECTIVE: Shelly needs someone *to advise her.*
> (*To advise her* modifies the pronoun *someone*.)
> ADVERB: Everyone came *to celebrate.*
> (*To celebrate* modifies the verb *came*.)
> ADVERB: Greg is afraid *to talk to Jessica.*
> (*To talk to Jessica* modifies the adjective *afraid*.)
> ADVERB: The ball flew too high *to catch.*
> (*To catch* modifies the adverb *high*.)

You can see that infinitives look like verbs but are not used as verbs. They function as nouns, adjectives, and adverbs.

The Split Infinitive

Sometimes a modifier is placed between the word *to* and the verb of an infinitive. A modifier in that position is said to *split* the infinitive. Usually, a split infinitive sounds awkward and should be avoided.

AWKWARD: Marietta tried to *patiently* wait.
BETTER: Marietta tried to wait *patiently*.

Diagraming Infinitives

To diagram an infinitive or infinitive phrase used as a noun, place it on a platform above the main line. *To,* the sign of the infinitive, belongs on a slanted line. The infinitive is shown on a horizontal line. Modifiers appear on lines slanted down from the infinitive. An object is shown on a horizontal line following the infinitive.

Dale tried to answer the questions correctly.

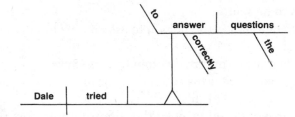

To diagram an infinitive or infinitive phrase used as a modifier, place it on a platform below the word modified. Modifiers and objects of the infinitive appear as explained above.

Sandpaper is used to smooth the wood.

559

Exercise A: Write each infinitive or infinitive phrase.

1. Don neglected to mention a few important facts.
2. The coat was too expensive to buy.
3. Ruth is too intelligent to believe entirely in luck.
4. Chief Joseph had hoped to lead his people to Canada.
5. To own her own horse is Sheila's dream.
6. I want to read more about the Mayan civilization.
7. All the candidates promised to find people jobs.
8. Our youth group plans to hike the Appalachian Trail.
9. Did Cynthia manage to find her way without a map?
10. To become a West Point cadet is Brian's goal.

Exercise B: Find the infinitive or infinitive phrase in each sentence. Then tell whether it is used as a subject, direct object, adjective, or adverb.

EXAMPLE: Deborah wants to tell her side of the story.
to tell her side of the story (infinitive phrase, used as direct object)

1. I never got a chance to thank Quentin for the birthday card he sent. adjective
2. The counselor is the person to ask about a job in the school office. adjective
3. We learned to program computers this year. direct object
4. Jeff tried to enter his cat in the dog show. direct object
5. To study cello at Julliard is Angela's dream. subject
6. The pigeons tried to avoid the spray of water from the fountain. direct object
7. Great tacos are not difficult to make. adverb
8. To walk to the stadium would take at least two and a half hours. subject
9. The forty-niners hoped to make their fortunes in California. direct object
10. The potter started to put glaze on the vase. direct object

Exercise C: Writing Write five sentences that describe some things you would like to do next summer. Include an infinitive in each sentence. Underline the infinitives and tell how they are used. Try to include several different uses.

Part 4   A Review of Verbals

Although verbals are verb forms, they are always used as other parts of speech.

The three kinds of verbals are gerunds, participles, and infinitives. All three kinds of verbals may be used alone or in phrases. These phrases are called gerund phrases, participial phrases, and infinitive phrases. Because they are like verbs, all three kinds of verbals may take objects or modifiers.

Gerunds are the verb forms used as nouns. Gerunds, which end in *-ing*, may be used in all the ways nouns are used.

> *Marching* tired us out. (subject)
> The troops began *marching along*. (direct object)
> The band makes designs by *marching in formation*.
>   (object of preposition)
> The next event is *precision marching*. (predicate word)

Participles are verb forms used as adjectives. Like adjectives, participles modify nouns and pronouns. Present participles end in *-ing*. Past participles of regular verbs end in *-d* or *-ed*. Past participles of irregular verbs are formed in various ways. (See Section 5, pages 483 to 489.)

> *Turning*, Richard skated back to his friends.
> The girl *turning sideways* is Nancy.
> The *broken* calculator was useless.
> Mario crossed the finish line, *breaking the record*.

Infinitives are the verbals that begin with the word *to*. Infinitives and infinitive phrases may be used as nouns, adjectives, or adverbs.

> *To say his lines right* was a challenge for Eric.
>   (noun used as the subject)
> The president asked us *to say our names*. (noun used as the direct object)
> Ms. Fields has a few words *to say*. (adjective)
> Everyone rose *to say the pledge*. (adverb)
> This tongue-twister is not easy *to say*. (adverb)

561

Optional Practice

Refer students to Exercise A on page 567. Have them identify every verbal in the paragraph.

Extending the Lesson

Have the class read the paragraph below and identify all verbals and verbal phrases. Ask them to tell how each one is used.

The training, care, and feeding of the jazz musician is something about which many of us ought to be more concerned. For jazz is a significant and vital musical language truly of our time. . . And its value has increased with the years as it has developed beyond its relatively humble and isolated beginnings to become a sophisticated art form, which speaks an international, world-wide language.

—*Jerry Coker*
Improvising Jazz

Exercise A: Write the verbal or verbal phrase in each sentence. Tell whether the verbal is a gerund, a participle, or an infinitive.

1. We were invited backstage to meet the cast. infinitive
2. The burglar entered through an unlocked window. participle
3. Jeans made in America are popular all over the world. participle
4. Where did you learn to speak Spanish? infinitive
5. Rita lugged the broken TV to the repair shop. participle
6. Reading the news is Dan Rather's occupation. gerund
7. Theresa tried juggling five oranges and failed. gerund
8. Martin woke to the smell of frying bacon. participle
9. The wagon master was responsible for leading the wagon train. gerund
10. It is too early to tell the outcome of the game. infinitive

Exercise B: Follow the directions for Exercise A.

1. The defeated candidate accused the winner of vote fraud. participle
2. Try to understand the lyrics of the song. infinitive
3. Talking before a group is hard for many people. gerund
4. Turning on the siren, the police officer drove her squad car through the busy intersection. participle
5. The wastebasket was filled with crumpled paper. participle
6. Separating Mexico from the United States, the Rio Grande flows to the Gulf of Mexico. participle
7. Reading science fiction stretches my imagination. gerund
8. Martha has saved enough money to buy a ticket. infinitive
9. Diving for the ball, the third baseman brought the fans to their feet. participle
10. Playing video games can develop your coordination. gerund

Exercise C: Writing As you can see from the examples below, many famous sayings contain verbals. Write five of your own "famous sayings" using at least one verbal in each. Underline the verbals and tell whether they are gerunds, participles, or infinitives.

> *Seeing* is *believing.*
> A *rolling* stone gathers no moss.
> A penny *saved* is a penny *earned.*
> *To be* or not *to be*, that is the question.

REINFORCEMENT EXERCISES
Using Verbals

Reinforcement Exercises

These Reinforcement Exercises may be used for additional practice of the concepts presented in this Section. Each exercise focuses on a single concept, and should be used after the page number indicated in parentheses.

Review

If you have not assigned these Reinforcement Exercises before this time, you can also use them as an excellent Section Review.

A. Recognize gerunds. Find each gerund phrase. Tell whether it is used as a subject, direct object, or object of a preposition.

(Use after page 553.)

1. Jonas tried pitching with his left hand. direct object
2. Sky diving looks like a thrilling sport. subject
3. A palette is used by artists for mixing paints. object of preposition
4. Twenty sound tracks were used in making this record. object of preposition
5. Nora suggested returning the carton of sour milk to the grocery store. direct object
6. Rabbits survive by running away from danger. object of preposition
7. Washing clothes in hot water might shrink them. subject
8. Gluing the pottery fragments together took several hours of tedious work. subject
9. There is an observation deck for viewing the city. object of preposition
10. Mark tried wrestling in the 130-pound weight class. direct object

B. Recognize participles. Write the participle or participial phrase in each sentence. Tell which word it modifies.

(Use after page 556.)

1. Overloaded with cargo, the freighter sank into the St. Lawrence Seaway. freighter
2. Screaming wildly, fans stormed the stage. fans
3. Sue found Tommy finger painting on the wall. Tommy
4. The hikers found a deserted cabin. cabin
5. We toasted marshmallows over the glowing embers of the campfire. embers
6. Hidden rocks could cut through the hull of the boat. rocks
7. Discouraged, the artist set the sketch aside. artist
8. Sitting on the levee, Mary Beth watched the barges move slowly down the river. Mary Beth
9. The wildflowers growing in the park are goldenrod, bee balm, and goatsbeard. wildflowers
10. Leaping out of the water, the dolphin sailed through the hoop. dolphin

C. Recognize Infinitives. Write the infinitive or infinitive phrase in each sentence. Tell whether it is used as a subject, direct object, adjective, or adverb. (Use after page 561.)

1. The displaced passenger had to take the next flight. direct object
2. Our environmental group has several exciting projects to complete. adjective
3. Each carrier has a certain amount of mail to deliver. adjective
4. Our mayor campaigned to become governor. adverb
5. To admit mistakes takes courage. subject
6. Spielberg's movies are always exciting to watch. adverb
7. I hope to see Waylon Jennings in Nashville. direct object
8. The government tries to warn us of health hazards. direct object
9. To hike in this heat would be foolish. subject
10. Laura hopes to find work picking strawberries. direct object

D. Identify verbals. Write the verbal or verbal phrase in each sentence. Label it *Gerund, Participle,* or *Infinitive.* Tell how it is used in the sentence. (Use after page 562.)

1. The diver tried to conserve his precious oxygen. infinitive, direct object
2. After baking two dozen cookies, we ate them all. gerund, object of preposition
3. Josh sat on a balcony overlooking Central Park. participle, modifies balcony
4. Delighted with the waterfall, Al stood under the cascade. participle, modifies Al
5. Hang gliding requires knowledge of air currents. gerund, subject
6. Moving West in the 1800's demanded toughness and stamina. gerund, subject
7. The audience persuaded the Beach Boys to sing an encore. infinitive, adverb
8. Forced out of their native country, the refugees sought protection in the United States. participle, modifies refugees
9. A gymnast training for the Olympics concentrates on little else. participle, modifies gymnast
10. This is the golf club to use in sand traps. infinitive, adjective

MIXED REVIEW
Using Verbals

Mixed Review

These exercises provide review of the concepts presented in this Section. Each exercise challenges the students to apply several of the skills they have acquired during previous study. Because the "mixed" feature of these activities makes them more difficult, the teacher may wish to have less-advanced students do them orally or in small groups.

A. Write the verbal or verbal phrase in each sentence. Label it *Gerund, Participle,* or *Infinitive.*

1. Leaving home was very difficult for Carlos. gerund
2. It was very difficult for Carlos to leave home. infinitive
3. Is that your grandmother dancing the Charleston? participle
4. Jim liked to sit in the first row at the theater. infinitive
5. It is foolish to ride a motorcycle without a helmet. infinitive
6. Living dangerously is normal for a stunt person. gerund
7. Janice looked forward to picking fresh strawberries in the field. gerund
8. She enjoyed watching the crowds on 42nd Street. gerund
9. Collecting samples, the amateur biologists combed the beach. participle
10. Jogging through the park, I saw two woodchucks. participle

B. Each sentence below contains an italicized verbal phrase. Read the three statements that follow each sentence, and choose the one that describes the verbal correctly.

EXAMPLE: Angela likes *to work jigsaw puzzles.*
      a. a prepositional phrase modifying *likes*
→ b. an infinitive phrase used as a direct object
      c. an infinitive phrase used as an adverb

1. *Trimming the hedges* is Sharon's least favorite chore.
   a. gerund phrase used as the subject
   b. participial phrase modifying *chore*
   c. infinitive phrase used as a subject

2. Felice likes *to design her own jewelry.*
   a. a gerund phrase used as the direct object
   b. an infinitive phrase used as the direct object
   c. a prepositional phrase modifying *likes*

3. The children *looking through the toy shop window* smiled.
   a. gerund phrase used as the subject
   b. gerund phrase used as the direct object
   c. participial phrase modifying *children*

565

4. Diana had wanted *to become a doctor* since her first visit to the emergency room.
   a. participial phrase modifying *Diana*
   b. infinitive phrase used as the direct object
   c. gerund phrase used as the direct object

5. His heart *thumping wildly*, Ramon ran the final ten meters.
   a. participial phrase modifying *heart*
   b. infinitive phrase used as the subject
   c. gerund phrase used as the subject

6. She called him *to explain her strange behavior*.
   a. infinitive phrase used as an adverb
   b. infinitive phrase used as an adjective
   c. infinitive phrase used as the direct object

7. Kathryn lost weight by *following her diet*.
   a. participial phrase modifying *weight*
   b. gerund phrase used as the object of a preposition
   c. gerund phrase used as the direct object

8. My grandmother bought a new suit *to wear on her first day at work*.
   a. participial phrase modifying *suit*
   b. infinitive phrase used as the direct object
   c. infinitive phrase used to modify *suit*

9. *Careful planning* is required in the selection of high school courses.
   a. participial phrase modifying *is required*
   b. gerund phrase used as the subject
   c. gerund phrase used as the predicate noun

10. Often, the best therapy for loneliness is *helping others*.
    a. participial phrase used as an adverb
    b. participial phrase used as an adjective modifying *loneliness*
    c. gerund phrase used as a predicate noun

USING GRAMMAR IN WRITING
Using Verbals

A. Imagine that, at age seventy, you have been asked by an editor of *Time* magazine to summarize the outstanding events, achievements, and successes of your distinguished career. The editor says to limit your list to seven items. Then she wants you to list three of your greatest disappointments or failures. The combined list will form the basis of an outline for the editor's "Person of the Year" cover story. The editor requests that you begin each statement with a gerund. Here is an example: *Graduating* from high school.

When your list is complete, choose the one item that you consider the most important and write a paragraph explaining it in detail.

B. What would you do if you had one year in which to do anything you pleased? Write a paragraph about your dream year (you may also assume that you have won a lottery and do not have to be concerned about money). Draw a line under each infinitive that you use. If you use a prepositional phrase that is introduced by the preposition *to*, mark it as a preposition to show that you know it is not part of an infinitive.

C. Imagine that you are a news announcer reporting on a huge outdoor concert given by your three favorite musical performers. Thousands of people have gathered to hear the concert, excitement is mounting, and you can see storm clouds and lightning approaching the concert grounds from the east. Write your moment-by-moment coverage of the event as the storm hits the assembled fans. Be sure to include participles and participial phrases in your description. If you also include any gerunds or infinitives in your report, mark them.

These exercises are designed to cover broad areas of grammar, usage, and mechanics. They require the application of skills taught thus far in the text. The exercises may be used for testing purposes, or as an excellent resource for review.

1. noun
2. adjective
3. verb
4. pronoun
5. pronoun
6. adjective
7. noun
8. preposition
9. infinitive
10. noun
11. adjective
12. preposition
13. interjection
14. pronoun
15. gerund
16. participle
17. adverb
18. adjective
19. adjective
20. preposition
21. adverb
22. verb
23. participle
24. conjunction
25. infinitive

CUMULATIVE REVIEW
The Parts of Speech

Recognizing the Parts of Speech and Verbals. Number your paper from 1 to 25. Decide whether each italicized word or phrase in the paragraph below is being used as a *Noun, Pronoun, Verb, Adverb, Adjective, Conjunction, Preposition, Interjection, Gerund, Infinitive,* or *Participle.* Write your answer next to the corresponding number. Remember that the part of speech a word is often depends on how it is used in the sentence. Answers in margin.

Volcanoes are *openings* in the earth's crust. From these openings, gases and lava are expelled under pressure. Lava is molten, *liquid* rock from far beneath the earth's surface. When the opening of a volcano *is blocked* by solid material, the various gases beneath the earth's surface force *themselves* up in a series of explosions. The gas and lava then erupt *from* the new opening.

One of *the* most famous volcanic eruptions in *history* took place in Italy *in* A.D. 79, when Mount Vesuvius, thought *to be* extinct, erupted. The explosion destroyed the towns of *Pompeii* and Herculaneum, among others. *Roman* observers wrote that there was a strong earth tremor *on* the first morning, followed by an explosion that sent a *tower* of ash and rock twelve miles into the sky. *Incredible!* After *this*, there was a fall of lava ash and cinders about *three* feet *deep*. *Fleeing* saved some; others took shelter inside, *thinking* that the catastrophe must *soon* be over. However, the next day there was *another* eruption that caused a rain of molten lava, pumice *rock*, and cinders that buried the town of Pompeii and killed more than *two* thousand citizens.

Since that time Mount Vesuvius has *never* been completely inactive. An eruption in 1631 killed eighteen thousand people. The last eruption *occurred* in 1944. Mount Vesuvius has been quiet since then, *emitting* only puffs of gas; *but* scientists do not expect it *to remain* quiet for long.

CUMULATIVE REVIEW
Usage (I)

Understanding How Words Are Used. A word or group of words can be used in different ways within a sentence. Number your paper from 1 to 20. Decide whether each italicized word or phrase in these sentences is being used as a *Subject, Verb, Adjective, Adverb, Predicate Noun, Direct Object, Indirect Object,* or *Object of a Preposition.* Write each word and your answers next to the corresponding number.

1. The curved spines of the *barrel* cactus once *were used* as fish hooks. adj. verb
2. Fred *nearly* forgot to turn the stove *off.* adv., adv.
3. The *Tyrolean* folk costumes were *colorful.* adj., adj.
4. Amy *patiently* turned the handle of the old ice cream *freezer.* adv. obj. of prep.
5. Mr. MacBride *plays* the *bagpipes* in a highland band. verb, dir. obj.
6. Juan *decided* to sign up for *soccer.* verb, obj. of prep.
7. What is your favorite *subject* at school *this* year? subj., adj.
8. The detective examined the *tire marks* left by the tires. direct object
9. The tracks were *finally clear* after the derailing of the train. adv., adj.
10. Those are *black* raspberry *bushes.* adj., pred. noun
11. *Swimming* is an excellent *form* of exercise. subject, pred. noun
12. That sergeant gives the *recruits* a tough but excellent *training* session. indirect obj., adj.
13. *Below* we could see the deserted *remains* of a town. adv., direct obj.
14. *Few* of the stable's horses were *thoroughbreds.* subject, pred. noun
15. *Below* the blossom hovered a *hummingbird.* prep., subject
16. I did not want *to arrive early.* direct object
17. The gawky giraffe can move *quite fast* when startled. adv., adv.
18. Athletes like him give *boxing* a bad *name.* indirect obj., direct obj.
19. The young marathon *runner* was not ashamed of *finishing* last. subject, object of prep.
20. In the near future, *becoming a space colonist* will no longer be an unrealistic *dream.* subject, pred. noun

Making Subjects and Verbs Agree

Read the following sentences. Do they sound correct to you?

> McCartney and Jackson sings together on that album.
> That guppy don't look healthy.

Both sentences have the same problem. In each, the verb does not agree with its subject. This is a common error in both speaking and writing. In fact, it is one of the most important things to look for whenever you are proofreading your written work.

This section will make you aware of some common problems of subject-verb agreement. Study them carefully so that you can avoid them in your own writing.

Part 1 Making Subjects and Verbs Agree in Number

The **number** of a word refers to whether the word is singular or plural. A word is **singular** when it refers to one thing and **plural** when it refers to more than one thing. If a subject and verb are the same in number, they agree.

A verb must agree in number with its subject.

If a subject is singular, its verb must be singular. If a subject is plural, then its verb must be plural.

SINGULAR	PLURAL
She *watches*.	They *watch*.
He *dances* well.	They *dance* well.
The monkey *chatters*.	The monkeys *chatter*.

You can see that in the examples, the singular form of each verb ends in -*s*. In each plural verb, there is no -*s*.

Agreement of subjects and verbs usually occurs naturally in speaking and writing. Problems arise, though, when it is not clear which word is the subject of the sentence.

The subject of the verb is never found in a prepositional phrase.

When you are trying to make subjects and verbs agree, watch out for phrases that appear between the subject and the verb.

The *tapes* on this shelf *are* mine.
That *book* of poems *is* by Robert Frost.
The *words* to that song *are* catchy.
One of the trains *is* late.

Remember that to find the subject, first find the verb. Then place *who* or *what* before the verb to form a question.

The papers in this folder are important.
    Verb: are
    What are? papers
    The subject is *papers*.

Objective

To use verbs that agree in number with their subjects

Presenting the Lesson

1. Read and discuss pages 571–572. Review with the class how to find the subject of a sentence. Point out that nouns in an intervening phrase should not be mistaken for the subject. Emphasize that mistakes in agreement of number only occur in the third person. There is no change in verb form for singular and plural in the first or second person.

2. Assign and discuss Exercises A and B on page 572.

Individualizing the Lesson

Less-Advanced Students

1. Have students decide whether the verb agrees with the subject in the sentences below. If there is an error, the students should rewrite the sentence.

1. The shoes in the closet needs polishing.
2. Tons of coal were dumped down the chute.
3. The children, as well as their teacher, is coming.
4. The paper in the boxes is for recycling.
5. Three members of the team has the flu.

2. Do Exercise A orally with the students. Discuss each answer. For Exercise B, you might suggest that students find and cross out all prepositional phrases before proceeding.

Advanced Students

Have students decide whether the verb agrees with the subject in the sentences below. If there is an error, the students should rewrite the sentence.

1. You, together with your family, are invited to the assembly.
2. Money, as well as gifts, were received.
3. A senator from each of the fifty states was present at the ceremony.
4. The scores for each contestant was recorded in lights.
5. I, as well as you, am guilty.

Reinforcement Exercise

Assign and discuss Exercise A on page 578.

Optional Practice

Ask students to choose two verbs, one regular and the other irregular. Have them write short sentences using first, second, and third person pronouns (both singular and plural) as the subjects for their chosen verbs. Point out how the verb form changes in the third person singular.

Extending the Lesson

Tell the class that certain sentences, though correct, sound awkward. Ask them to rewrite the following sentences to eliminate awkward constructions.

1. Jerome, as well as me, is going to the movies tonight.
2. You, together with him, are the winner.
3. The entire class, including them, completes its work on time.

Phrases beginning with the words *with, together with, including, as well as,* and *in addition to* are not part of the subject.

> A fire *truck*, in addition to the police car, *is* here.
> *Honesty*, as well as courage, *is* a virtue.
> The *meal*, including dessert, *costs* four dollars.

Exercise A: Choose the verb that agrees with the subject.

1. Even the best tennis players (try, tries) to improve their techniques.
2. The mission of those pilots (was, were) accomplished with the help of the ground personnel.
3. The radio, as well as the flashlights, (needs, need) batteries.
4. That row of the bleachers (is, are) almost empty.
5. Two of the bones in her foot (is, are) broken.
6. The oil on the waves (was, were) from the damaged tanker.
7. Homes near the river (has, have) to be evacuated before the dam breaks.
8. The woman in the red sandals (works, work) at the clinic.
9. Jane's rings, as well as her bracelet, (has, have) been stolen.
10. Those photographs, including the one of Jake, (is, are) in the album.

Exercise B: Follow the directions for Exercise A.

1. A person with third-degree burns (requires, require) immediate medical help.
2. Leslie, as well as many other students, (takes, take) the subway to school.
3. The mongrel with the brown spots (leads, lead) that pack.
4. The boats in the bay (sail, sails) every weekend in summer.
5. Some members of the committee (is, are) planning a skating party.
6. The keys on that piano (is, are) in need of dusting.
7. Only two theaters in town (shows, show) first-run movies.
8. The snow on the walks (needs, need) shoveling.
9. The pumpkins in this patch (is, are) ready to pick.
10. A doe, with her two fawns, (was, were) grazing in the meadow.

Part 2 Compound Subjects

As you have learned, a compound subject is two or more subjects used with the same verb.

A compound subject joined by *and* is plural. Therefore, it requires a plural verb.

The *radio* and the *stereo* **are playing** the same song.
Steve and *Marcella* **write** for the newspaper.

When the parts of a compound subject are joined by *or* or *nor*, the verb should agree with the subject nearer to the verb.

Neither Jan nor her *friends* **stay** for lunch.
Either the jugglers or the tightrope *walker* **performs** next.

Exercise A: Choose the verb that agrees with the subject.

1. Huck and Tom (was, were) creeping through the cave.
2. Janet and Beth (is, are) taking a dune buggy ride.
3. Either the seat or the handlebars (has, have) to be adjusted.
4. Boots and jeans (seems, seem) to be Mike's uniform.
5. Neither the potholes nor the curb (has, have) been repaired.
6. Neither the curb nor the potholes (have, has) been repaired.
7. Either the Smoky Mountains or Yellowstone (is, are) my choice for a vacation.
8. Ecuador and Colombia (exports, export) coffee.
9. Both Liz and Marilyn (bowls, bowl) at that alley.
10. Neither Joyce nor Pam (bowls, bowl) at that alley.

Exercise B: Writing Some of these sentences contain errors in subject-verb agreement. If a sentence contains no error, write *Correct*. If the sentence is incorrect, rewrite it correctly.

1. Neither the drugstore nor the grocery open until 8 A.M. opens
2. Either Ms. McGee or Mr. Baez teaches that math class. correct
3. Both hail and wind storms damage crops. correct

573

Part 2

Objective

To use verbs that agree with compound subjects

Presenting the Lesson

1. Read and discuss page 573. Point out that compound subjects joined by *and* do not sound awkward with a plural verb; however, sometimes compound subjects joined by *or* or *nor* may sound wrong even when they are right. Go over the examples on page 573.

2. Assign and discuss Exercises A and B on pages 573–574.

Individualizing the Lesson

Less-Advanced Students

Have students choose the correct verb form.

1. Michael and his brother (like, likes) to travel.
2. Either Dana or her sisters (has, have) the information.
3. Neither the roses nor the peony bush (has, have) bloomed.
4. The manager and their president (meet, meets) weekly.
5. Neither Freddi nor Beverly (is, are) qualified for the part.

Advanced Students

Have students write sentences in the present tense using the following subjects.

1. either the student or her teachers
2. neither you nor I
3. the actors and the director
4. both the chicks and the hen

Reinforcement Exercise

Assign and discuss Exercise B on page 578.

Optional Practice

Ask each student to write sentence beginnings such as those shown under **Advanced Students**. Have them exchange papers and write a predicate for each subject.

Extending the Lesson

Have students combine the following pairs of sentences into single sentences with compound subjects.

1. A raccoon is making the noise in the attic. On the other hand, some mice may be making the noise in the attic.
2. Two books were checked out. A volume of the encyclopedia was checked out.

Part 3

Objective

To use verbs that agree with indefinite pronoun subjects

Presenting the Lesson

1. Read and discuss pages 574–575. After going over the three kinds of indefinite pronouns, ask students to close their books. Give them the following pronouns and have them write short sentences with each as subject: *many, everyone, either, none, all.*

2. Assign and discuss Exercises A and B on page 575.

Individualizing the Lesson

Less-Advanced Students

1. Suggest that students memorize the list of singular indefinite pronouns.

4. Either the Pep Club or Student Council is selling homecoming mums. correct
5. Neither the mother panda nor her new cubs <u>is</u> on view yet at the zoo. are
6. Neither the parade nor the fireworks were as good as usual this year. correct
7. Cancer and TB <u>attacks</u> people of all ages and all occupations. attack
8. Either the piano or the singers <u>is</u> off-key. are
9. Neither the Cabinet members nor the President <u>are</u> available. is
10. Rockets and a mission to outer space were once only science fiction. correct

Part 3   Indefinite Pronouns

To make a verb agree with an indefinite pronoun used as the subject, you must determine whether the pronoun is singular or plural. As you have learned, an indefinite pronoun may be singular or plural. Some may be either, depending on the context in which they appear.

The following indefinite pronouns are **singular**:

another	each	everything	one
anybody	either	neither	somebody
anyone	everybody	nobody	someone
anything	everyone	no one	

Nobody here *knows* the answer.
Someone is clearing the creek of debris.
Each of the rooms *has* cable TV.
Everything was ready by 9:00 A.M.

The following indefinite pronouns are **plural**:

both	few	many	several

Several of the candidates *agree* on the issues.
Both of those countries *have* mild climates.

The following indefinite pronouns are **singular** if they refer to one thing and **plural** if they refer to several things.

all   any   most   none   some

All of the equipment *is* clean and new.
All of the representatives *are* in Washington.

Most of the lake *has* a mud base.
Most of the beaches *have* lifeguards.

Some of the money *is* Linda's.
Some of the boats *are* at the pier.

Exercise A: Choose the verb that agrees with the subject.

1. Most of the batteries (is, are) still good.
2. Each of the coaches (has, have) a different approach.
3. Few of the rumors (seems, seem) likely to be true.
4. (Is, Are) all of the islands inhabited?
5. Everyone here (has, have) heard that joke before.
6. Somebody upstairs (is, are) playing the piano.
7. Some of the wranglers (was, were) heading for Omaha.
8. Nobody in town (has, have) spoken to the stranger.
9. Most of the sunken treasure (is, are) still underwater.
10. Some of the spaghetti sauce usually (splatters, splatter) on the stove.

Exercise B: Follow the directions for Exercise A.

1. Most of the track (needs, need) repair.
2. Most of the roads (needs, need) repair.
3. Neither of the pens (has, have) a fine point.
4. Everybody in the band (is, are) playing at the festival.
5. All of the tribes (is, are) gathering for the ceremony.
6. Most of the raffle tickets (has, have) been sold.
7. Many of us (wants, want) to take archery.
8. One of the twins often (pretends, pretend) to be the other.
9. Everybody in the bleachers (was, were) cheering.
10. No one (know, knows) the true identity of the Lone Ranger.

2. Have students complete the following sentences.

1. Each of your grandparents _____.
2. Several of these exercises _____.
3. Most of the marbles _____.
4. Most of the milk _____.
5. Many of the drivers _____.

Advanced Students

Have students write two sentences for each of the following pronouns: *all, any, most, none, some.* Each pair of sentences should include one sentence with a plural subject and one with a singular subject.

Reinforcement Exercise

Assign and discuss Exercise C on page 519.

Optional Practice

Have students complete the following sentences.

1. Each of the meetings _____.
2. None of our streets _____.
3. Several of the eggs in the carton _____.
4. Some of the lemonade _____.
5. Either of the coaches _____.

Extending the Lesson

Have students rewrite the following sentences, replacing the noun subjects with indefinite pronouns.

1. Judy and Lloyd like sailing.
2. Sam and Arnice do not like dog-sitting.
3. About half of the milk is still fresh.
4. One hundred percent of the bread is moldy.
5. At least 50,000 people attended the game.

Objective

To avoid special problems of sub-ject-verb agreement

Presenting the Lesson

1. Read and discuss pages 576–577. Point out that *doesn't* and *don't* are contractions. They combine a verb change form in the third person singular like any other verb.

2. Tell the class that agreement problems with *Here*, *There*, and *Where* should not arise in writing because the writer has the opportunity to revise once the subject is written down.

3. Assign and discuss Exercises A and B on pages 576–577. When you are sure that students understand the concept, assign Exercise C.

Individualizing the Lesson

Less-Advanced Students

1. Ask students to choose the correct verb. Discuss the answers.

1. She (don't, doesn't) like to spend money.
2. Where (is, are) your slippers?
3. There (wasn't, weren't) any oranges left.
4. There (wasn't, weren't) any orange juice left.
5. It (don't, doesn't) seem like Sunday.

2. Suggest that students rewrite sentences that begin with *Here*, *There*, and *Where*, putting the subject before the verb.

Part 4 Other Problems of Agreement

Doesn't and *Don't* Used with Pronouns

The verb *doesn't* is singular. *Doesn't* is used with the subjects *she, he,* and *it.* All other personal pronouns are used with *don't.*

It *doesn't* matter to me.
He *doesn't* live near the city.
She *doesn't* speak Spanish.

I *don't* like jogging.
We *don't* watch much TV.
They *don't* play fairly.

Sentences Beginning with *There, Here,* or *Where*

When sentences begin with *There, Here,* or *Where,* the subject comes after the verb. You must look ahead to find the subject of the sentence. Then you must use the verb that agrees.

There *are* two *versions* of that song.
Here *is* the beach *towel.*
Here *are* an *ax* and a *saw.*
Where *are* the *peaches*?

Exercise A: Choose the verb that agrees with the subject.

1. Where (do, does) Paul Newman and Joanne Woodward live?
2. She (doesn't, don't) often lose her temper.
3. Here (is, are) some suspicious-looking pawprints.
4. Where (is, are) the Ionian Islands?
5. They (doesn't, don't) believe in ghosts.
6. (Doesn't, Don't) he look like Michael Landon?
7. (Doesn't, Don't) they go to Eagle River to camp?
8. There (is, are) some mail for you on the radiator.
9. Here (come, comes) that yellow Thunderbird with the sunroof.
10. There (doesn't, don't) seem to be a road up the mountain.

Exercise B: Follow the directions for Exercise A.

1. (Doesn't, <u>Don't</u>) they live near the ravine?
2. Here (is, <u>are</u>) cheese and mushrooms for the pizza.
3. (Isn't, <u>Aren't</u>) there submerged rocks along this pier?
4. Where (<u>is</u>, are) your backpack?
5. He (<u>doesn't</u>, don't) like lox and bagels.
6. Where (<u>is</u>, are) your new sweatshirt with the hood?
7. It (<u>doesn't</u>, don't) snow here at Christmas.
8. Here (is, <u>are</u>) the hooks and bait for your fishing trip.
9. She usually (don't, <u>doesn't</u>) appear with another singer.
10. There (was, <u>were</u>) several fire trucks heading for the wharf.

Exercise C: Writing Write two sentences that begin with each of the following words. Make sure that subjects and verbs agree.

doesn't	here	there
don't	where	

Advanced Students

Have students write a one-paragraph description in which at least two sentences begin with *Here* or *There*.

Reinforcement Exercise

Assign and discuss Exercise D on page 579.

Optional Practice

Ask students to choose the correct verb.

1. (Doesn't, Don't) it look stormy in the west?
2. There (is, are) strawberries for dessert.
3. The doors and windows (don't, doesn't) shut tight.
4. Here (come, comes) the garbage truck.
5. Mountain laurel and dogwood (don't, doesn't) grow in this region.

Extending the Lesson

Discuss with the class the fact that errors in subject-verb agreement are very common in song lyrics. Lines, such as *it don't matter to me* and *she don't love me any more*, are repeated over and over until they may begin to sound right. Ask the class for specific examples from songs they know. Revise the faulty sentences on the board.

Reinforcement Exercises

These Reinforcement Exercises may be used for additional practice of the concepts presented in this Section. Each exercise focuses on a single concept, and should be used after the page number indicated in parentheses.

Review

If you have not assigned these Reinforcement Exercises before this time, you can also use them as an excellent Section Review.

REINFORCEMENT EXERCISES
Making Subjects and Verbs Agree

A. Make verbs and subjects agree in number. Write the verb that agrees with the subject. (Use after page 572.)

1. The lane for bicycles (is, are) on the west side of the road.
2. A truckload of bananas (has, have) spilled onto the highway.
3. My recipe for brownies (is, are) unbeatable.
4. Two pieces of the puzzle (is, are) missing.
5. Several people, including Marion, (has, have) never tried skiing.
6. Victor, as well as his sisters, (play, plays) in a band.
7. The sounds of a foghorn (drift, drifts) across the harbor.
8. Our chances of winning (is, are) better than the other team's.
9. A bag of peanuts (is, are) my favorite movie snack.
10. All roads leading from town (is, are) flooded.
11. The purpose of the rigorous camping trips (was, were) to develop survival skills.
12. Roger, together with his brothers, (works, work) on a ranch each summer.
13. The monkeys in that cage (seems, seem) livelier than the chimpanzees.
14. The list of grievances (grow, grows) each month.
15. The photographs on this page (looks, look) very old.

B. Make verbs agree with compound subjects. Write the verb that agrees with the subject. (Use after page 574.)

1. Peanuts or popcorn (makes, make) a good snack.
2. Warm gloves and a down jacket (is, are) important for winter sports.
3. Both fog and rain (have, has) inspired painters and poets.
4. Tolerance and honesty (is, are) not always easy to practice.
5. Neither cardinals nor chicadees (fly, flies) south in winter.

6. In school, neither Thomas Edison nor Albert Einstein (was, were) considered a good student.
7. Neither white rice nor white bread (provides, provide) as much nutrition as brown rice.
8. Both salt water and chlorine (aggravate, aggravates) the infection.
9. Farming and ranching (has, have) replaced buffalo hunting for many Plains Indians.
10. Either Los Angeles or Chicago (is, are) second in size to New York City.

C. Make verbs agree with indefinite pronouns. Write the verb that agrees with the subject. (Use after page 575)

1. (Has, Have) any of the ice cream bars melted?
2. All of the snow (has, have) been blown into huge drifts.
3. All of the balloons (was, were) released at the rally.
4. Everyone in the stands (cheers, cheer) when the teams enter the stadium.
5. Each of the gondolas (carry, carries) ten passengers.
6. Both lacrosse and jai alai (require, requires) agility.
7. None of the coaches (allow, allows) players to skip practice.
8. Some of the fudge (is, are) for the bake sale.
9. Another of those old Westerns (is, are) on tonight.
10. Either logging or forest fires (has, have) leveled these hills.

D. Solve other problems of agreement. Write the verb that agrees with the subject. (Use after page 577)

1. It (doesn't, don't) take long to learn this dance.
2. He (doesn't, don't) remember much about the accident.
3. There (is, are) a swinging bridge across Capilano Canyon.
4. There (is, are) special box seats for famous visitors.
5. Where (is, are) the rental canoes?
6. Here (is, are) a wood-burning stove and some fuel.
7. Where (is, are) my running shorts?
8. She usually (don't, doesn't) complain like this.
9. (Doesn't, Don't) they have the lead roles?
10. Here (is, are) several abandoned miners' huts.

Mixed Review

These exercises provide review of the concepts presented in this Section. Each exercise challenges the students to apply several of the skills they have acquired during previous study. Because the "mixed" feature of these activities makes them more difficult, the teacher may wish to have less-advanced students do them orally or in small groups.

MIXED REVIEW
Making Subjects and Verbs Agree

A. Some of the following sentences contain errors in subject-verb agreement. If there are no mistakes, write *Correct*. If there is a mistake, rewrite the sentence correctly.

1. Don't the paintings in this exhibit look familiar? correct
2. Either the reporters or the editor need to check the facts more thoroughly. needs
3. Neither of the twins have ever been out of New York. has
4. A teenager with dental problems often benefit from braces. benefits
5. High technology, including various types of computers, has revolutionized many industries. correct
6. The winning teams in our division is in the playoffs. are
7. The vegetables in my neighbor's garden seem to grow better than mine. correct
8. My father and his co-workers plays racquetball during their lunch hour. play
9. There is the maps of the route for the bicycle race. are
10. Thousands of barrels of oil are imported into the United States every day. correct

B. Add words to complete each sentence. Make sure that your subjects and verbs agree. Write your sentences in the present tense.

1. Both Washington and Hawaii
2. Few in the crowded hall
3. Neither exercises nor diet
4. Each of the band members
5. The ringmaster, as well as several performers
6. Some of the caves in the Smoky Mountains
7. Lee, Ann, and Sara all
8. Swimming and jogging
9. Either my grandparents or my great-uncle
10. Several of the stray dogs

USING GRAMMAR IN WRITING
Making Subjects and Verbs Agree

A. Imagine that in order to select a group to perform at a school event, you have conducted a survey on musical tastes in your school. Your results are as follows:

	Students	Teacher
Do you enjoy music?	yes — 100%	yes — 100%
Do you enjoy loud music?	yes — 70% no — 30%	yes — 25% no — 75%
Would you prefer rock, new wave, or easy listening music?	Rock — 50% New Wave — 40% Easy Listening — 10%	Rock — 50% New Wave — 10% Easy Listening — 40%

Using indefinite pronouns such as *none, all, every, each, both, no one*, and *everyone*, write a paper reporting your results. Compare and contrast the results received from students and from teachers.

B. Zyxxt and Qlut are extraterrestrials who have just landed on earth. To make a good impression, Qlut has prepared a speech in English. She has, however, made some mistakes in subject-verb agreement. Rewrite the speech for her, correcting all <u>errors</u>.

> Greetings, Earth People: We, Zyxxt and Qlut, come in peace from the planet Thorax. We <u>doesn't</u> want to frighten you. Zyxxt <u>don't</u> mean harm, and I <u>doesn't</u> either. Where <u>are</u> your leader? We want to explain our mission. Here <u>is</u> some <u>gifts</u> of fruit from our planet. There <u>is</u> glimps, blyds, and flizzers for you to eat. <u>Doesn't</u> they look <u>delicious</u>? We <u>doesn't</u> plan to stay on earth very long, but we hope you will visit <u>our</u> home in the future. There <u>is</u> many interesting things to see and do on Thorax.

Using Grammar in Writing

These challenging and enjoyable activities allow the students to see how the concepts of grammar, usage, and mechanics may be applied in actual writing situations. Each exercise is designed to allow students practice in several of the skills they have acquired in this Section. The activities also provide opportunities for students to write creatively about a wide variety of interesting and unusual subjects.

Cumulative Review

These exercises are designed to cover broad areas of grammar, usage, and mechanics. They require the application of skills taught thus far in the text. The exercises may be used for testing purposes, or as an excellent resource for review.

CUMULATIVE REVIEW
Usage (II)

Using the Correct Form of Words. Number your paper from 1 to 10. Write the correct word from the two given in parentheses.

1. The lake had finally (froze, <u>frozen</u>) solid.
2. Everyone had drunk (<u>his or her</u>, their) water before we had hiked five miles.
3. Is it (<u>he</u>, him) whom everyone calls "Lightning"?
4. (Who, <u>Whom</u>) was the award presented to this year?
5. Of the last two governors, whom do you think was the (<u>better</u>, best)?
6. Did you finish painting all of (them, <u>those</u>) figures?
7. The stubborn camel walked very (slow, <u>slowly</u>).
8. It seems that (<u>we</u>, us) freshmen will have to plan the dance.
9. The President spoke to the press; his voice sounded sad and (<u>hesitant</u>, hesitantly).
10. The prize money was divided between Luis and (I, <u>me</u>).

Finding Errors in Usage. Eight of the following sentences contain at least one error in usage. Some are errors of agreement, and some are errors of form. Identify the <u>errors</u> and rewrite each incorrect sentence. Write *C* if a sentence is already correct.

1. The squirrels or that raccoon chews through that ~~there~~ screen door every summer.
2. The divers swam <u>careful</u> among the strange ocean plants. carefull
3. Who wants to see us squad leaders about last night's game? C
4. The costumes and the scenery <u>looks well</u> under the lights. look good
5. The speaker will attempt to <u>learn</u> us about the desert and <u>it's</u> strange beauty. teach, its
6. No one asked for his or her money back. C
7. <u>Was</u> the Samurai warriors ~~more~~ fiercer than modern soldiers? Were
8. The ranger had <u>saw</u> the smoke before Leah. seen
9. <u>Who</u> did you tell about <u>them</u> cracks in the bleachers? Whom, those
10. <u>Leave</u> me raise the sail of the boat this time. Let

582

Section 11

Using Compound and Complex Sentences

In preceding sections, you learned how the parts of a sentence work together. In this section, you will learn about four kinds of sentences that differ in their basic structure. They are called simple sentences, compound sentences, complex sentences, and compound-complex sentences.

Objective

To recognize the simple sentence and its possible compound parts

Presenting the Lesson

1. Read and discuss page 585. Ask volunteers for additional sentences for each of the six compound parts of a simple sentence. Be sure that students understand the term **simple sentence**, and encourage them to use it. Repeat the idea that the simple sentence has only one subject and one predicate even though either of these sentence parts may be compound.

2. Assign and discuss Exercises A and B on page 585.

Individualizing the Lesson

Less-Advanced Students

Complete Exercise B on pages 585–586 orally. Discuss with them the compound sentence parts. Point out that the sentences are all simple sentences.

Advanced Students

Have students write sentences containing the following parts: compound subject, compound predicate, compound direct object, compound· predicate word, compound subject and predicate.

Optional Practice

Have students diagram sentences 1, 3, 6, 7, and 10 of Exercise A on page 585. Be sure to point out how the diagrams emphasize the concept of the simple sentence.

Part 1 Review of the Sentence

The sentence is composed of two basic parts, the subject and the predicate.

SUBJECT	PREDICATE
Lights	flash.
Lights	flash a signal.
Blinking lights on the control panel	flash a signal.

The **subject** of a sentence names the person or thing about which something is said. The **predicate** is the idea that is expressed about the subject.

The **simple predicate** is the verb. The subject of the verb is called the **simple subject.**

Within the subject of the sentence are the simple subject and its modifiers. In the predicate of the sentence are the verb, objects, predicate words, and their modifiers.

Compound Parts of a Sentence

You have learned that all of the parts of the sentence may be **compound**. Each one, in other words, may have more than one part.

COMPOUND SUBJECT:	Neither sleep nor dreams are fully understood.
COMPOUND VERB:	The audience clapped, shouted, and cheered.
COMPOUND PREDICATE:	Derek cleaned the fish and then fried it on an open fire.
COMPOUND OBJECT:	Janelle designed the store decorations and window displays.
COMPOUND OBJECT OF THE PREPOSITION:	On holidays and weekends, the store is closed.
COMPOUND PREDICATE WORD:	That TV studio is large and empty.

The Simple Sentence

Even though sentences may have compound parts, they still express only one main idea. Such sentences, like all of those you have been studying, are called **simple sentences**.

A simple sentence is a sentence with only one subject and one predicate.

The subject and the predicate, along with any part of the subject or predicate, may be compound.

Now you are ready to distinguish simple sentences from other types of sentences.

Exercise A: Copy each of the following simple sentences. Then draw a line between the subject and the predicate.

1. Teresa and Nat|have social security cards.
2. Theodore Roosevelt and Franklin D. Roosevelt|were Presidents with strong personalities.
3. Dave|found the tuxedo and the top hat in a thrift shop.
4. Stevie Wonder and Brenda Lee both|began their singing careers as children.
5. China and Russia|border Mongolia.
6. Mr. Mendoza's two cats|are Siamese and Burmese.
7. Maria|carefully measured the space for the shelf and then sawed the plywood.
8. The figure skaters|were agile and daring.
9. The lifeguard|wears a whistle around her neck.
10. Sharon|keeps a flashlight and candles on hand for use during power failures.

Exercise B: Write the compound subjects, verbs, and objects you find in these simple sentences.

1. The crew <u>cleared</u> and <u>bulldozed</u> ten acres of wilderness. compound verb
2. <u>Vince Evans</u> and <u>Doug Williams</u> are both quarterbacks. compound subject
3. First <u>grate</u> and <u>measure</u> the cheese. compound verb
4. Fireflies blinked in the <u>trees</u> and <u>bushes</u>. compound object of preposition
5. South American Indians have unique <u>crafts</u> and <u>customs</u>. compound direct object
6. Early settlers made soap from <u>ashes</u>, <u>water</u>, and <u>grease</u>. compound object of preposition

585

7. Scrooge and Tiny Tim are two of Dickens's characters. *compound subject*
8. Theo feeds, grooms, and exercises horses at the stable. *compound verb*
9. Julia and Sandy left an hour ago. *compound subject*
10. Did you and Martha take snorkeling lessons? *compound subject*

Part 2

Objective

To recognize compound sentences and punctuate them correctly

Presenting the Lesson

1. Read and discuss **The Compound Sentence** and **Diagraming Compound Sentences** on pages 586–587. On the board put the diagram for *The press secretary spoke first.* Compare this to the diagram on page 587. The diagrams should illustrate for the class the difference between a compound sentence and a simple sentence. Repeat the illustration by diagraming the first two sentences in the revised paragraph on page 587 on the board. Point to the difference between a simple sentence and a compound sentence.

2. Assign and discuss Exercise A on page 587. Then assign Exercise B. Emphasize the usefulness of compound sentences in creating more interesting writing.

3. Read and discuss **Punctuating Compound Sentences** on pages 588–589. Tell the class that errors in punctuating compound sentences are among the most common punctuation errors in the written language. Put these pairs of simple sentences on the board and ask the

Part 2 The Compound Sentence

Sometimes two simple sentences express such closely related ideas that they are joined to form one sentence. The resulting sentence has more than one subject and more than one predicate. It is called a **compound sentence.**

A compound sentence consists of two or more simple sentences joined together.

The parts of the compound sentence may be joined by a coordinating conjunction (*and, or, but*) or by a semicolon (;).

The World Series is over, **and** the football season has begun.
This hill is small, **but** it's perfect for sledding.
Return your library books today, **or** you will have to pay a fine.
Special tags on the clothing can set off an alarm; they help to prevent shoplifting.

Compound sentences add variety and interest to a piece of writing. They break what might otherwise be monotonous strings of short, choppy sentences. Look at the following paragraph:

John Adams met Thomas Jefferson in 1775. Both men helped create the new government. They had opposing views about it. At first the men were close friends. Their political views drove them apart. They fought for the Presidency. They criticized each other's leadership. In their later years they began corresponding with each other. They patched up their differences. Jefferson died on July 4, 1826. Coincidentally, Adams died the same day.

The series of simple sentences, one after another, becomes dull and tiresome. Notice how much better the same paragraph sounds when some of the sentences are compound sentences.

586

John Adams met Thomas Jefferson in 1775. Both men helped create the new government, but they had opposing views about it. At first the men were close friends, but their political views drove them apart. They fought for the Presidency, and they criticized each other's leadership. In their later years they began corresponding with each other, and they patched up their differences. Jefferson died on July 4, 1826, and, coincidentally, Adams died the same day.

Diagraming Compound Sentences

If you can diagram simple sentences, you can diagram compound ones. The diagram simply demonstrates that a compound sentence is two or more simple sentences joined together. The simple sentences are diagramed one under the other. Then they are connected with a dotted line between the verbs. The conjunction sits on a "step" of the line.

The press secretary spoke first, and then the President held a press conference.

Exercise A: Label three columns *Subject*/*Verb*, *Conjunction*, and *Subject*/*Verb*. For each sentence, fill in the columns.

EXAMPLE: Nina sings well, but Angie and Ted sing better.

SUBJECT/VERB	CONJUNCTION	SUBJECT/VERB
Nina/sings	but	Angie, Ted/sing

1. The movie was dull, but the book was fascinating.
2. Do you have a radio, or should I bring one?

587

class how they could change them into compound sentences with correct punctuation.

The team was determied to win. Their practice games showed it.

Marla bought front row seats. She gave them to her grandparents.

4. Read and discuss **Compound Sentence or Compound Predicate?** on pages 589–590. Emphasize the difference between punctuating a compound sentence and a simple sentence with a compound predicate. Do Exercise A on page 591 orally with the class.

5. Assign and discuss Exercise B on page 591.

Individualizing the Lesson

Less-Advanced Students

Ask the students to turn the following pairs of simple sentences into compound sentences. Encourage them to use different methods of combining.

1. Fred worked last summer. He used the money to buy a bicycle.
2. Joanna broke her leg. She could not get to a doctor for three hours.
3. The movie begins at 8:00. I must work until 9:00.
4. You may go to summer camp in July. You may take a course in American History at the high school.
5. Did anyone call when I was out? Were there any deliveries?

Advanced Students

Prepare a paragraph such as the sample on page 586. Direct students to revise it by using compound sentences.

Reinforcement Exercises

Assign and discuss Exercises A and B on page 612.

3. I have lost my pen, or else somebody has borrowed it.
4. Montana is the Treasure State, and California is the Golden State.
5. The instructions confused me, but the nurse explained them.
6. Max cleared the fence, and I scrambled after.
7. The first vehicle with a steam engine worked well for a few hours, but then its engine failed.
8. The team is very strong this year, and we are almost sure to win the city championship.
9. The cavalry had ridden into Mexico on the trail of Chief Geronimo, but he evaded them.
10. The disc jockey talks to callers first, and then she plays records.

Exercise B: Writing Rewrite this paragraph, changing the italicized simple sentences into compound sentences.

> The oak tree is one of the most common trees in the United States. There is the white oak group and the black oak group. *The acorns of white oaks mature in one year. Those of the black oaks take two years.* The two trees differ, of course, in appearance. *White oaks have pale bark. Black oaks have dark bark.* Oak is used as hardwood timber for lumber and fuel. Oak is also used as timber for barrels and railroad ties.

Punctuating Compound Sentences

One of two punctuation marks is used in a compound sentence. Either a **comma** before a coordinating conjunction or a **semicolon** is needed to separate the two parts.

In a compound sentence, a comma is used before a coordinating conjunction. Notice how the comma is used in these compound sentences:

> s.   v.   s.   v.
> The subway car was nearly full, *but* all of us piled in anyway.

> s.   v.   s.   v.
> Sandra talked to her adviser, *and* he helped her with her schedule.

Note: Sometimes commas are not necessary in very short compound sentences.

      ^{s. v.}   ^{s. v.}
Either we're late or you're early.

     ^{s.}   ^{v.}   ^{s.}   ^{v.}
Alarms rang and everyone awoke.

Instead of a comma and a conjunction, a **semicolon** may be used alone to separate the parts of a compound sentence.

    ^{s.}   ^{v.}   ^{s.}   ^{v.}
Gil climbed the palm tree; he returned with a coconut.

             ^{s.}   ^{v.}
Mount McKinley is the highest point in the country;

        ^{s.} ^{v.}
Death Valley is the lowest.

A semicolon may also be used with a **conjunctive adverb**. A conjunctive adverb is an adverb like *therefore, however, moreover, consequently,* or *otherwise.* It joins the two parts of a compound sentence and shows the relationship between them.

    ^{s.}   ^{v.}   ^{s.}   ^{v.}
We missed our bus; *however,* we caught a later bus.

    ^{s.}   ^{v.}   ^{s.}
Heavy rains halted repairs on the highway; *therefore,* the crew

    ^{v.}
is behind schedule.

As you can see, a conjunctive adverb is used after a semicolon and is followed by a comma.

Compound Sentence or Compound Predicate?

In order to punctuate sentences correctly, you must be able to recognize the difference between a compound sentence and a simple sentence with a compound predicate. A compound predicate is composed of two verbs along with their complements and modifiers. Both verbs refer to the same subject. The parts of a compound predicate are joined by a coordinating conjunction. The conjunction is *not* preceded by any punctuation.

Alana *joined the team* and *made the starting lineup.*

A compound sentence, as you have just learned, is composed of two simple sentences, each with its own subject and verb. The two sentences are almost always separated by a comma and conjunction, or by a semicolon.

Alana *joined* the team, and **she** *made* the starting lineup.

As you compose your own sentences, you must be aware of whether a sentence is a compound sentence or a simple sentence with a compound predicate. If each verb has its own subject, then the sentence is compound. If the verbs share the same subject, then only the predicate is compound. Once you have determined what kind of sentence you are writing, you will know how to punctuate it correctly.

Kyle entered a baking contest and *won* first place.
(This simple sentence has a compound predicate. Both verbs, *entered* and *won,* have the same subject, *Kyle.* The conjunction is not preceded by a comma.)

Kyle entered a baking contest, and his *cheesecake won* first place.
(This is a compound sentence. The verb *entered* has its own subject, *Kyle.* The verb *won* has its own subject, *cheesecake.* The conjunction is preceded by a comma.)

The *clerk types* letters and *files* information.
(The conjunction *and* joins the compound predicate of this simple sentence. Both verbs, *types* and *files,* have the same subject, *clerk.* The conjunction is not preceded by a comma.)

The *clerk types* letters, and the *computer files* information.
(This compound sentence is actually two simple sentences joined by a comma and the conjunction *and.*)

Exercise A: For each sentence, write the two words between which the punctuation belongs. Put in the comma or semicolon. If a sentence needs no punctuation, write *Correct*.

1. You can make delicious pies from Concord grapes however, you must remove their seeds first. grapes; however
2. Dr. Jekyll was the kind doctor and Mr. Hyde was Jekyll's evil other self. doctor, and
3. The clouds parted and revealed a full moon. correct
4. Sharon writes the newsletter Jerome distributes it. newsletter; Jerome
5. I met Diana last week and liked her immediately. correct
6. Sal and Joy bought season tickets but they attended only the first and the last games. tickets, but
7. Vanilla extract and unsweetened chocolate both smell good but they taste bitter. good, but
8. The planet Mars has an average temperature of -45° and Martian winds can blow at 300 miles per hour. −45°, and
9. Cleo caught the trout and cleaned it. correct
10. Basketball players must wear appropriate shoes otherwise, they risk injury to their feet and ankles. shoes; otherwise,

Exercise B: Follow the directions for Exercise A.

1. My brother wrote a play and directed it. correct
2. Ivy hung like streamers and roses clambered up the wall. streamers, and
3. Sheila signaled an S.O.S. with her flashlight however, the people on the beach did not know Morse code. flashlight; however,
4. Sailors recognize an upside-down flag as an appeal for help and railroad engineers respond to a red flag by the track. help, and
5. Stories about vampires and monsters are popular and have been told for many centuries. correct
6. The judge heard the evidence and then dismissed the case. correct
7. Alligators look slow nevertheless, they can move very fast. slow; nevertheless,
8. Quilts and oak furniture were once used in many homes but now they are too expensive to be common. homes, but
9. Students in the work-experience program can get jobs with sponsor companies or they can find jobs themselves. companies, or
10. Mother Jones was a union organizer and an activist but earlier she had taught in a convent. activist, but

To recognize subordinate clauses and identify complex sentences

Presenting the Lesson

1. Read **The Complex Sentence, Clause or Phrase?** and **Subordinate Clauses** on pages 592–593. Be sure that students understand the meaning of *main clause* and *subordinate clause* and that they are the same as *independent clause* and *dependent clause*.

2. Use Exercise B on page 594 to illustrate how subordinate conjunctions may be used to make subordinate clauses. After volunteers have turned each simple sentence into a subordinate clause, ask them to complete the sentence by making up a main clause to go with it.

3. Point out that many of the subordinating conjunctions can also be used as other parts of speech. For example, *after* and *before* can be used as prepositions.

4. Assign and discuss Exercise A on page 594.

5. Read **Definition of the Complex Sentence** on page 595. When all students feel they grasp the definition, complete Exercise A on page 595 orally with the class.

6. Assign and discuss Exercise B on page 595.

Individualizing the Lesson

Less-Advanced Students

1. To make sure students understand the difference between a phrase and a clause, have them identify the following as phrases or clauses:

Part 3   The Complex Sentence

Now that you understand the structure of simple sentences and compound sentences, you are ready to study **complex sentences.** However, before you can understand the structure of a complex sentence, you must know what a clause is.

A clause is a group of words containing a verb and its subject.

According to this definition, a simple sentence is a clause. It contains a verb and its subject.

    s.   v.
Keith ran in the marathon.

       s.   v.
Many stores have clearance sales.

It will be easier to understand sentences, though, if you think of a clause as *a group of words within a sentence*. Compound sentences, for example, contain two or more clauses.

  s.   v.   s. v.
Lara demonstrated the loom, and she wove fibers for a rug.

  s.   v.   s. v.
Sherlock Holmes is a fictional character, but he has a large fan club.

Clause or Phrase?

Clauses differ from phrases. Like a clause, a phrase is part of a sentence. However, a clause has a subject and a verb. A phrase does not.

PHRASES: before the gold rush
          to cut the grass

                  s.   v.
CLAUSES: after the Bengals kicked off

                s.   v.
            before you left

Subordinate Clauses

Each of the clauses of a compound sentence can stand alone. In other words, each can function by itself as a sentence. Such a clause is called a **main clause**, or **independent clause**. A main clause is a clause that can stand by itself as a sentence.

Subordinate clauses, or **dependent clauses,** are clauses that cannot stand alone. A subordinate clause is not a complete sentence. Study these examples:

s.   v.

If you sign the contract

s.   v.

Before the gates close

Both of the subordinate clauses above contain subjects and verbs. However, neither of them expresses a complete thought, and neither can stand alone. Both leave you wondering *then what?*

The words that begin subordinate clauses have an important function. Without *if* and *before,* the clauses above become sentences. Words like *if* and *before* are called **subordinating conjunctions.** We say that they *subordinate,* or make *dependent,* the words they introduce. Many, though not all, subordinate clauses begin with subordinating conjunctions.

Words often used as subordinating conjunctions are shown here:

Words Often Used as Subordinating Conjunctions			
after	because	so that	when
although	before	than	whenever
as	if	though	where
as if	in order that	till	wherever
as long as	provided	unless	while
as though	since	until	

Note: The words above are subordinating conjunctions only when they begin clauses. Many of these words can be used in other ways.

Give students the following pairs of simple sentences. Have them rewrite the pair as a compound sentence when the ideas are of equal importance and as a complex sentence when one of the ideas is subordinate to the other.

1. Jacob returns from school for Thanksgiving. We will go to the football game together.
2. You play tambourine by sliding your fingers along the parchment. You can also hit it like a drum.
3. Sulphur dioxide has a suffocating odor. It is harmful to plant life.
4. You have done all your chores without being asked. We are going to double your allowance.
5. Many people can name all the presidents. Few can name all the vice-presidents.

Furthermore, not all subordinate clauses begin with subordinating conjunctions. Some clauses begin with words like these:

that	who, whom, whose
what, whatever	whoever, whomever
which	why
how	

Exercise A: Copy each sentence. Find the main clause and underline it. Then find the subordinate clause in each sentence and enclose it in parentheses.

1. Carla broke her glasses (when she fell off her bike.)
2. The prize would go to (whoever danced the longest)
3. (Although I prefer peach yogurt) I like strawberry yogurt, too.
4. (If the Braves lose this game,) they are out of the pennant race.
5. (When the smoke cleared,) we saw the charred ruins of the mansion.
6. We arrived (after the concert started.)
7. Do you know (where the Isle of Skye is located?)
8. The fans in the gallery were quiet (while the golfer putted)
9. Dr. Frankenstein smiled (as he entered the laboratory)
10. Our basement flooded (while we were on vacation.)

Exercise B: Writing Using *if, because, when, after,* and *since,* make subordinate clauses out of these sentences. Then use each subordinate clause in a sentence.

1. The bus was late.
2. The platform looks shaky.
3. Diane enjoys bowling.
4. There is a pinball machine in the back.
5. The juke box played only old songs.
6. This sundial is very accurate.
7. Flies were buzzing around the table.
8. Keith's contact lens is lost.
9. Strawberries are in season.
10. The cruise ship headed for the tropics.

Definition of the Complex Sentence

Now that you know the difference between main clauses and subordinate clauses, you can understand the complex sentence.

A complex sentence is a sentence that contains one main clause and one or more subordinate clauses.

MAIN CLAUSE	SUBORDINATE CLAUSE
We'll be out of the tournament	unless we win this game.
The real funs begins	when Anthony arrives.
King Kong is a fictional ape	that attacks New York.

Exercise A: Copy the (subordinate clause) in these complex sentences. Underline the subject once and the verb twice.

1. Roberto asked (if we liked oysters.)
2. Summer was over (before we knew it.)
3. These clothes are on sale (because they are unusual sizes.)
4. The plane ticket tells (when we will arrive.)
5. The orchestra tuned up (before the conductor appeared.)
6. Claudia looks (as if she knows the punchline.)
7. Mattie steadied the ladder (while Dawn replaced the bulb.)
8. The ham will spoil (unless you refrigerate it.)
9. (Unless it rains,) we'll go to the fair Monday.
10. (Although Bobbie disliked buckwheat pancakes,) she politely finished hers.

Exercise B: Follow the directions for Exercise A.

1. These windows stick (when the weather is humid.)
2. Jill climbed onto the top of a truck (so that she could see over the crowd.)
3. (As the Buick was turning left,) the light changed.
4. (When John is daydreaming,) he ignores everything else.
5. (Wherever there are wars,) there are refugees.
6. You can paint the room any color, (as long as it's not too dark)
7. Maria acted (as though she had not heard the news.)
8. Can't he remember (where the bases are?)
9. I don't know (if Juanita speaks Portuguese.)
10. Tina explained (how the controls of the kiln should be set.)

Objective

To recognize adverb clauses and their uses

Presenting the Lesson

1. Read and discuss page 596. Review the uses of adverbs. Emphasize that adverb clauses modify the same parts of speech as adverbs and they answer the same questions.

2. Assign and discuss Exercises A and B on page 597.

Individualizing the Lesson

Less-Advanced Students

Refer students back to Exercise A on page 594. Analyze each sentence with them, asking them to identify those that have adverb clauses. Ask them to explain their choices.

Advanced Students

Have students add a main clause to each of the following adverb clauses. Tell them to vary the position of the adverb clause in the sentences.

1. if the weather stays fair
2. because he forgot his keys
3. after the President spoke
4. unless you prefer pizza
5. since they will be late

Reinforcement Exercise

Assign and discuss Exercise D on page 613.

Optional Practice

For the sentences below, have students identify the adverb clause

Part 4 Adverb Clauses

Complex sentences contain subordinate clauses. These clauses may be one of three kinds. One type is the **adverb clause.** An adverb clause functions as any adverb or adverb phrase.

An **adverb** modifies a verb, an adjective, or another adverb. It tells *how, when, where,* or *to what extent.*

ADVERB: Marissa watched *intently.*

An **adverb phrase** is a prepositional phrase used as an adverb.

ADVERB PHRASE: Marissa watched *on the sidelines.*

An adverb clause is a subordinate clause used as an adverb.

ADVERB CLAUSE: Ed watched *while the gymnasts practiced.*

When the voters were polled, Al was leading.

Adverb clauses, like adverbs and adverb phrases, tell *how, when, where,* and *to what extent.* They modify verbs, adjectives, and adverbs.

Note that a clause, unlike a phrase, has a subject and a verb.

Diagraming Adverb Clauses

To diagram an adverb clause, place it on a separate horizontal line below the main line. A dotted line connects the adverb clause to the word it modifies in the main clause. The subordinating conjunction is shown on the dotted line.

When Carlos was twelve, he moved to New York.

Exercise A: Copy the (adverb clause) from each sentence. Underline the subject of each clause once and its verb twice.

1. We waited at the airport (until his plane departed.)
2. (If the treaty is signed,) the Secretary of State will return tomorrow.
3. (Although they're sisters,) they are different in every way.
4. Will school close (if the blizzard continues?)
5. The snow was twelve inches deep (before the city managers agreed upon a removal plan.)
6. The council objected (when the mayor proposed his plan.)
7. Helmets flashed in the sun (as the bikers roared past.)
8. Greg stirred the chili with one hand (while he answered the phone with the other.)
9. Walt Disney made his cartoon animals act (as though they were human.)
10. (Although there were storm warnings,) we foolishly took the boat out.

Exercise B: Follow the directions for Exercise A.

1. Nurses can usually find jobs (wherever they go.)
2. (Although Rita Gomez has not appeared in movies here,) she is a popular movie actress in the Philippines.
3. (When the President addressed the United Nations,) his speech was translated into many languages.
4. The doctor had to reset Linda's broken arm (because she fell on it again.)
5. (Before electricity became available,) many people went to sleep right after sundown.
6. (If the newsstand is out of papers,) try the drug store.
7. (Whenever Jeannie makes a winning basket,) she seems amazed.
8. (As Sam answered the questions,) the computer recorded the answers.
9. Mom learned German (when her dad was stationed near Heidelburg.)
10. (Because Gail had taken a first aid class,) she knew immediately what to do.

and the word it modifies. Also, ask the students to identify the subject and verb in each clause.

1. Whenever I drive, I wear a safety belt.
2. You can come to my house after I finish my homework.
3. Many people enjoy the Marx Brothers films when they are shown on television.
4. Since steak is on sale, we will have it for dinner.
5. Laura spoke as though she had not seen you in years.

Extending the Lesson

Have the students write sentences in which the adverb clauses modify adjectives or adverbs.

Part 5

Objective

To recognize adjective clauses and their uses

Presenting the Lesson

1. Read and discuss pages 598–600. Review the uses of adjectives. Emphasize that adjective clauses modify the same parts of speech as adjectives, and they answer the same questions.

2. Tell the class that adjective clauses may *not* be moved around to various positions in the sentence as adverb clauses can. Go over sentences 1, 2, 3, 8, 9, and 10 of Exercise A on page 601 with the class. Experiment with trying to move the adjective clauses. Point out that the sentence does not make sense unless the adjective clause follows the noun it modifies.

3. Caution students to be alert to *when* and *where* as introductory words for adjective clauses. They look like adverbs and are commonly used as subordinating conjunctions. When they are used in clauses that follow and explain time and place words, they are part of an adjective clause.

4. Take extra time to discuss Point 3 on page 599 and the examples that follow. Explain the use of *who* and *whom*, emphasizing that the relative pronoun should assume subject form if it is the subject or predicate word *within the adjective clause* and the object form if it is an object *within the adjective clause.* The case of the word the clause modifies is not what determines the case of the relative pronoun. Go

The second kind of subordinate clause is the **adjective clause.** An adjective clause has the same function as an adjective or an adjective phrase.

An **adjective** modifies a noun or pronoun.

ADJECTIVE: Melissa wears *big, round* sunglasses.

An **adjective phrase** is a prepositional phrase that modifies a noun or pronoun.

ADJECTIVE PHRASE: We glanced at the list *of sandwiches.*

An adjective clause is a subordinate clause used as an adjective to modify a noun or pronoun.

ADJECTIVE CLAUSE: A polygraph is a machine *that is used in lie detection.*

Anyone *who tries hard enough* can stay awake.

Adjective clauses, like adjectives and adjective phrases, tell *what kind* or *which one.* They usually come directly after the word they modify. Unlike adjective phrases, adjective clauses have subjects and verbs.

There are several words used to introduce adjective clauses. Two of them are *where* and *when.*

This is the studio *where recordings are made.*

This is the time *when the moon is full.*

Relative Pronouns

Besides *when* and *where,* the words *who, whom,* and *whose* are also used to begin adjective clauses. *Who, whom,* and *whose* are called **relative pronouns.** They relate a clause, called a **relative clause,** to a noun or pronoun in the sentence. Sometimes *that* and *which* are relative pronouns.

Words Used as Relative Pronouns				
who	whom	whose	that	which

Relative pronouns are special because they function in three different ways:

1. They introduce adjective clauses.
2. They link the clause to a word in the main clause of the sentence.
3. They have a function within the clause. They act as subject, object, or predicate pronoun of the verb within the adjective clause. They may also be the object of a preposition in the clause. *Whose* functions as an adjective.

Students *who work part-time* are dismissed early.
   (The adjective clause modifies *Students*, the subject of the main clause. *Who* is the subject of *work* within the adjective clause.)

The dentist's office plays music *that is soothing*.
   (The adjective clause modifies *music* in the main clause. *That* is the subject of *is* within the adjective clause.)

The person *whom we need most* is Anna.
   (The adjective clause modifies the word *person* in the main clause. *Whom* functions as the direct object of *need* within the adjective clause.)

The tall, blonde girl *with whom I chatted* turned out to be my distant cousin.
   (The adjective clause modifies the subject of the main clause, *girl*. *Whom* is the object of the preposition *with* within the adjective clause.)

Children *whose parents work here* may attend the day-care center.
   (The adjective clause modifies *Children* within the main clause. *Whose* modifies *parents*, the subject of the adjective clause.)

over sentences 4–7 of Exercise A on page 601 with the class, pointing out how the relative pronouns function in the main clause and in the subordinate clause.

5. Assign and discuss Exercise B on page 601.

Individualizing the Lesson

Less-Advanced Students

Complete Exercise A on page 601 orally.

Advanced Students

Have students complete the following by adding an adjective clause or a main clause.

1. Volkswagen is the car.
2. who had to leave the meeting early
3. a flat tire is the problem
4. Harrison Ford and Mark Hamil are the actors
5. the tour guide pointed out the spot
6. whom the mayor of Telluride appointed
7. that I like best
8. whose office is upstairs
9. that I read
10. Tuesday is the day

Reinforcement Exercise

Assign and discuss Exercise E on page 613.

Optional Practice

Have students rewrite each pair of sentences below as a complex sentence, using the italicized sentence as an adjective clause and the word in parentheses as the relative pronoun.

1. Where is the pen? *I just had it.* (that)
2. The new coach gave us some excellent advice. *He had played on a championship team.* (who)

3. The trees on our street had beautiful flowers this spring. *They were planted two years ago.* (that)
4. I want to see the movie. *It is playing at our local theater.* (that)
5. Linda won first prize. *She is a fine swimmer.* (who)

Extending the Lesson

Tell the class that some adjective clauses are restrictive; that is, they are necessary to identify or define the noun. Other adjective clauses are non-restrictive; that is, they simply add information. For more information on restrictive and non-restrictive clauses and how to punctuate them, they may consult Section 14.

Sometimes you may be confused about whether *who* or *whom* is the correct relative pronoun to use. To decide, see how the pronoun is used within the clause. Keep in mind that *who* is the subject form. *Whom* is the object form.

> She is the artist *who* painted the mural.
> (*Who* is the subject of *painted* within the clause.)

> She is the artist *whom* I most admire.
> (*Whom* is the direct object of *admire* within the clause.)

Diagraming Adjective Clauses

To diagram an adjective clause, use a separate line beneath the main line. A dotted line runs from the relative pronoun to the word in the main clause that the adjective clause modifies.

> The people who run the space program are in Houston.

> One of the players on whom we depend was injured.

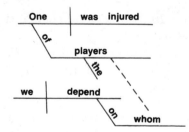

Exercise A: Copy the (adjective clause) from each sentence. Underline the subject once and the verb twice. Before the clause, write the word it modifies.

EXAMPLE: She is the teacher who wrote our textbook.

teacher—who wrote our textbook

1. It was the coldest winter (that New Yorkers had ever experienced.) winter
2. The maple tree (that Grandad planted) is over twenty feet tall. maple tree
3. Staph germs in the body head for tissue (that is damaged.) tissue
4. Donna is the cheerleader (who also plays baseball.) cheerleader
5. One American writer (who lived in Paris) was James Baldwin. writer
6. The man (who is wearing a neck brace) was in a car accident. man
7. The mayor is the person (to whom the petition should be sent.) person
8. Fireflies (which are really beetles,) produce cold lights. Fireflies
9. The milk (that is in this carton) smells sour. milk
10. This is the time of day (that I like best.) time

Exercise B: Follow the directions for Exercise A.

1. One of the cities (that produced early jazz) is New Orleans. cities
2. The carpenter (who made this cabinet) is eighty years old. carpenter
3. In almost every family there is someone (who cannot throw anything away.) someone
4. Panama, (which joins Central America and South America,) is a small but important country. Panama
5. The silo (in which the soybeans were stored) was struck by lightning. silo
6: The artist and her husband designed their own home, (which was made of steel and glass.) home
7. The manager gave the reporter a list of the players (whose contracts had been renewed.) players
8. The man (whose dog bit me) drove me to the hospital. man
9. Sunday night is the time (when television attracts the most viewers.) time
10. The window (which was broken) was repaired by a glazier. window

Objective

To recognize noun clauses and their uses

Presenting the Lesson

1. Read and discuss pages 602–603. Review with the class the various uses of nouns in sentences.

2. Call on volunteers to think of sentences in which noun clauses act as subject, predicate noun, direct object, and object of the preposition.

3. Point out that many of the words that introduce noun clauses may also be used to introduce adjective or adverb clauses. It is the use of the clause that determines whether it is a noun clause, an adjective clause, or an adverb clause.

4. Do Exercise A on page 604 orally with the class. Assign and discuss Exercise B.

Individualizing the Lesson

Less-Advanced Students

1. Using some of the noun clauses from Exercise A, show students how they may work as different parts of a sentence.

2. Allow students to work in pairs on Exercise B.

Advanced Students

Have students write complex sentences by using the following noun clauses in the ways indicated in parentheses.

1. that it would rain (subject)
2. what the owner hoped for (predicate noun)
3. whoever hit the fly ball (object of the preposition)

Part 6 Noun Clauses

The noun clause is the third kind of subordinate clause.

A noun clause is a clause used as a noun in a sentence.

Like a noun, a noun clause can be used as a subject, an object of the verb, a predicate word, or an object of a preposition. It can be used in any of the ways that nouns are used in a sentence. Unlike adverb and adjective clauses, however, noun clauses do not modify.

Uses of Noun Clauses

SUBJECT:	*Whoever sent the mayday alert* must need help urgently. *What concerns everyone* is inflation.
DIRECT OBJECT:	Scientists cannot always predict *when an earthquake will occur.* The controller radioed *that the runway was clear.*
OBJECT OF PREPOSITION:	Rod was impressed by *whatever Joyce said.* The signs point to *where the trail begins.*
PREDICATE NOUN:	City life is *what he wants.* The fact was *that the car was missing.*

As you can see from these examples, many noun clauses begin with the words *that* and *what.* The words *whatever, who, whoever,* and *whomever* can also signal noun clauses. *Where, when, how,* and *why* are used, too.

Diagraming Noun Clauses

To diagram a noun clause, extend a bridge from the place where the clause is used in the sentence. If the word that begins the clause functions simply as an introductory word, place it on a line over the clause. Look at the three examples on the next page:

1. Noun clause used as subject

What you need is a sense of humor.

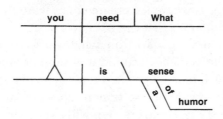

2. Noun clause used as object of the verb

Many people say that good times are ahead.

3. Noun clause used as object of a preposition

The candidate talked to whoever would listen.

4. what was really bothering him (direct object)
5. whatever the committee decides (object of a preposition)
6. where the marathon is run (predicate noun)
7. why the accident occurred (direct object)
8. whoever arrives first (subject)

Reinforcement Exercise

Assign and discuss Exercise F on page 614.

Optional Practice

Ask students to identify the noun clauses in the sentences below and tell how they are used in the sentences.

1. Claire asked when the movie was going to start.
2. Whoever came as a robot did a good job creating a costume.
3. Give this sandwich to whoever likes peanut butter.
4. The truth was that he didn't really want to play.
5. Take me to where your leader is.

Extending the Lesson

Have the students devise sentences in which there are phrase and clause constructions within other phrase and clause constructions. See who can come up with the most complex complex sentence that still makes good sense. Ask students to diagram their complex constructions.

Exercise A: Copy the noun clauses in these sentences. Underline the subject once and the verb twice. Tell how the clause is used.

1. Now I understand (why you left early.) direct object
2. Patrice explained (how yogurt is made.) direct object
3. St. Louis is (where ice cream cones were first sold.) predicate noun
4. The problem is (that the battery is dead.) predicate noun
5. You can make a scarf from (whatever fabric is left.) object of prepositio
6. (What the audience wanted) was another encore. subject
7. There will be enough food for (whomever you invite.) object of preposition
8. (Whoever made that statement) does not know the facts. subject
9. Mickie starts a conversation with (whoever sits next to her.) object o preposi
10. We all wondered (where the magician learned her tricks.) direct obje

Exercise B: Follow the directions for Exercise A.

1. The manager promised (that she would look for my jacket.) direct object
2. Hal asked (why the game had been delayed.) direct object
3. (How the pyramids were built) is a fascinating story. subject
4. Alex said (that high ozone levels give him headaches.) direct object
5. I wonder (who lost this watch.) direct object
6. (Whenever you must leave,) just let me know. direct object
7. Ken thinks (that he has the winning ticket.) direct object
8. The only solution is (that we raise the funds ourselves.) predicate nou
9. The minister spends her time with (whoever needs it.) object of preposition
10. (What the neighbors will think) bothers him too much. subject

Part 7

Objective

To review and compare the three types of subordinate clauses

Presenting the Lesson

1. Read and discuss page 604. Use the sentences in Exercise A on page 605 to review the various kinds of subordinate clauses.
2. Assign Exercise B.

Part 7 A Review of Subordinate Clauses

You have learned about the three kinds of subordinate clauses. They are the adverb clause, the adjective clause, and the noun clause.

You can identify the kind of clause by looking at its use in the sentence. A clause used as a noun is a noun clause. A clause used as a modifier is an adverb or adjective clause, depending on the word modified.

Exercise A: Write the (subordinate clause) in each sentence. If the clause is used as a noun clause, write how it is used in the sentence. If the clause is used as an adjective or adverb clause, write the word it modifies.

1. Nevada is one state (where wild horses still roam.) adjective, state
2. I wonder (where I stored my backpack.) noun, direct object
3. (When the movie was over,) the audience was silent. adverb, was
4. Mr. Chang, (who owns vegetable markets,) spoke to our JA club. adjective, Mr. Chang
5. Carol suddenly realized (who was on the phone.) noun, direct object
6. Tom always worries about (what he will say next.) noun, object of prep
7. The school days (that were lost during the snowstorm) will be made up in June. adjective, schooldays
8. Ellie remembered (that meteors would be visible in the early evening.) noun, direct object
9. Find a seat (wherever you can.) adverb, Find
10. Trees (that follow day-night cycles) may be injured by bright streetlights. adjective, trees

Exercise B: Follow the directions for Exercise A.

1. The ring, (which had belonged to her grandmother,) was Celia's most cherished possession. adjective, ring
2. Call the clinic right away (if the pain in your shoulder becomes worse.) adverb, Call   adjective, neighborhoods
3. Neighborhoods (that have no parks) are rare in Chicago.
4. The census taker (who visited our block) spoke Spanish and Polish. adjective, taker
5. I tried to sketch the scene (I saw from our cabin window.) adjective, scene
6. (Who will start) is the coach's decision. noun, subject
7. Julio will not eat junk food (while he is in training for the gymnastics team.) adverb, will eat
8. (While Glenda was rehearsing a loud scene from the play,) the people next door became worried about her. adverb, became
9. (As Rome was burning,) the emperor supposedly played his fiddle. adverb, played
10. The janitor said (that he would replace the doorknob tonight.) noun, direct object

Individualizing the Lesson

Less-Advanced Students

Have students identify the subject and verb in the main clause of each sentence in Exercise B. Then have them identify the subject and verb in the subordinate clause for each sentence.

Advanced Students

Have students write complex sentences in accordance with the instructions below.

1. a complex sentence with an adverb clause modifying an adjective
2. a complex sentence with a noun clause as direct object
3. a complex sentence with an adjective clause modifying a predicate word
4. a complex sentence with an adverb clause modifying a verb
5. a complex sentence with a noun clause as subject and an adjective clause modifying a predicate word

Optional Practice

Using reading materials in the classroom and the students' textbooks, ask students to find examples of the three types of subordinate clauses. Which type shows up most frequently?

Extending the Lesson

Ask students to write paragraphs that contain only simple or compound sentences. Then have them revise the paragraphs, using subordinate clauses to add more detailed information.

Objective

To prevent the use of subordinate clauses as sentence fragments

Presenting the Lesson

1. Read and discuss pages 606–607. Use Exercise A on page 606–607 for oral practice in distinguishing between fragments and sentences. Have students correct the fragments independently.
2. Assign and discuss Exercise B on page 607.

Individualizing the Lesson

Less-Advanced Students

Have students turn the following fragments into complete sentences.

1. while I was eating a popsicle
2. that the dog needs a bath
3. whoever knows how to get there
4. when the pirates roamed the seas
5. if the computer makes an error

Advanced Students

Have students use the words listed below to introduce the subordinate clauses given in parentheses. Use these clauses in complete complex sentences.

1. that (adjective clause modifying the subject)
2. where (noun clause as predicate word)
3. who (adjective clause modifying a direct object)
4. whomever (noun clause as subject)
5. when (adverb clause modifying the verb)

Optional Practice

Have students identify the fragments in the list below. Tell them to

Part 8   Clauses as Sentence Fragments

You have learned that a sentence fragment may lack a subject or verb or both.

Alone on the lake.   Played the jukebox.

The subordinate clause can be a sentence fragment, too. Even though it does have a subject and verb, it still does not express a complete thought. For that reason, it is a sentence fragment.

Notice the difference between these word groups:

The TV was on.   While the TV was on.

The first word group is a sentence. In the second group, the subordinating conjunction *while* creates a sentence fragment. The reader cannot tell *what was happening* while the TV was on. The subordinate clause should be used as part of a sentence.

A subordinate clause must not be written as a complete sentence. It must always be joined to a main clause.

MAIN CLAUSE   Australians are having summer.
AND FRAGMENT: When we are having winter.

SENTENCE: Australians are having summer when we are having winter.

Exercise A: Writing Number your paper from 1 to 10. Decide whether the groups of words below are sentences or fragments. Write *S* for *Sentence* and *F* for *Fragment*. Add words to make each fragment a complete sentence. Be sure to punctuate and capitalize where necessary.

s 1. what did the announcer say
s 2. when is the playoff game
f 3. what the fortune teller said
f 4. after the rain stops
s 5. after a while everyone returned
s 6. that showroom is filled with new cars

f 7. the book that you needed
f 8. before the dance started
s 9. why is the flag at half-mast
f10. why the dogs are barking

Exercise B: Writing Find the fragments in the paragraph below. Then rewrite the paragraph, eliminating all fragments.

Although Henry Ford has been credited with inventing the assembly line/, He really did not. He perfected the process, however. In 1908 the Model T could be sold for $850/, While other similar cars sold for $2,000 to $3,000. Although the price of the Model T was remarkable then/, Ford and his engineers were not content. When the last Model T's were produced on the assembly line in 1927/, The price was $290.

Part 9 Compound-Complex Sentences

You have already been introduced to simple, compound, and complex sentences. The fourth and final kind of sentence is the **compound-complex sentence.**

A compound-complex sentence consists of two or more main clauses and one or more subordinate clauses.

It may help you to think of a compound-complex sentence as a compound sentence plus a subordinate clause. Actually, the compound-complex sentence joins two main clauses, at least one of which has a subordinate clause. The subordinate clause may be an adjective, adverb, or noun clause. The main clauses are joined by either a coordinating conjunction or a semicolon.

| Main Clause | Main Clause | Subordinate Clause |

Yogurt is nutritious, and some say *that it brings good health.*

| Subordinate Clause | Main Clause | Main Clause |

When Dan called, he was angry; however, he soon calmed down.

607

write complex sentences that use the fragments as subordinate clauses.

1. whichever came first
2. that we all know and love
3. when you have the answer
4. that came with the kit

Extending the Lesson

Ask the students if they recognize any of the familiar sayings or titles from which the clauses below were taken. How are the clauses used?

When I was one (I was just begun—A. A. Milne)

Whom It May Concern (object of preposition *To* in standard salutation)

that I shall never see a poem lovely as a tree (I think. . .—Joyce Kilmer)

Part 9

Objective

To recognize compound-complex sentences

Presenting the Lesson

1. Read and discuss page 607. Review compound and complex sentences, asking students for examples of each.
2. Use the first three sentences in the Exercise on page 608 for oral practice with the class. Then assign sentences 4–10 to be completed individually.

Individualizing the Lesson

Less-Advanced Students

Write several simple sentences on the board, e.g., *The principal spoke.* Work with students at expanding the simple sentences into compound-complex sentences.

Advanced Students

Have students write three compound-complex sentences: one with a noun clause, one with an adjective clause, and one with an adverb clause.

Reinforcement Exercise

Assign and discuss Exercise G on page 614.

Optional Practice

Have students identify the main clauses and the subordinate clauses in the following sentences. They should identify both the type and function of the clauses.

1. Louis looked at his notes, and he realized what he had forgotten.
2. When the grocery bag ripped, everything fell to the ground, but nothing was broken.
3. The doctor told me that I should stay out of the sun; nevertheless, I want a tan.
4. The car backed out of the space where it had been parked, and it was hit by a delivery truck.

Extending the Lesson

Encourage students to experiment with the four types of sentences in their writing. Using examples from their own written work, show how writing can be improved by combining simple sentences.

Part 10

Objective

To recognize all four types of sentences

Exercise: Identify the two main clauses and the (subordinate clause) in these compound-complex sentences.

1. A bola is a rope (that has weights at the end;) it is used to catch cattle.
2. Larry tried the dance steps (that we demonstrated,) but he couldn't quite master them.
3. The instructor told us (how we could revive a heart attack victim,) and she demonstrated on a dummy.
4. Blair House is located across the street from the White House, and foreign leaders (who visit Washington) often stay there.
5. Hiawatha was the hero of a poem; moreover, he was a Mohawk chief (who organized tribes into the Five Nations.)
6. The election judges distribute the ballots, and then they count them (after the polls close.)
7. In earlier times, infants were wrapped snugly with strips of cloth; people thought (that this "swaddling" made babies feel secure.)
8. Al drives a snow-removal truck, and (whenever a heavy snow falls,) he is called to work.
9. Some television sets have tubes; however, newer models, (which are usually smaller,) are solid state.
10. I've just learned (that Dad's vacation was changed;) as a result, we'll leave earlier for Michigan.

Part 10   A Review of Sentences

There are four basic kinds of sentences.

A **simple sentence** contains one subject and one predicate. Parts of the simple sentence, however, may be compound. A simple sentence expresses one idea.

          s.   v.
The tower transmits radio signals.

     s.   v.   v.
Alexis was born in Alaska but grew up in the state of Texas.

A **compound sentence** is made up of two simple sentences. These simple sentences are connected by a comma and coordinating conjunction or by a semicolon. Sometimes a conjunctive adverb follows the semicolon. A compound sentence expresses two related ideas. Notice how the ideas are joined together in these sentences.

s.   v.   s.   v.
The tower is 300 feet tall, and it transmits radio signals.

s.   v.   s.   v.
Alexis was born in Alaska; however, she grew up in the state of Texas.

A **complex sentence** contains one main clause and one or more subordinate clauses. The subordinate clauses may be used as adverbs, adjectives, or nouns. A complex sentence expresses one main idea and one or more dependent ideas. Notice how the example sentences have changed.

s.   v.   s.   v.
Because the tower is the tallest structure in the city, it is used to transmit radio signals.

s.   v.   s.   v.
Although Alexis was born in Alaska, she grew up in the state of Texas.

A **compound-complex sentence** contains two main clauses and one or more subordinate clauses. The subordinate clauses may be adverb, adjective, or noun clauses. A compound-complex sentence expresses two main ideas, as well as one or more dependent ideas.

s.   v.   s.   v.
The tower is the tallest structure in the city, and it transmits

s.   v.
radio signals *that are heard throughout the Midwest.*

s.   v.   s.   v.
Although Alexis was born in Alaska, she grew up in the state

s.   v.
of Texas; now she is living in New York.

Presenting the Lesson

1. Read and discuss pages 608–609. Remind the students that parts of a sentence may be compound. Go over the punctuation of compound sentences carefully. See Exercise A on page 610 to work orally with the class on identifying the four sentence types.

2. Assign Exercises B and C on pages 610–611 to be completed individually. Give the students an opportunity to have troublesome sentences worked out on the board.

Individualizing the Lesson

Less-Advanced Students

Allow students to work on Exercise C in pairs. Discuss several of their answers, pointing out the reasons for any errors.

Advanced Students

Have students combine the simple sentences below into compound or complex sentences. Tell them to be ready to explain why they have punctuated their sentences as they have.

1. The custodian arrived. He fixed the broken desk.
2. You saved your money. You were able to go to Washington.
3. High heels are bad for the spine. Lynn insists on wearing them.
4. The concert began. Everyone relaxed and enjoyed it.
5. The book is copyrighted. You cannot photocopy it.

Optional Practice

Have students identify the following sentences as simple, compound, complex, or compound-complex.

1. The magazines that you need for your report are in the reference room.
2. Mother lit the candles and Father said the blessing before we ate.
3. Jessica and Sam have been rehearsing the dance number that they will perform at the talent show all quarter.
4. If this winter is cold, we may run out of natural gas; therefore, we must conserve gas now.
5. Many people have read some of Shakespeare's plays, but few have read them all.

Extending the Lesson

Have the class look for the four sentence types in their textbooks, including *Building English Skills*. Ask them to comment on the kinds of sentences they have found in the various texts. Which texts use predominantly simple sentences? Which ones use compound, complex, and compound-complex sentences regularly?

Exercise A: Number your paper from 1 to 10. For each sentence, write *Simple, Compound, Complex,* or *Compound-Complex* to show what kind it is.

1. Why did the governor veto that bill? simple
2. Bradley asked how high the waterfall was, and the forest ranger told her. compound-complex
3. The helicopter can carry thirty soldiers and some supplies. simple
4. The members of the Drama Club not only produce plays but they also write them. compound
5. When Cortez arrived in Mexico, the Aztecs mistook him for the god of the morning star, and they worshiped him. compound-complex
6. What a grotesque mask that is! simple
7. Helena hopes that one day she will become a chef. complex
8. Deep in space is a cloud of comets that are made of dust, rock fragments, and frozen gases. complex
9. The planet Pluto is very small and very far away; it was not discovered until 1930. compound
10. Does the discovery of a new planet influence astrology? simple

Exercise B: Follow the directions for Exercise A.

1. Tracy sings while she plays the banjo. complex
2. The paramedics arrived as soon as they could, but it was too late. compound-complex
3. The planner interviewed the neighborhood residents, and then she wrote her recommendations. compound
4. After I wrote the report, I proofread it. complex
5. After this exercise you should flex your shoulders and stretch. simple
6. The man in the pinstriped, three-piece suit looked odd with the wet dog in his arms. simple
7. Do you like the pudding, or are you just being polite? compound
8. Do you drink diet drinks, which might contain a harmful substance, or do you drink sugared drinks, which are fattening? compound-complex
9. General MacArthur said that he would return. complex
10. The airlines know that some passengers will not show up; therefore, extra tickets are sold for each flight. compound-complex

Exercise C: Writing Rewrite each of the following sentences or sets of sentences. Follow the directions in parentheses. Use correct punctuation. Answers in margin.

1. People expect Peru's coast to be a jungle. The coastline is actually arid. (Combine the two sentences with *but* to make a compound sentence.)

2. The wind died. We were sailing near the cove. (Combine the two sentences with *when* to make a complex sentence.)

3. The sun set. The wind started up. The temperature dropped to 65°. (Using *when* and *and*, combine these three sentences to make a compound-complex sentence.)

4. Sara sprained her ankle. She completed the marathon. (Combine these sentences with *although* to make a complex sentence.)

5. Connie read the novel. She did not see the movie. (Combine the two sentences with *but* to make a compound sentence.)

6. Keith preferred ball point pens. He tried a fine line marker. (Combine the sentences with *until* to make a complex sentence.)

7. Karen doodles on the phone book. Jason twists the phone cord. They talk on the telephone. (Combine these sentences with *and* and *while* to make a compound-complex sentence.)

8. The hurricane hit Galveston, Texas. Many people were left homeless. (Combine the sentences using *after* to make a complex sentence.)

9. An airplane flight from Chicago to Orlando takes less than three hours. An auto trip takes about twenty-four hours. A train trip the same distance takes thirty-six hours. (Combine these sentences using *and* and *but* to make a compound sentence.)

10. School closed. The community swimming pool has been open daily. (Combine these sentences using *since* to make a complex sentence.)

Exercise C

1. People expect Peru's coast to be a jungle, but the coastline is actually arid.
2. We were sailing near the cove when the wind died.
3. When the sun set, the wind started up, and the temperature dropped to 65°.
4. Although Sara sprained her ankle, she completed the marathon.
5. Connie read the novel, but she did not see the movie.
6. Until he tried a fine line marker, Keith preferred ball point pens.
7. While they talk on the telephone, Karen doodles on the phone book, and Jason twists the phone cord.
8. After the hurricane hit Galveston, Texas, many people were left homeless.
9. An airplane flight from Chicago to Orlando takes less than three hours, and an auto trip takes about twenty-four hours, but a train trip the same distance takes thirty-six hours.
10. Since school closed, the community swimming pool has been open daily.

REINFORCEMENT EXERCISES
Using Compound and Complex Sentences

A. Analyze simple and compound sentences. Number your paper from 1 to 10. Write *Simple* or *Compound* to show what kind each sentence is. (Use after page 585.)

1. At this airport, a plane departs or lands every minute. simple
2. Janna loves tennis and has won many medals. simple
3. The map is old, but it will serve as a general guide. compound
4. The hubcap fell off and clattered down the road. simple
5. Debra applied for a job at the stables, and she got it. compound
6. Peter, Paul, and Mary have sung together for over twenty years. simple
7. Some Islamic women wear veils, but others do not. compound
8. This beanbag chair is extremely comfortable; I almost fell asleep in it. compound
9. Ernie ordered dessert, but he couldn't finish it. compound
10. This restaurant is always open and always full. simple

B. Analyze and punctuate compound sentences. Copy these compound sentences. Underline each subject once, and each verb twice. Punctuate correctly. (Use after page 591.)

1. Marshmallows are candy; marsh mallows are plants.
2. Many players dislike artificial turf; nevertheless, they must play on it.
3. We must catch that train; it is the last one today.
4. Houses collapsed, and trees were uprooted.
5. Ron's final dive was superb, but he still didn't win the contest.
6. Will you telephone Mom, or shall I call?
7. The snow has melted, and soon the trees will bud.
8. The truck weighs three tons; it cannot stop very fast.
9. The factory has closed; however, it will reopen soon.
10. Rachel seems shy and introverted, but she has a wonderful sense of humor.

C. Distinguish clauses and phrases. Tell whether the italicized words in each sentence are a *Clause* or a *Phrase*.   (Use after page 594.)

1. The pool doesn't open *until Memorial Day*. phrase
2. The passenger was nervous *until the plane landed.* clause
3. *As Jerry made a basket,* the backboard shattered. clause
4. *As a special reward,* John received twenty dollars. phrase
5. The coach gave us a pep talk *before the second half.* phrase
6. *Before we pitched the tents,* Marla chopped firewood. clause
7. We have lived in Juneau *since last May.* phrase
8. *Since Joshua's braces are off,* he smiles more. clause
9. *After the alarm rang,* firefighters dashed to their trucks. clause
10. *After the concert,* fans waited by the stage door. phrase

D. Recognize adverb clauses. Write each (adverb clause.) Underline its subject once and its verb twice. Then write the word modified by the clause.   (Use after page 597.)

1. (Although <u>we</u> <u><u>came</u></u> to Boston for a weekend,) we stayed there for two weeks. stayed
2. Carolyn spilled the paint (as <u>she</u> <u><u>reached</u></u> for the brush.) spilled
3. (Because <u>Ed</u> <u><u>has</u></u> practice every day,) he values his free time. values
4. (Since <u>Ian</u> <u><u>had been benched,</u></u>) Cal got a chance to play.   got
5. Dan fixed his lunch (before <u>he</u> <u><u>left</u></u> for school.) fixed
6. Our radio doesn't play well (unless <u>it</u> <u><u>is facing</u></u> south.) does play
7. The editor spliced the film (after <u>she</u> <u><u>cut</u></u> a scene.) spliced
8. The courtroom artist sketched (as the <u>witness</u> <u><u>talked.</u></u>) sketched
9. We will need canteens (if <u>we</u> <u><u>hike</u></u> all day.) will need
10. After her defeat, Sue trained harder (than <u>she</u> <u><u>had</u></u> before.) harder

E. Recognize adjective clauses. Write each (adjective clause.) Underline its subject once and its verb twice. Then write the word modified by the clause.   (Use after page 601.)

1. One animal (<u>that</u> <u><u>can live</u></u> more than fifty years) is the raven. animal
2. February 2 is the day (when the <u>groundhog</u> <u><u>looks</u></u> for its shadow.) day
3. One artist (whom <u>I</u> <u><u>admire</u></u>) is Georgia O'Keeffe. artist
4. The candidate (<u>who</u> <u><u>receives</u></u> the most electoral votes) wins. candidate
5. Pavarotti is the only opera singer (to whom <u>I</u> <u><u>enjoy</u></u> listening.) singer

613

6. The cabinet (where the <u>supplies</u> <u>are kept</u>) is in here. <small>cabinet</small>
7. The coach, (who <u>had</u> once <u>played</u> professional basketball,) brought the team to first place. <small>coach</small>
8. Where did Karen put the card (that <u>I</u> <u>brought</u>?) <small>card</small>
9. The priest calmed the people (who <u>had been hurt</u>.) <small>people</small>
10. Here is the telescope (that <u>I</u> <u>borrowed</u>.) <small>telescope</small>

F. Recognize noun clauses. Write each (noun clause.) Underline the subject once and the verb twice. Tell whether the clause is used as a subject, direct object, object of a preposition, or predicate noun.
<small>(Use after page 60</small>

1. Nicole explained (how <u>glaciers</u> <u>create</u> valleys.) <small>direct object</small>
2. (Whatever <u>was making</u> the noise) <u>has stopped</u>. <small>subject</small>
3. In the fog, Liz could hardly see (where <u>she</u> <u>was going</u>.) <small>direct objec</small>
4. The problem is (that the <u>boat</u> <u>has</u> a leak.) <small>predicate noun</small>
5. A trophy was made for (whoever <u>won</u> the contest.) <small>object of preposit</small>
6. The newspapers told (how the <u>crime</u> <u>was committed</u>.) <small>direct objec</small>
7. Dan commented (that the <u>Steelers</u> <u>had</u> a strong defense.) <small>direct o</small>
8. (Whoever <u>answered</u> the phone) <u>was</u> rude. <small>subject</small>
9. The President listened to (what the <u>Senator</u> <u>said</u>.) <small>object of prepositi</small>
10. David told us only (what <u>we</u> <u>wanted</u> to hear.) <small>direct object</small>

G. Identify sentences. For each sentence, write *Simple, Compound, Complex,* or *Compound-Complex.* <small>(Use after page 611.)</small>

1. Paula shoveled the drive, and Megan did the walk. <small>compound</small>
2. After school Jerome has a paper route. <small>simple</small>
3. Jane steered the jeep down the muddy road to the river, <small>compoun</small> and then she discovered that the bridge had collapsed. <small>complex</small>
4. The callouses on her hands are not from work; they are from climbing the rope in gym. <small>compound</small>
5. Long ago, soldiers bit on bullets while they were having surgery. <small>complex</small>
6. The young recruits lined up and listened for their orders. <small>simple</small>
7. If you place the avocado pit in water, it will soon sprout. <small>complex</small>
8. When Superman arrives, outlaws haven't a chance. <small>complex</small>
9. Eric Heiden won five Olympic gold medals, and his sister Beth won a bronze medal. <small>compound</small>
10. Our van holds more people than a station wagon does. <small>complex</small>

MIXED REVIEW

Using Compound and Complex Sentences

A. Copy each sentence, adding any necessary punctuation. Then tell whether each sentence is *Simple, Compound, Complex,* or *Compound-Complex.*

1. When Sandy came to the plate,the bases were loaded,and there were two outs. compound-complex
2. Linda participated in the Outward Bound program and learned a great deal about herself. simple
3. Every Saturday Lila does her chores at home,goes to dance class,cooks dinner,and visits friends. simple
4. The medical profession is always making breakthroughs in disease control. simple
5. How often does Halley's Comet enter the atmosphere of the earth? simple
6. Many people have a fear of closed places,but some can overcome their fear through therapy or hypnosis. compound
7. After he met his graduation requirements in summer school,Raymond applied to the paramedic program. complex
8. The control tower received the message,and the pilot who sent the information waited for instructions. compound-complex
9. She went on most of the really terrifying rides,but she wouldn't go near the Ferris wheel. compound
10. Benjamin loves any game that deals with words. complex

B. Find the (subordinate clause) in each of the following sentences. Copy it onto your paper. Then, write the letter of the phrase that best describes the clause.

1. (Because of the foul weather,)we canceled our picnic.
   a. Adjective clause modifying *picnic*
   <u>b.</u> Adverb clause modifying *canceled*
   c. Noun clause used as the subject
2. The umpire ruled (that the ball was out of bounds.)
   a. Adjective clause modifying *umpire*
   b. Adverb clause modifying *ruled*
   <u>c.</u> Noun clause used as the direct object

615

Mixed Review

These exercises provide review of the concepts presented in this Section. Each exercise challenges the students to apply several of the skills they have acquired during previous study. Because the "mixed" feature of these activities makes them more difficult, the teacher may wish to have less-advanced students do them orally or in small groups.

3. (If you don't tie up the bundle of food,) the bears will
        steal it.
        a. Adjective clause modifying *bears*
        b. Noun clause used as the subject
        c. Adverb clause modifying *will steal*
4. Phil is very interested in carpentry, (which is the vocation of
        his father and his sister.)
        a. Adjective clause modifying *carpentry*
        b. Adjective clause modifying *Phil*
        c. Noun clause used as the subject
5. (That we would have a hot summer) was predicted by the
        Farmer's Almanac.
        a. Adverb clause modifying *was predicted*
        b. Noun clause used as the subject
        c. Adjective clause modifying *summer*
6. The person (whom Elena respects most) is her great-
        grandmother.
        a. Noun clause used as the direct object
        b. Adjective clause modifying *Elena*
        c. Adjective clause modifying *person*
7. (By the time the flood waters receded,) several homes had
        been evacuated.
        a. Adverb clause modifying *had been evacuated*
        b. Adjective clause modifying *homes*
        c. Noun clause used as the subject
8. She acted (as though she had been on the stage all of
        her life.)
        a. Adjective clause modifying *She*
        b. Adverb clause modifying *acted*
        c. Noun clause used as the object of a preposition
9. The students (who volunteer at the nursing home) enjoy the
        companionship of the residents.
        a. Noun clause used as the direct object
        b. Adjective clause modifying *students*
        c. Adjective clause modifying *home*
10. My younger brother asked me (what causes sonic booms.)
        a. Adjective clause modifying *brother*
        b. Adverb clause modifying *asked*
        c. Noun clause used as the direct object

C. Rewrite each sentence or group of sentences, following the directions shown in parentheses. You may have to add, rearrange, or delete words. Answers may vary.

1. Karen enjoyed watching the Steelers' games on television/ and ~~she~~ attended as many home games as possible. (Rewrite as a simple sentence.)

2. Tom cut three lawns/ ~~H~~e used the money he earned to buy [, and h] a birthday gift for his cousin. (Rewrite as a compound sentence using *and*.)

3. [If t] ~~T~~he computer breaks down/ ~~T~~he company loses a lot of [, t] [When it is] money. (Rewrite as a complex sentence using *if*.)

4. ~~On~~ a clear night, many of the constellations can be seen with the naked eye. (Rewrite as a complex sentence [Unless] using *when*.)

5. ~~Either~~ we study the past, ~~or~~ we will repeat the mistakes of our ancestors. (Rewrite as a complex sentence using *unless*.)

6. The theme of this year's science fair is "Alternate Energy Sources"; several students are doing projects ~~that~~ involv~~e~~ ing solar energy. (Rewrite as a compound sentence.)

7. ~~After~~ [W]e developed the pictures, [and] we sent them to a newspaper. (Rewrite as a compound sentence.) [because]

8. Thousands of people gathered at Cape Canaveral/ they wanted to see the re-entry and landing of the space shuttle. (Rewrite as a complex sentence using *because*.)

9. The recipe called for butter/ [which] Juan did not have ~~any~~/ [so/] ~~H~~e [h] [so] used margarine. (Rewrite as a compound-complex sentence using *which* and *so*.)

10. [Although] Mara's family was not rich, ~~but~~ they were wealthy in many ways. (Rewrite as a complex sentence using *although*.)

617

Using Grammar in Writing

These challenging and enjoyable activities allow the students to see how the concepts of grammar, usage, and mechanics may be applied in actual writing situations. Each exercise is designed to allow students practice in several of the skills they have acquired in this Section. The activities also provide opportunities for students to write creatively about a wide variety of interesting and unusual subjects.

USING GRAMMAR IN WRITING
Using Compound and Complex Sentences

A. The following article contains only simple sentences. Rewrite the article, making some of the sentences compound and some complex. You may also include simple sentences with compound predicates.

> The earliest cameras were invented in the 1500's. They were difficult to use. They were very large, bulky, and awkward. Few people wanted to bother with them. Very few photographers existed. For over three hundred years after its invention, photography was almost unknown.
>
> During the mid-1800's Mathew Brady became a well-known photographer. He captured striking scenes of the U.S. Civil War. He took many formal portraits of President Lincoln. Brady stimulated public interest in photography.
>
> Few people had Brady's patience with large, complicated cameras. Then, in 1888, there was a great improvement. George Eastman invented the first box camera. It was much simpler than earlier cameras. It could easily be held in the hand. The camera cost $25. It had a leather case. It came with Eastman's new roll film.
>
> By 1900 the camera was even smaller and simpler. It sold for $1. More people could now afford one. Photography became the latest rage.
>
> Today, photography is a national hobby. We owe it all to George Eastman. Strangely enough, he was a terribly shy man. He rarely allowed his own picture to be taken.

B. Imagine that you are given the plans for an important new product to guard for a day. Spies from other companies are trying to steal these plans. What precautions would you take to be sure that they would not succeed? Write your ideas first in simple sentences only. Then go back and combine some of these sentences into compound or complex sentences for a more mature and fluid style.

CUMULATIVE REVIEW
The Sentence (I)

Kinds of Sentences. The paragraphs below contain simple sentences, compound sentences, complex sentences, and compound-complex sentences. Number your paper from 1 to 15. Next to each number, write either *S, CD, CX,* or *CD-CX* to identify the type of sentence it is. Also write *INT* next to the numbers of the interrogative sentences, and *E* next to the numbers of the exclamatory sentences.

1. S   (1) You have probably heard of the seven wonders of the an-
2. CX-INT cient world. (2) Did you know, though, that only one of these
3. CX   seven wonders is still standing? (3) That wonder is the Egyp-
          tian Pyramids, which were originally built as tombs for kings.
4. S   (4) The second wonder was the Hanging Gardens of Babylon.
5. CD-CX (5) These gardens hung about seventy-five feet above the
          ground, and they were irrigated by slaves who hauled up water
6. CD   from the Euphrates River. (6) The third wonder was the gold
          and ivory statue of the god Zeus at Olympia; the fourth was a
7. CX   temple of the goddess Artemis. (7) Archaeologists in Turkey
          recently found a few fragments of the temple, which was once
8. CX-E famous for its decoration and extensive use of marble. (8) How
          excited they must have been when these pieces were unearthed!
9. S
10. CX   (9) No traces of the other three wonders remain. (10) One
          was a tomb, or mausoleum, built for Mausolus, who was an of-
11. CD-CX ficial of the Persian empire. (11) There was also a colossal statue
          of Apollo in the harbor of Rhodes, Greece; this was said to be
12. CX   so huge that ships could pass between its legs. (12) Finally, there
          was a huge lighthouse of white marble, which stood for one
          thousand years and was finally toppled by an earthquake.
13. S   (13) Ancient builders contributed many marvels to the civ-
14. CX-E ilized world. (14) How much more awesome, though, are the
          events of nature that destroyed even these magnificent struc-
15. CD-INT tures! (15) Which of our own modern wonders will survive these
          powerful natural forces, and which will most impress future
          generations?

CUMULATIVE REVIEW
The Sentence (II)

Correcting Fragments and Run-ons. On your own paper, rewrite the following passage. Correct all sentence fragments and run-on sentences. You may have to add a few words, but most of the errors can be corrected with punctuation and <u>capitalization</u> changes only. Answers may vary.

Every day articles about the advantages and disadvantages of different types of energy are found In newspapers, magazines, and on television. There is so much information on these subjects that we find it hard to decide what would be the best course of action.

The fuel most used in the United States and throughout the world is oil; this is the same fuel that most experts believe will be exhausted within thirty years. Natural gas and coal and other sources of fossil fuels/ These are more abundant than oil, but, like oil, they will eventually be exhausted. In addition, coal produces harmful products when burned; these particles increase pollution of air and water.

Nuclear reactors currently produce about one-tenth of the energy in the United States/ And could easily supply more; many people, however, feel that the dangers of radioactivity are too high a price to pay for this form of energy.

Renewable energy sources, such as solar power and wind, are used very little at present. Solar collectors and wind turbines are expensive to build/, But some experts say that such sources could provide about one fourth of the United States' energy needs by the year 2000. Until the many problems of energy sources are solved/, Conservation, or using less energy, seems to be the best policy for ourselves and for the world.

CUMULATIVE REVIEW
The Sentence (III)

Writing Good Sentences. Rewrite each sentence on your own paper. Follow the directions given in parentheses. Answers will vary.

1. Sally looks like a powerful soccer player. (Change this N LV N sentence to one with an N V N pattern.)
2. Suddenly, somebody turned off all the stage lights. (Change the active verb to a passive verb.)
3. An eruption at Mount St. Helen's took place in 1980. About two thousand people were evacuated from the path of its destruction. (Change these simple sentences to one complex sentence.)
4. Repairs are needed on this highway. Accidents could occur. (Change these simple sentences to one compound sentence by adding the word "otherwise" and the proper punctuation.)
5. The slime monster was subdued by the furious chemist. (Change this passive verb to an active verb.)
6. Stephen made chili for dinner, and Sarah made a tossed green salad. (Change this compound sentence to a simple sentence with a compound subject and a compound direct object.)
7. I hope to become an oceanographer. (Add a prepositional phrase to this sentence.)
8. That omelet has a strange taste. (Change this N V N sentence to one with a N LV Adj. pattern.)
9. Maria tossed the Frisbee to Jeremy. (Change this N V N sentence to one with an N V N N pattern.)
10. Dr. Steinman treated Chuck for his broken collarbone. (Add the prepositional phrase "with the nurse's assistance.")

These exercises are designed to cover broad areas of grammar, usage, and mechanics. They require the application of skills taught thus far in the text. The exercises may be used for testing purposes, or as an excellent resource for review.

Section 12

The Right Word

You have studied the different parts of a sentence and how they function together to communicate ideas. The correct use of certain troublesome words is also necessary for writing clear, standard English.

Standard English is the language of educated people. It is the language that would be judged correct or appropriate in nearly all situations. **Nonstandard English**, on the other hand, is not generally considered correct or acceptable in all situations.

In this section you will study some specific words that can cause problems for writers. Learning to use these words correctly will help you write standard English.

Part 1 Words Often Confused

The words listed in this section are often misused. The words in each pair or group may look alike or have similar meanings. However, one word cannot replace another. Study the following words, and try to use the right word at the right time.

capital means "most important." It is used to refer to an upper case letter. It also names the city or town that is the official center of government for a state or country.

capitol refers to the building where a state legislature meets.

The **Capitol** is the building in Washington, D.C., where the United States Congress meets. Notice that the *c* is capitalized.

> The *capital* of New York is Albany.
> The state *capitol* dome can be seen for miles.
> Farmers protested outside the *Capitol* in Washington.

des′ ert means "a dry, barren region."
de sert′ means "to abandon."
des sert′ (note the difference in spelling) is a sweet food at the end of a meal.

> The explorers were stranded in the *desert*.
> Did the soldier *desert* his company?
> Our *dessert* tonight is banana cake.

hear means "to listen to" or "to receive sound by the ear."
here refers to this place.

> Did you *hear* the screeching brakes?
> A new record store will open *here*.

its is a possessive, meaning belonging to *it*.
it's is the contraction for *it is* or *it has*.

> The band has *its* own sound system.
> *It's* almost midnight.

loose means either "not tight" or "free and untied."
lose means "to be unable to find or keep." It is also the opposite of *win*.

Objective

To distinguish between words often confused

Presenting the Lesson

1. Read and discuss pages 623–625. Go over the differences in spelling for each of the pairs or groups of words. Give the students hints about how to remember the spellings. For example, they can remember that *stationery* with the *-er* is the one that has to do with *paper*, which also has an *-er*. Ask the students for any similar mnemonic devices that they have come up with. Also point out that the *its* that is a possessive does *not* have the *-'s* which they commonly associate with possessives.

2. Assign and discuss Exercises A and B on page 625.

Individualizing the Lesson

Less-Advanced Students

Provide additional practice by going over the following sentences with the students. Ask them to find errors and tell how they should be corrected.

1. We didn't know weather the whether would improve.
2. It's so hot in the desert that your likely to become ill.
3. The principle reason I went out was to buy stationery, but it was too expensive.
4. Your foolish not to visit the state capitol during your vacation.
5. Whose going to be the winner? I know I will lose.
6. The crew did not want to dessert the ship, but it became too dangerous to stay on board.

623

7. The pipe is supposed to be stationary, but its loose.
8. Do you mean your to full for dessert?
9. The protesters remained at the capital on principle.
10. The Congress is voting in the Capitol on the issue of capital punishment; their deciding whether it is to harsh a punishment for any crime.

Advanced Students

Have students write their own sentences that include the following word pairs.

1. whether, weather
2. capital, capitol
3. your, you're
4. lose, loose
5. whose, who's
6. too, to
7. its, it's
8. their, there

Optional Practice

Have students fill in the blanks in the paragraph below with words presented in Part 1.

Our class visited the state _____ last spring, but the _____ was _____ cold for us to enjoy the outdoor sights. However, we did get to _____ the state senators debate the passage of an important law. While we were _____ we saw the _____ of democratic government in action.

Extending the Lesson

Ask students to write a paper that includes as many of the twenty-six words presented in Part 1 as possible.

Several snakes from the zoo are *loose*.
I *lose* my balance when I spin on skates.
Did the wrestlers *lose* the meet?

principal means "leading," "chief," or "highest in importance, rank, or degree."
principle refers to a basic truth, rule, or law.

The *principal* industry here is steel-making.
The basic *principle* of this country is a free and democratic society.

stationary means "not moving, fixed."
stationery refers to writing paper and envelopes.

The trailer can move, but right now it's *stationary*.
The drugstore sells boxes of *stationery*.

their shows possession by *them*.
there means "in that place."
they're is the contraction for *they are*.

The steelworkers have *their* own union.
The bus route ends *there*.
They're losing their courage.

to means "toward" or "as far as."
too means "also" or "extremely."

Tracy slid *to* home plate.
I read the book, and I saw the movie *too*.

weather refers to the condition of the atmosphere, such as its heat or cold, wetness or dryness.
whether indicates a choice between two things.

The *weather* in Hawaii is usually pleasant.
Ask Stacy *whether* she is going or staying.

who's is the contraction for *who is* or *who has*.
whose is the possessive form of *who*.

Who's running the computer?
Whose sandwich is this?

your shows possession by *you*.

you're is the contraction for *you are* or *you were*.

When is *your* birthday?

You're on the team, aren't you?

Exercise A: Choose the right word from the words given.

1. From the top of the Washington Monument, we looked down at the white dome of the nation's (capital, capitol, Capitol).
2. The (deserted, desserted) building was about to be demolished.
3. Sand dunes in the (desert, dessert) are always shifting due to wind and rain.
4. We could (hear, here) the alarm four blocks away.
5. The computer at our school can correct some of (its, it's) own mistakes.
6. (Its, It's) time to leave for the show.
7. Ballet slippers should be tight, not (loose, lose).
8. I don't want to (loose, lose) this match.
9. The (principals, principles) stated in the Hippocratic Oath are still important to doctors.
10. The letter was typed on official (stationary, stationery).

Exercise B: Follow the directions for Exercise A.

1. We ate (their, there) for Mom's birthday.
2. Sometimes the players get careless when (their, there, they're) ahead.
3. All the students in the speech class have heard (their, there, they're) own voices on tape.
4. The bowling ball veered (to, too) far to the left.
5. The Rosens drove (to, too) Syracuse for Thanksgiving.
6. Are you getting off at this stop, (to, too)?
7. I wonder (weather, whether) I should call her or write her a letter.
8. (Who's, Whose) responsible for that decision?
9. (Who's, Whose) story do you believe?
10. (Your, You're) too worried about how you look.

Part 2

Objective

To distinguish verbs in troublesome pairs

Presenting the Lesson

1. Read and discuss pages 626–628. Give special emphasis to the principal parts of *lie* and *lay*. After going over all of the pairs of verbs, call on students to think of sentences for the following: *sit*, *lay*, *bring*, *may*, *take*, *let*, *set*.

2. Assign and discuss Exercises A and B on page 629. Suggest that they view Exercise C as a proofreading activity.

Individualizing the Lesson

Less-Advanced Students

Conduct an oral drill of the three principle parts of each problem verb. Concentrate on any that seem to be a result of dialect.

Advanced Students

Have students write sentences in which they use the following verb pairs.

1. raise, can   4. rise, bring
2. lie, teach   5. lie, sit
3. take, may   6. lay, set

Reinforcement Exercises

Assign and discuss Exercises A and B on page 634.

Optional Practice

Present the following sentences and go over them orally with the students, correcting any errors in verb usage.

Part 2   Troublesome Verbs

These pairs of verbs are often confused. Notice how they differ.

Bring and *Take*

Bring refers to movement toward the person speaking. Example: The pipeline *brings* water here to the desert.

Take refers to motion away from the speaker. Example: Did you *take* those books back to the library?

Here are the principal parts of these verbs:

bring, brought, brought

PRESENT: *Bring* that hammer to me, please
PAST: We *brought* Janet with us.
PAST PARTICIPLE: No one *has brought* enough money.

take, took, taken

PRESENT: When you leave, *take* some cake.
PAST: I *took* my cycle there to be fixed.
PAST PARTICIPLE: Someone *has taken* my keys.

Learn and *Teach*

Learn means "to gain knowledge or skill." Example: Did you *learn* the words to that song?

Teach means "to help someone learn." Example: Will you *teach* me to dribble?

Here are the principal parts of these verbs:

learn, learned, learned

PRESENT: *Learn* the metric system.
PAST: Cal *learned* karate.
PAST PARTICIPLE: We *have learned* Spanish.

teach, taught, taught

PRESENT: Mrs. Rivera *teaches* music.
PAST: Kelly *taught* me about photography.
PAST PARTICIPLE: This course *has taught* us about carpentry.

Let and Leave

Let means "to allow or permit." Example: *Let* her go.
Leave means "to go away from" or "to allow something to remain." Example: *Leave* us alone.
The principal parts of these verbs are as follows:

let, let, let

PRESENT:	*Let* the motor run for a minute.
PAST:	Dad *let* the dog out.
PAST PARTICIPLE:	The landlord *has let* us stay.

leave, left, left

PRESENT:	*Leave* your jacket on.
PAST:	Jennifer *left* in a hurry.
PAST PARTICIPLE:	The robbers *had left* with the cash.

Lie and Lay

Lie means "to rest in a flat position" or "to be in a certain place." Example: *Lie* still.
Lay means "to place." Example: *Lay* the wreath here.
Here are the principal parts of these verbs:

lie, lay, lain

PRESENT:	*Lie* down on this mat.
PAST:	Jason *lay* in bed all day.
PAST PARTICIPLE:	The patient *has lain* very still.

lay, laid, laid

PRESENT:	*Lay* the baby in her crib.
PAST:	The nurse *laid* a bandage on the wound.
PAST PARTICIPLE:	Workers *have laid* the foundation.

May and Can

May refers to the granting of permission. *May* also refers to something that is possible. *Might* is the past tense of *may*.

May we *have* dessert?   It *may* snow.   I *might be* wrong.

1. Use my car to bring the books back to the library.
2. You can stay up till midnight on New Year's Eve.
3. Frank learned me how to play chess.
4. If you lay in the sun too long, you will get a burn.
5. At school we rise the flag every morning.
6. Until the doctor arrives, you must set in the waiting room.
7. Ask George to set the package on the porch.
8. You may lie your books on the stage.
9. The trainer is learning the dogs to sit.
10. When you go to Aunt Suzie's house, take some of these cookies.

Extending the Lesson

Explain that some nonstandard usages may be the result of the dialect, or speech pattern, of a particular area or group of people. Challenge students to find examples of such variations in the dialogue of a TV show, story, or novel. Emphasize that this variety of language adds color to our spoken language but should be avoided in formal situations.

Can means being physically or mentally able to do something. *Could* is the past tense of *can*.

> *Can* you *do* a push-up?   We *could* not *remember*.

May and *might* and *can* and *could* are never used alone. They are used as helping verbs.

Rise and *Raise*

Rise means "to go upward." Example: The sun *rises*.
Raise means "to lift" or "to make something go up." Example: *Raise* your right hand.
The principal parts of these verbs are as follows:

rise, rose, risen

PRESENT:	The steam *rises* and disappears.
PAST:	The choir *rose* from their seats.
PAST PARTICIPLE:	The drawbridge *has risen*.

raise, raised, raised

PRESENT:	Please *raise* the window shade.
PAST:	Kim *raised* the ladder to reach the roof.
PAST PARTICIPLE:	Inflation *has raised* the cost of living.

Sit and *Set*

Sit means "to occupy a seat." Example: *Sit* on this bench.
Set means "to place." Example: *Set* the tools there.
The principal parts of these verbs are as follows:

sit, sat, sat

PRESENT:	*Sit* near me, please.
PAST:	We *sat* in the waiting room.
PAST PARTICIPLE:	All of the passengers *have sat* down.

set, set, set

PRESENT:	*Set* your toothbrush on the sink.
PAST:	John *set* the books in his new bookcase.
PAST PARTICIPLE:	We *have set* the costumes backstage.

Exercise A: Choose the right verb from the two given.

1. We (sat, set) aside some money in a savings account.
2. The sales tax has (raised, risen) to 6 percent.
3. Litter (lay, laid) all over the park.
4. Stranded passengers (sat, set) in the airport.
5. You can't (bring, take) your bike in here.
6. The dog (learned, taught) to obey simple commands.
7. Someone (let, left) the computer turned on.
8. (May, Can) I use Dad's jigsaw?
9. The photographer (sat, set) the film in a jar to develop.
10. Mom's boss (raised, rose) her pay.

Exercise B: Follow the directions for Exercise A.

1. Leonne insists she (may not, cannot) carry a tune.
2. (Take, Bring) those books to the library, please.
3. Mr. Ross (laid, lay) a new kitchen floor today.
4. Who (learned, taught) you judo?
5. When (may, can) you cut the grass?
6. The gymsuit has (lain, laid) in that locker all year.
7. Will you (let, leave) us skate on your pond?
8. Jenny says we (may, can) have the party here.
9. Annie Sullivan (taught, learned) Helen Keller to speak.
10. The factory (raised, rose) its level of production.

Exercise C: Writing Find the errors in the following sentences. Rewrite the sentences correcting the errors. If a sentence has no errors, write *Correct*.

1. Mrs. Motosaka learned me the art of origami. taught
2. Can I look through your scrapbook? May
3. Set the tray on the kitchen counter. correct
4. The cat was laying on the rug near the woodburning stove. lying
5. When you go to the zoo, bring your camera. correct
6. It took four years to lay the transcontinental railroad. correct
7. The curtain has raised, and the play has begun. risen
8. The palace guard leaved the ambassador enter the gates. let
9. Aunt Lydia set down in the seat behind the bus driver. sat
10. May dolphins live indefinitely underwater, without surfacing? Can

629

Objective

To use problem words correctly

Presenting the Lesson

1. Read and discuss pages 630–631. Complete Exercise A on page 631 orally with the class.

2. Read and discuss page 632. Complete Exercise A on page 633 orally with the class.

3. Assign Exercise B on page 631 and Exercise B on page 633 to be completed individually.

Individualizing the Lesson

Provide additional practice. Go over the following sentences with the students, asking them to correct any errors.

1. A good friend will always borrow you what you need.
2. I cannot except such an expensive gift.
3. Let's keep this information between the three of us.
4. There were fewer empty seats than there should of been.
5. John acted like there was some sort of a problem.
6. Everyone filed into the gym accept the graduating seniors.
7. Labor Day is a ways off, sometime in September.
8. Alright, we'll divide the prize money among the two winners.
9. I don't agree with the plan the committee outlined.
10. Less noise in the study hall led to less errors on assignments.

Advanced Students

Have students write sentences that include the following word pairs.

Part 3 Usage Problems

The words in this section are often used incorrectly. Notice the standard usages for these problem words.

accept means "to agree to something" or "to receive something willingly."

except means "to leave out." *Except* also means "not including."

> "I *accept* the blame," Todd said.
> "We'll *except* you from this rule," the counselor said.
> We bought all the supplies *except* glue.

agree on means "to come to an understanding." You and others agree *on* a plan.

agree to means "to consent to." You agree *to* something, such as a plan.

agree with means "to have the same opinion as someone else." You agree *with* somebody. *Agree with* may also be used in a colloquial sense to refer to something being suitable, as when foods don't *agree with* you.

all right is the correct spelling. The spelling *alright* is nonstandard English and should not be used.

> *All right*, I'll turn off the TV.
> Ariel felt *all right* after she got off the boat.

among refers to a group of more than two people or things.
between refers to two people or things.

> We divided the food *among* the four of us.
> There is a treaty *between* the two countries.

anywhere, nowhere, somewhere, and **anyway** are standard usages. The words *anywheres, nowheres, somewheres*, and *anyways* are nonstandard. The final *s* should be dropped.

> NONSTANDARD: She wasn't anywheres in sight.
> STANDARD: She wasn't *anywhere* in sight.

> NONSTANDARD: I know that clip is here somewheres.
> STANDARD: I know that clip is here *somewhere*.

between each, followed by a singular noun, is incorrect. *Between* should not be used with a singular noun.

> NONSTANDARD: Between each game, the Bears practiced hard.
> STANDARD: *Between games*, the Bears practiced hard.

> NONSTANDARD: The elevator stopped between every floor.
> STANDARD: The elevator stopped *between floors*.

borrow means "to receive something on loan." Don't confuse it with *lend*, meaning "to give out temporarily."

> NONSTANDARD: Will you borrow me your pen?
> STANDARD: Will you *lend* me your pen?
> STANDARD: May I *borrow* your pen?

Exercise A: Writing Look for sentences with nonstandard usage. Rewrite those sentences, using the right words.

1. Between each quarter of the game, the band plays. Between quarters
2. Every block accept ours has sidewalks. except
3. Will you borrow me your bicycle? lend
4. Do you feel all right? correct
5. TV time was divided equally among the three candidates. correct
6. Did you agree on what that columnist wrote? with
7. Scott couldn't find his calculator anywheres. anywhere
8. The jury agreed on a verdict. correct
9. My purse has to be around here somewheres. somewhere
10. Jane found it hard to except praise. accept

Exercise B: Writing Follow the directions for Exercise A.

1. Bill borrowed me his new video game. lent
2. The shoe store has every size accept the one I need. except
3. Did Jessica and David agree with the best route to take? on
4. Alright, tell me what's bothering you. All right
5. The family chose among the two sailboats. between
6. Rock walls stood between each field. between fields
7. The vice-president agreed with the plan. to
8. Anyways, I'm heading for home. Anyway
9. Ken borrowed my hat for the costume party. correct
10. The President excepted the resignation of his aide. accepted

fewer refers to numbers of things that can be counted.
less refers to amount or quantity.

> Did Nicklaus win *fewer* tournaments than Snead?
> We hear *less* noise in the country.

in means "inside something."
into tells of motion from the outside to the inside of something.

NONSTANDARD:	The performers went in the studio.
STANDARD:	The performers went *into* the studio.

NONSTANDARD:	Joe hit the hockey puck in the goal.
STANDARD:	Joe hit the hockey puck *into* the goal.

kind of a and **sort of a** are nonstandard. The *a* is not necessary.

NONSTANDARD:	What kind of a radio do you have?
STANDARD:	What *kind of* radio do you have?

NONSTANDARD:	There is some sort of a problem here.
STANDARD:	There is some *sort of* problem here.

like can be a preposition. Using *like* as a conjunction before a clause is not fully accepted. Especially in writing, it is better to use *as* or *as if*.

NONSTANDARD:	*Like* I said, you can depend on Sara.
STANDARD:	*As* I said, you can depend on Sara.

NONSTANDARD:	Ramon talked *like* he had a cold.
STANDARD:	Ramon talked *as if* he had a cold.

of is sometimes incorrectly used in phrases like *could of, shouldn't of,* and *must of.* The correct word is *have* or its contraction: *could have, could've, shouldn't have, must have, might have, might've.*

NONSTANDARD:	Darryl should of locked his bike.
STANDARD:	Darryl *should have* locked his bike.

ways does not refer to distance. *Way* is correct.

NONSTANDARD:	We drove a short ways down the road.
STANDARD:	We drove a short *way* down the road.

Exercise A: Writing Rewrite the sentences that contain nonstandard usage. If a sentence is correct, write *Correct*.

1. Chris acted <u>like</u> the world was ending. as if
2. I make <u>less</u> phone calls than Penny. fewer
3. Carolyn stuffed her change <u>in</u> her pocket. into
4. A dalmatian is less nervous than a poodle. correct
5. <u>Like</u> the President says, we must conserve energy. As
6. There are <u>less</u> new TV programs this season. fewer
7. The center should <u>of</u> practiced her lay-up shots. have
8. What <u>kind of a</u> penalty did the ref call? kind of
9. The stadium is <u>a ways farther</u> south. farther
10. Cautiously, they stepped <u>in</u> the deserted house. into

Exercise B: Writing Follow the directions for Exercise A.

1. Kate has <u>less</u> lines to memorize in this play. fewer
2. The council must <u>of</u> held some sort of a meeting. have
3. The movie ended just <u>like</u> I thought it would. as
4. Lauren slipped a message <u>in</u> our mailbox. into
5. Fewer radio stations are playing the top ten songs now. correct
6. The reservoir is quite <u>a ways</u> from here. a way
7. <u>Less</u> people go to the later show. Fewer
8. Jim looks <u>like</u> he needs more time. as if
9. What kind of sausage goes on the pizza? correct
10. We should <u>of</u> stopped at the park for our picnic. have

These Reinforcement Exercises may be used for additional practice of the concepts presented in this Section. Each exercise focuses on a single concept, and should be used after the page number indicated in parentheses.

Review

If you have not assigned these Reinforcement Exercises before this time, you can also use them as an excellent Section Review.

REINFORCEMENT EXERCISES
The Right Word

A. Use confusing pairs of words correctly. Choose the correct word from the two given. (Use after page 625.)

1. Did you (loose, lose) your ticket stub?
2. Have you worn (your, you're) down vest yet?
3. The fish had jumped out of (it's, its) bowl.
4. Proper nouns begin with (capitol, capital) letters.
5. The schools were closed because of severe (weather, whether) conditions.
6. When Amie moved (here, hear), she didn't know anyone.
7. (Who's, Whose) going to the Science Fair on Saturday?
8. That house has been (desserted, deserted) for years.
9. (Principles, Principals) of Modern Agriculture is my brother's favorite college class.
10. (There, They're, Their) are many people who disagree with that statement.

B. Use troublesome verbs correctly. Choose the correct word. (Use after page 629.)

1. The alarm didn't go off because you (set, sat) it incorrectly.
2. Can you (learn, teach) me how to windsurf?
3. (Leave, Let) me do this by myself.
4. Please (bring, take) me the desk calendar.
5. (May, Can) you play a musical instrument?
6. Mr. Kim (learned, taught) us Tae-Kwon-Do.
7. You shouldn't (let, leave) your camera in the car.
8. The test pilot (sat, set) at the controls.
9. Meredith (lay, laid) awake and couldn't sleep.
10. The oil has (raised, risen) to the surface of the sea.

C. Use problem words correctly. Choose the correct answer. (Use after page 633.)

1. Denver is a long (way, ways) from Baltimore.
2. What (kind of a, kind of) truck is this?
3. Tim jumped (in, into) the lake from the pier.

4. (All right, Alright), we'll agree (with, on, to) a rematch.
5. Will you (borrow, lend) me your Bill Cosby tape?
6. The Eskimos divided their catch (between, among) all the villagers.
7. Juan graciously (excepted, accepted) my apology.
8. Trisha looked (as if, like) she didn't feel well.
9. There is a curb (between, between each) parking spaces.
10. I should (have, of) eaten (fewer, less) pretzels.

D. Use standard English. Rewrite these sentences. Correct all nonstandard usage. (Use after page 633.)

1. The art league hear announced it's annual contest. here, its
2. I don't know weather the conductor will except the ticket. whether, accept
3. Do you get homesick when your a long ways from home? you're, way
4. You should of taken an earlier ferry. have
5. Raise the cage door and leave the dog run lose. let, loose
6. In England, the driver of a car sets on the right side. sits
7. Is it to late too buy tickets for the concert? too, to
8. Alright, I'll meet you somewheres if we can agree on a place. All right, somewhere
9. My sister always carries less books than I do, but she goes to her locker between each class. fewer, between classes
10. Before they're events, the swimmers laid on the pool deck. their, lay

635

These exercises provide review of the concepts presented in this Section. Each exercise challenges the students to apply several of the skills they have acquired during previous study. Because the "mixed" feature of these activities makes them more difficult, the teacher may wish to have less-advanced students do them orally or in small groups.

MIXED REVIEW
The Right Word

A. Choose the correct answer from those given in parentheses.

1. (Whose, Who's) idea was it to display the posters (here, hear)?
2. The (capitol, capital) of Nova Scotia is Halifax.
3. Arizona is a healthy place for some people to live because of (its, it's) (desert, dessert) climate.
4. Next year we will (lose, loose) our (principle, principal) volleyball player because she is transferring to another high school.
5. For thousands of years, people thought that the earth was (stationary, stationery).
6. Since the freshmen were successful with (they're, their, there) car wash, the sophomores decided to have one (to, too, two).
7. Visitors to Hawaii report that the (whether, weather) (there, their, they're) is ideal.
8. (Your, You're) supposed to make (less, fewer) mistakes on a retest, not more!
9. (Its, It's) pleasant to (sit, set) back and watch the clouds roll overhead.
10. He asked if it would be (alright, all right) if he (laid, lay) his books on my desk.
11. Everyone (agrees on, agrees with, agrees to) the plan (except, accept) Tim.
12. If you're tired you can (lay, lie) down over (here, hear) on the sofa.
13. Evan (could have, could of) stayed on his diet if he hadn't eaten that (dessert, desert).
14. That baby is older, but it has (fewer, less) hair on (it's, its) head.
15. Vic jumped (in, into) the van and sat down (between, among) Zach and Chris.

B. Find the errors in the following sentences. Then, rewrite the sentences correctly. If a sentence has no errors, write *Correct*.

1. Jennifer asked her brother to let her alone for a few minutes. leave
2. We should be able to resolve this problem between the four of us. among
3. It is often difficult for parents and children to agree on a curfew. correct
4. The shy players were reluctant to except there awards. accept, their
5. Jackie acts like she's angry at the world today. as if
6. May I have some extra time to finish this report? correct
7. Chris laid in bed until she felt all right. lay
8. The Mid-Atlantic Ridge, a mountain range of 10,000 miles long, raises from the floor of the Atlantic Ocean. rises
9. I set your shoes near the door like you asked me. as
10. Beth could of made the traveling team if she hadn't broken her ankle. have
11. A guard was positioned between each column of the Capitol. between columns
12. What kind of a radio do you have? kind of
13. Rick shouldn't of lain his wallet on the table. have, laid
14. The manager left us stay for the next show because the theater was empty. let
15. Put the album I borrowed you in its jacket so it doesn't get dusty. lent

USING GRAMMAR IN WRITING
The Right Word

The great American tall tale is being revived these days in stories that are being told about the fast-growing vine, *kudzu*. Originally planted to prevent erosion in the South, the kudzu vines
quickly spread over trees, telephone poles, houses, barns, and
abandoned cars. Kudzu grows as much as a foot a day, and is now
moving toward the West. Below is a typical tall tale of the kudzu,
containing many incorrectly used words. Read through the story
and then revise it, correcting all nonstandard English.

       ^{As}
Like I started to tell that agriculture expert who came down
^{here} hear from the Capitol, the kudzu's not a plant: <u>Its</u>^{It's} a kind of a
green monster. Anywhere you go around <u>hear</u>,^{here} you may see
whole farms with nothing left on them but the tip of a silo <u>rais</u>-
^{rising} ing up out of a mountain of kudzu. <u>Their</u>'s^{There's} no stopping it be-
^{weather} cause these vines grow as fast in bad <u>whether</u> as in good, though
^{there} ^{fewer} I've heard it said that <u>their</u> are <u>less</u> leaves on them when the
temperature drops under fifty below zero. Now, you may think
^{have} I'm exaggerating, but you should <u>of</u> seen what happened to that
^{teach} agriculture man when he tried to <u>learn</u> the farmers around <u>hear</u>^{here}
how to get rid of this pesky weed. That so-called expert took a
^{way} can of weedkiller to a farm just a short <u>ways</u> down the road from
my place, and I guess he figured that that kudzu was just going
^{lie there} to <u>lay</u> their <u>stationery</u> while he sprayed it. However, as soon as
^{stationary}
^{into} he walked <u>in</u> that kudzu field, the vine saw what he was doing
^{raised} and grabbed him. It was a sight. That plant <u>rose</u> him right off
^{set} the ground and <u>sat</u> him down <u>in</u>^{into} the top of a sycamore tree. We
called the volunteer fire department to get him down, but when
^{heard} that vine <u>hered</u> the sirens, it grabbed him again and <u>rose</u>^{raised} him
up higher and higher until his head hit the underside of a cloud.
^{there too} I imagine he's still up <u>their, to</u>. I guess he would <u>of</u>^{have} starved to
^{lent} death if I hadn't <u>borrowed</u> the fire department my shotgun so
they could shoot biscuits up to him. That kudzu's mean. <u>Ex</u>-
^{Accept} cept my word for it. I was <u>their</u>. ^{there}

638

Section 13

Capitalization

Section Objectives

1. To capitalize all proper nouns and adjectives

2. To capitalize the first word in various written constructions

Preparing the Students

Put the following sentence on the board.

*m*other and *f*ather are driving south to the *c*alifornia side of the *w*hite *m*ountains to see *m*ethuselah and the other bristlecone pines that date back to the third millenium *b.c.*

Ask the students to say which words in the sentence should be capitalized. If they are not sure about some of them, tell them that the Section they are about to study will answer these and many more questions about capitalization.

Additional Resources

Diagnostic Test — See page 8 in the test booklet. Recommended for use before teaching the Section.

Mastery Test — See pages 71–72 in the test booklet. Recommended for use after teaching the Section.

Additional Exercises — See pages 651–655 in the student text.

Skills Practice Book — pages 181–187.

Duplicating Masters — pages 181–187.

Special Populations — See special section at the front of this Teacher's Edition.

Like most other conventions of language, capital letters help make writing easier to read. They call attention to certain special words and indicate the beginnings of sentences.

There are specific rules for capitalizing words. This section will show you the rules. You can refer to this section at any time if you have questions about capitalization.

Objective

To capitalize all proper nouns and adjectives

Presenting the Lesson

1. Read and discuss pages 640–641. Spend extra time on family relationships. Assign and discuss Exercise A on page 642.

2. Read and discuss pages 643–644. Spend extra time on sections of the country vs. directions on the compass. Assign and discuss Exercise A on page 644.

3. Read and discuss pages 645–646. Emphasize the difference between the general name of a school subject and the specific name of a course. Assign and discuss Exercise A on page 646.

4. Assign and discuss Exercise B on page 642, Exercise B on page 644, and Exercise B on page 647 as a cumulative review of this part.

Individualizing the Lesson

Less-Advanced Students

Present the following sentences for additional practice. Have students capitalize words when necessary.

1. My sister, juliette, was born on valentine's day, february 14, 1970. That was a joyful spring in my family.
2. Cancer research is being conducted at st. jude's hospital in tennessee.
3. The treaty of versailles, signed when woodrow wilson was president, ended world war I.
4. I cashed my check at sears bank and trust company.

Part 1 Proper Nouns and Adjectives

Capitalize proper nouns and proper adjectives.

As you learned in Section 3, a **proper noun** is the name of a particular person, place, or thing. In contrast, a **common noun** is the name of a whole group of people, places, or things. A **proper adjective** is an adjective formed from a proper noun.

COMMON NOUN	PROPER NOUN	PROPER ADJECTIVE
queen	Victoria	Victorian
country	Ireland	Irish
government	Congress	Congressional

There are many different kinds of proper nouns. The following rules will help you to identify the types of nouns that should be capitalized.

Names of People

Capitalize people's names. Also capitalize the initials or abbreviations that stand for names.

F. D. Roosevelt	**F**ranklin **D**elano **R**oosevelt
Susan **B. A**nthony	**S**usan **B**rownell **A**nthony

Capitalize the titles used with people's names. Also capitalize the initials or abbreviations that stand for those titles.

The titles *Miss, Ms., Mrs.,* and *Mr.* are always capitalized.

Gov. R. T. Alberg	**M**ajor Edward J. Brooks
Ms. Susan Manzano	**D**r. Evelyn Santucci
Judge Ellen O'Brien	**R**ev. L. K. Jenkins

Do not capitalize a title that is used without a name. It is a common noun.

Barbara Sloan is president of the bank.
The judge in this courtroom is Justice Black.

Capitalize titles of very high importance, even when they are used without names.

the **P**resident of the United States
the **C**hief **J**ustice of the Supreme Court
the **P**rime **M**inister of Canada
a **C**ongresswoman
the **P**ope

Family Relationships

Capitalize such family words as *mother, father, aunt,* **and** *uncle* **when they are used as names. If the noun is preceded by a possessive word or by** *a, an,* **or** *the,* **it is not capitalized.**

What was **D**ad like when he was sixteen, **G**randma?
Jessica's **m**other is here, **M**om.
We call our **a**unt and **u**ncle **U**ncle Hy and **A**unt Lo.
My **m**om's car needs a new battery.
The **f**ather in the show was played by James Stewart.

The Pronoun *I*

Capitalize the pronoun *I.*

He and **I** saw a movie.   **I** work after school.

The Supreme Being
and Sacred Writings

Capitalize all words referring to God, to the Holy Family, and to religious scriptures.

the **A**lmighty   the **B**ible   the **S**on of **G**od
the **L**ord   the **T**almud   the **N**ew **T**estament
the **B**lessed **V**irgin   **A**llah   the **B**ook of **J**ob

Capitalize personal pronouns referring to God.

They asked the Lord for **H**is blessing.

5. The month of july is named after julius caesar, who died in 44 b.c.
6. The psalms have some of the most beautiful poetry in the old testament.
7. Ask your mother if you can take latin as well as german this fall.
8. The panama canal links the atlantic and pacific oceans.
9. Uncle george and father bought a model t ford and restored it.
10. The east is famous for its colleges, but i am heading west for a school in oregon.

Advanced Students

Have students try to write a newspaper story using the following words correctly

1. east   6. Queen
2. West   7. President
3. brother   8. vice-president
4. Mother   9. the car
5. queen   10. Le Car

Reinforcement Exercises

Assign and discuss Exercises A, B, and C on pages 651–652.

Optional Practice

Have the students correct the capitalization in the sentences below.

1. My sister, margretta, learned to play the harp from sister angelina of st. matthew's convent.
2. The president of our club insisted that we all listen to the president's state of the union address.
3. Every winter my family goes south to enjoy the southern hospitality of my aunt belva and uncle wendell.
4. The workers of the third century b.c. could have used an organization like the a.f.l.–c.i.o.
5. I would like to study sub-atomic physics and swahili, but they are not offered at central high school.

6. A song was written about the train they called the city of new orleans.
7. Even-number highways, like route 80, go east and west.
8. The neo-classical period in literature is sometimes called the augustine era.
9. Attila the hun ruled much of northern asia and europe during the 5th century a.d.
10. Our minister, rev. barkin, read from kings, job, and chronicles in the old testament.

Extending the Lesson

Ask the students if they know what the abbreviations A.D. and B.C. mean. If not, have them find out.

Exercise A: Copy the following sentences. Change small letters to <u>capital</u> <u>letters</u> wherever necessary.

1. A hurricane hit the town that dad and i were visiting.
2. My mother's medical doctor is dr. herrera and her dentist is dr. alexander.
3. If you enjoy being scared, read the horror stories of h.p. lovecraft.
4. The new testament of the bible was written many years after christ died.
5. Yesterday ms. turner told me that i could now call her sgt. turner.
6. The pope visited his homeland in 1983.
7. The director of st. christopher hospital is my cousin, rowine hayes brown.
8. Some religions honor god by not speaking his name.
9. In her lecture, professor bailey explained how laws are made.
10. State sen. dawn clark netsch sponsored the bill to protect consumers against fraud.

Exercise B: Follow the directions for Exercise A.

1. Can nate tell mr. banzali the most direct route from grand rapids to memphis?
2. The best-known leader of the dakota tribes was chief sitting bull.
3. The ten commandments are recorded in the book of exodus.
4. Did lorene help with the work on your brother's bike?
5. Few people who write to the president of the united states receive a personal answer.
6. Ms. eppie lederer gives advice under the name of ann landers.
7. My cousin dale and i work at mr. j. j. vernon's downtown office.
8. Did dad make an appointment with dr. case?
9. According to the gospels, adam and eve disobeyed god.
10. Will the president meet with governor ray?

Geographic Names

In a geographical name, capitalize the first letter of each word except articles and prepositions.

If the article *the* appears before a place name, it is not part of the name and is therefore not capitalized.

CONTINENTS: Africa, North America, Europe, Asia

BODIES OF WATER: the Atlantic Ocean, the Ohio River, the Gulf of Mexico, the South China Sea, Hudson Bay, the Panama Canal, Lake Michigan

LAND FORMS: Mount McKinley, Aleutian Islands, Death Valley, Cadillac Mountain, the Black Hills, Cape Lookout

POLITICAL UNITS: Florida, Denver, Province of Ontario, Republic of Kenya, State of Israel, Thirteenth Congressional District

PUBLIC AREAS: Glacier National Park, Fort Sumter, Badlands National Monument, Ford Theater, Dunes State Park, Fallen Timbers Battlefield

ROADS AND HIGHWAYS: Route 66, Interstate Highway 610, Hampton Road, Thornwood Avenue, Main Street

Directions and Sections

Capitalize names of sections of the country.

The West has several old trading posts.
The South is sometimes called "Dixie."
The Sorensons moved from New England to the West Coast.

Capitalize proper adjectives that come from names of sections of the country.

a Midwestern town   Western saddle
Southern food   East Coast company

Do not capitalize directions of the compass.

Barrow, Alaska, is north of all other United States cities.
Drive east on Interstate 80 to New York.

Do not capitalize adjectives that come from words showing direction.

> The parking lot is on the north side of the building.
> The southerly breeze turned into a fierce wind.

Exercise A: Number your paper from 1 to 10. Find the words in the following sentences that should be capitalized. Write the words after the proper number, using the necessary capital letters.

1. The tenth congressional district is north of chicago.
2. There is an extinct volcano called mount shasta in california.
3. The yucatan channel connects the gulf of mexico with the caribbean sea.
4. The andes mountains are in south america.
5. The district of columbia's biggest park is rock creek park.
6. Some southern foods are now popular in the north.
7. Hurricanes attacked the southeast, and tornadoes hit the southwest.
8. Both interstate 90 and route 20 run from albany to buffalo, new york.
9. The north defeated the south in a key battle at gettysburg, pennsylvania.
10. In japan, the cities are extremely crowded.

Exercise B: Writing Rewrite the following paragraph, adding capital letters where necessary.

A trip to the east coast isn't complete without a visit to the boston area. The capital of massachusetts, this old new england town is rich in historical and scenic attractions. The famous freedom trail wends among such landmarks as faneuil hall, the old north church, and the old state house. A walk on beacon street will take one past boston common, the oldest park in america. Among the tourist attractions outside the city is the village of concord, on route 2. Going south of boston on route 28 will bring you to cape cod, a tourist haven in summer, with its quaint atlantic villages and its beautiful national seashore park.

Organizations and Institutions

Capitalize the names of organizations and institutions, including political parties, governmental bodies or agencies, schools, colleges, churches, hospitals, clubs, businesses, and abbreviations of these names.

Republican Party	Children's Memorial Hospital
Federal Trade Commission	American Medical Association
Stevenson High School	National Urban League
St. Joseph's Church	AFL-CIO

Do not capitalize such words as *school*, *company*, *church*, and *hospital* when they are not used as parts of names.

Several people from our church work at the hospital.

Events, Documents, and Periods of Time

Capitalize the names of historical events, documents, and periods of time.

Battle of Concord	Panama Canal Treaty
Vietnam War	the Middle Ages
United States Constitution	the Reformation

Months, Days, and Holidays

Capitalize names of months, days, and holidays, but not the names of seasons.

July   Thursday   Halloween   winter

Races, Languages, Nationalities, Religions

Capitalize the names of races, languages, nationalities, and religions. Also capitalize any adjectives that come from these names.

Greek	Oriental	Catholicism	Protestant
German	Hinduism	Puerto Rican	Polish

School Subjects

Do not capitalize the names of school subjects, except course titles followed by a number.

history   Reading Workshop I
industrial arts   Math 300

Remember that the names of languages are always capitalized.

French   Spanish   Japanese   English

Ships, Trains, Airplanes, Automobiles

Capitalize the names of ships, trains, airplanes, and automobiles.

U.S.S. *Constellation*   *Concorde*   Buick Skyhawk

B.C., A.D.

Capitalize the abbreviations *B.C.* and *A.D.*

The Pyramids of Egypt were begun about 300 **B.C.**
Mohammed was born in **A.D.** 570.

Exercise A: Write the words in each sentence that should be capitalized. Use the necessary capital letters.

1. The national basketball association begins its playoffs in march.
2. Every june, elizabeth seton high school holds a carnival.
3. The high school is across the street from lakeview hospital.
4. There are many different protestant religions.
5. In the middle ages, people believed that a woman would dream of her future husband on st. agnes's eve, january 20.
6. The battle of antietam was one of the fiercest in the american civil war.
7. Montezuma II, the last aztec ruler of mexico, died in a.d. 1520.

8. Amtrak's *southwest limited* travels over eighty miles per hour on some runs.
9. King tut, the egyptian ruler, was buried in 1344 b.c.
10. The marzo family spent august traveling through europe in a volkswagen van.

Exercise B: Follow the directions for Exercise A.

1. The second monday in october is celebrated as columbus day.
2. Both the french and the americans celebrate their independence in july.
3. The democratic party received contributions from many unions.
4. The united mineworkers' union is a member of the afl-cio.
5. We are reading the declaration of independence in my history class.
6. Cheryl could not sign up for german I because it conflicted with her math class.
7. The national language of the israelis is hebrew.
8. The alaskans make the most of their short summer.
9. After graduating from howard university, judy received job offers from ibm and general foods corporation.
10. After looking at many different trucks and vans, the powells bought a new datsun.

Part 2   First Words

Sentences and Poetry

Capitalize the first word of every sentence and the first word of most lines of poetry.

The disc jockey began her show. She played a new album.

Listen my children, and you shall hear
Of the midnight ride of Paul Revere,
"Paul Revere's Ride"—HENRY WADSWORTH LONGFELLOW

Part 2

Objective

To capitalize the first word in various written constructions

Presenting the Lesson

1. Read and discuss pages 647–649. Spend extra time explaining divided quotations, being sure that students are confident about how to use capitals in them.

2. Assign and discuss Exercises A and B on pages 649–650.

Individualizing the Lesson

Less-Advanced Students

Have students write a short letter in which they order a record album by name from a record company. They may make up the name of the person to whom the letter is addressed and the company name, too, if necessary. Remind them before they write the letter of the places where capital letters are required.

Advanced Students

Have the students write an outline of a chapter from their social studies or science text. They may use the headings and subheadings that appear in the Section. Point out before they make the outline where capital letters are required.

Reinforcement Exercise

Assign and discuss Exercise D on page 652.

Optional Practice

Have the students compile a list of the ten best things they have ever read. Have them discuss these lists in class and use the opportunity to go over the capitalization rules for titles.

Extending the Lesson

Below are two passages from English literature: the first from Sir Philip Sidney's *Arcadia* written in the 16th century, and the second from William Blake's *Songs of Experience* written in the 18th century. Have students study the capitalization in

Sometimes, especially in modern poetry, the lines of a poem do not begin with capital letters.

Quotations

Capitalize the first word of a direct quotation.

A **direct quotation** tells the exact words of a speaker or writer.

Emerson said, "**T**he only way to have a friend is to be one."

In a **divided quotation,** a direct quotation is broken into two parts by words like *he said* or *she explained.* Do not capitalize the first word of the second part unless it starts a new sentence.

"I agree," Tim said, "**t**hat a good friend is rare."
"I agree," Tim said. "**A** good friend is rare."

Letter Parts

Capitalize the first word in the greeting of a letter. Also capitalize the name of the person addressed, or words like *Sir* and *Madam* that stand for names.

Dear **M**s. **V**aldez: **D**ear **M**r. **N**ash: **D**ear **S**ir:

In the complimentary close, capitalize only the first word.

Very truly yours,   **S**incerely yours,

Outlines

Capitalize the first word of each item in an outline. Also capitalize the letters before each line.

    I. **H**olidays
        A. **C**hief legal holidays
            1. **N**ational
            2. **S**tate or local
        B. **R**eligious holidays

Titles

Capitalize the first word and all important words in the titles of chapters, magazine articles, short stories, essays, poems, television or radio episodes, and songs or short pieces of music.

CHAPTER TITLE:	Chapter 3, "Food and Health"
MAGAZINE ARTICLE:	"Today's Changing Family"
SHORT STORY:	"To Build a Fire"
ESSAY:	"The Seeing See Little"
POEM:	"The Base Stealer"
SONG:	"Oh, What a Beautiful Morning!"

Capitalize the first word and all important words in titles of books, newspapers, magazines, plays, movies, television and radio programs, works of art, and long musical compositions.

BOOK TITLE:	*Where the Lilies Bloom*
NEWSPAPER:	*Los Angeles Times*
MAGAZINE:	*Ebony*
PLAY:	*You Can't Take It with You*
MOVIE:	*Return of the Jedi*
TELEVISION PROGRAM:	*Wide World of Sports*
WORK OF ART:	*The Sunflowers*
LONG MUSICAL COMPOSITION:	*Carmen*

Exercise A: Number your paper from 1 to 10. Write the words that should be capitalized. Use the correct capital letters.

1. dear ms. kruger:
   your two tickets to a special showing of the *star wars* trilogy are enclosed. thank you for your order.
   sincerely yours,
2. television movies about athletes such as "brian's song," always seem to have popular appeal.
3. the action photography in *sports illustrated* is excellent.
4. I. finding a cure for the common cold
   A. difficulties
      1. more than 200 cold viruses
5. our school library has back issues of several newspapers, including *the washington post*.
6. rachel chose the poem "a dream deferred" to memorize.

each and comment on the changes that have taken place in the rules for 20th century English.

1. About his neck he wore a broad and gorgeous collar whereof the pieces interchangeably answering, the one was of Diamonds and pearl, set with a white enamel so as by the cunning of the workman it seemed like a shining ice and the other piece, being of Rubies and Opals, had a fiery glistering which he thought pictured the two passions of Fear and Desire wherein he was enchained.
2. The modest Rose puts forth a thorn,
   The humble Sheep a threat'ning horn;
   While the Lilly white shall in Love delight,
   Nor a thorn, nor a threat, stain her beauty bright.

7. "dave," joyce called, "watch while I try a half-gainer."
8. "i keep forgetting my locker combination," said adam. "maybe i should write it down."
9. mary cassatt's painting *the letter* shows a sad woman sealing an envelope.
10. john p. davis and the russian author gogol both wrote short stories titled "the overcoat."

Exercise B: Follow the directions for Exercise A.

1. the last song of the beach boys' concert was "surfin' u.s.a."
2. it was many and many a year ago,
   in a kingdom by the sea,
   that a maiden there lived whom you may know
   by the name of annabel lee;
           —edgar allan poe, "annabel lee"
3. we discussed the chapter called "two images of the future" from the book *this endangered planet.*
4. "i'm not sure," said gerard, "what we should do now."
5. i read the article "new research in dental care" in *prevention* magazine.
6. megan asked, "have you seen the latest issue of *time*?"
7. george lucas made *american graffiti* before he made *star wars.*
8. my little sister insisted that i turn to "fraggle rock."
9. the song "some enchanted evening" is from the musical *south pacific.*
10. dear sir:
    i would like two tickets to monday night's performance of *the messiah.*
                          yours truly,

Exercise C: Writing Every week, your school paper includes a feature article on ten students. This week, you are one of the ten. To complete the article, the paper needs to know the titles of your favorite song, book, and movie. They would also like you to include either a quotation or a few lines of poetry that you find especially meaningful. Write the information in a letter to Alice Evans, the paper's editor. Use correct capitalization throughout.

REINFORCEMENT EXERCISES
Capitalization

Reinforcement Exercise

This Reinforcement Exercise may be used for additional practice of the concepts presented in this Section.

Review

If you have not previously assigned this Reinforcement Exercise, you can use it as an excellent Section Review.

A. Use capital letters with proper nouns and adjectives. Copy these sentences, adding <u>capitals</u> where necessary. (Use after page 642.)

1. Reg dwight changed his name to elton john.
2. My brother saw harrison ford at the airport.
3. Margaret thatcher became prime minister in 1979.
4. One writer of the new testament was st. matthew.
5. Rabbi levy and father krause compared their impressions of moses.
6. How can uncle gene get to ames by noon?
7. When he was rescued, capt. john smith thanked god.
8. Last year my mother and i took an auto repair course.
9. Jean and i met state's attorney mary m. newton.
10. Who was vice-president during president ford's term?

B. Use capital letters correctly. Copy these sentences, adding <u>capitals</u> where necessary. Some sentences may already be correct.
(Use after page 644.)

1. The okefenokee swamp is in georgia and florida.
2. We drove south through brown county into kentucky.
3. Unseasonal rains drenched the southwest.
4. The northern border of poland faces the baltic sea.
5. Motocross races are held on the east side of town. Correct
6. I've never seen the south or the west coast.
7. Our favorite spot in the west is the grand tetons.
8. The largest lake in the united states is lake superior.
9. Sanibel island is west of fort myers.
10. We waterskied on lake tahoe in california.

C. Use capital letters correctly. Copy these sentences, adding <u>capitals</u> where necessary. (Use after page 647.)

1. Next saturday the anti-cruelty society will move to a new building.
2. Are volvos made only in sweden?

3. The republican candidate fought in world war II.
4. Students in spanish III have lab sessions on thursdays.
5. Will revell industries be closed on december 24?
6. The scanners at many food stores are made by ibm.
7. My cousin graduated from roberto clemente high school.
8. Our history class toured the united nations building.
9. Most catholic schools are closed on good friday.
10. When is the jewish holiday of yom kippur celebrated?

D. Capitalize words correctly. Write the words that should be capitalized. Use capital letters correctly. (Use after page 650.)

1. my sister auditioned for a part in *annie*.
2. a TV show based on true experience is "all creatures great and small."
3. naomi said, "this is ridiculous!"
4. tom wolfe's book *the right stuff* is about astronauts.
5. hazlitt said, "no really great man ever thought himself so."
6. "hold the ladder," said mark. "it's not too steady."
7. "hopes," pindar said, "are but the dreams of those who are awake."
8. dear mr. ortega:
   your order will be shipped immediately.
                              very truly yours,
9. tammy asked, "do you subscribe to *runner's world*?"
10. dogs display reluctance and wrath
    if you try to give them a bath.
                              —ogden nash

MIXED REVIEW

Capitalization

A. Rewrite the following sentences on your paper, capitalizing words where necessary.

1. prince charles and princess diana of england are often in the news.
2. has the pope made more than one trip to his native country of poland?
3. "dad, mom's birthday is next thursday," reminded diane.
4. in iran, egypt, and several other mideastern countries, people worship allah, the supreme being in the islamic religion.
5. our band trip took us through the ohio valley, over the blue ridge mountains, and across the rolling hillsides of maryland to our destination of washington, d.c.
6. when we visited california last year, we drove south on highway 1 from san francisco to the baja peninsula.
7. at central high school, students are only permitted to enter on the south side of the building.
8. susan is a volunteer at the local branch of the a.s.p.c.a. on lincoln avenue.
9. in 1066, the normans conquered britain in the battle of hastings.
10. the u.s.f.l. has approved several new franchises, including one in tulsa, oklahoma.
11. the best-selling car produced by general motors is the chevrolet, followed in sales by the oldsmobile.
12. the united nations was founded on october 24, 1945.
13. the french celebrate their independence on bastille day, july 14.
14. freshmen at brockman college are required to take composition 101, a science course, a computer course, and a foreign language course.
15. "would you like to go to the beach?" asked gina, "or should we try the central park zoo?"

This exercise provides review of the concepts presented in this Section. The exercise challenges the students to apply several of the skills they have acquired during previous study. Because the "mixed" feature of this activity makes it more difficult, the teacher may wish to have less-advanced students do the exercise orally or in small groups.

B. Proofread the following letter for incorrect capitalization. Rewrite the letter correctly.

624 Washtenaw avenue
Ypsilanti, michigan 48109
july 4, 1985

dear Lynn,

I received your letter this afternoon, and i'll be happy to accept your invitation! I've always wanted to see the southwest, and traveling with you and aunt Pat sounds like the perfect way to do it! When I asked my mom if I could go, she said, "only if I can go along, too!" She was just teasing, because she has a new job at sears and is not eligible for a vacation until next spring. My summer school classes, chemistry 2 and the math class I told you about, will be completed next thursday. After those, I'll need a vacation!

I look forward to hearing from you concerning the details of our trip. I have already made a reservation for a flight on eastern airlines that leaves detroit on saturday, july 30, at 10:00 a.m. and arrives in tulsa at 3:10 p.m. Please let me know if Aunt Pat or rev. Thomas can meet me. (Did he replace his old buick yet?)

your cousin,

Anita

USING MECHANICS IN WRITING
Capitalization

A. If you could travel across the United States, what states, historical places, recreational areas, or natural wonders would you want to visit? The Rocky Mountains? Disney World? Zion National Park? Plan and write out a route that would take you to at least five of the places you would most like to visit in the United States. If you know the particular roads you would have to take to get you there, be sure to include them in your paper. Remember that sections of the country such as the East and the Midwest are capitalized, as well as the names of towns, parks, individual land formations, and bodies of water. You may want to consult a map or an atlas.

B. Write an essay about your favorite musical group. Where are the members from? What is the best song the group has ever recorded? What is the worst? Compare the two songs. If you can, tell when the songs were written and how they reflect the group's development as performers. Don't forget to capitalize all of the important words in the titles of the songs.

C. The year is 2000. You are on a space mission and have discovered a new planet. As your reward, the government has given you the honor of naming the planet, its land forms and bodies of water, the various creatures it contains, and so on. You may create any sort of strange new world you like. Tell about it in a few paragraphs.

Section Objectives

1. To use end marks correctly
2. To use commas correctly
3. To use semicolons and colons correctly
4. To use dashes correctly
5. To use hyphens correctly
6. To use apostrophes correctly
7. To use quotations marks correctly

Preparing the Students

Ask students how a speaker helps his or her listeners understand when one idea ends and another begins, when a particular word is very important, or when he or she is quoting someone. How can a speaker let his or her listener know that he or she is asking a question or feeling strong emotion or surprise? Mention voice intonation, volume, pause, and facial expression. Remind students that writers do not have these means available. However, the writer is able to use punctuation to indicate some of the same kinds of things in writing.

Additional Resources

Diagnostic Test — See page 9 in the test booklet. Recommended for use before teaching the Section.

Mastery Test — See pages 73–74 in the test booklet. Recommended for use after teaching the Section.

Additional Exercises — See pages 685–690 in the student text.

Skills Practice Book — pages 188–201.

Duplicating Masters — pages 188–201.

Special Populations — See special section at the front of this Teacher's Edition.

Section 14

Punctuation

Road signs and traffic lights guide a driver. Similarly, punctuation marks guide a reader. **Punctuation marks** show readers where to stop, slow down, or change direction.

When you write, your punctuation signals your reader. It marks groups of words that belong together and tells how a sentence should be read. Correct punctuation, above all, helps prevent the kind of confusion that can result from a sentence such as the following:

> Lee likes rock music new wave however is his
> girlfriends favorite.

Correctly punctuated, the message reads:

> Lee likes rock music; new wave, however, is his
> girlfriend's favorite.

In your own writing, be careful to punctuate sentences correctly, to prevent confusion.

Part 1   End Marks

End marks are the punctation marks that indicate the end of a sentence. The three kinds of end marks are the **period,** the **question mark**, and the **exclamation point**.

The Period

Use a period at the end of a declarative sentence.

A **declarative sentence** is a sentence that makes a statement.

The streets are covered with ice.✓

Use a period at the end of most imperative sentences.

An **imperative sentence** is a sentence that orders or requests someone to do something.

Use the revolving door, please.✓

At times, imperative sentences express strong excitement or emotion. Then an exclamation point, rather than a period, is used at the end of the sentence.

Get away!✓   Hurry up!✓

Use a period at the end of an indirect question.

An **indirect question** indicates that someone has asked a question. However, it does not give the reader the exact words of the question.

The captain asked whether the ship was on course.✓

Notice how a **direct question** differs:

The captain asked, "Is the ship on course?✓"

A direct question shows the exact words of the person asking the question. A direct question ends with a question mark.

Use a period at the end of an abbreviation or an initial.

657

Part 1

Objective

To use end marks correctly

Presenting the Lesson

1. Read and discuss pages 657–659. Review with the class the various types of sentences and be sure they know which end mark is appropriate for each type. Encourage students to use the correct terms when discussing **declarative, imperative, interrogative,** and **exclamatory** sentences.
2. Assign and discuss Exercises A and B on page 659.

Individualizing the Lesson

Less-Advanced Students

For additional practice, have students supply the necessary punctuation in·the following sentences.

1. Help   These bookshelves are falling
2. Did your watch stop   It is 1:00 AM
3. The Russian skaters earned a perfect score
4. Where were you able to find shoes for $900
5. Carlos asked if Mr   Garcia was in his office
6. What a shock that was
7. The baby weighed 7 lbs, 3 oz and was named Ernest M   Miller, Jr
8. Stop   Your time is up
9. Do you like Italian food, Tina
10. Summerdale Ave   isn't north of here, is it

Advanced Students

Have students write the following kinds of sentences and insert appropriate punctuation: two imperative sentences, two exclamatory sentences, two interrogative sentences, two declarative sentences, two sentences using initials or abbreviations, two sentences with indirect quotations.

Optional Practice

Have students change the following direct quotations to indirect quotations.

1. Mrs. Cruz said, "Does anyone want to go for a swim?"
2. "How many volunteers can we get for clean-up?" asked David.
3. "When is the next full moon?" inquired Dr. Stahl.
4. "Are you ready for your final exams?" Marion asked.
5. The speaker demanded, "Which one of us is truly educated?"

Extending the Lesson

Discuss the term *acronym*. Explain that an acronym uses the initial letters of an abbreviated name to form a word. Give examples such as SALT and UNICEF. Point out that the periods have been eliminated from acronyms, and often people do not realize that they are abbreviations at all. Ask them if they know what the words *laser* and *radar* actually mean. If not, have them look them up. Ask the class for other examples of acronyms. (HUD, AWOL, CORE, NOW, etc.)

An **abbreviation** is a shortened form of a word. An **initial** is a first letter that stands for a word.

| Gov. James R. Thomas | 4 P.M. on Aug. 4 |
| Lt. Margaret B. Hill | 6 lb., 12 oz. |

Certain abbreviations do not use periods. To check whether or not to use a period with an abbreviation, look up the abbreviation in your dictionary.

CIA (*Central Intelligence Agency*)
CB (*Citizens' Band*)
UN (*United Nations*)

Use a period after each number or letter for an item in an outline or a list.

(An Outline)	(A List)
I. Sports	1. nails
A. Contact	2. hammer
1. Football	3. putty

Use a period between dollars and cents and before a decimal.

$13.64   3.14

The Question Mark

Use a question mark at the end of an interrogative sentence.

An **interrogative sentence** is a sentence that asks a question.

What do you want for dinner?

The Exclamation Point

Use an exclamation point at the end of an exclamatory sentence.

An **exclamatory sentence** expresses excitement or other strong emotion.

That's terrific!   How nice you look!

Use an exclamation point after an interjection.

An **interjection** is one or more words that show strong feeling. Sometimes the interjection is a sound.

Nice! Ouch! Not again! Super!

Exercise A: Copy the following sentences, adding the necessary punctuation. Be prepared to tell what punctuation marks you used and why you used them.

1. Where is Lt.Moseley stationed?
2. Vince asked why the car had a fiberglass hood.
3. Fantastic ！Those twenty-dollar shirts have been marked down to $9.99.
4. Did she want to call at 8:15 A.M.or P.M.?
5. Say！Where have you been?
6. I.Foods containing calcium
    A.Dairy products
       1.Milk
7. The initials WHO stand for the World Health Organization.
8. Is your appointment with Dr.Sam Williams, Jr.or with Dr.Sam Williams, Sr.?
9. Gena's new address is P.O.Box 12, Altoona, Pennsylvania.
10. The *USS.Pueblo* was captured by North Korea.

Exercise B: Follow the directions for Exercise A.

1. Aaron asked if China bordered the U.SSR.
2. Please send all complaints to Brown, Brooks, and Co.in New York.
3. Is that an AM radio?
4. Darryl Fields, R.N., helps his patients to keep smiling.
5. Oh, no！Why did you do that?
6. Should I make the check out to Dr.Sara Bosco or to Sara Bosco, M.D.?
7. If the amount is $9.91 or more, round it off to ten dollars.
8. The NEA is an educational organization. (or N.E.A.)
9. Does the winter sun really set by 3 P.M.in Alaska?
10. Halt！Who's there?

Part 2   The Comma

Objective

To use commas correctly

Presenting the Lesson

1. Read and discuss pages 660–666, being sure that students understand what is meant by *series*, *introductory words*, *interrupters*, *direct address*, *appositives*, *direct quotations*, and *compound sentences*. Point out that commas are not just sprinkled around arbitrarily in a sentence. Every comma must have a reason for being there.

2. Assign the A Exercises on pages 660, 663, and 666 after each section is discussed. Assign the B Exercises as a cumulative review.

3. Read and discuss pages 667–669. Allow extra time to discuss the difference between restrictive and non-restrictive clauses. It is often difficult for students to grasp the difference between the two, and it will probably be necessary to provide many examples. (See **Optional Practice**.)

4. Assign and discuss Exercises A, B, and C on pages 669–670.

Individualizing the Lesson

Less-Advanced Students

Dictate the following sentences and ask the students to write them, using commas where necessary. Then go over the sentences with the students and ask them which rule applies to each comma.

1. I was exposed to German measles, but I didn't catch them.

Part 2   The Comma

A comma is used to indicate pauses and breaks in thought. In this way, commas help you to communicate clearly.

Using Commas in a Series

Use a comma after every item in a series except the last one.

A series is three or more items of the same kind. Your writing may contain a series of words, phrases, or clauses.

WORDS: Woody Allen is a writer, an actor, and a director.

PHRASES: We searched under beds, inside drawers, and in closets.

CLAUSES: The doctor explained how the blood test is made, what it tells, and why it is necessary.

Use commas after *first, second, third,* and so on, when these adverbs introduce a series.

There are four steps to any house painting job: first, scrapping; second, sanding; third, priming; and fourth, painting.

When there are two or more adjectives before a noun, use commas between them.

The vet treated the cold, wet, sick dog.

Exercise A: Number your paper from 1 to 10. Copy the following sentences and add commas where necessary.

1. January, February, and March are cold, bitter months here.
2. Jeff plays baseball in spring, tennis in summer, and basketball in winter.
3. Nan wanted to know three things about the car: first, its gas mileage; second, its cruising speed; and third, its price.
4. Tired crews of workers picked grapes in the hot, dusty fields.

5. Ron groped for the alarm, shut it off, and went back to sleep.
6. The radio squawked out news of a fire, an airplane crash, and a bus strike.
7. Kerry lifted the phonograph needle, removed the dust, and set the needle back down.
8. Seth has had three part-time jobs: first, as a newspaper carrier; second, as a cook; and third, as an usher.
9. His eyes widened, brightened, and seemed to smile.
10. A pleasant guide told the tourists where Libya is, when it was founded, and how it is governed.

Exercise B: Follow the directions for Exercise A.

1. The building inspector listed these problems: first, falling plaster; second, cracked windows; third, peeling paint.
2. Lightning flashed, black clouds billowed, and leaves whirled.
3. To make a soda, mix syrup, ice cream, and soda water.
4. Baking soda and water make a cheap, effective toothpaste.
5. Betty climbed the wall, gripped the ledge, and threw the rope.
6. Tall, thin, gray lockers lined the halls.
7. Hondas, Yamahas, and Harley-Davidsons glittered in the lot.
8. Denny looked for work at supermarkets, theaters, restaurants, and amusement parks.
9. First, I checked the plug; second, I looked at the fuse box; third, I fiddled with the antennas; fourth, I gave up.
10. The plumber stood up, stretched, and flexed her fingers.

Exercise C: Writing You have just returned from a shopping mall where you visited the following stores:

> an exotic pet store
> a gourmet grocery store
> a sporting goods store

Write a sentence about each store that includes a list of three or more things you saw inside. Use commas correctly.

Then write sentences about each item you listed above. Use at least two adjectives to describe each item. Use commas correctly.

2. On January 12, 1984, Andrea and her family moved to St. Paul, Minnesota.
3. Sanka Knox, who reported the story, placed great emphasis on the unusual, complicated details.
4. The gardeners raked the leaves, pruned the hedges, and turned the soil.
5. Howard, come and eat your dinner.

Advanced Students

Have students write the following kinds of sentences: two with direct quotations, two with commas to avoid confusion, two with non-restrictive clauses, two with appositives, two with nouns of direct address, two compound sentences.

Reinforcement Exercise

Assign and discuss Exercise A on page 685, which reviews end marks and commas.

Optional Practice

Have students identify the clauses in the sentences below as restrictive or non-restrictive. Then ask them to punctuate the sentences accordingly.

1. Joseph Guillotin was not actually the person who invented the guillotine.
2. Chief Hooshtogl who was also called Tom Hill was a leader of the Shahaptian-Nez Perce Tribe.
3. New televisions that use microchips to produce a perfect picture are making other televisions obsolete.
4. For people in Brooklyn, baseball lost its thrill the year that the Dodgers left Ebbets Field.
5. Bayard Taylor who was born in Pennsylvania in 1825 travelled extensively and wrote books about his voyages.

Using Commas with Introductory Words

Use a comma to separate an introductory word, long phrase, or clause from the rest of the sentence.

No, I'm not leaving yet. (introductory word)

After four rounds with the champ, Diaz was knocked down. (prepositional phrase)

Laughing wildly, Lauren threw down the necklace and ran offstage. (verbal phrase)

When you pay the toll, the gate goes up and a green light goes on. (adverb clause)

As you can see, commas are used after introductory words like *yes* and *no*. They are also used after prepositional phrases, verbal phrases, and adverb clauses that begin sentences.

Sometimes the comma may be left out. When there would be almost no pause in speaking, no comma is used.

At noon the auction will begin.

Using Commas with Interrupters

Use commas to set off one or more words that interrupt the flow of thought in a sentence.

The judge, in any event, sentenced the man.

William, moreover, made the all-state squad.

The bus lines, I think, have increased the fare.

The cost of some foods, however, has gone down.

The following words are additional examples of interrupters. Set them off with commas.

therefore	I believe	of course
for example	by the way	furthermore
I suppose	in fact	nevertheless

662

Exercise A: Number your paper from 1 to 10. Copy the following sentences. Add commas where necessary.

1. Yes, the first ELO album was titled "No Answer."
2. After dialing Tony's number, Rita had second thoughts.
3. Waiting outside, the reporter overheard a startling conversation.
4. Carlos, I believe, deserves our support.
5. Dazed from lack of sleep, the swimmer finally reached the beach.
6. No, I haven't been to Williamsburg.
7. You and your brother will be at the Valentine's Day dance, I suppose.
8. To tell the truth, this pie could have used more time in the oven.
9. After he talked with the coach, Glenn felt better about the loss.
10. As other nations get more industry, they will share our pollution problems.

Exercise B: Follow the directions for Exercise A.

1. Campbell's interception was, I think, the high point of the game.
2. Brenda, on the other hand, is a computer whiz.
3. Yes, that is the quickest route to Indianapolis.
4. The British, however, do not like iced tea or any other chilled drink.
5. On the way home from the dentist's office, Fran chipped her tooth.
6. Although Marguerite seems aloof, she is just shy.
7. Delighted at the prospect of a summer on the beach, Carmen took the job.
8. Whenever a new mail carrier delivers the mail, we get somebody else's letters.
9. The rust, I am afraid, has eaten completely through the hood and doors of the car.
10. Because the public pool was closed, we had no place to swim.

Using Commas with Nouns of Direct Address

Use commas to set off nouns of direct address.

Sometimes when you speak or write to someone, you use the person's name. The name of someone directly spoken to is a **noun of direct address**.

> Marsha, call a time-out!
>
> In the hallway, Mark, is a package for you.
>
> Did anybody call, Cynthia?
>
> After you leave, boys, lock the garage.

As in the last example, nouns of direct address may be common nouns.

Using Commas with Appositives

Use commas to set off most appositives.

An **appositive** is one or more words that explain or identify another word. The appositive directly follows the word it explains.

> Art Buchwald, a humorous writer, has a column in this newspaper.
>
> Our assistant coach, Mr. Wagner, played with the Jets.
>
> The Superbowl, the biggest football game of the year, is held in January.

As in the final example, an appositive may contain a prepositional phrase.

Nouns used as appositives are called **nouns in apposition**. When the noun in apposition is a single name, it is not usually set off by commas.

> My sister Jennifer works here.
> Dave's cousin Stan is spending the summer.

Using Commas with Quotations

Use commas to set off the explanatory words of a direct quotation.

The explanatory words are the statements like *he said, Greg replied,* or *Sheila asked.* They are not part of the quotation. Explanatory words often precede the quotation. Use a comma after the explanatory words.

Rich said, "Take the expressway to the third exit."

Now look at this quotation:

"Take the expressway to the third exit," Rich said.

In the sentence above, the explanatory words come after the quotation. Notice that the comma belongs at the end of the quotation inside the quotation marks.

Sometimes a quotation is broken into two parts. The explanatory words separate the two parts. Here is an example of a *divided quotation*:

"Take the expressway," Rich said, "to the third exit."

In a divided quotation, a comma is used within the quotation marks at the end of the first part of the sentence. A comma is also used after the explanatory words.

Indirect quotations do not tell the speaker's exact words. No commas are used.

Rich said that we should take the expressway to the third exit.

Using Commas in Compound Sentences

Use a comma before the conjunction between the two main clauses of a compound sentence.

The Dodgers won the pennant, but they lost the World Series.

The comma is not necessary when the main clauses are very short and are joined by *and.*

We worked and then we relaxed.

Sometimes very short main clauses are joined by *but* or *or*. A comma is used since the words *but* and *or* mark a change in the flow of thought.

Ken works, but he isn't paid much.

Do not confuse compound sentences with compound subjects or compound predicates. There is no comma before the *and* that joins a compound subject or predicate.

Beth dove into the pool *and* retrieved her wallet.

Exercise A: Copy these sentences. Add commas as needed.

1. Lincoln Logs,the building blocks for children,were designed by a famous architect's son.
2. The orthodontist,a kind woman,always puts her patients at ease.
3. Ms. Calder,that is my cousin James.
4. Here is the hockey stick you lost,Cory.
5. Don's sketch,a realistic drawing of the park,was displayed at the library.
6. Please submit your application to Dr. Vasquez,the director of the project.
7. Shawn said,"The breakfast will be held in the church."
8. "I was at that show myself," said Vic.
9. "The sun," whined the pitcher,"was in my eyes."
10. Martin called several times,but Nathan's line was busy.

Exercise B: Follow the directions for Exercise A.

1. Is Molly still first chair in the clarinet section,or is Brian?
2. Coleman built a cabinet for the stereo,and then he tucked all the wires out of sight.
3. Captain William Kidd,a well-known pirate,buried treasure in New York.
4. Melissa found her information at the library,and Ben got his from City Hall.
5. Jackie said,"I need a volunteer for my experiment."
6. "You have to watch the ball and keep your elbow straight Cindy," explained Travis.

7. "These recruits already act like professionals," said Sergeant Willis.
8. Gary likes knockwurst,a sausage with lots of seasoning.
9. "Your engine," said the mechanic,"needs a lot of work."
10. The coach said,"Keep up the good work girls."

Using Commas in Dates

In dates, use a comma between the day of the month and the year.

Feburary 22,1976   May 8,1945

When a date is part of a sentence, a comma follows the year.

The first talking picture was shown on July 6,1928,in New York.

Using Commas in Place Names

Use a comma between the name of a city or town and the name of its state or country.

Detroit,Michigan   Santiago,Chile

Athens,Greece   Houston,Texas

When an address is part of a sentence, use a comma after each item.

For more information, write to the National Wildlife Federation,1412 Sixteenth Street,Washington,D.C. 20005.

Do not put a comma between the state name and the ZIP code.

Using Commas in Letters

Use a comma after the salutation of a friendly letter. Use a comma after the complimentary close of a friendly letter or a business letter.

Dear Gretchen,   Yours truly,

Using Commas with Nonrestrictive Clauses

Use commas to set off nonrestrictive clauses.

A **nonrestrictive clause** is a clause that merely adds an idea to the sentence. The sentence would be complete, and the meaning would be clear without it.

A **restrictive clause** is a clause that is essential to the meaning of a sentence. The clause is needed for the sense of the sentence. If a restrictive clause is dropped out of a sentence, the meaning changes.

NONRESTRICTIVE CLAUSE: Terry Reese, *who is the center for the Wildcats,* scored the most points.

Terry Reese scored the most points. (The clause can be dropped from the sentence.)

RESTRICTIVE CLAUSE: Terry Reese is the player *who scored the most points*.

Terry Reese is the player. (The clause cannot be dropped.)

To see if a clause is nonrestrictive, read the sentence without it. If the meaning doesn't change, the clause is nonrestrictive. Use commas before and after it.

Restrictive clauses are often used to identify or to point out the person or thing they modify. Without this identification, the meaning of the sentence would not be clear. Nonrestrictive clauses, on the other hand, add no essential meaning to the sentence.

RESTRICTIVE CLAUSE: Janice is the girl *who found the money*. (The clause tells which girl.)

NONRESTRICTIVE CLAUSE: Janice, *who is very alert,* found the money.

Janice found the money. (The clause is not needed.)

RESTRICTIVE CLAUSE: This is the book *that has the map*. (The clause tells which book.)

NONRESTRICTIVE CLAUSE: This book, *which has pictures,* is my
                          choice.
                          This book is my choice. (The clause
                          is not needed.)

Using Commas To Avoid Confusion

Use a comma whenever the reader might otherwise be confused. Sometimes no rule applies, but a sentence might be misread without commas.

Without commas, the following sentences could be misunderstood:

> Inside everything was a mess.
> Whoever called called twice.

With commas, the sentences are clearer.

> Inside, everything was a mess.

> Whoever called, called twice.

Exercise A: Copy the following sentences. Add commas where necessary.

1. The walking catfish was first reported near Clearwater, Florida, on May 25, 1968.
2. Dear Nicole,
     My summer address will be 205 Linden Street, Ladysmith, Wisconsin 54848.
     I hope to hear from you.
                         With best wishes
                         Katy
3. On May 24, 1844, the first telegraph message was sent.
4. Taconite, Minnesota, is one city that produces much iron ore.
5. The album was made in Nashville, a city with many recording studios.
6. On November 1, 1835, Texas declared its independence from Mexico.

7. Coins are made in Denver, Colorado, and Philadelphia, Pennsylvania.
8. John Brown's raid on Harper's Ferry, West Virginia, began on October 16, 1859, and was crushed on October 18.
9. Write to Lynn Brown at 665 California Avenue, Ames, Iowa 50010.
10. Outside, the wind blew fiercely.

Exercise B: Follow the directions for Exercise A.

1. On December 3, 1967, a doctor successfully transplanted a human heart.
2. Dear Caroline,
   My Aunt Betsy's new address is Rural Route 3, Ridgeway, Virginia 62321.
          Sincerely,
          Michael
3. On August 27, 1859, Edwin Drake struck oil near Titusville, Pennsylvania.
4. The intruder you saw, saw you.
5. Martin Luther King, Jr., was assassinated on April 4, 1968, in Memphis, Tennessee.
6. The school is located at 6900 South Stewart Avenue, Chicago, Illinois.
7. Do you come from Barcelona, Venezuela, or Barcelona, Spain?
8. He seems to believe the saying, "Whatever is, is right."
9. The first American automobile, which was called a "gasoline buggy" by some, was completed on April 19, 1892.
10. Mary's grandmother, who lives downstairs, left Warsaw, Poland, in 1935.

Exercise C: Writing Write ten sentences that illustrate the correct use of commas. The following items should be included at least once.

 commas in dates
 commas in place names
 commas in nonrestrictive clauses
 commas to avoid confusion

Part 3   The Semicolon

Use a semicolon to join the parts of a compound sentence if no coordinating conjunction is used.

The operator interrupted the call; our time was up.

When there are several commas in the parts of a compound sentence, separate the clauses with a semicolon.

On this diet I can eat bread, fruits, and vegetables; but candy, soft drinks, and desserts are forbidden.

When there are commas within parts of a series, use semicolons to separate the parts.

In the Olympics the first place winner gets a gold medal; second place, a silver medal; and third place, a bronze medal.

Use a semicolon before a conjunctive adverb that joins the clauses of a compound sentence.

You have learned that the parts of a compound sentence are sometimes joined by such words as *therefore, however, so, consequently, besides, nevertheless, then, yet,* and *moreover*. These words, called **conjunctive adverbs**, are preceded by a semicolon and followed by a comma.

The Rams have a fine offense; however, their defense is weak.

Justin has a cold; therefore, he will not be able to go swimming this weekend.

Part 4   The Colon

Use a colon after the greeting of a business letter.

Dear Ms. Nolan: Dear Sir or Madam:

Use a colon between numerals indicating hours and minutes.

4:30 P.M.   8:15 A.M.

Objective

To use semicolons and colons correctly

Presenting the Lesson

1. Read and discuss pages 671–672. Review compound sentences with the class, and discuss the various ways they may be punctuated. Emphasize that a semicolon is a stronger pause than a comma but not so strong as a period.

2. Discuss the uses of a colon. Caution students that a colon must never be preceded by a sentence fragment.

3. Assign and discuss Exercises A and B on pages 672–673.

Individualizing the Lesson

Less-Advanced Students

For additional practice, have students insert semicolons and colons where needed in the following sentences.

1. The twins look identical moreover, they have the same habits.
2. Dear Mayor Feinstein
   The parade will begin at Union Square at 900 A.M. therefore, additional traffic control will be required.
3. The garden contained the following flowers tulips, daffodils, roses, mums, and hyacinths.
4. The primary contests were very close in Milwaukee, Madison, and Green Bay, Wisconsin, Albany and Rochester, New York and Chicago, Rockford, and Springfield, Illinois.
5. Heidi loves to watch the soaps she catches up on them when she does not have school.

Advanced Students

Have students write the following sentences: one introducing a list of items, one compound sentence without a coordinating conjunction, one compound sentence with a conjunctive adverb, one sentence with an hour of the day, one sentence with a series in which the parts contain commas.

Optional Practice

Go back to Section 11, Exercise A on pages 587–588. Ask the students to decide which of the compound sentences there could be punctuated with a semicolon instead of a comma and coordinating conjunction. For those sentences where they think the comma and coordinating conjunction are better, have them tell why.

Extending the Lesson

Have students write a brief business letter in which they include the following: a formal salutation, a sentence that introduces a list, a time of the day, and a compound sentence with conjunctive adverbs.

Use a colon to introduce a list of items.

The colon indicates a pause before the items that follow.

> The FBI investigates the following federal crimes: spying, treason, kidnaping, and counterfeiting.

If there would be no pause in speaking, a colon is not used before a list.

> The term "mass media" refers to television, radio, newspapers, magazines, and books.

Exercise A: Number your paper from 1 to 10. Copy the word before and after each missing semicolon or colon. Add the correct punctuation mark.

1. The fullback outran the ball; the fans went wild.
2. Some people object to the following clothes made from animal skins; leopard furs, sealskin coats, and alligator shoes.
3. Dear Madam;
   The item that you ordered is out of stock; consequently, we are unable to fill your order at this time.
4. Skaters, cyclists, and joggers crowded the path; it was not a good place to stroll.
5. From the road, the ocean looked blue; however, it was dull brown at the shore.
6. The Community Center requests the following foods; dry milk, canned meat, canned soup, coffee, flour, sugar, and cereals.
7. The flight to Honolulu was scheduled to depart from Los Angeles at 7: 30; however, we did not even board the airplane until 8: 15.
8. There were many cars on the road; consequently, the smog was thick.
9. The following cities are growing quickly; Calcutta, India; San Juan, Puerto Rico; Sao Paulo, Brazil and Mexico City, Mexico.
10. Willie Nelson was not a typical country and western singer; nevertheless, he became quite popular.

Exercise B: Follow the directions for Exercise A.

1. The two sides could not reach an agreement; therefore, a third party was called in.
2. The picnic tables held bowls of thick, tangy barbecue sauce; platters of warm, crisp, fried chicken; and big, shiny loaves of fresh-baked bread.
3. Karen built a large, roaring fire, and we roasted hot dogs, corn, and marshmallows.
4. Barbara works after school; therefore, she will not be home until 6:30.
5. Some popular home remedies for colds include the following: fruit juices, chicken soup, garlic cloves, and aspirin.
6. Dear Resident:
   Would you like to win $500 a week for life?
7. Rafael Septein has an amazing kick; besides, he thinks quickly.
8. On Labor Day at 7:30 P.M., the lifeguard closes the pool.
9. Spices are used in cooking for the following reasons: they preserve food, they add variety to meals, and they are flavorful.
10. This year, a serious flu is widespread; flu shots are being given at the clinic.

Part 5   The Dash

Using Dashes with Interrupters

You have learned about using commas with words or short phrases, like *however* and *I think*, that interrupt a sentence. A dash is used with a long explanation that interrupts the thought.

An electric car—its battery must be recharged every 1,000 miles—was introduced by one auto maker.

A TV crew—a noise truck, huge cameras, complex sound equipment, and eager reporters—arrived at the scene.

673

Part 5

Objective
To use dashes correctly

Presenting the Lesson
1. Read and discuss pages 673–674.
2. Assign and discuss Exercise A on page 674.

Individualizing the Lesson
Less-Advanced Students
Do Exercise A on page 674 orally, explaining where the dashes are required.

Optional Practice

Have students insert dashes as needed in the following sentences.

1. Feeding, bathing, diapering, and dressing the baby these were my responsibilities as a mother's helper.
2. Traffic was so heavy at least a thousand cars were lined up at the bridge that we turned around and came home.
3. All of the laundry even the brand new sheets, blankets, and towels was ruined by the dye from the jeans.
4. Elvis Presley, Chubby Checker, The Everly Brothers, The Big Bopper these were the favorites in my parents' day.
5. Our family stopped early so early it was still daylight to be sure we could get a motel room.

Extending the Lesson

Point out that the dash does not appear on typewriter keyboards. However, typed papers use two hypens with no space before or after to approximate the dash.

Using the Dash Before a Summary

Use a dash after a series to indicate that a summary statement will follow.

> Edsels, Packards, Studebakers, Hudsons—these cars are no longer made.
>
> Chocolate milkshakes, hamburgers, and potato chips—this is the diet of some teen-agers.

Be careful not to overuse dashes. They should not be used to replace semicolons or periods.

Exercise A: Number your paper from 1 to 10. Copy these sentences. Insert dashes as needed.

1. Layoffs a nearby factory cut 100 workers are one way to lower costs.
2. Taxi fares, school busing, and a new shopping district these issues were decided by the city council.
3. The Boston Red Sox what a great season they're having will play here next week.
4. That magazine the new one I told you about is in the library.
5. The coach talked about team work, timing, concentration the keys to any victory.
6. Trains, cars, buses, planes all of them were halted by the snowstorm.
7. The winter of 1982 there were not enough trucks to remove the snow set records for snowfall.
8. We can take the elevator unless it is broken again to the tenth floor.
9. Parks, beaches, shops, interesting sights Toronto has them all.
10. Trumpets, drums, saxophones, trombones the band has all these instruments.

Exercise B: Writing Write five of your own sentences, illustrating the correct use of dashes.

Part 6   The Hyphen

Use a hyphen if part of a word must be carried over from one line to the next.

Words are separated by hyphens only between syllables.

> The FBI has about 195,000,000 finger-
>   prints on file.

Only words having two or more syllables can be broken by a hyphen. Never divide one-syllable words like *growl* or *weight*. Check your dictionary to learn the syllables of a word.

A single letter should not be left at the end of a line. For instance, this division of *election* would be wrong: *e- lection*. A single letter should not begin a line either.

Use a hyphen in compound numbers from twenty-one to ninety-nine.

> forty-six chairs   sixty-five lockers

Use a hyphen in fractions.

> a two-thirds majority   one-fourth of the votes.

Use a hyphen in certain compound nouns, such as *brother-in-law, drive-in*, and *great-grandmother*.

> The *editor-in-chief* of the local paper is my *sister-in-law*.

Use a hyphen or hyphens between words that make up a compound adjective used before a noun.

> The radio announcer gives a play-by-play account of the game.
> *but*: The radio announcer describes the game play by play.

When compound adjectives are used after a noun, they are not usually hyphenated.

A dictionary will tell you if a word needs a hyphen. These are some examples of compound adjectives:

> five-year-old boy   well-oiled machine
> beat-up truck   best-selling book
> little-used street   long-legged spider

675

Part 6

Objective

To use hyphens correctly

Presenting the Lesson

1. Read and discuss page 675. Emphasize the point that compound adjectives use hyphens only when they appear before the noun. Tell the class that adjective phrases that include an *-ly* adverb (perfectly tuned piano) do not have hyphens.

2. Assign and discuss the Exercise on page 676.

Individualizing the Lesson

Less-Advanced Students

Use the following list of words to have students practice finding correct syllabification in the dictionary.

1. combination   4. seventeen
2. democracy   5. claimed
3. fielded   6. agreeable

Advanced Students

Ask students to rewrite the first five sentences in the Exercise on page 676 in such a way that the hyphenated compound adjectives no longer require hyphens.

Reinforcement Exercise

Assign and discuss Exercise B on pages 685–686 which reviews semicolons, colons, dashes, and hyphens.

Optional Practice

Have students look up the following words to see whether or not they require hyphens.

1. halfback   4. laborsaving
2. pearshaped   5. hasbeen
3. nickname   6. hardshell

A proofreader's job includes checking for proper syllabification of words that are hyphenated at the ends of lines. Have the students use a dictionary to check the syllabification on a page of printed text that includes at least five words that are broken at the ends of lines. See if anyone in the class can discover an error of this kind in a printed book.

Part 7

Objective

To use apostrophes correctly

Presenting the Lesson

1. Read and discuss pages 676-677. Give special emphasis to the fact that 's is used to indicate possession for nouns, but that no apostrophe is used to indicate possession for pronouns. Emphasize the difference between *its* and *it's*.

2. Make sure that students understand the use of an apostrophe to form the plurals of letters, figures,

Exercise: Number your paper from 1 to 15. After the proper number, write the word or words that should be hyphenated, and add the necessary hyphens. Use your dictionary if necessary.

1. This out-of-date map is no help.
2. Have you ever heard a twenty-one-gun salute?
3. That is a half-baked idea.
4. Turn-of-the-century houses lined the street.
5. The old library had built-in bookcases.
6. My great-grandmother sent me twenty-five dollars.
7. Only one-third of the students at that school have up-to-date health records.
8. The used paperbacks are forty-five cents each, or three for one dollar and twenty-five cents.
9. About fifty-one out of every 100 babies born each year are boys.
10. Carl prefers his make-believe world to the real one.
11. One-half of those surveyed were younger than twenty-two.
12. Three-fourths of the students walk to school.
13. Most of my friends headed for the drive-in.
14. The patient had a wild-eyed look.
15. The editor-in-chief of that newspaper writes the editorials himself.

Part 7   The Apostrophe

The apostrophe is frequently used to form the possessive of nouns. To use the apostrophe correctly, you should know whether a noun is singular or plural.

To form the possessive of a singular noun, add an apostrophe and an -s.

student + 's = student's   Les + 's = Les's
baby + 's = baby's   Vanessa + 's = Vanessa's

To form the possessive of a plural noun that does not end in -s, add an apostrophe and an -s.

women + 's = women's   frogmen + 's = frogmen's

To form the possessive of a plural noun that ends in -s, add only an apostrophe.

racers + ' = racers'   players + ' = players'
Reeses + ' = Reeses'   sponsors + ' = sponsors'

To form the possessive of indefinite pronouns, use an apostrophe and an -s.

everybody + 's = everybody's   someone + 's = someone's

Do not use an apostrophe with a personal pronoun to show possession.

hers   ours   yours   its   theirs

The team changed *its* attitude.

Use an apostrophe in a contraction.

In contractions words are joined and letters are left out. An apostrophe replaces one or more letters that are left out.

she's = she is   hasn't = has not
we'll = we will   won't = will not
they're = they are   I'm = I am
it's = it is   shouldn't = should not

Use an apostrophe to show the omission of numbers in a date.

the spring of '79 (the spring of 1979)
a '71 Ford (a 1971 Ford)

Use an apostrophe and s to form the plurals of letters, figures, and words used as words.

ABC's   two *n's*   three *4's*   *yes's* and *no's*

Exercise A: Number your paper from 1 to 10. Write the words that need apostrophes. Insert apostrophes where they are needed.

1. Experts cannot tell the difference between a mans handwriting and a womans. man's, women's
2. Ive already met Russs sister. I've, Russ's
3. Its going to rain before we reach the Carlsons porch. It's, Carlsons'
4. The class of 70 is holding its reunion in the gym. '70

677

3. Assign and discuss Exercises A and B on pages 677–678.

Individualizing the Lesson
Less-Advanced Students

Have students form the possessive of the following words and use five of them in sentences.

woman   anyone   horses
people   fish   Amy
bus   Jones   Chris

Advanced Students

Have students form the possessive and plural possessive of the following words and then use them in sentences.

child   bus
sister-in-law   editor-in-chief
Jones   Wilkins

Optional Practice

Have students form contractions from the following words and use five of them in sentences.

it is   could not   she had
he will   I will   have not
we have   will not   you are

Extending the Lesson

Point out that an apostrophe takes the place of something that is missing. In Old English, a regular way to form possession was by adding -es. When the -e- was dropped, the apostrophe was included to mark where a letter was left out. For example, in Old English the word for *stone* was *stan,* and the possessive *stone's* was *stanes.* Therefore, the use of apostrophe for possession and the use of apostrophe for contraction are not really different.

5. Thats Sandras favorite team. That's, Sandra's
6. Im sure the brakes on my bike are in good shape. I'm
7. Anybodys guess is as good as mine. Anybody's
8. Theyve admitted that the fault is theirs. They've
9. DeeAnnes name is spelled with three *es*. DeeAnne's, e's
10. The trainer didnt at first notice the gorillas absence.
   didn't, gorilla's

Exercise B: Follow the directions for Exercise A.

1. Is that Suzys book youre reading? Suzy's, you're
2. How would you describe the 1980s? 1980's
3. His *maybes* arent the same as *yess*. maybe's, aren't, yes's
4. The coachs jacket was a gift from her team. coach's
5. Dont the Reeses dogs ever stop barking? Don't, Reeses'
6. The band lost some of its best musicians when the class of 83 graduated. '83
7. Arent the clinics hours from 2:00 until 8:00? Aren't, clinic's
8. The two scientists conclusions were the same. scientists'
9. This is everyones park, not just yours. everyone's
10. My little sister hasnt learned to tell the *ds* from the *bs*.
   hasn't, d's, b's

Part 8   Quotation Marks

Use quotation marks at the beginning and at the end of a direct quotation.

Quotation marks tell your reader that a speaker's exact words are being given. Here is an example:

Linda said, "Someone is following me."

Quotation marks are *not* used with indirect quotations. An indirect quotation does not tell the speaker's exact words.

Linda said that someone was following her.

At the beginning of a sentence there are often explanatory words. Use a comma directly after these words. Then begin the quotation with quotation marks. A period at the end of a sentence belongs *inside* the quotation marks.

Objective

To use quotation marks correctly

Presenting the Lesson

1. Read and discuss pages 678–680. Be sure that students understand when to place punctuation marks inside of quotation marks and when to place them outside.

2. Have selected students complete Exercise A on page 680 on the board. Have students explain where each item of punctuation should go and why. Then assign the Exercise at the top of page 680 and Exercise B on page 681.

The pilot said, "Fasten your seat belts."

Sometimes explanatory words end the sentence. Then the quoted statement at the beginning of the sentence is followed by a comma. The comma belongs inside the quotation marks.

"Fasten your seat belts," the pilot said.

When it is necessary to write a quote within a quote, use single quotation marks to enclose the inside quotation.

"It was Captain James Mugford who originally said, 'Don't give up the ship,'" Mr. Gomez told us.

Using Divided Quotations

Sometimes a quotation is divided by explanatory words. Then, each part of the quotation is enclosed by quotation marks.

"One very healthful food," Pamela said, "is granola."

When the divided quotation is a single sentence, the second part begins with a small letter. Look at the example above. At times, however, the second part begins a new sentence. Then a capital letter is used at the beginning of the second part.

"There is entertainment at halftime," Toby noted. "The band will play."

The first part of a divided quotation is followed by a comma. Commas always appear inside quotation marks.

"On the way," Derek said, "we will pick up Kelly."

The explanatory words in the middle of a divided quotation are followed by either a period or a comma. A period is used if the first part completes a sentence. A comma is used if the sentence continues after the explanatory words.

"At the plant," Eric said, "we work in shifts."

"First, we spread paste on the wallpaper," Ginger explained. "Then we hang the paper and cut it to size."

3. Read and discuss pages 681–682. Have each student complete the Exercise on page 682 individually. Then go over the passage orally to be sure everyone understands how to punctuate dialogue.

4. Read and discuss **Punctuating Titles** on page 682. Explain that underlining (italics in print) is used for titles of sizable works that are published separately, such as books, magazines, and plays. Quotation marks are used for titles of shorter selections within publications, such as articles, chapters, and songs.

5. Assign and discuss Exercises A and B on pages 683– 684. Assign Exercise C as a creative writing exercise.

Individualizing the Lesson

Less-Advanced Students

For additional practice, have students punctuate the following sentences.

1. Wow exclaimed Helen That was the best game we've ever played
2. Janis asked Are you going to the museum tomorrow
3. Can you give me a hand asked Bill I could really use some help
4. Our history teacher said Please review last week's notes before the test
5. May I have the directions for getting to your house requested Mr. Brian

Advanced Students

Ask students to re-create and correctly punctuate a conversation they heard in school or on TV.

Reinforcement Exercises

Assign and discuss Exercises C and D on pages 686–687.

Optional Practice

Have students turn the following indirect quotations into direct quotations. Direct them to add quotation marks and underlinings where necessary. Encourage them to vary the position of the words describing the speakers.

1. Mrs. Marsh asked whether anyone had read the book Pride and Prejudice.
2. Janice begged her sister to let her read the latest issue of Seventeen.
3. Paulo suddenly screamed that today was his mother's birthday and he had forgotten all about it.
4. Mark K. announced that he was going to play Slaughter On Tenth Avenue in the concert.
5. Marla asked her father if she could see Flashdance, and he said she could only if she had finished her homework by 6:00.

Extending the Lesson

Have the students examine a passage of dialogue from a novel or short story by their favorite author. Ask them to describe how the author uses speaker tags to let the reader know how the speaker is feeling.

Exercise: Writing Write each of the following sentences three ways as a direct quotation. Try to use words other than *said* in some of your sentences. Answers will vary.

> EXAMPLE: I need an honest answer.
>
>> a. "I need an honest answer," she stated.
>> b. She said, "I need an honest answer."
>> c. "I need," she declared, "an honest answer."

1. Don't talk to me while I'm working.
2. Yes, Stevie Wonder writes many of his own songs.
3. I'm sorry that I forgot to call you.
4. In the last two minutes, the Cowboys took the lead.
5. Finally, a wrecking crew attacked the vacant building.

Using Punctuation with Quotation Marks

Place question marks and exclamation points inside the quotation marks if they belong to the quotation itself.

> Andrew asked, "Who sent you a telegram?"
> Andrea screamed, "Move fast!"

Place question marks and exclamation points outside the quotation marks if they do not belong to the quotation.

> Did Keith say, "Meet me at school"?
> What a surprise it was when our drama coach said, "You made the lead role"!

Commas and periods, as you have seen, always appear within quotation marks.

Exercise A: Copy the following sentences. Punctuate them correctly with quotation marks, end marks, and commas. (There are three indirect quotations that need only end punctuation.)

1. "Watch out for the hornet's nest" yelled Pat.
2. "Do you like that yellow Datsun" asked Mindy?
3. "Oh well" said Angie "a little glue will fix that."
4. Ms. Pappas explained why copper wiring is used.

5. "I have finally had my ice skates sharpened," Tisha said.
6. Terry announced proudly, "I knocked down all ten pins."
7. Adam said that he was on a diet.
8. "We locked this door when we left," said Harris nervously. "Why is it open now?"
9. Did Dr. Korshak say that you should tape your ankle?
10. Did the dentist say, "I think your tooth must be pulled"?

Exercise B: Writing Write each of the following sentences as a direct quotation. In some examples, put the quotation first. In others, put the quotation last. Also, divide some quotations. Answers will vary.

1. Is Costa Rica part of Central America?
2. Don't say that!
3. I called the fire department from a neighbor's house.
4. There's a restaurant by the bowling alley.
5. I never know what Merle will say next.
6. By next June, I will have finished repairing the roof.
7. We swam in the quarry.
8. Stand back!
9. Was that snake a copperhead?
10. This weekend I have to help my cousin.

Using Long Quotations

When two or more sentences are spoken by the same person, do not use an end quotation mark until after the final sentence. Look at the following example:

> "When you keep accounts, there are credits and debits," Stacy explained. "Debits are amounts that you owe. Credits are amounts that are paid to you."

Using Quotation Marks for Dialogue

Dialogue is conversation between two or more people. It is punctuated in a special way. Begin a new paragraph each time the speaker changes.

"What are your favorite TV commercials?" Christy asked.

"I like the commercials for Coca-Cola," replied Ted.

"My favorites are Dr. Pepper and Pepsi commercials," Delia said. "Which ones do you like, Christy?"

"I like most of them," Christy answered. "Some of them are better than the TV programs that come in between."

If one speaker's words continue for more than a paragraph, each paragraph begins with a quotation mark. However, the closing quotation mark is not used until the end of the entire quotation.

Tony said, "The movie star who was nominated for an Academy Award more often than any other was Katharine Hepburn. She was nominated twelve times, and won four times.

"Bette Davis was the next most-nominated star. Nominated ten times, she won two Oscars."

Exercise: Writing Rewrite the following conversation. Make correct paragraph divisions, and use the right punctuation. (¶ = new paragraph)

The interviewer, Mr. Brown, asked Stevie Wonder How did you learn to cope with your handicap? The singer-composer replied I've never seen my blindness as the handicap others do." Why is that? pursued Mr. Brown. Being blind," said Stevie Wonder, you don't judge books by their covers . . . The people I feel sorry for are those who have sight but still don't see."

Punctuating Titles

Use quotation marks to enclose the titles of magazine articles, chapters, short stories, essays, poems, television and radio episodes, songs, and short pieces of music.

MAGAZINE ARTICLE:	"Fads of the Eighties"
CHAPTER TITLE:	Chapter 2, "The New World"
SHORT STORY:	"Clothes Make the Man"
ESSAY:	"The Dog That Bit People"
POEM:	"The Raven"
TELEVISION EPISODE:	"Radar Writes Home"
SONG:	"Jingle Bells"

Underline the titles of books, newspapers, magazines, plays, movies, television series, works of art, and long musical compositions.

In writing or typing, such titles are underlined, like this: <u>The Chocolate War.</u> In print, these titles appear in italics.

BOOK TITLE:	*The Pigman*
NEWSPAPER:	*New Haven Register*
MAGAZINE:	*Field and Stream*
PLAY:	*The Miracle Worker*
MOVIE:	*Raiders of the Lost Ark*
WORK OF ART:	*Mona Lisa*
LONG MUSICAL COMPOSITION:	*The Pirates of Penzance*

Exercise A: Copy the following sentences, adding quotation marks around titles or underlining titles where necessary.

1. The story "Saving the Pieces" was published in <u>Audubon</u> magazine.
2. "Old Abe Lincoln Came Out of the Wilderness" was a popular marching song during the Civil War.
3. I reported on Althea Gibson's article, "I Always Wanted To Be Someone."
4. The article appeared in the book <u>Out of the Bleachers.</u>
5. Our city was featured on the TV show <u>60 Minutes.</u>
6. Of all the Frankenstein movies, I like <u>Young Frankenstein</u> most.
7. The <u>Post-Dispatch</u> is a St. Louis newpaper.
8. The musical <u>West Side Story</u> is a modern version of Shakespeare's play <u>Romeo and Juliet.</u>
9. Monet's painting <u>Waterlilies</u> has been reproduced on bedsheets.
10. Many people recognize the eerie notes of the ballet music <u>The Firebird.</u>

Exercise B: Follow the directions for Exercise A.

1. Surely you can think of a better title for your essay than "What I Did During My Summer Vacation."
2. I like Langston Hughes's poem "Dreams."

3. Julia Ward Howe wrote the song "The Battle Hymn of the Republic."
4. Please read Chapter 10, "The Last Frontier."
5. John Tenniel, who illustrated the book <u>Alice in Wonderland</u>, also drew cartoons for the magazine <u>Punch</u>.
6. <u>The Time Machine</u> was first a novel and then a movie.
7. <u>The Searchers</u> was a famous Western.
8. The first New York newpaper was called the <u>Gazette</u>.
9. <u>The Devil's Dictionary</u> is a book of humorous definitions.
10. Our school play last year was <u>A Raisin in the Sun</u>.

Exercise C: Writing Imagine that you are a famous writer who has published books, magazine articles, and song lyrics. You are on tour promoting your latest novel. A talk show host who is interviewing you asks about the new book as well as your earlier work. Write the conversation that takes place. Be sure to use quotation marks and underlining correctly.

REINFORCEMENT EXERCISES
Punctuation

A. Use end marks and commas. Rewrite the following sentences, adding the missing punctuation. (Use after page 670.)

1. Skates are becoming more popular, and skateboards have almost been forgotten.
2. How thin you are!
3. How thin are you?
4. Should Carol bring her own pliers, wrench, and wire?
5. Joan of Arc, the French heroine, was declared a saint in 1920.
6. Ms. Doyle, Dr. Antonelli, and Mr. McCoy are holding a meeting at 8:00 P.M. on Saturday, September 3.
7. On March 13, 1852, the first newpaper cartoon of Uncle Sam appeared.
8. Robin bought the tickets, but then she lost them.
9. Yes, Mel, I remembered to bring my new album.
10. Georgia looked in her address book, rummaged through a stack of old mail, and finally found this address: 215 Main Street, Carthage, Illinois 62321.
11. When the balloon burst, my cat jumped straight into the air.
12. On Tuesday, by the way, you'll meet Ann Archer, the co-captain of the team.
13. "Are you done, Ron? Mike said. "We want to leave."
14. Dear Tommy,
       Here is the clipping that you asked for.
                     Sincerely,
15. Renee, who lived in France for two years, can speak French fluently.

B. Use semicolons, colons, dashes, and hyphens. Add semicolons, colons, dashes, and hyphens as you rewrite these sentences. (Use after page 676.)

1. Racquetball, tennis, squash, and badminton—Mark can play them all well.
2. The Cougars will need the following players: pitchers, infielders, and left-handed batters.

685

Reinforcement Exercises

These Reinforcement Exercises may be used for additional practice of the concepts presented in this Section. Each exercise focuses on a single concept, and should be used after the page number indicated in parentheses.

Review

If you have not assigned these Reinforcement Exercises before this time, you can also use them as an excellent Section Review.

3. At eighty‸six, my great‸grandmother still has a happy‸go‸ lucky view of life.

4. Deidre can remember everything she reads ; furthermore, she understands the material.

5. The commander‸in‸chief, the general, and the prime minister‿these people will arrive at 7:15 P.M.

6. Three‸fourths of the students listed these long term goals : more education, an interesting job, and a happy family life.

7. Dear Madam :
   We have received your letter ; it will be published in next week's column.

8. This weekend‿I can hardly wait‿we'll be leaving for the lake.

9. Seventy‸five people have entered the five‸mile race.

10. Margie had only a four‸week course in self‸defense ; however, she is already very good at it.

C. Use apostrophes, quotation marks, and underlining.

each sentence, putting in necessary apostrophes, quotation marks, and underlining. (Use after page 684.)

1. Rachel said,"I like the TR-7's that were made in the early 1970's."

2. The students' theme for their dance will be from the play Grease.

3. The song "Fire Lake" reminds me of the spring of '80.

4. Did the teacher say that we would discuss Tillie Olsen's story, "I Stand Here Ironing"?

5. "Get out of the way!" yelled Lee.

6. "Is it true," asked Gloria's brother, "that the injured player is my sister?"

7. "It's somebody's problem, but not yours," said Ms. Kane emphatically.

8. Chris's contact lens can't be found anywhere.

9. All three teachers' classes are reading the novel Ordinary People.

10. "I don't see Meryl Streep's picture in this copy of People," said Beth. "Maybe it's in last week's issue."

D. Use apostrophes, quotation marks, and underlining.

each sentence, putting in necessary apostrophes, quotation marks, and underlining. (Use after page 684.)

1. Walt Disney's feature cartoon films, like <u>Cinderella</u> and <u>Bambi</u>, are shown every seven years.
2. "Most American families have two or more TV's," Mr. Lloyd said.
3. The freshmen's lockers are on the first floor.
4. John Ciardi's poem "Beagles" in the book <u>Introduction to Poetry</u> is one of my favorites.
5. Jenny asked, "Isn't Jason's dog much older than yours?"
6. Jody's grandpa recalls the stock market crash of '29.
7. Ken shouted, "Somebody's car is rolling down the hill!"
8. Didn't you see this week's "Mystery Theater" on TV?
9. <u>Eubie</u>, Bonnie explained, "is a musical about ragtime musician Eubie Blake."
10. "Do most students' parents help them with homework?" Ms. Richardson asked.

Mixed Review

These exercises provide review of the concepts pre-
sented in this Section. Each
exercise challenges the students to apply several of the
skills they have acquired during previous study. Because
the "mixed" feature of these
activities makes them more
difficult, the teacher may wish
to have less-advanced students do them orally or in
small groups.

Punctuation

A. Proofread the following letter for incorrect or missing punctuation. Rewrite the letter correctly.

> 3006 Merton Road
> Palo Alto, California/ 94306
> November 23, 1985

Sales Manager
Rockinwell Corporation
680 Broadway
New York, New York 10006

Dear Sir or Madam/:

On April 26, I ordered twenty-three songbooks from your company for my mother-in-law, who is seventy-eight years old. These songbooks were ordered from your catalog entitled Tunes from the 40's. For some reason, the books that I received contained music such as the following/:rock songs by the Bee Gees, the Rolling Stones, and Men at Work/;Broadway show tunes from Pippin, The Wiz, and Annie/;and blues songs by Muddy Waters.

Despite your company's error, my mother-in-law's choral group has enjoyed these books immensely. As she said to me after her last rehearsal,"Son, these books are definitely going to liven things up around here."

Thank you, therefore, for your error, and please send me a copy of your new catalog.

> Sincerely,
>
> Martin E. Hudnut

B. Proofread the following passage for incorrect or missing punctuation. Rewrite the passage correctly.

If Olympic games were held for birds, the winners of the flight contests would be the swift, the falcon, and the tern. Swifts, the earth's fastest birds, have been clocked at 106 miles-per-hour in level flight. However, peregrine falcons, which are related to eagles, occasionally fly even faster. Diving for prey, this bird has been known to reach the incredible speed of 217 miles-per-hour. The Arctic tern, according to biologist David Attenborough in his book Life on Earth, is another great flyer. In 1955, one Arctic tern was tracked/over 12,000 miles from the White Sea Coast of the U.S.S.R. to the city of Fremantle, Australia?.

Using Mechanics in Writing

These challenging and enjoyable activities allow the students to see how the concepts of grammar, usage, and mechanics may be applied in actual writing situations. Each exercise is designed to allow students practice in several of the skills they have acquired in this Section. The activities also provide opportunities for students to write creatively about a wide variety of interesting and unusual subjects.

Exercise A

"Don't touch me!" Crawley cried, shrinking back in mock terror."

"All right, laugh," said Wheldon, forcing the words out between clenched teeth, "but there's one thing you're afraid of and I'm not."

Crawley stopped laughing. "What's that?" he demanded fiercely.

"Spooks," said Wheldon.

"Spooks?" All of a sudden Crawley sounded as uncertain as a kid trying to recite a poem he'd had to learn for homework.

"Yes, Spooks," said Wheldon, drawing the word out like chewing gum. "I thought that'd wipe the smile off your face."

USING MECHANICS IN WRITING
Punctuation

A. The following passage is a dialogue between two characters, from the short story "Wheldon the Weed" by Peter Jones. Rewrite the dialogue, adding necessary punctuation and paragraph divisions.

Answers in margin.

Don't touch me Crawley cried shrinking back in mock terror. All right laugh said Wheldon forcing the words out between clenched teeth but there's one thing you're afraid of and Im not. Crawley stopped laughing. Whats that he demanded fiercely. Spooks said Wheldon. Spooks? All of a sudden Crawley sounded as uncertain as a kid trying to recite a poem hed had to learn for homework. Yes spooks said Wheldon drawing the word out like chewing gum. I thought thatd wipe the smile off your face.

B. You are an agent for Dan D. Tripps travel agency. A client wants you to put together an itinerary for an exciting five-day vacation. For each day, include the following information:

The date
Starting place and destination
Times of departure and arrival
Places of interest
Activities planned, including admission or ticket fees
Names and addresses of hotels

Include in the itinerary at least one series of items; several introductory words, such as *first* and *next*; one or more compound sentences; a possessive noun; and a compound word. Your itinerary may be realistic or highly imaginative. Following is a sample entry:

Saturday, July 1: Leave Des Moines, Iowa, at 8:40 a.m. Travel by United Airlines to Los Angeles, arriving 11:18 a.m. Take shuttle bus to Holiday Inn in Anaheim. Arrive at Disneyland at 1:00 p.m. The gate admission for Disneyland is $15.00.

690

CUMULATIVE REVIEW
Capitalization and Punctuation

Using Capitalization and Punctuation Correctly. Copy the following paragraphs. Change small letters to capital letters or capital letters to small letters wherever necessary. Add the correct punctuation marks. Leave out incorrect marks.

Last saturday my mother's youngest brother, uncle jack, went with me to the Museum of science and Industry. On exhibit was a collection of some artistic, scientific, and Technological inventions of the chinese. This exhibit had been recommended by three of my teachers; my english teacher, my Industrial Arts I teacher, and my Science teacher.

We saw a waterclock made in A.d. 1,068 that had many gears and stood two stories high. Because I am especially interested in astronomy, I most enjoyed the planetarium, in which a chinese astronomer could sit and be surrounded by a view of the stars. I was amazed to learn that this device was built more than 1,000 years ago. We also saw irrigation machines, compasses, looms, fireworks, printing presses, and even a seismograph.

There were also demonstrations of ancient Arts and Crafts. Most of the visual arts developed during four dynasties: the han, the T'ang, the sung, and the ming. I asked one man, who was demonstrating chinese ink painting, to write my name in chinese characters. He asked, "how do you pronounce your name?" When he had finished the painting, he stamped it with a red seal that showed, I think, his own name.

We also saw a silkworm exhibit. According to Chinese Legend, silk was discovered in 2700 b.c. in the garden of emperor huang-ti. One five-year old girl really enjoyed watching the silkworms produce silk fibers. She asked if she could take a worm home to play with, but she was given a sample of silk thread instead.

After viewing the exhibit, we browsed through a special shop. This shop contained many products made in china. Their beauty made me sorry that I didn't have more time and money to spend at the exhibit.

Cumulative Review

These exercises are designed to cover broad areas of grammar, usage, and mechanics. They require the application of skills taught thus far in the text. The exercises may be used for testing purposes, or as an excellent resource for review.

1. To develop a plan to improve spelling skills
2. To develop a plan to master the spelling of a particular word
3. To understand and apply common spelling rules

Preparing the Students

To demonstrate the frustrating problem of unpredictable variation in English spelling, write the word *ghoti* on the board. Ask the class if anyone knows what the letters spell or how to pronounce the word. After they volunteer some guesses, tell them that the word spells *fish: gh* as in *enough, o* as in *women,* and *ti* as in *action.* Tell students that this Section will give them help in spelling words correctly; however, sometimes they will have to use the dictionary to check spelling. They should consider a dictionary as important a tool to writing as paper and pen.

Additional Resources

Diagnostic Test — See page 10 in the test booklet. Recommended for use before teaching the Section.

Mastery Test — See pages 75–76 in the test booklet. Recommended for use after teaching the Section.

Additional Exercises — See pages 701–705 in the student text.

Skills Practice Book — pages 202–206.

Duplicating Masters — pages 202–206.

Special Populations — See special section at the front of this Teacher's Edition.

Section 15

Spelling

Good spelling is a skill that is important in all writing, from school reports to messages, letters, and job applications. On the job, too, you will often need to write. Accurate spelling is essential to communicate clearly and to create a favorable impression on paper.

Becoming a good speller is not an easy task, though. The spelling of many English words does not seem logical, and many words are not spelled the way they sound.

Learning to spell well is not hopeless, however. There are certain patterns of spelling that many English words follow. There are general rules that make spelling easier, and there are methods of attacking spelling problems. With such tools, you can avoid many problems and improve spelling. This Section will show some solutions.

Part 1 How To Improve Your Spelling

1. **Locate and conquer your own specific spelling problems.** What spelling errors do you make over and over? Study your past written assignments and make a list of the misspelled words. Work on mastering those words.

2. **Pronounce words carefully.** Occasionally people misspell words because they don't pronounce them correctly. If you are writing *famly* for *family*, for instance, you are probably mispronouncing the word. Try to pronounce your words more precisely.

3. **Try to remember the letters in new words.** The habit of really looking at the spelling of new or difficult words can help imprint the correct spelling on your memory. After examining a word carefully, write the correct spelling several times.

4. **Always proofread your writing.** Many misspellings are actually careless mistakes. By examining your writing, you may catch such errors. Read over your work slowly, word by word.

5. **Look up difficult words in a dictionary.** Reach for the dictionary when you're unsure of a spelling. Get into the habit of letting the dictionary help you to spell well.

6. **Learn the few important spelling rules explained in this section.**

Part 2 How To Spell a Particular Word Correctly

1. **Look at the word and say it to yourself.** Make sure to pronounce the word correctly. Say it twice, looking at the syllables as you say them.

2. **Look at the letters.** Close your eyes and try to visualize the word. Then look at the word again. Notice any structural aspects of the word, such as prefixes, suffixes, and double letters, that are important to the correct spelling.

Part 1

Objective

To develop a plan to improve spelling skills

Presenting the Lesson

1. Read and discuss page 693. Ask students which words are particularly troublesome to them. Have students begin their own lists of trouble words.
2. Call the class's attention to the **List of Commonly Misspelled Words** on pages 699–700 in the text. Go over the words on this list observing any peculiarities that might make spelling difficult. Tell students that they should try to master a few words from this list each week until the whole list is covered.

Extending the Lesson

Discuss the importance of good spelling to composition. Emphasize how crucial proofreading is to the revision process.

Part 2

Objective

To develop a plan to master the spelling of a particular word

Presenting the Lesson

Read and discuss pages 693–694. Have students practice these steps using their own lists of troublesome words.

Extending the Lesson

Have the students review previously written work that has already been corrected and returned. Have them write down all of the spelling errors on these papers and use the five steps to master their spellings.

Part 3

Objective

To understand and apply common spelling rules

Presenting the Lesson

1. Read and discuss page 694. Give special emphasis to the exceptions and point out what makes them exceptions. Assign and discuss the Exercise on top of page 695.

2. Read and discuss page 695. Assign the Exercise at the bottom of page 695.

3. Read and discuss page 696. Assign Exercises A and B on pages 696–697.

4. Read and discuss page 697. Assign the Exercises on page 698. Use Exercise B as an opportunity for creative writing.

Individualizing the Lesson

Less-Advanced Students

Dictate the following words and have the students write them, using the rules presented in this Part.

1. slipping	8. praying
2. tasteful	9. succeed
3. niece	10. lovely
4. either	11. rotting
5. saving	12. ceiling
6. thinness	13. misplace
7. hiking	14. unnatural

---

3. **Write the word without looking at your book or list.**

4. **Check to see if you spelled the word correctly.** Look back at your book or list. If you spelled the word correctly, repeat the process.

5. **If you made an error, note what it was.** Then repeat steps 3 and 4 until you have written the word correctly three times.

Part 3   Spelling Rules

Adding Prefixes

When a prefix is added to a word, the spelling of the word remains the same. When the addition of a prefix creates a doubled letter, be careful not to drop one of them.

im + perfect = imperfect	ir + rational = irrational
re + entry = reentry	mis + use = misuse
inter + action = interaction	mis + spell = misspell
dis + agree = disagree	il + legal = illegal

Suffixes with Silent e

When a suffix beginning with a vowel is added to a word ending in a silent e, the e is usually dropped.

save + ing = saving	value + able = valuable
style + ish = stylish	rate + ing = rating
grace + ious = gracious	imagine + ation = imagination

When a suffix beginning with a consonant is added to a word ending in a silent e, the e is usually retained.

time + less = timeless	strange + ly = strangely
like + ly = likely	amaze + ment = amazement
same + ness = sameness	hope + ful = hopeful

The following words are **exceptions.** Study them.

truly   argument   ninth   wholly   judgment

Exercise: Find the <u>misspelled</u> words. Spell them correctly.

1. Dorothy was <u>gazeing</u> at the graceful skaters. gazing
2. They found the sameness of the plains <u>boreing</u>. boring
3. The missile exploded upon <u>rentry</u> to the atmosphere. reentry
4. These <u>arguements</u> are not <u>solveing</u> the problem. arguments, solving
5. The man <u>mistated</u> several facts about the <u>ilegal</u> exports. misstated, illegal
6. That penalty was wholly <u>unecessary</u>. unnecessary
7. Our district <u>relected</u> that <u>insincere</u> politician. reelected
8. Tim has trouble <u>wakeing</u> up on these <u>freezeing</u> days. waking, freezing
9. A <u>fameous</u> surgeon performed the <u>operateion</u>. famous, operation
10. Leaving <u>everthing</u> to chance is <u>imature</u>. everything, immature

Suffixes and Final *y*

When a suffix is added to a word ending in *y* preceded by a consonant, the *y* is usually changed to *i*.

carry + er = carrier	fury + ous = furious
worry + ed = worried	thirty + eth = thirtieth
silly + est = silliest	holy + ness = holiness

Note this exception: When *-ing* is added, *y* does not change.

hurry + ing = hurrying	study + ing = studying
rally + ing = rallying	cry + ing = crying

When a suffix is added to a word ending in *y* preceded by a vowel, the *y* usually does not change.

play + ing = playing	destroy + er = destroyer
decay + ed = decayed	annoy + ing = annoying

Exercise: Add the suffixes as shown and write the new word.

1. dizzy + ness dizziness
2. carry + ing carrying
3. ready + ness readiness
4. heavy + er heavier
5. witty + est wittiest
6. marry + ing marrying
7. marry + age marriage
8. fifty + eth fiftieth
9. employ + able employable
10. stay + ed stayed
11. terrify + ing terrifying
12. creepy + est creepiest
13. relay + ed relayed
14. glory + ous glorious
15. cozy + er cozier
16. history + an historian
17. joy + ful joyful
18. enjoy + able enjoyable
19. tiny + ness tininess
20. fry + ed fried

Adding the Suffixes -*ness* and -*ly*

When the suffix -*ly* is added to a word ending in *l*, both *l*'s are kept. When -*ness* is added to a word ending in *n*, both *n*'s are kept. When any suffix creates a double consonant, keep both letters.

cruel + ly = cruelly   even + ness = evenness
general + ly = generally   lean + ness = leanness

Doubling the Final Consonant

In words of one syllable that end in one consonant preceded by one vowel, double the final consonant before adding -*ing*, -*ed*, or -*er*.

beg + ing = begging   thin + er = thinner
flap + ed = flapped   grab + ing = grabbing

Some two-syllable words follow a similar rule. If the final syllable is accented and ends in one consonant preceded by one vowel, double the final consonant before adding -*ing*, -*ed*, or -*er*.

admit + ing = admitting   regret + ed = regretted

In words of one syllable that end in one consonant preceded by two vowels, the final consonant is not doubled.

steer + ing = steering   lead + er = leader
join + ed = joined   fool + ing = fooling

Exercise A: Find the misspelled words. Spell them correctly.

1. Lana foolled everyone by speaking truthfuly. fooled, truthfully
2. Chris spoted the actress and beged for her autograph. spotted, begged
3. I finaly stopped the driping of the water faucet. finally, dripping
4. Something is cloging the bathtub drain. clogging
5. Angela is hopping to become a space scientist. hoping
6. The Richardsons usually go sailling on Sunday afternoons. sailing
7. The miser Scrooge is generaly known for his meaness. generally, meanness
8. We were permited to use only bamboo fishing poles. permitted
9. The openess of this building makes it especialy cool. openness, especially
10. Are you realy digging a new trench? really

696

Add the suffixes as shown and write the new word.

1. green + ness — greenness
2. tip + ed — tipped
3. boom + ed — boomed
4. lag + ed — lagged
5. top + ed — topped
6. awful + ly — awfully
7. grim + est — grimmest
8. playful + ly — playfully
9. brag + ing — bragging
10. plain + ness — plainness
11. cook + ed — cooked
12. sob + ed — sobbed
13. run + ing — running
14. clip + ed — clipped
15. stern + ness — sternness
16. cheerful + ly — cheerfully
17. groan + ing — groaning
18. pat + ed — patted
19. stop + ing — stopping
20. stoop + ing — stooping

Words with the "Seed" Sound

There is only one English word ending in *sede: supersede*. Three words end in *ceed: exceed, proceed, succeed*. All other words ending with the sound of *seed* are spelled *cede*:

recede   precede   concede   secede

Words with *ie* and *ei*

There is a general rule for words with the long *e* (*ē*) sound. The word is spelled *ie*, except after *c*. If the vowel combination sounds like a long *a* (*ā*) spell it *ei*.

I before *E*

piece   fierce   field   grief   chief
believe   relief   niece   reprieve   retrieve

Except after *C*

perceive   deceit   ceiling   receipt
conceive   conceit   receive   deceive

Or when sounded as *ā*

neighbor   weigh   reign

The following words are exceptions to the rule.

either   leisure   seize
weird   species   neither

Exercise A: Find the <u>misspelled</u> words in these sentences and spell them correctly.

1. This new law <u>superceeds</u> the old one. supersedes
2. South Carolina <u>seceded</u> from the Union in 1860 and <u>siezed</u> Fort Sumter in 1861. seized
3. My <u>neice</u> Meredith received a <u>wierd</u> surprise. niece, weird
4. Sal <u>beleives</u> that he can clear that field in his <u>liesure</u> time. believes, leisure
5. The warden <u>conceeded</u> that the prisoner should get a reprieve. conceded
6. Erin <u>succeded</u> in tying the boat to the pier. succeeded
7. <u>Niether peice</u> of land is big enough for an apartment building. Neither, piece
8. The forged <u>reciept</u> did not deceive the sales clerk, who <u>proceded</u> to call the detective. receipt, proceeded
9. In some cultures the period of grieving <u>excedes</u> two years. exceeds
10. That species of owl has a <u>peircing</u> shriek. piercing

Exercise B: Writing Compose a poem or a set of song lyrics of at least eight lines. Use "seed" words and *ie/ei* words. Note that many of these words rhyme: exceed-secede, grief-chief, neither-either.

A List of Commonly Misspelled Words

abbreviate	committee	fascinating	nickel
accidentally	courageous	February	ninety
achievement	courteous	financial	noticeable
across	criticize	foreign	nuclear
address	curiosity	fourth	nuisance
all right	cylinder	fragile	obstacle
altogether	dealt	generally	occasionally
always	decision	government	occur
amateur	definitely	grammar	opinion
analyze	despair	guarantee	opportunity
anonymous	desperate	guard	original
answer	dictionary	gymnasium	outrageous
apologize	dependent	handkerchief	parallel
appearance	description	height	particularly
appreciate	desirable	humorous	permanent
appropriate	different	imaginary	permissible
argument	disagree	immediately	persuade
arrangement	disappear	incredible	picnicking
associate	disappoint	influence	pleasant
awkward	discipline	intelligence	pneumonia
balance	dissatisfied	interesting	politics
bargain	efficient	knowledge	possess
beginning	eighth	laboratory	possibility
believe	eligible	lightning	practice
bicycle	eliminate	literature	prejudice
bookkeeper	embarrass	loneliness	preparation
bulletin	emphasize	maintenance	privilege
bureau	enthusiastic	marriage	probably
business	environment	mathematics	professor
cafeteria	equipped	medicine	pronunciation
calendar	especially	minimum	propeller
campaign	exaggerate	mischievous	psychology
candidate	excellent	missile	quantity
certain	exhaust	misspell	realize
changeable	expense	mortgage	recognize
characteristic	experience	municipal	recommend
column	familiar	necessary	reference

referred
rehearse
repetition
representative
restaurant
rhythm
ridiculous
sandwich
schedule
scissors
secretary

separate
sergeant
similar
sincerely
sophomore
souvenir
specifically
strategy
strictly
success
surprise

syllable
sympathy
symptom
temperament
temperature
thorough
throughout
together
tomorrow
traffic
tragedy

transferred
truly
Tuesday
twelfth
undoubtedly
unnecessary
vacuum
vicinity
village
weird
writing

REINFORCEMENT EXERCISES
Spelling

Reinforcement Exercise

This Reinforcement Exercise may be used for additional practice of the concepts presented in this Section.

Review

If you have not previously assigned this Reinforcement Exercise, you can use it as an excellent Section Review.

A. Add prefixes and suffixes. Add the prefix or suffix as shown. Write the new word. (Use after page 697.)

1. thin + ness thinness
2. hot + er hotter / dissatisfied
3. dis + satisfied
4. shop + ing shopping
5. rusty + est rustiest / engagement
6. engage + ment
7. true + ly truly
8. spine + less spineless
9. stage + ing staging
10. move + ment movement

11. un + necessary unnecessary
12. excite + able excitable
13. angry + er angrier
14. destroy + ing destroying
15. stain + ed stained
16. continual + ly continually
17. luxury + ous luxurious
18. merry + ment merriment
19. un + attractive unattractive
20. ninety + eth ninetieth

B. Add prefixes and suffixes. Add the prefix or suffix as shown. Write the new word. (Use after page 697.)

1. join + ed joined
2. natural + ly naturally
3. slim + est slimmest
4. include + ing including
5. early + er earlier / disappoint
6. dis + appoint
7. happy + ly happily / regulatory
8. regulate + ory
9. copy + ing copying
10. like + ness likeness

11. in + voluntary involuntary
12. hope + less hopeless
13. forty + eth fortieth
14. even + ness evenness
15. grin + ed grinned
16. usual + ly usually
17. employ + er employer
18. submit + ing submitting
19. argue + ment argument
20. mis + judge misjudge

C. Spell words with _ie, ei,_ or the _seed_ sound. Find the misspelled words. Write them correctly on your paper. (Use after page 698.)

1. Feirce winds knocked the pier into the lake. Fierce
2. The doctor conceeded that there was only one way to relieve the pain. conceded, relieve
3. In the preceeding weeks we enjoyed our leisure time. preceding

4. "Procede with your weird tale," Gail said. Proceed
5. She defended her cheif loyally, I beleive. chief, believe
6. Niether of the advertisements is meant to decieve us. Neither, deceive
7. Unbeleivable! Martin has finally succeeded in making that radio work. Unbelievable
8. Sam hurried over to his crying neice. niece
9. We recieved directions to the new baseball field. received
10. Gus has succeded in putting the peices together. succeeded, pieces

D. Spell words correctly. Find the misspelled words in each sentence. Write them correctly on your paper. (Use after page 698.)

1. The feirce cougar dissappeared into the cave. fierce, disappeared
2. Marcy's horse gracefully steped and trotted around the ring. stepped
3. Annie is planning to send out the inviteations today. invitations
4. The wide reciever was completly unaware of the new plan. completely, receiver
5. David shouted angryly at his friends but immediatly was sorry. angrily, immediately unaware
6. Some taxpayers worryed that the money was mispent. worried, misspent
7. The uneveness of the slope makes skiing unusualy hard. unevenness, unusually
8. Police cars generaly preceed the President's car in a parade. generally, precede
9. In all of the excitment we accidentaly misplaced our tickets. excitement, accidentally
10. The weight of the ship's cargo excedes ten tons. exceeds

702

MIXED REVIEW
Spelling

A. Copy each sentence. Add the suffixes and prefixes in parentheses to the words with which they are paired.

1. Susan said that none of her answers were (in + correct). incorrect
2. Who was the (win + er) of the masquerade contest? winner
3. Roger Ebert and Gene Siskel always (dis + agree) on that type of movie. disagree
4. We found an insect (imbed + ed) in a piece of amber. imbedded
5. The explorers (final + ly) reached their destination. finally
6. Most of Inspector Clouseau's actions were completely (il + logical). illogical
7. A lighthouse operator has to combat (lonely + ness). loneliness
8. A (fury + ous) storm ravaged the tiny island. furious
9. We raised money to pay for (bus + ing) our team to the Bears' exhibition game. busing or bussing
10. At the age of ten, she began (write + ing) her memoirs. writing
11. The plan called for more (inter + action) among members of different departments. interaction
12. That dog will have to stop (bury + ing) its bones in my petunias. burying
13. Playwright George Kaufman first became known for the (witty + ness) of his newspaper columns. wittiness
14. Those thunderclouds definitely aren't (line + ed) with silver. lined
15. His new job may be causing his uncharacteristic (mean + ness). meanness
16. Sheila is (plan + ing) on (study + ing) (biology + cal) science. planning, studying, biological
17. She has been (save + ing) money for college. saving
18. Has anyone (broke + en) Babe Ruth's home run record? broken
19. What was his (bat + ing) average? batting
20. No plants or animals relieve the (barren + ness) of the moon's surface. barrenness

703

B. Proofread these sentences for spelling <u>errors</u>. Write each misspelled word correctly. One sentence has no errors.

1. It was the silliest <u>arguement</u> we had ever had. argument
2. Mary Chase's play *Harvey* is <u>truely</u> amusing. truly
3. All <u>merryment</u> stopped when the host began <u>braging</u>. merriment, bragging
4. Bill was cooking dinner, and Monica was <u>bakeing</u> dessert. baking
5. The losing candidate <u>finaly</u> decided to <u>consede</u> the election. finally, concede
6. Which occurrence are you <u>refering</u> to? referring
7. To the <u>amazment</u> of onlookers, the <u>feirce</u> winds uprooted a huge tree. amazement, fierce
8. To ensure the <u>eveness</u> of each coat of paint, we used a paint <u>thiner</u>. evenness, thinner
9. Coach Marowitz spoke meaningfully about the need for modifying our defensive strategy. correct
10. The dog <u>proceded</u> to retrieve the Frisbee and bite a huge hole in it. proceeded

USING MECHANICS IN WRITING
Spelling

A. Pretend that you are a student in another country who has only recently learned English. You have just written the following letter to your American pen pal. One of your teachers suggests that you check your letter for <u>spelling errors</u>. Follow that teacher's advice and rewrite the letter correctly. There are nineteen mistakes. You may have to refer to the *List of Commonly Misspelled Words* on pages 699 and 700.

Dear <u>Freind</u>, Friend

received I <u>recieved</u> your letter of <u>Febuary</u> 4 and read <u>happyly</u> about February, happily what you have been doing. Your family happenings <u>especialy</u> made me smile. especially

The story about when your brother was preparing dinner as clipping your sister was <u>cliping</u> the dog in the kitchen <u>realy</u> was the fun- really, funniest <u>nyest</u> I've read. When the dog <u>tiped</u> over the chair that your tipped brother had set the spaghetti sauce on, I can imagine how he yelled! Has your brother recovered from his <u>greif</u>? grief

Our weather has been so <u>changable</u> recently. One day it is changeable pleasant raining, and the next day it is hot. On <u>plesent</u> days my brother sailing and I go <u>sailling</u>. Do you like to sail? We like <u>raceing</u> our boat racing on the ocean. It is summer here now, you know, so we enjoy being in the water. In winter we will be <u>plaing</u> soccer. playing

I have so many questions to ask you. What is the <u>tempature</u> temperature now? What athletics do you enjoy? You said your sister is a <u>sophmore</u>. What is that? sophomore

Please write soon, I appreciate hearing about the wonderful <u>missadventures</u> of your family. misadventures

Yours <u>truely</u>, truly

B. Write a story in which a mad professor and his assistant, Igor, are working in a laboratory on one of their typically horrifying projects. Use at least fifteen words from the *List of Commonly Misspelled Words* in your story. You should be able to use many more.

Cumulative Review

These exercises are designed to cover broad areas of grammar, usage, and mechanics. They require the application of skills taught thus far in the text. The exercises may be used for testing purposes, or as an excellent resource for review.

CUMULATIVE REVIEW
Spelling

Spelling Words with *ei, ie, ede,* and *eed*. Number your paper from 1 to 15. Write each word correctly by adding the letters *ei, ie, ede,* or *eed*.

1. c _e i_ ling
2. ch _i e_ f
3. rec _e i_ ve
4. l _e i_ sure
5. prec _e d e_

6. dec _e i_ ve
7. rel _i e_ f
8. n _e i_ ther
9. bel _i e_ ve
10. _e i_ ther

11. proc _e e d_
12. rec _e i_ pt
13. ach _i e_ vement
14. succ _e e d_
15. n _i e_ ce

Adding Prefixes and Suffixes. Number your paper from 1 to 15. Write the word formed by adding the prefix or suffix.

1. de + code — 1. decode
2. re + entry — 2. reentry
3. thirty + eth — 3. thirtieth
4. strange + ly — 4. strangely
5. study + ing — 5. studying

6. im + mature — 6. immature
7. value + able — 7. valuable
8. copy + s — 8. copies
9. nine + th — 9. ninth
10. general + ly — 10. generally

11. thin + er — 11. thinner
12. mis + spell — 12. misspell
13. coach + s — 13. coaches
14. decay + ed — 14. decayed
15. potato + s — 15. potatoes

Using the Correct Word. Number your paper from 1 to 10. Next to each number, write the correct word from those in parentheses.

1. If (your, <u>you're</u>) going to see Kate, say hello for me.
2. Equal opportunity is a basic (principal, <u>principle</u>) of a democracy.
3. An elephant uses (<u>its</u>, it's) trunk to dig.
4. If I'd waited ten more minutes, I (could of, <u>could have</u>) seen John Travolta in person.
5. Betty (<u>set</u>, sat) the test tubes in the rack.
6. Everyone agreed (<u>on</u>, to, with) pepperoni pizza.
7. In 1979, Mother Teresa (excepted, <u>accepted</u>) the Nobel Peace Prize for her aid to the poor of India.
8. The curtain (<u>rose</u>, raised) and the play began.
9. The four neighboring farmers shared several pieces of large equipment (between, <u>among</u>) them.
10. Is it (alright, <u>all right</u>) to bring my cousin to the picnic?

Section 16

The Correct Form For Writing

Section Objectives

1. To use accepted form for headings, titles, margins, and spacing

2. to use the correct form for writing numbers

3. To use abbreviations correctly in writing

Preparing the Students

Tell the students that good writing always requires more than one draft. The first draft is often very messy because the writer must go back and correct mistakes, rearrange sentences, and change words. However, the final form of a paper must be neat, legible, and as close to error free as possible. Tell the class that this Section will provide guidelines and information that will help them turn out papers in standard, acceptable form.

Additional Resources

Additional Exercises — See pages 713–715 in the student text.

Skills Practice Book — pages 207–208.

Duplicating Masters — pages 207–208.

Special Populations — See special section at the front of this Teacher's Edition.

An effective writer needs to be as concerned with the form of his or her papers as with the content. Careless or sloppy form can muddle a writer's message, confuse and annoy the reader, and even prevent someone from making the effort to read the material at all.

Good form is careful, neat, and consistent. Some schools set their own specific rules for the correct form for written work. In this section you will learn about the kind of form that is accepted by many schools.

Objective

To use accepted form for headings, titles, margins, and spacing

Presenting the Lesson

Read and discuss pages 708–709, modifying the suggestions in the text, if necessary, to include your school's standard form.

Optional Practice

Put the following paper titles in the correct title form.

the history of a school
an a b c of micro-computers
what is electromagnetism
food from the sea
man's place in his environment

Extending the Lesson

Have students rewrite a previously written assignment, following all the guidelines given in this Part.

Part 1   Acceptable Form

Your papers must always be neat and legible. Neatness shows that you care about your work. Whether typewritten or handwritten in ink, give your papers that extra bit of attention that will make your reader *want* to read what you have to say.

Of course, the correct form for writing means more than a neat appearance. In a paper with acceptable form, the various parts are positioned correctly. Headings, titles, margins, and spacing should be in the correct form.

The Heading

A heading identifies your paper. It is usually placed in the upper right-hand corner of the first page. Place your name on the first line. Write the name of your class on the second line. Write the date on the third line. In a paper with a title page, the heading is placed in the upper right corner of that page.

Each page, except for page one, should be numbered. Beginning with page two, place the page number in the upper right-hand corner. To identify all pages, you might want to put your name under the page number.

Some teachers may require a different form for labeling your paper. Follow any special instructions you are given.

The Title

The title of a paper should appear near the top of the first page. In general, place the title two lines down from the last line of the heading. Begin the first line of your paper two lines below the title.

Correct form for a title also means proper capitalization. The first word and all important words in the title should be capitalized. Use capitals for only the first letters of words, not for every letter. Do not underline your title or place it in quotation marks.

When a paper is more than three pages long, a title page may be used. This page precedes the paper.

Margins and Spacing

Use correct margins and spacing to achieve an attractive appearance. Margins of one inch at the top, bottom, and left side of the paper look pleasing.

Try to keep the right-hand margin fairly even. Do not break too many words with hyphens, though, to keep the margin straight. Try to avoid hyphens in more than two lines in a row.

Double-spacing makes typed papers look neat and makes them much easier to read. Paragraphs are usually indented five spaces. Skip two spaces after the end of a sentence.

Part 2   Writing Numbers

The form for writing numbers should be consistent. Numbers that can be expressed in fewer than four words are usually spelled out. Larger numbers are written in figures.

> These jeans cost *twenty-four* dollars.
> The National League consists of *twelve* teams.
> Ticket sales amounted to *$2,125*.

A number at the beginning of a sentence is always spelled out.

> *Thirty thousand* people attended the game.
> *One thousand* millimeters make up one meter.
> *Four hundred* dollars was stolen.

Figures rather than spelled-out words are used for these numbers: dates, street and room numbers, telephone numbers, temperature, page numbers, decimals, and percentages.

> The Battle of Concord took place on April *19, 1775*.
> The clinic is at *66* West Schiller in Room *35*.
> Matthew's phone number is *328-6610*.
> Last night the temperature went down to *10* degrees.
> Did you see that article about vans on page *16*?
> Ann ran the hurdles in *15.8* seconds.
> The new sales tax is *4* percent.

---

subject. Then have them write up the results, using numbers in their reports.

Optional Practice

Have students try to write a report on an appropriate subject in which they use all of the kinds of numbers mentioned in this Part.

Extending the Lesson

Have students look at a variety of cookbooks to see if some texts vary in their writing of numbers. Have them bring in examples of other systems and note how they vary from the one given in this Part.

Part 3

Objective

To use abbreviations correctly in writing

Presenting the Lesson

Read and discuss pages 710–711. Assign the Exercises on 712.

Individualizing the Lesson

Less-Advanced Students

For additional practice, have students correct the abbreviations,

In large sums of money or large quantities, use commas to separate the figures. Commas are not used in dates, serial numbers, page numbers, addresses, or telephone numbers.

CORRECT: The Statue of Liberty cost $500,000.
CORRECT: The Milky Way has 200,000,000,000 stars.
INCORRECT: The first World Series was in 1,903.
CORRECT: The first World Series was in 1903.

Exercise: Copy these sentences, correcting any errors.

1. A movie shows fourteen hundred and thirty-five frames of film per minute. 1,435
2. The serial number of the typewriter is 20,002. 20002   First,
3. 1st prize is one thousand two hundred and fifty dollars. $1,250
4. About ninety percent of the patients who have this operation recover fully within 6 months. 90, six
5. Although the temperature was actually 30 degrees, the wind chill factor lowered it to two degrees. 2
6. The profit of twelve thousand two hundred and five dollars is ten percent higher than last year's. $12,205, 10
7. 3 years ago the Chandlers moved to 1,682 Garfield Street.
8. 1 barrel of oil is equal to 31 gallons. One, thirty-one   Three, 1682
9. 1000 grams equals a little more than three pounds. One thousand
10. On March eighteenth, 1,959, Hawaii became our 50th state.
    18, 1959, fiftieth

Part 3   Using Abbreviations

Abbreviations are shortened forms of words. In formal writing, abbreviations are usually not acceptable. Abbreviations, however, may be used for most titles before and after names. Abbreviations may also be used for government agencies and for time.

TITLES BEFORE PROPER NAMES: Mrs., Mr., Ms., Gen., Dr., Rev., Sgt., Fr., Sen.
TITLES AFTER PROPER NAMES: Jr., M.D., D.D.S., Ph.D.
GOVERNMENT AGENCIES: FBI, VA, EPA, FTC
DATES AND TIMES: A.M., P.M., B.C., A.D.

Notice that periods are omitted in some abbreviations, such as those for government agencies. If you are not sure whether an abbreviation should be written with or without periods, look up the abbreviation in your dictionary.

A title is abbreviated only when it is used with a person's name, as in *Dr. Lauren Sherwood*. The following, for example, would not be acceptable: The dr. found a cure for the disease.

Abbreviations are not used for certain titles. *Honorable* and *Reverend* are not abbreviated when preceded by *the: the Reverend Lee Withers*. Abbreviations are not used for the titles of the President and Vice-President of the United States.

In most writing, abbreviations are not acceptable for the following: names of countries and states, months and days of the week, addresses, and firm names.

INCORRECT: The Hon. John Evans was the guest.
CORRECT: The Honorable John Evans was the guest.

INCORRECT: Both the Pres. and the Vice-Pres. were there.
CORRECT: Both the President and the Vice-President were there.

INCORRECT: The Mayans built pyramids in Mex.
CORRECT: The Mayans built pyramids in Mexico.

INCORRECT: Detroit, Mich., is called "Motor City."
CORRECT: Detroit, Michigan, is called "Motor City."

INCORRECT: Tues., Nov. 2, is Election Day.
CORRECT: Tuesday, November 2, is Election Day.

INCORRECT: The bottling co. has a plant on Oak Ave.
CORRECT: The bottling company has a plant on Oak Avenue.

In ordinary writing, abbreviations are not acceptable for the following: names of school courses, and the words *page, chapter,* and *Christmas*. Abbreviations for measurements, like *ft., in., min., hr., oz., qt., mi.,* are also unacceptable.

INCORRECT: The story "A Xmas Memory" begins on pg. 108 of our literature book.
CORRECT: The story "A Christmas Memory" begins on pg. 108 of our literature book.

where necessary, in the following sentences.

1. The Pres. of the U.S. must be at least thirty-six years old.
2. N.Y.C. is famous for its skyscrapers.
3. This recipe calls for a qt. of milk and an oz. of chocolate.
4. Read up to chapt. 3, pg. 230.
5. My grandfather was a sgt. in the army and now works for the F.B.I.

Advanced Students

Have students find the proper abbreviations for the following words. Tell them to use the dictionary if necessary.

1. ante meridiem
2. gram
3. pound
4. cash on delivery
5. répondez s'il vous plaît
6. post script
7. Maine
8. versus
9. et cetera
10. anno Domini

Optional Practice

Have the students look up the currently accepted form of abbreviation for each of the fifty states. Suggest that they check with the post office, if necessary.

Extending the Lesson

Introduce the concept of acronyms if it was not introduced earlier. (See **Extending the Lesson** for Section 14.1 on page 658.) Point out that sometimes the word formed by the acronym expresses some aspect of the organization it stands for. For example, NOW (National Organization of Women) conveys the idea of immediacy and modernity. Similarly, CORE (Congress on Racial Equality) conveys the sense of being at the heart of something. Ask the students to think of acronyms for imaginary organizations that somehow convey (comically, perhaps) the spirit of the group.

Exercise A: Correct the errors in abbreviation in these sentences.

1. The secy. of H.E.W. is usually not a medical dr. secretary, HEW, doctor
2. The Pres. met with the Secy. of Defense at Camp David, Md. President, Secretary, Maryland
3. The Rev. Amelia Gleason gave a sermon about the true meaning of Xmas. Reverend, Christmas
4. McDonald's Corp. has its headquarters on Twenty-second Ave. in Oakbrook, Ill. Corporation, Avenue, Illinois
5. Mr. Frank Ransom, Jr., is applying for a govt. grant to start a center for sr. citizens. government, senior
6. Benito Juarez, a nineteenth-century pres. of Mexico, is described in Ch. 10. President, Chapter
7. Last Fri., our home ec. class visited Mercy Hosp. Friday, economics, Hospital
8. I lost two lbs. in forty-eight hours on the diet Dr. Rossi gave me. pounds,
9. Cleopatra ruled Egypt in the first cent. B.C. century
10. Pres. Roosevelt closed all banks in the U.S. on Mar. 6, 1933. President, United States, March

Exercise B: Writing Write each of the items described below. Use abbreviations correctly only where indicated.

1. Describe yourself. Include your full name, age, height, and weight.
2. Make up a guest list for an important White House dinner. Each guest has a title. You may use abbreviations.
3. Describe this textbook. Include its size, subject matter, number of pages, and number of chapters.
4. Write a party invitation. Include the time, date, and address.
5. Make up an itinerary for an around-the-world trip. Include dates, departure times, and the names of the cities and countries you plan to visit. You may use abbreviations.

REINFORCEMENT EXERCISES
The Correct Form for Writing

A. Understand proper manuscript form. Tell whether the following statements are true or false.   (Use after page 710.)

F 1. Your name, the date, and the name of your class should be placed on the first line of the first page of your paper.

F 2. Each page, beginning with page one, should be numbered in the top right-hand corner.

T 3. The title of a paper should appear near the top of the first page, two lines below the last line of the heading.

F 4. All words in a title should be capitalized.

F 5. Titles should be placed in quotation marks.

F 6. All written work should be accompanied by a title page.

T 7. Use a one inch margin at the top, bottom, and left side of your paper.

F 8. Hyphens may be used at the end of every line.

T 9. Double-spacing makes typewritten papers look neat and increases their readability.

F 10. Paragraphs are usually indented three spaces.

B. Correct errors in manuscript form. Rewrite the following sentences, correcting all errors.   (Use after page 712.)

1. The pres. flew to Peking from Washington, D C, a trip of six thousand nine hundred and sixty-five miles. President, D.C., 6,965

2. The Yangtze River, in China, is three thousand four hundred and thirty-four miles long. 3,434

3. The Pacific Ocean is a little over 36,000 feet deep. thirty-six thousand

4. 469 million people live on the continent of China. Four hundred sixty-nine

5. The sun is 1 of 100 billion stars in our galaxy. one, one hundred

6. Ms Beth Henley won the Pulitzer Prize for her play *Crimes of the Heart* in nineteen hundred and eighty-one. Ms., 1981

7. The Rev. Thomas McKay started a Xmas fund. Reverend, Christmas

8. Does the Ewing Oil Co. have an office in Houston, Tex? Company, Texas

9. Last Wed. our eng. class read chpt. 12 of *Stories of the Amer. Civil War.* Wednesday, English, Chapter, *American*

10. The dr. told me to drink 8 oz. of water with every meal. doctor, ounces

713

Reinforcement Exercises

These Reinforcement Exercises may be used for additional practice of the concepts presented in this Section. Each exercise focuses on a single concept, and should be used after the page number indicated in parentheses.

Review

If you have not assigned these Reinforcement Exercises before this time, you can also use them as an excellent Section Review.

Mixed Review

These exercises provide review of the concepts presented in this Section. Each exercise challenges the students to apply several of the skills they have acquired during previous study. Because the "mixed" feature of these activities makes them more difficult, the teacher may wish to have less-advanced students do them orally or in small groups.

MIXED REVIEW

The Correct Form for Writing

The following short composition contains several <u>errors</u> in manuscript form and in the use of numbers and abbreviations. Rewrite the composition correctly.

> Patricia Smith
> Social Studies
> Jan. 11, 1984
>
> ○ <u>Mount Rushmore</u> (Center title and move body down one line.)
>
> Gutzon Borglum created his famous masterpiece on the face of <u>mt.</u> Rushmore in the Black [Mount] Hills of <u>S.D.</u> On it he carved the [South Dakota] busts of <u>4</u> great <u>Amer.</u> Presidents: [four] [American] <u>Geo.</u> Washington, <u>Thos.</u> Jefferson, [George] [Thomas] Abraham Lincoln, and Theodore Roosevelt.
>
> ¶Borglum began this project in 1927 and <u>cont.</u> until his death <u>14</u> years [continued] [fourteen] later. The sculpture was completed ○ by his son, Lincoln, and was hailed as the world's largest sculpture, standing <u>60</u> <u>ft.</u> high. [sixty] [feet] <u>1000's</u> of sightseers visit the <u>mt.</u> [Thousands] [mountain] every <u>yr.</u> [year]

USING PROPER FORM IN WRITING
The Correct Form for Writing

A. Listed below are words and expressions that are frequently abbreviated. Using a dictionary, give the correct abbreviations for each. Be careful to capitalize where necessary.

sergeant Sgt.   A.M. ante meridiem   incorporated Inc.
doctor Dr.   anno domini A.D.   limited Ltd.
february Feb.   united states U.S.   senator Sen.
environmental EPA   new jersey N.J.   adjective adj.
    protection agency junior Jr.   assistant asst.

B. According to *The Book of Firsts,* the first roller skates were worn to a costume party in 1760 by a man named Joseph Merlin. Merlin skated into the ballroom playing a violin and crashed into a mirror worth over $1,000. Write this story from the point of view of one of the other guests at the party. Revise and proofread your paper, and then rewrite it. Use your neatest handwriting and observe proper margins. When you have finished, exchange it with another student. See if your classmate can find any errors in form.

C. Imagine that you are living in prehistoric times and that the hunters from your clan have just come back to your cave with a woolly mammoth for you to prepare for dinner. Write a recipe for mammoth dinner, giving special attention to the proper form for numbers. Be sure to include the temperature at which your recipe must be cooked and how many it will serve.

Using Mechanics in Writing

These challenging and enjoyable activities allow the students to see how the concepts of grammar, usage, and mechanics may be applied in actual writing situations. Each exercise is designed to allow students practice in several of the skills they have acquired in this Section. The activities also provide opportunities for students to write creatively about a wide variety of interesting and unusual subjects.

715

1. To organize ideas for an outline
2. To know how and when to use a topic outline
3. To use correct form in a topic outline

Preparing the Students

Ask the students to imagine that they are going to write an essay on "The Best Movies I Have Ever Seen." The movies must be organized by category. Write the following outline on the board.

I. Science fiction
   A.
   B.
II. Comedy
   A.
   B.
III. Westerns
   A.
   B.
IV. Horror
   A.
   B.

Ask the class to supply further major headings and ask them how they would go about filling in the subheadings. Point out how this simple outline could help them organize the ideas in a paper and help the reader follow the points being made.

Additional Resources

Additional Exercises — See pages 721–724 in the student text.

Skills Practice Book — pages 209–210.

Duplicating Masters — page 209–210.

Special Populations — See special section at the front of this Teacher's Edition.

Section 17

Outlining

One very common problem in longer compositions and speeches is weak organization. You may have collected a wealth of interesting information on your subject. Unless your facts, examples, and other information are carefully organized, however, your reader or listener may have difficulty understanding you.

From beginning to end, your ideas should flow smoothly. One point should lead logically to the next, rather than be presented in a random order.

One useful method of organizing your thoughts and facts into a logical order is an **outline**. After you have "brainstormed" your topic and gathered all your information, making an outline will help you sort and organize your ideas. That is why so many experienced writers use outlines to prepare for writing.

Outlining can also be used for several purposes other than in writing. You may use an outline to record important information from a lecture. You can use it to take notes when you do research. You can even use outlining as a study device to help clarify the main points and organization of a chapter.

In this section, you will learn the rules and guidelines for writing an outline. Familiarize yourself with them so that outlining can become a useful and comfortable organizational aid.

Organizing an Outline

To begin an outline, you should have a clear idea of the purpose of your composition. Then determine the main ideas that you want to develop. These main ideas will be the **main points** in your outline.

Next, consider how you can develop or explain each main point. The supporting ideas for these points will become **subpoints** in the outline. Consequently, related ideas will be grouped together.

Finally, decide which scheme to use for ordering the main points. While time sequence works well for some topics, order of importance or spatial order is better for others. The best order is the one that makes your topic clearest and easiest to understand.

When your outline is complete, you will have the skeleton for a composition. Fill in details and build paragraphs around related ideas to create a solid, well-organized composition.

Writing Topic Outlines

A **topic outline** is an informal kind of outline. Topic outlines use words or phrases instead of complete sentences. Topic outlines are effective for organizing compositions.

Study the topic outline on the following page. Notice that it does not use complete sentences. Pay particular attention to the grouping of subpoints under related main ideas.

Organizing an Outline

Objective

To organize ideas for an outline

Presenting the Lesson

Read and discuss **Organizing an Outline** on page 717. Stress that all subpoints should support the main point they come under and all main points should support the purpose of the composition. Discuss how the outline on page 718 fulfills these requirements.

Optional Practice

Select a topic for a paper, such as "Popular Music," and develop an outline with the class. Write main points and subpoints on the board. Ask the students to come up with similar topics and have the class develop an outline for a paper.

Writing Topic Outlines

Objective

To know how and when to use a topic outline

Presenting the Lesson

Read and discuss pages 717–718. Ask the class if they can add any main points and subpoints to the outline on page 718.

Go over the outline on pages 719–720 with the class, filling in the blanks with the words provided.

Optional Practice

Present a topic for a paper, such as "Parts of a Newspaper" and develop a topic outline with the class, writing main points and subpoints on the board.

Using Outline Form

Objective

To use correct form in a topic outline

Presenting the Lesson

Read and discuss **Using Outline Form** on pages 718–719. Point out how each of the rules applies to the sample outline on page 718. Give special emphasis to the point that a heading cannot have just one subheading. There must be at least two subheadings or none at all, since nothing can be divided into fewer than two parts. Do the Reinforcement Exercise on pages 721–722 as

The Arctic

I. Arctic lands
  A. The true arctic
  B. The subarctic
    1. Is not part of true arctic
    2. Has warmer summers
II. Natural resources
  A. Soil
  B. Minerals
    1. Coal
    2. Radioactive minerals
      a. Thorium
      b. Uranium
    3. Petroleum
  C. Plants
  D. Animals
III. Arctic peoples
  A. Eskimos
  B. Americanoids

Using Outline Form

Outlines use a precise form that does not vary. Here are some rules to follow:

1. Write the title of your composition at the top of the outline. The introduction and the conclusion are usually not considered parts of the outline.
2. Arrange numbers and letters of headings in the following order: first, Roman numerals for main points, then capital letters for subpoints. Next, Arabic numerals are used. Small letters are used for details under these ideas, then numbers in parentheses for details developing the details, and, finally, small letters in parentheses for subdetails. The arrangement on the next page shows clearly which ideas belong together. Note the placement of periods.

```
I.  A.
    B.
        1.
        2.
            a.
            b.
                (1)
                (2)
                    (a)
                    (b)

II.
    A.
    B.
    (and so on)
```

3. Indent all headings in the outline. Place letters and numbers of all headings directly underneath the first word of the larger heading above.
4. Do not use a single subheading. A heading should not be broken down if it cannot be divided into at least two points.
5. Use the same kind of word or phrase for all headings of the same rank. If, for example, *A* is a verb, then *B* should be a verb, too.
6. Begin each item in the outline with a capital letter. In a topic outline, do not end headings with periods or other punctuation.

Exercise: Look at the partial outline on the next page. Copy it on your paper, leaving blank spaces as indicated. Then complete the outline by inserting the following headings after the appropriate numbers and letters.

Diet	Famous archaeological finds
Botanists	History courses
Excavating sites	Classification
Provides careers in four fields	Writing

Individualizing the Lesson

Less-Advanced Students

Have students prepare an outline for the steps in preparing a dish or making something.

Advanced Students

Have students write an outline for a chapter in one of their text books. A science text or a history text will probably provide manageable material.

Optional Practice

Emphasize the usefulness of outlines in notetaking. Have students attend a lecture or listen to a speech on the radio or television. Ask them to take notes and then prepare an outline of the speech.

Extending the Lesson

Have the students go to a store that sells greeting cards and take notes on the classifications of cards they find there. Then ask them to prepare an outline for a paper on "Types of Greeting Cards." They will undoubtedly discover that there is more than one way to classify the cards. Have the students read their outlines and discuss the various methods of classification. See if there is group consensus about which method of classification is best.

Archaeology

I. How archaeologists gather information
   A. Surveying sites
   B. Excavating sites
      1. Varied methods
      2. Range of tools
   C. Recording and preserving materials

II. How archaeologists interpret finds
   A. Classification
   B. Dating
      1. Absolute chronology
      2. Relative chronology
   C. Evaluation
      1. Can help explain lifestyles
         a. Diet
         b. Work
         c. Social class
      2. Aided by specialists from other fields
         a. Zoologists
         b. Botanists

III. Famous archaeological finds
   A. Discovery of Troy, 1870
   B. Discovery of King Tut's tomb, 1922
   C. Discovery of treasure ship off
      coast of England, 1939

IV. Futures in archaeology
   A. Require specific college preparation
      1. Languages
      2. History
      3. Anthropology
      4. Biology
      5. Geology
   B. Provides careers in four fields
      1. Museum work
      2. Government service
      3. Teaching
      4. Writing

REINFORCEMENT EXERCISE
Outlining

Complete an outline. Copy the partial outline. Then insert the following headings where they belong in the outline.

Two meals eaten each day	Nobles
Brought by missionaries	Thor
No windows	Clothing
Shipbuilding	Religion
	Marriage

Viking Life

I. Ancestry and population
   A. Germanic background
   B. Three social classes
      1. Nobles
      2. Freemen
      3. Slaves

II. Economic activities
   A. Farming
   B. Fishing
   C. Trading
   D. Shipbuilding
      1. Trading ships
      2. Warships

III. Daily life
   A. Marriage
      1. Parents arranged
      2. Several wives
   B. Food
      1. Two meals eaten each day
      2. Food provided by husbands
         a. Wild game
         b. Farm produce
   C. Clothing

721

Reinforcement Exercises

These Reinforcement Exercises may be used for additional practice of the concepts presented in this Section. Each exercise focuses on a single concept, and should be used after the page number indicated in parentheses.

Review

If you have not assigned these Reinforcement Exercises before this time, you can also use them as an excellent Section Review.

      D. Housing
          1. Stone or wooden walls
          2. Sod or straw roofs
          3. No windows
IV. Religion
      A. Worshipped several gods
          1. Odin
          2. Thor
      B. Christianity
          1. Brought by missionaries
          2. Ended Norse religion

MIXED REVIEW

Outlining

Mixed Review

These exercises provide review of the concepts presented in this Section. Each exercise challenges the students to apply several of the skills they have acquired during previous study. Because the "mixed" feature of these activities makes them more difficult, the teacher may wish to have less-advanced students do them orally or in small groups.

Revise this outline, correcting all errors in outline form.

The First Submarines

I. Description of modern submarine
   A. Can remain submerged for almost unlimited time
   B. Has underwater speeds of above 20 knots
   C. Holds large crews

II. The First Submarine
   A. Built by C.J. Drebbel in 1620
   B. In 1620
   C. Had strange design
      1. Was rowboat covered with leather
      2. Was propelled by twelve oarsmen
      3. Had oars that went through flexible leather seals

III. The first combat submarine
   A. Built by David Bushnell in 1776
   B. Also had unusual design
      1. Small, egg-shaped craft
      2. All wood
   C. Operated by a man turning a propeller
   D. how it submerged
      1. Pumped water in to submerge and pumped water out to surface

IV. Robert Fulton's submarine built in 1800
   A. Called the Nautilus
   B. Was forerunner of the modern submarine
   C. The Nautilus Could remain submerged for six hours
   D. Pumped in air through a tube that went to the water's surface
   E. Used compressed air in later versions

USING MECHANICS IN WRITING
Outlining

Use the outline below as the basis of a short report on the impact of the horse on early Native American cultures. Add your own introduction and conclusion. Follow all of the steps of the Process of Writing.

The Arrival of the Horse

Purpose: The impact of the horse on early Native American cultures was as strong as that of the automobile on modern society.

I. Arrival of the horse
  A. Brought to America by Spanish conquistadors in 1519
  B. Left behind by these Spaniards and later explorers
  C. Gradually turned wild and formed herds
  D. Spread northward across the Great Plains
  E. Seen all over western America by late 1800's

II. Initial reaction of natives
  A. Heard accounts of "big dogs" used to the south
  B. Were wary of the huge animals
  C. Accepted horses gradually
  D. Learned to train them for many useful tasks

III. Uses of horses by Native American tribes
  A. Pulled heavy loads during tribe migration
  B. Used for transporation
  C. Used in battle
    1. Added speed
    2. Gave psychological advantage over tribes on foot
  D. Used on buffalo hunts
    1. Allowed easier tracking of herds
    2. Provided speed during a chase
    3. Were used as lures
      a. Disguised with a buffalo skin
      b. Lured herds within easy bow-and-arrow range

Sources of Quoted Materials

Cover

Homage to the Square: Apparition, 1959. Josef Albers. The Solomon R. Guggenheim Museum, New York. Cover photographer, Carmelo Guadagno.

Editorial Credits

Editor-in-Chief: Joseph F. Littell
Editorial Director, English Programs: Joy Littell
Managing Editor: Kathleen Laya
Assistant Managing Editor: Geraldine Macsai
Senior Editor: Bonnie Dobkin
Assistant Editor: Robert D. Shepherd

Associate Designer: Mary E. MacDonald
Handwritten Art: Kenneth Izzi
Cover Design: Joy Littell, Debbie Costello
Production Assistant: Julie Schumacher

Index